2010-2011

KJV
Standard
LESSON COMMENTARY®

Edited by
Ronald L. Nickelson

KING JAMES
VERSION

Jonathan Underwood,
Senior Editor

Volume 58

Standard®
PUBLISHING
Cincinnati, Ohio

IN THIS VOLUME

Cover design by Brigid Naglich
Lessons based on International Sunday School Lessons © 2007 by the Lesson Committee.

INDEX OF PRINTED TEXTS

The printed texts for 2010–2011 are arranged here in the order in which they appear in the Bible.

CD-ROM AVAILABLE

The *Standard Lesson Commentary*® is available in an electronic format in special editions of this volume. The compact disk contains the full text of the King James *Standard Lesson Commentary*® and *The NIV® Standard Lesson Commentary*® powered by the Libronix Digital Library System, and a collection of presentation helps that can be projected or reproduced as handouts. Order #020510110.

If you have any questions regarding the installation, registration, or activation of this CD-ROM, please contact Logos **Customer Service** at (800) 875-6467.

If you have problems with the CD, *Technical Support* is available by telephone at *(360) 679-4496,* by e-mail at *tech@logos.com,* or online at *www.logos.com/support.*

LESSON CYCLE CHART

International Sunday School Lesson Cycle, September 2010—August 2016

Year	Fall Quarter (Sep, Oct, Nov)	Winter Quarter (Dec, Jan, Feb)	Spring Quarter (Mar, Apr, May)	Summer Quarter (Jun, Jul, Aug)
2010-2011	The Inescapable God (Exodus, Psalms)	Assuring Hope (Isaiah, Matthew, Mark)	We Worship God (Matthew, Mark, Philippians, 1 & 2 Timothy, Jude, Revelation)	God Instructs His People (Joshua, Judges, Ruth)
2011-2012	Tradition and Wisdom (Proverbs, Ecclesiastes, Song of Solomon, Matthew)	God Establishes a Faithful People (Genesis, Exodus, Luke, Galatians)	God's Creative Word (John)	God Calls for Justice (Pentateuch, History, Psalms, Prophets)
2012-2013	A Living Faith (Psalms, Acts, 1 Corinthians, Hebrews)	Jesus Is Lord (Ephesians, Philippians, Colossians)	Beyond the Present Time (Daniel, Luke, Acts, 1 & 2 Thessalonians, 1 & 2 Peter)	God's People Worship (Isaiah, Ezra, Nehemiah)
2013-2014	First Things (Genesis, Exodus, Psalms)	Jesus and the Just Reign of God (Luke, James)	Jesus' Fulfillment of Scripture (Deuteronomy, Zechariah, Malachi, Matthew)	The People of God Set Priorities (Haggai, 1 & 2 Corinthians)
2014-2015	Sustaining Hope (Job, Isaiah, Jeremiah, Ezekiel, Habakkuk)	Acts of Worship (Psalms, Daniel, Gospels, Ephesians, Hebrews, James)	Work of the Spirit (Mark, John, Acts, 1 Corinthians, 1, 2, & 3 John)	God's Prophets Demand Justice (Isaiah, Jeremiah, Ezekiel, Amos, Micah, Zechariah, Malachi)
2015-2016	The Community of Believers Comes Alive (Matthew, John, 1 John)	Traditions of Israel (Leviticus, Numbers, Deuteronomy)	The Gift of Faith (Mark, Luke)	Toward a New Creation (Genesis, Psalms, Zephaniah, Romans)

"God"   "Hope"   "Worship"   "Community"   "Tradition"   "Faith"   "Creation"   "Justice"

NEW AND IMPROVED!

by Ronald L. Nickelson

Welcome to your "new and improved" *Standard Lesson Commentary!* There are many changes for the 2010–2011 edition—some obvious, some not so obvious. But there are some things that haven't changed. You deserve an explanation, so here goes.

New Size and Styling

The most obvious, outward change to the SLC is in its physical dimensions. Those using the regular print version will notice a slight reduction in height and width; those using the large print version will notice fewer pages. This change allows for a more economical conversion from regular print to large print, which in turn helps us hold the line on price increases—something everyone appreciates! It also means you can use both the regular size and the large print edition in the same class; the two editions contain exactly the same information and are paginated identically.

Another obvious change is in the way discussion questions are presented. In place of the familiar "answers," the SLC now offers "talking points"; these are designed to foster genuine discussion. The questions now occur at the appropriate points in the running commentary, thus eliminating the need to turn to the back of each lesson. Changes in fonts, artwork, and various other design elements also add to increased usability.

Downloadable Reproducible Pages

Reproducible student activity pages are now available for KJV users as a free download from www.standardlesson.com. This full-color feature is a major enhancement for teachers who like to use learning activities. The "Involvement Learning" section of each lesson (renamed from "Learning by Doing") offers guidance on how to use the reproducible pages. You can also find this new resource on the *Adult Resources* CD and in the *Standard Lesson eCommentary.*

New Cycle, More Topics

Our six-year cycle of International Sunday School Lessons begins anew with the 2010–2011 SLC. The new cycle features eight topics compared with the six topics of the 2004–2010 cycle (see the chart at left).

What Has Not Changed

The strength of the SLC has always been its reliable verse-by-verse explanation of the lesson text. This has not changed. Many other old favorites also continue to present themselves: the opening Scripture text page for each lesson, pronunciation guides, the quarterly quiz, daily Bible readings, etc. Also here to stay is the cumulative index of passages studied (although you won't see it in this 2010–2011 edition since this is the first year of the cycle).

The SLC also continues to be the best-resourced lesson commentary available for teaching the International Sunday School Lessons. Our on-line (downloadable) resources, the *Adult Resources* packet (containing full-color posters plus a CD), the *Teacher's Convenience Kit,* the student book *Adult Bible Class, SEEK*® take-home papers, and the quarterly or annual *Devotions*® support multiple teaching and learning styles. Within these resources you can find the maps, charts, posters, PowerPoint® slides, etc., as your "must have" additional resources for preparing both your heart and your lesson for teaching. Additional comments and teaching ideas can be found on the Web sites for *Christian Standard*® (www.christianstandard.com) and *The Lookout*® (www.lookoutmag.com).

We should mention one other thing that has not changed: the need for your learners to "grow in grace and in the knowledge of our Lord and Saviour Jesus Christ" (2 Peter 3:18). Every aspect of the SLC is designed with that goal in mind!

Aaron *Air*-un.
Abimelech Uh-*bim*-eh-lek.
Abraham *Ay*-bruh-ham.
acacia uh-*kay*-shuh.
Achan *Ay*-kan.
Achor *Ah*-core.
Aegean A-*jee*-un.
Ai *Ay*-eye.
Alpha *Al*-fa.
Amalekites *Am*-uh-leh-kites or
    Uh-*mal*-ih-kites.
Ammonites *Am*-un-ites.
Amorites *Am*-uh-rites.
Anakims *An*-a-kims.
Antiochus An-*tie*-oh-kus.
Aramaic *Air*-uh-**may**-ik.
Arimathaea *Air*-uh-muh-**thee**-uh.
Aristotle Eh-rih-*stah*-tul.
Aroer Uh-*row*-er.
Artemis *Ar*-teh-miss.
Asaph *Ay*-saff.
Asherah Uh-*she*-ruh.
Ashtaroth *Ash*-tuh-rawth.
Askelon *Ash*-ke-lon or *As*-ke-lon.
Assyrian Uh-*sear*-e-un.
Astarte A-*star*-te (first *a* as in *had*).
Augustus Caesar Aw-*gus*-tus
    See-zer.

Baal *Bay*-ul.
Baalgad *Bay*-ul-gad (gad with a
    short "a" as in *bad*).
Babel *Bay*-bul.
Babylonian Bab-ih-*low*-nee-un.
Bar Kochba Bahr Kokh-*bah*.
Barnabas *Bar*-nuh-bus.
Beatitudes Bee-*a*-tuh-toods (*a* as
    in *mat*).
Bethany *Beth*-uh-nee.
Bethel *Beth*-ul.
Bethlehem *Beth*-lih-hem.
Bethphage *Beth*-fuh-gee.
Bethshemesh Beth-*she*-mesh.
Beulah *Bew*-luh.
Bildad *Bill*-dad.

Boaz *Bo*-az.
Byzantine *Bih*-zen-teen
    (*i* as in *tip*).

Caesar Augustus *See*-zer Aw-*gus*-
    tus.
Caesarea Maritima Sess-uh-*ree*-uh
    Mar-uh-*tee*-muh.
Caesarea Philippi Sess-uh-*ree*-uh
    Fih-*lip*-pie or *Fil*-ih-pie.
Cambyses Kam-*bye*-seez.
Canaan *Kay*-nun.
Chaldeans Kal-*dee*-unz.
Chemosh *Kee*-mosh.
cherubim *chair*-uh-bim.
Chilion *Kil*-ee-on.
Cornelius Cor-*neel*-yus.
covenant *kuv*-nent or *kuh*-vuh-
    nent.
Cyrus *Sigh*-russ.

Dagon *Day*-gon.
Damascus Duh-*mass*-kus.
Darius Duh-*rye*-us.
Davidic Duh-*vid*-ick.

Ecclesiastical Ih-klee-zee-*as*-tih-
    kul.
Egyptian Ee-*jip*-shun.
Ehud *Ee*-hud.
Elias Ee-*lye*-us.
Elijah Ee-*lye*-juh.
Elimelech Ee-*lim*-eh-leck.
Elohim *(Hebrew)* El-o-*heem*.
Elyon El-*yon*.
Emmanuel Eh-*man*-you-el.
Engedi En-*gee*-dye.
Epaphroditus Ee-*paf*-ro-**dye**-tus .
ephah *ee*-fah.
Ephesian Ee-*fee*-zhun.
Ephesus *Ef*-uh-sus.
ephod *ee*-fod.
Ephraimites *Ee*-fray-im-ites.
Epiphanes Ih-*piff*-a-neez.
Esau *Ee*-saw.

Ethiopian E-thee-*o*-pee-un.
eunuch *you*-nick.
Euphrates You-*fray*-teez.
Eusebius You-*see*-be-us.

Gadites *Gad*-ites.
Galilee *Gal*-uh-lee.
Gentiles *Jen*-tiles.
Gershom *Gur*-shom.
Gethsemane Geth-*sem*-uh-nee
    (G as in *get*).
Gilead *Gil*-ee-ud (G as in *get*).
Gilgal *Gil*-gal (G as in *get*).
Goliath Go-*lye*-uth.

Hadrian *Hay*-dree-un.
Hagar *Hay*-gar.
Hazor *Hay*-zor.
Hephzibah *Hef*-zih-bah.
Heraclitus Her-uh-*klee*-tus.
Hermon *Her*-mun.
Herod *Hair*-ud.
Herodias Heh-*roe*-dee-us.
Herodotus Heh-*rod*-uh-tus.
Hesiod Hee-*see*-ud.
Hezekiah Hez-ih-*kye*-uh.
Horeb *Ho*-reb.
Hur Her.
Hymenaeus Hi-meh-*nee*-us.

infidel *in*-fuh-dell.
Isaac *Eye*-zuk.
Ishmaelites *Ish*-may-el-ites.
Israelite *Iz*-ray-el-ite.

Jahaziel Juh-*hay*-zuh-el.
Jehoshaphat Jeh-*hosh*-uh-fat.
Jephthah *Jef*-thuh (*th* as in *thin*).
Jericho *Jair*-ih-co.
Jeroboam Jair-uh-*boe*-um.
Jerusalem Juh-*roo*-suh-lem.
Jethro *Jeth*-ro.
Jezebel *Jez*-uh-bel.
Jordan *Jor*-dun.
Josephus Jo-*see*-fus.

Judaea Joo-*dee*-uh.
Judah *Joo*-duh.
Judas Iscariot *Joo*-dus Iss-*care*-ee-ut.
Judea Joo-*dee*-uh.
Julius Caesar *Joo*-lee-us *See*-zer.

Keturah Keh-*too*-ruh.
koinonia *(Greek)* koy-no-*nee*-uh.
Korah *Ko*-rah.

Laish *Lay*-ish.
levirate *leh*-vuh-rut.
Levites *Lee*-vites.
Lydia *Lid*-ee-uh.

Maccabees *Mack*-uh-bees.
Magdalene *Mag*-duh-leen or Mag-duh-*lee*-nee.
Mahlon *Mah*-lon.
Manasseh Muh-*nass*-uh.
Manoah Muh-*no*-uh.
Maon Muh-*own*.
Maonites *May*-on-itz.
Masada Muh-*saw*-duh.
maschil mass-*kill*.
Melchizedek Mel-*kiz*-eh-dek.
Meribah *Mehr*-ih-buh.
Mesopotamians *Mes*-uh-puh-*tay*-me-unz.
Messiah Meh-*sigh*-uh.
messianic mess-ee-*an*-ick.
Methuselah Muh-*thoo*-zuh-luh
Michal *My*-kal.
Midianites *Mid*-ee-un-ites.
Minnith *Min*-ith.
Miriam *Meer*-ee-um.
Moabites *Mo*-ub-ites.
Moabitess *Mo*-ub-*ite*-ess.
Molech *Mo*-lek.
Mosaic Mo-*zay*-ik.
Moses *Mo*-zes or *Mo*-zez.
Mycenaean *My*-suh-*nee*-un.

Naphtali *Naf*-tuh-lye.
Nazareth *Naz*-uh-reth.
Nazarite *Naz*-uh-rite.
Nero *Nee*-row.
Nineveh *Nin*-uh-vuh.

obeisance oh-*bee*-suntz.
Omega O-*may*-guh or O-*mee*-guh.
omnipotent ahm-*nih*-poh-tent.
omnipresent *ahm*-nih-*prez*-ent.
omniscience ahm-*nish*-unts.
omniscient ahm-*nish*-unt.
Orion O-*rye*-un.
Orpah *Or*-pah.
Othniel *Oth*-ni-el.

paganism *pay*-guh-nih-zum.
Paran *Pair*-un.
Patmos *Pat*-muss.
patriarchs *pay*-tree-arks.
Pax Romana *(Latin)* Paks Row-*mah*-nah.
Pentateuch *Pen*-ta-teuk.
Pentecost *Pent*-ih-kost.
Persian *Per*-zhuhn.
Pharaoh *Fair*-o or *Fay*-roe.
Pharez *Fair*-ezz.
Pharisees *Fair*-ih-sees.
Philetus Fuh-*lee*-tus.
Philippi Fih-*lip*-pie or *Fil*-ih-pie.
Philistine Fuh-*liss*-teen or *Fill*-us-teen.
Pilate *Pie*-lut.
Pleiades *Plee*-uh-deez.
Polycarp Paw-lee-*karp*.

rabbis *rab*-eyes.
Rahab *Ray*-hab.
Ramoth *Ray*-muth.
Reubenites *Roo*-ben-ites.
Reuel *Roo*-el.
Rosh Hashanah Rosh Huh-*shu*-nuh.

Sabaoth *Sab*-a-oth.
Sabeans Suh-*be*-unz.
Sadducees *Sad*-you-sees.
Samaria Suh-*mare*-ee-uh.
Sanhedrin *San*-huh-drun or San-*heed*-run.
Seba *See*-buh.
Sebaste Seh-*bas*-tee.
Seir *See*-ir.
Seirath Seh-*eye*-rath.

Selah *(Hebrew)* *See*-luh.
Sennacherib Sen-*nack*-er-ib.
Septuagint Sep-*too*-ih-jent.
sepulchre *sep*-ul-kur.
seraphim *sair*-uh-fim.
Shaddai *(Hebrew)* *Shad*-eye.
shalom *(Hebrew)* shah-*lome*.
Shamgar *Sham*-gar.
Sheol *She*-ol.
Shephelah She-*fuh*-lah.
Shinar *Shye*-nar.
shofar *show*-far.
Silas *Sigh*-luss.
Sinai *Sigh*-nye or *Sigh*-nay-eye.
Solomon *Sol*-o-mun.
synagogue *sin*-uh-gog.
syncretism **sin**-kruh-*tih*-zem.

tabernacle **tah**-burr-*na*-kul.
Tabor *Tay*-ber.
Tamar *Tay*-mer.
Tarot *Ter*-oh.
Tetrach *Teh*-trark or *Tee*-trark.
tetragrammaton teh-truh-*grah*-muh-tawn.
theophany the-*ah*-fuh-nee.
Tigranes Tie-*gran*-us.
Titus *Ty*-tus.
torah *(Hebrew)* *tor*-uh.
tsunami sue-*nah*-me.

Uzziah Uh-*zye*-uh.

whoremongers *hor*-mon-gers (g as in get).

Yahweh *(Hebrew)* *Yah*-weh.

Zabdi *Zab*-dye.
Zebedee *Zeb*-eh-dee.
Zebulun *Zeb*-you-lun.
Zechariah Zek-uh-*rye*-uh.
Zerubbabel Zeh-*rub*-uh-bul.
Zeus Zoose.
Zidonians Zye-*doe*-nee-uns.
Zimri *Zim*-rye.
Ziph *Zif*.
Zipporah Zi-*po*-ruh.
Zorah *Zo*-ruh.

THE INESCAPABLE GOD

Special Features

Lessons

Unit 1: God Reveals

Unit 2: God Sustains

Unit 3: God Protects

QUARTERLY QUIZ

Use these questions as a pretest or as a review. The answers are on page iv of This Quarter in the Word.

Lesson 1

1. What was Jethro's vocation? (tent maker, camel trader, priest?) *Exodus 3:1*

2. The voice from the burning bush told Moses to remove his shoes. T/F. *Exodus 3:5*

Lesson 2

1. In the Ten Commandments, God describes himself as "a jealous God." T/F. *Exodus 20:5*

2. The seventh day of the week is called the _____. *Exodus 20:10*

Lesson 3

1. The people were very patient in waiting for Moses to come down from the mountain. T/F. *Exodus 32:1*

2. What was the main source of gold that Aaron used to make the golden calf? (coins, earrings, idols?) *Exodus 32:2*

Lesson 4

1. The second pair of stone tablets for the Law was made by _____. *Exodus 34:1, 4*

2. At one point, God came down in a cloud and stood with Moses. T/F. *Exodus 34:5*

Lesson 5

1. The psalmist says that God made human beings a little lower than _____. *Psalm 8:5*

2. God made human beings to have dominion over creation. T/F. *Psalm 8:6*

Lesson 6

1. The psalmist says that the law of the Lord is perfect. T/F. *Psalm 19:7*

2. Gold and what else are deemed less desirable than God's law? (health, honey, air?) *Psalm 19:10*

Lesson 7

1. The psalmist says the voice of the Lord has the power to _____ the earth. *Psalm 46:6*

2. The Lord is identified as God of _____, whose other name is "Israel." *Psalm 46:7*

Lesson 8

1. The psalmist pictures God going up in triumph with a _____. *Psalm 47:5*

2. The psalmist recognizes that God is yet to exert His reign over pagans. T/F. *Psalm 47:8*

Lesson 9

1. The psalmist says that the loving-kindness of the Lord is better than _____. *Psalm 63:3*

2. The psalmist pictures his soul as following "hard" after the Lord. T/F. *Psalm 63:8*

Lesson 10

1. The people of Israel were tested like what? (copper, salt, silver?) *Psalm 66:10*

2. Psalm 66 pictures Israel as having been caught in the Lord's net. T/F. *Psalm 66:11*

Lesson 11

1. The psalmist says that a thousand years are as a single tomorrow for the Lord. T/F. *Psalm 90:4*

2. The average life of a human being is said to be how many years? (50, 60, 70?) *Psalm 90:10*

Lesson 12

1. What are the things of night and of day that the psalmist says he has no fear of? (terror/arrow, dark/lion, death/betrayal?) *Psalm 91:5*

2. What does the psalmist say shall be trampled underfoot? (owl, young lion, bear?) *Psalm 91:13*

Lesson 13

1. The psalmist praises the Lord because the psalmist is fearfully and _____ made. *Psalm 139:14*

2. The psalmist asks God to search his heart to see if there is any righteousness in his soul. T/F. *Psalm 139:23, 24*

Quarter at a Glance

by A. Eugene Andrews

WE SEEM TO HAVE a love/hate relationship with the concept of *extreme*. On the one hand, people enjoy "pushing the envelope" in extreme ways. Think of "extreme sports" and "extreme makeovers." On the other hand, to be branded *an extremist* is to be dismissed as a kook or impugned as a terrorist.

But the Bible offers us many positive examples of extremists. The ultimate extremist is, of course, God himself. This series of lessons reveals both the extreme things God does and the extreme nature of His being. We will meet the God who reveals in extreme ways (Unit 1), sustains in extreme ways (Unit 2), and protects in extreme ways (Unit 3). We will see that God is all-powerful, all-knowing, and always present. You can't get any more extreme than that!

Woven within these studies is the challenge for an extreme faith-response by God's people. An encounter with God should make an extreme difference in the way we live. Recognizing truths about God and about ourselves should result in extreme makeovers of our lives. Let us consider how these next 13 weeks can and should cause us to change.

Unit 1: God Reveals

The various false religions of the world try to explain humanity's attempts to find God. The Bible, by contrast, shows us God's attempts to find us. He does this as He reveals His nature, His abilities, and His expectations. We will see all these in this unit's four lessons from Exodus.

These concepts cannot be separated from one another. For example, a key attribute of the nature of God is His *holiness*. This is the basis of His expectation of holiness on our part. This interconnection comes right to the fore in Lesson 1 when Moses is told "Draw not nigh hither: put off thy shoes from off thy feet, for the place whereon thou standest is holy ground" (Exodus 3:5).

Unit 2: God Sustains

God goes further than revealing himself and His expectations. He also makes clear that He is the one who sustains us. The five lessons of this unit focus on psalms that sing of God's majesty, sovereignty, and steadfast love. We are powerless to sustain ourselves, but He is powerful to do so.

Understanding that God is forever, that He has always been and always will be, should cause us to trust in His ability to sustain. He will sustain us to make the lifestyle changes that are necessary to honor Him instead of promoting self. He sustains us so that we can live a life that honors Him. This will (or should) lead to a humbling of self.

Unit 3: God Protects

In the final four lessons of the quarter, we study in the psalms what it means to take refuge in Him. When we acknowledge that the Lord has "been our dwelling place in all generations" (Psalm 90:1), we will encounter the God who loves us and desires to protect and comfort us.

This encounter challenges us to remain true to Him. That happens when our fears and failures give way to faithfulness, when our doubts give way to determination and devotion to the one

> **"Encounters with God are God-sized."**

who protects us in ways that we cannot protect ourselves.

A certain Christian author observes that "Encounters with God are God-sized." When we encounter the God who is always there, the God with all knowledge, the God with all power, it should strike a chord of awe in our lives that leads to extreme worship. This kind of worship focuses solely on the eternal one who is present in our midst.

by Mark S. Krause

Exodus, Lessons 1–4

Exodus is the second of five books in an Old Testament collection called the *Pentateuch* or the *Books of Law.* These five books of Moses were the earliest Scriptures of the nation of Israel. They were already being used long before the rest of the Old Testament was completed. For example, in 2 Kings 14:6 a king is commended for his adherence to a certain commandment "written in the book of the law of Moses."

If we understand the Pentateuch as five connected books, then we are able to gain perspective on the purpose of Exodus. The story of the exodus of the people of Israel from Egypt and their formation into a covenant nation of the Lord God is the primary story of the Old Testament. We might say that when the Pentateuch gets to Exodus 1:1, it has arrived at the story it most wants to tell. The accounts in Genesis lead up to this fact.

The lesson texts from Exodus included in this quarter are among the most important in all the Bible. Exodus 3 relates the calling of Moses and the revelation of God's personal name. Exodus 20 is the giving of the Ten Commandments at Mt. Sinai, a defining act for the nation of Israel. Exodus 32 and 34 tell the horrible story of the unfaithfulness of the people of Israel and how God forgives them and starts over.

Mt. Sinai (also called "Horeb") is a major location for the book of Exodus. It is where Moses sees the burning bush. It is where the law is given. It is where Israel makes and worships the notorious golden calf. Today we are not sure exactly which mountain this is, but

many have identified it as *Jabal Musa*, the mountain towering over Saint Catherine's Monastery in the Sinai Peninsula.

Psalms, Lessons 5–13

There are 150 psalms in the Old Testament's *Book of Psalms.* It is natural for us to try to classify or subdivide this collection in various ways. Traditionally, students of the Bible acknowledge that the psalms fall into five subbooks. Another way to classify the psalms is by author. See the discussions of these classifications on page 43.

Still another way to classify the psalms is by function. One such category is that of *worship,* including psalms written for use in public worship and for private worship by an individual; Psalms 8, 19, 46, 47, and 66 (Lessons 5, 6, 7, 8, and 10, respectively) seem to fit this category. Such psalms contain praise and blessing for God.

Other psalms have a more specific focus of *thanksgiving.* Psalms 63 and 91 (for Lessons 9 and 12, respectively) fit this designation; they have a strong sense of gratefulness for God and His mercies. Still other psalms are *laments,* or cries of complaint to God. These ask for God's grace and help in discouraging times; Psalms 90 and 139 (for Lessons 11 and 13, respectively) are examples of this type.

We acknowledge that such functional categories are not "airtight." For example, Psalm 8 has been called *a creation psalm* in addition to being *a worship psalm.* But no matter the category, all the psalms, in some way, are expressions of our relationship to the Almighty God. Jesus took the psalms seriously (Luke 20:42), and so should we.

THIS QUARTER IN THE WORD

Answers to the Quarterly Quiz on page 2

Lesson 1—1. priest. 2. true. **Lesson 2**—1. true. 2. Sabbath. **Lesson 3**—1. false. 2. earrings. **Lesson 4**—1. Moses. 2. true. **Lesson 5**—1. angels. 2. true. **Lesson 6**—1. true. 2. honey. **Lesson 7**—1. melt. 2. Jacob. **Lesson 8**—1. shout. 2. false. **Lesson 9**—1. life. 2. true. **Lesson 10**—1. silver. 2. true. **Lesson 11**—1. false. 2. 70. **Lesson 12**—1. terror/arrow. 2. young lion. **Lesson 13**—1. wonderfully. 2. false.

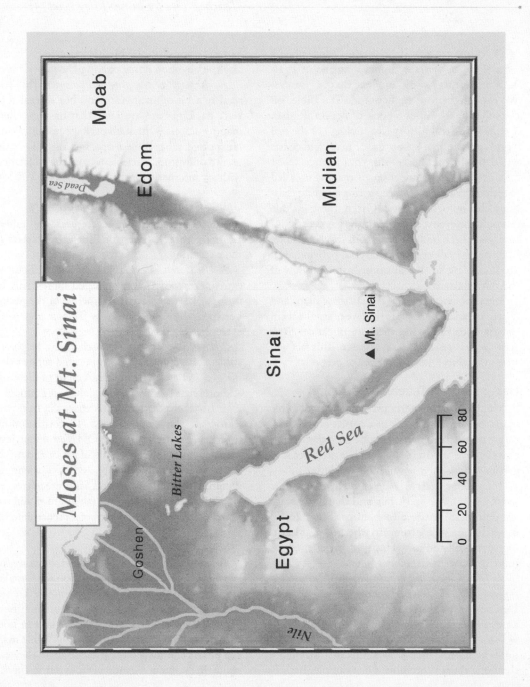

Moses at Mt. Sinai

Moab

Edom

Dead Sea

Midian

Sinai

▲ Mt. Sinai

Red Sea

Bitter Lakes

Goshen

Egypt

Nile

80
60
40
20
0

MAPS AND CHARTS

Teacher Tips by James Riley Estep, Jr.

Stories that start out with "Once upon a time" or perhaps "Long, long ago in a galaxy far, far away" are just that . . . stories. We expect them to be fictional. The Bible, on the other hand, is not a book of fiction. Rather, it reflects the real history (chronology) of the real world (geography). Proper use of maps and charts will drive this fact home with your learners.

Most Bibles include a set of maps. So-called "Study Bibles" may go deeper in providing elaborate chronological charts. Often, these include not only the events recorded in the pages of Scripture, but also parallel events from secular history. The rise and fall of Egypt, Assyria, Babylon, etc., are important to the salvation-historical flow of the Bible narrative.

The problem, however, is that these maps and charts are *so* commonplace that we may take them for granted, forgetting their significance. *Bible events intersect with real-world events!* This fact will strengthen our faith if approached properly.

Using Maps in Teaching Scripture

Many church classrooms have a set of Bible maps. But often it stands in a corner of the classroom untouched. They may be so old and frail that they are almost unusable. Here are three suggestions for using maps in Bible teaching.

1. Use large, colorful maps. I realize that some maps are in black-and-white and that some maps are designed for use on tabletops. But colorful maps that are visible from anywhere in your learning space will add to the learning experience, far more so than small, colorless ones.

2. Identify on the map movements and locations noted in the Bible text as your lesson progresses. Demonstrating the path of the exodus journey is an example. An inexpensive laser pointer works well for doing this. While you're at it, be sure to note the significance of locations that play more than one role in the Bible. For example, Bethle-

hem was not only the birthplace of Jesus, it was also the boyhood home of King David.

3. Use digital mapping technologies. This will require a bit of an investment, but several software packages are available that have excellent map functions. One such package not only contains projectable Bible maps, but also allows the user to draw lines, circle items, and show distances with an automatic display.

Using Charts in Teaching Scripture

Charts include timelines, figures, and tables. Here are three suggestions for using charts in Bible teaching.

1. Use charts to explain. Concepts difficult to explain verbally may be grasped more easily by using a chart to clarify. A timeline of the period between the Old and New Testaments is an example.

2. Use charts to simplify. A chart can help your students comprehend a complicated subject that involves intersecting threads. A chart of the kings and prophets of Israel and Judah is an example.

3. Use charts to organize. A chart can help your learners see how a large mass of information fits together. For example, the Old Testament Jewish calendar is a dizzying mix of major and minor feasts, overlapping religious and civil calendars, unfamiliar month names, and Scripture references. Such information placed in a table of rows and columns will allow "at a glance" comprehension.

Final Thoughts

Good teaching accounts for the fact that we live in a visual age. That's why this lesson series makes available the *Adult Teacher's Convenience Kit* and *Adult Resources* to enhance your teaching; both contain maps, charts, and other visuals in both hard copy and on CD for projection. While maps and charts cannot replace Bible content, they can make that content memorable for your learners.

GOD CALLS
MOSES

BACKGROUND SCRIPTURE: Exodus 3
PRINTED TEXT: Exodus 3:1-6, 13-15

EXODUS 3:1-6, 13-15

1 Now Moses kept the flock of Jethro his father-in-law, the priest of Midian: and he led the flock to the back side of the desert, and came to the mountain of God, even to Horeb.

2 And the angel of the LORD appeared unto him in a flame of fire out of the midst of a bush: and he looked, and, behold, the bush burned with fire, and the bush was not consumed.

3 And Moses said, I will now turn aside, and see this great sight, why the bush is not burnt.

4 And when the LORD saw that he turned aside to see, God called unto him out of the midst of the bush, and said, Moses, Moses. And he said, Here am I.

5 And he said, Draw not nigh hither: put off thy shoes from off thy feet; for the place whereon thou standest is holy ground.

6 Moreover he said, I am the God of thy father, the God of Abraham, the God of Isaac, and the God of Jacob. And Moses hid his face; for he was afraid to look upon God.

. . . .

13 And Moses said unto God, Behold, when I come unto the children of Israel, and shall say unto them, The God of your fathers hath sent me unto you; and they shall say to me, What is his name? what shall I say unto them?

14 And God said unto Moses, I AM THAT I AM: and he said, Thus shalt thou say unto the children of Israel, I AM hath sent me unto you.

15 And God said moreover unto Moses, Thus shalt thou say unto the children of Israel, The LORD God of your fathers, the God of Abraham, the God of Isaac, and the God of Jacob, hath sent me unto you: this is my name for ever, and this is my memorial unto all generations.

KEY VERSE

[God] said, I am the God of thy father, the God of Abraham, the God of Isaac, and the God of Jacob. And Moses hid his face; for he was afraid to look upon God. —**Exodus 3:6**

THE INESCAPABLE GOD

Unit 1: God Reveals

LESSON AIMS

After participating in this lesson, each student will be able to:

1. Summarize God's call of Moses and Moses' response.

2. Explain why it is important to serve God on His terms, not ours.

3. Identify one area where he or she is resisting God's leading, and write a prayer of acceptance for that call.

LESSON OUTLINE

Introduction

A. Getting Reacquainted

In 1999, Vern Jones was living alone at the Fort Washington Hotel in Cincinnati, Ohio. One particular Sunday, he found himself surrounded by a family he had forgotten. Jones, who had been living in the single-room occupancy hotel for nine years, was "discovered" by his family. They saw his picture on the front page of the *Cincinnati Enquirer* newspaper in an article about a possible sale of the hotel. They had not seen him in 31 years!

Jones, age 63 at the time the article appeared, had disappeared from his family's life some three decades earlier after he divorced his wife. Then he had suffered a stroke and lost some of his memory. One of his daughters, who was only age 3 at the time she lost contact with her father, was quite overwhelmed by this unexpected news.

This kind of reunion is quite touching to read about. So also is the record of the "reunion" between God and His people described in the book of Exodus, as He provided a dramatic deliverance from bondage to freedom. This is not to say that God had somehow lost contact with His people in Egypt. But 400 years of bondage had no doubt caused many Israelites to give up hope, wondering whether the God of their fathers had disowned them (compare Judges 6:13).

That time period, however, had been noted by God himself to Abraham (Genesis 15:13, 14). The God of whom David said "My times are in thy hand" (Psalm 31:15) had the times of His people in His hand as well.

B. Lesson Background

The lessons to be studied through the month of September will emphasize the theme *God Reveals*. That God reveals himself to humanity is one of the most pivotal doctrines of the entire Bible. It has often been pointed out that the Bible is not a record of humanity's attempts to find God. It is, rather, God's revelation of himself to humanity. It is a revelation of His desire to enter into a relationship with those created in His image, even though people are often rebellious and more concerned

God Calls Moses

with pursuing their own agendas than God's. As today's lesson will show, Moses was a prime example of such an attitude.

From the start of the account of his life, it appears that Moses was destined for greatness in being spared from Pharaoh's murderous edict and raised by Pharaoh's own daughter. Acts 7:22 tells us, "Moses was learned in all the wisdom of the Egyptians, and was mighty in words and in deeds."

At the age of 40, Moses came upon an Israelite being mistreated by an Egyptian. He killed the Egyptian, thinking by doing so that "his brethren would have understood how that God by his hand would deliver them; but they understood not" (Acts 7:25). The next day, when Moses saw two Israelites fighting and tried to be a peacemaker, he was chastised by one of the Israelites who angrily asked him, "Who made thee a ruler and a judge over us? Wilt thou kill me, as thou diddest the Egyptian yesterday?" (vv. 27, 28).

Moses then fled to Midian, where he stayed for 40 years (Acts 7:30). This is where we find him at the beginning of our printed text for today. More important than Moses' location geographically, however, was where he was spiritually. Perhaps he had resigned himself to the fact that he had mistaken his calling. Exodus 2:21, 22 tells us that he married while in Midian and named his firstborn son Gershom (meaning "an alien there") declaring, "I have been a stranger in a strange land."

HOW TO SAY IT

Abraham	*Ay*-bruh-ham.
Canaan	*Kay*-nun.
Gershom	*Gur*-shom.
Horeb	*Ho*-reb.
Jethro	*Jeth*-ro.
Keturah	Keh-*too*-ruh.
Malachi	*Mal*-uh-kye.
Midian	*Mid*-ee-un.
Moses	*Mo*-zes or *Mo*-zez.
patriarchs	*pay*-tree-arks.
Reuel	*Roo*-el.
Sinai	*Sigh*-nye or *Sigh*-nay-eye.
Zipporah	Zi-*po*-ruh.

But Moses had not mistaken his calling—only the timing of it. That had to be God's and God's alone.

I. Sight of a Bush
(Exodus 3:1-3)
A. God's Man at Work (v. 1)

1. Now Moses kept the flock of Jethro his father-in-law, the priest of Midian: and he led the flock to the back side of the desert, and came to the mountain of God, even to Horeb.

At this point Moses has taken on the responsibility of tending *the flock of Jethro his father-in-law.* Not long after Moses had first arrived in Midian, he had come to the aid of Jethro's seven daughters. They were drawing water from a well for their flocks but were being harassed by some other shepherds (Exodus 2:16, 17). Moses married Zipporah, one of Jethro's daughters, and he began to learn the shepherd's task. (Moses probably figured there were few other options left for him.)

What Do You Think?
If you're married, how have you seen God at work in your relationship with your in-laws?
Talking Points for Your Discussion
- Genesis 38; Exodus 18; Judges 19:1-10; Ruth; Luke 12:53
- Marrying not just a person, but "into a family"
- Sitcom depictions of relationships with in-laws: a grain of truth?
- We, or our in-laws, may have accepted Christ or grown as Christians through our relationship.

Jethro is also given the name Reuel in Exodus 2:18. Some suggest that Reuel (meaning "friend of God") is this man's given name, while Jethro (meaning something like "his excellency") may be a title. The nature of Jethro's priesthood is something of a mystery, since the Bible does not specifically say that he is a priest of the Lord, only *the priest of Midian.*

Midian was named after one of the sons of Abraham born to him through Keturah, whom he married following Sarah's death (Genesis 25:1,

2). Whether Abraham's faith in the true God was eventually passed on to the Midianites or how many of them embraced it is difficult to know. In Jethro's case, he may worship the true God alongside other gods, for later he will declare "Now I know that the Lord is greater than all gods" (Exodus 18:11) after he learns of what the Lord has done for the Israelites.

The territory covered by Midian is a vast desert area. Often a shepherd has to travel for some time before coming to an area sufficient for grazing the flock. As Moses tends Jethro's flock, he leads them *to the back* (more distant) *side of the desert* and to *Horeb*, the *mountain of God.*

Theories about Horeb are that it is either (1) another name for Mount Sinai, (2) another peak in the Sinai Peninsula, or (3) the designation for an entire range of mountains, with Mount Sinai designating a specific mountain. (Compare Exodus 33:6; Deuteronomy 1:6.) Horeb may be called *the mountain of God* because God speaks to Moses and later gives His law there; or perhaps the Midianites have given the mountain that name for reasons unknown to us.

B. God's Messenger at Work (vv. 2, 3)

2. And the angel of the Lord appeared unto him in a flame of fire out of the midst of a bush: and he looked, and, behold, the bush burned with fire, and the bush was not consumed.

Visual for Lesson 1. *Keep this map posted for the first four lessons of the quarter. This will help your learners keep a geographical perspective.*

There is also a bit of mystery surrounding the identity of *the angel of the Lord*. In this passage, there seems to be little distinction between the angel and the Lord himself as verse 4 indicates, and that close relationship must be respected. Some propose that the angel of the Lord is a preincarnate appearance of Jesus.

That something supernatural is occurring before Moses is clear from the sight of a *bush* that burns but is *not consumed.* Moses and the Israelites will witness a far greater fiery presence when they come to Mount Sinai following the exodus (Exodus 19:16-18).

Some students attach a symbolic meaning to the burning bush, seeing the fire to represent the affliction of God's people in Egypt (compare Deuteronomy 4:20; 1 Kings 8:51; Jeremiah 11:1-4). They note the imagery of fire to signify affliction in Psalm 66:10-12. Just as the bush is not consumed by the fire, God's people are not consumed or destroyed by their Egyptian oppressors. God intends to carry out His holy purpose for them. Such a symbolic meaning, however, is not specifically affirmed in the Scriptures.

What Do You Think?
How do we evaluate claims of God's encountering people today?
Talking Points for Your Discussion
- Regarding claims of miracles
- Regarding claims of "being led" to do something
- Regarding near-death experiences

3. And Moses said, I will now turn aside, and see this great sight, why the bush is not burnt.

Naturally Moses is curious as to the nature of the *great sight* before him. A closer look at the *bush* is certainly warranted.

❧ GETTING OUR ATTENTION ❧

Fire has a way of getting our attention, doesn't it? That seems particularly true for highly destructive fires. People sit in stunned silence as they watch TV reports of wildfires destroying thousands of square miles of forest. Occasionally, a city will suffer the tragic loss of a historic building to

God Calls Moses

fire. It's painful to watch, and yet we can't look away. Fire is destructive, but it is also fascinating.

Moses demonstrated the natural human reaction when he turned aside to see the burning bush. But it was not the fire itself or the fire's destructive nature that got his attention. Rather, it was the fact that the fire was *nondestructive* that piqued his curiosity. That's just not what one expects of fire!

We serve a God who acts in unexpected ways. Moses discovered that, as did many who came after him. Think of Gideon, Daniel, and Paul. When God acts in an unexpected way in your life, will He have your undivided attention?

—C. R. B.

II. Sound of a Voice
(EXODUS 3:4-6)
A. Calling Moses' Name (v. 4)

4. And when the LORD saw that he turned aside to see, God called unto him out of the midst of the bush, and said, Moses, Moses. And he said, Here am I.

The unusual sight of a burning (yet unconsumed) bush is now followed by unexpected words: Moses hears his name called from *out of the midst of the bush*. What a shock this must be! No doubt with some uncertainty, Moses answers *Here am I.* It is the first time that the Lord will speak to Moses, though it will not be the last.

B. Commanding Moses (v. 5)

5. And he said, Draw not nigh hither: put off thy shoes from off thy feet; for the place whereon thou standest is holy ground.

To remove one's shoes expresses humility or reverence. Joshua, Moses' successor, will be told to do the same in Joshua 5:13-15. Moses' action is recounted in Acts 7:33.

C. Confirming the Speaker (v. 6)

6. Moreover he said, I am the God of thy father, the God of Abraham, the God of Isaac, and the God of Jacob. And Moses hid his face; for he was afraid to look upon God.

By referring to himself as *the God of thy father, the God of Abraham, the God of Isaac, and the God*

of Jacob, God establishes His ties with Moses' ancestors. Abraham has been dead for over 500 years at this point. Both Abraham's son Isaac and Isaac's son Jacob have been dead over 400 years. We recall that Levi was one of Jacob's 12 sons, and Exodus 2:1, 2 establishes that Moses is descended from that tribe. God has initiated a special relationship with Moses' ancestors, whom we often call *the patriarchs.*

Exodus 2:24 says that God "remembered his covenant" with Abraham, Isaac, and Jacob. The word *remembered* in a passage such as that suggests that God is about to act in fulfillment of a promise He has made. He had promised to Abraham, Isaac, and Jacob that He would give their descendants the land of Canaan as their home. He had revealed to Abraham that this would occur only after 400 years of enslavement (Genesis 15:13). The time for fulfilling that promise has come!

> **What Do You Think?**
> What do you appreciate most about your family's faith heritage?
> *Talking Points for Your Discussion*
> - An ancestor who was a spiritual anchor for the family
> - Lessons from blessings and tragedies
> - The legacy of godly or ungodly family values

Of course, Moses likely is thinking about none of this at this point. He is too awestruck by the sight and sound before him to make any of those connections to history just yet. All he can do is hide his face, for he is aware enough of who God is that he is *afraid to look upon* Him (compare Genesis 32:30).

In verses 7-12 (not in today's printed text), God assures Moses that He is indeed aware of His people's suffering in Egypt. He tells Moses that He has "come down" (v. 8) to help them. Perhaps Moses takes heart at hearing such an announcement. But the Lord's words to him in verse 10 likely deflate whatever sense of hope he possesses to that point: "Come now therefore, and I will send thee unto Pharaoh, that thou mayest bring forth my people the children of Israel out of Egypt."

III. Supremacy of God
(Exodus 3:13-15)
A. Moses' Reservation (v. 13)

13. And Moses said unto God, Behold, when I come unto the children of Israel, and shall say unto them, The God of your fathers hath sent me unto you; and they shall say to me, What is his name? what shall I say unto them?

Verse 11 (not in today's text) presents Moses' first objection to God's plan with the question, "Who am I?" Moses' second objection, in the text before us, can be summarized by the question, "Who are You?" Moses believes that the *children of Israel* will want to know the specific identity of the God whom Moses will say has spoken to him.

Most of the people will understand that the fathers include Abraham, Isaac, and Jacob. But the people have been in bondage in a foreign land for 400 years. Many probably have lost touch with their spiritual roots. Whatever deity these people believe in seems to have forgotten them and left them to languish in their misery. For a desert shepherd to show up out of nowhere with a claim to have a word from on high undoubtedly will be a bit much to many!

B. God's Revelation (vv. 14, 15)

14. And God said unto Moses, I AM THAT I AM: and he said, Thus shalt thou say unto the children of Israel, I AM hath sent me unto you.

God's revelation of himself to Moses as *I Am That I Am* is one of the simplest yet most profound descriptions of Him in the Bible. Essentially this phrase expresses the self-existence of God; He simply *is*. In other words, there has never been a time when God did not exist; and there will never be a time when He does not exist—a concept that is beyond the finite human mind's ability to grasp. The name may also call attention to God's unchanging nature (Malachi 3:6).

Some have suggested alternative meanings of the Hebrew word rendered as *I Am,* including "I will be what I will be." This idea highlights how God reveals himself "at sundry times and in divers manners" (Hebrews 1:1). But in light of Jesus' frequent use of the phrase "I Am," the previous understanding is probably the most acceptable. Jesus' use of the term is likely meant to echo its use by God and is part of Jesus' "making himself equal with God" (John 5:18).

> **What Do You Think?**
> How can we be encouraged by God's self-description *I Am*?
> *Talking Points for Your Discussion*
> - Look up the definition of the rare word *aseity*
> - Contrast God's *I Am* with the various ways culture uses *I am* (song lyrics, etc.)

15. And God said moreover unto Moses, Thus shalt thou say unto the children of Israel, The LORD God of your fathers, the God of Abraham, the God of Isaac, and the God of Jacob, hath sent me unto you: this is my name for ever, and this is my memorial unto all generations.

The name *the Lord* is actually the third person form of the Hebrew verb translated "I Am" in the previous verse. Thus the meaning is "He is," since this will be spoken about the Lord by Moses to the people instead of being spoken by the Lord about himself. In Hebrew, the name is spelled with four consonants that are usually rendered in English as YHWH. Since ancient Hebrew does not have written vowels, we cannot be sure of how the name should be pronounced. Some suggest it should be pronounced *Yahweh*. In many English editions of the Bible, the name is printed as LORD, in small capital letters.

The Lord then describes himself as He did earlier: as *the God of Abraham, the God of Isaac, and the God of Jacob* (v. 6). Here He uses the phrase *God of your fathers* (plural), rather than "God of thy father" (singular), as He had with Moses (again, v. 6). Earlier God was referring to Moses' personal heritage; in the verse before us He is describing the heritage of all the Israelites.

Twice in verses 14, 15 God mentions sending Moses to *the children of Israel.* Previously Moses had acted as a deliverer, or so he thought, when he killed an Egyptian. But Moses was not acting as a sent person at that time. Only as one truly sent by God, acting according to God's plan and timing, can Moses fulfill what he is being called to do.

God also instructs Moses to tell the Israelites that the name of the Lord ("He is") *is my name for ever* and is His *memorial unto all generations.* Every generation of Israelites is to accept the Lord as He reveals himself to Moses, for He will be no less their God than He is to any other generation of Israelites. As noted earlier, the use of the phrase *I Am* by Jesus makes that name significant for Christians of any and every time and place. We come to know that Jesus Christ is Lord (Acts 2:36; 10:36) and that He is "the same yesterday, and to day, and for ever" (Hebrews 13:8).

What Do You Think?

In what ways can you help ensure that God's name is a memorial to future generations?

Talking Points for Your Discussion
- Family Life
- Church involvement
- Missions support
- Prayer

❧ CORRECT IDENTITY ❧

At least eight million Americans are victims of identity theft each year. Annual losses run into the billions of dollars. The personal cost in time and money for "rescuing" one's stolen identity can itself be quite steep. According to the Federal Trade Commission's *2006 Identity Theft Survey Report,* 10 percent of identity-theft victims incurred costs of $1,200 or more in attempting to correct the misuse of their identities.

One's identity can be stolen in many ways. Typical methods include "dumpster diving" to find personal information, stealing credit card numbers with cell phone cameras in checkout lines, and "phishing" (which involves using e-mail to fool people into revealing personal data).

Identity fraud is common in the spiritual realm also (2 Corinthians 11:13-15). But God absolutely will not allow His identity to be hijacked! God knows us by name (John 10:3), and He expects us to know Him by name as well. When people observe our speech and actions, they should be able to identify the divine source correctly. Do they?
—C. R. B.

Conclusion
A. Getting Educated

Stephen described Moses as "learned in all the wisdom of the Egyptians" (Acts 7:22). Moses likely became quite a scholar in his day. As the son of Pharaoh's daughter, he was a prince in the royal court with great possibilities ahead of him.

Yet there were certain vital lessons that not even the wisdom of the Egyptians could teach Moses. This is not to downplay formal education; it is simply to acknowledge that formal education has its limitations in one's spiritual development. As educated as Moses was in the culture of his time, he seems to have been that ignorant in regard to spiritual matters. Stephen also pointed out that when Moses killed the Egyptian who was mistreating one of the Hebrews, he firmly believed that his countrymen would recognize him as their hero and fall in step behind his leadership. This highly educated man was badly mistaken in that regard.

It would take another 40 years of watching sheep in the desert country before Moses was deemed "educated enough" by the Lord for the task of being a deliverer. By then Moses had learned that the one who believes himself unworthy of being used by God is really in the best position to be shaped and molded toward His holy purpose. Regardless of one's level of formal education, this is probably the toughest "school" of all!

B. Prayer

Father, we admit that we are not very good at waiting. Help us to trust You to accomplish Your good purpose in us, to complete in us what You have begun. We pray in Jesus' name. Amen.

C. Thought to Remember

God's work is best done in His way and timing.

VISUALS FOR THESE LESSONS

The visual pictured in each lesson (example: page 12) is a small reproduction of a large, full-color poster included in the *Adult Resources* packet for the Fall Quarter. That packet also contains the very useful *Presentation Helps* on a CD for teacher use. Order No. 020019210 from your supplier.

INVOLVEMENT LEARNING

Some of the activities below are also found in the helpful student book, Adult Bible Class.
Don't forget to download the free reproducible page from www.standardlesson.com to enhance your lesson!

Into the Lesson

Distribute copies of the Called by Name activity from the reproducible page for learners to work on as they arrive. (This page is available as a free download at www.standardlesson.com and it is on the *Adult Resources Presentation Helps* CD.)

Next, distribute handouts of the following true-false quiz. 1. Moses was extremely familiar with the pagan and idolatrous worldview of the Egyptians. 2. Moses committed murder. 3. Moses was reluctant to submit to God's will. 4. Moses was age 80 years before he took on his ultimate leadership role for God's purposes. 5. Moses was reared from infancy in a privileged environment, at least partly. 6. Moses sinned against God on occasion. 7. Moses was buried in an unmarked and unknown grave. *[Answers: 1. true, Acts 7:22; 2. true, Exodus 2:11, 12; 3. true, Exodus 3:11, 13; 4:1, 10, 13; 4. true, Acts 7:23, 30; 5. true, Exodus 2:1-10; 6. true; for example, Numbers 20:12; 7. true; Deuteronomy 34:1-6.]*

The class will soon notice the pattern that all are true. That will serve as a lead-in for this affirmation: "All these are true of Moses, and yet God saw in him the potential for leadership of His people at a pivotal time in His redemptive plan."

You may wish to stop and discuss the implications of these truths about Moses for your own class. For example, old age does not necessarily prohibit one from leading; being reared in an ungodly household and culture does not determine one's destiny; hesitancy is not refusal; sin is forgivable; etc. You may wish to come back to these truths about Moses for an Into Life discussion regarding the Like Moses? activity there.

Into the Word

Assign each learner a verse of today's text. Since there are nine verses, repeat the verse assignments if you have fewer than nine students, or assign more than one verse per student if you have fewer than nine. Say, "I'm going to ask a series of ques-

tions. If your verse will answer it, jump right in and read it aloud."

The expected responses are in italics following the questions, so make sure you don't read those aloud. The questions are given in random order, although some teachers may prefer to give them in the order that the answers occur in the text. Add any questions you choose that can be answered by the reading of a verse.

1. What words did God use to get Moses' attention? *[v. 4]* 2. Before Moses agreed to confront the children of Israel with God's plan, what question did he anticipate their asking? *[v. 13]* 3. In what manner did the angel of the Lord appear to Moses? *[v. 2]* 4. What human characteristic did Moses exhibit when he first saw the burning bush? *[v. 3]* 5. What were Moses' first words when God called him? *[v. 4]* 6. In what way did the miracle of the burning bush set aside the laws of nature? *[v. 2]* 7. What simple act was Moses commanded to do when he neared the bush? *[v. 5]* 8. Why was Moses commanded to take off his shoes? *[v. 5]* 9. What was Moses doing when God first spoke to him? *[v. 1]* 10. Whose names did God use in identifying himself to Moses? *[v. 6]* 11. What natural reaction did Moses make to God's identification of himself? *[v. 6]* 12. What name did God tell Moses to use for Him? *[v. 14]* 13. What other designation, in addition to "I Am," was Moses to use to identify God to the Israelites? *[v. 15]* 14. Other than sheep owner, what was Jethro's position? *[v. 1]*

After (or as) the questions are answered, introduce the commentary ideas of the lesson writer. Make sure to include the notes in the Introduction and Lesson Background as appropriate.

Into Life

Distribute copies of either the Like Moses? or Which Way Will You Go? activities from the reproducible page. Open a time of voluntary sharing after learners complete the exercise.

God Calls Moses

GOD MAKES A COVENANT WITH ISRAEL

BACKGROUND SCRIPTURE: **Exodus 20**

PRINTED TEXT: **Exodus 20:1-11**

EXODUS 20:1-11

1 And God spake all these words, saying,

2 I am the LORD thy God, which have brought thee out of the land of Egypt, out of the house of bondage.

3 Thou shalt have no other gods before me.

4 Thou shalt not make unto thee any graven image, or any likeness of any thing that is in heaven above, or that is in the earth beneath, or that is in the water under the earth.

5 Thou shalt not bow down thyself to them, nor serve them: for I the LORD thy God am a jealous God, visiting the iniquity of the fathers upon the children unto the third and fourth generation of them that hate me;

6 And shewing mercy unto thousands of them that love me, and keep my commandments.

7 Thou shalt not take the name of the LORD thy God in vain: for the LORD will not hold him guiltless that taketh his name in vain.

8 Remember the sabbath day, to keep it holy.

9 Six days shalt thou labour, and do all thy work:

10 But the seventh day is the sabbath of the LORD thy God: in it thou shalt not do any work, thou, nor thy son, nor thy daughter, thy manservant, nor thy maidservant, nor thy cattle, nor thy stranger that is within thy gates:

11 For in six days the LORD made heaven and earth, the sea, and all that in them is, and rested the seventh day: wherefore the LORD blessed the sabbath day, and hallowed it.

KEY VERSE

I am the LORD thy God, which have brought thee out of the land of Egypt, out of the house of bondage. Thou shalt have no other gods before me. —**Exodus 20:2, 3**

THE INESCAPABLE GOD

Unit 1: God Reveals

LESSONS 1–4

LESSON AIMS

After participating in this lesson, each student will be able to:

1. Recite or paraphrase the first four of the Ten Commandments.

2. Compare and contrast the ethic of the Ten Commandments with the ethic that seems to drive society today.

3. Measure his or her life against the standard of the Ten Commandments and determine one specific change that he or she will make in the coming week.

LESSON OUTLINE

Introduction
    A. Life with Limits
    B. Lesson Background
 I. God's Truths (Exodus 20:1, 2)
    A. He Speaks (v. 1)
    B. He Acts (v. 2)
II. Humans' Response (Exodus 20:3-11)
    A. Recognizing His Uniqueness (v. 3)
    B. Respecting Him in Worship (vv. 4-6)
      Worship Enhancements or Distractions?
    C. Revering His Name (v. 7)
    D. Remembering His Day (vv. 8-11)
      Blue Laws
Conclusion
    A. Respect the Law
    B. Prayer
    C. Thought to Remember

Introduction

A. Life with Limits

In June of 2008, my wife and I took a trip to a state park not far from our home. We hiked over several trails and saw various caves and waterfalls. At one of the waterfalls was a stand with a plaque attached to it. Part of the message warned hikers not to wade or swim in the streams or climb on any of the rocks or ledges. "We love to see everyone having a great time," the words continued, "but please use caution when hiking these rugged areas. Stay on the trails at all times so that we may maintain these areas for generations to come." The implied message was that a "great time" is possible only when the trail boundaries are respected.

Acknowledging the existence of "trails" and limits is important to living a satisfying, fulfilling life that is free from the heartaches that result from ignoring such limits. This is true whether the topic is hiking a trail, driving a car, playing a sport, or making moral decisions.

Under the leadership of Moses, the Israelites were set free from 400 years of bondage in Egypt. But what did that freedom mean for them? How were they to exercise it? Some three months after the exodus, God brought the people to Mount Sinai. There He gave them His laws. Were the Israelites being ushered into another kind of bondage by being told how they had to live from day to day? Some who see any kind of moral restriction or limit as confining might say *yes*. However, learning to obey God is not the pathway to bondage. It is the "trail" to true freedom.

B. Lesson Background

Following their dramatic deliverance from Egypt, the Israelites were led by Moses to Mount Sinai. That accorded with the "token" or sign that God had provided to Moses when He first spoke to him from the burning bush (Exodus 3:12). Traditionally the location of Mount Sinai is believed to be at the southern end of the Sinai Peninsula.

A primary purpose for taking the people to such a setting seems to have been to provide a kind of "retreat" environment. There God's people could be separated from distractions and could focus on

God Makes a Covenant with Israel

what He had to say. (Even so, as we will see in next week's study, such a setting did not guarantee that sin would not wreak havoc among the people.)

Exodus 19:1 tells us it was in the third month following the exodus that the Israelites arrived at Mount Sinai. Moses went up the mountain, where God gave him a message to relay to the people. That included His desire to establish a special covenant with them (vv. 5, 6). When Moses returned and delivered the message, the people responded with the promise "All that the Lord hath spoken we will do" (v. 8).

Then Moses again climbed the mountain, and the Lord told him that He himself would come to the people. The Lord gave special instructions as to how the people must prepare for such a sacred occasion—instructions which Moses relayed to the people (Exodus 19:9-15). On the third day after the Lord had spoken to Moses (vv. 10, 11), the people witnessed a spectacular display of both sights and sounds, indicating God's mighty presence on the mountain.

God then spoke to Moses and commanded him to climb to the top of the mountain. As Moses began to ascend, God sent him back to the people to warn them not to go beyond the barrier that had been set at the foot of the mountain. Moses came down and conveyed this message. At this point, it appears that the Lord himself spoke to the people the Ten Commandments; for after the commandments were given, the people begged for only Moses to speak to them (Exodus 20:19; see also Deuteronomy 4:12, 13). Thus Moses was also listening as God issued the commandments. This was appropriate, for he was as responsible to obey them as any other Israelite.

HOW TO SAY IT

Aaron	*Air*-un.
Byzantine	*Bih*-zen-teen (*i* as in *tip*).
Deuteronomy	Due-ter-*ahn*-uh-me.
Egypt	*Ee*-jipt.
Ezekiel	Ee-*zeek*-ee-ul or Ee-*zeek*-yul.
Israelites	*Iz*-ray-el-ites.
Moses	*Mo*-zes or *Mo*-zez.
Sinai	*Sigh*-nye or *Sigh*-nay-eye.

I. God's Truths
(Exodus 20:1, 2)
A. He Speaks (v. 1)
1. And God spake all these words, saying.

The Ten Commandments, as we refer to them, are mentioned in the Hebrew text of Exodus 34:28 and Deuteronomy 4:13 as literally the "ten words." Here the source of these words is made clear: *God spake all these words.* The Ten Commandments do not reflect man-made opinions about human conduct; they are, rather, the instructions of our loving Creator, who knows what is necessary in order for us to live life to the fullest.

B. He Acts (v. 2)
2. I am the LORD thy God, which have brought thee out of the land of Egypt, out of the house of bondage.

Before God gives the Ten Commandments, He establishes His authority to give those rules: *I am the Lord thy God, which have brought thee out of the land of Egypt.* God's powerful actions establish the powerful authority of His words. It is sadly ironic that when Aaron and the people construct the golden calf while Moses is on the mountain, God's mighty act of delivering His people from bondage is attributed to the calf (Exodus 32:4, 8)!

What Do You Think?
What are some popular false gods of our society? How do we resist the urge to "bow down" to these?
Talking Points for Your Discussion
- Things that secular advertising promotes
- Deities that various religions promote
- 1 Corinthians 1:12, 13; Colossians 2:18

II. Humans' Response
(Exodus 20:3-11)
A. Recognizing His Uniqueness (v. 3)
3. Thou shalt have no other gods before me.

Our allegiance must be directed toward only one God—the true God. Other gods are mentioned not because they exist, but because the idea of worshiping them will be a temptation to God's people (a temptation to which they will yield all too frequently). Because God alone is "I Am" (Exodus 3:14), any other supposed god or goddess automatically "is not" (compare Jeremiah 2:11).

B. Respecting Him in Worship (vv. 4-6)

4. Thou shalt not make unto thee any graven image, or any likeness of any thing that is in heaven above, or that is in the earth beneath, or that is in the water under the earth.

This commandment concerns the "how" of worship: God is not to be represented by *any likeness* of any being anywhere in the created world. Thus idolatry is forbidden. As Moses later will recall when addressing the Israelites on the verge of entering the promised land, "The Lord spake unto you out of the midst of the fire: ye heard the voice of the words, but saw no similitude; only ye heard a voice" (Deuteronomy 4:12). God reveals himself to the Israelites primarily through His Word; to construct an idol is to draw the people's focus away from that Word.

> **What Do You Think?**
> Does this commandment forbid the use of religious art in worship? Why, or why not?
> *Talking Points for Your Discussion*
> - Exodus 37:7-9; Numbers 21:4-9; 2 Kings 18:4; Acts 17:23
> - Distinction between an "aid to worship" and an "object of worship"
> - Relevance of distinction between two-dimensional and three-dimensional art

❧ WORSHIP ENHANCEMENTS OR DISTRACTIONS? ❧

Christian history certainly has seen its share of controversy over the use of religious imagery! In AD 726, Leo III, emperor of the Byzantine Empire, ordered that the image of Christ be removed from a gate of his palace. Decades of debate ensued, and in AD 787 the Council of Nicaea sanctioned the use of religious art "in painting and mosaic as of other fit materials." Attendees condemned those who did not hold their viewpoint.

But the controversy did not go away. For example, in 1643–44 William Dowsing, an ardent Christian, became (in)famous for his path of destruction involving dozens of church buildings in England. His original commission from Parliament of August 1643 (later expanded) authorized him to destroy "all Monuments of Superstition and Idolatry," to include "fixed altars, altar rails, chancel steps, crucifixes, crosses, images of the Virgin Mary and pictures of saints or superstitious inscriptions." He did so with great zeal.

Today, all this is pretty much a nonissue. Crosses and stained glass are common in church buildings. Objects of idolatry today are likely to be more abstract: the desire for fame, fortune, etc. How do we guard ourselves? —C. R. B.

5. Thou shalt not bow down thyself to them, nor serve them: for I the LORD thy God am a jealous God, visiting the iniquity of the fathers upon the children unto the third and fourth generation of them that hate me.

Some of the Ten Commandments are simply stated, with no additional comments. With this commandment, however, the Lord adds a statement of why He does not want His people to bow down to or serve any images or idols: it is because *I the Lord thy God am a jealous God.*

Jealousy is usually considered a negative quality, so how can it be descriptive of God's character? Here jealousy is used in a positive manner to describe the high degree of God's love and concern for His people. God desires the allegiance of His people to Him and to no other gods. This is not for selfish reasons (which we often associate with jealousy), but because He knows that this kind of allegiance is best for His people.

So seriously does God take the violation of this commandment that He punishes *the iniquity of the fathers upon the children unto the third and fourth generation of them that hate me.* At first glance, this seems to contradict other Scriptures that stress individual responsibility for sin (example: Ezekiel 18:4-20). Perhaps the best way to understand the verse before us is to consider the impact of sinful behavior on succeeding generations. A person who is thrown in jail for a crime is the one whom the law is punishing, but the children suffer too when the family breadwinner is absent.

God Makes a Covenant with Israel

By including this particular warning with this commandment, God may be challenging His people to think about the long-term consequences of embracing idolatrous practices. Those practices will affect not only the ones engaging in them, but also will have a bearing on future generations. The Babylonian captivity will result in punishment of the guilty, but also will affect negatively their offspring who are born into that captivity.

A pattern of sinful behavior need not be repeated by succeeding generations. Any individual at any point can choose a different course of action. He or she can begin a pattern of obedience to God. That pattern produces a far more positive and beneficial legacy, which is described in the next verse.

> *What Do You Think?*
> What cycles of intergenerational sin do we need to break? How do we do that?
> *Talking Points for Your Discussion*
> - Societal legacies (racism, class distinctions)
> - Family legacies (alcoholism, spousal abuse)
> - Personally "owning" the sin (Nehemiah 1:5-7)

6. And shewing mercy unto thousands of them that love me, and keep my commandments.

The use of the word *thousands* points to the bountiful nature of God's love. His earnest desire is always to demonstrate His love, not His judgment. Ezekiel 18:32 says this well: "For I have no pleasure in the death of him that dieth, saith the Lord GOD: wherefore turn yourselves, and live ye."

C. Revering His Name (v. 7)

7. Thou shalt not take the name of the LORD thy God in vain: for the LORD will not hold him guiltless that taketh his name in vain.

This commandment deals with another facet of reverence for God: how we talk about Him. The Hebrew word translated *in vain* is actually the source of the word *schwa,* which describes a lightly pronounced vowel in a word (for example, the letter *a* in the word *balloon*). The term refers to taking God's name lightly, which can be done through profanity or cursing but is certainly not limited to that.

For the Israelites, this commandment may also prohibit using God's name in ways in which the pagans use the names of their deities—to cause harm to others (by casting spells, for example) or to try to manipulate Him to comply with their wishes. Any time the Lord's name is used casually or carelessly with little or no reverence in mind constitutes a violation of this commandment. Examples are the oft-heard exclamation "Oh, my God!" and its shortened version "OMG."

> *What Do You Think?*
> How can we ensure that we are not taking the name of God lightly?
> *Talking Points for Your Discussion*
> - How we use God's name in prayer
> - How we use God's Word to instruct others

D. Remembering His Day (vv. 8-11)

8. Remember the sabbath day, to keep it holy.

In this commandment, God designates the seventh day of the week (our Saturday) as the *Sabbath,* a word meaning "rest." God had prepared the people for this observance in His instructions on how to collect manna (Exodus 16:21-23).

9. Six days shalt thou labour, and do all thy work.

The regulations concerning this commandment must be understood in light of ancient Israel's being an agricultural society rather than a modern industrialized one. As any farmer will attest, farming is truly a full-time activity. It is easy to justify working every day because there is always some job or task that needs to be addressed.

Time is a gift from God. Like all of His other gifts, it must be used according to the giver's guidelines in order to be enjoyed to the fullest extent. The commandment recognizes that work is also a gift of God, but it must be balanced by an appropriate time of rest.

10. But the seventh day is the sabbath of the LORD thy God: in it thou shalt not do any work, thou, nor thy son, nor thy daughter, thy manservant, nor thy maidservant, nor thy cattle, nor thy stranger that is within thy gates.

ONE HOLY GOD

Visual for Lesson 2. Point to this visual as you discuss the concept of holiness as it relates to God and each of His commandments.

Here the scope of the commandment is clarified: it includes all members of a household, animals, and any stranger who may be passing through the area when the Sabbath is observed. To include the animals in the Sabbath observance recognizes that they too are to be given proper rest.

Specific tasks either allowed or prohibited on the Sabbath are not laid out in this commandment. By the time of Jesus, an entire body of rather complex regulations had been developed to specify acceptable and unacceptable actions on the Sabbath. These "traditions" created no small measure of controversy between Jesus and the religious leaders of His day. Jesus brought clarity by focusing on the bigger picture: "The sabbath was made for man, and not man for the sabbath" (Mark 2:27).

11. For in six days the LORD made heaven and earth, the sea, and all that in them is, and rested the seventh day: wherefore the LORD blessed the sabbath day, and hallowed it.

God bases the observance of the Sabbath day on the fact that in six days He accomplished the work of creation, then *rested the seventh day.* Of course, God does not need to rest in the way that human beings must rest. That God rested simply means that He ceased His creative activity.

Another reason for observing the Sabbath is given later by Moses in Deuteronomy 5:14, 15: the fact that the Lord brought the Israelites out of bondage in Egypt. This reason and the one given in the verse before us should not be seen as contra-dictory, but as complementary. Keeping the Sabbath recognizes God's activity in creating Heaven and earth and everything within them, and it also honors His activity in creating His people Israel and establishing His special covenant with them.

Should Christians observe the Sabbath? The New Testament seems to indicate that first-century Christians respect the Sabbath principle, but apply it to the first day as a way of recognizing that as the day Jesus rose from the dead (see Matthew 28:1-6; Acts 20:7; 1 Corinthians 16:1, 2). Some early Christians who came from a Jewish background probably continued to observe the seventh-day Sabbath. Paul describes that as a matter of personal preference—one in which each person should be "fully persuaded in his own mind" (Romans 14:5; compare Colossians 2:16).

What Do You Think?

How should we include the principle of Sabbath-rest in our lives, if at all? Why?

Talking Points for Your Discussion
- Occupations that require working seven days per week
- Occupations that require work on Sunday
- What does and does not count as *rest*
- Genesis 2:2, 3; 2 Corinthians 7:5; Colossians 2:16, 17; Revelation 14:11

Not included in today's text are the remaining six commandments. It has often been noted that the first four of the Ten Commandments deal primarily with one's relationship with God, while the last six cover one's relationship with others. Together the Ten Commandments encompass the gamut of human behavior. They are part of that law that serves as a "schoolmaster" to point out every person's need for a Savior (Galatians 3:24, 25). Christians can and should obey God's commandments out of gratitude for the grace that forgave and forgives our failures to obey them.

❧ BLUE LAWS ❧

America has an interesting history in relating the Old Testament Sabbath (Saturday) with the Lord's Day of the New Testament (Sunday). This mixture has come across into the culture at large

God Makes a Covenant with Israel

most notably in the form of so-called *blue laws*. Such laws restrict various commercial activities on Sunday, including the sale of alcoholic beverages.

Blue laws in America date back to the Puritans in the seventeenth century. Over time, however, many such laws have gone unenforced or have been repealed outright. This trend is due more to the increasing secular and pluralistic nature of society rather than to any recognition of doctrinal error in equating the Old Testament Sabbath with the Lord's Day of the New Testament.

Regardless of how such political struggles turn out, each Christian needs to wrestle personally with how to treat the Lord's Day. How can or should the concept of Sabbath-rest come over into the New Testament era? Should we allow our children to participate in sports on Sunday morning? Is attending a Saturday night worship service acceptable if we have something else we want to do on Sunday morning? Are there activities that are "improper" after church lets out on Sunday that are permissible the other six days of the week? As we ask ourselves such questions, we remember that the ultimate goal is to honor the Lord.—C. R. B.

Conclusion

A. Respect the Law

Today, the Old Testament law by which the ancient Israelites were to live is treated frequently like the late comedian Rodney Dangerfield: "it gets no respect." This is because in many people's thinking the Old Testament law is set against the concept of grace. It is true that Christ's work of grace served to blot "out the handwriting of ordinances that was against us, which was contrary to us, and took it out of the way, nailing it to his cross" (Colossians 2:14). Even so, we must take care not to treat the Old Testament law unfairly.

We start by considering what the law was intended to mean to the ancient Israelite. Most ancient peoples worshiped gods and goddesses that were seen to be capricious and unpredictable in their behavior. (After all, many of those so-called gods were constructed in the image of man, in contrast with what Genesis 1:26 says.) Such gods demonstrated almost no consistency in their requirements and often left worshipers groping in the dark, as it were, for any kind of stability.

How different was Israel's God! Here was a God who wanted to establish a covenant relationship with His people. Here was a God who was not unpredictable, but refreshingly consistent in His actions and expectations. The Israelites were not left groping in the dark as to what God required. His laws were clear, and obedience to them was designed to enhance His people's witness to the nations around them (see Deuteronomy 4:5-8).

This is why we read, particularly in the Psalms, of such a deep and passionate appreciation for the law of the Lord. Psalm 119 is especially outstanding in expressing that appreciation. Nearly every one of the 176 verses in that psalm contains some reference to the law of God. Consider, for example, the words of verse 97: "O how love I thy law! it is my meditation all the day."

How is it possible to *love* the Old Testament law? It is possible because the ancient Israelites were supposed to understand that God had done for them what no other god of any other people had done— spoken His words clearly and plainly. When He spoke, it was with only the best and noblest of intentions for the people with whom He had established His covenant (see Psalm 147:19, 20).

When we read the Old Testament laws today, we can give thanks for the better covenant of grace that we have in the cross of Christ (Hebrews 7:22). But we shouldn't make the mistake of thinking that the concept of grace is absent from the Old Testament. The law itself was a wonderful gift of grace to God's people of the Old Testament era. "How sweet are thy words unto my taste! yea, sweeter than honey to my mouth" (Psalm 119:103).

B. Prayer

Thank You, Father, for the gracious gift of Your commandments. Even as followers of Jesus in the New Testament era, we can receive timeless instructions from them. May we declare, "I seek thy precepts" (Psalm 119:45). We pray in Jesus' name. Amen.

C. Thought to Remember

God's laws liberate.

INVOLVEMENT LEARNING

Some of the activities below are also found in the helpful student book, Adult Bible Class.
Don't forget to download the free reproducible page from www.standardlesson.com to enhance your lesson!

Into the Lesson

Write the numeral *10* on the board. After learners assemble, say, "Today's class is brought to you by the number 10 and the letter C." (Some will smile as they recognize the *Sesame Street* allusion.) Say, "Anyone who can think of items that come in tens, please come forward and write it on the board." Allow time for volunteers to do so. Expect responses such as, "human toes," "yards for a first down in football," "players in a basketball game," and "cents in a dime."

Reiterate that the lesson is brought today by the number 10, then ask, "But how does the letter C belong?" Someone will suggest (or may have already written on the board) the word *commandments.* Next, have the class turn to today's text in Exodus 20.

Into the Word

Ask learners to finish this sentence with appropriate adjectives and verbs (one- or two-word responses only): "God is the God who (is) _____." Take about five minutes to compile an extensive list. Your learners will have many ideas, but if they need a stimulus, give these as examples: "God is the God who is all-knowing" and "God is the God who cares."

After you have a list of 20 or so, say, "Our text today, recording four of the Ten Commandments, reveals much about God. Take a look at the text and identify which characteristics of God are revealed. See what we have included in our list and what we have not."

You can approach this by going verse by verse. A different approach is to go entry by entry in your list as you try to match those ideas to the text. Though you can expect a variety of responses, here is a sampling, verse by verse:

Verse 1: God who speaks, reveals himself, expects. *Verse 2:* God who is powerful, purposive, redemptive; God who cares, who is personal, rela-tional. *Verse 3:* God who is alone, one of a kind, unique. *Verse 4:* God who is supreme, unrivaled. *Verse 5:* God who is jealous, just, lovable, hateable (by those who reject His moral standards). *Verse 6:* God who is merciful, loving, expectant, authoritative. *Verse 7:* God who is worthy, holy, moral. *Verse 8:* God who is Creator (related to Sabbath rest), holy. *Verse 9:* God who is active, expectant. *Verse 10:* God who rests, is expectant, cares (about the well-being of his creatures). *Verse 11:* God who creates, blesses, sanctifies.

Though not here related to a specific verse, the fact that God loves is evident in the thought of verse 2 and in His concern for people's well-being in verses 9-11. Your class will probably have made a variety of initial responses that can be related to the text. For those you cannot relate, ask the class to explain on the basis of other Scriptures. (*Option:* Follow this activity with the Seven Deadly Sins exercise from the reproducible page.)

Into Life

Distribute copies of The Ten Commandments and Me activity from the reproducible page. Have learners work individually to complete the exercise. Then ask for volunteers to share their conclusions with the class as a whole or in small groups.

In advance, make photocopies of a wooden ruler, one copy per learner; trim each ruler image down to a 10-inch length. As you distribute them, ask, "What is special about your ruler?" The answer will be obvious to all.

Say, "Put your special ruler where you will see it each day this week. When you see it, run your finger along the numbers and recall the Ten Commandments. Give yourself a list, if you need to. When your finger passes a number representing God's will at a point where you struggle, pause to say a brief prayer of petition and commitment. Remember that a look at God's Word and will is always an exercise in how we 'measure up.'"

God Makes a Covenant With Israel

GOD REJECTS IDOL WORSHIP

BACKGROUND SCRIPTURE: Exodus 32

PRINTED TEXT: Exodus 32:1-10

EXODUS 32:1-10

1 And when the people saw that Moses delayed to come down out of the mount, the people gathered themselves together unto Aaron, and said unto him, Up, make us gods, which shall go before us; for as for this Moses, the man that brought us up out of the land of Egypt, we wot not what is become of him.

2 And Aaron said unto them, Break off the golden earrings, which are in the ears of your wives, of your sons, and of your daughters, and bring them unto me.

3 And all the people brake off the golden earrings which were in their ears, and brought them unto Aaron.

4 And he received them at their hand, and fashioned it with a graving tool, after he had made it a molten calf: and they said, These be thy gods, O Israel, which brought thee up out of the land of Egypt.

5 And when Aaron saw it, he built an altar before it; and Aaron made proclamation, and said, To morrow is a feast to the LORD.

6 And they rose up early on the morrow, and offered burnt offerings, and brought peace offerings; and the people sat down to eat and to drink, and rose up to play.

7 And the LORD said unto Moses, Go, get thee down; for thy people, which thou broughtest out of the land of Egypt, have corrupted themselves:

8 They have turned aside quickly out of the way which I commanded them: they have made them a molten calf, and have worshipped it, and have sacrificed thereunto, and said, These be thy gods, O Israel, which have brought thee up out of the land of Egypt.

9 And the LORD said unto Moses, I have seen this people, and, behold, it is a stiffnecked people:

10 Now therefore let me alone, that my wrath may wax hot against them, and that I may consume them: and I will make of thee a great nation.

KEY VERSE

They have turned aside quickly out of the way which I commanded them: they have made them a molten calf, and have worshipped it, and have sacrificed thereunto. —**Exodus 32:8**

THE
INESCAPABLE GOD

Unit 1: God Reveals

LESSONS 1–4

LESSON AIMS

After participating in this lesson, each student will be able to:

1. Summarize the sequence of events in the golden calf episode.

2. Explain how the sin of idolatry is still a threat to Christians today.

3. Identify a modern golden calf in the student's own life or in the church and suggest a way to destroy it.

LESSON OUTLINE

Introduction

A. Getting Egypt out of Israel

"You can take the boy out of the country, but you can't take the country out of the boy" is a familiar saying. It means that when a person has been brought up in rural surroundings, the learned habits, attitudes, and expressions of that environment are not easily forgotten. This writer readily agrees with the statement; I often find myself longing for the simpler, slower-paced country life that I knew growing up in south central Indiana.

The exodus was the event that brought the nation of Israel out of Egypt. But getting Egypt out of Israel was quite another matter. It involved the removal of all ties to that previous way of life. The practices of Egyptian culture were no longer appropriate (if they ever were) for the Israelites, given their covenant with God (Exodus 19:5, 6). Getting Israel out of Egypt was a geographical step; getting Egypt out of Israel was a spiritual issue.

In a way, the latter transition was far more challenging. The Israelites had to be willing to sever ties with their past. God's power had delivered them from physical bondage. Did the Israelites have the willpower and resolve to avoid spiritual bondage?

The incident recorded in today's printed text reveals that getting Egypt out of Israel was not going to happen overnight. A high price would be paid in the process of learning that lesson.

B. Lesson Background

Last week's study focused on God's provision of the Ten Commandments to His people. After the Lord had given these commandments, the people, who were fearful because of the accompanying display of overwhelming sights and sounds, pleaded with Moses that he rather than the Lord speak to them (Exodus 20:19). Moses then approached the Lord (v. 21), and God proceeded to give him the laws recorded in Exodus 21–23.

Following this, Moses led in conducting a ceremony during which the covenant was confirmed by the shedding of blood (Exodus 24:1-8). Twice during this ceremony, the people voiced their desire to obey whatever the Lord had commanded them (vv. 3, 7). There followed a special time of fellowship with the Lord that included Moses, Aaron, two of Aaron's sons, and 70 of the elders of Israel (vv. 9-11). Apparently, though it is not specifically stated in the text, these men returned to the foot of the mountain after this.

The Lord then told Moses alone to come to Him so that He could give further instructions and write His commandments on "tables of stone" (Exodus 24:12). But while Moses was on the mountain receiving God's laws, a tragic irony was unfolding below: the Israelites proceeded to break those laws, particularly the commandment against idolatry.

I. Israelites' Concern
(EXODUS 32:1)
A. Moses' Delay (v. 1a)

1a. And when the people saw that Moses delayed to come down out of the mount.

At this point, Moses has been on Mount Sinai for 40 days (Exodus 24:18). When he announced his plan earlier to ascend the mountain, he had not given any specific time that he would come back. He had simply told the elders to wait until he and Joshua returned (24:13, 14).

The word *delayed* implies that the people are becoming impatient with Moses. Forty days must seem like more than enough time for him to stay on the mountain! When will he return so they can resume their journey to the promised land?

B. People's Demand (v. 1b)

1b. The people gathered themselves together unto Aaron, and said unto him, Up, make us gods, which shall go before us; for as for this Moses, the man that brought us up out of the land of Egypt, we wot not what is become of him.

As previously noted, Moses had told the elders, before he went up the mountain, that Aaron and Hur would be available to consult should any issues arise (Exodus 24:14). Aaron is probably approached on this occasion because of his previous role as Moses' spokesman (4:14-16; 7:1, 2). *The people* who come to him probably are representatives of all 12 tribes.

The demand of the people likely catches Aaron off guard: *Up, make us gods, which shall go before us.* It seems inconceivable to us as we read this account that these people want to abandon the Lord, who has done so much for them in recent memory. It seems inconceivable to us that they insist that Aaron make idols. How can they reject the Lord so completely and so quickly—with all the evidence that they have witnessed?

The Bible does not analyze the people's rebellion in great detail. It does warn us that we too can follow the same destructive pattern if we become complacent and fail to learn from the Israelites' example (see 1 Corinthians 10:6-13).

The Hebrew word translated *gods* in the verse before us is *Elohim*. While this word can be rendered as *gods,* it is also one of the primary names for the true God in the Old Testament. When used of God, the word is accompanied by a singular verb (as in Genesis 1:1). Here in the people's demand of Aaron, *Elohim* is used with a plural verb *(go before).* It seems that the people want Aaron to make not only a representation of the Lord but of other gods as well. Those gods may include Apis, an Egyptian god whose form is that of a bull. Images of this god were probably a common sight for the Israelites when they were slaves in Egypt. Yet why do they want a god such as this to replace the God who has freed them from their slavery?

The people's use of *go before* is noteworthy, for the Lord himself already "went before" them toward the Red Sea by means of the pillar of a cloud by day and the pillar of fire by night (Exodus 13:21). Similar language is used of the angel of God (14:19; 23:20-23). But the people are prepared

HOW TO SAY IT

Aaron	*Air* un.
Corinthians	Ko-*rin*-thee-unz (*th* as in *thin*).
Elohim *(Hebrew)*	El-o-*heem.*
Galatians	Guh-*lay*-shunz.
Hur	Her.
Israelites	*Iz*-ray-el-ites.
Moses	*Mo*-zes or *Mo*-zez.
Yahweh *(Hebrew)*	*Yah*-weh.

to reject such leadership and replace it with something abysmally inferior.

Not only is the people's demand a rejection of the Lord's authority, they also demonstrate great contempt for His appointed messenger. They scornfully refer to him as *this Moses, the man that brought us up out of the land of Egypt.* They seem to have forgotten that Moses is only the human instrument who led them out of Egypt. Their ultimate deliverer is the Lord!

> **What Do You Think?**
> How should Christians respond when majorities in democratic societies enact laws that conflict with God's law?
> *Talking Points for Your Discussion*
> ▪ In manner of prayer
> ▪ In making "a holy noise"
> ▪ In acts of civil disobedience (Acts 4:19; 5:29)

❧ THE RESULTS OF PATIENCE ❧

Although Scripture acknowledges the value of patience, this trait is often lacking. Christians are not immune to this problem. However, at times God's people have shown great patience (and its companion virtue, perseverance). The great cathedrals of Europe are a testimony to this fact.

Generation after generation took part in erecting these striking houses of worship. Many who helped had no hope that they would ever see the finished results of their efforts. Construction of the cathedral in Cologne, Germany, began in 1248. One of the church's towers had reached only one-third of its ultimate height 200 years later. After 300 years, the roof still had only a board covering. The building was completed in 1880, over 600 years after the foundation was laid!

The people Moses was leading had no such patience. Moses had been on the mountain six weeks when they began clamoring for a different god who would satisfy their longings immediately. So, which are we more like: the Israelites or the cathedral builders? When change in the church, society, or even our personal lives is not moving at the pace we think it should, we need to remember what Israel's impatience led to!   —C. R. B.

II. Aaron's Counsel
(EXODUS 32:2-6)
A. Collecting Materials (vv. 2, 3)

2. And Aaron said unto them, Break off the golden earrings, which are in the ears of your wives, of your sons, and of your daughters, and bring them unto me.

While Aaron appears all too eager to yield to the people's desires, some suggest that initially he is very troubled by what the Israelites are saying. Some believe that he is attempting to dissuade them from carrying out their idolatrous intentions by asking them to provide the necessary resources: the golden earrings that they are wearing.

Under this theory, Aaron is thinking, "Once they see what their idea will cost them, they'll change their minds." But this is just a theory, as the text doesn't tell us what Aaron is thinking. No doubt the items of gold are part of the plunder that the people took when the Pharaoh finally allowed them to leave (Exodus 11:1, 2; 12:33-36).

3. And all the people brake off the golden earrings which were in their ears, and brought them unto Aaron.

If Aaron thinks that the people will not want to part with their wealth, he is wrong. If the theory we mentioned above is correct, it means that the people have called Aaron's bluff. If only they were this eager to obey the Lord's commands!

> **What Do You Think?**
> What are the costs of sin, and why do people seem so willing to pay those costs?
> *Talking Points for Your Discussion*
> ▪ In terms of spiritual costs
> ▪ In terms of physical costs
> ▪ In terms of psychological costs
> ▪ In terms of financial costs

B. Crafting an Idol (v. 4)

4. And he received them at their hand, and fashioned it with a graving tool, after he had made it a molten calf: and they said, These be thy gods, O Israel, which brought thee up out of the land of Egypt.

At this point Aaron can still object to what the people want him to do. He can refuse to go through with it. But the further along he proceeds in acceding to the people's demand, the harder it becomes for him to stop the process. (Possibly he is hoping that Moses will suddenly return from the mountaintop and rescue him from having to pursue this act any further.)

It should be noted that Aaron fashions one calf, not multiple calves or gods. Is he trying to cover for his mistake by limiting the people to one "god" who will represent the Lord? However this question may be answered and whatever Aaron's motives may be, it cannot be denied that he allows the violation of the commandment prohibiting "any graven image" (Exodus 20:4). That Aaron is held responsible for his part in this sin is clear from Moses' later account in Deuteronomy 9:20.

The people's words reflect the high regard in which they hold the golden calf that Aaron has constructed: *These be thy gods, O Israel, which brought thee up out of the land of Egypt.* This statement blatantly, brazenly denies what the Lord had declared to the people just prior to giving them the Ten Commandments: "I am the Lord thy God, which have brought thee out of the land of Egypt, out of the house of bondage" (Exodus 20:2).

In a sense, this is the ultimate blasphemy (and amounts to breaking the commandment concerning taking the Lord's name in vain): the people are attributing God's mighty act of deliverance through the exodus to a golden calf! One may compare this with altering the Good Confession of faith to say, "I believe that Buddha is the Son of God."

What Do You Think?

How do we resist giving in to ungodly pressures?

Talking Points for Your Discussion

- As preteens
- As teenagers
- As adults

⅔ *CURSED TREASURE?* ⅔

A 14-pound gem known as the *Pearl of Allah* reputedly carries a curse with it. Legend has it that the pearl once belonged to a Chinese philosopher some 2,500 years ago. It was lost in a shipwreck, but in 1934 a diver found it in Philippine waters. When he reached into a huge clam to get it, the clam closed on his hand and he drowned. When his body and the clam were recovered, the chief of the island—a Muslim—gave the pearl its name. Five years later, the chief gave the pearl to a man who saved his son's life. So goes the legend.

In 1980 the pearl was sold to two California men, who formed a corporation seeking investors. At this point, the story gets murkier yet. One of the investors was alleged to be involved in at least one contract killing. Heirs of the victim sued. The pearl has been appraised at over $90 million.

The idea of "cursed treasure" certainly makes for good story lines! But real curses come about by the behavior of people. Deuteronomy 27:15 says, "Cursed be the man that maketh any graven or molten image, an abomination unto the Lord." The Israelites had left Egypt with physical treasure taken from the Egyptians. When they used that treasure to build the golden calf, they revealed what they treasured in their hearts.   —C. R. B.

C. Calling a Feast (vv. 5, 6)

5. And when Aaron saw it, he built an altar before it; and Aaron made proclamation, and said, To morrow is a feast to the LORD.

Aaron may be said to have broken the first part of the Second Commandment by building a graven image. He now proceeds to violate the second part with his next action: promoting the actual worship of the calf (Exodus 20:5). Is Aaron once more trying to "save face" by encouraging the people to celebrate a *feast to the Lord,* since the word for *Lord* that Aaron uses is *Yahweh*?

Even if that is true, Aaron should realize that with the construction of a pagan symbol will come the observance of pagan practices. If Aaron is going to encourage doing something *to the Lord,* he should have done so at the outset by refusing to comply with the people's demand to "make us gods" (v. 1).

6. And they rose up early on the morrow, and offered burnt offerings, and brought peace offerings; and the people sat down to eat and to drink, and rose up to play.

Visual for Lesson 3. Use this visual to start a discussion about the things we allow to displace our devotion to God.

Burnt offerings and *peace offerings* were part of the ceremony confirming God's covenant, as recorded in Exodus 24:1-8. Ironically, that was one of the occasions on which the Israelites had promised their obedience to all that the Lord commanded (v. 7). Here they follow their offerings by a time of eating and drinking, which accompany peace offerings (compare Leviticus 7:11-36).

But the words about rising up *to play* carry a far more ominous meaning. The Hebrew verb often has sexual connotations. Illicit sexual activity is often part of pagan worship ceremonies (compare Numbers 25:1, 2). The people's earlier pledge to obey the Lord has become nothing but a farce.

> **What Do You Think?**
> How and why do people rebel against God today?
> *Talking Points for Your Discussion*
> - Issues of personal freedom
> - Wrong views of God's love and justice
> - Hebrews 3:7-19

III. Lord's Command
(Exodus 32:7-10)
A. Instruction (vv. 7, 8)

7. And the LORD said unto Moses, Go, get thee down; for thy people, which thou broughtest out of the land of Egypt, have corrupted themselves.

Now the scene shifts from the people's rebellion at the foot of the mountain to the Lord's word to Moses, who had ascended the mountain. Whatever thrill Moses experienced at receiving the Lord's commandments is now tempered by the bad news that the people *have corrupted themselves* by acting in total defiance of these commandments.

In addressing Moses, the Lord refers to the Israelites as *thy people, which thou broughtest out of the land of Egypt*. Why doesn't the Lord say, "Whom I brought out of Egypt" (compare Exodus 20:2)? Perhaps the Lord is indicating His wrath toward the people (32:11) and distancing himself from them by such language.

8. They have turned aside quickly out of the way which I commanded them: they have made them a molten calf, and have worshipped it, and have sacrificed thereunto, and said, These be thy gods, O Israel, which have brought thee up out of the land of Egypt.

The Lord describes to Moses exactly what the Israelites have done and professed concerning the molten calf. One may compare the language *have turned aside quickly* to what Paul writes about the Galatian Christians: "I marvel that ye are so soon removed from him that called you into the grace of Christ unto another gospel" (Galatians 1:6).

As noted in the comments on verse 1b, Paul uses the incident of the golden calf to warn the Corinthians against developing the same attitude. (He quotes Exodus 32:6 in 1 Corinthians 10:7.) We dare not be too quick to criticize them for their lack of faith; as Paul cautions, "Let him that thinketh he standeth take heed lest he fall" (1 Corinthians 10:12).

B. Intention (vv. 9, 10)

9. And the LORD said unto Moses, I have seen this people, and, behold, it is a stiffnecked people.

When the Lord called Moses to lead the people out of bondage, He spoke of seeing their affliction and being moved to do something about it (Exodus 3:7, 8). Now, however, the Lord sees something else about the Israelites: they are *stiffnecked*. As such, they are determined not to obey Him despite the good intentions they previously expressed (19:8;

24:3, 7). They have not really grasped what it means to be a "holy nation" (19:6).

10. Now therefore let me alone, that my wrath may wax hot against them, and that I may consume them: and I will make of thee a great nation.

The Lord now announces a most dramatic change in His plans for the Israelites: He is prepared to destroy them. In so doing, the Lord plans to start anew using Moses as the founder of *a great nation* (compare similar language in Genesis 12:1, 2). The very mountain where the Lord provided as a "token" of the fulfillment of His promise (Exodus 3:12) is now to be a token of His judgment. It is a stunning reversal of the Lord's intentions. But He has made it clear that the Israelites' position before Him hinges on their obedience (19:5).

> *What Do You Think?*
> What are some signs that you are becoming "stiffnecked" toward God? What corrective action do you take?
> *Talking Points for Your Discussion*
> ▪ In the church
> ▪ At home
> ▪ At work

Exodus 32:11-14 (not in today's text) records Moses' intercessory appeal for the wayward Israelites. Moses raises three critical concerns. First, the Lord has already (and quite recently) displayed His power on behalf of the people (v. 11); despite the people's twisted thinking in attributing their deliverance to the golden calf, that does not change the fact of what the Lord has accomplished. Second, the Egyptians will claim that the Lord has delivered the people from bondage with the ultimate aim of destroying them (v. 12); thus His reputation in the sight of the nations will be tarnished.

Third, the Lord has made a covenant with Abraham, Isaac, and Israel (Jacob), promising that their descendants will be as numerous as the stars of Heaven (v. 13). God established a link with the patriarchs when He called Moses and sent him to the Israelites in their suffering (Exodus 3:6, 15, 16). Will He sever that link now?

The Lord hears Moses' plea and refrains from destroying the people (Exodus 32:14). However, the Israelites are not given a complete exemption from judgment. Their sin results in bitter consequences (Exodus 32:15-35). What should have been a joyous occasion has become a heartbreaking reminder of the high cost of disobedience.

Conclusion
A. Idol Words

An idol has been defined as "anything that comes between a person and God." That simple description is hard to improve on. An idol does not have to be a "graven image" such as the golden calf.

In Colossians 3:5, Paul defines covetousness as idolatry. Thus idolatry can include violation of not only the Second Commandment (as in the case of the Israelites) but also of the Tenth. Looked at from this perspective, idolatry becomes an issue not only for primitive tribes in a remote jungle but also for highly educated people. Modern advertising constantly bombards us with messages about all the "stuff" we need to make our lives more rewarding. Such messages distract us from God's perspective.

Any act of idolatry, whether it involves a graven or computer-generated image, ultimately begins in the human heart. Idolatry was King Solomon's ruin, but it began when the king's heart "was turned from the Lord God of Israel" (1 Kings 11:9). The king failed to heed his own advice found in Proverbs 4:23: "Keep thy heart with all diligence; for out of it are the issues of life." In staying with the focus of this study, perhaps the verse could be paraphrased as follows: "Keep thy heart with all diligence; for out of it are the *idols* of life."

B. Prayer

Father, we realize that the account of the Israelites' idolatry is for our benefit (1 Corinthians 10:11). May we examine ourselves to see what idols we have allowed to displace You. Help us destroy them before they destroy us. In Jesus' name, amen.

C. Thought to Remember
No Christian is exempt
from the temptation of idolatry.

INVOLVEMENT LEARNING

Some of the activities below are also found in the helpful student book, Adult Bible Class.
Don't forget to download the free reproducible page from www.standardlesson.com to enhance your lesson!

Into the Lesson

Write the following letter sequence on the board: *I E S G R Y A P E T L*. Get the learners' attention to what you are doing, then slowly erase the letters *E, T, Y, P, G* one at a time in that sequence. (The word *ISRAEL* will be left.)

Ask, "What did you see me doing?" The answer you want is "getting Egypt out of Israel." Summarize the lesson writer's Introduction as the lead-in to the lesson. Say, "The pervasive idolatry of Egypt had tainted the religious thinking of the Hebrews. But God said strongly, 'Idolatry must go!'"

Into the Word

Responsive reading. Class members will represent the people of Israel, and you (or someone you designate) will represent the Word. Create handouts of the following "quotes" for three of your students to use (the "quotes" are related to specific verses, as noted). Say, "I want you three to represent the people of Israel in the situation that today's text concerns. In our verses, they speak up against God and Moses. Please read your 'quotes,' then I will read the verse it applies to."

Reader 1: He's been gone over a month. *Reader 2:* I think he died. He was old. *Reader 3:* I'm tired of waiting. *Reader 1:* Let's tell Aaron how we feel. *Reader 2:* We need gods we can see. *Reader 3:* This Moses . . . so he led us out of Egypt, but to what?! [for v. 1]

Reader 1: Tell us what to do, Aaron. *Reader 2:* We've got the riches of Egypt. What will new gods cost? *Reader 3:* Our families are fed up. We'll all cooperate. [for v. 2]

Reader 1: Aaron's going to do what we asked. But he will need things from each of us. *Reader 2:* We'll pile 'em up in front of Aaron. He will see how serious we are. *Reader 3:* Children, you're in on this too. They'll be your gods as well. [for v. 3]

Reader 1: Stand back and watch Aaron work. *Reader 2:* Whew, that fire's hot. *Reader 3:* It didn't look like anything but a blob of gold until Aaron put his magic hands to work. Now look! [for v. 4]

Reader 1: Aaron, it's not complete until we have an altar for sacrifice. *Reader 2:* What a leader Aaron is! *Reader 3:* Wow, what we need is an all-out feast and party! [for v. 5]

Reader 1: Get up, you sleepy heads! Things are about to happen! *Reader 2:* Now we've got a place to sacrifice. Let's do it! *Reader 3:* Hurry, children. Bring the lamb and the grain. [for v. 6]

Reader 1: Moses and his God—they're clueless. *Reader 2:* A good sacrifice makes me feel so right. *Reader 3:* Moses thought we were "his people." Well, I'm not. [for v. 7]

Reader 1: We gave Moses' God a chance, but patience lasts only so long. *Reader 2:* We know a god who delivers when we see one. *Reader 3:* Ah, now that looks just like the gods who sent us on our way from Egypt. [for v. 8]

Reader 1: I'm going to bow my head to the god of my own choosing. *Reader 2:* Just call me open-minded. *Reader 3:* That God on Moses' mountain doesn't think twice about me. [for v. 9]

Reader 1: Moses' God certainly isn't going to stop us, is He? *Reader 2:* Does Moses think we're just going to hang around and be "his people"? *Reader 3:* Where's that promise of a "great nation"? We're stuck out here in the middle of nowhere. [for v. 10]

Once the "quotes" and text are read, allow learners to express their reactions.

Into Life

Have a learner read 1 Corinthians 10:1-13. Note that this passage quotes today's lesson text. Then distribute copies of the Bad Examples activity from the reproducible page for learners to complete in study teams. Allow about eight minutes, then discuss. Distribute copies of the Earrings and Idolatry activity from the reproducible page as take-home work as learners depart.

GOD PROMISES AN AWESOME THING

BACKGROUND SCRIPTURE: Exodus 34:1-10
PRINTED TEXT: Exodus 34:1-10

EXODUS 34:1-10

1 And the LORD said unto Moses, Hew thee two tables of stone like unto the first: and I will write upon these tables the words that were in the first tables, which thou brakest.

2 And be ready in the morning, and come up in the morning unto mount Sinai, and present thyself there to me in the top of the mount.

3 And no man shall come up with thee, neither let any man be seen throughout all the mount; neither let the flocks nor herds feed before that mount.

4 And he hewed two tables of stone like unto the first; and Moses rose up early in the morning, and went up unto mount Sinai, as the LORD had commanded him, and took in his hand the two tables of stone.

5 And the LORD descended in the cloud, and stood with him there, and proclaimed the name of the LORD.

6 And the LORD passed by before him, and proclaimed, The LORD, The LORD God, merciful and gracious, longsuffering, and abundant in goodness and truth,

7 Keeping mercy for thousands, forgiving iniquity and transgression and sin, and that will by no means clear the guilty; visiting the iniquity of the fathers upon the children, and upon the children's children, unto the third and to the fourth generation.

8 And Moses made haste, and bowed his head toward the earth, and worshipped.

9 And he said, If now I have found grace in thy sight, O LORD, let my LORD, I pray thee, go among us; for it is a stiffnecked people; and pardon our iniquity and our sin, and take us for thine inheritance.

10 And he said, Behold, I make a covenant: before all thy people I will do marvels, such as have not been done in all the earth, nor in any nation: and all the people among which thou art shall see the work of the LORD: for it is a terrible thing that I will do with thee.

KEY VERSE

The LORD passed by before him, and proclaimed, The LORD, The LORD God, merciful and gracious, longsuffering, and abundant in goodness and truth. —**Exodus 34:6**

THE INESCAPABLE GOD

Unit 1: God Reveals

LESSON AIMS

After participating in this lesson, each student will be able to:

1. Summarize what occurred both visually and verbally when the Lord revealed His name to Moses.

2. Tell why it is important to accept the Lord's revelation of himself as a God of both mercy and judgment.

3. Thank God for the combination of both mercy and judgment at the cross of Jesus in order to provide salvation for lost humanity.

LESSON OUTLINE

Introduction
  A. Our Father in Heaven
  B. Lesson Background
 I. Moses' Preparation (EXODUS 34:1-4)
  A. Getting Two Tablets (v. 1)
  B. Going Alone (vv. 2, 3)
  C. Giving Obedience (v. 4)
 II. Lord's Proclamation (EXODUS 34:5-7)
  A. Sight of a Cloud (v. 5)
  B. Sound of a Voice (vv. 6, 7)
   "It's a Good Idea, but . . ."
 III. Moses' Prayer (EXODUS 34:8, 9)
  A. His Posture (v. 8)
  B. His Plea (v. 9)
 IV. Lord's Promise (EXODUS 34:10)
  A. Action (v. 10a)
  B. Outcome (v. 10b)
  Handling a Paradigm Shift
Conclusion
  A. Inescapable Evidence
  B. Prayer
  C. Thought to Remember

Introduction

A. Our Father in Heaven

A man once drove a nice-looking sports car through a poorer neighborhood of his city. He stopped at a gas station to make a phone call. While on the phone, he noticed another man about his age who approached the car and looked it over closely, obviously quite fascinated by it.

When the man got off the phone, the other man asked him, "Where did you get a car like this?" The man replied, "Well, actually my dad gave it to me." He waited a moment, thinking the other fellow might say something like, "I wish I had a dad like that." Instead, the man's response was, "I wish I could be a dad like that."

We live in a time when fathers are often that only in a biological sense. Many men have abandoned the daily responsibilities of being true fathers. As a result, they leave behind youngsters who desperately need the love, support, and stability that faithful fathers supply to a home.

When the Lord sent Moses to Egypt, He told him to tell Pharaoh, "Thus saith the Lord, Israel is my son, even my firstborn" (Exodus 4:22). God wanted the children of Israel to know that their heavenly Father still cared deeply for them and had come to deliver them from their bondage.

This is the same God who sent His Son to this world to let all humanity know that their heavenly Father cares deeply for them and wants to deliver them from the spiritual bondage caused by sin. That is why Jesus gave His life for us and took our punishment at the cross. What a Father we have!

B. Lesson Background

Last week's printed text concluded with the Lord's declaration of His intention to destroy the Israelites as a result of their worship of the golden calf. Moses, however, interceded for the people and became (again) an instrument of their deliverance. Such was his passion for them that he even requested that the Lord blot his (Moses') name out of the Lord's book if that would result in the Israelites being spared punishment (Exodus 32:31, 32; compare Romans 9:3, 4). The Lord did not destroy the people. But He did tell Moses that

God Promises an Awesome Thing

those who had participated in the sin against Him would not escape punishment (Exodus 32:33).

The beginning of Exodus 33 records the Lord's instructions to Moses to proceed toward the promised land. The Lord's angel would go before the people to lead the way and drive out the land's inhabitants (vv. 1, 2). The Lord himself, however, would not go lest He determine at some point to destroy the people for being "stiffnecked" (v. 3).

Once again Moses demonstrated his intercessory spirit. He expressed to the Lord his personal desire to know the Lord more fully, but added his concern for the people's welfare (Exodus 33:12, 13). The Lord indicated that He would accompany Moses to the promised land (v. 14), but Moses was not satisfied with that response. He desired the presence of the Lord on behalf of *all* the people—not just Moses. The Lord answered, "I will do this thing also that thou hast spoken: for thou hast found grace in my sight, and I know thee by name" (v. 17).

It was then that Moses voiced perhaps his boldest request of the Lord: "I beseech thee, shew me thy glory" (Exodus 33:18). The Lord promised that He would "proclaim the name of the Lord before" Moses (v. 19) and allow him to see a portion of His glory (vv. 20-23). The printed text for today records how the Lord granted Moses this very sacred encounter.

Moses had come a long way from the fear he showed when the Lord first appeared to him (Exodus 3:6). He had reached the same level of desiring God as expressed by the psalmist: "As the hart panteth after the water brooks, so panteth my soul after thee, O God" (Psalm 42:1).

I. Moses' Preparation
(Exodus 34:1-4)
A. Getting Two Tablets (v. 1)

1. And the Lord said unto Moses, Hew thee two tables of stone like unto the first: and I will write upon these tables the words that were in the first tables, which thou brakest.

Prior to the special encounter with the Lord, Moses is to cut two new tablets of stone similar to the first two tablets. Moses had broken those first two tablets in his anger at the people's disobedience in building and worshiping the golden calf (Exodus 32:19). The Lord himself had provided the first set of tablets (31:18); but Moses is to supply this second set, most likely because he was responsible for breaking the first set. It is important to note that what the Lord will write on these new tablets will not be a new message. They will be the same words that were written on the first set of tablets—the Ten Commandments (34:28).

> **What Do You Think?**
> When should we wait for God to fix what we have broken in our lives as opposed to going ahead with our own fix?
>
> *Talking Points for Your Discussion*
> - Issues involving other people (Matthew 5:23, 24; Luke 19:8)
> - Issues of personal behavior (Colossians 3:5-10)
> - Issues that can't be fixed in this life (Revelation 21:4)

B. Going Alone (vv. 2, 3)

2, 3. And be ready in the morning, and come up in the morning unto mount Sinai, and present thyself there to me in the top of the mount. And no man shall come up with thee, neither let any man be seen throughout all the mount; neither let the flocks nor herds feed before that mount.

Previously, Moses had ascended Mount Sinai with Aaron, 2 of his sons, and 70 of the elders of

HOW TO SAY IT

Aaron	*Air*-un.
Deuteronomy	Due-ter-*ahn*-uh-me.
Egypt	*Ee*-jipt.
Jericho	*Jair*-ih-co.
Levites	*Lee*-vites.
Moses	*Mo*-zes or *Mo*-zez.
paradigm	*pair*-uh-dime.
Pharaoh	*Fair*-o or *Fay*-roe.
Rahab	*Ray*-hab.
Sinai	*Sigh*-nye or *Sigh*-nay-eye.

Israel (Exodus 24:1, 9, 10), and later with Joshua (24:13, 14; 32:15-17). For this sacred occasion, however, Moses is to come alone. It is only he who has made the bold request to see the Lord's glory; thus only he will participate in the experience. The fact that the flocks and herds are to keep their distance from the mountain stresses that the limits previously set (19:12, 13) are still in place.

> **What Do You Think?**
> Do you feel closer to God in times of solitude or when worshiping with others? Why?
> *Talking Points for Your Discussion*
> - Matthew 4:25; 6:6; Luke 5:16; 22:41; John 4:20, 21; Hebrews 10:25
> - The value of "stretching" yourself to appreciate the one that is less preferred
> - Individual personality

C. Giving Obedience (v. 4)

4. And he hewed two tables of stone like unto the first; and Moses rose up early in the morning, and went up unto mount Sinai, as the LORD had commanded him, and took in his hand the two tables of stone.

Moses complies fully with the Lord's instructions. This is a characteristic of Moses' life, with a notable exception at Numbers 20:12 (compare Numbers 20:24; 27:14; Deuteronomy 32:51).

II. Lord's Proclamation
(EXODUS 34:5-7)
A. Sight of a Cloud (v. 5)

5. And the LORD descended in the cloud, and stood with him there, and proclaimed the name of the LORD.

A cloud had been one indicator previously of the Lord's presence with the Israelites (Exodus 13:21, 22; 14:19, 20; 19:16; 24:15-18). Later, a cloud will envelop the tabernacle after Moses finishes setting it up (40:34-38).

It is difficult to read this account and picture exactly what occurs next. The text simply declares the Lord to be standing with Moses as a proclamation takes place. In what form does the Lord appear when He "stands" with Moses? (Com-

pare 1 Samuel 3:10.) When the Lord tells Moses, "I will make all my goodness pass before thee" (Exodus 33:19), we wonder how "goodness" can "pass before" someone! Perhaps on occasions such as these, human language simply fails in explaining what is going on. Whatever words are used will always fall far short in describing a holy experience such as the one granted to Moses.

We may also wonder what it means to "proclaim" *the name of the Lord.* We can at least conclude that the idea of a name in the Scriptures is often much more than just a label to identify someone. A name also says something about one's character. God had told Moses previously, "I know thee by name" (Exodus 33:12, 17). God knows Moses' heart. God knows that the request Moses makes to see His glory is not done flippantly or for mere sake of curiosity. Moses' request comes from a true seeker after God.

Even before this experience, the Lord is described as having spoken to Moses "face to face, as a man speaketh unto his friend" (Exodus 33:11). Such language is not to be understood literally (see 33:20). Rather, it is a way of capturing the special intimacy that exists between the Lord and His servant.

> **What Do You Think?**
> Why does God not grant a visible manifestation of His presence to everyone who asks?
> *Talking Points for Your Discussion*
> - Issues of faith (John 20:29; 1 Peter 1:8; etc.)
> - Issues of purpose (Acts 10:41; 1 Corinthians 9:1; etc.)

B. Sound of a Voice (vv. 6, 7)

6, 7a. And the LORD passed by before him, and proclaimed, The LORD, The LORD God, merciful and gracious, longsuffering, and abundant in goodness and truth, keeping mercy for thousands, forgiving iniquity and transgression and sin.

The phrase *the Lord passed by before him* indicates the fulfillment of the promise made in Exodus 33:21-23. The visual revelation is combined with a verbal revelation of a listing of the Lord's characteristics. The combination of the visual and

God Promises an Awesome Thing

verbal revelations must be extraordinarily powerful to Moses.

The words in verses 6, 7 of our text might be considered the Old Testament's "Good Confession," similar in importance to "Thou art the Christ, the Son of the living God" (Matthew 16:16). The fact that this description of the Lord is reflected elsewhere in the Old Testament indicates its significance (see Numbers 14:18; Nehemiah 9:17; Psalms 86:15; 103:8; 145:8; Joel 2:13; Jonah 4:2).

It is easy for Christians reading this passage today to miss the significance of this moment in the record of God's revelation of himself. The fact that the Lord is merciful, gracious, and forgiving is well known to us. But for Moses to hear the Lord speak of himself with these terms is a spiritual milestone. The Lord has not described himself in this manner before this point in time.

Moses had learned the Lord's identity when God spoke to him from the burning bush (Exodus 3:14, 15). But to hear the Lord expand on this in the way Moses witnesses and hears Him do so is a singular privilege indeed. Such self-revelation by God will be surpassed only when the Word becomes flesh and dwells among us (John 1:14) and when the Lord's servants actually "see his face" in Heaven (Revelation 22:4).

> **What Do You Think?**
> Why is it important to see *grace* as characteristic of God in the Old Testament?
> *Talking Points for Your Discussion*
> - Old Testament as preparation for the Messiah
> - Old Testament records of catastrophic judgment and punishment
> - Galatians 3:23-25

7b. And that will by no means clear the guilty; visiting the iniquity of the fathers upon the children, and upon the children's children, unto the third and to the fourth generation.

When we read the previous words about the Lord's mercy and compassion, some might wonder how to interpret them in light of how the Lord has just dealt with the Israelites. Following the sin of worshiping the golden calf, the Levites were commanded to put to death some of the guilty.

About 3,000 were slain (Exodus 32:25-29). A later plague results in more deaths (32:35).

Although the Lord is indeed a God of mercy and compassion, He also reveals himself to be a God of judgment. The holiness of the Lord demands that sin be punished. The Lord possesses the knowledge to determine when judgment must be administered. Even in the case of the idolatry at Mount Sinai, we recognize God's mercy when we recall that His first intention was to destroy the entire nation (Exodus 32:9, 10).

The fact that Lord visits *the iniquity of the fathers . . . unto the third and to the fourth generation* is similar to the language used in Exodus 20:4-6. See the discussion of that passage in Lesson 2.

❧ "IT'S A GOOD IDEA, BUT . . ." ❧

Since making a right turn after stopping for a red light was made legal many years ago, the "rolling stop" has become a common occurrence. The attitude of many seems to be, "This law is a good thing, but I'm free to 'interpret' it for my situation." That "interpretation" often results in outright disobedience.

Few would actually express that attitude so blatantly, but many live by that creed nonetheless. They like the law when it keeps others from crashing into them. They just don't like limits to be placed on their own freedom. Within each of us is the tendency to act selfishly at the expense of others. The law places limits on all of us so that society can function for the general good.

How interesting it is that God's proclamation of His mercy, grace, and forgiveness comes in the context of giving His law! Does the reality of God's grace move us to do any better in the area of obedience than it did the ancient Israelites? —C. R. B.

III. Moses' Prayer
(EXODUS 34:8, 9)
A. His Posture (v. 8)

8. And Moses made haste, and bowed his head toward the earth, and worshipped.

How else should one react to an experience of this magnitude? Reverent worship is Moses' immediate response.

B. His Plea (v. 9)

9. And he said, If now I have found grace in thy sight, O LORD, let my LORD, I pray thee, go among us; for it is a stiffnecked people; and pardon our iniquity and our sin, and take us for thine inheritance.

Moses returns to the issue of whether or not the Lord will accompany the Israelites as they proceed toward the promised land. He brings before the Lord two realities: the people's nature (they are *stiffnecked*) and the Lord's nature (He is one who is willing to *pardon our iniquity and our sin*). Moses is keenly aware that the people cannot inherit the promised land unless the Lord accepts them as His and blesses their future endeavors. Thus Moses pleads with God to *take us for thine inheritance*.

IV. Lord's Promise
(EXODUS 34:10)
A. Action (v. 10a)

10a. And he said, Behold, I make a covenant: before all thy people I will do marvels, such as have not been done in all the earth, nor in any nation.

The Lord's response to Moses' request for pardon is stated in terms of a promised covenant. It is through this covenant that the Lord intends to grant His blessing to Moses and the people. The Lord's leading in this regard will be unmistakable, because the Lord will confirm His covenant with

Visual for Lesson 4. As you discuss verse 10, point to this visual and ask, "What are some 'awesome' ways the Lord works in the church today?"

marvels, or wonders, that have never been done anywhere else.

B. Outcome (v. 10b)

10b. And all the people among which thou art shall see the work of the LORD: for it is a terrible thing that I will do with thee.

The Lord also calls what He will do with Moses *a terrible thing*. The Hebrew word translated *terrible* comes from a word meaning "to fear." It conveys the idea of "something causing terror" or "awe" in the response of those who witness it.

What is this work that the Lord declares that He will do through Moses? In Exodus 34:11 (not in today's text), the Lord promises to drive out the inhabitants of the land where the Israelites are going. He also warns the people not to be seduced by the gods those people worship (vv. 12-14); this is counsel that they should take to heart, based on what has just happened with the golden calf!

Moses, however, is not the one who guides the Israelites into the promised land. Because of his later disobedience, he is not permitted to do that (Numbers 20:1-13). It will be left to Joshua, his successor, to lead the people in crossing the Jordan River and carrying out the promise given in Exodus 34:11. But Moses does begin the process of conquest. Under his leadership, the Israelites take territory east of the Jordan River, which is then allotted to some of the tribes of Israel (Numbers 21:21-35; 32:1-33).

Those victories leave their mark on the thinking of people such as Rahab of Jericho, who acknowledges to the two Israelite spies that "your terror is fallen upon us" (Joshua 2:9). She also recounts to them the victories of the Israelites "on the other side [of the] Jordan" (v. 10) and testifies that when she and her people heard of these events their "hearts did melt, neither did there remain any more courage in any man, because of you: for the Lord your God, he is God in heaven above, and in earth beneath" (v. 11).

Clearly, Moses leaves a legacy that is unsurpassed by any future leader of God's people except Jesus. The closing verses of Deuteronomy note that "there arose not a prophet since in Israel like unto Moses, whom the Lord knew face to face, . . . in all

God Promises an Awesome Thing

that mighty hand, and in all the great terror which Moses shewed in the sight of all Israel" (Deuteronomy 34:10, 12). The man who once asked, "Who am I, that I should go unto Pharaoh?" (Exodus 3:11) will leave this world with no doubt of who he is and, more importantly, who his God is.

> **What Do You Think?**
> Is it legitimate to compare God's "marvels" of the exodus with the "awesome" things we think He is doing in our church? Why, or why not?
> *Talking Points for Your Discussion*
> - Outreach ministries (evangelism, benevolence)
> - Inreach ministries (spiritual nurture)
> - Upreach ministries (worship)

❧ *HANDLING A PARADIGM SHIFT* ❧

Nanotechnology, which deals with the control of matter at the atomic and molecular level, is said to be the wave of the future. If that prediction is true, everything about our lives will change—clothing, cars, houses, food, medicine, computers, etc. Scientists predict that in just a few years more than half of all new products will be developed using nanotechnology. Some even suggest that we are right now in the beginning days of a new industrial revolution, one that will make the industrial revolution of the nineteenth century seem—shall we say—terribly old-fashioned!

The results are already being seen in lens coatings on eyeglasses, bonding agents on dental crowns, stain-resistant clothing, and tennis balls that last longer. Among the most amazing advances is chemotherapy medicine that attaches only to cancer cells!

This is an example of a *paradigm shift*, which is a change from one way of thinking to another. Handling paradigm shifts properly can be tricky. Take ancient Israel, for example. With the exodus, their thinking needed to change from slavery to freedom, from false gods to the true God. God promised to lead them to—and help them conquer—a land that would become theirs. However, Israel did not handle the paradigm shift well, and things went terribly wrong. It's a caution we need to hear as we contemplate our own future.   —C. R. B.

Conclusion
A. Inescapable Evidence

The four lessons that have been covered thus far are part of a quarter of studies under the topic *The Inescapable God*. It is instructive to consider today's lesson in particular in light of that theme.

That God is "inescapable" can be either comforting or frightening, because as today's study has noted He is a God of both mercy and judgment. David took great encouragement from knowing that the Lord had "beset me behind and before, and laid [His] hand upon me. Such knowledge is too wonderful for me; it is high, I cannot attain unto it" (Psalm 139:5, 6). Jonah found out that it is a good thing that God is inescapable! Though the reluctant prophet was tossed into the sea, the Lord knew exactly where he was.

On the other hand, the thought of standing in judgment before God should fill us with a sense of foreboding. Revelation 6:15-17 describes the anguish of those who are filled with terror at the wrath of the Lamb, "for the great day of his wrath is come; and who shall be able to stand?"

Thank God that in Jesus we see the mercy and the judgment of God displayed in a way that only God himself could have arranged! Paul summarizes the combination as follows: "For [God] hath made [Jesus] to be sin for us, who knew no sin; that we might be made the righteousness of God in him" (2 Corinthians 5:21). God's mercy toward sinners is made available because Jesus took humanity's judgment upon himself at the cross.

The cross is inescapable evidence of God's passion to demonstrate grace. If we ignore that evidence, judgment is inescapable.

B. Prayer

Father, thank You for revealing yourself to us as You have, especially in Jesus—the Word who became flesh and gave His life for us. May we offer ourselves to You each day in a lifestyle of grateful and reverent worship. In Jesus' name, amen.

C. Thought to Remember

All that the Lord revealed himself to be to Moses is seen in Jesus.

INVOLVEMENT LEARNING

Some of the activities below are also found in the helpful student book, Adult Bible Class.
Don't forget to download the free reproducible page from www.standardlesson.com to enhance your lesson!

Into the Lesson

Several occasions in today's lesson development call for a learner to read Bible texts related to the study. You may wish to preassign those, either earlier in the week or as learners arrive.

As each learner enters, direct him or her to the board where you have written *Write your name here.* Ask each learner to do so.

As class begins, have assigned readers read Exodus 33:17 and John 10:3. Then issue this old evangelist's challenge: "And all God's people said?" After you get the expected *Amen,* tell the class that's not the response you wanted. Turn things around and ask your learners to say the challenge in unison so that you (the teacher) can give the desired response. As soon as your class does so, articulate the sheep's sound: *Baa-a-a!*

The smiles (or groans) will draw attention to John 10:3 and, by extension, back to Exodus 33:17. There God prepares Moses for the experience of chapter 34, the source of today's text.

Into the Word

Have a learner read Exodus 33:11. Repeat the ideas in the verse. Say, "We all should desire such a closeness with God wherein He would consider us His friend." Have a learner read John 15:12-15.

Ask your class to define the word *awesome.* If one of your students does not mention it, point out that this word is used rather casually in the culture. As a result, a deeper, spiritual sense is difficult to maintain. Note that verse 10 of today's text uses the word *terrible* in the *King James Version,* a usage that is intended to convey the idea of *awe.*

Ask the class to examine today's text and suggest elements of awe that are implied in some way. Allow answers freely, but expect such elements as these: God's sanctification of the mountain (v. 3); the Lord coming down in a cloud (v. 5); the declarations of God (vv. 6, 7); Moses' reaction by bowing to the ground and worshiping (v. 8); Moses asking God to forgive the people (v. 9); God's promise to make a covenant to reveal himself in marvels/wonders (v. 10).

Then ask, "What wonderful work of God is most awesome to you?" Accept all answers, but expect one to be "the incarnation of the Son for our redemption." See if your class agrees with the proposition that that is indeed His most awe-inspiring deed.

Have a class member read Hebrews 1:1-3 as a statement of God revealing His glory. Return to Exodus 33:18 where Moses asked God to show him His glory. Affirm that we have seen God's glory in ways Moses could not imagine in his day. Have a learner read John 1:11-14. Shift from a discussion of God's deeds to a consideration of God's nature by breaking the class into study teams to complete the Who God Is activity on the reproducible page.

Into Life

Refer back to your Into the Lesson activity, in which learners wrote their names on the board. Remind the class that God indeed knows each of us by name. Reinforce the idea by having your class sing the following words to the tune of "Jesus Loves Me":

> *Jesus knows me, this I love;*
> *The Good Shepherd from above;*
> *Knows my name and knows my need;*
> *With grace and mercy, He will lead.*
> *Yes, Jesus knows me [3X]*
> *The Bible tells me so.*

Distribute copies of the Alone with God exercise from the reproducible page. Have learners complete this individually or in pairs. After an appropriate amount of time, ask for volunteers to share their successes and struggles in having "alone time" with God.

GOD'S MAJESTY AND HUMAN DIGNITY

BACKGROUND SCRIPTURE: Psalm 8
PRINTED TEXT: Psalm 8

PSALM 8

1 O LORD our Lord, how excellent is thy name in all the earth! who hast set thy glory above the heavens.

2 Out of the mouth of babes and sucklings hast thou ordained strength because of thine enemies, that thou mightest still the enemy and the avenger.

3 When I consider thy heavens, the work of thy fingers, the moon and the stars, which thou hast ordained;

4 What is man, that thou art mindful of him? and the son of man, that thou visitest him?

5 For thou hast made him a little lower than the angels, and hast crowned him with glory and honour.

6 Thou madest him to have dominion over the works of thy hands; thou hast put all things under his feet:

7 All sheep and oxen, yea, and the beasts of the field;

8 The fowl of the air, and the fish of the sea, and whatsoever passeth through the paths of the seas.

9 O LORD our Lord, how excellent is thy name in all the earth!

KEY VERSE

Thou madest him to have dominion over the works of thy hands; thou hast put all things under his feet.
—**Psalm 8:6**

41

THE INESCAPABLE GOD

Unit 2: God Sustains

LESSONS 5–9

LESSON AIMS

After participating in this lesson, each student will be able to:

1. Summarize what the text says about the place of humans in God's created universe.

2. Compare and contrast the Bible's view of humanity with the extremes prevalent today—exalting humans to god-like status on the one hand or as no better than animals on the other.

3. Make a statement of self-worth that recognizes God's order of creation.

LESSON OUTLINE

Introduction

A. Ultimate Questions

Poetry has power. The artistic expression of human observations, emotions, and desires retains influence over the passage of the years in poetry. We all have observed others moved to tears by hearing just a line of a beloved poem or song. Think of "In Flanders fields . . ."; "On a hill far away . . ."; "The Lord is my shepherd . . ." These words have power to move us. This week we begin a two-month series of lessons taken from the greatest of all poetry books, the Psalms. Here we find both questions and answers to the vital issues of life.

The Greek philosopher Aristotle (384–322 BC) began his classic treatise *Metaphysics* with this statement: "All humans naturally desire to know." But what do we—or what should we—desire to know? What are the ultimate questions? From a human perspective, we may boil down the critical questions to three. First, "Where did we come from?" Second, "Why are we here?" And third, "Where are we going?" These are the questions of *origin, purpose,* and *destiny.* (Some thinkers expand these three to four: *origin, condition, salvation,* and *destiny.*) Psalm 8 deals directly with the first two of the three questions, providing answers that still resonate nearly 3,000 years after David wrote it.

Naturalistic science sometimes tries to avoid these questions altogether. Some nonreligious people might say that to ask *Why are we here?* is ridiculous. But to dismiss the tough questions does not answer them. The great thinkers throughout history have grappled with these questions.

A vital question in Psalm 8 is *Why does God care about human beings?* This question is not posed for the discussion of the learned person, however. Rather, it is asked of God himself. The answer given forms the bedrock basis for our understanding of our relationship with God. When we have understood and appreciated this answer, all the other questions begin to find answers too.

B. Lesson Background

The Psalms contain some of the most-loved Scriptures in the entire Bible. Little children are taught to memorize Psalms 23 and 100 at an early age.

God's Majesty and Human Dignity

Passages from Psalms are quoted approximately 80 times in the New Testament, more than any other Old Testament book. Today's worship and praise songs are filled with words taken from Psalms.

It is best, however, not to think of Psalms as a "book" like most other Bible books. It is actually a collection of material from many different authors and periods in the history of Israel. This collection is divided into five subbooks, each ending with a similar statement of praise to God (see Psalms 41:13; 72:18, 19; 89:52; 106:48; and 150:6). Many people think that King David, "the sweet psalmist of Israel" (2 Samuel 23:1), wrote the psalms. Indeed, we find his name attached to 72 psalms, but that is fewer than half of them. David is just 1 of 7 authors we can identify. In addition to him, we find psalms written by Asaph, the Sons of Korah, Solomon, Moses, Heman, and Ethan. Moreover, 51 psalms (about one-third) do not identify the author, thus remaining anonymous.

Today's text, Psalm 8, is ascribed to David. We are told in the psalm's superscription that it is to be performed according to the *Gittith,* but we are not sure what a *Gittith* was. Some believe it is related to the word for *winepress.* If this is the case, the directions are to sing it using the melody from the "Song of the Winepress," although we do not have this tune.

Another explanation is that the *Gittith* was some type of musical instrument, perhaps a stringed instrument. Again, this is possible, but we do not know what such an instrument looked like or what type of sound it produced. Regardless, we recognize the influence of this psalm in such well-known hymns as "How Great Thou Art," "For the Beauty of the Earth," and "This Is My Father's World."

Psalm 8 is sometimes designated as *a creation psalm.* Others in this category include Psalms 19, 29, 65, and 104. They all contain parallels to Genesis 1 and meditate on the marvel and power of God's creation. Many other passages present God as the Creator (see Job 38, 39; Isaiah 42:5; Amos 4:13; compare Colossians 1:15-17). Psalm 8 is the best-known creation psalm, and it still serves to help us understand the mysteries of God's purposes in creating the universe.

I. Divine Excellency
(PSALM 8:1, 2)
A. Preeminence in Earth and Heaven (v. 1)

1. O LORD our Lord, how excellent is thy name in all the earth! who hast set thy glory above the heavens.

David begins by marveling at the Lord's excellence. The word *excellent* conveys a sense of royal majesty. David distinguishes the Lord from earthly kings, though, by proclaiming that God's glory extends far beyond the human realm to be the preeminent name in all the universe, higher than any created reality, even that of *the heavens.*

It is a quirk of our English translations that the word *Lord* is repeated here for no apparent reason. However, the careful reader will note that the first *LORD* is in small capital letters while the second is not. The small-capital rendering is the conventional way of translating the divine, personal name of God, which is *Yahweh.* This is sometimes called *the Tetragrammaton,* meaning "four letters." Without vowels (which is how Hebrew is written), *Yahweh* shortens to *YHWH,* which are the four letters. A long-standing tradition in English translations is to indicate this word by using small capital letters in the text, thus *LORD.* The second *Lord* is the word of respect that means "lord" in any context, whether addressed to God or one's superior.

> ### What Do You Think?
> If God's glory is already "above the heavens," how can we glorify Him as other psalms call us to do?
> #### Talking Points for Your Discussion
> - Isaiah 42:12; Jeremiah 13:16; Revelation 4:9; 14:7
> - Glory as "stuff" vs. glory as "recognition"
> - Obedience, praise, and worship as they relate to glory

B. Paradoxical Power (v. 2)

2. Out of the mouth of babes and sucklings hast thou ordained strength because of thine enemies, that thou mightest still the enemy and the avenger.

Sometimes the best way to understand the attributes of God is to speak in a paradox. Here David presents the example of the weakest human beings: *babes and sucklings.* His point is that the majesty of the Lord is so overwhelming that even these wee ones can be empowered to acknowledge God and do His work. This is a power that routs any who would stand as an enemy of God or His people. The weakest people who trust in the Lord are more powerful than the strongest of the godless.

This paradox is enacted during Jesus' last public ministry in Jerusalem. At that time, the children and common people acclaim Him as Messiah while the powerful leaders of the city reject Him. Jesus quotes this verse to explain the apparent contradiction (Matthew 21:16).

II. Human Insignificance
(Psalm 8:3, 4)
A. Speck in the Universe (v. 3)

3. When I consider thy heavens, the work of thy fingers, the moon and the stars, which thou hast ordained.

Human understanding of the immensity of the universe has grown dramatically since the time of David. What has not changed is the awe that we feel (or should feel) when gazing at a clear sky on a dark, cloudless night. This is even more spectacular if we are removed from the lights of a city and away from any pollution in the air. If we are at high altitude, this is magnified to another level.

We can see the fabulous phenomenon we call *the Milky Way,* and yet we understand that it is not white liquid in the sky. It is comprised of stars in such number and concentration that they look like white blotches. Some scientists believe there are more than 100 billion stars in our galaxy alone, with more than 400 billion galaxies in the universe. Most calculators cannot process these numbers, and neither can our minds fully grasp them.

David understands all this humbling magnificence to be the careful and delicate creation of his Creator. It is the work of God's fingers, an intimate act. David's ancestors understood "the finger of God" as having written words on stone tablets for Moses, giving Israel its law (Exodus 31:18). David is not saying that our God is a glorified human with a physical body, but that our Creator is personal and deliberate beyond our greatest imaginings.

> **What Do You Think?**
> What comes to mind when we think of someone working with his or her fingers? What could this imply about the creation and the Creator?
> *Talking Points for Your Discussion*
> - Attention to detail
> - Advance planning

God's creation is with purpose. It is not the bored experiment of a capricious deity. God has created men and women to be in fellowship with Him. God also has created a beautiful, meaningful universe to be our home (Isaiah 45:18).

Today, some scientists cannot imagine that humanity is the center and purpose of the universe. They want, desperately, to find intelligent beings on other planets. To such scientists, we are an insignificant speck in this enormous universe. Their faith in the randomness of nature and the known extent of the universe causes them to doubt the uniqueness of humanity.

All this can be understood only if we realize that God is the Creator of all, and He answers to no scientist as to why and how He has ordered His creation. David would agree that we are a tiny

Visual for Lesson 5. Use this visual to start a discussion regarding where your learners have seen the fingerprint of God.

God's Majesty and Human Dignity

crumb (size wise) in the universe, but this does not drive him to the despair of unbelief. Instead, it pushes him to greater depths of faith.

B. Puzzle in the Cosmos (v. 4)

4. What is man, that thou art mindful of him? and the son of man, that thou visitest him?

Having extolled God's glory as revealed in His creation, David now narrows his focus to one of the great questions: *What is man?* By extension, why would the Creator of the marvelous universe care about human beings?

This central question occurs elsewhere in the Bible. Job asks the question out of his misery, trying to understand why God has afflicted him with such great suffering (Job 7:17). Later, Job's question is thrown back to him by his "friend" Bildad, who challenges Job's assumption that human beings are any more important than a worm (Job 25:6). Psalm 144:3 offers another example of David asking this question. There, the psalmist-king does not offer an answer to the question "What is man?" but uses it to show the profound contrast between frail humanity and mighty God.

We acknowledge that we are used to seeing the phrase *son of man* as a title for Jesus. However, the descriptor *son of man* occurs in the Old Testament over 100 times in reference to human beings—usually to the prophet Ezekiel.

❧ *Who Am I?* ❧

The world of secular psychology seems to have a fancy word for just about everything dealing with human nature. Consider the word *individuation*. This word sums up the process by which children establish their own identities, particularly in distinction from their parents.

This often is not a "pretty" process, as parents of teenagers can attest. Actually, the process begins very early in life. The two-year-old who has learned to use the words *no* and *mine* has started on the long road toward individuation, for better or for worse. The ensuing years involve a series of choices by which a child asserts his or her independence in various ways. These choices involve accepting and rejecting various foods, clothing,

friendships, and values. It's all a part of the process of answering the question *Who am I?*

The most important aspect of that question is found in the way the psalmist phrased it. By using the word *thou*, the psalmist recognized that *Who am I?* must be answered in terms of our relationship with the God who created the universe. That's the proper starting point! Those who attempt to answer the question *Who am I?* without reference to the Creator will not come to a correct answer.

—C. R. B.

III. Human Responsibility
(Psalm 8:5-9)

A. Position of Dignity (v. 5)

5. For thou hast made him a little lower than the angels, and hast crowned him with glory and honor.

David begins his answer to the question by reflecting on the position of humanity in the created order. He teaches us that there is a ceiling for us, and this can be defined in reference to the angels of God. They are special creatures of God, designed to perform crucial tasks of ministry for the Almighty (Hebrews 1:14).

We should admit that we do not fully understand the exact nature and position of angels. In some ways, the Bible presents angels as extensions or representatives of God himself. For example, when Jacob receives the message from God that it

HOW TO SAY IT

Aristotle	Eh-rih-*stah*-tul.
Asaph	*Ay*-saff.
Bildad	*Bill*-dad.
Ezekiel	Ee-*zeek*-ee-ul or Ee-*zeek*-yul.
individuation	in-dih-vid-you-*a*-shun.
Jean-Jacques	Zhahn-zhahk
Rousseau	Roo-*soh*.
Korah	*Ko*-rah.
Marquis de Sade	Mar-key deh *Sod*.
Moses	*Mo*-zes or *Mo*-zez.
Solomon	*Sol*-o-mun.
Tetragrammaton	Teh-truh-*grah*-muh-tawn.
Yahweh *(Hebrew)*	*Yah*-weh.

is time for him to leave Laban and return home, it is presented as a revelation through an angel (Genesis 31:11), yet the message Jacob receives is presented as the voice of God himself (Genesis 31:13).

What we do know, however, is that angels are not glorified human beings. We do not become angels when we die, although we become "equal unto the angels" in certain respects (Luke 20:35, 36). Angels are a created order of beings distinct from humans. They are not described as being made in God's image, as humans are (Genesis 1:27). The fact that "we shall judge angels" (1 Corinthians 6:3) indicates that being *a little lower than the angels* is a temporary situation.

What Do You Think?

How does popular culture view angels? What's wrong and right with those ideas?

Talking Points for Your Discussion

- Cultural ideas that match the Bible
- Cultural ideas that contradict the Bible
- Cultural ideas that cannot be confirmed or refuted by the Bible

---

B. Position of Responsibility (vv. 6-8)

6. Thou madest him to have dominion over the works of thy hands; thou hast put all things under his feet.

David presents the true position and purpose of humanity. While on earth, we are created to function in a position below the angelic beings of God's Heaven, but above all other created things. This is acknowledged to be a place of *dominion,* a position of power and control.

Dominion is not permission to exploit, however. Herein lies the stewardship responsibility of the human race. Genesis records that God created a man and placed him in a beautiful garden "to dress it and to keep it" (Genesis 2:15). God has given us a marvelous home in which to live. Will we treat the earth with respect or with contempt?

7, 8. All sheep and oxen, yea, and the beasts of the field; the fowl of the air, and the fish of the sea, and whatsoever passeth through the paths of the seas.

David lists the three realms of living beings as understood by ancient people: land, air, and sea (compare Genesis 1:28). His description includes both domesticated and wild animals. These are the areas of human dominion.

Reductionist science is uneasy with this biblical perspective. Some scientists want to see the human race as just another species among many. Yet that viewpoint is unable to explain the vast difference in intelligence between human beings and the rest of the animal species. No other animal species even approaches the human capacity for knowledge.

The Bible also teaches that we are unique in our spiritual nature, and therefore our relationship with God. While we may share DNA and genes with other animals, humans are created with a dignity and purpose that no other mortal life form possesses. To assert that human life is no more important or valuable than any other living creature is a direct contradiction of David's teaching here.

What Do You Think?

What are some ways you can exercise your "dominion" role in a godly manner?

Talking Points for Your Discussion

- Stewardship of renewable resources
- Stewardship of nonrenewable resources
- Proper relationship to pets

❧ *BANKRUPT PHILOSOPHY* ❧

Two eighteenth-century European philosophers illustrate two of secular society's perspectives on human nature. Jean-Jacques Rousseau (1712–1778) is commonly credited with speaking of humans as "noble savages" (although that term actually was first used by John Dryden in 1692). By this designation, Rousseau believed that humans are good when in the state of nature that characterizes all the other animals (as he would have phrased it), but we become increasingly corrupted by society.

The Marquis de Sade (1740–1814) also believed that man is governed by his nature. But his viewpoint was that this nature is "intrinsic," and thus not to be fought against. Rather, it is to be enjoyed to the fullest. In that light, he advocated radical freedom in the way people treat each other, including the freedom to abuse them. He was imprisoned many times for rape, torture, sodomy, and poisoning. His name is the source of our word *sadism*.

Neither view offers us the perspective that is stated by the psalmist. Being made in the image of God gives us a status that neither philosopher acknowledged. Human identity is not decided by philosophers, but by the Creator.　　—C. R. B.

C. Position of Praise (v. 9)

9. O LORD our Lord, how excellent is thy name in all the earth!

The final line of the psalm repeats the first line. Thus we have come full circle. We are reminded that it is not about us. It is about God. It is foolish to praise the glories of the universe without remembering the Lord (Romans 1:20). It is futile to worship the creation and not the Creator (1:21, 22).

The final word of the psalm is a good reminder for us too. The earth is the home of the human race. We were created for the earth. The earth was created for us. It is our venue for appreciating and worshiping the Lord. There is a perfect match, provided by the wisdom of God. When we really understand this, we are naturally moved to proclaim, *how excellent is thy name!*

What Do You Think?

What can you do this week to proclaim the excellent nature of God's name?

Talking Points for Your Discussion
- At home
- At work or school
- During recreational activities

Conclusion

A. Human Animals?

Why is human dignity important? Why do even secularists speak of the "sacredness" of human life? Is human life any more sacred than the life of, say, a cow or a salmon? These are important questions.

The consensus for many millennia that human beings are a distinct and higher order of earth's life is now challenged. Some would reduce humanity

to merely another branch of the animal kingdom. Others would elevate all animals to a position of sacred dignity that sees humanity without special privilege. Psalm 8 places human beings properly in relation to God, angels, and animals.

The book of Hebrews gives us a further implication of the high position of humans in God's created order. To be a "little lower than the angels" was a position of dignity suitable for the incarnation (Hebrews 2:6-9). God became human in the person of Jesus. It was necessary for Jesus to be human for two primary reasons. First, as a man He was able to communicate God to us in a direct and credible way (John 1:18). God did not come as a talking monkey. He came as a man.

Second, it was important that Jesus be human in order for Him to die for our sins (Hebrews 2:9). Angels spoke to men and women in various places in the Bible (Luke 1:26-28; Hebrews 2:2; etc.). But no angel could die for human sins. Animal sacrifices for sin were good but inadequate. Only the sacrifice of the Son of God as the Son of Man was sufficient and "once for all" (Hebrews 10:10).

If we ponder this, we may begin to understand why we were created with certain capacities. These capacities were needed by God to impart His revelation effectively. A cat sleeping in the sun may have a vague appreciation for God's provision for its comfort. But that is a quantum leap removed from the human enjoyment of the fellowship and love of God in which we participate. God did not create a perfect cat to save all catdom. He did not send a flawless pine tree to redeem all treedom. He sent a perfect man, the human Jesus, to liberate us from the bondage of sin and be restored to Him.

B. Prayer

O Lord, how excellent is Your name! How majestic is Your creation. How marvelous is Your plan. May we come to You today as persons with whom You have provided great dignity, but who willingly submit ourselves to You. We pray this in the excellent name of Your Son, amen.

C. Thought to Remember

God has granted us
both authority and responsibility.

INVOLVEMENT LEARNING

Some of the activities below are also found in the helpful student book, Adult Bible Class.
Don't forget to download the free reproducible page from www.standardlesson.com to enhance your lesson!

Into the Lesson

Download the reproducible page and put in chairs copies of the Five Books, One Theme activity for learners to begin working on as they arrive. *Alternative:* Distribute copies of the What Is Man? activity from the reproducible page instead.

Ask several class members in advance to come prepared to quote or read their favorite short poem. This will introduce the concept of poetry as power and passion encapsulated in few words. As class begins, ask your assigned learners to stand and present their verses.

Alternative. Display a variety of books of poetry, both those for children and for adults. (A library will have several poetry anthologies on its shelves.) As your class assembles and notices your collection, paraphrase the first paragraph of the lesson introduction's "Ultimate Questions."

Into the Word

Say to your class, "It has been said that poetry is a way to wrap big ideas in very small but beautiful packages." Distribute paper and pencils. Ask learners to make two columns, one headed *Big Things* and the other headed *Little Things.* Say, "I am going to read to you a list of words from Psalm 8. Write each into one of the two columns." Then read the following list; pause between words to give learners time to decide and write.

Lord; name; earth; glory; heavens; mouth; babes; strength; enemies; avenger; fingers; moon; stars; man; angels; honor; dominion; hands; feet; beasts; fowl; fish; sea; paths.

At the end say, "Now let's read today's familiar text and see if you change your mind on any words." Do a double antiphonal reading of the text wherein you read one segment of a verse, then one side of the class repeats it, followed by the other side of the class doing the same. For example, in verse one you would read, "O LORD, our Lord, how excellent is thy name in all the earth."

Then one side would read the same thing, then the other. Continue through the nine verses in this manner, in repeatable segments of your choosing. This threefold repetition will well fix the words for your continuing discussion.

Next, give class members an opportunity to identify words they put in each column. Discuss differences among answers.

At the end, ask how one could consider this psalm to follow a "big-little rhythm." Let students examine the text and suggest answers. If no one gets the class started, point out that God (a BIG concept) is the emphasis and subject of verse 1. You may see that children (little, in a relative sense of size) are in the second verse; verse 3 returns to the universe (big); verse four turns to man (little, in a relative sense); verse 5 goes to angels (big); verses 6-8 note animals and other creatures (little) and verse nine restates God's glory (BIG). All this is to get learners to think about humanity's position in God's creation and plan of redemption.

Into Life

Give each learner a card with the following:
Big I, Little i—Lord, how big am I?
Am I You, God? Am I all-powerful, the Lord of all I see and do?
Am I just another animal, Lord, a bundle of random instincts?
Why, O Lord, do I count to You?
Yet, while I was living life in sin, You said, "O _____, you can be a child of God."
You, O Lord, said "_____, I love you!"
You, Lord, paid the price of my redemption: one crucified Son.
O Lord, my Lord, how excellent and majestic is Your name!

Have learners put their names in the blanks. Suggest that each one place his or her card where it can be read to start each day with a biblical sense of self-worth.

God's Majesty and Human Dignity

GOD'S
PERFECT LAW

BACKGROUND SCRIPTURE: Psalm 19

PRINTED TEXT: Psalm 19:7-14

PSALM 19:7-14

7 The law of the LORD is perfect, converting the soul: the testimony of the LORD is sure, making wise the simple.

8 The statutes of the LORD are right, rejoicing the heart: the commandment of the LORD is pure, enlightening the eyes.

9 The fear of the LORD is clean, enduring for ever: the judgments of the LORD are true and righteous altogether.

10 More to be desired are they than gold, yea, than much fine gold: sweeter also than honey and the honeycomb.

11 Moreover by them is thy servant warned: and in keeping of them there is great reward.

12 Who can understand his errors? Cleanse thou me from secret faults.

13 Keep back thy servant also from presumptuous sins; let them not have dominion over me: then shall I be upright, and I shall be innocent from the great transgression.

14 Let the words of my mouth, and the meditation of my heart, be acceptable in thy sight, O LORD, my strength, and my redeemer.

KEY VERSE

The law of the LORD is perfect, converting the soul: the testimony of the LORD is sure, making wise the simple. The statutes of the LORD are right, rejoicing the heart: the commandment of the LORD is pure, enlightening the eyes. —Psalm 19:7, 8

THE INESCAPABLE GOD

Unit 2: God Sustains

LESSONS 5–9

LESSON AIMS

After participating in this lesson, each student will be able to:

1. List several benefits or values of God's Word ("law").

2. Contrast the psalmist's view of the unchanging Word of God with the relativism of postmodern culture.

3. Commit to reading the Bible through in a year.

LESSON OUTLINE

Introduction

A. The Curse of Lawlessness

The school experience involves more than learning how to read, write, and do math. It also involves learning to follow rules of the classroom. In an earlier generation, this included such basics as no gum-chewing, lining up correctly, and addressing teachers with respect. Teachers seem to have other battles to fight these days. Rules now include no text-messaging in class, no gang-related clothing, and no inappropriate touching.

Recently I was waiting in line to be served by a clerk at a local drugstore photo counter. The person in front of me was confused and was demanding an accounting of his bill to the last penny. As I tried to wait politely for the young clerk to finish with this persistent customer, another man came up who was obviously impatient. He initially waited behind me. But as the first customer continued to fuss and linger, the second man was soon standing beside me.

When my turn came, the clerk turned to me, but Mr. Impatient asserted himself and demanded to be waited upon, disregarding me. I chose not to make a scene, but thought, "This man never learned the basics. He doesn't even know the rule about lining up and waiting your turn. He needs to go back to kindergarten."

Any ordered society needs rules that guide public behavior. Because we always have rule breakers among us, we need laws and police to enforce them. Enforcement requires judges and penalties, and so a legal system is born. The best societies, however, are ones in which the enforcement of laws is seen as a personal responsibility rather than a police task. The citizenry follows the law, even when there is no possibility of police detection or prosecution.

In a lawless society, rules are spurned and disregarded by individuals. If this becomes too widespread, the result is either chaos or the imposition of a draconian police state. The answer is not really to have more laws and law enforcers. The ultimate and only answer is to have people with the integrity to strive to obey the laws without the threat of a watching police officer.

A problem in all of this, however, is that human laws are always imperfect and may favor one citizen at the expense of another. A notorious example in the history of the United States is the Fugitive Slave Act of 1850. It required people who abhorred slavery to assist in the tracking down and capturing of runaway slaves. This law perpetuated injustice on several levels and contributed to the societal breakdown of America's Civil War.

In the Old Testament, Israel was privileged to be both the people of God and the people of God's laws. They had a legal code to regulate their religion and society, but it was more than the product of the best legal minds and traditions of their day. It was God's law, delivered to Israel through God's chosen representatives. It was perfect, for it gave humans guidance from the Creator on how humans should live. It has been referred to as an "owner's manual," written by the great designer.

From this perspective, then, lawlessness is more than a penchant to break the rules of a society. It is a disregard for the expressed and intended will of God in the realm of human behavior. This understanding of the relationship between God, God's laws, and human beings is at the heart of today's lesson.

B. Lesson Background

Hebrew poetry is unlike traditional English poetry. Whereas we are accustomed to poetry that uses rhyme, rhythm, alliteration, and repetitive structure, the poetry we find in Psalms relies more on a balance of ideas and repetition of thoughts. We call this feature of Hebrew poetry *parallelism*.

It is important to recognize this parallel arrangement when we read the Bible. If we do not, we may not recognize that two lines of poetry are saying the same thing. Instead, we may think there are two points being made and impose an incorrect interpretation on the text. Our lesson today looks at the last half of Psalm 19, which features several good examples of parallelism.

The superscription of Psalm 19 presents this work as a composition of David "to the chief Musician." This could mean that the psalm was originally a private composition of King David that eventually became a resource to be used in public worship. It begins with the same theme as last week's psalm (Psalm 8) in extolling the wonders of God's creation. The theme of Psalm 19:1-6, just before today's lesson text, is the witness that is given to God's glory through the beauty of the heavens and the earth. Its sense of the verbal proclamation of creation reminds us of God speaking creation into existence as portrayed in Genesis 1.

In the last half of the psalm (today's text), this verbal aspect of God's creative powers is directed toward the divine laws given to the people of God. As God's creation is beautiful and perfect, so are His laws.

I. Seeking Legal Perfection
(PSALM 19:7-11)
A. Appreciating God's Law (vv. 7, 8)

7, 8. The law of the LORD is perfect, converting the soul: the testimony of the LORD is sure, making wise the simple. The statutes of the LORD are right, rejoicing the heart: the commandment of the LORD is pure, enlightening the eyes.

These two verses have a total of four parallel lines. (It may look like eight parallel lines if your edition of the Bible uses narrow columns, but in Hebrew it's really just four.) Each of the four lines begins with the same general subject: some expression of *the law of the Lord*.

The first line's word for *law* is the famous word *torah*, which Jews today use to refer to the first five books of the Old Testament. *Torah* has a broader sense than law as legal code. It is the expression of God's will for human beings as revealed in His recorded words and actions.

This expanded sense of law is variously seen in the three companion terms. The first of these

HOW TO SAY IT

covenant	*kuv*-nent or *kuh*-vuh-nent.
Maimonides	My-*mah*-nuh-deez.
medieval	me-*dee*-vul or me-dee-*ee*-vul.
Moses	*Mo*-zes or *Mo*-zez.
Nazarite	*Naz*-uh-rite.
rabbi	*rab*-eye.
torah	*tor*-uh.

three is *testimony*. It is also a legal term that has a sense of "witness." It is sometimes synonymous with "covenant" and can be used to refer to the actual tablets of stone inscribed by God and given to Moses. These are housed in the ark of the covenant, which is sometimes called "the ark of the testimony" (Exodus 25:22; 26:33, 34; etc.).

The second of these companion terms is *statutes*. It brings the sense of specific laws that go together to form a legal code. The Hebrew word behind this term is used only in the Psalms, and it is a favorite in Psalm 119, where it appears 21 times.

The third companion term for *law* is *commandment*. This carries the implication of something that must be obeyed. The Bible often speaks of "keeping" God's commandments (example: Psalm 78:7). This indicates an active response.

The four parallel terms *law, testimony, statutes,* and *commandment* are followed by four descriptive designations: *perfect, sure, right,* and *pure,* respectively. These set the Lord's law apart from any human creation. We might say that God's law is always complete, always stable and trustworthy, always correct, and always above corruption. It needs no adjustment for changing times. It shares a quality of eternality with its Creator.

Finally, each of the four descriptive terms is followed by a result. These are *converting the soul, making wise the simple, rejoicing the heart,* and *enlightening the eyes*. These reveal the remarkable power available to those who follow God's will as revealed in His Scriptures. They will find inspiration, wisdom, joy, and clarity. They need not live an existence of depression, foolishness, sadness, and ignorance. God's law is for their benefit.

❧ *IMPERFECT LAW AND PERFECT LAW* ❧

Some argue that the American system of representative government is *the* best approach to governing society ever developed. Yet we see from history that it is not perfect. The fact that the U.S. Constitution has been amended numerous times is evidence of imperfection.

Take, for example, the issue of Prohibition. One of the most argued-over constitutional amendments in America's history is the eighteenth, ratified in 1919. It forbade the manufacture, sale, and transportation of "intoxicating liquors." It was repealed by the Twenty-first Amendment in 1933. Regardless of which amendment was "better," this back-and-forth revision reveals that human laws are subject to the whims of human nature and the changing political winds.

Not so with the laws of God. God's law glistens in its perfection. It is absolutely trustworthy. God's law is right, which brings joy to the hearts of upright people. It is like a brilliant light that enables us to see the nature of moral perfection. Is that how you perceive God's law? —C. R. B.

B. Internalizing God's Law (vv. 9-11)

9a. The fear of the LORD is clean, enduring for ever.

Having described the law from an impersonal, objective viewpoint, David now turns to the personal, subjective side. What is our response to this powerful gift of the Lord?

David begins the answer with a well-known starting place for Bible students: *the fear of the Lord.* The person who seeks to live wisely knows that "the fear of the Lord is the beginning of wisdom" (Psalm 111:10). This attitude of reverence and respect for God and the things of God are presented with two important qualities: purity and eternity. The word *clean* emphasizes the necessary attitude of holiness involved in the fear of the Lord. There is no need for later modification of this response, for it is *enduring for ever.*

> *What Do You Think?*
> How do you balance fearing God with loving God?
> *Talking Points for Your Discussion*
> ▪ Deuteronomy 10:12; 1 John 4:18
> ▪ Relationship between children and parents

9b. The judgments of the LORD are true and righteous altogether.

The judgments of the Lord should not be seen as something distinct from the law discussed above. The sense of this term is what we would refer to as "case law." These are prior decisions of a judge that have become precedents and are legally binding. In point at hand, the quality of the judgments and the character of the judge are flawless, so the judgments are always true, with no taint of falseness. Furthermore, these judgments are *righteous altogether,* a phrase that lifts up the perfect, uncorrupted justice present in the expressed will of God in the laws delivered to Israel.

10. More to be desired are they than gold, yea, than much fine gold: sweeter also than honey and the honeycomb.

Here the psalmist expresses an attitude that is generally absent in today's world: the desirability of the law. We often see contempt for laws and the desire to bend, abolish, or avoid them.

David uses two comparisons to highlight the desirability of which he speaks. First, the guidance of the Lord through His laws is more attractive than the finest *gold,* the ultimate in material possessions for the ancient world (compare Psalm 119:127). Second, God's laws are *sweeter* than *honey,* an extremely precious food commodity. Honey is virtually the only source of intense sugar available. Chocolate, a modern favorite "source" of sugar after sugar is added, is unknown to David, for its origins are in Central and South America.

Gold and honey, the high points of human luxury, thus are considered inferior to God's commandments. Nothing in the earthly realm can compare with the desirability of the law of the Lord (compare Psalm 73:25).

> **What Do You Think?**
> How would our church be different if we truly valued God's law more than gold?
> *Talking Points for Your Discussion*
> - What we talk about
> - How we behave
> - What our budget priorities would be
> - How we schedule our time

11. Moreover by them is thy servant warned: and in keeping of them there is great reward.

David ends his analysis of human response to the law of the Lord by invoking the common Old Testament theme of the blessing and curse. We find fulfillment, even great reward, for obedience. At the same time, we are warned. There are nega-

Visual for Lesson 6. Point to this visual as you introduce the discussion question that is associated with verse 10.

tive consequences for disregard and disobedience. The law is inherently both a stick and a carrot. It will punish wrongdoers and reward those serving it faithfully (see Deuteronomy 30:19, 20).

> **What Do You Think?**
> In what ways do you benefit from keeping God's law?
> *Talking Points for Your Discussion*
> - Health issues
> - Relationship issues
> - Conscience issues

Although we cannot be sure when this psalm is written as far as David's life is concerned, we know that David experiences both sides of this promise. David is called a man after God's own heart (1 Samuel 13:14; Acts 13:22), yet David and the nation are punished because of his presumptuous, sinful pride (1 Chronicles 21:17). Therefore, there may be a personal element behind the words *by them is thy servant warned.*

II. Seeking Personal Perfection
(PSALM 19:12-14)
A. Recognizing Our Blind Spots (v. 12)

12. Who can understand his errors? Cleanse thou me from secret faults.

Having looked at the law from both an objective and a subjective standpoint, David now begins to examine the practical side of his relationship with God's commands. First, he lifts up the introspective power of the law: it assists us in identifying our *errors*. Many years later, the apostle Paul will echo this thought when he says that he never would have understood the sin of covetousness without the law (Romans 7:7).

In the midst of this appreciation for the law, David breathes a simple prayer to the Lord: *cleanse thou me*. This is something the law cannot do. The commandments of God are perfect in their function of defining and identifying sin, but there is no power in the law to bring forgiveness.

To the contrary, the law makes us realize the depth of our sinfulness, the magnitude of our spiritual uncleanness. It is only God who can create a clean heart (Psalm 51:10). Only He can wash our sins so that they are as white as snow (Isaiah 1:18).

B. Asking for Assistance (v. 13)

13a. Keep back thy servant also from presumptuous sins.

Recognizing his weakness, David pleads for God's assistance in a dangerous sin territory: that of *presumptuous sins*. This is the category of deliberate, intentional sin. Once we are informed as to what constitutes sinful behavior in the eyes of God, what excuse do we have for continuing such behavior?

13b. Let them not have dominion over me.

David well knows that certain types of sin may exert a powerful sway over people. He describes this influence as *dominion* (compare Psalm 8:6 from last week's lesson). We are wise to recognize that the devil may have strongholds of sin in our lives (see 2 Corinthians 10:4).

Modern psychology may label such things as pathologies or addictions. We might tag someone as a "pathological liar," a "sex addict," or as "incurably greedy." But these are more than psychological disorders. We should recognize that while the law helps us understand these ungodly and destructive sin patterns, we need God's assistance in breaking down these strongholds. We pray that we will not let sin have dominion over us (Romans 6:14).

13c. Then shall I be upright, and I shall be innocent from the great transgression.

David's final desire is that he be upright and that he avoid profound, life-wrecking sin. He calls this *great transgression*. This is not "great" in the sense of a single, colossal sin-mistake that destroys one's marriage or career. It is, rather, "great" in the sense of an ongoing, willful, defiant life-pattern that privately thumbs its nose at God and believes itself to be untouchable or undetectable.

C. Focusing Our Efforts (v. 14)

14. Let the words of my mouth, and the meditation of my heart, be acceptable in thy sight, O LORD, my strength, and my redeemer.

David ends with a prayer of submission, the expression of the desire to conform his thoughts and his words to God's standards. His final description of God reveals his strategy for accomplishing this desired result: God is his strength.

David knows his inability to live up to God's law with his own strength. Without God's empowering Holy Spirit, he is lost (compare Psalm 51:11). In the end, David also knows that even with God's help, he will fail and sin. For this reason he looks

God's Perfect Law

to God as his *redeemer,* the one who must "come and save" him (Isaiah 35:4).

The television age has introduced us to *the sound bite.* This is a snippet of someone's comments or speech. Often, sound bites are used to summarize a person's thoughts fairly. But sometimes sound bites are used deliberately to take a person's thoughts out of context, with the intent of defaming or discrediting that person.

The Internet has added another way for harming others, and anyone can disseminate false information widely using that medium. The fact that false information can be spread anonymously in this manner shields the perpetrator from accountability for actions intended to harm or deceive. Thus the temptation to do so increases.

If David were offering his ancient prayer today, he might have to update it! Today it could read something like "and may the output of my fingers on the keyboard be acceptable in your sight, O Lord." Technology gives us new outlets for the meditations of our hearts. Christians, of all people, should use it to glorify God.   —C. R. B.

Conclusion

A. A Religion of Rules?

What is the Christian to do with the Old Testament law? Moses Maimonides, the medieval Jewish rabbi, counted 613 separate commandments in the laws of Moses. Maimonides catalogued these laws in two divisions. One set consisted of the negative, "thou shalt not" directives. Maimonides listed 365 of these, significant for him because it is the number of days in a solar year. The other set consisted of the positive, "thou shalt" directives. Maimonides found 248 of these and linked them to the segments in the human body.

Every commandment on Maimonides's list can be found in the Old Testament, but we certainly ignore a lot of them today. For example, #606 is the instruction to provide each soldier with a shovel in order to dig a latrine (Deuteronomy 23:13). Commandment #221 forbids those taking a Nazarite vow to eat raisins (Numbers 6:3). Commandment #69 forbids men to shave their beards (Leviticus 19:27). These and many others are seen as either irrelevant or nonbinding to the Christian.

But we don't want to toss out the figurative baby with the bathwater! The church must work hard to understand the value of the Old Testament law and its application for us today. The gospel frees us from the tyranny of the law and its hopelessness (Romans 8:2; Colossians 2:14). No one in training is successful if the coach offers nothing but criticism. The law tends to highlight our flaws and weaknesses, whereas the gospel allows us to transcend sin and live for the Lord without dread.

This does not mean we have no more rules. Paul described his own duty to the law of Christ (1 Corinthians 9:21), meaning Paul still had high moral expectations for his own lifestyle. Freedom from the law is not a license to sin. It is a move from service motivated by dread to service motivated by love. The psalmist understands this when he exclaims "O how I love thy law!" (Psalm 119:97).

Christianity, at its core, is not a religion of rule-keeping. In fact, the central message of the gospel is that keeping rules will never earn salvation. We just cannot obey all the rules all the time, whether there be 613 of them (per Maimonides), or 10 (Exodus 20:2-17), or just 2 (Matthew 22:36-40).

Paul advises us to think about those things that are true, honest, just, pure, lovely, and of good report (Philippians 4:8). David's description of the law of the Lord in Psalm 19 meets all of these criteria. We would do well to ponder God's law in all of its beauty and glory.

B. Prayer

Heavenly Father, Creator of all the universe, You have revealed Your will to us through Your Holy Scriptures. In them we may learn Your rules for serving You. O God, may You continue to be our strength as we seek daily to live according to Your will. We pray this in the name of the one who kept Your law perfectly, Jesus. Amen.

C. Thought to Remember

Honor God's law.

INVOLVEMENT LEARNING

Some of the activities below are also found in the helpful student book, Adult Bible Class.
Don't forget to download the free reproducible page from www.standardlesson.com to enhance your lesson!

Into the Lesson

Download and put in chairs copies of the A Lamp and a Light exercise from the reproducible page for learners to work on as they arrive. From an approaching or past election, secure the text of a proposed ballot initiative. Make a copy for each learner. Get an issue that is worded in a complex and convoluted way, one that is filled with the "legalese" that characterizes such initiatives.

Draw your learners' attention to the draft and say, "Here is a law only a lawyer could love." Allow time for reactions. Then hold up a Bible and say, "Here is a Law we all can love . . . and should." Have selected readers (or at least four) prearranged to read aloud these segments from Psalm 119: verses 14-16; verse 18; verse 24; verses 46-48; verse 54; verse 62; verse 72; verse 97; verse 103; verse 111; verses 163, 164.

Into the Word

Divide the class into two groups, *Group A* and *Group B,* for a responsive reading of today's text. This will work best if you prepare handouts with the text divided appropriately as follows:

A. The law of the LORD is perfect
  B. Converting the soul
A. The testimony of the LORD is sure
  B. Making wise the simple
A. The statutes of the LORD are right
  B. Rejoicing the heart
A. The commandment of the LORD is pure
  B. Enlightening the eyes
A. The fear of the LORD is clean
  B. Enduring for ever
A. The judgments of the LORD are true
  B. And righteous altogether
Both. More to be desired are they than gold
A. Yea, than much fine gold
  B. Sweeter also than honey and the honeycomb
A. Moreover by them is thy servant warned
  B. And in keeping them there is great reward
A. Who can understand his errors?
  B. Cleanse thou me from secret faults
A. Keep back thy servant also from presumptuous sins
  B. Let them not have dominion over me
A. Then shall I be upright
  B. And I shall be innocent from the great transgression
Both. Let the words of my mouth and the meditation of my heart
A. Be acceptable in thy sight
  B. O LORD, my strength
Both. And my redeemer

Now let your two groups assemble for the following discussion/response items. (Subdivide to get manageable groups of four to six.)

Group A: Make a listing of all the synonyms today's text uses for "the law of the Lord." What is distinctive about each term? How have you experienced God's Word in each way in your own life?

Group B: Make a listing of all the descriptors today's text uses of "the law of the Lord." In what way do you see the words of the Bible to be each of these? What are the effects of each characteristic in your own life?

After a time for deliberation, ask groups to share their conclusions with the whole class. *Option:* Have these two lists ready to display: (A) for synonyms: *law, testimony, statutes, commandment, fear, judgments;* (B) for descriptors: *perfect, converting, sure, wise, right, joyful, pure, enlightening, clean, enduring, true, righteous, desired, rewarding.*

Into Life

Locate and distribute one or more Bible reading programs designed to take the reader through the Bible in a year. Also distribute the Read It! exercise from the reproducible page. Discuss both. Distribute copies of the Think About It! exercise from the reproducible page as learners depart.

GOD'S SAFE REFUGE

BACKGROUND SCRIPTURE: Psalm 46:1-7
PRINTED TEXT: Psalm 46:1-7

PSALM 46:1-7

1 God is our refuge and strength, a very present help in trouble.

2 Therefore will not we fear, though the earth be removed, and though the mountains be carried into the midst of the sea;

3 Though the waters thereof roar and be troubled, though the mountains shake with the swelling thereof. Selah.

4 There is a river, the streams whereof shall make glad the city of God, the holy place of the tabernacles of the most High.

5 God is in the midst of her; she shall not be moved: God shall help her, and that right early.

6 The heathen raged, the kingdoms were moved: he uttered his voice, the earth melted.

7 The LORD of hosts is with us; the God of Jacob is our refuge. Selah.

KEY VERSE

God is our refuge and strength, a very present help in trouble. —**Psalm 46:1**

THE INESCAPABLE GOD

Unit 2: God Sustains

Lessons 5–9

LESSON AIMS

After participating in this lesson, each student will be able to:

1. List three things the psalmist says God is able to do to protect us.

2. Use a contemporary situation to illustrate the idea of God's strength and protection.

3. Use Psalm 46 in daily devotions for a week.

LESSON OUTLINE

Introduction
A. Cliff-hanger Lives
B. Lesson Background
I. Confidence in God's Power (Psalm 46:1)
A. Holy Fortress (v. 1a)
   An Inclusionary and Exclusionary Refuge
B. Active Intervention (v. 1b)
II. Confidence in God's Protection (Psalm 46:2, 3)
A. Fellowship of the Fearless (v. 2a)
B. Bravery in Cataclysm (vv. 2b, 3)
   When Things Shake
III. Confidence in God's Presence (Psalm 46:4-7)
A. River of Joy (v. 4)
B. City of Stability (v. 5)
C. Voice of Power (v. 6)
D. Refuge of Security (v. 7)
Conclusion
A. The Mighty Fortress
B. Prayer
C. Thought to Remember

Introduction

A. Cliff-hanger Lives

Many novels use "the cliff-hanger" as a literary device. In such cases, a chapter ends with the hero in a precarious situation. Death or disaster seems inevitable. This causes the reader to continue reading to learn how the crisis is resolved. This device may be traced back to a time as early as the classical Greek tragedies. Today this style has found a happy home in television shows, where a cliff-hanger ending makes it more likely that viewers will watch the next installment of a program.

Many people see a cliff-hanger aspect to their own lives. We seem to stagger from one crisis to another, never completely escaping the perilous feeling of looming disaster. We weather financial pressure only to be confronted with family disaster. We have illness followed by loss of employment. We lose a friend and barely recover from our grief before we have a serious accident ourselves.

Even our church family changes and adds stress to our lives. The preacher leaves. The budget is out of whack. The worship leader commits adultery. The city imposes new regulations on our parking lot. The congregation fights over something that causes a split. It never ends. We may keep it to ourselves, but our lives seem to be cliff-hangers, with disaster waiting just around the corner.

Sometimes a crisis is self-inflicted. But often we cannot control the coming of a crisis—it just happens. This seems to be our lot in life. But we can find the strength to endure the present storm and prepare for the next onslaught. This is not from our inner reserves, for they are quickly depleted. It is from our relationship to the rock, the God of our salvation. The Bible does not promise believers that their lives will be trouble-free. The promise is that God will provide stability for us and help us weather the storms that arise. This is not a new strategy. Today's lesson derives the same message from a psalm written three millennia ago, and its truth still speaks today.

B. Lesson Background

Psalm 46 is an expression of victory, relief, and thanksgiving. Although the author is not specifi-

God's Safe Refuge

cally named, the psalm appears to have been written in the aftermath of a significant threat to the city of Jerusalem that had been overcome. The psalm ascribes this wholly to the Lord, showing us the hopeless situation that prevailed.

A possible setting for this is during the time of King Hezekiah, who reigned over Judah about 727–696 BC. Hezekiah's Jerusalem was besieged by the mighty host of Assyria's King Sennacherib in 701 BC. Sennacherib and his armies had raged through Syria (capital city, Damascus) and northern Palestine, crushing all opposition.

The prospect of being conquered by the ruthless Assyrians terrified the trapped residents of the city. Sennacherib later claimed to have confined Hezekiah "like a bird in a cage." But the people were delivered by one of the mightiest miracles recorded in the Old Testament: the angel of the Lord slew 185,000 of Sennacherib's troops in their sleep, causing him to retreat to Nineveh (2 Kings 19:35, 36). This surprising rescue was immortalized much later in Lord Byron's poem "The Destruction of Sennacherib":

> *Like the leaves of the forest when Summer is green,*
> *That host with their banners at sunset were seen;*
> *Like the leaves of the forest when Autumn hath blown,*
> *That host on the morrow lay withered and strown.*

We can imagine the relief and celebration that followed such a victory. However, there were no armies to fete and no generals to acclaim. The victory was entirely the work of God, and the desire to praise Him was overwhelming. In this, Psalm 46 has similarities to Psalms 47 and 48, all connected with the "sons of Korah" (in the superscriptions).

Psalm 46 is unique in its directive to sing it "upon *Alamoth*," which occurs in the superscription. This rare word may refer to young women, thus indicating the psalm was intended to be sung by soprano voices (compare 1 Chronicles 15:20). Since this psalm was intended to be sung for a special service of thanksgiving in the temple, it may be an indication that women participated in the musical ministrations of the temple.

I. Confidence in God's Power
(PSALM 46:1)
A. Holy Fortress (v. 1a)
1a. God is our refuge and strength.

The psalm begins with a bold statement of two major characteristics of God. First, He is *our refuge*. A refuge is a place of safety. In the Bible, this is often associated with a military fortress (see Psalm 61:3; 91:2). It can also refer to a place of protection from extreme weather (Isaiah 4:6).

God is also affirmed as our *strength*. This is a frequent perspective of the psalms. Here, it is not that God makes us stronger, but that God *is* our strength (see Psalm 28:7). We are reminded of Paul's paradoxical claim that "when I am weak, then am I strong" (2 Corinthians 12:10). Human strength is finite and failing, whether from exhaustion, aging, or natural limitation. This is true for both physical and spiritual strength. The singers of this psalm understand that power that does not fluctuate or fail must come from the Lord.

These two words together thus portray God as a "strong refuge" or "mighty fortress." The citizens of ancient Jerusalem know that while the fortifications of their city are strong, they are not impregnable. Only God provides an absolute mighty fortress whose walls cannot be breached.

What Do You Think?
  How do we actualize God's strength in our lives?
Talking Points for Your Discussion
- In terms of how we pray
- In terms of how we persevere
- In terms of what we fear
- Zechariah 4:6

❧AN INCLUSIONARY AND EXCLUSIONARY REFUGE❧

No girls aloud! Even though misspelled, the rough, hand-painted sign on the tree house left no doubt as to the intention of the boys who placed it there. There is a time in most boys' lives when that inscription seems to be exactly what is needed to protect the way things "should" be. At a certain age, girls are "the enemy." Young boys feel the need to have a refuge from the world of sisters.

We smile at the childhood attitude behind this exclusionary practice. The attitude is amusing as long as it doesn't continue into adulthood. Sadly, there are times when it does. Most of us have heard of "clubs" that functioned to promote business opportunities for men only—and often men only of a specific race or nationality. Thus women and various minorities were excluded from the economic advantages those fraternities provided.

These cultural antagonisms that have characterized life almost since the Garden of Eden do not characterize the refuge of which the psalmist speaks. God's refuge is both inclusionary and exclusionary, but it is we who decide whether we are included or excluded. Those who have trusted God through the centuries have found in Him the strength they need in life's struggles.   —C. R. B.

B. Active Intervention (v. 1b)
1b. A very present help in trouble.

The second line of this verse expands on the image of God as a protective fortress to extol the Lord's active role in our troubled lives. The psalmist sees God as much more than a wall to hide behind for shelter. God is *a very present help,* one who fights alongside of us. Our relationship with God involves more than safety. It involves assistance. When this is fully grasped, its comfort is immense. We are not called to run away from harsh realities. Instead, we can face life without being paralyzed by fear (see Isaiah 41:13).

Visual for Lessons 7 & 12. Point to this visual as you introduce the discussion question that is associated with verse 1.

Sometimes we find ourselves sinking in the quicksand of life. God does not come and scold us, "If you had listened to me, this would not have happened." God just helps us get out of the quicksand. The psalmist celebrates God's help rather than His condemnation (see Isaiah 50:9).

II. Confidence in God's Protection
(Psalm 46:2, 3)
A. Fellowship of the Fearless (v. 2a)
2a. Therefore will not we fear.

The *therefore* reveals the result of recognizing the fact of God's help in verse 1. Fear is a horrible reality in the lives of many people. Fear can freeze us into inaction. Fear can haunt our every waking moment, even disrupt our sleep. In some countries, Christians have valid reason to fear brutal repression. Governments that see Christianity as a threat may have no compunction about creating a climate of fear for believers.

What power, then, behind these simple words *will not we fear*! This is not a solitary comfort, since the psalmist uses the plural: *we.* The church finds strength in God and through the mutual faith of fellow believers. We stand united and fearless, protected by the king of the universe.

> *What Do You Think?*
> How does being part of a fellowship of believers help you overcome fear?
> *Talking Points for Your Discussion*
> - Mutual accountability
> - Positive examples
> - Intercessory prayer

It is a paradox of the Bible that this fearlessness in our lives is founded on a very real fear or reverence for God. We are wise to remember our own fear of the Lord (Psalm 34:11). Elsewhere, another psalmist reminds us that "God is greatly to be feared" (Psalm 89:7).

B. Bravery in Cataclysm (vv. 2b, 3)
2b, 3. Though the earth be removed, and though the mountains be carried into the midst

of the sea; though the waters thereof roar and be troubled, though the mountains shake with the swelling thereof. Selah.

A well-known symbolic act is that of a person bowing and kissing the earth after surviving a harrowing plane ride or ocean voyage. This person has lived through great danger and now claims the stability of solid ground. What is the reaction, then, when even the ground becomes unstable? This is what the psalmist now pictures. The first lines describe a situation where a mountainous coastal area slides into the ocean. The following lines portray a colossal earthquake accompanied by tsunami-like waves from the sea.

We expect that natural disasters will strike terror in the hearts of those affected. Yet all of these are connected with the psalmist's earlier affirmation "therefore will not we fear." There is no imaginable circumstance that should shake our trust in the Lord (compare Hebrews 12:27). Whether our tsunamis and earthquakes are caused by people or nature, we are secure in God's protective hands.

The psalmist ends this section with the Hebrew word *Selah*. We do not know exactly what this word means, but it seems to be some type of musical direction related to the public performance of a psalm. It may indicate a planned pause or that a different group of singers is to begin its part. *Selah* occurs again at the end of verses 7 and 11.

❧ WHEN THINGS SHAKE ❧

The San Francisco earthquake of 1906 is probably the most famous temblor to strike the United States. The loss of life has been estimated at 3,000. Also severe (though with less loss of life) were the succession of New Madrid quakes in the Mississippi Valley in 1811 and 1812. The shocks were felt in many places across the continent. Even the course of the mighty Mississippi River was altered. Stronger yet was the Alaska earthquake of 1964.

Of course, earthquakes happen worldwide. Undersea quakes can be the most deadly, as we saw in the one that struck offshore from Indonesia on December 26, 2004. It caused a tsunami that killed 300,000.

Thus *terra firma* is not so firm after all! In fact, the mountains shake and the waters of the sea are troubled all the time. Despite our attempts to mitigate the effects of disaster, the only sure refuge is the Lord. This is true of both literal shakings of the ground and the figurative shakings of cultural upheaval, personal tragedy, etc. The psalmist looked to Him, and so should we. —C. R. B.

III. Confidence in God's Presence
(PSALM 46:4-7)
A. River of Joy (v. 4)

4. There is a river, the streams whereof shall make glad the city of God, the holy place of the tabernacles of the most High.

The psalmist continues his celebration of victory by musing on the abode of God. The word *tabernacles* has the sense of tents that are dwelling places (see Psalm 84:1, 2). The people of Israel consider Jerusalem and its temple to be an earthly residence of the Lord and a type or representation of Heaven itself (compare Psalm 76:1, 2, where *Salem* and *Zion* equate to Jerusalem). That this is more than earthly Jerusalem is seen in the reference to *a river*, for there is no river that flows through it. In the book of Revelation, Heaven is pictured as a place with a wonderful river coming from the throne of God (Revelation 22:1).

In the dry climate found in much of the Middle East, there is nothing more precious than a river bringing water necessary for growing crops and quenching thirst (see Psalm 65:9). Such a provision is seen as a tangible, joyous gift of God.

HOW TO SAY IT

Assyria	Uh-*sear*-ee-uh.
Assyrian	Uh-*sear*-e-un.
Damascus	Duh-*mass*-kus.
Hezekiah	Hez-ih-*kye*-uh.
Jacob	*Jay*-kub.
Judah	*Joo*-duh.
Korah	*Ko*-rah.
Nineveh	*Nin*-uh-vuh.
Sabaoth	*Sab*-a-oth.
Sennacherib	Sen-*nack*-er-ib.
tsunami	sue-*nah*-me.

Sufficient water means life and is a sign of God's blessing (as is a military victory).

B. City of Stability (v. 5)

5. God is in the midst of her; she shall not be moved: God shall help her, and that right early.

The psalmist skillfully shifts the imagery at this point, from that of a joyous, yet fluid, river to the immovable stability of the city. The foundation is God himself, and His presence allows the writer to claim *she [the city] shall not be moved.*

The reasoning behind this claim is that God promises to *help her,* and that His assistance will come before disaster overtakes them *(right early).* If this psalm is written in the context of the deliverance of Jerusalem from the Assyrian horde, we can understand the power in these words. Imagine the relief the city feels after it had first cowered in fear when threatened by this overwhelming, hostile military force!

David, the most well-known of the psalmists, celebrates these themes often in his musical poems. After he is delivered from his enemies, including King Saul, he breaks out in ecstatic praise and piles up many images of God's immovability in his life. God is his "rock," his "fortress," his "deliverer," his "shield," his "horn of . . . salvation," his "high tower," his "refuge," and his "saviour" (2 Samuel 22:2, 3; compare Psalm 18:2). God is powerful to deliver us from danger or threat. God's presence in our lives brings a stability that we cannot duplicate on our own.

C. Voice of Power (v. 6)

6. The heathen raged, the kingdoms were moved: he uttered his voice, the earth melted.

The stability and protection provided by the Lord is contrasted here with the ungodly nations that are helpless before God's power. God is more than the protector of Jerusalem; He is the master of all nations. Before His power, the pagans are in turmoil. They are not stable, for they have no rock in their midst. To the contrary, they are *moved* in various ways. Even the earth itself is helpless before the power of the Lord. In a remarkable word picture, the psalmist describes the ground melting as a result of God's voice.

The voice of God is often representative of both the creative and destructive power of the Lord. The power of His utterances is shown by the frequent connection between His voice and the sound of thunder (example: Job 37:4, 5). This makes sense to the ancient person who believes that Heaven, God's abode, is located somewhere beyond human perception. Thunder comes from above, and it is easy to associate it with God's speaking. Here this concept is coupled with the mastery of the heavenly over the earthly, so that the voice of God from above is mighty to melt the earth below.

D. Refuge of Security (v. 7)

7. The LORD of hosts is with us; the God of Jacob is our refuge. Selah.

The final verse of today's lesson text includes a dramatic title for God: *Lord of hosts.* This phrase occurs more than 250 times in the Old Testament and means "master of the heavenly armies." No earthly army can stand against the angelic hosts of God. Consider that the 185,000 soldiers of Sennacherib were killed by 1 angel (2 Kings 19:35). What earthly army can stand against 12 legions of angels mentioned in Matthew 26:53 or against the 10,000 times 10,000 angels of Revelation 5:11?

Sometimes the armies of ancient Israel are seen as a part of these angelic battalions (see 1 Samuel 17:45). For this psalmist, however, the potential of military power is not the most important thing. The key concept is that the commander of these armies *is with us*. His presence ensures victory. It is OK to be under martial law if your commander is the Lord, perfectly just and invincibly powerful. In this sense, military rule is a refuge.

This perspective is important for us in understanding the protective power of God as it applies to us today. Although this psalm may have been written to celebrate an ancient military victory, it has resonated throughout the centuries for the people of God who look heavenward for help in times of distress and discouragement.

The psalmist reminds the people of their heritage in his phrase *the God of Jacob*. That founding ancestor had his name changed from *Jacob* to *Israel* (Genesis 32:28). This may have special poignancy for the original hearers of the psalm if they are in Jerusalem. If the occasion that calls the psalm into being is the Assyrian campaign of 701 BC, they know that their sister nation to the north already has been destroyed and carried into captivity by Assyria (see 2 Kings 15:29; 17:3-6).

> **What Do You Think?**
> Is the description of God as *the God of Jacob* meaningful or relevant to you? Should it be? Explain.
> *Talking Points for Your Discussion*
> - God's interactions with Jacob in Genesis 28:10-22; 32:22-32; etc.
> - Jesus' statements in Matthew 8:11; 22:32; etc.

The final demise of Samaria, the capital city of the northern tribes, occurred in 722 BC. In those days, the northern kingdom had retained the name *Israel*, while the southern kingdom was called *Judah*. The Assyrian crisis for Judah during the time of Hezekiah takes place 21 years after the deportation of Israel. The people are reminded that the nation called *Israel* may be no more, but they are still the people of the God of Israel/Jacob. National affairs may have shifted, but God is the same. He does not change.

Conclusion
A. The Mighty Fortress

The most famous hymn to come out of the Protestant Reformation was Martin Luther's "A Mighty Fortress Is Our God," written around 1527. It is still sung regularly in churches nearly 500 years later. Luther drew the basic ideas for this hymn from Psalm 46, our focus text for this lesson. Luther transformed the victory over the Assyrians to the Christian victory over Satan.

We may see evidence of this in several phrases. Luther's description of God as a "mighty fortress" is derived from Psalm 46:1. Luther pictures God as "our Helper" in the flood of "mortal ills," a paraphrase of the psalm's description in verse 1 of God as "a very present help in trouble." Luther identifies God as "Lord Sabaoth" (46:7, same as the "Lord of hosts"). Luther states that the devil's "rage" can be endured, for "his doom is sure," a reference to the rage of the "heathen" who are powerless before the Lord (46:6). Luther recognizes the might of the voice of the Lord when he claims, "One little word shall fell [the enemy]" (compare 46:6).

Luther's final phrase sums up the message of the psalm: "His kingdom is forever." Kingdoms and nations may come and go. Families, careers, and fortunes may wax and wane. But the eternal kingdom of God Almighty does not change and will never fail. There is no end to the reign of our king (Luke 1:33; compare Revelation 11:15). When we are part of the people of God, we are citizens of the eternal city. Our hope and future are secure in the rock of our salvation.

B. Prayer

Holy God, Lord of hosts, You are our rock, our fortress, and our refuge. Though the storms of life assail us, may we trust in You. Though the attacks of the devil bear down on us, may we be loyal to You. In the turmoil of our lives, may we be still and acknowledge that You are God. May we exalt You above everything in our world. We pray this in the name of Your Son, Jesus. Amen.

C. Thought to Remember

God still provides an unassailable refuge.

INVOLVEMENT LEARNING

Some of the activities below are also found in the helpful student book, Adult Bible Class.
Don't forget to download the free reproducible page from www.standardlesson.com to enhance your lesson!

Into the Lesson

To relate the lesson's introduction about cliff-hangers, show a short video clip from one of the serial adventures of the 1930s to 1950s that ends in a formulaic cliff-hanger. An Internet search for "cliffhanger serials" will identify many titles, and a video rental store probably will have collections. *Flash Gordon* is just one example.

You can also find cliff-hangers in more recent TV shows, although the cliff-hangers in these often are found only in the season finale. These are designed to create a summer-long "can't wait" expectation before new shows premier several months later. The idea is to give your learners an example of danger and rescue.

Make a transition to the lesson by saying, "Cliff-hangers make great entertainment. But cliff-hangers are not nearly as much fun when they happen in our own lives. Let's see what Psalm 46 has to say about this."

Into the Word

Establish three groups. Name them *The Power Group, The Protection Group,* and *The Presence Group.* (*Option:* Establish *The Voice Group* as a fourth.)

Give the Power Group a copy of Martin Luther's "A Mighty Fortress Is Our God." Include the notation that Luther based the title on the "refuge and strength" phrase of Psalm 46:1, etc. Direct the group to compare Luther's conclusions in his hymn with the conclusions the psalmist reaches. Ask the group to clarify how the concept of God's power is critical to the believer.

Give the Protection Group these written directions: "*Fear* and *help* are two key words in Psalm 46. What is it that people are most afraid of? How does (or should) the protection of God relieve those fears?"

Give the Presence Group these written directions: "As Matthew 1:18-23 describes the words

of the angel to Joseph, the Gospel writer cites Isaiah's words regarding Immanuel (or Emmanuel) in Isaiah 7:14. What is the significance that God is 'with us'? How does Psalm 46 describe and value the presence of God in the psalmist's life?"

If you have established the optional Voice Group, give its members copies of the His Voice activity from the reproducible page. Have the group complete it according to printed directions.

Allow at least eight minutes for the groups to consider their responses. Then ask a representative from each group to read their directions aloud and report conclusions. Summarize the conclusions on the board for all to see.

Say, "The psalmist inserts the word *Selah* three times: after verses 3, 7, and 11. Most students consider this to be a musical notation, in line with the idea that Psalm 46 is to be sung in public performances." Ask class members to look at the psalm and suggest hymns and/or praise choruses that are brought to mind by the psalm's phrasing.

If responses are slow in coming, you can offer one or more of these examples: "A Mighty Fortress Is Our God" (related to v. 1); "God Is Our Refuge and Our Strength" (sung to the tune of "America the Beautiful"; related to v. 1); "Like a River Glorious" and "Shall We Gather at the River?" (related to v. 4); and "In the Calm" (related to v. 10). After compiling a short list, recruit someone to lead the class in singing one or more of the songs.

Into Life

Say, "Study should lead to application. If you were to pick just one verse of Psalm 46 as your primary application text, which one would it be?" There may be a variety of responses, but be sure to draw attention to verse 10 if no one else does. Discuss. Then distribute copies of the Applying Psalm 46 exercise from the reproducible page that you have downloaded. Allow learners to complete it during class or as a take-home activity.

GOD'S UNIVERSAL REIGN

BACKGROUND SCRIPTURE: Psalm 47

PRINTED TEXT: Psalm 47

PSALM 47

1 O clap your hands, all ye people; shout unto God with the voice of triumph.

2 For the LORD most high is terrible; he is a great King over all the earth.

3 He shall subdue the people under us, and the nations under our feet.

4 He shall choose our inheritance for us, the excellency of Jacob whom he loved. Selah.

5 God is gone up with a shout, the LORD with the sound of a trumpet.

6 Sing praises to God, sing praises: sing praises unto our King, sing praises.

7 For God is the King of all the earth: sing ye praises with understanding.

8 God reigneth over the heathen: God sitteth upon the throne of his holiness.

9 The princes of the people are gathered together, even the people of the God of Abraham: for the shields of the earth belong unto God: he is greatly exalted.

KEY VERSE

Sing praises to God, sing praises: sing praises unto our King, sing praises. For God is the King of all the earth: sing ye praises with understanding. —**Psalm 47:6, 7**

THE INESCAPABLE GOD

Unit 2: God Sustains

LESSONS 5–9

LESSON AIMS

After participating in this lesson, each student will be able to:

1. List three reasons or ways to praise God.

2. Explain the connection between the sovereignty of God and our need to praise Him.

3. Plan a worship service that incorporates Psalm 47 in various ways.

LESSON OUTLINE

Introduction
  A. Appropriate Applause
  B. Lesson Background
 I. Celebrating God's Reign (PSALM 47:1-4)
  A. Clapping for the Lord (v. 1)
  B. Looking Up to the Lord (v. 2)
  C. Anticipating the Lord (vv. 3, 4)
II. Understanding God's Reign (PSALM 47:5-9)
  A. Acclaim of the Victorious Warrior (v. 5)
    We'll Sing and Shout the Victory
  B. Center of Joyous Praise (vv. 6, 7)
  C. Focus of International Attention (vv. 8, 9)
    Defense Systems
Conclusion
  A. National Praise
  B. Prayer
  C. Thought to Remember

Introduction

A. Appropriate Applause

Classical music lovers know that there are unwritten rules when it comes to live performances. One of these has to do with the proper times to applaud. The tradition is that applause is appropriate only at the end of a piece of music, not between the piece's sections. For example, a Beethoven symphony may have four movements. The audience is expected to be silent when the orchestra pauses after the first, second, and third movements, and to clap only at the end of the fourth movement.

Often, however, there will be appreciative but uninitiated audience patrons who begin to clap after the first movement. This quickly dies, however, when they realize they are not being joined by the bulk of the audience. According to the traditions of symphony halls, this applause is inappropriate even if well intended.

Churches too may have unwritten rules when it comes to applause. For example, there may be various reactions to a musical presentation in a worship service. Some in attendance may applaud enthusiastically, not realizing that the tradition of that particular congregation is to view applause as out of kilter with the purpose of worship.

The heart of this matter, of course, is understanding the purpose of hand clapping. In today's entertainment culture, clapping is most commonly used as a response to outstanding performance. When we clap in this sense, we are physically saying, "You are really a great singer, and we want to let you know that we recognize it." But there are other purposes for clapping too. Sometimes we clap in appreciation. For example, a beloved speaker may receive a long ovation when being introduced. This is saying, "We appreciate you."

Since ancient times, people have combined these two purposes (recognition of greatness and heartfelt appreciation) to use clapping as a form of worship. Clapping is associated with exuberant joy, and this may be channeled into praise for God. We must remember that all humans are participants in a worship service. The only "audience" is God, for He alone is worthy of praise (see Revelation 4:11). Applause in praise of God is both appropriate and exciting. Our applause need not die an embarrassed death like the clapping between the movements of a Beethoven symphony.

B. Lesson Background

Psalm 47 lends itself to public worship and praise. Its enduring qualities are shown by its current place in the celebration of Rosh Hashanah (New Year's Day) in some Jewish congregations today. By tradition, Psalm 47 is recited seven times before the blowing of the *shofar* (ram's horn) to mark the beginning of the New Year and its celebration.

Psalm 47 is the fifth in a series of seven psalms associated with "the sons of Korah." Descendants of Korah seem to have been important pioneers in the liturgical worship of the temple in Jerusalem (see 1 Chronicles 9:19; 2 Chronicles 20:19).

As we noted in the Background of Lesson 5, the psalms traditionally are divided into five "books." Seven psalms of the sons of Korah begin Book II, which consists of Psalms 42–72. Originally, Psalms 42 and 43 were one unit, so the seven are 42/43, 44, 45, 46, 47, 48, and 49 (Psalms 84–88 comprise another collection of Korah psalms).

The superscription of Psalm 47 calls it *A Psalm*. By contrast, some other Korah psalms are identified as *maschil*. We are not sure what a *maschil* is. One theory is that this title is given to song-poems of a personal, contemplative nature, while the designation *A Psalm* is attached to works written as expressions of praise to God for use in public worship. We note, however, that Psalm 88 features

HOW TO SAY IT

Assyria	Uh-*sear*-ee-uh.
Babylon	*Bab*-uh-lun.
Beethoven	*Bay*-toe-ven.
Canaan	*Kay*-nun.
Korah	*Ko*-rah.
Manasseh	Muh-*nass*-uh.
maschil	mass-*kill*.
Melchizedek	Mel-*kiz*-eh-dek.
Rosh Hashanah	Rosh Huh-*shu*-nuh.
shofar	*show*-far.
Solomon	*Sol*-o-mun.

both designations. Psalm 47, for its part, combines words of praise to the Lord with active participation from the congregation.

We do not know the precise historical context of Psalm 47, but it has allusions to the history of Israel. For example, the reference to "a trumpet" in verse 5 reminds us of the miraculous victory of Joshua over the walled city of Jericho (Joshua 6). The psalm, then, combines praise of God with a patriotic celebration of the victories of the nation of Israel.

I. Celebrating God's Reign
(PSALM 47:1-4)
A. Clapping for the Lord (v. 1)

1. O clap your hands, all ye people; shout unto God with the voice of triumph.

There are certain human practices that predate recorded history because they are instinctive. We smile. We laugh. We cry. We stomp our feet. And we slap the palms of our hands together to make noise. Clapping, among other things, is an auditory gauge as measured by its loudness and length. Clapping is a physical act that requires active involvement.

This is a participatory psalm. It is not intended to be droned out in a monotone voice to an unresponsive crowd. It begins by encouraging the worshipers to clap and shout. Such crowd noise is reminiscent of the celebration after a military victory. It is not praise for an army, though, but a tribute to the mighty God of Israel.

What Do You Think?

How are you able to shout "with the voice of triumph" even when you don't feel triumphant?

Talking Points for Your Discussion
- The long view vs. the short view
- Understanding the nature of feelings

The psalms are not always written in metered poetry, but this verse seems to be. Each line of this verse contains four "beats" in the original language: ***Clap*** your **hands**, **all** ye **people**. **Shout** unto **God** with the **voice** of **triumph!** This arrangement makes it easy for the congregation to both chant and clap as it uses the psalm in its worship. Naturally, it's harder to see these beats in translating from one language to another.

B. Looking Up to the Lord (v. 2)

2a. For the LORD most high is terrible.

Verse 2 uses some fabulous descriptions for God. The Bible's first use of the title *Lord most high* appears in the record of Abraham's encounter with Melchizedek, the king of Salem (Jerusalem; Genesis 14:18). During this episode, Abraham confessed an oath to "the Lord, the most high God" (Genesis 14:22). The sense of this phrase is not to say that the God of Israel is the greatest among a large group of competing gods. It is to affirm, rather, that the Lord is on a unique plane and has no rivals.

Other supernatural beings exist, such as angels and demons, but none are "gods." This is reinforced when the psalm asserts that the Lord is terrible. In this context, the word *terrible* is not a negative term, as in "awful." Rather, it denotes the one who strikes terror in those who encounter Him. This is not terror associated with a fear of evil, but a reverential awe of the mighty power of God.

2b. He is a great King over all the earth.

The second line of verse 2 affirms the unlimited sovereignty of God. The description *great king* is sometimes extended to earthly, human kings in the Bible (compare 2 Kings 18:19; Ezra 5:11). In an absolute sense, however, God is the ultimate king, the unrivaled and unquestioned king of the universe (see Malachi 1:14). We are wise to remember that while we may have an intimate, personal relationship with God, He is still the King of kings and Lord of lords (see 1 Timothy 6:15).

What Do You Think?

How difficult is it for people who live in democratic societies to appreciate God as king? In what ways can that be a positive image for us?

Talking Points for Your Discussion

- Faults of human tyrants
- Expectation of choice in the selection of leaders
- Long-term rule vs. frequent change

C. Anticipating the Lord (vv. 3, 4)

3. He shall subdue the people under us, and the nations under our feet.

Verses 3, 4 are set in the future tense *(shall)*, but they have a larger sense: the people's anticipation of great victories in the future are based on the mighty triumphs in the past. This is what allows them to expect God's continuing assurance of protection and success.

The two clauses here are parallel, saying the same thing in different ways. They share the image of a vanquished foe. This picture of submission has important implications. An enemy that is *under our feet* no longer poses a threat to Israel. While some of the kings and people of Israel no doubt have delusions of a military empire and world conquest from time to time, most are more concerned with the peace that comes when enemies are subdued. Verse 4 (next) offers more implications.

4. He shall choose our inheritance for us, the excellency of Jacob whom he loved. Selah.

With peace comes prosperity. Rather than worry about the looming threat of war caused by a foreign invasion, the people can truly look to enjoyment of their inheritance, a land chosen for them by God. The people of Israel remain aware of their heritage, tying this to their ancestor Jacob. God's promises to Jacob are of the possession of the land of Canaan and of a vast multitude of descendants. In addition, Jacob's descendants are to be a blessing for all peoples (Genesis 28:13-15). This is a marvelous heritage, worthy of celebration with all the clapping and shouting that the crowd can muster!

II. Understanding God's Reign
(PSALM 47:5-9)

A. Acclaim of the Victorious Warrior (v. 5)

5. God is gone up with a shout, the LORD with the sound of a trumpet.

The psalm now moves to a celebratory picture drawn from the world of military acclamation. After a great victory, the Israelite army would march back to Jerusalem in triumph. Upon approaching and entering the city, the army naturally would ascend the "holy hill" to the temple, the focal point of the city (Psalm 24:3; 43:3).

In this case, the ascending victor is an army of one, God, for it is the Lord who has gone up to the applause and shout of the crowd and with the ringing *sound of a trumpet.* The scene being pictured is one of near pandemonium, of joy and exuberance directed to God for His victory.

We speak sometimes of the "roar of the crowd" as when a collection of people has a single voice like a lion. You might have experienced this in a large sports stadium when an unexpected yet brilliant play on the field moves the crowd to a spontaneous combination of yelling, whistling, stomping, and clapping. The people rise to their feet as one without any direction. You can feel a wave of emotion sweep the stadium. It can bring goose bumps to any spectator.

To be recognized in this way is breathtaking for the shouters and for the player who caused the uproar. To be the focus of the loud, spontaneous praise of 50,000 fans is a thrill like no other. This is the phenomenon that the psalm describes here, but all the praise and focus is for the Lord.

What Do You Think?
Should the celebratory sounds we make in a worship setting be different from those we make at sporting events? Why, or why not?
Talking Points for Your Discussion
- Volume
- Motivation
- Intelligibility
- Luke 19:37, 38; 1 Corinthians 14:40

✾ WE'LL SING AND SHOUT THE VICTORY ✾

America's first ticker-tape parade was held on October 29, 1886, as part of the dedication celebration of the Statue of Liberty in New York City. This kind of celebration involves a parade through the streets that is accompanied by shredded paper (originally paper tapes that contained stock quotes from stock "tickers") being thrown from the windows of office buildings. Among others, war heroes, sports heroes, and astronauts have been lauded in this fashion.

The countries of the world have different means of honoring their heroes. Some are welcomed into the royal palace of their country's leader, others receive medals, monetary gifts, or have buildings or streets named for them. They may also be recognized by having statues raised in their honor or shrines built in their memory. All this, of course, is nothing new. The Romans had their triumphal processions for victorious military commanders. Jesus was honored with His own triumphal entry when He arrived in Jerusalem (Luke 19:28-40).

An important part of our worship celebrations is our recognition of Jesus' victory over death. The joy that marks a ticker-tape parade should be eclipsed by the joy of Christians as we sing and shout that victory. Is it that way at your church? —A. E. A.

B. Center of Joyous Praise (vv. 6, 7)

6, 7. Sing praises to God, sing praises: sing praises unto our King, sing praises. For God is the King of all the earth: sing ye praises with understanding.

At the end of his life, as he was turning the reins of power over to Solomon, King David organized 38,000 Levites into various categories of service. One grouping consisted of 4,000 Levites who were to offer praise using instruments made for that purpose (1 Chronicles 23:1-5). Clearly, praise of God was a high priority! In this section, the people are enjoined five times to sing praises. This is praise of celebration and submission, for it is in recognition that *God is the King of all the earth.* The Lord does not share His position with any earthly king.

Visual for Lesson 8. Point to this visual as you ask, "In what situations is it especially appropriate to sing praises to God?"

There is a qualifier here: the people are enjoined to sing praises *with understanding* (1 Corinthians 14:15). If a time of praise devolves into mindless chaos, the purpose is lost. Some may enjoy such bedlam, but praise without focus and understanding is not what this psalm is advocating. The more we know about God, the more effective and satisfying our times of praise will be. We do not need to park our intellect at the door when we come to praise the Lord. We should bring both our heads and our hearts to the service of praise.

C. Focus of International Attention (vv. 8, 9)

8. God reigneth over the heathen: God sitteth upon the throne of his holiness.

The psalm moves toward its conclusion with a picture of God enthroned in holiness. His reign is not confined to Israel, but extends to pagan nations. The psalmist does not make the mistake of elevating his own nation, Israel, to a position of power over all the nations of the earth. To do so would be historically inaccurate and doctrinally erroneous. Israel is never a dominating world power, even during its heyday of Solomon. Ancient Israel never challenges Egypt, Assyria, Babylon, or Rome for world domination.

9. The princes of the people are gathered together, even the people of the God of Abraham: for the shields of the earth belong unto God: he is greatly exalted.

Rather than picturing other nations as subservient to Israel, the psalm pictures a gathering of all nations at the throne of God (compare Revelation 7:9). Israel is among them, *even the people of*

the God of Abraham. These many nations are represented by their *princes* and their *shields*. In this context, these two terms are equivalent. The legitimate king of any nation has an obligation to protect his people from foreign invasion, and thus is a shield to that nation's sovereignty. However, all of these guardians are subservient to the dominant, all-powerful reign of God. There is no shield from His wrath and no challenge to His authority.

The final line of the psalm is a fitting summation: *he is greatly exalted*. The reality of God's exaltation is not in question, only our understanding of it. At some point, however, we must confess our inadequacy to comprehend fully the reign of God over the earth (see Romans 11:33). Our limited understanding does not lessen God's eternal power. When words fail and comprehension falters, we may always fall back on praise. We may yield to our inborn, created function and give Him all the honor and glory of which we are capable.

❧ DEFENSE SYSTEMS ❧

A staple of science-fiction movies such as *Star Trek* is the "force field" that provides protection from enemy attacks. On a more down-to-earth level, we have windshields to protect us against the elements as we drive, lead aprons to provide protection while getting an X-ray, and sunglasses to shield our eyes from the sun's glare.

The use of shielding as protection in time of war has a long history. The metal armor used by the Roman legions finds its parallel in a modern soldier's ceramic body armor. The steel plating on modern ships of war hearkens back to the iron-clads of the nineteenth century. The list goes on.

All of this shielding is useful to varying degrees, but none is foolproof. At some point any of these shields can be breached, resulting in harm or even death to those being protected. But there is one shield that can never be breached, one that is guaranteed to provide the ultimate protection: God himself. "Thou art my hiding place and my shield" (Psalm 119:114). Remember that fact the next time you put on your sunglasses! —A. E. A.

Conclusion

A. National Praise

Americans are familiar with the arguments about a "wall" of separation between church and state. But there was no such wall in ancient Israel. Likewise, there was no freedom of religion as we know it. Israel was not a pluralistic society that welcomed spiritual diversity; it was not multifaith in its ideal. The head of state, the king, had controlling influence over the religious affairs of the nation. The central focus of Jerusalem was the temple, and it was financed by the national treasury. Temple employees were like our modern civil servants. The high priests had final say in temple matters, although kings seemed to interfere repeatedly (examples: 2 Kings 21:1, 4, 5; 2 Chronicles 26:16).

Such a configuration is far removed from the situation in most modern democratic nations. In such countries, the government has a hands-off attitude when it comes to religion in order to ensure individual freedom. Further, people who are antagonistic toward religion use the court systems and bureaucracies to place limits on religious activity. The result is that sacred elements in public ceremonies have nearly disappeared. For example, to whom do we pray in the pluralistic environment of such ceremonies? Do we pray to the God of Israel? to Jesus? to Allah? to Vishnu? to Gaia? Even the attempt to allow personal prayer by schoolchildren via a moment of silence has been attacked in the courts and sometimes ruled as illegal.

To ponder these things helps us gain perspective on the teaching and practice of Psalm 47. The history of Israel itself proves how difficult it is to turn back the clock when religious decline begins. As the kings of Israel and Judah became unfaithful, their nations followed. Reforms under righteous kings like Hezekiah didn't last. Heze-

kiah's reign was followed by the 55-year rule of Manasseh, the most evil of all the kings of Judah (2 Kings 21:11, 12). For us the days are gone when a political leader like Abraham Lincoln can refer to "this nation, under God" without a storm of protest. There is no longer a correlation between religious preference and national identity.

Psalm 47, then, no longer has a place in the worship of a nation. It is unlikely we will ever see a pageant of worship in which presidents, prime ministers, senators, generals, and governors join with the citizens to clap their hands and shout to God with a voice of triumph. Some may still blame God for national disasters, but do we ever praise Him for national success?

The doctrines and purpose of Psalm 47 remain unchanged though. It still has a place in the worship of God's people, the church. Here we can sing and praise to our utmost. We can be told repeatedly to "sing praises" and agree by our joyous obedience. And we know that the final picture of the psalm still rings true. Our God is more than the God of ancient Israel whom Christians have adopted. He is, rather, the God over all nations and all princes and all peoples. This is true whether the leaders and citizens of any given nation choose to acknowledge it or not. He is the only God, the true God. May we sing His praises!

> What Do You Think?
> What are some of the advantages and disadvantages of church and state being kept apart?
> Talking Points for Your Discussion
> - Promotion of one religion over another
> - Issue of freedom of conscience
> - Viability of uniformity of belief

B. Prayer

O Lord God, all-powerful Ruler of the universe, to You we bring our praise and honor. May You reign from the mighty throne of Your holiness and from the tiny thrones of our hearts. May our clapping and shouting be for Your glory. We pray this in the name of Your Son Jesus, amen.

C. Thought to Remember

Bring joyous praise to His throne.

INVOLVEMENT LEARNING

Some of the activities below are also found in the helpful student book, Adult Bible Class.
Don't forget to download the free reproducible page from www.standardlesson.com to enhance your lesson!

Into the Lesson

Display four blank lines on the board like this: ___ ___ ___ ___. Say that you want the class to join in a childhood game of *Hangman*. Alternate between the two sides of the classroom as learners guess the letters in the word. Fill letters as they are given correctly. Before you begin, give a clue by saying, "This key word is part of today's study."

The word the class is to discover is *clap*, from verse 1 of the text. Ask for examples of times when we strike our palms together to make the noise that results.

Into the Word

Distribute copies of the following word-find puzzle, which uses words and concepts from Psalm 47.

```
P P S G O D D E T L A X E P
I A N L M F O R T W Y S R I
H I E V Y L B M E S S A E H
S I N G N N Q S A Z I M O S
R Q O G Y D O G T S C L E R
O Y X E O M O E E V I L E O
W K P G E D N G T N N E A W
P I S A N O L M E G F L O P
I N R T R I Y S P S N B E I
H G I H V E S I M N P I S H
S O T A A L M N U F O R S S
R D R Q Y N S G R E V R E R
O N X S G O D A T L M E F O
W O X T Y S E S H O U T V W
```

Include these directions: Locate 30 words and concepts from Psalm 47. One word of 4 letters, a key word in the psalm and a key element in worship, is included 5 times—the same number of times it appears in the psalm. One word of 3 letters, the most important word in the psalm, occurs 8 times. What is significant about the direction of the word that occurs in the far left and far right columns, twice in each column?

You can have students work in pairs or small teams to see who can finish first. Award token prizes to the winning pair or team. Providing a list of the words to be found will make the puzzle easier to solve. Not providing a list of the words to be found will encourage your students to look closely at the text, although this will require more time.

Words to be found are *assembly, awesome, clap, exalted, God* (eight times), *hands, high, holiness, king, praise, shout, sing* (five times), *terrible, throne, trumpet, worship* (four times). The word *worship* is the one appearing twice in the far left column and twice in the far right; the significance is that this word goes upward, as does our actual worship. Have an extra prize available for anyone who notices that the unused, "filler" letters of the puzzle's first four lines spell out *Psalm Forty-seven*.

After the word-search is completed, discuss the significance of each word as it relates to the object of worship (God) and to the worshiper. Note to your class one potential way Psalm 47 is structured: first a call for acts of worship (v. 1); then an explanation of how/why God is worthy (vv. 2-5); then another call for worship (v. 6); followed by an additional statement of God's worthiness (vv. 7-9).

Ask, "What is the connection between God's sovereignty and our need to praise Him?" After responses, ask, "How can our private and corporate times of worship incorporate that connection?" List the typical elements of your congregation's worship assemblies to see whether the class can relate them to these two questions. (If you have time for deeper study, use the Israel's Heavenly King . . . and Ours activity from the reproducible page.)

Into Life

Download the reproducible page and distribute copies of the What's Your Inheritance? activity from it. Allow time to complete and discuss. Distribute copies of the Sing Praises activity from the reproducible page as take-home work.

God's Universal Reign

GOD'S COMFORTING
PRESENCE

BACKGROUND SCRIPTURE: **Psalm 63**

PRINTED TEXT: **Psalm 63**

PSALM 63

1 O God, thou art my God; early will I seek thee: my soul thirsteth for thee, my flesh longeth for thee in a dry and thirsty land, where no water is;

2 To see thy power and thy glory, so as I have seen thee in the sanctuary.

3 Because thy lovingkindness is better than life, my lips shall praise thee.

4 Thus will I bless thee while I live: I will lift up my hands in thy name.

5 My soul shall be satisfied as with marrow and fatness; and my mouth shall praise thee with joyful lips:

6 When I remember thee upon my bed, and meditate on thee in the night watches.

7 Because thou hast been my help, therefore in the shadow of thy wings will I rejoice.

8 My soul followeth hard after thee: thy right hand upholdeth me.

9 But those that seek my soul, to destroy it, shall go into the lower parts of the earth.

10 They shall fall by the sword: they shall be a portion for foxes.

11 But the king shall rejoice in God; every one that sweareth by him shall glory: but the mouth of them that speak lies shall be stopped.

KEY VERSE

O God, thou art my God; early will I seek thee: my soul thirsteth for thee, my flesh longeth for thee in a dry and thirsty land, where no water is. —**Psalm 63:1**

THE
INESCAPABLE GOD

Unit 2: God Sustains

LESSONS 5–9

LESSON AIMS

After participating in this lesson, each student will be able to:

1. Tell how David praised God in the midst of trials.

2. Explain how people experience or sense the presence of God in different settings.

3. Use Psalm 63 to counsel someone who feels trapped in a figurative wilderness.

LESSON OUTLINE

Introduction

A. Sleeping Rough

"Sleeping rough" is an expression I first encountered while living briefly in England during the 1990s. It has a mildly romantic tinge, and I first equated it with the American expression "roughing it." Americans might say they are roughing it if slightly inconvenienced. If I run out of coffee filters and substitute a paper towel, I am roughing it. If my water heater is out and I have a cold shower, that is certainly roughing it! But this is not what "sleeping rough" means. The English people use this euphemism for the urban homeless.

I am writing this from my office in Los Angeles, a city dubbed the "homeless capital of the United States." It is estimated that there are upwards of 100,000 people who are "sleeping rough" every night in Los Angeles County. The mild weather makes this somewhat tolerable, but there is nothing romantic or exotic about living on the streets without a home. Homelessness is a persistent issue that affects both large and small cities all over the world. Christians and churches may respond differently to the homeless in their community, but we are united in wishing that street people had decent housing and were not forced to "sleep rough."

Homelessness is not a new issue. Jesus and His disciples were often given the hospitality of staying as guests in homes as they traveled about, but it also seems that they slept rough at times (see Matthew 8:20). Jacob used a rock as his pillow while sleeping rough at Bethel (Genesis 28:11). When Moses fled from Egypt, he spent nights sleeping rough before he found refuge in the household of Jethro, the priest of Midian (Exodus 2:15).

Before David ascended to the throne as king of Israel, he spent many months in the wilderness hiding from King Saul (see 1 Samuel 23:14). He had others with him, but there is no indication that they stayed in hotels or inns. They were most certainly sleeping rough.

Those were tense times, periods of great hardship and distress. David's early days as a shepherd had prepared him for this homeless life, for shepherds were expected to be with their flocks 24/7, often far from their homes. David was well acquainted with homelessness. Yet, out of these wilderness experiences came some of David's greatest poetry, available to us in the Psalms. Today's lesson comes from one of these, Psalm 63.

B. Lesson Background

The story of Israel's first king is not a happy one. When the people clamored for a king in order to be "like all the nations" (1 Samuel 8:20), it was a sad day in God's eyes, for God saw this as a rejection (8:7). The first king, Saul, might have been a magnificent and militarily inspiring physical specimen, but he was a moral failure. His disobedience caused God to reject him (15:26) and terminate the right of his sons to succeed him on the throne. Instead, God directed the prophet Samuel to anoint David the shepherd boy as the future king (16:13).

David eventually became a part of Saul's household. He served as the king's armor bearer (1 Samuel 16:21). He played the harp and sang for Saul to ease his troubled mind (16:23). David was even permitted to marry one of Saul's daughters, Michal (18:20, 21). But at some point Saul perceived David as a threat to his throne and sought to kill him (19:10). This caused the future king to flee to the wilderness (23:14).

Psalm 63 comes from this period in David's life. (Some students think this refers to a different period of David's life, when he fled from Absalom's rebellion; see 2 Samuel 15:23, 28 and Psalm

3). The superscription of Psalm 63 tells us that it was written while David was "in the wilderness of Judah," which is a broad category. David apparently lived in various parts of this rugged hill country in central Israel.

Some of these locations were more specifically called *Ziph* (1 Samuel 23:14), *Maon* (23:25), and *Paran* (25:1). One of these locations that scholars can locate today is an oasis on the western shores of the Dead Sea called *Engedi* (24:1). Here David and his men were safe because of their isolation, and they had sufficient water and food. Engedi is a likely location for the writing of Psalm 63.

Those were difficult and dangerous times for David—times that surely tried his faith. He must have questioned the anointing he had received from Samuel. Would he ever be king? Would he die in the wilderness? Would he be betrayed by one of his men? Would he be forced into a showdown with King Saul, perhaps even forced to slay the king out of self-preservation? Would he ever have a normal, settled, secure life again?

Perhaps David longed for the days of shepherding, when at least he knew he was welcome in his father's house and was loved by his family. But David had become a fugitive, a homeless leader of a band of homeless men. Understanding these circumstances causes us to marvel at the great faith expressed in the psalm.

I. Seeking God's Comfort
(Psalm 63:1-3)

A. Longing and Dryness (v. 1)

1. O God, thou art my God; early will I seek thee: my soul thirsteth for thee, my flesh longeth for thee in a dry and thirsty land, where no water is.

David begins with a simple yet profound confession of faith: *O God, thou art my God.* David does not say this with the attitude that he has made a careful survey of the various deities and has chosen God rather than, say, Dagon of the Philistines or Molech of the Ammonites. The God whom David has prayed to since he was old enough to pray is the God of Israel. It is the Lord, the God of his ancestors Abraham, Isaac, and Jacob.

HOW TO SAY IT

Ammonites	*Am*-un-ites.
Bethel	*Beth*-ul.
Dagon	*Day*-gon.
Engedi	En-*gee*-dye.
euphemism	*you*-fuh-mizm.
Maon	Muh-*own*.
Michal	*My*-kal.
Midian	*Mid*-ee-un.
Molech	*Mo*-lek.
Paran	*Pair*-un.
Philistines	Fuh-*liss*-teenz or *Fill*-us-teenz.
Sheol	*She*-ol.
Ziph	*Zif*.

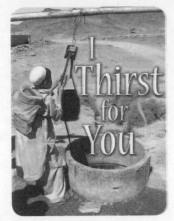

Visual for
Lesson 9

Point to this visual as you ask, "What does a lack of thirst for God imply?"

Being in the wilderness, pursued by the king of Israel, has not caused David to change his religious allegiance. God is still God for David, whether in the desert, the city, or the mountains.

David likens his need for God to the man dying of thirst in a desert. David applies this imagery to his spiritual condition, using the striking metaphor of the thirsty soul (see Psalm 143:6, also by David). Jesus uses similar language when He blesses those who "hunger and thirst after righteousness" (Matthew 5:6).

The physical realities of David's situation in the wilderness contribute to this language. He rises *early*, for in the desert this is the coolest daylight time, the best time. He seeks God first, before he becomes preoccupied with the day's tasks. He wants to quench his thirst for God as the one arising from bed needs liquids after a night of sleep. His relationship with God is vital and sustaining. Nothing else will meet his desire for spiritual refreshment.

> *What Do You Think?*
> What is the best time of the day for you to seek God? Why?
> *Talking Points for Your Discussion*
> - Allowing "the urgent" to squeeze out "the important"
> - Frequency of seeking God
> - Amount of time spent seeking God

B. Eyes and Lips (vv. 2, 3)

2. To see thy power and thy glory, so as I have seen thee in the sanctuary.

Sanctuary means "holy place." David is not using this word to refer to a specific physical location, but to the utter holiness of God. David's spiritual eyes have experienced the glorious *power* of the Lord. In this early morning time, David does not approach God casually, wanting a quick sip from the heavenly water bottle to slake his spiritual thirst. Rather, David approaches God in full awareness of His holiness, power, and glory.

3. Because thy lovingkindness is better than life, my lips shall praise thee.

David now offers another phrase of great depth: God's *lovingkindness is better than life*. David would rather enjoy the sweet fellowship of God in the dawn hours than any other aspect of living. His spiritual needs take priority over his physical needs. Water and food can wait, for he requires this time to praise the Lord with his lips.

> *What Do You Think?*
> Have you ever tried fasting for spiritual reasons? If so, how did things turn out? If not, why not?
> *Talking Points for Your Discussion*
> - Fasting for right reasons (Acts 13:2, 3; 14:23)
> - Fasting for wrong reasons (Matthew 6:16; Luke 18:11, 12)
> - Different kinds of fasts

God has created us with impulses that help ensure our survival. We thirst because our bodies need water. We hunger because our bodies need food. But most of all, our souls have a longing because we need God (compare Ecclesiastes 3:11).

II. Resting in God's Presence
(Psalm 63:4-7)
A. Hands and Mouth (vv. 4, 5)

4. Thus will I bless thee while I live: I will lift up my hands in thy name.

What are David's morning devotions like? Here we get a little insight. For one thing, he seems to do this alone, for his language is *I* rather than *we*. Second, he spends time in simple praise. To bless

God's Comforting Presence

the Lord is a form of praise coupled with thankfulness. Third, he understands this to be a lifelong task, done daily *while I live.* Fourth, David praises actively and physically, lifting his hands toward Heaven in a posture of prayer.

5. My soul shall be satisfied as with marrow and fatness; and my mouth shall praise thee with joyful lips.

David finds satisfaction in this devotional period. He compares it with *marrow and fatness,* considered delicacies to the meat eaters of David's day. They are not interested in low-fat diets! They enjoy the rich taste of an animal's fat, crispy from roasting over an open fire. (The prohibition of Leviticus 7:23-25 apparently does not apply here, since the context there is offerings.) They crack the cooked bones to be able to get the tasty marrow out of them. This is feasting at its highest level for a band of homeless men in a wilderness hideout.

Finally, David acknowledges that this early morning praise of God brings him great joy. He does not sing to the Lord with a reluctant or jaded spirit, but with *joyful lips.* He approaches his private time with God with anticipation and leaves with joy to sustain him throughout the day. David doesn't see his devotional time as burdensome.

What Do You Think?

Why do many Christians in comfortable settings struggle to find joy in their walk with God?

Talking Points for Your Discussion

- The mind-set of being in need (Philippians 4:10-13; 1 Timothy 5:5)
- The mind-set of having plenty (Daniel 4:28-37; Luke 12:13-21)
- Expectations and appreciation

B. Day and Night (vv. 6. 7)

6, 7. When I remember thee upon my bed, and meditate on thee in the night watches. Because thou hast been my help, therefore in the shadow of thy wings will I rejoice.

David now shifts to the other end of his day, the time before sleep. This is not so much a time of praise, but of meditation and remembering. He can look back on the day and count its blessings, ways in which God has been his *help.* To do this

on a regular, daily basis causes one to appreciate more fully the constant care that God provides.

This period of David's life is stressful beyond expression. Will there be enough food today? Will Saul find David's place of refuge and take his life? What of his family members who are apart from any protection he might give them? Will foreign invaders (like the Philistines) see this conflict between Saul and David as an opportunity to attack and conquer Israel?

In stressful times, we might begin our day saying, "How will I ever get through this?" At the end of the day we should remember that we have survived and God has not abandoned us. As the mother hen gathers her young brood of chicks under her wings for protection as they sleep, we may end our day and take our rest knowing that we are always under God's loving protection.

❧ *UNDER HIS WINGS* ❧

An article was circulated on the Internet in the year 2000 that related an inspirational story from *National Geographic* magazine regarding a mother bird's self-sacrifice to protect her young. As a forest fire swept through Yellowstone National Park one year, the mother protected her chicks by covering them with her wings. Eventually, a park ranger found the remains of the mother bird. When he knocked the dead bird over with a stick, three young birds emerged alive.

The story is very touching, and it was circulated to illustrate how God protects His children under His wings. There is only one problem: the story is not true. Editors at *National Geographic* say that no such story ever appeared in their magazine. Yellowstone National Park authorities say they have no record of such an event having taken place. Per www.snopes.com, this story is an urban legend.

Christianity maintains its credibility when it speaks truth. We truthfully speak of God's protection, but it's false to propose that no earthly harm will ever befall us (Acts 12:2; Revelation 6:9; etc.). God's protection refers to God's blessings. That is a universal truth for those who love Him. It is in that sense that we can face the fires of this world with confidence; we know that we are protected by our Father's wings for eternity.   —A. E. A.

III. Following God's Direction

(PSALM 63:8-11)

A. Assisted Pursuit (v. 8)

8. My soul followeth hard after thee: thy right hand upholdeth me.

To "follow hard" is an old expression that means to follow very closely, right behind. It does not imply that it is difficult for David to follow God's leading. David is more than willing to follow and not strike out on his own. This sense of proximity is reinforced by the image of the active, supportive presence of the leader's *right hand*. David understands that he will fall without the support of the Lord. The right hand is presumably the stronger hand, the hand of power.

David does not see his relationship with God to be static and unchanging. He is being led to places that he may not anticipate. In this case, he does not know how God's promise of David's becoming king will play out. He must hold onto God's hand for his future. This is the grasp of faith.

B. Vanquished Pursuers (vv. 9, 10)

9. But those that seek my soul, to destroy it, shall go into the lower parts of the earth.

David momentarily takes his eyes off God and looks around. He knows that there are those who seek his soul. Saul is not named, but that king and his henchmen may be whom David has in mind. The word *soul* in this context does not have an eternal sense, but simply refers to human life (compare Genesis 2:7). David's enemies want to kill him.

David does not see his enemies prevailing over him. They will end up going to the *lower parts of the earth*. This is a roundabout way of referring to *Sheol*, which is the Hebrew designation of the realm of the dead in the Old Testament (although the Hebrew word *Sheol* does not occur in this passage). Since only the dead are in this place, David's vision of his enemies in residence there foresees their deaths rather than his. The phrase "lower/lowest parts of the earth" also occurs in Psalm 139:15 and Isaiah 44:23, although those contexts are more positive in nature.

10. They shall fall by the sword: they shall be a portion for foxes.

David's prediction is reinforced by two gruesome details. First, his enemies are seen to die *by the sword*, which implies violently, as in battle. The story of King Saul ends with his choice for suicide rather than capture by the Philistines (1 Samuel 31:4). Saul and all who were with him were killed that day (31:6). This left their bodies exposed to carrion-eating animals such as foxes.

Second is the result. Saul's body lay in that state all night and was discovered by the Philistines on the next day. It is not unreasonable to speculate that his corpse had been violated by hungry animals. The Philistines desecrated the body further and hung it from a city wall (1 Samuel 31:8-10).

When all that happens later, David will take no joy in the death of Saul, for he recognizes him to be the Lord's anointed (see 2 Samuel 1:17-27). Saul's tragic death is among the grim realities that David endures. There is no sense of joy in this psalm at the future demise of David's enemies. The joy, rather, is in David's trust that God will safeguard him. It is this relationship that always encourages David, that brings him to praise God with joyful lips.

C. Necessary Joy (v. 11)

11. But the king shall rejoice in God; every one that sweareth by him shall glory: but the mouth of them that speak lies shall be stopped.

The psalm ends on a note of assurance for future vindication. David is looking forward to what his reign as king should be like. He will be a king who acknowledges the preeminence of God. David will be a leader of many who give glory to the Lord.

David also foresees the end of false, hypocritical worship. Ideally, there will be no more time for lies, for truth-twisting. People will give no place to falsehood, but be swept up in pure, ongoing praise for the Lord. One of the greatest word pictures of worship in the Bible is of the joyous celebrations David leads (example: 2 Samuel 6:5, 16).

❧ TELLING THE TRUTH ❧

U.S. Senator Ted Stevens was on trial for corruption in October 2008. During jury deliberations, one juror said that her father had died and that she had to go to California because of this. The judge allowed her to do so. But suspicions grew when she failed to return. Eventually the truth came out: her father hadn't died. The juror merely had decided that she wanted to attend a horse race.

Sadly, lying is so common that often we are not surprised when it happens. We have even developed various ways to categorize lies. The *little white lie* is meant to look out for the good of someone. The *manipulative lie* is an attempt to control someone or get things to work out for one's own purposes. The *lie of omission* leaves out certain bits of information in order to create a false impression.

God's people are called to be people of truth. As children of the God of all truth, lying goes against our spiritual heritage. Speaking the truth is part of maturing in Christ. "Speaking the truth in love, [we] may grow up into him in all things, which is the head, even Christ" (Ephesians 4:15; see also Colossians 3:9; 1 Timothy 4:2).   —A. E. A.

Conclusion

A. Not Just on Sunday

When do you recognize your relationship with God? How often? Do you praise Him on Sunday, but not during the week? If your time of communion with your Creator is limited to once a week, what happens if you miss a couple of weeks? Can you maintain a strong relationship if you neglect it for 7 or 14 or 21 days? What if you miss a couple of months, maybe during a sports season or due to a change in shifts at your job?

The answer to this is obvious: any relationship withers if it is not cultivated. David understood this, even in his times of deepest distress. He languished as a fugitive in a remote wilderness hideout, far from his family and his old childhood stomping grounds. Whatever his family worship patterns had been as he grew up, they would have been difficult to maintain. There must have been days when he was confused, wondering why Samuel would have promised him the throne of Israel only to have King Saul seek his death. But today's psalm shows us that David did not despair of his strong, sustaining relationship with the Lord.

A mature, growing relationship with God will not be confined to Sunday. It will spill over into the other days. It can begin as we seek time alone with the Lord every morning and/or evening. We do not need a carefully planned program with people designated to pray and read Scripture. There is nothing wrong with these things, but worshiping "only on Sunday" is not enough.

As our relationship grows deeper, we will begin to understand what David learned: that God's "lovingkindness is better than life." We will begin to acknowledge that our souls have a deep, unquenchable thirst for God and that we need to experience His presence to sustain us.

B. Prayer

Holy God, lover of our souls, we praise You with lips of joy. We want to seek You in the morning, in the evening, and all the day through. Our souls are destitute without Your presence. They are like the parched ground in a desert during a long-term drought. They need and seek the living water that comes from You. May You continue to bless us with Your presence and comfort. In the name of Jesus we pray. Amen.

C. Thought to Remember

God is always available.

INVOLVEMENT LEARNING

Some of the activities below are also found in the helpful student book, Adult Bible Class.
Don't forget to download the free reproducible page from www.standardlesson.com to enhance your lesson!

Into the Lesson

If your budget allows, provide a bottle of water for each learner as he or she arrives. If your budget does not allow this, have small disposable cups of water set out on a table. Have the question *Are You Thirsty?* visible on the board. As class begins, add this question: "What exactly are you thirsty for?" Compare and contrast physical thirst with David's spiritual thirst for God's presence, per today's text.

Into the Word

Prepare handouts of the statements below. Distribute copies to small study-groups or pairs. Say, "First see whether you agree with these statements as principles of life and worship. Then decide whether Psalm 63 supports your position." (The statements are given here in random order; following the statement is the applicable verse or verses, which you may wish to leave off.)

1. True worship is truly satisfying. [v. 5]
2. Truth conquers lies. [v. 11]
3. Worship acknowledges God's greatness. [v. 2]
4. God's love cannot but spur our praise, if we are honest. [v. 3]
5. Early in the day is a good time to approach God. [v. 1]
6. Worship never ends; first it is here, then it is in eternity. [v. 4]
7. The only safe place is in God's care. [v. 7]
8. Raised hands symbolize both petition and receptiveness. [v. 4]
9. True devotion to God involves a sense of true closeness. [v. 8]
10. Expressions of praise should be loud. [v. 3]
11. Sleep comes easier to those who dwell on God's presence. [v. 6]
12. We're in good hands with God. [v. 8]
13. Fear dissipates in the submission of worship. [v. 9]
14. We honor God when we have confidence in His justice. [vv. 9, 10]
15. A commitment to God's lordship involves giving Him glory. [v. 11]
16. It is appropriate in dire straits to elicit humble worship rather than anxiety and distress. [v. 1]

After an appropriate amount of time, call for teams to express their conclusions. Some may want to qualify certain statements as being too broad. For example, #2 may have to await God's consummation of all things before it is fully realized. Students may suggest other principles of life and worship that they see in Psalm 63.

Into Life

Continue discussing the principles of life and worship you used in Into the Word. Ask, "For any of these principles, identify a life situation that we might call 'a spiritual wilderness.' For one trapped in such a wilderness, how can he or she be strengthened and blessed by the powerful truth of the principle?"

For example, suggest that the principle of *humble worship* (#16) for one in dire straits (as seen in the life of David) is just what is needed to counter the rationalization "I am so low spiritually that going to a worship assembly will be a waste of my time and God's." Recommend that the class work through the whole list for themselves as "ready counsel" when someone reveals a spiritual need to them. *Alternative:* The exercise Faith in a Forest of Failures and Fears on the reproducible page is a similar application activity; however, that exercise works from situation back to principle rather than from principle to situation, as here.

If time allows, also have learners complete the Wilderness exercise from the reproducible page that you have downloaded; otherwise distribute copies as a take-home activity. If you distributed bottles of water at the outset, encourage learners to let their bottles sit in a conspicuous place for a few days. This can remind them of today's study.

God's Comforting Presence

GOD IS AWESOME

BACKGROUND SCRIPTURE: Psalm 66
PRINTED TEXT: Psalm 66:1-12

PSALM 66:1-12

1 Make a joyful noise unto God, all ye lands:

2 Sing forth the honour of his name: make his praise glorious.

3 Say unto God, How terrible art thou in thy works! through the greatness of thy power shall thine enemies submit themselves unto thee.

4 All the earth shall worship thee, and shall sing unto thee; they shall sing to thy name. Selah.

5 Come and see the works of God: he is terrible in his doing toward the children of men.

6 He turned the sea into dry land: they went through the flood on foot: there did we rejoice in him.

7 He ruleth by his power for ever; his eyes behold the nations: let not the rebellious exalt themselves. Selah.

8 O bless our God, ye people, and make the voice of his praise to be heard:

9 Which holdeth our soul in life, and suffereth not our feet to be moved.

10 For thou, O God, hast proved us: thou hast tried us, as silver is tried.

11 Thou broughtest us into the net; thou laidst affliction upon our loins.

12 Thou hast caused men to ride over our heads; we went through fire and through water: but thou broughtest us out into a wealthy place.

KEY VERSE

Come and see the works of God: he is terrible in his doing toward the children of men. —**Psalm 66:5**

THE INESCAPABLE GOD

Unit 3: God Protects

LESSON AIMS

After participating in this lesson, each student will be able to:

1. List some of God's mighty acts for which the psalmist expresses praise to God.

2. Compare and contrast the tenor of praise in Psalm 66 with the praise he or she typically offers to God.

3. Paraphrase the worship expressions of Psalm 66:1-12 for a modern call to worship.

LESSON OUTLINE

Introduction

A. "Awesome God" Story

Some years ago, I was an interim preacher for a church in Grand Rapids, Michigan, for about a year. The worship minister also was an interim. We both stayed in the basement of the home of one of the leaders on Saturday evenings. During those times we planned the sermons and the worship services so that a unified biblical theme could be developed and presented for the congregation.

On one occasion the worship minister asked me to create a sermon to match a new song he had written just a few weeks earlier. And so I preached a sermon on Isaiah 40:28-31 and called it the same title as the song: "Our God Is an Awesome God!" Yes, it was Rich Mullins who was the worship minister, and little did either of us know that this song eventually would become a classic of Christian music.

I chose Isaiah as my text because Rich was in the habit of reading Isaiah once a month for inspiration to write music. Yet I could have preached from a number of biblical texts to match that song title! Indeed, God is awesome, and both Old and New Testaments proclaim His awesome deeds. Psalm 66 is one of those texts that proclaim that *God is awesome!*

B. Lesson Background

Psalm 66 is a hymn praising God for awesome deeds in the present as well as in the past. The hymn is divided into two parts. The first part (vv. 1-12) is a communal exhortation to praise God for His awesome works on behalf of His people, even during times of testing instigated by God. The second part (vv. 13-20) is characterized by a representative figure (a king? a priest?) who offers thanksgiving offerings on behalf of the congregation. The two parts are mutually dependent.

What is interesting about this psalm is the placement of *Selah* at various places (at the end of vv. 4 and 7 for part one and at the end of v. 15 for part two). Scholars do not know the meaning of *Selah,* but here it clearly is used at the logical breaks in the thought of the text. Part one (vv. 1-12) is divided into three stanzas (vv. 1-4, 5-7, 8-12). These are the texts for our lesson. Part two (vv. 13-20) is clearly divided into two stanzas (vv. 13-15 and vv. 16-20), with verse 20 as a benediction.

No one knows what crisis (if any) is the background for this psalm. Most scholars suggest two possibilities. One is the Assyrian crisis of 701 BC, involving Sennacherib's siege of Jerusalem and King Hezekiah's faithfulness to God to trust in His deliverance (Isaiah 36, 37; 2 Kings 18:13, 17-37; 2 Chronicles 32:9-19). Only by the intervention of God was the city of Jerusalem spared. To this end Hezekiah had prayed the words we see in Isaiah 37:16-20. If the words of Psalm 66:13-20 are from Hezekiah's lips, then we can see their deep significance. The praise and sacrifice offered by the king are not on his own behalf alone, but for the people whom God has rescued.

The second possible background is the release from Babylonian captivity. The date under this possibility would have to be after the rebuilding of the temple in 516 BC since Psalm 66:13 refers to that structure. But no one knows which theory (if either) is correct. Yet this uncertainty does not rob this psalm of its power and dynamic. It can be applied to any "deliverance" the people of God experience in any circumstance.

Neither do we know who wrote the psalm. Both Psalms 66 and 67 are without a named author, but both are surrounded by "Davidic" psalms. This uncertainty does not, of course, prevent our appreciation for the content of the psalm.

I. Sing to an Awesome God
(PSALM 66:1-4)
A. With Joy (v. 1)

1. Make a joyful noise unto God, all ye lands.

I have to chuckle at the exhortation to *make a joyful noise* because I know a number of godly saints who cannot carry a tune in a bucket. Their singing is indeed "a joyful noise"!

But disharmonious noise is not what this exhortation is about. Literally, it is about a shout, and it is to be done with joy. When a multitude of people are raising their voices together, distinct words are hard or impossible to differentiate. Often one hears only a loud noise. (The mob scenes in Acts 19:32 and 21:34 are negative examples.) But even if distinct words and phrases cannot be distinguished, the tone of the noise is still recognizable. Is it joyful? Is it fearful? Is it angry? One knows without being told.

What Do You Think?
What are some ways, other than singing, to make a joyful noise unto the Lord?
Talking Points for Your Discussion
- In private time with God
- In family settings
- During small-group fellowship
- During corporate worship

In the Hebrew, the phrase *all ye lands* is precisely the same as the phrase "all the earth" in verse 4 (considered below). Together they emphasize the fact that the God of the Hebrews is also the God of the whole earth. Thus the tone of the psalm is universal. The peoples of the earth cannot refuse to recognize God's awesome deeds. His sovereignty demands universal worship and obedience. This should be done with joy.

❧ THE LOUDEST NOISE IS YET TO COME ❧

In 1883, the volcanic island of Krakatau, Indonesia, exploded with the force of 13,000 Hiroshima atomic bombs. The sound of the explosion was heard some 3,000 miles away. The volume hit 180 decibels within 100 miles of the epicenter, louder than a jet engine at close range. Some claim that it was the loudest noise in human history.

Yet there are louder noises to come. God will wake the dead at the sound of the last trumpet (1 Corinthians 15:52). The heavens will disappear with "a great noise" (2 Peter 3:10). Christ, the King of kings, will appear to lead the armies of Heaven (Revelation 19:11-16). People of every tribe, tongue, language, and nation, along with the multitudes of angels and heavenly beings, will gather before God's throne and shout, "Alleluia: for the Lord God omnipotent reigneth" (Revelation 19:6). The echoes of *that* noise will never end!

May the joyful noise we make in worship anticipate the joy of that final day. —A. R. W.

B. For Glory (v. 2)

2. Sing forth the honour of his name: make his praise glorious.

This verse is parallel to verse 1, but adds the idea of singing to the shouting for joy. The one being referred to by the phrase *his name* is not in doubt: it is God, per verse 1. How do we *make his praise glorious*? By singing in such a way as to exalt, honor, and glorify God's great name, for He is an awesome God! The worship leader who can lead the people in doing this is valuable indeed.

There is a play-on-words here that is evident only in the original Hebrew. The words *honour* and *glorious* are translations of the same Hebrew word, derived from a root meaning "weightiness." Honor and glory are "heavy"! The apostle Paul undoubtedly has this play-on-words in mind when he writes, "For our light affliction, which is but for a moment, worketh for us a far more exceeding and eternal weight of glory" (2 Corinthians 4:17). Our worship must include music that "gives weight" to God's name.

C. By a Statement (v. 3)

3. Say unto God, How terrible art thou in thy works! through the greatness of thy power shall thine enemies submit themselves unto thee.

We move from the "noise" of verse 1 (unintelligible but joyful nonetheless) to the "music" of verse 2 (beautifully crafted songs that honor and glorify God's name) to a "statement" here in verse 3. The statement is an acknowledgment of the greatness of God's power to accomplish His pur-

poses. And perhaps these are the words to be used in praising God. The word *terrible* as used here has the sense of something that elicits terror, fear, or awe. Hence one should view the works of God with a great deal of fear and reverence.

Since God is awesome, His works and deeds are awesome. An example of this is in the way the disciples of Jesus responded to His command to let down their nets once more even though they had caught nothing all night long (Luke 5:1-11). The resulting great catch of fish was awesome, and Simon Peter seems to have been terrified (v. 8)! When one reviews all the works of God in the Old Testament and the great deeds of Jesus in the New Testament, the large catch of fish is a small thing compared with the other awesome works of God.

God's power is so great that when it is manifested, the enemies of God have no choice but to submit themselves to His authority (example: Revelation 6:15-17). Those who do not worship God willingly will do so unwillingly. A good way to say it is: "They will cower before God!" (See Psalm 18:44, 45; 81:15.) They will indeed cringe with fear.

D. Prophetically (v. 4)

4. All the earth shall worship thee, and shall sing unto thee; they shall sing to thy name. Selah.

All the earth should be taken prophetically. At present only about a third of the earth's population calls itself "Christian," and that number undoubtedly includes many who are Christian in name only. Not until some future day will all the earth worship God the Father as revealed through Jesus and as known by His Spirit (compare Romans 14:11; Philippians 2:10).

The verse has now come full circle so that we see a vision of a future people singing unto God and honoring His name. God's people in their present circumstances do not yet see the whole earth either bowing down in homage to God or singing to Him. But by faith we can envision at least the saved of Revelation 15:3, 4 doing so: "And they sing the song of Moses . . . saying, Great and marvelous are thy works, Lord God Almighty; just and true are thy ways, thou King of saints." See the Lesson Background for discussion of *Selah*.

HOW TO SAY IT

Assyrian	Uh-*sear*-e-un.
Baal	*Bay*-ul.
Babylonian	Bab-ih-*low*-nee-un.
Davidic	Duh-*vid*-ick.
Hezekiah	Hez-ih-*kye*-uh.
Malachi	*Mal*-uh-kye.
Miriam	*Meer*-ee-um.
Moses	*Mo*-zes or *Mo*-zez.
Selah *(Hebrew)*	*See*-luh.
Sennacherib	Sen-*nack*-er-ib.
Zechariah	Zek-uh-*rye*-uh

II. See the Works of God
(Psalm 66:5-7)
A. They Are Awesome (v. 5)

5. Come and see the works of God: he is terrible in his doing toward the children of men.

The invitation to *come and see* God's activities or works is also offered in Psalm 46:8. If one worships an awesome God, it must be because He has done awesome works. This is the reason for our worship. The invitation to "come and see" in this part of Psalm 66 is balanced by "come and hear" down in verse 16.

As with our comments of verse 3 above, we should relate the word *terrible* to the word *terrifying*. Indeed, it can be a terrifying experience when God begins to work on behalf of His people, such as He did during the exodus events. Think of the 10 plagues (Exodus 7–11). Think of the Passover meal on that climactic night (Exodus 12). Think of the crossing of the Red Sea (Exodus 13, 14). The Israelites had been terrified by the Egyptians (14:10-12). But as God revealed His awesome power, the Israelites feared Him instead (14:31). The reader is invited to see what the Israelites saw (next verse).

B. They Are Well-known (v. 6)

6. He turned the sea into dry land: they went through the flood on foot: there did we rejoice in him.

God has shown His awesome power in the past by delivering His people from the Egyptian army by opening a way through the Red Sea. The movie *The Ten Commandments* depicts the sea dividing almost instantly, but the Bible reveals that God "caused the sea to go back by a strong east wind all that night" (Exodus 14:21). I envision God directing a strong jet stream of air onto the waters, piling up a frozen wall of water on each side until there is a wide frozen mud path left for the Israelites to hurry to the other side (see Exodus 14:29; 15:8; Psalm 78:13).

The path then becomes thick mud when the temperature increases, which causes the chariot wheels to become stuck and some even to fall off (Exodus 14:25; compare 15:4, 5). At just the right moment, with the Egyptian soldiers and chariots

caught in the mud, God causes the frozen walls of water to crack, releasing the deadly waters upon the path (Exodus 14:26-28; compare 15:1, 4, 5, 10, 12, 19, 21). Although the text doesn't mention water freezing and ice forming, this is a possible way that this supernatural, miraculous event manifested itself. The exodus is ancient Israel's most beloved and well-known story of salvation.

Verse 6 is typical Hebrew poetry in that it features what we call *synonymous parallelism*. We see the parallel between the words *sea* and *flood*. Literally in Hebrew the words are *sea* and *river*. These two words are used in ancient pagan societies to refer to water gods or chaos gods who are overcome by Baal's ascendancy to kingship over nature.

Here, instead, it is God who is victorious over these fictitious chaos monsters (see Psalm 77:16-19; 78:13; 136:13-15). God's awesome power controls the chaotic waters. Some might think that the word *river* may refer to the Jordan River, which the Israelites miraculously crossed (Joshua 3:14-17), based on the parallel of *sea* with *Jordan* in Psalm 114:3, 5. But it is best to see these two words as referring to the Red Sea event in the text at hand.

The rejoicing after this awesome event refers to the songs of Moses and Miriam (Exodus 15:1-18, 20, 21). Moses' song became a pattern for such rejoicing at great events ever since.

> *What Do You Think?*
> How do you rejoice in God's deliverance in ways that are similar to and different from the ways the ancient Israelites rejoiced?
> *Talking Points for Your Discussion*
> - By the use of your financial resources
> - By the use of your time
> - Through your relationships

C. They Are Powerful (v. 7)

7. He ruleth by his power for ever; his eyes behold the nations: let not the rebellious exalt themselves. Selah.

The song of Moses ends with this declaration: "The Lord shall reign for ever and ever" (Exodus 15:18). It is God who is the king of all the earth. In that capacity He rules with great power and His accomplishments are awesome (see Exodus 14:31). The divine king is always watching the nations, for He is sovereign over them as well as over Israel. Any nation can suffer the consequences of being an enemy of God (see Psalm 66:3, above) when it refuses to honor God's name or acknowledge His awesome power and great deeds. Look at what happened to the Egyptians! No nation should dare try to exalt itself above God's sovereign power. See the Lesson Background for a discussion of *Selah*.

What Do You Think?
In what ways do the rebellious exalt themselves?
Talking Points for Your Discussion
- By the use of their financial resources
- By the use of their time
- Through their relationships

III. Suffer the Testing of God
(Psalm 66:8-12)
A. With Loud Praise (v. 8)

8. O bless our God, ye people, and make the voice of his praise to be heard.

What "all ye lands" are compelled to do in verse 1, the present generation of God's people (in terms of this psalm) are to do as well: praise God loudly! All the nations are to hear God's people praising Him for deliverance. The generation this psalm is written to is to identify itself with the exodus generation. We in the twenty-first century must do so as well (compare 1 Corinthians 10:1-13).

B. For Great Deliverance (v. 9)

9. Which holdeth our soul in life, and suffereth not our feet to be moved.

This is a pivotal point of the psalm. The God of the Hebrews is a life-giving God, and we identify with Him. The psalmist's generation perhaps has experienced a life-threatening event (see the Lesson Background), and yet God sustains them.

The imagery of slipping feet reminds us of Psalm 73:2: "But as for me, . . . my steps had well nigh slipped." Instead, it is the evildoers whom God places in slippery locations (see 73:18). Life is always both precarious and precious. Without God's constant care we are dead. Our generation needs to understand this principle.

C. By Fiery Trials (vv. 10, 11)

10. For thou, O God, hast proved us: thou hast tried us, as silver is tried.

No one really knows what kind of character a person has until that person is tried by difficult circumstances, even divine testing. David asks God to test his character in Psalm 17:3; 26:2; 139:23 (compare Romans 5:3-5; 2 Corinthians 2:9; 8:8; 13:5-7). Without such testing, no one will know our true commitment.

What Do You Think?
What example have you seen of someone whose faith has proven true during a crisis?
Talking Points for Your Discussion
- During times of personal sickness
- During times of family sickness
- Through the pain caused by a rebellious child
- In times of financial devastation
- When falsely accused

Visual for Lesson 10

Praise God even in times of testing.

Point to this visual as you ask, "How do we know when God is testing us?"

The smelting of metals such as silver is a well-known practice. Figuratively, it refers to being disciplined by God to remove the dross and impurity of sin (compare Isaiah 1:25; 48:10; Jeremiah 9:7; Zechariah 13:9; Malachi 3:3). The exile of Judah in 586 BC is the primary example of this. If God is to be experienced at all, He must be experienced as a "consuming fire," which purges our sins (Deuteronomy 4:24; quoted in Hebrews 12:29).

❧ FROM IMPURE TO PURE ❧

It's hard to imagine that two such opposite metals as lead and silver can coexist. Lead is dark and dull; silver is so reflective it is used in the highest quality optical mirrors. Lead is a poor electrical conductor; silver is one of the best conductors. Lead is used as a common construction material; silver is a precious metal.

In ancient times, metallurgists painstakingly separated the two by applying heat and skimming off the refined silver. What an apt image for God's purifying activity in our lives! He finds us spiritually dull, inert, and base. Through tests and trials, He melts away sin and pride. The result is something that is spiritually bright, active, and pure.

The soul refined by God reflects His image. Such a soul faithfully transmits His message, brings life, and becomes a vessel suitable for noble purposes (2 Timothy 2:20, 21). Will you embrace God's refining or try to avoid it?   —A. R. W.

11. Thou broughtest us into the net; thou laidst affliction upon our loins.

The second metaphor is that of an animal being caught in a net, also used by Ezekiel in describing the exile of a Judean king (Ezekiel 12:13; 17:20). We suggested in the Lesson Background that this is one of the possible historical circumstances of the psalm. If this is the correct backdrop, then the people may see their Babylon servitude as something of a repeat of what they underwent in Egypt.

D. Toward a Flourishing Place (v. 12)

12. Thou hast caused men to ride over our heads; we went through fire and through water: but thou broughtest us out into a wealthy place.

What some people see as disaster, the psalmist sees as God's purifying process. God has caused others to ride roughshod over His people, but this is for a purpose. The presence of trials of fire and water does not mean that the Lord is absent (see Isaiah 43:2). While cosmic and human powers seek the death of God's people, God delivers them *into a wealthy place.* God provided water and manna in the wilderness. The ultimate goal was a land "flowing with milk and honey" (Exodus 3:8, 17, etc.). Only those who live by faith will experience this abundant life (Psalm 23:5; John 10:10; Romans 1:17; 5:17).

> **What Do You Think?**
> When was a time God brought you from a very bad situation into a very good one?
> *Talking Points for Your Discussion*
> • After allegations against you were proven false
> • When a prodigal child returned to the Lord
> • When you got a job after unemployment

Conclusion
A. Our God Is an Awesome God

Indeed, our God is an awesome God, and His works are awesome! Creation itself testifies to this characteristic of God. But bending nature to His will seems easy compared with shaping a people for God's purposes. A slave-nation in Egypt, the Hebrews were to become a holy nation, a kingdom of priests, and God's most-prized treasure. God led His fickle people through the wilderness and across the Jordan River to conquer the promise land.

Eventually, a nation became a kingdom with eternal and unconditional promises given to David. That kingdom thrived until sin divided it. Yet a remnant returned from exile, and God's awesome deeds were recognized by a renewed people.

Finally, the Messiah came. It is the resurrection of Jesus that causes us to declare most completely that our God is an awesome God! Even the Jewish scholars who translated the Hebrew Bible into Greek about 200 years before Christ entitled Psalm 66 as "a song of resurrection." Our God is an awesome God.

B. Prayer

O God, You have given us new life and kept our feet from slipping. Purify us for Your purposes and lead us through fire and water to You. We pray in Jesus' name. Amen.

C. Thought to Remember

Worship only the awesome God.

INVOLVEMENT LEARNING

Some of the activities below are also found in the helpful student book, Adult Bible Class.
Don't forget to download the free reproducible page from www.standardlesson.com to enhance your lesson!

Into the Lesson

Option #1: Prepare for a simplified game of *Bible Jeopardy* by writing these two categories on the board: *God's Deliverers* and *Israel's Enemies*. Underneath each one write the point values 20, 40, 60, 80, 100 vertically. Divide the class into two teams, and have each team select a spokesperson. Randomly decide which team goes first. Then have teams alternate in selecting a category and amount. By the end each team will have had five chances. Remind the players that the response should be in the form of a question (but don't deduct points if they forget).

Answers for GOD'S DELIVERERS: (20) Brought down a giant with a slingshot. (40) Died when he brought down the house on his enemies. (60) Won the battle with 300 men armed with pitchers and torches. (80) She told Barak that because he was afraid to go to battle without her, a woman would have the honor. (100) Without telling Saul, he climbed up with his armor bearer and slew 20 Philistines. *Questions:* Who was (20) David? (40) Samson? (60) Gideon? (80) Deborah? (100) Jonathan?

Answers for ISRAEL'S ENEMIES: (20) Said no to God's demand, "Let my people go." (40) Had Goliath as their champion. (60) These 450 men were defeated on Mount Carmel by Elijah's God. (80) The people of this city were defeated when Rahab, one of its citizen's, assisted Israel's two spies. (100) Daniel prophesied that the king of this nation would lose his mind and become like an animal. *Questions:* Who/What was/were (20) Pharaoh? (40) the Philistines? (60) the prophets of Baal? (80) Jericho? (100) Babylon?

Option #2: Download the reproducible page and distribute copies of the activity Special Delivery by God from it. Students are to solve the letter substitution crypto-quiz to come up with a list of ways that God helped the Israelites when He took them out of Egypt into the promised land.

To lead into Bible study, say, "The Israelites had abundant reasons for being grateful to the Lord for delivering them from their enemies. The psalm we will be studying is an excellent example of how to praise the Lord for His awesome deeds."

Into the Word

Have learners form small groups to complete the following matching activity. Distribute handouts with the following list of "Puny Paraphrases" from Psalm 66:1-12 down the left side, with verse numbers 1 through 12 down the right side. Have them find the verse that is the best match for each one.

1. "I almost lost my footing, but You saved me." 2. "You just got to come and see the amazing things God has done for us!" 3. "All you people need to open up and let your praises of God be heard." 4. "Bow down, earth, and sing out your praise and worship." 5. "Being melted down has its benefits." 6. "What a name You have, Lord, full of honor and glory!" 7. "We were almost run over, burned, and drowned, but it paid off." 8. "Every place on earth needs to make a racket in praise of God." 9. "I am so happy to tell you that God dried up the sea so we could walk right through it!" 10. "Caught in a trap and locked up, we were in for a rough time of it." 11. "Enemies slink." 12. "God is watching the nations like a hawk!

Answers: 1, v. 9; 2, v. 5; 3, v. 8; 4, v. 4; 5, v. 10; 6, v. 2; 7, v. 12; 8, v. 1; 9, v. 6; 10, v. 11; 11, v. 3; 12, v. 7.

When groups have finished, ask for volunteers to tell the match for each one and read the verse aloud.

Into Life

Download the reproducible page and distribute copies of the exercise Increase the Volume! from it. Ask students to complete the self-evaluation of how well they praise God. Then have them suggest one way they can do better in the coming week.

God Is Awesome

GOD IS FOREVER

BACKGROUND SCRIPTURE: Psalm 90
PRINTED TEXT: Psalm 90:1-12

PSALM 90:1-12

1 Lord, thou hast been our dwelling place in all generations.

2 Before the mountains were brought forth, or ever thou hadst formed the earth and the world, even from everlasting to everlasting, thou art God.

3 Thou turnest man to destruction; and sayest, Return, ye children of men.

4 For a thousand years in thy sight are but as yesterday when it is past, and as a watch in the night.

5 Thou carriest them away as with a flood; they are as a sleep: in the morning they are like grass which growth up.

6 In the morning it flourisheth, and groweth up; in the evening it is cut down, and withereth.

7 For we are consumed by thine anger, and by thy wrath are we troubled.

8 Thou hast set our iniquities before thee, our secret sins in the light of thy countenance.

9 For all our days are passed away in thy wrath: we spend our years as a tale that is told.

10 The days of our years are threescore years and ten; and if by reason of strength they be fourscore years, yet is their strength labor and sorrow; for it is soon cut off, and we fly away.

11 Who knoweth the power of thine anger? even according to thy fear, so is thy wrath.

12 So teach us to number our days, that we may apply our hearts unto wisdom.

KEY VERSE

Before the mountains were brought forth, or ever thou hadst formed the earth and the world, even from everlasting to everlasting, thou art God. —**Psalm 90:2**

THE
INESCAPABLE GOD

Unit 3: God Protects
LESSONS 10–13

LESSON AIMS

After participating in this lesson, each student will be able to:

1. List some characteristics of human frailty that contrast with the nature of God.

2. Tell how the world tries to deal with human frailty and why those efforts are ultimately doomed to fail.

3. Make a statement of faith in God, who gives his or her life meaning and significance.

LESSON OUTLINE

Introduction

A. Life Is Short

My father passed away on April 1, 2008, of leukemia at age 90. He had lived 10 years beyond the 80 years of Psalm 90:10 (part of today's text). The year before, I had the opportunity to take him on a trip back to his roots in southeast Alabama. He showed me where he was born and grew up. There's a marker on the side of the road that tells the story of my great-grandfather and the settlement named after him. The old three-room schoolhouse where my dad received all of his formal education still stands, but with a tree growing through the porch roof.

As we left that place, he commented "Life is short!" Indeed—one day you are a child and the next day an adult and another day you are old.

Dad's earthly claim to fame was his induction into Georgia's Country Music Hall of Fame. He was a fiddler. He was happy with that, but I wished for more. In his 90 short years, my dad chose not to be a Christian.

B. Lesson Background

We noted in Lesson 5 that the Psalms are divided into five "books." Psalm 90, today's text, begins the fourth of these five. Many scholars consider this section of the Psalms (that is, Psalms 90–106) to be the answer to the problem presented in the first three books: the Davidic dynasty established, Psalm 2; the flourishing of that dynasty, Psalm 72; and the failure of that dynasty, Psalm 89. The emphasis in this fourth section is simply *Yahweh reigns!* (see Psalms 93, 96–99).

Here, finally, the problem presented in the first three books is stated. Human kings may disappoint us, but Yahweh is our king, and He reigns forever. He is the king who through Moses led the children of Israel out of Egyptian bondage.

In this light, Book IV of the Psalms has something of a Mosaic flavor (notice that the superscription of Psalm 90 attributes it to Moses). Book IV ends with two views of the wilderness wandering, which was led by Moses: God's viewpoint (Psalm 105) and Israel's viewpoint (Psalm 106). The former is about God's faithfulness to the covenant promises, while the latter is about Israel's sinfulness and failure to obey God and keep the covenant.

Evaluating the connection between Book III and Book IV, we see Psalm 89 connected with Psalm 90 by the common topics of the brevity of life (89:47, 48; 90:3-6) and divine wrath (89:46; 90:7-10). Notice too the question *How long?* that they have in common (89:46; 90:13). Thus some lines of thought at the end of Book III carry into the beginning of Book IV.

Psalm 90 is a community's lament asking God for divine favor (vv. 13-17), lest God's wrath prevail over the people's short lives (vv. 1-12). What the distress is about no one knows for sure. Whatever the distress, it affects the whole community.

I. Eternal God
(PSALM 90:1, 2)
A. Our Dwelling Place (v. 1)

1. Lord, thou hast been our dwelling place in all generations.

The word *Lord* is *Adonai,* which is not God's personal name, but rather is a title (example: Psalm 8:1). He is our Master and Ruler. This is the designation the psalmist uses to end the psalm as well (90:17).

In addition to being our Lord, God is our *dwelling place.* The word originally referred to a shelter for animals. Then it came to be used for God's dwelling (Psalms 26:8; 68:5). As a result, that dwelling is a shelter for those who trust in the Lord. The word becomes *refuge* just by changing the last letter in Hebrew. Perhaps there is a play on words here. In this area of the world, visitors receive both hospitality and protection in homes

where they stay (compare Genesis 19:1-8). Thus the dwelling places are places of refuge for guests.

God's own dwelling place is Heaven (1 Kings 8:30). But His dwelling place is also seen to be the temple (Psalm 74:7). This visible reminder of God's presence is a source of comfort.

> **What Do You Think?**
> Where was your *dwelling place* as a child, the place where you went for refuge? How is such a dwelling place similar to and different from the *dwelling place* of God?
> **Talking Points for Your Discussion**
> - To escape from annoying siblings
> - To escape from authority figures
> - To escape from bullies

B. From Everlasting to Everlasting (v. 2)

2. Before the mountains were brought forth, or ever thou hadst formed the earth and the world, even from everlasting to everlasting, thou art God.

The Lord was God before there was a temple. He was God before any part of creation existed. We should note that verse 1 refers to "dwelling place in all generations." That goes back only to the creation of either humanity in general or the people of God in particular. The psalmist now declares that God is eternal—*from everlasting to everlasting.* No beginning, no end! He is the one and only powerful God. This eternal attribute of God is contrasted with human weakness in the verses that follow.

> **What Do You Think?**
> In what situations have you been helped by recalling that God is "from everlasting to everlasting"? Why are those meaningful?
> **Talking Points for Your Discussion**
> - Job situations
> - Church situations
> - Political situations

HOW TO SAY IT

Davidic	Duh-*vid*-ick.
Isaiah	Eye-*zay*-uh.
Jeremiah	Jair-uh-*my*-uh.
Lamentations	Lam-en-*tay*-shunz.
Mosaic	Mo-*zay*-ik.
Moses	*Mo*-zes or *Mo*-zez.
Septuagint	Sep-*too*-ih-jent.
Yahweh (Hebrew)	*Yah*-weh.

❧ TO BE AGELESS ❧

Many of us feel shocked the first time a store clerk calls us *sir* or *ma'am,* the first time we see wisps of gray in our hair, or when we're offered our first senior citizen's discount. Even though we can't fathom how *we* could be aging, there are some people who by definition are "supposed" to be old—grandparents, for example.

Another example is God. In the popular imagination, God is an ancient man with gray hair and beard. His face may show some wrinkles. At least that's the way He is portrayed in cartoons.

But God does not age. He is as ageless today as the day He created the universe. He never grows tired or weary (Isaiah 40:28). The ageless God has the power to grant us resurrected bodies that will never wear out, and He will do so (1 Corinthians 15:42). Praise Him!   —A. R. W.

II. Frail Humanity
(Psalm 90:3-6)
A. Cursed Life (v. 3)

3. Thou turnest man to destruction; and sayest, Return, ye children of men.

The word *destruction* refers to pulverized dirt. Thus this verse echoes Genesis 3:19. After Adam and Eve disobeyed God's command of Genesis 2:17, curses were placed on every aspect of that disobedience. The declaration *Return [to dust], ye children of men* is certainly part of that curse. The Genesis 3 story behind this verse prevents humanity from participating in the "tree of life" in order to "live for ever" (3:22). Genesis 3 in a nutshell reveals the reality of a cursed existence due to sin.

B. Contrast with God (v. 4)

4. For a thousand years in thy sight are but as yesterday when it is past, and as a watch in the night.

Humans experience the effects of aging, but God has no such experience. A thousand years are nothing to God, a trifle to be compared with *yesterday when it is past* (see 2 Peter 3:8). A *watch in the night* is a segment of time between sunset and sunrise, a time of service for a watchman. Such periods of time may seem very long to us when we can't get to sleep or choose not to sleep (compare Psalm 63:6; 119:148; Lamentations 2:19), but we have no sensation of time passing while we are

asleep. A millennium is a long time for us but not for God. The contrast is stark.

God never sleeps, yet a thousand years is no more a length of time to Him than watches in the night. This is not to say that time has no meaning for God. After all, the eternal God is Lord of history as well as Lord of the present and future (compare Isaiah 46:10). Time is passing for us, and God knows it.

C. Short Life (vv. 5, 6)

5a. Thou carriest them away as with a flood; they are as a sleep.

Verse 5 is notoriously difficult to understand from the original Hebrew text. All English versions have settled on the best that the translators could do. If we were to summarize with a single word the phrase *carriest them away as with a flood,* that word could be *engulf.* Thus we have a picture of God who can and does "engulf men in sleep." The word *sleep* is a figure of speech for death (compare John 11:11-14). All of us are swept away by God into the sleep of death as if by a flood (see Psalm 76:5, 6). That seems to be the gist of verse 5a.

5b, 6. In the morning they are like grass which groweth up. In the morning it flourisheth, and groweth up; in the evening it is cut down, and withereth.

The latter half of verse 5 begins a metaphor that emphasizes the shortness of human life. The metaphor of short-lived *grass* is used often in the Scriptures (see Job 8:12; Isaiah 15:6; 40:6-8 [quoted in 1 Peter 1:24, 25]; 51:12; Psalm 102:3, 4, 11; 103:15, 16; compare Psalm 129:6; Matthew 6:30).

> *What Do You Think?*
> What was a time when the brevity of life became most real to you? How did this affect your relationship with God?
> *Talking Points for Your Discussion*
> ▪ A personal situation
> ▪ A family situation
> ▪ A national situation

This metaphor makes great sense in the hot, dry climate of Israel and most of the Middle East. The small sprigs of grass that grow in the morning by means of the heavy dew are dried up and withered by the hot sun by the evening. This imagery declares the shortness of human life. But why is human life consigned to such a short expectancy, even if a person lives to be over 80? The next section tells us.

III. Wrath of God
(Psalm 90:7-10)
A. Consumes Life (v. 7)

7. For we are consumed by thine anger, and by thy wrath are we troubled.

Humanity's sin and guilt have a consequence that consumes all of life. This consequence is the wrath of God. This is one of God's responses to human sin. This wrathful, angry response includes God's command to all humanity to "turn back to dust!" (see v. 3, above). The rebellious humans are cast out of the Garden of Eden to till the ground during their short lives, eventually to die in the "dust of death" (see Genesis 3:19, 23).

The best commentary on the verse before us is Romans 1:18-32. There Paul writes "For the wrath of God is revealed from heaven against all ungodliness and unrighteousness of men, who hold the truth in unrighteousness" (v. 18). Paul says God gave them up to their own lusts (v. 24), to vile affections (v. 26), and to a reprobate mind (v. 28).

God is saying, in effect, "Live the way you want to live and see just how short life can be!" and "Have it your way and see what the result is!" (Compare Jeremiah 44:24-27.) The wrath of God consumes life just as the grass withers in the heat. This is not to say, of course, that those who are relatively less evil automatically live longer lives than those who are relatively more evil.

B. Reveals Sin (v. 8)

8. Thou hast set our iniquities before thee, our secret sins in the light of thy countenance.

This verse represents beautiful Hebrew parallelism. The word *iniquities* matches *secret sins* while *before thee* represents the same as *light of thy countenance,* although the Hebrew words are not exactly the same. Iniquity always implies guilt, wrongdoing, and vileness.

The word for *secret sins* really is just *secret,* with the idea of *sins* implied. Those who think their secret sins are hidden from God are only fooling themselves (see Psalm 44:21; 101:5; Jeremiah 16:17, 18). "The light which streams out from the divine face illumines the dark places of human culpability; God knows human beings—all of us—as they actually are" (Marvin Tate).

God desires that we confess sins and seek His face instead (see Psalm 38:18; 51:2-17). Which will we hide in our hearts: our sins or God's Word? Psalm 119:11 says that we hide God's Word in our hearts that we might not sin.

> **What Do You Think?**
> What was a situation where a public figure tried to hide his or her sin? What tactic did he or she use? How does this serve as a warning to you personally?
> *Talking Points for Your Discussion*
> - Rationalizing
> - Blame-shifting
> - Claiming victim status
> - Denying the reality of the sin

❧ Undead Foxes ❧

"Look out, there's a dog in the road!" <Screech . . . THUMP!> My dad pulled the car off the highway and walked back to see if the dog was dead, but it wasn't a dog. Dad came back to the car holding a limp grey fox by the tail. To my mother's chagrin, he threw the carcass in the trunk, a trophy to take to his taxidermist friend.

Twenty minutes later, Dad pulled into the garage and opened the trunk . . . but there was no fox! Then from the dark recesses of the trunk we heard a demonic growl, and we caught a glimpse of two bright eyes. In a flash of gray, our "dead" fox sprung out and disappeared into the junk of the garage. Dad grabbed a shovel, Mom grabbed the children, and 15 minutes of screaming chaos later the fox was dead for good.

Sin can be like that. We defeat a problem, or so we think. Rather than getting rid of all vestiges of it, we hang on to a few trophies. An unhealthy friendship. A questionable Web site.

A hidden resentment. Suddenly, what seemed dead and defeated growls menacingly to life again and wreaks havoc. Even the great apostle Paul confessed his inability to conquer sin (Romans 7:14-24). What hope then is there for us? The same hope that he had: "I thank God through Jesus Christ our Lord" (Romans 7:25).   —A. R. W.

C. Pervades All (v. 9)

9. For all our days are passed away in thy wrath: we spend our years as a tale that is told.

The concept of *time* is a major theme throughout this psalm: "in all generations" (v. 1); "from everlasting to everlasting" (v. 2); "a thousand years" (v. 4); "yesterday" (v. 4); "a watch in the night" (v. 4); "morning" (vv. 5, 6); "evening" (v. 6); "days" (vv. 9, 12, 14, 15); "years" (vv. 9, 10, 15); "soon" (v. 10); and "how long" (v. 13). Here our life span is measured in terms of *days* and *years*.

Noting parallelism in this verse will help interpret it; thus, we should stay alert to places where various ideas, such as those involving different ways of expressing time, reflect each other. But we should not force ourselves to see parallelism where it may not exist. For example, we may expect *in thy wrath* to be parallel to *a tale that is told*. But parallelism between those two phrases is hard to see.

The difficulty is traced to a difference between the Hebrew and the ancient Greek version known as the Septuagint. The *King James Version* apparently has followed the Septuagint, which reads the last half of the verse as "our years have spun out their tale as a spider." The parallel here, if it exists, could be the idea that whatever it is that constitutes the story of our life (*a tale*) is spent under the outflowing of God's fury against our sin.

D. Brings Sorrow (v. 10)

10. The days of our years are threescore years and ten; and if by reason of strength they be fourscore years, yet is their strength labor and sorrow; for it is soon cut off, and we fly away.

Threescore years and ten computes to the number 70, while *fourscore* means 80. Those who live in the U.S. are used to hearing annual updates to life expectancies. The expectancies creep up a little each year due to improvements in health care,

but the 70 to 80 range that the psalmist mentions is still pretty close, even many hundreds of years after the psalmist writes.

The overall life expectancy in the psalmist's day is probably only about 40 or 50 years, but that average includes a very high infant mortality rate. If a person can reach age 5 in the psalmist's day, then the chances of living to age 70 are very good. We all know, however, that even if a person is healthy up to very old age, the curse of death eventually will take the body. Like the flight of a bird, the years of life quickly take off *and we fly away.*

Before we move on, we should take care to note that life expectancy deals with averages. Some people live to be over 100, while others don't live to see their teenage years. But no matter how long we live, we do well to remember the observation of James 4:14: "For what is your life? It is even a vapour, that appeareth for a little time, and then vanisheth away."

> *What Do You Think?*
> What thoughts come to your mind when you think of dying? Why?
> *Talking Points for Your Discussion*
> - When a person "should" die
> - How you will be remembered
> - Your "bucket list"
> - What will happen to your family
> - Where you will end up

IV. Prayer for Wisdom
(PSALM 90:11, 12)
A. To Fear God (v. 11)

11. Who knoweth the power of thine anger? Even according to thy fear, so is thy wrath.

The context of this psalm as a whole reveals the meaning of this verse. The psalm is not just about encouraging us mortals generally to brace up against the trials of life that are caused by our own sins and imposed on us by God's wrath. Rather, the community being addressed is suffering extensively from some particular adversity (see the Lesson Background), and the question *Who knoweth the power of thine anger?* indicates that nobody knows the ultimate extent of the affliction (compare 2 Samuel 12:22; Proverbs 24:22). Thus we have the question "How long?" in verse 13 (not in today's text). The community wants relief for as many days as it has been afflicted (v. 15).

The second phrase here in verse 11 means that God's wrath should be matched by our fear of Him (see Proverbs 9:10). When we approach God in prayer, we should do it with reverence and humility. Let God be God and humans be humans.

B. To Number Our Days (v. 12)

12. So teach us to number our days, that we may apply our hearts unto wisdom.

The emphasis throughout verses 3-11 has been how mortals live under the wrath of God. All of life has its sorrows. It is the attitude we take toward all the toil and trouble we face daily that makes the difference.

The attitude should be that we are to petition God to *teach us to number our days, that we may apply our hearts unto wisdom.* The ability to number our days is one of the most important discernments we may have! When we have this discernment, we will not waste the life process. Life is too precious to waste on counterproductive pursuits.

A wise heart seeks God's will in life; when that happens, one can deal properly with life's brevity and sorrow. To number our days is to evaluate and make judgments concerning our thoughts, attitudes, and actions every waking day! Are we consciously trying to please God or ourselves?

What Do You Think?
What are some ways that people "number their days" properly and improperly?
Talking Points for Your Discussion
- Luke 12:15-21; Philippians 1:21
- What they include in their wills
- How they react when diagnosed with a terminal disease

Conclusion

A. Make Time for God

Ecclesiastes 12:1-8 is a sober look at growing old and dying. The shortness of human life requires that we take seriously our relationship with the eternal God as He is known to us through Jesus the Christ and present to us in the Holy Spirit.

The church I attend promotes this relationship through small groups for fellowship, Bible study, and spiritual growth. My wife and I join several other couples in a weekly meeting. In March 2007, one of our members had a seizure and was diagnosed with a brain tumor. Within seven months he was gone. Bill was only 64 years old. For our group he was "young" and just at the point of enjoying years of retirement. But we were comforted by the fact that he had a great relationship with God, the Scriptures, the church, and his family.

We all miss Bill. But I am confident that Bill had "numbered his days" correctly, because in his 64 years he had made time for God. Bill now has eternity with Him and the certain hope of a coming resurrection. I wish my dad in his 90 years had made time for God.

B. Prayer

Eternal Father, teach us to number our days so that we don't waste our lives in trivial pursuits or sinful living. Be our dwelling place throughout all generations so that we may experience Your unfailing love forever in eternity. In Jesus' name we pray, amen.

C. Thought to Remember

Seek God in all circumstances.

Teach us to number our days.
—Psalm 90:12

Visual for
Lesson 11

Point to this visual as you introduce the discussion question associated with Psalm 90:12.

INVOLVEMENT LEARNING

Some of the activities below are also found in the helpful student book, Adult Bible Class.
Don't forget to download the free reproducible page from www.standardlesson.com to enhance your lesson!

Into the Lesson

Option #1: Early in the week, contact an older individual who has served the Lord for many years; ask if he or she would be willing to be interviewed about life as a Christian. Supply the person with a list of questions to be asked, such as the following: "When and how did you become a Christian?" "How did that make a difference in your life?" "What was one occasion when the Lord was with you through a hard time?" "Considering Psalm 90:12, what words of wisdom can you share with us that will help us to number our days better?" Feel free to substitute other questions based on your knowledge of the person's life.

Thank your volunteer for sharing his or her life story. Then say, "We need to make the most of a life that goes by all too quickly. Let's take a look at Psalm 90 and learn how to do that."

Option #2: Hang inflated balloons around the classroom. Wear a party hat, blow a roll-out party favor, and display other visual effects that suggest a birthday party. Ask students to think about how the families in which they grew up celebrated birthdays; have them share one of their traditions, either with the group as a whole or in small groups.

Then say, "How did it feel as a child to wait for your next birthday to come around?" Then ask, "How has that changed today? Does it feel like your birthday comes around too quickly or not quickly enough?" Make the point that birthdays help us realize how quickly our lives are going by. State that Psalm 90 gives us good advice on how to deal with that fact.

Into the Word

Prepare enough copies of the following two assignments so that each small group has a copy of one of them. As you distribute the assignments say, "Some of you will be looking at what Psalm 90 teaches us about humans and the rest of you will be considering what it teaches us about God."

Assignment #1: Humans. Read through Psalm 90:1-12 and answer these questions: 1. What happens to our bodies when we die? (v. 3) Why does that happen? (see Genesis 3:17-19). 2. What images does the psalmist use to show how short and difficult our lives are? (vv. 5, 6, 10). 3. How does sin make our lives harder? (vv. 7-9, 11). 4. Why does the psalmist ask God to teach us to "number our days"? How can that help us be wise and make the most of our lives? (v. 12)

Assignment #2: God. Read through Psalm 90:1-12 and answer these questions: 1. What phrases does the psalmist use to teach us that God is eternal? How should this affect your life? (vv. 1, 2) 2. How is God's view of time different from ours? (v. 4). 3. How well does God know us? (v. 8) 4. What is God's response to sin? (v. 11). 5. What can God teach us so we can "number our days" and live with wisdom? (v. 12)

After an appropriate amount of time for discussion, ask each group to share one or more things they learned about humans or about God.

Into Life

Option #1: Download the reproducible page and distribute copies of the Would You Agree? activity from it. Have learners complete this individually, according to directions. Encourage them to use Psalm 90 to support their ideas. Allow time for discussion.

Option #2: Relate the following story; then have learners work in small groups to discuss how they would respond. "You have a friend at work named Chris. He has certain bad habits that can lead to an early death. When you question these habits, Chris replies, 'Life is short, and I'm going to enjoy it to the fullest while I can.' How do you respond?"

Option #3: Distribute copies of the From Everlasting to Everlasting activity from the reproducible page. Allow learners time to write in their answers. Ask for volunteers to share.

God Is Forever

GOD IS
PROTECTOR

BACKGROUND SCRIPTURE: **Psalm 91**
PRINTED TEXT: **Psalm 91:1-6, 9-16**

PSALM 91:1-6, 9-16

1 He that dwelleth in the secret place of the most High shall abide under the shadow of the Almighty.

2 I will say of the LORD, He is my refuge and my fortress: my God; in him will I trust.

3 Surely he shall deliver thee from the snare of the fowler, and from the noisome pestilence.

4 He shall cover thee with his feathers, and under his wings shalt thou trust: his truth shall be thy shield and buckler.

5 Thou shalt not be afraid for the terror by night; nor for the arrow that flieth by day;

6. Nor for the pestilence that walketh in darkness; nor for the destruction that wasteth at noonday.

. . . .

9 Because thou hast made the LORD, which is my refuge, even the most High, thy habitation;

10 There shall no evil befall thee, neither shall any plague come nigh thy dwelling.

11 For he shall give his angels charge over thee, to keep thee in all thy ways.

12 They shall bear thee up in their hands, lest thou dash thy foot against a stone.

13 Thou shalt tread upon the lion and adder: the young lion and the dragon shalt thou trample under feet.

14 Because he hath set his love upon me, therefore will I deliver him: I will set him on high, because he hath known my name.

15 He shall call upon me, and I will answer him: I will be with him in trouble; I will deliver him, and honour him.

16 With long life will I satisfy him, and shew him my salvation.

KEY VERSE

Because he hath set his love upon me, therefore will I deliver him: I will set him on high, because he hath known my name. —**Psalm 91:14**

THE
INESCAPABLE GOD

Unit 3: God Protects
LESSONS 10–13

LESSON AIMS

After participating in this lesson, each student will be able to:

1. List some elements of the protection imagery of today's text.

2. Describe how the figurative imageries of God's protection are seen daily in practical ways.

3. Identify one way he or she can be an agent of God's protection to someone else and act on that awareness.

LESSON OUTLINE

Introduction
    A. My Security Blanket
    B. Lesson Background
 I. Asylum of Protection (PSALM 91:1, 2)
    A. Place and Shadow (v. 1)
    B. Refuge and Fortress (v. 2)
 II. Assurances of Protection (PSALM 91:3-6)
    A. From Snare and Pestilence (vv. 3, 4)
    B. From Terror and Arrow (v. 5)
    Are You Scelerophobic?
    C. From Pestilence and Destruction (v. 6)
 III. Angels of Protection (PSALM 91:9-13)
    A. Conditional Provision (vv. 9, 10)
    B. Supernatural Protection (v. 11)
    C. Protection Along the Way (v. 12)
    D. Power over Deadly Creatures (v. 13)
 IV. Affirmation of Protection (PSALM 91:14-16)
    A. "I Will Protect Him!" (v. 14)
    In Need of Protection
    B. "I Will Answer Him!" (v. 15)
    C. "I Will Satisfy Him!" (v. 16)
Conclusion
    A. Let God Be Your Security Blanket
    B. Prayer
    C. Thought to Remember

Introduction
A. My Security Blanket

I have a granddaughter who is going through her second security blanket, and it is about gone. In fact, it is gross! There is hardly anything left but tattered threads. It is dirty, for she refuses to let anyone touch it. She resists having it washed. If it were washed, it would probably disintegrate. In her little world, this security blanket represents her asylum from the stress of parents, siblings, etc. Unfortunately, this has gone on for several years now, and I am beginning to worry that the fading blanket is there to stay!

While I am concerned about a granddaughter's clinging to a piece of cloth for security, I wonder about my own "security blanket." What do I cling to when times get tough? At my age of 67, I can worry if there is enough money put away in investments and Social Security benefits to pay for expenses of a home, food, medicine, taxes, gas, and inflation. Perhaps keeping a good job and income at this age is a security blanket. I also lean on my spouse for security.

We tend to seek security in a variety of sources. These include pension plans, a job, a spouse, or even our children. Any of these can end up being a security blanket in a negative sense. But there is only one place where real security can be found: God! We need to discover that God's ability to sustain us is greater than the evils that beset us. Psalm 91 will help us discover that God is our protector.

B. Lesson Background

Last week's lesson from Psalm 90 starkly pointed out the difference between the eternal God and frail humanity as God's wrath overrides all human sin. Today's lesson from Psalm 91 moves us forward in emphasizing the fact that God's protection and grace are sufficient in times of great distress if we take refuge in Him. Psalm 91 is a song of trust. Its aim is to encourage the individual to put trust in a God who cares and protects those committed to Him.

The structure of Psalm 91 is based on a certain Hebrew conjunction that can be translated in various ways. Depending on context, some possibilities for translating this word are "for," "that," "if," and "when." It also can be an emphatic "indeed," "truly," or "surely." In today's lesson, we see it used in verse 3 as "surely," in verse 9 as "because," and in verse 14 as "because."

Thus, the structure of the psalm is divided into identifiable parts: verses 1 and 2 form an introduction to the psalm as a whole; verses 3-13 give assurances of God's protection, as subdivided into the two repetitious sections of verses 3-8 and verses 9-13; verses 14-16 function as a concluding oracle of God in affirming His promise of protection to those who love Him.

I. Asylum of Protection
(Psalm 91:1, 2)
A. Place and Shadow (v. 1)

1. He that dwelleth in the secret place of the most High shall abide under the shadow of the Almighty.

The theme of Psalm 91 is stated clearly and concisely here in verse 1. There is a beautiful parallelism evident, with *dwelleth* being parallel to *abide,* and *the secret place of the most High* being parallel to *the shadow of the Almighty.*

This parallelism establishes the fact that the only place where one can find protection and security in the midst of threats is the secret place of God. By the thinking of most scholars, this is the temple. This is a protective area (see Psalm 27:5; 31:20; 61:4). Some even think the shadow of the Almighty is the secure area underneath the wings of the cherubim over the ark of the covenant in the Holy of Holies (compare 1 Kings 8:6). Perhaps the imagery anticipates the strong use of the "wings" metaphor in verse 4, below (compare Exodus 19:4).

B. Refuge and Fortress (v. 2)

2. I will say of the Lord, He is my refuge and my fortress: my God; in him will I trust.

With the theme stated in verse 1, the psalmist now gives a personal testimony as he makes the theme his own. This forms the basis for the exhortations to follow in verses 3-13.

The four names for God in these first two verses are well known in the ancient traditions of Isra-el's history. For "most High" *(Elyon)* of verse 1, see Genesis 14:18-20; Deuteronomy 32:8. For "Almighty" *(Shaddai)* of verse 1, see Genesis 17:1; 28:3; 49:25; Exodus 6:3; etc. While these two names along with "God" *(Elohim)* are also used in pagan circles, the personal name of God is "Lord" *(Yahweh).* To express God's personal name is somehow to have a more intimate relationship with Him (see Exodus 3:18; 6:2-6). By this personal name of God, Yahweh, the Israelites were delivered from Egyptian slavery. Now by this same name the Israelites addressed in the psalm will be protected.

The *refuge* is that secret or hidden place of verse 1 where God guarantees His presence and protection (see Psalm 14:6; 46:1; 62:7; 71:7; 94:22). The word *fortress,* used as a figure of speech, reinforces the idea of protection, for it stands for "a stronghold, a fastness" (see Psalm 18:2; 31:3; 71:3; 144:2). From this word comes the name *Masada,* the great fortress that Herod built in southern Judea. (Perhaps some reading this will remember the TV miniseries of the same name, released in 1981.) The psalmist's emphatic declaration *in him will I trust* implies that his readers should do the same!

What Do You Think?
How has God been a fortress and refuge for you?
Talking Points for Your Discussion
- In times of trouble and doubt (Psalm 46:1)
- In providing a way of escape (1 Corinthians 10:13)
- In times of grief (Isaiah 51:11)

II. Assurances of Protection
(Psalm 91:3-6)
A. From Snare and Pestilence (vv. 3, 4)

3. Surely he shall deliver thee from the snare of the fowler, and from the noisome pestilence.

Verses 3-8 present a list of adversities. Since these are stated in general terms and bold imagery, the reader undoubtedly can identify with at least one of the metaphors. *The snare of the fowler* is a trap used for catching birds (compare Psalm 124:7; Hosea 9:8). The psalmist sometimes refers to himself as a defenseless bird (see Psalm 11:1;

Visual for Lessons 7 & 12. Point to this visual as you ask the discussion question that is associated with verse 2.

102:6, 7). This metaphor thus represents persecution by others.

Pestilence, by contrast, is not something we normally think of as being inflicted on one person by another (although there are cases of that happening). Rather, pestilence or plague is seen as being inflicted by God (see Exodus 5:3; 9:3, 15; Psalm 78:50; Habakkuk 3:5). It can be deadly *(noisome)*. Just as birds are helpless before a well-constructed trap, so human beings are helpless before destructive pestilence. This is particularly true in a time before antibiotics and vaccines, which is most of human history.

Even today there are many diseases that are beyond our control. A literal pestilence can be terrifying (see v. 6, below). God is the one able to deliver from both persecution and plague.

4. He shall cover thee with his feathers, and under his wings shalt thou trust: his truth shall be thy shield and buckler.

Yahweh is portrayed as a mother hen that protects her brood with outspread wings (see Psalm 17:8; 36:7; 57:1; 63:7; also see Jesus' use of this metaphor in Matthew 23:37-39 and Luke 13:34, 35). The imagery is a strong one for protection, but the believer in Yahweh must willingly seek the refuge under His wings! That's the idea of *shalt thou trust*. Notice that Jesus says "ye would not" in the two New Testament passages above.

When we willingly seek that protection, we discover that God is true to His promise of providing it. His faithfulness is like a *shield and buckler*. A shield is the perfect symbol for protection. The Hebrew word translated *buckler* appears only here in the Old Testament, which makes its meaning more difficult to determine. Perhaps the idea is that of a "wall" or "bulwark" that protects a city.

B. From Terror and Arrow (v. 5)

5. Thou shalt not be afraid for the terror by night; nor for the arrow that flieth by day.

Our next two verses use the contrasting imagery of night/darkness and day/noonday to indicate dangers that may occur at any time. We saw in verse 3 that the reader simply receives God's promise of deliverance, while in verse 4 the reader must seek the "wings" of the Lord for protection. These lead to the command to *not be afraid*.

What is this *terror by night* that we are not to fear? This seems to be a general expression for "a dreadful thing." This came home to me in a personal way the night before writing this. I was driving through a vicious storm. It was night, the clouds were dark and swirling, the rain came down in sheets, and lightning lit up the sky continually. To make things worse, the tornado sirens went off when we reached the outskirts of town. I was terrified! It was indeed "a dreadful thing" to experience. On the other hand, some have suggested that the *terror by night* is really a "night terror," that is, a demonic power of some kind that attacks humans (compare Song of Solomon 3:8).

The Bible sometimes uses the word *arrow* figuratively to refer to flashes of lightning in storms (see Psalm 18:14; 77:17, 18; 144:6). Thus it may not be far off to suggest that the expression *the arrow that flieth by day* refers to "the storms of life" as we speak of it today.

> **What Do You Think?**
> What terrifies you? How do you draw on God's strength to allay your fears?
> *Talking Points for Your Discussion*
> - Job issues
> - Family issues
> - Church issues
> - National and political issues

· God Is Protector

Scelerophobia is the name of the condition for those who have a fear of evil persons, such as burglars. However, even such phobics should not be afraid of Brittany McDermott and Russell Bloss. This inept pair allegedly robbed a Salt Lake City Bank in late 2003 by handing the teller a note demanding money.

Even though the two escaped with $1,300, they didn't have time to enjoy it. In her hurry to commit the crime, Brittany had written the holdup note on the back of her own personal check. The police merely went to her home address and arrested the two.

While stories of incompetent thieves are amusing, we know that our lives can be in danger from the evildoers in the world. Yet fear of evil people should not preoccupy our minds. To allow that to happen would indicate a lack of trust in Almighty God. Instead, we face life confidently, knowing that we rest safely in His shadow.   —C. J. F.

C. From Pestilence and Destruction (v. 6)

6. Nor for the pestilence that walketh in darkness; nor for the destruction that wasteth at noonday.

We have already encountered the word *pestilence* in verse 3. The deadly implications of that word are enhanced by the acknowledgment that it *walketh in darkness*. The idea seems to be that no one sees it coming.

What Do You Think?

Why do we often continue to fear when the Scripture encourages us not to? How do we overcome this problem?

Talking Points for Your Discussion
- The issue of not being "in control"
- The issue of pain
- The issue of doubt
- Misunderstanding the nature of God

The certainty of death is associated with these metaphors. If we fear the threat of diseases and plagues today, even with knowledge of modern medicine, think of how much more the ancient peoples fear such attacks on the body! Ultimately,

however, the threat of pestilence or *destruction that wasteth*—whether at night or noonday—is irrelevant to those who trust God. We are not to fear such things, for God is with us and we are with God—under His wings!

III. Angels of Protection
(PSALM 91:9-13)
A. Conditional Provision (vv. 9, 10)

9, 10. Because thou hast made the LORD, which is my refuge, even the most High, thy habitation; there shall no evil befall thee, neither shall any plague come nigh thy dwelling.

The Hebrew word translated *because* is the structural word for the psalm that we mentioned in the Lesson Background. The overall context here is that of something being conditional. The people to whom the psalmist is speaking are to fear none of the things mentioned in verses 3-8 because of the fact that they already have put their trust in Yahweh. They are seeking Him as their refuge (the theme of the psalm). The condition for receiving the promised deliverance from evil is to make the Lord one's refuge or habitation.

B. Supernatural Protection (v. 11)

11. For he shall give his angels charge over thee, to keep thee in all thy ways.

Some propose that verses 3-8 relate to the exodus events. Exodus 19:4 depicts the people being brought out "on eagles' wings" from Egypt to the foot of Mount Sinai. In that light, the section at hand also may use the exodus tradition to communicate God's protection for the reader's own "exodus journey."

We may compare the verse before us with Exodus 23:20, 23a: "Behold, I send an Angel before thee, to keep thee in the way, and to bring thee into the place which I have prepared. . . . For mine Angel shall go before thee" (see also Exodus 32:34; 33:2). God protects us during our daily walk. He has many ways of doing this, one of which is through the sending of angels. The following texts mention angels providing protection from harm: Genesis 24:7; 48:16; Exodus 14:19; Psalm 34:7; Isaiah 63:9; Matthew 4:11; Acts 12:7; Hebrews 1:14.

C. Protection Along the Way (v. 12)

12. They shall bear thee up in their hands, lest thou dash thy foot against a stone.

Wherever we go in life, there is always the possibility of stubbing one's toe against a rock, either physically or spiritually (see Psalm 35:15; 37:24; 38:16; Proverbs 3:23; etc.). In Israel, that is an easy metaphor to understand. Rocks are everywhere! To have angels help you keep your balance when you are about to stumble is a great assurance.

However, we must take care not to misapply this promise. Jogging down the street the other day, I saw a woman posting on the edge of her yard a copy of today's text, Psalm 91. She was trying to use it as a protective "hedge" against unwanted intruders on her property. Others have placed this text in amulets to provide magical protection from evil when worn.

Perhaps the greatest misuse of this text is from the devil himself. He used Psalm 91:11, 12 to tempt Jesus to jump from the pinnacle of the temple. Surely if Jesus were the Son of God, then God would charge angels to protect the Son from such an impact on the stones (see Matthew 4:5-7). Jesus responded with another text: "It is written again, Thou shalt not tempt the Lord thy God" (Matthew 4:7; compare Deuteronomy 6:16).

We must pay careful attention to Jesus' response to the devil! We must never take the promised protection of God into our own hands in an attempt to force God to do our will and match our idea of destiny. It is our will versus God's will! Trying to force God to bend to our will may just land us on a crushing stone (see Isaiah 8:14, 15; 28:16; Matthew 21:42-44). There is a big difference between faithfully trusting God's promises and skeptically testing them.

What Do You Think?

What was a time when you were spared from what appeared to be certain harm? What do you think God's role in that incident was?

Talking Points for Your Discussion

- A "near miss" traffic situation
- Deliverance in a war zone

D. Power over Deadly Creatures (v. 13)

13. Thou shalt tread upon the lion and adder: the young lion and the dragon shalt thou trample under feet.

No one doubts it: *the lion* is "king of the beasts." The *adder* or cobra is an extremely poisonous snake (see Job 20:14, 16; Psalm 58:4; Isaiah 11:8). *The young lion* is one that is at the beginning of its strength. *The dragon* is a large snake or serpent in this context (see Deuteronomy 32:33; etc.). Thus, these creatures are used figuratively to represent any and all persons and powers that threaten human existence, especially that of God's people.

HOW TO SAY IT

Allah	*Ah*-luh.
Baal	*Bay*-ul.
cherubim	*chair*-uh-bim.
Elohim *(Hebrew)*	El-o-*heem*.
Elyon	El-*yon*.
Herod	*Hair*-ud.
Hosea	Ho-*zay*-uh.
Judea	Joo-*dee*-uh.
Masada	Muh-*saw*-duh.
scelerophobia	skuh-lair-uh-*foe*-bee-uh.
scelerophobic	skuh-lair-uh-*foe*-bic.
Shaddai *(Hebrew)*	*Shad*-eye.
Sinai	*Sigh*-nye or *Sigh*-nay-eye.
Yahweh *(Hebrew)*	*Yah*-weh.
Zeus	Zoose.

IV. Affirmation of Protection
(PSALM 91:14-16)
A. "I Will Protect Him!" (v. 14)

14. Because he hath set his love upon me, therefore will I deliver him: I will set him on high, because he hath known my name.

Here we have another *because,* which we noted in the Lesson Background to indicate a new part of the psalm's structure. Verses 14-16 represent what is called *an oracle of God.* It is the climax of the psalm, for God is giving His own assurance of protection from every conceivable evil that is hurled at those who take refuge in Him. The oracle confirms the psalmist's assertions in verses

God Is Protector

3-13. God delivers those who cling to Him! He delivers them by setting them securely on a high place out of the way of harm (compare 2 Samuel 22:34; Psalm 18:33; Habakkuk 3:19). God, indeed, protects and defends His people because they know His name. His name is not Allah, Baal, Zeus, or "the man upstairs." His name is God—Yahweh. To know Yahweh is to trust Him.

❧ *IN NEED OF PROTECTION* ❧

There are a few people who seem to be so able to take care of themselves that they apparently don't need anyone to protect them. André the Giant was one of those. His appearance was intimidating. Billed as being 7'4" and weighing 500 pounds, he was one of the world's most famous professional wrestlers in the 1980s and early 1990s.

In private life, he could also hold his own. On one occasion, four men in a bar were hassling him. Although he tried to avoid a confrontation, he eventually chased the hecklers out to their car. André grabbed the car and turned it over with the four men inside.

Yet, this big man suffered a premature death at age 46, as a result of the medical condition that caused his abnormal size. Even this powerful man was powerless in the face of death. May we have no illusions that we can protect ourselves in that regard! There is still only one who is able to deliver us from these frail bodies into eternal life.   —C. J. F.

B. "I Will Answer Him!" (v. 15)

15. He shall call upon me, and I will answer him: I will be with him in trouble; I will deliver him, and honour him.

When Christians make God their prayer refuge, God answers. Notice that God does not promise to take the trouble away from us. Rather, He will be with us *in trouble*. So once again God promises to deliver, even honor, His people. God grants us His favor in all phases of the distress.

C. "I Will Satisfy Him!" (v. 16)

16. With long life will I satisfy him, and shew him my salvation.

Psalm 90:12 (last week's lesson) challenges us to "number our days" aright. We do this by trusting daily in God as a refuge, especially when distress and trouble come. In return, God delights in showing us long life.

But even better than that, He wants to reveal His salvation. Jesus' name means "saves." It is to Him we must cling. God is our protector, both now and through eternity. The length of our eternal life will certainly be enough to satisfy anyone!

What Do You Think?
In what ways can you use your experience of God's care to encourage and help others?
Talking Points for Your Discussion
- Mentoring (Titus 2:3)
- Testimony (Joshua 24:17)

Conclusion
A. Let God Be Your Security Blanket

The presence of evil in this world is a fact of life for all, but especially for God's people who seek to live righteously. Sometimes the danger includes premeditated entrapment by evil people or epidemic diseases of a fallen world (Psalm 91:3, 6). Some attacks come in the dead of night, others at midday (vv. 5, 6). Harm and disaster is never far away (v. 10).

There is no time or place on this earth when we are not endangered by evil. Yet for all these threats God is still our protector. His promises are certain. He will rescue and protect those who know His name (v. 14). When we cry out for help, He will answer by being with us, delivering us, and even honoring us in the end (v. 15). How can we not trust God to be our refuge and fortress (vv. 2, 9)?

B. Prayer

Almighty God, hear our prayer for protection. We are bombarded continually by evil. Shelter us in the shadow of Your wings. Be our shield and wall of protection. Give us victory over those who would harm us. Show us Your salvation. For the sake of Your kingdom and in the name of Jesus Christ our Lord we pray, amen.

C. Thought to Remember

God is greater than the evils that beset us.

INVOLVEMENT LEARNING

Some of the activities below are also found in the helpful student book, Adult Bible Class.
Don't forget to download the free reproducible page from www.standardlesson.com to enhance your lesson!

Into the Lesson

Divide the class into two groups. Then say, "Today we're going to play a game to see how well you know your superheroes." Ask each group to appoint a spokesperson. Say, "You will be given four clues for each superhero, and you can have one guess after each clue. The clues will descend in value from 4 to 1." Record the points on the board. Give all the clues for one superhero to a group, allowing for one guess as each clue is offered. Then start new clues for the other group.

A: 4. No superpowers but skilled in martial arts. 3. Saw parents murdered. 2. Inventor billionaire. 1. Robin. [Answer: Batman]; *B:* 4. Invisible plane. 2. Bullet-deflecting bracelets. 2. Superstrength female. 1. Lynda Carter. [Answer: Wonder Woman]; *C:* 4. Absent-minded detective. 3. Fights the evil organization MAD. 2. Has bionics built into anatomy. 1. Inspector for the Metro City police. [Answer: Inspector Gadget]; *D:* 4. On earth when it was bombarded by fiery meteors. 3. Starships faster than light. 2. Ming the Merciless. 1. Dale Arden. [Answer: Flash Gordon]; *E:* 4. A reserved physicist. 3. Immense feats of strength. 2. Emotional distress is the trigger. 1. Dr. Bruce Banner. [Answer: The Incredible Hulk]; *F:* 4. Grew up on a Kansas farm. 3. Knows people with the initials *L. L.* 2. "The Big Blue Boy Scout." 1. Has X-ray vision. [Answer: Superman].

Lead into the lesson by saying, "As Christians we serve a God who has powers far beyond those of even the most fantastic superhero. He has given us many promises to protect us from the dangers of life. Let's take a look at Psalm 91 to discover what some of those are."

Alternative. Place in chairs copies of the Lions and Arrows and Snares—Oh My! activity from the reproducible page for learners to work on as they arrive. After an appropriate amount of time, say, "Now let's take a closer look at Psalm 91 and all the promises it contains of God's protection."

Into the Word

Have learners break into small groups. Give each group one of the following three assignments. Provide groups with the necessary materials: dictionaries (Assignment A); construction paper, scissors, glue, and markers (Assignment B); index cards (Assignment C).

Assignment A: Dangers. 1. Make a list of the dangers mentioned in Psalm 91:3, 5, 6, 10, 12, 13, 15. 2. Use the dictionary to look up any words with which you are not familiar. 3. Name common dangers today that might correspond to those in the text.

Assignment B: Designations. 1. Make a list of descriptive words for God, our protector, from Psalm 91:1, 2, 4, 9. 2. Use the art materials to create an illustration of the protection God provides from the dangers in the world. 3. Use one of the words selected and give an everyday example of how God protects us.

Assignment C: Deliverance Promises. 1. Make a list of God's promises in Psalm 91:4, 9-15. 2. List some of the conditions we must meet in order to be eligible for God's promises. 3. Ask each person in the group to select one of the promises and write it on an index card to take home.

Give the groups plenty of time to work on their assignments (15 to 20 minutes). If there is time, ask each group to name one thing they learned from the assignment.

Into Life

Lead a discussion of how God protects us from danger. Questions you can ask: 1. What are some dangers that cause us to be fearful? 2. What are some practical ways we make ourselves more aware of God's promises of protection?

Option: Download the reproducible page and use the Under His Wings activity from it to enhance this segment of the lesson. Ask for volunteers to share what they have written.

GOD IS
OMNISCIENT

BACKGROUND SCRIPTURE: Psalm 139
PRINTED TEXT: Psalm 139:1-6, 13-16, 23, 24

PSALM 139:1-6, 13-16, 23, 24

1 O LORD, thou hast searched me, and known me.

2 Thou knowest my downsitting and mine uprising; thou understandest my thought afar off.

3 Thou compassest my path and my lying down, and art acquainted with all my ways.

4 For there is not a word in my tongue, but, lo, O LORD, thou knowest it altogether.

5 Thou hast beset me behind and before, and laid thine hand upon me.

6 Such knowledge is too wonderful for me; it is high, I cannot attain unto it.

. . . .

13 For thou hast possessed my reins: thou hast covered me in my mother's womb.

14 I will praise thee; for I am fearfully and wonderfully made: marvellous are thy works; and that my soul knoweth right well.

15 My substance was not hid from thee when I was made in secret, and curiously wrought in the lowest parts of the earth.

16 Thine eyes did see my substance, yet being unperfect; and in thy book all my members were written, which in continuance were fashioned, when as yet there was none of them.

. . . .

23 Search me, O God, and know my heart: try me, and know my thoughts:

24 And see if there be any wicked way in me, and lead me in the way everlasting.

KEY VERSE

There is not a word in my tongue, but, lo, O LORD, thou knowest it altogether. —**Psalm 139:4**

105

THE
INESCAPABLE GOD

Unit 3: God Protects

LESSONS 10–13

LESSON AIMS

After participating in this lesson, each student will be able to:

1. Describe the completeness and intimacy of God's knowledge about humans.

2. Explain how God's absolute knowledge of his or her life relates to His care.

3. Use verses 23, 24 daily in prayer in the week ahead.

LESSON OUTLINE

Introduction
   A. "He Knows My Name"
   B. Lesson Background
 I. God's Knowledge (PSALM 139:1-6)
   A. Facts of His Knowing (vv. 1-4)
   B. Results of His Knowing (vv. 5, 6)
 II. God's Works (PSALM 139:13-16)
   A. Origin and Awareness (vv. 13, 14)
      The Lowly, Lovely Appendix
   B. Unhidden and Foreknown (vv. 15, 16)
 III. Psalmist's Invitation (PSALM 139:23, 24)
   A. To Search and Know (v. 23)
   B. To See and Lead (v. 24)
      Stop Thinking?
Conclusion
   A. God Knows!
   B. Prayer
   C. Thought to Remember

Introduction

A. "He Knows My Name"

Each year the music department of the Bible college where I teach presents its *Christmas Celebration* during the first week in December. The program is an integrated drama and music presentation. One year the program was based on the American Civil War and how it liberated the slaves. In so doing, the program provided a backdrop for the message of the Christian's liberation from the "slavery of sin" when Jesus came.

During the presentation of one scene, picture after picture of African slaves—beaten, starved, tortured, and nameless—were on the screen. During these scenes of humanity's inhumanity, one of our African students sang the song "He Knows My Name." Tears fell from my eyes as I remembered my own upbringing in the South, where cultural prejudices had demeaned and segregated the African-American population among us.

I can be the lowliest of slaves, but God knows my name. God knows and cares. I can be attacked by enemies who press false charges or be falsely accused by "friends" or family, yet God knows my heart. He knows the truth, and He even knows me better than I know myself. He will vindicate me and declare me innocent. These are the circumstances that best fit Psalm 139.

The emphasis, however, will be that God is omniscient (meaning "all knowing"). As the Creator, He knows everything there is to know about each and every one of us. How could it be otherwise?

B. Lesson Background

The superscription of Psalm 139 tells us that it was written by David. The difficulty of understanding this psalm is in determining how verses 19 and following (dealing with vengeance) relate to verses 1-18 (dealing with praise) since the tones of the two sections are so different. Some scholars have proposed excising verses 19-24, declaring that they do not belong with the psalm. This is surely wrong. All of Psalm 139 must be considered.

There are examples throughout the psalms that feature much praise of God along with condemnation of enemies and "the wicked" (see Psalms 5, 7, 17; 104:35). The unity of Psalm 139 can be seen in various ways. We begin by noting that verses 23, 24 function as an *inclusion* with verses 1, 2; this is seen as we observe the use of *search, know, Yahweh/God,* and *thoughts* in both places. Within verses 23, 24 we find a possible accusation by the enemies of the psalmist. The phrase "wicked way" in verse 24 can refer to idolatry; such an accusation can mean death if the accused cannot defend himself. Therefore, the psalmist submits to a divine judgment, with verses 1-18 describing the scrutiny that is requested in verses 23, 24.

Thus one must account for verses 19-24 and not dismiss them. The psalmist has encountered enemies who seek his harm, perhaps his life, if they can make the charge of idolatry stick. God can examine the accused in the most thorough manner because He is omniscient ("all knowing," vv. 1-6), omnipresent ("present everywhere," vv. 7-12), and omnipotent ("all powerful," vv. 13-18).

Standing alongside these characteristics of God is the fact that we are always being known, accompanied, and fashioned by God. God knows us and cares for us. Indeed, He is fearfully wonderful! That is why we are dependent on Him and praise Him.

I. God's Knowledge
(Psalm 139:1-6)
A. Facts of His Knowing (vv. 1-4)

1. O Lord, thou hast searched me, and known me.

The psalmist addresses the Lord by His personal name, which in Hebrew is "Yahweh" (also in vv. 4, 21). Perhaps the psalmist does so because of the intimacy of the action described: Yahweh already has searched him thoroughly (compare Job 13:9; Jeremiah 12:3; 15:15; 17:10). This is the kind of searching that only the Almighty God, Yahweh, can do.

The searching means God knows the psalmist (compare Psalm 44:21; Romans 8:27). This verse is a theme for the rest of the section, as it summarizes the fact of God's ability to know.

2. Thou knowest my downsitting and mine uprising; thou understandest my thought afar off.

Yahweh knows the daily routine of the psalmist. Since God knows when the psalmist sits down after a hard day's work and when he gets up in the morning, it's logical to conclude that God also knows everything in between! This is a literary technique known as a *merism,* which involves naming two contrasting parts to refer to the whole. For instance, when we say that something appeals to both "young and old," we really mean "young, old, and all ages in between." The merism of downsitting at night and uprising in the morning thus embraces all points of time between those two.

To have such knowledge is not difficult for God, since He sees all things at all times. This knowledge extends not only to what the psalmist does, but also to what he thinks. Every unspoken word is clear to God. The fact that Christians believe this is seen in our practice of silent prayer. God hears every word of such unverbalized prayers.

What Do You Think?
 What comforts and convictions are yours
   because God understands your very thoughts?
Talking Points for Your Discussion
- Comforts: issues of God's patience and provisions (2 Corinthians 1:3-7; 7:5-7)
- Convictions: issues of things I know I need to change or do (John 16:8; Jude 15)

---

3. Thou compassest my path and my lying down, and art acquainted with all my ways.

The rare word *compassest* is difficult to grasp. In that verb form, it has the range of meanings "to

HOW TO SAY IT

Corinthians	Ko-*rin*-thee-unz (*th* as in *thin*).
doxological	docks-uh-*lah*-jih-kul.
Jeremiah	Jair-uh-*my*-uh.
merism	*mah*-rizm.
omnipotent	ahm-*nih*-poh-tent.
omnipresent	*ahm*-nih-**prez**-ent.
omniscient	ahm-*nish*-unt.
Septuagint	Sep-*too*-ih-jent.
Yahweh (*Hebrew*)	*Yah*-weh.

devise, to bring about, to get into one's possession." Its Hebrew original involves the idea of winnowing, as one separates wheat from chaff. Thus God is able to distinguish the good parts from the bad parts of the psalmist's path. To be walking on a path is the opposite of lying down. If being out on a path is a reference to going out in the morning to work, then we have another merism: the two opposites of "work" and "rest" include everything in between.

The phrase *art acquainted* reflects a rare usage of the Hebrew. Normally, this Hebrew word is used in the sense of "be of use or benefit" (example: Job 22:2). In its causative form in the Hebrew, which is what we have here, it takes the idea of "know intimately." Therefore, God knows intimately not only our work habits, but also when we turn in for the night as well as every other habit we may have. We sometimes call these habits our *ways*. What we may think of as routine activities are scrutinized by God closely on a daily basis.

4. For there is not a word in my tongue, but, lo, O LORD, thou knowest it altogether.

This is the height of God's capabilities or knowledge as they relate to every human being. He knows the very thoughts of an individual before those thoughts can be expressed in audible words. Considering that there are over six billion people on the face of this earth, that is impressive! (See also 1 Kings 8:39; Psalm 11:4, 5; 14:2; 33:13-15.)

What Do You Think?

How is your relationship with God affected by realizing that He knows your thoughts even before they are on your lips?

Talking Points for Your Discussion

- Issues of appreciation: God's capabilities
- Issues of self-control: what I ought to do/think
- Issues of perspective: awareness of my position in relation to God's

---

B. Results of His Knowing (vv. 5, 6)

5. Thou hast beset me behind and before, and laid thine hand upon me.

The word *beset* means "to encircle, barricade, lay siege to." It can be used as a word of judgment. In that sense, it would mean that the psalmist cannot escape, as if he were in a city besieged by an enemy (see Jeremiah 21:4, 9, where the same root word is used). It can also be used as a comfort word, where God surrounds and protects the psalmist. Both ideas of judgment and protection are also true for the second phrase: *laid thine hand upon me.*

Some may think that this reveals God's absolute control of a person's movements. A better idea is that it refers to God's abilities to know all and be everywhere. God surrounds all our habits and even has His hand on us—either in protection or in judgment.

Taking a bird's-eye view of verses 2-5, we notice that verse 2 is related to verse 4 in the sense of God's ability to know our thoughts. Verse 3 is related to verse 5 by the common theme of God knowing our ways or our habits. If verse 1 is the theme of this section, then verse 6 (next) is a doxological (praise) conclusion as the psalmist exults on his contemplation of God's ability to know.

6. Such knowledge is too wonderful for me; it is high, I cannot attain unto it.

God's ability to know everything is too wonderful and high for the psalmist to grasp. Even with all the extra knowledge we have today, this should still be our confession. We still have to struggle to understand even a little of what God knows.

The doxological use of *wonderful* is placed in the first position in the original Hebrew (literally, "wonderful knowledge above me; too high I am not able to it") to emphasize the amazement of the psalmist (see also v. 14, below). It is good to pause in wonderment over God's knowledge and ability to know. It is this attribute of God that makes possible an intimate, loving relationship with Him. The same attribute also makes God's justice absolutely fair. The righteous are comforted by that fact, while the wicked should be fearful.

II. God's Works
(PSALM 139:13-16)
A. Origin and Awareness (vv. 13, 14)

13. For thou hast possessed my reins: thou hast covered me in my mother's womb.

The section consisting of verses 13-16 emphasizes the power of God as well as His knowledge

—the power to create a human being and the knowledge to do so. However, the psalmist does not use the normal word for creating that we see in Genesis 1:1. He is using a word that has broad meanings of "to buy, acquire, create, produce" (see Proverbs 8:22, 23, referring to the creation of wisdom; and Exodus 15:16; Deuteronomy 32:6; Psalm 74:2, referring to the creation of God's people).

Reins translates the literal word for kidneys. In ancient times, these organs are associated with the seat of the conscience, the innermost feelings of the human will (compare Psalms 7:9; 26:2; Jeremiah 11:20; 17:10; 20:12). God has produced within each of us our own, personal conscience. The importance of conscience is seen in Genesis 20:5, 6; 1 Peter 3:21; etc. Problems of conscience are seen in 1 Corinthians 8:7, 10; 1 Timothy 4:2; etc.

The phrase *hast covered me* is the idea of "weaving together." Job 10:11 offers the same idea: "Thou hast clothed me with skin and flesh, and hast fenced me with bones and sinews." In other words, God is the one who skillfully creates people by forming them in the *mother's womb*. This thought is so amazing that the psalmist must stop and praise God for it (next verse)!

14. I will praise thee; for I am fearfully and wonderfully made: marvellous are thy works; and that my soul knoweth right well.

One way to look at this verse is to understand the psalmist's meaning as something like, "God has made me in a fearful and wonderful manner. Since this is part of God's work of creation, I call it marvelous. I know it because it is part of my life consciousness. I know it well!"

This may indeed be the meaning of the verse. But the Septuagint, which is the Greek version of the Old Testament that came into being before Christ, offers another possibility that we should consider. In place of *I will praise thee; for I am fearfully and wonderfully made,* one translation of the Septuagint has "I will give thee thanks; for thou art fearfully wondrous." The reason for this uncertainty is because there is no word for "I am . . . made" in the Hebrew text.

Thus we see in the Septuagint translation the ideas of "fearful" and "wonderful" being applied to God himself rather than to the way the psalmist

has been created. This second interpretation is possible. But the *King James Version* translation seems better given that the psalmist naturally is one of God's *marvelous . . . works,* which the second half of the verse mentions. God is to be praised for His amazing power to create the human being.

What Do You Think?
  How do you praise the Lord who made you?
Talking Points for Your Discussion
  ▪ In the songs you sing
  ▪ In the prayers you pray
  ▪ In the way you serve
  ▪ In the way your talk matches your walk

❧ THE LOWLY, LOVELY APPENDIX ❧

For years, the human appendix has been under attack by evolutionists. They have called it a functionless organ, a remnant from a more complete organ of our "animal" ancestors.

Today, however, most scientists agree that the appendix serves useful functions. This specialized organ contributes to a healthy immune system. At its strategic location, the appendix provides a barrier of protection as it produces antibodies that act against bacteria that would be harmful if allowed to escape into the bloodstream. The appendix helps the body recognize that certain foods, bacteria, and enzymes need to be tolerated, not attacked, during early childhood. The list goes on.

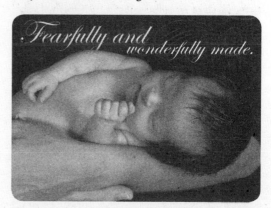

Visual for Lesson 13. Point to this visual as you ask, "How will realizing that you are 'fearfully and wonderfully made' affect your life this week?"

Once again the arrogance of human presumption is overturned. Again we realize how limited is human knowledge and how infinite is the wisdom of God. He carefully created even the small appendix to provide protection. How can we not marvel at the works of God?   —C. J. F.

B. Unhidden and Foreknown (vv. 15, 16)

15. My substance was not hid from thee when I was made in secret, and curiously wrought in the lowest parts of the earth.

The word translated *substance* refers to "bones." Therefore, the psalmist is talking about the skeletal framework of a person and thus the strongest part of one's physical substance. Even the formation of the bones of a child in the womb is not hidden from God's eyes.

We are not quite sure what the psalmist means by referring to being *made in secret*. This phrase seems to be parallel to the last phrase, *curiously wrought in the lowest parts of the earth*. Thus if we can figure out what that last phrase means, we may get a good idea of what *made in secret* means. Some students think that the *curiously . . . earth* phrase refers to an ancient idea about humanity originating deep in the earth (compare Genesis 2:7; Job 10:9). However, the psalmist seems to use this phrase as a figure of speech for the mother's womb. This idea is supported by the fact that the psalmist has just talked about the womb in verse 13.

Today, doctors and scientists are able to observe the growth of an embryo into a fully formed baby. Expectant parents can see their unborn child on ultrasound. It is wonderful to see what God has always been able to see!

16. Thine eyes did see my substance, yet being unperfect; and in thy book all my members were written, which in continuance were fashioned, when as yet there was none of them.

The Hebrew word that is behind the translation *substance* here is different from the Hebrew word behind *substance* in verse 15. The word at issue here is used only once in the Hebrew text, and it clearly means "embryo." Thus the beginning stages of a living and growing embryo are within the realm of God's knowledge and sight. This says something to all who believe that life does not begin until there is a birth, which is the rationale used to support abortion. Life begins at conception, and God knows it! See also Psalm 22:9, 10.

Scripture refers to God's book as the heavenly record of the deeds of people. This book lists the names of those who will dwell in the heavenly city. This book is the book of life (see Exodus 32:32, 33; Psalm 56:8; 69:28; Revelation 3:5; 17:8; 20:12, 15; 21:27). These images come from the fact that in the ancient world official registers are kept of citizens. When citizenship is forfeited for any reason, the name is blotted out of the register. The psalmist seems to be saying that even before his embryo is mature, his name is registered by God in His book. God knows what we will do and choose.

III. Psalmist's Invitation
(Psalm 139:23, 24)
A. To Search and Know (v. 23)

23. Search me, O God, and know my heart: try me, and know my thoughts.

Verses 23, 24 directly follow the "cursing" portion of the psalm (which is vv. 19-22, not in today's text). Often these "cursing texts" are left out of liturgical readings in many church groups. But they should not be. In verses 19-22, the psalmist rails against the wicked. Seen against this backdrop, verses 23, 24 is the psalmist's request for God to see that he (the psalmist) is not one of the wicked.

In that light, the psalmist cries out for vindication. Thus the invitation for God to search the psalmist's heart, test his life, and know his thoughts to see if there is any "wicked way" in him (see the next verse). The innocent person has no problem asking God to do this (see Job 7:17, 18; Psalm 11:4-7; Jeremiah 17:10). The words in verse 23 function as inclusion with verse 1 of this psalm (see the Lesson Background).

What Do You Think?
As God searches your heart and knows your thoughts, what does He see and hear?
Talking Points for Your Discussion
- Your fears, struggles, and frustrations
- Your hopes, aspirations, and motives

B. To See and Lead (v. 24)

24. And see if there be any wicked way in me, and lead me in the way everlasting.

Whatever the charge—whether it is idolatry or some other kind of wickedness—the charge is not true of the psalmist. Thus he seeks God's help in his declaration of innocence (compare Psalms 7:3-5; 18:20-24; 101:2-4 for other claims of innocence). For the psalmist, to think of God in terms of being all-knowing, all-powerful, and present everywhere are not abstract doctrines, but are part of the lifestyle of the believer who walks with God every day. Who else is able to lead the psalmist *in the way everlasting?*

We sometimes call this willingness to follow God "practicing the presence of God." Sometimes God may lead us in a path we would rather not take. That can be a fearful experience, and our instinct may be to flee or hide (compare the actions of Jonah). But ultimately *the way everlasting* can be found only in God. "Lord, to whom shall we go? thou hast the words of eternal life" (John 6:68).

> **What Do You Think?**
> What particular sin has God delivered you from? How did that happen?
> *Talking Points for Your Discussion*
> - Sins of commission (example: Mark 10:12)
> - Sins of omission (example: James 4:17)
> - Sins of thoughts (example: Ezekiel 14:7)
> - Sins of the tongue (example: James 3:1-12)

❧ *STOP THINKING?* ❧

In 2007, Finance Minister Christine Lagarde of France made a statement that shocked that country's intellectual community. Trying to encourage the French people to abandon what she called their "old national habit," she stated, "France is a country that thinks. . . . We have in our libraries enough to talk about for centuries to come. This is why I would like to tell you: Enough thinking, already. Roll up your sleeves."

Ms. Lagarde made her remarks in an effort to revitalize the French economy by encouraging people to work longer and harder. Her message agrees with the outlook of French President Nicolas Sarkozy, whose theme is doing, not philosophizing. He has encouraged his people to "work more to earn more."

In an entertainment-driven culture such as America's, few would say that "too much thinking" is one of the "wicked ways" that needs to be overcome! Yet all of us have things in our daily routines of work and leisure that can hamper our Christian growth. We should take advantage of the fact that God is completely familiar with every aspect of our lives. We can ask Him to search our hearts to see if there is "any wicked way" in us. Then we will be in the best position to surrender it to Him so He can change it.   —C. J. F.

Conclusion

A. God Knows!

Are you convinced that "God knows"? I hope you are. But merely acknowledging that God knows us better than we know ourselves is not enough. We should go further: part of our conviction that "God knows" should involve inviting the Holy Spirit's examination of our hearts and actions so that we might grow in sanctification. God created us and He cares. When we are innocent, He can and will vindicate us because of His fearfully wonderful abilities—His ability of knowledge, presence, and power.

Even if we find that our hearts condemn us, "God is greater than our heart, and knoweth all things" (1 John 3:20). For the innocent, the thought of an all-knowing God is a comfort. For the wicked the thought should bring fear—real fear of judgment, if not now, then on Judgment Day. The intimacy we seek with God is possible because He knows us better than we know ourselves.

B. Prayer

Search me, O God, and know my heart; test me and know my thoughts. See if there is any sinful way in me and lead me in the way everlasting. It is Jesus who makes that way possible. In His name we pray. Amen.

C. Thought to Remember

Know that God knows.

INVOLVEMENT LEARNING

Some of the activities below are also found in the helpful student book, Adult Bible Class.
Don't forget to download the free reproducible page from www.standardlesson.com to enhance your lesson!

Into the Lesson

Prepare handouts of the following activity, which is designed to find out how well your students know one other. Put *Who . . . ?* at the top. Then include the following statements below it.

1. Has seen "Old Faithful" in Yellowstone Park. 2. Can play the piano. 3. Never had a speeding ticket. 4. Has a cat. 5. Was born in February. 6. Drives a green vehicle. 7. Is left-handed. 8. Has been to Rome. 9. Has an older sister. 10. Has a redheaded child. 11. Went to church camp as a child. 12. Likes classical music.

Use the size of your class to determine the number of items listed; feel free to change the items to make them more appropriate for your class. Distribute the handouts and say, "Find people in the class who fit the categories; ask them to write their name on the correct line. If possible, find a different person for each one."

To conclude, go down the list and have people call out the names of those who fit the categories. Then say, "Although we know some things about each other, there's a lot we don't know. But our heavenly Father knows everything about us. Today's lesson will describe that knowledge."

Alternative: Have students pair off and take the quiz Your Amazingly Wonderful Body from the reproducible page. Or divide the class into two teams and alternate asking each team one of the questions. Then say, "Because God made us, He knows us very well. Let's find out just how well."

Into the Word

Prepare the following instructions for three groups (duplicate assignments if your class is large enough to have more than three groups).

Group A: Read Psalm 139:1-6, 16 aloud and make a list of all the things the psalmist says God knows about us. Discuss these questions: 1. Think about someone you know well; how did you get to know him or her so well? 2. How is God able to know us so well? (See Hebrews 4:13.) 3. According to Psalm 139:16, what special knowledge does God have about your life that even you don't know? Do you find this fact comforting? Why, or why not? 4. How does God use His knowledge to bless us?

Group B: Read Psalm 139:13-16 and make a list of the phrases that describe God as our Creator. Discuss the following questions: 1. How would you respond to someone who says, "Each person is just an accident resulting from a combination of genes"? 2. What clues do we have from these verses about why God is so interested in us from the moment of conception? 3. What aspects of God's close attention to you make you feel comforted and uncomfortable? Why? 4. In what ways does God use His knowledge to bless us?

Group C: Read Psalms 33:13-15; 139:23, 24. Make a list of the things we try to hide from others. Discuss the following questions: 1. How is God able to know things about us that others don't? 2. Why is God interested in the details of each person's life? (See also Psalm 139:13.) 3. Why does the psalmist invite God to take an even closer look at his life? Is that something you are willing to do? Why, or why not? 4. In what ways does God use His knowledge to bless us?

Ask groups to express answers for question #4.

Into Life

To conclude, say, "Even with all the surveillance equipment available today, no one is able to read our thoughts. Yet we know that God hears all our thoughts and knows what's in our hearts. As a result, He is able to purify us and help us change. Psalm 139:23, 24 offers a wonderful prayer to ask God to search us and put our thoughts to the test."

Distribute index cards and ask your students to write out those two verses to take with them for use as part of their daily prayers this week. Distribute copies of the Praise the Creator! activity from the reproducible page as take-home work.

God Is Omniscient

ASSURING
HOPE

Special Features

Lessons

Unit 1: Comfort for God's People

Unit 2: A Future for God's People

Unit 3: The Fulfillment of God's Promise

QUARTERLY QUIZ

Use these questions as a pretest or as a review. The answers are on page iv of This Quarter in the Word.

Lesson 1

1. Isaiah says that Jerusalem can be comforted because her warfare is over. T/F. *Isaiah 40:2*

2. While grass withers and flowers fade, what abides forever? (God's Word, the temple, stupidity?) *Isaiah 40:8*

Lesson 2

1. Who is described as God's friend? (Moses, Abraham, David?) *Isaiah 41:8*

2. Isaiah prophesies that the Servant of the Lord will bring judgment to the _____. *Isaiah 42:1*

Lesson 3

1. The Branch will come from the roots of whom? (Jesse, Solomon, Jesus?) *Isaiah 11:1*

2. *Emmanuel* means "____ with ____." *Matthew 1:23*

Lesson 4

1. What nation did God give as a ransom for Israel? (Babylon, Egypt, Greece?) *Isaiah 43:3*

2. Isaiah informs Israel that their God is the best of many possible saviors. T/F. *Isaiah 43:11*

Lesson 5

1. What has the Lord blotted out "as a cloud"? (sins, doubts, Babylon?) *Isaiah 44:22*

2. God says of Cyrus that "he is my shepherd." T/F. *Isaiah 44:28*

Lesson 6

1. Isaiah says God is one who hides himself. T/F. *Isaiah 45:15*

2. Isaiah promises a time when every _____ will bow. *Isaiah 45:23*

Lesson 7

1. If Israel had heard and obeyed the Lord's commandments, then the nation would have had peace as a _____. *Isaiah 48:18*

2. There is no peace for whom? (the wicked, the oppressed, the king?) *Isaiah 48:22*

Lesson 8

1. The Lord made Isaiah's mouth like a sharp what? (stick, razor, sword?) *Isaiah 49:2*

2. Israel was to be a light to the _____. *Isaiah 49:6*

Lesson 9

1. Isaiah portrays the Messiah as a man of sorrows who is acquainted with _____. *Isaiah 53:3*

2. In what way does Isaiah compare the Messiah to a sheep? (whiteness of wool, doesn't open his mouth, bleats loudly?) *Isaiah 53:7*

Lesson 10

1. Mark records that _____, one of the disciples, was brazen enough to "rebuke" Jesus for something He said. *Mark 8:32*

2. Jesus promises that He will be ashamed of some when He comes again. T/F. *Mark 8:38*

Lesson 11

1. What two Old Testament figures appeared on the mount of transfiguration? (Elias and Moses, David and Job, Adam and Eve?) *Mark 9:4*

2. The disciples heard the voice of God while on the mount of transfiguration. T/F. *Mark 9:7*

Lesson 12

1. The two who asked to sit at Jesus' right and left were _____ and _____. *Mark 10:35-37*

2. Jesus stressed the importance of being "servant of all." T/F. *Mark 10:44*

Lesson 13

1. Jesus advised His followers to flee when they saw the "_____ of desolation." *Mark 13:14*

2. Jesus says that false prophets will be able to show "signs and wonders." T/F. *Mark 13:22*

by Douglas Redford

His oath, His covenant, His blood,
Support me in the whelming flood;
When all around my soul gives way,
He then is all my hope and stay.
On Christ, the solid Rock, I stand;
All other ground is sinking sand,
All other ground is sinking sand.
—Edward Mote ("The Solid Rock")

OLD TESTAMENT PROPHETS were not just messengers of gloom and doom. They were also harbingers of hope for God's people. Isaiah, whose prophecies make up much of the printed text in this quarter's lessons, pictured how the weakened condition of the "stem of Jesse" would be transformed through the coming of the Messiah: "a Branch shall grow out of his roots" (Isaiah 11:1-5).

It is important to see Isaiah's words of hope in light of the circumstances facing God's people in the prophet's day. In addition to the Assyrian threat (see "Get the Setting," page 116), significant areas of life were in disarray. Leaders were ineffective (Isaiah 3:14). Social abuses were rampant; groups such as orphans and widows were being neglected (1:23). Worship had degenerated into mere performance (1:10-15). The promise to Abraham of a "great nation" (Genesis 12:1-3) and to David of an everlasting throne (2 Samuel 7:16) seemed empty words.

Even so, the prophet Isaiah boldly declared his hope and stay to be in the Lord. One of the most significant themes in Isaiah is God's knowledge of the future and His ability to declare that future. By contrast, the pagan gods have no life whatever (Isaiah 42:8, 9; 43:10-12). As the Lord's inspired messenger, Isaiah named Cyrus as the ruler whose "right hand" God would take hold of in using him to end the Babylonian captivity (Isaiah 45:1). Cyrus is even described as the Lord's "shepherd" (44:28) and as His "anointed" (45:1)—though Cyrus did not come on the scene of history until some 150 years after Isaiah!

However, Isaiah's prophetic insight and his message of hope were not limited to the captives returning from Babylon. Isaiah heralded news of a coming age of salvation that involved deliverance from an enemy that was much worse than Babylon. That foe was sin, and the instrument of deliverance would be the Servant of the Lord.

Three of the lessons in this quarter (2, 8, and 9) are taken from the portions of Isaiah that include the Servant passages. Isaiah 53:1-12 (Lesson 9) is the most beloved and impressive of Isaiah's messianic glimpses. There the Servant's death is described as vividly as if Isaiah were watching the events of the crucifixion himself.

Although those who actually witnessed the crucifixion saw it as a hopeless end, Isaiah declared the endless hope brought about by Jesus' death. The hopeful conclusion of Isaiah 53 is the hopeful outcome for all who place their faith in the risen Servant, whose death paid the penalty for their sins.

Today there is much in our world that appears to be "giving way." Economic concerns cause significant stress in individuals, families, and in many of our most important institutions. Constant conflict and instability in various parts of the

> One of the most significant themes in Isaiah is God's knowledge of the future and His ability to declare that future.

world rarely seem to decrease. Leaders offer polished speeches and glowing promises, but seem to achieve little in terms of real results. In such times, hope seems out of the question.

Christians cannot allow themselves to be swayed by the negative situations around them. As you study this quarter's lessons, encourage your learners not to lose hope because of what is going on "all around" lest they forget the one who remains our "hope and stay."

by Douglas Redford

THE BOOK OF ISAIAH has been labeled by some as *the Fifth Gospel*. This statement is made because of the numerous messianic prophecies included in the record of Isaiah's messages. To see how the life and ministry of Jesus fulfills Old Testament prophecies such as those of Isaiah is one of the most compelling evidences for the inspiration and trustworthiness of Scripture.

Sometimes, however, readers focus so much on the prophets' messianic predictions that they overlook the extremely messy times in which most of the prophets carried out their ministries. Isaiah, for example, served as the Lord's spokesman during one of the most frightening times in the history of Old Testament Israel. The northern kingdom fell to the Assyrians in 722 BC. The southern kingdom appeared destined for a similar fate.

Isaiah counseled two kings of Judah (Ahaz, then his son Hezekiah) on how to address the crisis. His advice to each was the same: trust the Lord and do not fear the empty threats of earthly rulers. Ahaz rejected the prophet's counsel (Isaiah 7). The other king, Hezekiah, heeded Isaiah's message. Because this king chose faith rather than fear, the Lord brought about a miraculous deliverance of Jerusalem (Isaiah 37:36).

When Isaiah's prophecies experienced their fulfillment in Jesus' day, the situation confronting the nation of Israel was just as messy. Israel chafed under the control of the Roman Empire, anticipating the day when the Messiah would do away with that menace and restore Israel to its former greatness. God's response? To send a child—the very child predicted by Isaiah, born of the virgin Mary and destined to be and do all that Isaiah 9:6, 7 said He would be and do. And as this child grew to manhood and began His ministry, He began to demonstrate a power that no Roman ruler or army could overcome or decree out of existence.

But Jesus did not come to recreate the defeat of the Assyrians at Jerusalem. Rather, Jesus came to set up a different kind of kingdom—a kingdom "not of this world" (John 18:36). The enemy Jesus came to do battle with was not Rome; it was Satan. Jesus came to address a bondage that was not political in nature; it was spiritual. That was the bondage to sin. And Jesus came not only for Israel but other peoples. This was just as Isaiah had predicted (Isaiah 45:14, 22-25; 49:6).

The weapons Jesus used were hardly the kind employed by the Assyrians or Romans. Jesus came to conquer people's hearts, not through force or might, but by mercy and compassion. The "bruised reed" and "smoking flax" (the hurt, the injured, the downtrodden, the rejected) would not be shown further abuse (Isaiah 42:3). A quiet spirit, not the loud, brash arrogance of Assyria or Rome, characterized Jesus' demeanor (Isaiah 42:2; 53:7). Not only did He live this way, He also died this way, giving himself to be "wounded" and "bruised" for the transgressions of others (Isaiah 53:5).

Even after Jesus' resurrection, the power of Rome remained firmly in control of the Jewish people. Perhaps it seemed as though little had changed. But a revolution was under way nonetheless. It has outlasted the Roman Empire. It is destined by God to bring all kingdoms under His authority (Isaiah 49:7; Revelation 11:15). As "messy" as our present day is, we are in the unshakable kingdom of the Messiah (Hebrews 12:28).

THIS QUARTER IN THE WORD

Mon, Nov. 29	God's Glory Revealed	Deuteronomy 5:22-27
Tue, Nov. 30	God's Glory Declared	1 Chronicles 16:28-34
Wed, Dec. 1	God's Glory Praised	2 Chronicles 5:11-14
Thu, Dec. 2	God's Glory Beseeched	Psalm 79:5-10
Fri, Dec. 3	God's Glory Above the Nations	Isaiah 40:12-17
Sat, Dec. 4	God's Glory Above the Earth	Isaiah 40:18-24
Sun, Dec. 5	God's Coming Glory	Isaiah 40:1-8, 25, 26, 29-31
Mon, Dec. 6	A God of Love	1 John 4:13-19
Tue, Dec. 7	A God of Grace and Mercy	2 Chronicles 30:6-9
Wed, Dec. 8	A God Ready to Forgive	Nehemiah 9:16-21
Thu, Dec. 9	A God of Hope	Psalm 71:1-6
Fri, Dec. 10	The Lord, First and Last	Isaiah 41:1-7
Sat, Dec. 11	Do Not Fear	Isaiah 41:11-16
Sun, Dec. 12	The Lord's Promise to Protect	Isaiah 41:8-10; 17-20; 42:1-4, 9
Mon, Dec. 13	The God of Peace	Romans 15:25-33
Tue, Dec. 14	The Gospel of Peace	Ephesians 6:13-17
Wed, Dec. 15	Peace with God	Romans 5:1-5
Thu, Dec. 16	Peace Given to You	John 14:25-31
Fri, Dec. 17	A Child Is Born	Isaiah 9:1-6a
Sat, Dec. 18	His Mission—Our Mission	Matthew 28:16-20
Sun, Dec. 19	The Prince of Peace	Isaiah 9:6b, 7; 11:1-8

Mon, Feb. 14	Serving like a Slave	Luke 15:25-32
Tue, Feb. 15	Choosing the Better Part	Luke 10:38-42
Wed, Feb. 16	As One Who Serves	Luke 22:24-30
Thu, Feb. 17	Come, Follow Me	Mark 10:17-22
Fri, Feb. 18	Serving and Following	John 12:20-26
Sat, Feb. 19	An Example Set	John 13:3-16
Sun, Feb. 20	Greatness Through Service	Mark 10:35-45
Mon, Feb. 21	Terror for the Proud and Lofty	Isaiah 2:5-12
Tue, Feb. 22	Peril in Distressing Times	2 Timothy 3:1-9
Wed, Feb. 23	The Day of Judgment	2 Peter 3:1-10
Thu, Feb. 24	What You Ought to Be	2 Peter 3:11-18
Fri, Feb. 25	Beware!	Mark 13:1-13
Sat, Feb. 26	Be Watchful!	Mark 13:28-37
Sun, Feb. 27	Coming of the Son of Man	Mark 13:14-27, 31

Answers to the Quarterly Quiz on page 114

Lesson 1—1. true. 2. God's Word. Lesson 2—1. Abraham. 2. Gentiles. Lesson 3—1. Jesse. 2. "God with us." Lesson 4—1. Egypt. 2. false. Lesson 5—1. sins. 2. true. Lesson 6—1. true. 2. knee. Lesson 7—1. river. 2. the wicked. Lesson 8—1. sword. 2. Gentiles. Lesson 9—1. grief. 2. doesn't open his mouth. Lesson 10—1. Peter. 2. true. Lesson 11—1. Elias (Elijah) and Moses. 2. true. Lesson 12—1. James and John. 2. true. Lesson 13—1. abomination. 2. true.

FULFILLMENT OF PROPHECY
ISAIAH 53:1-12

Verse	Text	References
53:1	Who hath believed our report? and to whom is the arm of the LORD revealed?	JOHN 12 ROMANS 10:16
53:4	Surely he hath borne our griefs, and carried our sorrows: yet we did esteem him stricken, smitten of God, and afflicted.	MATTHEW 8:17 1 PETER 2:24
53:5	But he was wounded for our transgressions, he was bruised for our iniquities: the chastisement of our peace was upon him; and with his stripes we are healed.	MATTHEW 26:67 ROMANS 4:25 1 PETER 2:24
53:6	All we like sheep have gone astray; we have turned every one to his own way; and the LORD hath laid on him the iniquity of us all.	1 PETER 2:25
53:7	He was oppressed, and he was afflicted, yet he opened not his mouth: he is brought as a lamb to the slaughter, and as a sheep before her shearers is dumb, so he openeth not his mouth.	MATTHEW 26:63; 27:12 MARK 14:60, 61; 15:4, 5 ACTS 8:32
53:8	He was taken from prison and from judgment: and who shall declare his generation? for he was cut off out of the land of the living: for the transgression of my people was he stricken.	ACTS 8:33
53:9	And he made his grave with the wicked, and with the rich in his death; because he had done no violence, neither was any deceit in his mouth.	1 PETER 2:22 1 JOHN 3:5
53:11	He shall see of the travail of his soul, and shall be satisfied: by his knowledge shall my righteous servant justify many; for he shall bear their iniquities.	ROMANS 5:19
53:12	Therefore will I divide him a portion with the great, and he shall divide the spoil with the strong: because he hath poured out his soul unto death: and he was numbered with the transgressors; and he bare the sin of many, and made intercession for the transgressors.	MATTHEW 27:38 LUKE 22:37; 23:33, 34 HEBREWS 9:28 1 PETER 2:24

TESTING AS TOOL

Teacher Tips by James Riley Estep, Jr.

THE WORD *TEST* may conjure up bad memories of a teacher strolling down a classroom aisle, slowly handing anxious students their midterm exams. With such a negative association, why would we consider using testing with our Bible lessons?

We certainly do not wish to inflict "test anxiety" on our learners! But with a bit creativity, we can use testing as a tool of instruction.

"Before"

Testing can be used to introduce the Bible lesson. Testing at the outset of the lesson helps learners see gaps in their knowledge, showing them why they need the lesson. For example, Bible teachers often distribute a "Christmas Quiz" to start a lesson during that season. A typical question on such a quiz is, "How many Magi were there?" Answer: "The Bible doesn't say." Missing such a question can create an eagerness to fill in the gaps.

"During"

Testing also can be used in the middle of the Bible lesson as a way to measure students' understanding of the lesson as it progresses. Such a test can take many forms: true/false, multiple choice, matching, and listing are typical. But testing need not take the form of a written quiz. It also can be in the form of questions you pose verbally to the class as a whole.

You should keep in mind, however, that there are different types of questions. Some deal with *knowledge* (recall of facts), others deal with *comprehension* (understanding how facts fit together), while others address *application* (what difference it should make in the student's life). Questions of knowledge and comprehension have "right" answers, while questions involving application tend to be open-ended. Application questions thus lend themselves more to discussion than to testing as we are using that term here. Each type of question has its place, and the distinctions among them should be recognized.

"After"

Testing at the end of the lesson can reveal if your learning goals have been met. One common posttest is to ask students to summarize the lesson (or a series of lessons on a common theme). For example, you can ask learners to jot on index cards their responses to a certain question that an unbeliever might ask on the subject of the lesson or lessons at hand. Volunteers can share their answers as you create a joint, classroom response.

Some teachers use a pretest before the unit or quarter begins, then distribute the very same test questions at the end of the unit or quarter. This procedure alerts the student to what he or she should expect to learn in the weeks ahead, then provides a way to self-discover what the progress has been in that regard at the end. The Quarterly Quiz included with each quarter of study in this commentary is useful for this.

Obstacles

Some teachers are not comfortable with using testing as a teaching method. The first obstacle, therefore, is the teacher's own willingness to try something new! Try using testing only periodically at first. This will help you develop a feel for what works best with your class.

A second obstacle involves the students. Let's face it: adults do not like to "be wrong" in front of other adults! When using written tests, you can minimize anxiety and fear of embarrassment at "being wrong" by informing your learners that (1) they are going to score the quizzes themselves and (2) you, the teacher, are not going to collect the completed quizzes. Anxiety with verbalized test questions can be minimized by posing the questions to the class as a whole, then allowing volunteers to respond.

GOD GIVES STRENGTH

BACKGROUND SCRIPTURE: Isaiah 40
PRINTED TEXT: Isaiah 40:1-8, 25, 26, 29-31

ISAIAH 40:1-8, 25, 26, 29-31

1 Comfort ye, comfort ye my people, saith your God.

2 Speak ye comfortably to Jerusalem, and cry unto her, that her warfare is accomplished, that her iniquity is pardoned: for she hath received of the LORD's hand double for all her sins.

3 The voice of him that crieth in the wilderness, Prepare ye the way of the LORD, make straight in the desert a highway for our God.

4 Every valley shall be exalted, and every mountain and hill shall be made low: and the crooked shall be made straight, and the rough places plain:

5 And the glory of the LORD shall be revealed, and all flesh shall see it together: for the mouth of the LORD hath spoken it.

6 The voice said, Cry. And he said, What shall I cry? All flesh is grass, and all the goodliness thereof is as the flower of the field:

7 The grass withereth, the flower fadeth; because the spirit of the LORD bloweth upon it: surely the people is grass.

8 The grass withereth, the flower fadeth: but the word of our God shall stand for ever.

· ·

25 To whom then will ye liken me, or shall I be equal? saith the Holy One.

26 Lift up your eyes on high, and behold who hath created these things, that bringeth out their host by number: he calleth them all by names by the greatness of his might, for that he is strong in power; not one faileth.

· ·

29 He giveth power to the faint; and to them that have no might he increaseth strength.

30 Even the youths shall faint and be weary, and the young men shall utterly fall:

31 But they that wait upon the LORD shall renew their strength; they shall mount up with wings as eagles; they shall run, and not be weary; and they shall walk, and not faint.

KEY VERSE

He giveth power to the faint; and to them that have no might he increaseth strength. —**Isaiah 40:29**

ASSURING HOPE

Unit 1: Comfort for God's People
LESSONS 1–5

LESSON AIMS

After participating in this lesson, each student will be able to:

1. List three ways God comforts and strengthens His people.

2. Explain the importance of Isaiah's promises for the New Testament era.

3. Tell how he or she can use Isaiah's promises to comfort a fellow believer.

LESSON OUTLINE

Introduction

A. Highway Engineering

Highways are often built over the route of older roads. The older roads may have been based on old footpaths or even older animal paths. Such paths usually took the easiest route, zigzagging to avoid steep inclines, etc. They almost never went "as the crow flies," a straight line in one direction from place to place. Older roads in the country often followed property boundaries, sometimes detouring hundreds of yards in order not to bisect a piece of prized farmland.

Isaiah, the Israelite prophet of the eighth century BC, was well acquainted with such wandering paths and roads. He undoubtedly experienced soft roadways with deep wagon ruts, poorly drained stretches that turned to mud in the rainy season. He knew about poorly maintained roads that could cause a turned ankle or a tumble for the traveler who did not exercise appropriate caution.

In today's lesson text, however, Isaiah has a vision of a better transportation system. He envisions a royal roadway, laboriously prepared as the pathway for the coming king. Roads are not self-preparing. To make them smooth and flat takes planning and work. It takes a sense of appreciation that the king deserves better than to walk a narrow goat path. It is with this in mind that Isaiah cries out, "Prepare ye the way of the Lord."

B. Lesson Background

Isaiah 40 begins a new section in the book. Chapters 36–39, immediately preceding, tell of Jerusalem's deliverance from the Assyrian army of King Sennacherib as well as other events from the time of King Hezekiah (ruled approximately 727–695 BC). Those were dark days for the little nation of Judah, for powerful foreign nations threatened her sovereignty. This narrative section ends in chapter 39 with an ill-advised action by Hezekiah: the king welcomed Babylonian envoys to Jerusalem and gave them a private viewing of all his wealth. Isaiah then gave Hezekiah a dire prophecy that the Babylonians would carry Judah and all her treasures into captivity (Isaiah 39:5-7; compare 2 Kings 20:12-19).

Chapter 40 marks a turning point. There is still a sense of impending doom for Judah, but Isaiah saw beyond that to a time of restoration. He gave hope, even before the disaster, that God would not abandon Israel. Moreover, Isaiah saw beyond the fate of the nation to the coming of God's Messiah to accomplish an even bigger work.

I. Reassuring Voice
(ISAIAH 40:1-5)
A. Speaking Comfort (vv. 1, 2)

1. Comfort ye, comfort ye my people, saith your God.

Isaiah begins the chapter with a command to comfort the people. This is a group command, as indicated by the *ye* in the *King James Version*. As such, it is probably directed to the leaders of Judah, meaning Hezekiah and his associates.

Comfort is a strong theme in Isaiah. For Isaiah, comfort is the alleviation of suffering. The comfort of the Lord is pictured as the opposite of the anger of the Lord (Isaiah 12:1). In this, comfort follows punishment, like the mother who hugs her son after spanking him (compare 66:13). The comfort of the Lord also is expressive of God's restoration of His people and their land (see 51:3; 52:9).

What Do You Think?

How would you describe the comfort you have received from God? What has been your response to that peace?

Talking Points for Your Discussion
- Peace that involves relationships
- Peace that involves spiritual issues
- Peace that involves physical issues

---

2. Speak ye comfortably to Jerusalem, and cry unto her, that her warfare is accomplished, that her iniquity is pardoned: for she hath received of the LORD's hand double for all her sins.

The basis for comfort is now explained a little further. The danger of military destruction is depicted as past, but there are at least two ways to interpret that perspective.

First, the danger may be in the past from Isaiah's point of view. Jerusalem underwent a threat by the Assyrians in 701 BC, and there was no comfort while the city was under siege (see Isaiah 22:4). But the Lord saved Jerusalem (2 Kings 19:35, 36; Isaiah 37:36, 37). Isaiah tells us that during this time King Hezekiah was also delivered from a deadly illness (Isaiah 38:5). Although Hezekiah was a righteous king in many ways, he had a problem with pride. This ungodly pride was at least part of the reason for his illness and the near-destruction of Jerusalem (see 2 Chronicles 32:24-26). Naturally, comfort came when the threat had passed.

The second possibility is that the danger is in the future from Isaiah's point of view. Under this viewpoint, the reference is to the Babylonian captivity of 586 BC. This is many decades in the future from Isaiah's perspective. The comfort, then, is what the Jews will experience when they return from exile. This viewpoint is supported by Isaiah 44:28; 45:1, 13, which predicts the role of Cyrus in this deliverance (compare Ezra 1:1-4).

In neither case does God forget His people. Sin has its price, but God comforts and forgives.

❧ *COMFORT IN THE FACE OF CALAMITY* ❧

Extended times of prosperity tend to make people think that the good days will never end. But 2008 brought the meltdown of the U.S. housing market that was based on risky mortgage instruments; this caused many to lose their homes to foreclosure. The stock market plunged to its lowest point in years. A highly trusted financial adviser

HOW TO SAY IT

Ammonites	*Am*-un-ites.
Assyrian	Uh-*sear*-e-un.
Babylonian	Bab-ih-*low*-nee-un.
Chemosh	*Kee*-mosh.
Cyrus	*Sigh*-russ.
Hezekiah	Hez-ih-*kye*-uh.
Messiah	Meh-*sigh*-uh.
Moabites	*Mo*-ub-ites.
Molech	*Mo*-lek.
Orion	O-*rye*-un.
Pleiades	*Plee*-uh-deez.
Zerubbabel	Zeh-*rub*-uh-bul.

was discovered to have been working a multi-billion-dollar Ponzi scheme for decades; numerous investors—including charities—lost their large investments. In the midst of it all, millions lost their jobs, and unemployment rolls rose to levels unseen in decades.

Where is the comfort when such things happen?

There is no easy solution, no panacea that will make everything right quickly. To someone who has lost job and home, hearing that "Things will get better" is of little comfort. Yet that is what Isaiah said to his people. They had to pay the price for (and hopefully learn a lesson from) their sin. Sin always has its price, and God does not change that fact. What can *we* learn from this?   —C. R. B.

B. Crying Preparation (vv. 3, 4)

3. The voice of him that crieth in the wilderness, Prepare ye the way of the LORD, make straight in the desert a highway for our God.

Isaiah now looks ahead to the time when Jerusalem will be visited by the ultimate king, the Lord God himself. This is not to be a surprise visit. It is proclaimed by the voice crying *in the wilderness* in order for proper preparations to be made. This verse exhorts the people to be prepared for the visitation of their king, the Lord God. This requires advance and extensive planning. Not just the city is to be prepped, but even the wilderness outside the city. There the highway should be improved, straightened for the king and His entourage.

Ultimately, however, this verse points to the preparatory ministry of John the Baptist, the forerunner of the Messiah (compare Malachi 3:1). Isaiah 40:3 is so important that it is quoted in all four Gospels in reference to John (Matthew 3:3; Mark 1:3; Luke 3:4; John 1:23). In God's plan, John's purposes are to raise the expectations of the people for a Messiah (Luke 3:16, 17), to spur them to prepare their hearts (Luke 1:76-79), and to be God's designated revealer of Jesus as the Messiah at the proper time (John 1:29-34).

4. Every valley shall be exalted, and every mountain and hill shall be made low: and the crooked shall be made straight, and the rough places plain.

This verse continues the imagery of road construction activities. Valleys along the route will be exalted, meaning that any large dips in the road will be corrected through fill or bridges. Making low the topographical high places will require laborious modification by digging and cutting through the rock of the hills. The twisted curves of the roadway shall be made straight. The rough places are those stretches of roadway where minor rocks and ridges make for a bumpy ride. Such parts will be made like a smooth plain.

C. Returning Glory (v. 5)

5. And the glory of the LORD shall be revealed, and all flesh shall see it together: for the mouth of the LORD hath spoken it.

The revelation of *the glory of the Lord* reminds us of the dedication of Solomon's temple, when there was a stupendous display of God's presence (2 Chronicles 7:1). Isaiah can see that this temple, still standing in his day, will cease to be a focal point for the glory of Israel's God. Isaiah's words here look beyond the temple's destruction to a new era of the glory of the Lord.

When the temple is rebuilt by Zerubbabel and dedicated in 515 BC, there is no record of a visitation of the glory of the Lord (see Ezra 6:14-18). Thus we should understand this text as referring to something other than a rebuilt temple. Isaiah indicates the certain nature of the revelation of God's glory by including the authoritative phrase *the mouth of the Lord hath spoken it.* The apostle John's visions of Heaven include glimpses of the glory of God in the eternal temple (Revelation 15:8) and anticipate that the glory of God will permeate the new Jerusalem (21:23). This best fits what *all flesh shall see.*

God Gives Strength

II. Enduring Voice
(Isaiah 40:6-8)
A. Flesh That Fades (vv. 6, 7)

6. The voice said, Cry. And he said, What shall I cry? All flesh is grass, and all the goodliness thereof is as the flower of the field.

In the midst of this grand prophetic vision, Isaiah is called to remember his mortality. He is an instrument of God's communication, a vessel of hope for the future. At the same time, he is a temporary tool akin to the cyclical vegetation.

7. The grass withereth, the flower fadeth; because the spirit of the Lord bloweth upon it: surely the people is grass.

Like Isaiah, his hearers are subject to this mortal nature. Here we should understand *spirit* in the sense of "breath" or "wind." In Israel, the hot winds of the dry season quickly cause the unwatered grass and flowers to wither. Their glory is momentary and fleeting. Isaiah draws a direct correlation to this seasonal pattern and the fate of human beings. We are made of the dust of the earth, eventually to die, decompose, and become dust again (Genesis 3:19; compare Job 34:15).

B. Word That Lasts (v. 8)

8. The grass withereth, the flower fadeth: but the word of our God shall stand for ever.

In contrast with the fleeting, impermanent nature of vegetation and human beings stands the eternal, permanent nature of God's Word. This includes Isaiah's prophetic message but also looks forward to the "everlasting gospel" (Revelation 14:6), the good news of salvation preached to the world. Indeed, Peter quotes this very sequence of verses some 700 years after Isaiah and applies it directly to the gospel message (1 Peter 1:24, 25).

Understanding the eternal nature of God's Word is essential for appreciating the concept of prophecy. The only way a word can be spoken in the eighth century BC and find fulfillment in the first century AD is through the divine power this word embodies. Likewise, the only way the Word of God remains an infallible authority for us today is through this eternal, timeless quality. Men and women come and go. Teachers of the church live and die. The constant, consistent anchor for our lives is found in the Word of God.

> **What Do You Think?**
> In what ways have you experienced the enduring nature of God's Word?
> *Talking Points for Your Discussion*
> - As you consider promises made in the Word
> - As you reflect on prophecies fulfilled
> - As you live by the principles taught in the Word
> - 2 Timothy 3:16, 17

❧ *Fading Away* ❧

Has middle age brought the dreaded sagging of your anatomy? Are "laugh lines" and "crow's feet" beginning to make you look your age, and you find it neither to be a laughing matter nor something to crow about? Does the person in the mirror look like one of your grandparents?

Fear not—cosmetic surgery can solve your problems! Laser resurfacing can take care of all those wrinkles on your face for a mere $1,500 to $6,500. If you need a major face lift, add another $2,000 to that higher figure. A tummy tuck will cost you only $7,500, not counting the $2,300 to $7,000 for the liposuction that reveals how much you need that tummy tuck!

We fool ourselves if we think that repeated cosmetic surgeries will stop us from getting older. The flower fades away, and so do we! Rather than spending money on cosmetic surgery, we could use that money in ways that result in treasures in Heaven—treasures that will never fade (Matthew 6:20).
—C. R. B.

III. Strengthening Voice
(Isaiah 40:25, 26, 29-31)
A. Powerful Source (vv. 25, 26)

25. To whom then will ye liken me, or shall I be equal? saith the Holy One.

The final section of this marvelous chapter presents the Lord speaking more directly to us. He is *the Holy One*, untainted by sin and perfect in righteousness. He poses two rhetorical questions, two questions for which the answer is obvious.

First, who (or what) is a worthy object of comparison with the Lord? God might be called king, Father, or judge (see Psalm 5:2; 68:5). These are categories of human existence that are transcended by God in an absolute way. Thus, the answer to this first question must be "no one."

Second, we are queried as to who might be equal to the Lord. This question is parallel to the first, but with a twist. In the ancient world, it is common for a nation to be identified by its national god. For example, the national god of the Moabites is Chemosh, while Molech is the national deity of the Ammonites (see 1 Kings 11:7). The power and glory of these localized gods is judged by the success of their nations. The truth behind Isaiah's message, however, is that there is no real comparison in this area. Such fictitious gods are not in any way equal to the God of Israel, for He is the true God, the Creator of all things. The answer to this question is also "no one."

26. Lift up your eyes on high, and behold who hath created these things, that bringeth out their host by number: he calleth them all by names by the greatness of his might, for that he is strong in power; not one faileth.

We are now told why the God of Israel is beyond comparison: He, and He alone, is the one who created the host of the heavens. This is a reference to the stars and planets, which give witness to God's glory by their constant shining (Psalm 19:1). These heavenly bodies are completely subject to God, for he *calleth them all by names*. We are reminded of God's challenge to Job, asking if he is able to reposition the constellations of the Pleiades or Orion (Job 38:31).

> **What Do You Think?**
> What specific things in creation most cause you to acknowledge the power of God?
> *Talking Points for Your Discussion*
> - Very, very small things
> - Very, very large things

B. Needed Invigoration (vv. 29, 30)

29. He giveth power to the faint; and to them that have no might he increaseth strength.

We move from the power required to fuel the stars to the power needed to empower a weak and falling people—*them that have no might*. The point is that with God there is always a surplus of strength. He experiences no brownouts or empty fuel tanks. The same God who placed the blazing sun in our sky can restore our strength. We can draw on our inner resources only for so long, and then we are empty and spent. We are called to "lift up [our] eyes" to God, for He "made heaven and earth," and He has the power to remake us in our weakness (Psalm 121:1, 2). We are called to look outside of ourselves for the necessary spiritual vigor to survive our times of trial.

30. Even the youths shall faint and be weary, and the young men shall utterly fall.

The universal nature of this need for God's empowerment is stressed. Even the young, the healthy and athletic, will run out of strength at some point. Our refrigerators may run day and night for 20 years without failing. But even these most reliable of appliances require an outside power source to continue functioning. We may run without God or away from God for a long time, but eventually we will *utterly fall* if we do not allow Him to come into our lives in a powerful, healing way.

C. Soaring Renewal (v. 31)

31. But they that wait upon the LORD shall renew their strength; they shall mount up with wings as eagles; they shall run, and not be weary; and they shall walk, and not faint.

To *wait upon the Lord* is not to give up in complete passivity. "Waiting," in this biblical sense, is an act of faith, a move of trust. It is to change the focus of our empowerment from ourselves to the Lord. Isaiah tells us that this commitment of faith is rewarded, using one of the most striking metaphors in all of Scripture: we are to be given *wings as eagles*. We are blessed with the ability to soar above the daily troubles that beset and discourage us.

Furthermore, we become the tireless runner and ceaseless walker. When we yield to God's power and control in our lives, we may not immediately be a soaring spiritual eagle. We might not even be a relentless runner. But all of us can at least be a tireless walker, journeying with God in faith and assurance that we do not walk alone.

> **What Do You Think?**
> What was a circumstance when waiting on the Lord brought you renewed strength?
> *Talking Points for Your Discussion*
> - A personal trial (James 1:2-4)
> - A family issue
> - A church conflict

Conclusion

A. Spiritual Eagles

The soaring eagle has been an inspiring sight since ancient times. They have enormous wing-spans. This is combined with precision eyesight in their quest for food. Eagles may cover as much as 100 miles in this daily search, and some claim that they may reach an altitude of 10,000 feet. From this vantage point, they are able to see a wide ter-ritory, locate their prey, and quickly swoop down to seize it. Yet eagles do not attain these incredible heights merely by flapping their wings. They find updrafts in the atmospheric patterns, stretch their wings fully, and soar.

Our age of aircraft has taken away some of the wonder of soaring eagles, for many of us have looked out an airplane window at 30,000 feet. Yet we can still look at the soaring eagle with a sense of longing, a desire to use our personal wings to rise above the trees and buildings and roads. What freedom that would be! How exhilarating! How empowering!

Isaiah promises that if we trust in the Lord, we will soar like spiritual eagles. This will not come from laborious flapping of our spiritual wings, but by catching God's updraft and riding its power to new heights. Our perspective then will change. What seemed so big and intimidating on the ground will look tiny at 10,000 feet. We still must deal with the hard issues of life. But we can gain a little bit of God's perspective, the large view that He is in control and we draw on His strength.

The Messiah provides that strength. He is God's ultimate servant in bearing the sins of people as an atoning sacrifice (Isaiah 53:5). This promise is for

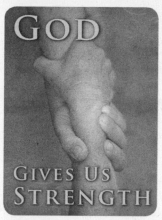

Visual for Lessons 1 & 2

Point to this visual as you introduce the discussion question associated with verse 31.

everyone. Even the dispossessed and "he that hath no money" can "come . . . , buy, and eat" at the table of the Lord (55:1). When the time comes for us to enjoy the Christmas season, we should remember that the season is possible because of those who prepared the way for the king who has come. We remember Isaiah, who was given a glimpse of the Messiah's future glory. And we remember John the Baptist, who seized Isaiah's messages as a definition of his own ministry of preparing the way for the ministry of Jesus (see Matthew 3:3). What role will you play in preparing an unbeliever's heart to receive the Messiah?

B. Prayer

Heavenly Father, grant that we might take "the long view" of history. It is there we will find comfort because we realize that history will end when Your Son returns. In His name we pray, amen.

C. Thought to Remember

Test your God-given spiritual wings!

VISUALS FOR THESE LESSONS

The visual pictured in each lesson (example: page 127) is a small reproduction of a large, full-color poster included in the *Adult Resources* packet for the Winter Quarter. That packet also contains the very useful *Presentation Helps* on a CD for teacher use. Order No. 292 from your supplier.

INVOLVEMENT LEARNING

Some of the activities below are also found in the helpful student book, Adult Bible Class.
Don't forget to download the free reproducible page from www.standardlesson.com to enhance your lesson!

Into the Lesson

Write the words *Children* and *Adults* on the board. Ask learners to brainstorm a list of activities and objects that people use to comfort themselves when they are frightened or troubled.

Write answers on the board as they are called out, in the correct column. Answers for children might include holding on to a favorite blanket, sucking a thumb, or crawling into a parent's lap. Answers for adults could include eating "comfort" foods, sleeping, shopping, and smoking. Say, "While most adults have found ways to comfort themselves beyond thumb-sucking, we all seem to need ways to find relief from the stresses of life. Today's text contains several wonderful promises from God to comfort and strengthen His people."

Optional: Download the reproducible page and introduce the activity No God Like Our God by saying, "When times are tough, remembering God's qualities can give us faith in His ability to help us. Complete this matching activity that shows the kind of God we serve."

Into the Word

Form your learners into three small groups of no more than four or five each. (Use duplicate assignments if your class is large enough to have more than three groups; smaller classes can use study pairs.) Distribute the following assignments along with the indicated resources.

Group A: Promises for the Israelites. Read Isaiah 40:1, 2. Use the reference material provided to discuss these questions: (1) From what peril had the Lord delivered His people? (2) What would the people suffer in the future at the hands of the Babylonians because of sin? (3) How could these verses have given the people hope? (4) How do these verses show God's love for His people? [Resources needed: a copy of the Lesson Background and the commentary on verses 1, 2.]

Group B: Promises for the Early Christians. Read Isaiah 40:3-5. Use the reference material provided to discuss these questions: (1) What kind of work was done to make a "straight highway" for Jesus? (2) How might the fulfillment of this and other Old Testament prophecies have given the early Christians confidence in God's promises? [Resources needed: a copy of the Introduction and the commentary on verses 3-5.]

Group C: Promises for All Believers. Read Isaiah 40:6-8, 25, 26, 29-31. Use the reference material provided to discuss these questions: (1) In contrast with vegetation and people, what is the nature of God's Word? (2) How do the works of creation give us confidence in God's power and uniqueness? (3) What are God's promises for those who are feeling helpless? (4) Why should we learn to wait on the Lord? [Resources needed: a copy of the commentary on verses 6-8, 25, 26, 29-31.]

Into Life

Alternative 1: Discussion. Distribute copies of the following scenario to the previously formed groups. Say, "Read through this scenario and find a verse or verses from today's text that might provide guidance to the person described. Decide on one way you could introduce the verse to the person. Be prepared to share conclusions with the class as a whole."

Collin has never been a believer, but has recently started attending a Bible study with a Christian friend. His opinion is that the Bible is an outdated book full of irrelevant information that has no use in today's world.

Alternative 2: Prayer. Distribute copies of the activity Soar Like Eagles from the reproducible page. Have your learners work individually to write in a current problem and a verse from today's text that gives them comfort and hope. Form learners into pairs to share their burdens (if appropriate) and pray for each other.

God Gives Strength

THE LORD IS OUR GOD

BACKGROUND SCRIPTURE: Isaiah 41:1–42:9
PRINTED TEXT: Isaiah 41:8-10, 17-20; 42:1-4, 9

ISAIAH 41:8-10, 17-20

8 But thou, Israel, art my servant, Jacob whom I have chosen, the seed of Abraham my friend.

9 Thou whom I have taken from the ends of the earth, and called thee from the chief men thereof, and said unto thee, Thou art my servant; I have chosen thee, and not cast thee away.

10 Fear thou not; for I am with thee: be not dismayed; for I am thy God: I will strengthen thee; yea, I will help thee; yea, I will uphold thee with the right hand of my righteousness.

. . . .

17 When the poor and needy seek water, and there is none, and their tongue faileth for thirst, I the LORD will hear them, I the God of Israel will not forsake them.

18 I will open rivers in high places, and fountains in the midst of the valleys: I will make the wilderness a pool of water, and the dry land springs of water.

19 I will plant in the wilderness the cedar, the shittah tree, and the myrtle, and the oil tree; I will set in the desert the fir tree, and the pine, and the box tree together:

20 That they may see, and know, and consider, and understand together, that the hand of the LORD hath done this, and the Holy One of Israel hath created it.

ISAIAH 42:1-4, 9

1 Behold my servant, whom I uphold; mine elect, in whom my soul delighteth; I have put my spirit upon him: he shall bring forth judgment to the Gentiles.

2 He shall not cry, nor lift up, nor cause his voice to be heard in the street.

3 A bruised reed shall he not break, and the smoking flax shall he not quench: he shall bring forth judgment unto truth.

4 He shall not fail nor be discouraged, till he have set judgment in the earth: and the isles shall wait for his law.

. . . .

9 Behold, the former things are come to pass, and new things do I declare: before they spring forth I tell you of them.

KEY VERSE

Fear thou not; for I am with thee: be not dismayed; for I am thy God. —**Isaiah 41:10**

ASSURING HOPE

Unit 1: Comfort for God's People
LESSONS 1–5

LESSON AIMS

After participating in this lesson, each student should:

1. Tell how the work of the Lord and His servant brings assurance to the people.

2. Explain why Jesus is the fulfillment of the servant of the Lord prophecies.

3. Write a prayer that asks for God's comforting presence to allay fears that beset his or her life.

LESSON OUTLINE

Introduction

A. Unneeded Gifts

Buying gifts for friends and family can be an unwelcome chore. Why is this? At least one reason is that we dislike giving a gift that may end up being unappreciated. When a gift fails to please its recipient, we feel we have wasted our time, money, and effort. Worse, we may feel that rejection of a gift is, in a small way, a rejection of us.

I have a tongue-in-cheek personal rule for this: if I do not know what to get someone, I get something I like. That way, at least one person will like the gift! I learned this as a youngster from my friend Mike. He did not know what to get his sister for Christmas one year, so he gave her a left-handed baseball mitt he really liked. It helped that Mike was the only leftie in his family and that his sister didn't play baseball. He knew that at least one person would use that gift!

On the other side, we have all received unneeded gifts. A man might get another tie when he already has dozens. A woman might receive another kitchen gadget to add to her drawerful.

The Bible teaches that our God is a giving God, and His gifts are never unneeded. They might be unwanted or underappreciated, but not unneeded. God is the giver of all good and perfect gifts (James 1:17). If we do not want or appreciate what God gives us, the problem lies with us, not with the gift. In today's lesson, Isaiah presents this giving side of God in a twofold way. He sees God as the one who gives us a role, a task; in this, God gives purpose to our lives. Isaiah also sees God as the one who gives us the resources to fulfill our roles. He is both sustainer and provider for those who serve Him. He is our Lord and Master, the one whom we serve. But He is also our source, the rock that anchors and supports us (Psalm 18:2).

B. Lesson Background

Isaiah's ministry as a prophet of the Lord lasted more than 40 years. He prophesied under at least four kings of Judah (Isaiah 1:1). This was a period in Israel's history dominated by the Assyrian menace from the north. Assyrian activities during Isaiah's lifetime included an invasion in about 740 BC

(2 Kings 15:19). Assyria eventually destroyed the northern kingdom, Israel, in 722 BC and deported her people (15:29). Jerusalem itself was threatened by the Assyrians, surviving only because of God's miraculous rescue in 701 BC (19:36).

The second half of the book of Isaiah, from chapter 40 onward, has the perspective of a nation that has been through terrible crisis and yet survived. The southern kingdom, Judah, knew what could happen because she had seen her sister nation to the north, Israel, wiped off the map.

Judah had experienced the terror of foreign invasion firsthand. In this context, Isaiah began to reveal the future that God had planned for the nation of Judah. (Note: Sometimes the Bible uses the term *Israel* to refer to the totality of the Jewish people, and sometimes it uses *Israel* to refer only to the northern kingdom as distinct from the southern kingdom, *Judah*. Context usually makes clear which usage is intended.)

I. The Lord Elects
(ISAIAH 41:8-10)
A. Servant Selector (vv. 8, 9)

8. But thou, Israel, art my servant, Jacob whom I have chosen, the seed of Abraham my friend.

There are three names in this verse, each accompanied by a descriptive tag. But all apply to the people of Israel, Isaiah's people. Isaiah uses the national name *Israel*, the name given to Jacob after his experience of wrestling with a man whom we believe was an angel (Genesis 32:28). The word *Israel* means "God prevails." This reminds us that the function of the nation of Israel was to be God's servant, empowered to do His will.

The people of Israel have been given a covenant with God and are intended to be a "light of the Gentiles" (Isaiah 42:6). This is God's purpose in choosing Israel as His people. God is not working to fulfill national ambitions or maintain traditions. Rather, He is protecting and enabling Israel so that it can be His servant, His instrument for making himself known to all peoples (see 49:6). For this reason, Isaiah 40–66 has frequent references to the Lord's "servant" (see 41:9; 49:3). In its

ultimate sense, however, this concept is expanded and fulfilled not by the nation of Israel, but by the Messiah, Jesus (see Matthew 12:18).

Isaiah also describes his people as *Jacob whom I have chosen*. Genesis tells how Jacob was chosen over his older brother, Esau, to be the father of the nation of Israel. Likewise, the nation that came from Jacob did not earn a position of favor based on merit. Rather, they had been selected by the Lord out of all the nations to be an instrument for fulfilling God's plan for human redemption.

Finally, the people are called the *seed of Abraham*. This is a reminder of their heritage. The relationship between the Lord and Israel is not a business partnership or military alliance entered into by equals by mutual agreement. It is instead based on the plan, purpose, and affection of the sovereign God.

9. Thou whom I have taken from the ends of the earth, and called thee from the chief men thereof, and said unto thee, Thou art my servant; I have chosen thee, and not cast thee away.

God's selection of Israel now receives fuller explanation. Israel has been chosen out of the vast field of all nations, for God has surveyed *the ends of the earth*. Furthermore, this people-group has been chosen after consideration of the finest earth has to offer: its *chief men*.

The words of God reinforce what is said in the previous verse: Israel was chosen by the Lord to serve Him. Now, however, a new detail is added, for God promises not to *cast thee away*. God's choice of Israel is not a short-term appointment. There are no qualifiers here. God simply promises never to

HOW TO SAY IT

acacia	uh-*kay*-shuh.
Assyria	Uh-*sear*-ee-uh.
Esau	*Ee*-saw.
Hezekiah	Hez-ih-*kye*-uh.
Jacob	*Jay*-kub.
Malachi	*Mal*-uh-kye.
Manasseh	Muh-*nass*-uh.
Messiah	Meh-*sigh*-uh.
messianic	mess-ee-*an*-ick.

abandon His commitment to Israel. Although it is not stated here, we know from history that there is a good reason for this: the Messiah is to be ushered into the world through Israel.

❧ CALLED TO BE SERVANTS ❧

The world has a long history of looking down on those who serve others. The phrase *indentured servant* describes a type of servanthood that goes back at least to Old Testament times. Such a servant was, in effect, a slave to the one to whom a debt was owed. The kind of slavery that was known in the Western world from the 1600s to the 1800s (and is still found in many parts of the world today) is especially notorious.

Jesus changed the outlook on servanthood when He came as God's ultimate servant. As a result, there are many organizations today that promote servanthood in the name of Christ. The focus may range from disaster relief to the problems brought on by poverty, warfare, or disease in many regions of the world. Other agencies offer humanitarian aid from a secular concern for education, sanitation, and medical advancement.

Our impetus for servanthood as Christians originates with God and His example. Through His supreme act of service—the incarnation of His Son—He also calls us to be servants to the world (Mark 9:35).   —C. R. B.

B. Strong Sustainer (v. 10)

10. Fear thou not; for I am with thee: be not dismayed; for I am thy God: I will strengthen thee; yea, I will help thee; yea, I will uphold thee with the right hand of my righteousness.

This verse gives a double command and a triple promise to Israel. The people are commanded not to fear or be dismayed. The sense of dismay here is to look around with anxiousness. They are not to live in dread of the future, for they have the Lord, the master of the universe, as their God.

Furthermore, Israel is promised that God will strengthen, help, and uphold them. God vows not to abandon them or to stand back and watch them flounder. God is present in their affairs. This is not an arbitrary display of power, however. It is the righteousness of God that drives these promises.

II. The Lord Provides
(ISAIAH 41:17-20)
A. Water in the Drought (vv. 17, 18)

17. When the poor and needy seek water, and there is none, and their tongue faileth for thirst, I the LORD will hear them, I the God of Israel will not forsake them.

People have always faced water shortages. If weather patterns do not produce regular rain in a timely manner, a drought is the result. This is more of a problem in cultures that are not technologically advanced. Sometimes deep wells may be the only source of water. If these are privatized and the water is hoarded by the wealthy, the less fortunate are left with no water resources.

In times of extreme drought, it is not uncommon (even today) for people to walk miles each day for water. This is a life-and-death situation. Israel is assured that *the Lord will hear them* in a time of need. The people may be in distress, but they are not abandoned (compare Deuteronomy 8:15). This is true even in times when the Lord uses drought as a punishment.

18. I will open rivers in high places, and fountains in the midst of the valleys: I will make the wilderness a pool of water, and the dry land springs of water.

Isaiah pictures God's abundant provision of water in a paradoxical way. We usually expect rivers in the valleys but fountains (meaning "springs") in the mountains, not the other way around. We don't expect open pools of water in the desert wilderness, and we anticipate no water sources at all in *the dry land* just by definition. God's provisions are surprising and generous. As He provides the needy with more water than they can use, His grace to Israel is beyond what they deserve or expect. So it is with God's people today.

What Do You Think?

What was a time when God has provided spiritual water in "a dry place" for you?

Talking Points for Your Discussion

- During a severe illness
- During a family crisis
- When enticed by sin

B. Trees in the Desert (vv. 19, 20)

19. I will plant in the wilderness the cedar, the shittah tree, and the myrtle, and the oil tree; I will set in the desert the fir tree, and the pine, and the box tree together.

The wilderness is a barren region (see Leviticus 16:22) and is generally defined by a lack of trees. Yet the Lord promises to plant the wilderness with a variety of prized trees. We are not sure of the exact identification of all of these trees, so there are differences in some of the translations of this verse. We can see two groups, though.

First is the grouping *cedar, shittah* (probably the acacia), *myrtle,* and *oil tree* (probably the olive tree). These are sometimes found in the wild, but often cultivated for wood, fruit, or both. Isaiah presents a future where such trees are not only found around the cities, but flourish in the wilderness.

The second set is a list of evergreen trees: *fir, pine,* and *box* (probably the cypress). These are normally found in the hills, not in the barren desert. This description contributes further to Isaiah's promise of God's overwhelming, unfettered, and unexpected provisioning in Israel's future.

20. That they may see, and know, and consider, and understand together, that the hand

GOD GIVES US STRENGTH

Visual for Lessons 1 & 2

Point to this visual as you introduce the discussion question associated with verse 18.

of the LORD hath done this, and the Holy One of Israel hath created it.

God will do the things of verses 18, 19 in such a way that Israel cannot question their source. They will *see* (physically experience), *know* (come to a realization), *consider* (ponder and think through), and *understand* (make sense of) these striking phenomena. The only possible conclusion will be that *the Lord hath done this.* Such acts are those in which the Creator of the universe has helped His chosen people in their distress in a mighty way.

What Do You Think?

How do we make sure we give God the credit when great things happen?

Talking Points for Your Discussion

- On a personal level
- With regard to your church
- On a national level
- Psalms 71:19; 106:21; 126:2, 3

We are reminded here of the ultimate fulfillment of this type of prophecy: God's provision for His people in a Savior, Jesus the Messiah. In Him, the grace of God is lavished on a sinful and needy people, people dying of spiritual thirst. He becomes the chief cornerstone of God's new spiritual temple, and those who observe Him must come to the inevitable conclusion that "this is the Lord's doing" (Psalm 118:23, quoted in Matthew 21:42).

III. The Lord Determines

(ISAIAH 42:1-4, 9)

A. Servant of Judgment (vv. 1-4)

1. Behold my servant, whom I uphold; mine elect, in whom my soul delighteth; I have put my Spirit upon him: he shall bring forth judgment to the Gentiles.

For the third time in our lesson, Isaiah employs the image of the servant of the Lord. It is in this chapter that Isaiah shifts his focus from the nation of Israel to the ultimate servant of the Lord. In so doing, Isaiah casts a prophetic vision about a key person in God's plans. This helps us understand that while the ancient nation of Israel is intended to be God's special servant, its role in this context is a preparatory pattern of the Messiah. This is a person chosen by God, *mine elect,* and a person who brings delight and joy to God. God delights when His servants act with love, justice, and righteousness (see Jeremiah 9:24). His servant will epitomize these and other godly characteristics.

This future servant is projected to have two important functions. First, He is the one to bring God's Spirit in a new and dynamic fashion. Jesus claims this role when He reads Scripture in Nazareth (Luke 4:16-21). Jesus teaches and does many things, but one of the things that impresses those who observe Him is the mighty presence of God's Spirit in His life (see Luke 4:1, 14; Acts 10:38).

The second function of this messianic servant is to *bring forth judgment to the Gentiles.* This role of the Messiah as judge is found many times in the Bible (example: Acts 17:31; compare Isaiah 2:4). However, the sense of judgment here is not harsh condemnation, but of true justice. This is seen as a blessing, an enlightenment for those who do not have the law of God as Israel does (compare Isaiah 9:2). They will understand that God is holy and that wickedness will not go unpunished.

2. He shall not cry, nor lift up, nor cause his voice to be heard in the street.

Isaiah presents the Servant-Messiah in unusual terms of humility and gentleness in our next two verses. He will not be one who purposely calls attention to himself by shouting in the street (contrast Matthew 6:2).

3. A bruised reed shall he not break, and the smoking flax shall he not quench: he shall bring forth judgment unto truth.

Similarly, the Messiah will treat people with compassion and tenderness (compare Matthew 9:36; Luke 7:13). Isaiah employs two striking metaphors to illustrate this compassionate servant. First, He will not even break *a bruised reed;* this describes a damaged plant stalk, a condition that might result in the death of the plant. Our expression, "He wouldn't hurt a fly" is similar. This is not about plants or insects, however. It is about people. In other words, the Messiah's function is to comfort the oppressed, not to crush them. By His ministry, the bruised reed (or person) may be healed (compare Malachi 4:2).

> **What Do You Think?**
> As servants of the ultimate servant, Jesus Christ, what are some circumstances that require us to display His tenderness and compassion rather than confrontation?
> *Talking Points for Your Discussion*
> - Matthew 25:37-40
> - Matthew 3:7-10; 23:13-36

Smoking flax is an image of a very crude way of giving a little light to the house after dark. Poor people cannot afford candles or oil, so they use rushlights, a plant stalk (like flax) soaked in animal fat. This is a picture of the poor person with a weak but still burning hope. The function of the Messiah will not be to snuff out this hope, but to fan it into full flame. The fact that this imagery fits the Messiah is confirmed in Matthew 12:17-21, which quotes this section of verses.

❧ *A DIFFERENT KIND OF LEADER* ❧

The Holocaust, which took place under the Hitler regime in Nazi Germany, resulted in the deaths of six million Jews. Stalin engaged in a similar campaign in the same era of history. There were thousands of forced-labor camps in Russia and Siberia, and Stalin was responsible for the deaths of millions.

Genocide did not stop with the deaths of Hitler and Stalin. Following those regimes, 1.7 million people were killed in Cambodia (one-fifth of the nation's population) in 1975–79; 800,000 were butchered in Rwanda's tribal violence of 1994; and "ethnic cleansing" resulted in 200,000 murders in Bosnia-Herzegovina in 1992–95.

This is the world's way of dealing with the problem of "undesirable" people: get rid of them. God's servant Jesus takes an entirely different approach. This is illustrated by the metaphors of tenderness, gentleness, and compassion that Isaiah uses in telling of the Messiah's character. Do we who follow the Messiah imitate His concern for the world's suffering, unsaved multitudes?   —C. R. B.

4. He shall not fail nor be discouraged, till he have set judgment in the earth: and the isles shall wait for his law.

The mission of the coming Servant-Messiah simply will not be thwarted. He will never give up nor will His opponents be able to stop Him. This is because the Messiah is not acting alone but is carrying out the will and plan of the Lord. God's judgment (justice) will prevail on the earth. Even those dwelling in the most remote regions, *the isles,* will be confronted with the righteous law of the Lord. His justice will extend everywhere.

B. Controller of Destiny (v. 9)

9. Behold, the former things are come to pass, and new things do I declare: before they spring forth I tell you of them.

This remarkable verse helps us understand the nature of prophecy and Isaiah's role as a prophetic voice. Isaiah clearly knows that other things must *come to pass* first before these stirring prophecies are fulfilled. Then the *new things* will come. But these should not be a complete surprise, for this new era of salvation is foretold by men like Isaiah. The messianic age that he looks forward to is a deliberate plan of God, so much so that God can reveal details about it before it is inaugurated.

When the Christmas season comes around, we should remember that the birth of the Messiah has been both long awaited and long expected. Those who understand that Jesus fulfills the prophecies of Isaiah and other prophets know that He does so according to God's preordained plan.

Conclusion
A. Chosen to Serve

In 1884, General William T. Sherman was being considered as a possible U.S. presidential candidate. This veteran of America's Civil War had no interest in this, knowing that he had neither the skills nor the temperament to be a successful politician. Thus Sherman famously declared that if drafted, he would not run; if nominated, he would not accept; if elected, he would not serve.

Sherman understood better than some of his contemporaries that election to public office was accompanied with the expectation of competent service. That was an era where some understood it differently. Many who were elected or appointed to office viewed it as an opportunity to enrich themselves through graft and other corrupt practices. They acted as if they were elected to *be* served.

The ancient Israelites occupied a special place in God's plans. They were intended to provide the moral and religious foundation for God's revelation of His Messiah. The nation was to show the world that there is one God, not many. They were to be examples of service to the one true God. The record in this regard was mixed. There were kings like Hezekiah who "did that which was right" (2 Kings 18:3), but there were many kings like Hezekiah's son, Manasseh, who "did that which was evil" (2 Kings 21:2). Kings in the latter category forgot the covenant that Israel had with God.

We, today, as the chosen people of God also have a covenant with Him. This is the new covenant of grace and salvation purchased by the blood of Jesus our Savior. He has promised to protect and empower His people. Our status should not be abused. It should result in yielding to God's will and serving Him.

B. Prayer

Father, we marvel at Your grace, Your concern for us. We thank You for Your protection and provision and, most of all, for Your greatest gift: Jesus Your Son. We pray in His name. Amen.

C. Thought to Remember
You are called to serve the Lord God Almighty.

INVOLVEMENT LEARNING

Some of the activities below are also found in the helpful student book, Adult Bible Class.
Don't forget to download the free reproducible page from www.standardlesson.com to enhance your lesson!

Into the Lesson

Open class by saying, "Assume that you have less than two weeks to prepare for a major event (Christmas, wedding, etc.). How afraid are you? Turn to the person next to you and tell him or her your greatest fear or anxiety related to not having everything ready." After a few minutes, say, "Of course, there are things in life that are much worse than not being ready for an important event. Today's memory verse tells us that we don't have to be afraid of anything, because the Lord is our God. Let's take a few minutes to memorize it."

Write the text of Isaiah 41:10 on the board. Then have the class read it in unison twice. Call on someone to select two words from the verse for you to erase. After you do so, have the class say the verse again. Repeat this process until all the words are gone.

Into the Word

Ask three learners to read aloud the following passages from the lesson text: Isaiah 41:8-10; Isaiah 41:17-20; Isaiah 42:1-4, 9. Using the lesson commentary for Isaiah 41:8, 9 and Isaiah 42:1, prepare a brief lecture on how the nation of ancient Israel is the "servant" referred to in 41:8, 9, while the Messiah is the "servant" in 42:1-4, 9. *Option:* Download the reproducible page and have learners complete the Who Is My Servant? activity.

For a closer look at the Scripture text, have learners form into groups of four to six and complete the following activity. Prepare a handout in advance that has the two column headings *People Say* (left column) and *God Says* (right column). In the left column, list the following items: 1. "I am scared to death." 2. "How can I know there is a Creator God who cares about me?" 3. "My boss is loud, obnoxious, and unfair. Are all authority figures like that?" 4. "I'm nobody special." 5. "I'm poor and have no clean water." 6. "I'm so discouraged by my failures. Whom can I look to as an

example?" 7. "I'm weak and helpless." 8. "I've been treated so unfairly. Where can I go for justice?" 9. "I loved someone, and he [or she] rejected me." 10. "I have no shelter and no resources. Can anyone help me?"

Say, "Search the verses of today's text and complete the right-hand column by writing in statements (either quotes or paraphrases) that God might say to each person. Also include the number of the verse(s) you used. Try to use all the verses."

Let your learners know that there can be a variety of acceptable answers. For your reference, here are some possible responses: 1. "Don't be afraid; I am with you" (41:10); 2. "I want you to understand that I am your Creator, and I will take care of you" (41:20); 3. "My servant (my Son), who has all authority, is quiet and gentle" (41:2, 3); 4. "I have chosen you to be my servant" (41:8); 5. "I can make rivers, springs, and pools appear anywhere" (41:17, 18); 6. "My Servant never fails nor is discouraged" (42:4); 7. "I will strengthen, help, and uphold you" (41:10); 8. "My Servant judges fairly; He provides justice" (42:1); 9. "I will never reject you or throw you away!" (41:9); 10. "I can make any resources that you need (such as cedar, olive, and pine trees) available for you" (41:19).

Into Life

Have the class remain in groups. Distribute the following questions for them to discuss. 1. "Whom do you ask for help when you have a problem that you can't handle yourself? Why that person? 2. When did you experience a problem that was so tough that no one seemed able to help? 3. At that time did you ask God for help? If so, what help did He provide?

Conclude by having learners complete individually the activity Praying God's Words Back to Him from the reproducible page. After a few minutes, ask for a volunteer to pray his or her prayer for the class.

The Lord Is Our God

A Child
Is Born

BACKGROUND SCRIPTURE: Isaiah 9:1-7; 11:1-9; Matthew 1:18-25
PRINTED TEXT: Isaiah 9:6, 7; 11:1-8; Matthew 1:21-23

ISAIAH 9:6, 7

6 For unto us a child is born, unto us a son is given: and the government shall be upon his shoulder: and his name shall be called Wonderful, Counsellor, The mighty God, The everlasting Father, The Prince of Peace.

7 Of the increase of his government and peace there shall be no end, upon the throne of David, and upon his kingdom, to order it, and to establish it with judgment and with justice from henceforth even for ever. The zeal of the LORD of hosts will perform this.

ISAIAH 11:1-8

1 And there shall come forth a rod out of the stem of Jesse, and a Branch shall grow out of his roots:

2 And the spirit of the LORD shall rest upon him, the spirit of wisdom and understanding, the spirit of counsel and might, the spirit of knowledge and of the fear of the LORD;

3 And shall make him of quick understanding in the fear of the LORD: and he shall not judge after the sight of his eyes, neither reprove after the hearing of his ears:

4 But with righteousness shall he judge the poor, and reprove with equity for the meek of the earth: and he shall smite the earth with the rod of his mouth, and with the breath of his lips shall he slay the wicked.

5 And righteousness shall be the girdle of his loins, and faithfulness the girdle of his reins.

6 The wolf also shall dwell with the lamb, and the leopard shall lie down with the kid; and the calf and the young lion and the fatling together; and a little child shall lead them.

7 And the cow and the bear shall feed; their young ones shall lie down together: and the lion shall eat straw like the ox.

8 And the sucking child shall play on the hole of the asp, and the weaned child shall put his hand on the cockatrice' den.

MATTHEW 1:21-23

21 And she shall bring forth a son, and thou shalt call his name JESUS: for he shall save his people from their sins.

22 Now all this was done, that it might be fulfilled which was spoken of the Lord by the prophet, saying,

23 Behold, a virgin shall be with child, and shall bring forth a son, and they shall call his name Emmanuel, which being interpreted is, God with us.

KEY VERSE

Righteousness shall be the girdle of his loins, and faithfulness the girdle of his reins. —Isaiah 11:5

ASSURING HOPE

Unit 1: Comfort for God's People
LESSONS 1–5

LESSON AIMS

After participating in this lesson, each student will be able to:

1. List some of the titles and descriptions of Jesus.

2. Compare and contrast the spiritual and secular concepts of "peace."

3. Tell how Christ has brought peace to his or her life.

LESSON OUTLINE

Introduction

A. Shalom

Most of us are familiar with the term *shalom*, generally translated "peace." To think of *shalom* as merely "peace," though, misses its richness. We see the full beauty of this word in today's lesson text.

We tend to think of peace as being the absence of hostilities. If two nations are not having a war, they are at peace, even if their troops are on high alert. If a husband and wife are not fighting, they are at peace, even if there is deep animosity in their relationship. This one-dimensional view ignores the presence of profound, underlying tension: a war is waiting to happen. When the Bible speaks of peace as given by God, it means more than a lack of fighting. It refers to a healthy, reconciled relationship. It means that the things that cause conflict have been resolved. There is no more need or desire to fight. A situation of peace as granted by God is a promise for future health and prosperity (compare Judges 6:23).

Peace is a major topic in Isaiah. The prophet can speak of a "perfect peace," which can come only from God (Isaiah 26:3). Isaiah often looks forward to a time of peace and healing as part of God's plan for the future (55:12; 57:19; contrast 48:22). Isaiah's future era is a period both of prosperity and the flourishing of righteousness (32:17). All things that cause a breakdown in the peace between God and humans will be gone.

This universal peace will never be the result of all the warring parties of the world working out peace treaties. It will come when all are under the rule of the Prince of Peace and are like-minded in their allegiance to Him. Then, and only then, will the nations "learn war" no more (Isaiah 2:4).

B. Lesson Background

Some of the earliest Greek philosophers believed that war was inevitable and that nations at war was the norm rather than the exception. Heraclitus of Ephesus, one such philosopher, wrote about 200 years after Isaiah. Heraclitus summed up the thinking of many before and after him when he said, "War is the father and king of all." Heraclitus is most known for his theory that everything is in

A Child Is Born

a state of flux, constantly changing. The only constant, for him, is change. "You cannot step into the same river twice," because it will have changed between your steppings. This dynamic view of the universe is reflected in his understanding of war. For Heraclitus, nations could not live in static, peaceful coexistence. They constantly bickered, postured, and warred.

To a large degree, Isaiah and his countrymen would have agreed with these observations. They had kings who used brief times of peace to rearm and prepare for war. They experienced the mighty, marauding armies of Egypt and Assyria marching across their lands. There seemed to be no other existence than war or the threat of war.

This brutal geopolitical situation continued up until the time of Jesus. In the decades before His birth in Bethlehem, the Mediterranean basin was rocked repeatedly by the foreign and civil wars of the Romans. In 27 BC, these wars ended when the great-nephew of Julius Caesar emerged triumphant and began to reign as Caesar Augustus.

A peace then spread over the Roman territories, including Palestine. This is known as the *Pax Romana*, the Roman Peace. It lasted for about 200 years. Yet it was an uneasy peace that was enforced by the stationing of Roman legions throughout the empire—a peace enforced by military threat. It was marred by various rebellions such as the Jewish Revolt of AD 66–73, which resulted in the destruction of Jerusalem and its temple.

Our world is not much different today. Countries still have large armies and arsenals of weapons. War can, and does, erupt with little warning (compare Matthew 24:6). True peace will come only from God's intervention, from the universal reign of His chosen Messiah, the Prince of Peace.

I. Peaceful Prince
(ISAIAH 9:6, 7)
A. The Kingdom of Peace (v. 6)

6. For unto us a child is born, unto us a son is given: and the government shall be upon his shoulder: and his name shall be called Wonderful, Counsellor, The mighty God, The everlasting Father, The Prince of Peace.

HOW TO SAY IT

Bethlehem	*Beth*-lih-hem.
Caesar Augustus	*See*-zer Aw-*gus*-tus.
Ephesus	*Ef*-uh-sus.
Heraclitus	Her-uh-*klee*-tus.
Emmanuel	Eh-*man*-you-el.
Julius Caesar	*Joo*-lee-us *See*-zer.
Mediterranean	*Med*-uh-tuh-*ray*-nee-un.
Messiah	Meh-*sigh*-uh.
Pax Romana *(Latin)*	Paks Row-*mah*-nah.
shalom *(Hebrew)*	shah-*lome*.

This is a favorite verse of the Christmas season, giving a prophetic taste of the coming Messiah. Isaiah proclaims a coming child, meaning someone yet to be born from his perspective. This person is to be given as a provision of God's plan for His people. This extraordinary person will bear the burden of governing the people as part of God's intended purposes.

Isaiah follows this announcement with four marvelous descriptions of this one to come. First, He will be known as the *Wonderful Counsellor*. Some have separated these into two names, but Isaiah most likely intended us to hear him speak of a *Counsellor* who is *Wonderful*.

We have weakened the meaning of *wonderful* in the English language. Today this word means something like "really, really good." The original intent, though, is something that causes a jaw-dropping sense of astonishment. When one experiences the wonderful in this sense, one knows that this is a miraculous work of God Almighty (see Isaiah 29:14). To combine this with the function of counselor means that Isaiah foresees someone who knows all the questions and has all the answers. This can be only God himself (compare 25:1).

The second prophetic designation amplifies this by saying the coming child will be *The mighty God*. The descriptive word *mighty* is drawn from the world of war heroes (compare Genesis 10:8). We might liken this to our term *invincible*, the one who cannot be defeated. The coming child will not be bested by any army, either human or demonic, in the reign of His universal government (see Isaiah 42:13).

Third, the child is to be given the title of *The everlasting Father,* identifying Him even more specifically with the Lord God of Israel. The concept of eternity was difficult to grasp in Isaiah's day and remains so for us. The eternality of God, however, is a characteristic that sets Him apart in a decisive way (see Isaiah 57:15). The Old Testament rarely uses the term *Father* to refer to God (for a few places where it does, see Psalm 68:5; 89:26; Malachi 2:10). It remains for Jesus to teach humans that God is our Father in a universal, loving way. It is to our heavenly Father that we are taught to pray for His gracious daily provisions (Matthew 6:11). Isaiah prophesies that, in a way that is beyond our complete understanding, the child is to be the embodiment of the Father.

Fourth, the child to come will be *The Prince of Peace.* This is not *prince* in the sense of a junior king or a king-in-waiting. Rather, it is *prince* in the sense of ruler of a people, a virtual synonym with "king" or "monarch." Jesus' dominion will be characterized by peace, not war. His agenda will be reconciliation and *shalom.*

What Do You Think?
In what specific ways has Jesus been the Prince of Peace in your life?
Talking Points for Your Discussion
- In calming a certain storm of life
- In calming you rather than calming a life storm
- Luke 12:51; John 14:27; 16:33

B. The Unending Peace (v. 7)

7. Of the increase of his government and peace there shall be no end, upon the throne of David, and upon his kingdom, to order it, and to establish it with judgment and with justice from henceforth even for ever. The zeal of the LORD of hosts will perform this.

It is easy to imagine that Isaiah's original hearers think that he is talking about a coming king who will reign in Jerusalem. To be sure, this will be an extraordinary ruler. The coming child is to be in a different category from any earthly monarch. His reign is to be characterized in five ways that no normal human ruler can ever measure up to.

First, His reign is to be endlessly increasing, as opposed to the rise and fall of empires throughout history. Second, it is to be endlessly peaceful, never at war or preparing for war. Third, it is to be tied to the most beloved ruler of Israel, King David. Fourth, it is to be established on true justice, not on the "might makes right" philosophy. Fifth, its existence and increase are guaranteed by *the zeal of the Lord.* This is to be a primary matter for the all-powerful God of Israel. Such zeal cannot be thwarted by anyone or anything.

What Do You Think?
How does the fact that the Lord's kingdom is one of eternal peace affect how you respond to various situations in life?
Talking Points for Your Discussion
- In minor situations (rude drivers, bad service)
- In major situations (being physically assaulted)

❧ THE HOPE OF PEACE ❧

Frances, the wife of poet Henry Wadsworth Longfellow, died tragically on July 10, 1861. Her dress had caught fire the previous day in an accident involving a candle.

Longfellow sank into a depression. It deepened late in 1863 when he received word that his son Charles had been wounded in battle during the American Civil War. Finally, as the war was nearing its end, Longfellow's spirits seemed to improve. For Christmas 1864, Longfellow penned the lines of "I Heard the Bells on Christmas Day," one of the most famous Christmas carols. Part of the carol tells of the tragedy of war, but also of the hope that Christmas brings:

And in despair I bowed my head:
"There is no peace on earth," I said.
"For hate is strong, / And mocks the song
Of peace on earth, good-will to men."
Then pealed the bells more loud and deep:
"God is not dead; nor doth he sleep!
The wrong shall fail, / The right prevail,
With peace on earth, good-will to men."

May that be the message that is ever in our hearts! May the Prince of Peace reign among us!
—C. R. B.

II. Blessed Branch
(ISAIAH 11:1-8)

A. Spiritual Authority (vv. 1-3a)

1. And there shall come forth a rod out of the stem of Jesse, and a Branch shall grow out of his roots.

Isaiah's vision of the Messiah in chapter 9 is of a perfect ruler. Here in chapter 11, Isaiah uses a different way of describing the coming one: as *a Branch* growing from *the stem of Jesse*. This ties the Messiah to King David, the physical son of a man named Jesse (compare Luke 2:4).

2, 3a. And the spirit of the LORD shall rest upon him, the spirit of wisdom and understanding, the spirit of counsel and might, the spirit of knowledge and of the fear of the LORD; and shall make him of quick understanding in the fear of the LORD.

The branch prophecy focuses on personal attributes. The coming one will be endowed with the *spirit of the Lord,* an infallible guide. The result will be an astonishing package of spiritual maturity: *wisdom, understanding, counsel, might,* and *knowledge.* Isaiah reminds us here of the wisdom tradition of Israel as found in the book of Proverbs. That book teaches that these attributes originate in a person's *fear of the Lord* (see Proverbs 1:7; 9:10; compare Isaiah 33:6).

The *fear of the Lord* is not lingering terror of God that causes us to hide and avoid Him. Rather, it is a profound reverence for our Creator. It is a recognition of the vast difference between mortals and the master of the universe. It does not prevent us from loving God and knowing that He loves us, because in so doing we appreciate the great gulf that is bridged for our salvation (Romans 5:8).

What Do You Think?

How does the fact that Jesus has the spirit of wisdom, understanding, etc. influence you?

Talking Points for Your Discussion

- Regarding your decisions and lifestyle (see Proverbs 16:33; James 3:13)
- Regarding the way you treat the Word of God (see 2 Timothy 3:15)

B. Judicial Perfection (vv. 3b-5)

3b. And he shall not judge after the sight of his eyes, neither reprove after the hearing of his ears.

The fear of the Lord brings a sense of accountability. This is sharpened by the realization that the divine judge is not prone to subjective mood swings. There is an objective standard for judgment based on His revealed will.

4. But with righteousness shall he judge the poor, and reprove with equity for the meek of the earth: and he shall smite the earth with the rod of his mouth, and with the breath of his lips shall he slay the wicked.

The Messiah will not be influenced by a person's economic status, etc. This judge, God's holy branch, will be a champion of the poor and oppressed in their constant battle against the wicked.

The Messiah's power will not be in armies, but in a message. The prophet gives a double description of this concept: *the rod of his mouth* and *the breath of his lips.* This is Spirit-empowered proclamation, the gospel news of peace and of the reign of God (Isaiah 52:7). Earthly sources of power will fail, but the Spirit of the Lord provides inexhaustible power to the Messiah (see Zechariah 4:6).

5. And righteousness shall be the girdle of his loins, and faithfulness the girdle of his reins.

This verse depicts the Messiah in terms of spiritual clothing (compare Ephesians 6:14). The girdle around the waist is the item of clothing that holds everything tight and ready for action. For a man wearing a loose, robe-like garment, the hems will be pulled up and tucked into this belt so he can engage in strenuous activity. This leaves the legs unencumbered, minimizing the possibility of tripping.

For the Messiah, everything is held together by righteousness and faithfulness. This is a consistency of message based on the character of God himself. There is no false note here, no change or modification based on future circumstances.

C. Adversarial Reconciliation (vv. 6-8)

6. The wolf also shall dwell with the lamb, and the leopard shall lie down with the kid; and the calf and the young lion and the fatling together; and a little child shall lead them.

The messianic peace is portrayed as a cessation of the violent patterns of the natural world. Isaiah foresees well-known predators from the animal kingdom in peaceful coexistence with animals that are normally their prey. The young pastoral animals mentioned have no effective natural defenses against aggressive and hungry predators. Most surprisingly, this mixed flock will be shepherded by a little child, not by an experienced shepherd who is armed with sling and staff.

7. And the cow and the bear shall feed; their young ones shall lie down together: and the lion shall eat straw like the ox.

The underlying tension of the animal world is based on the instinctive desire of some animals to survive by killing and eating other animals. This "kill or be killed" mentality also characterizes the world of many people, who see life as a survival test where the strongest prevails. This will not do in the messianic kingdom. Even the ferocious lion *shall eat straw* like a grazing animal.

If we see these verses as a justification for vegetarianism, we have missed the point. Isaiah is simply telling us again that the messianic kingdom will be a kingdom of peace, a world without violence. This is because the underlying causes for violence will be eliminated as the Prince of Peace reigns.

8. And the sucking child shall play on the hole of the asp, and the weaned child shall put his hand on the cockatrice' den.

Isaiah gives one more striking image of the kingdom of peace. In this future world, a baby will be able to play near the den of poisonous snakes without fear or danger. Two names are given for these deadly serpents.

The first, *asp,* is a general term for various venomous snakes. The second, *cockatrice,* is an English term for a legendary serpent that is a horrific combination of a snake and a rooster. This "bird-snake" image is drawn from medieval tradition. Isaiah's original word does not suggest a mythological creature, but is another term for various poisonous snakes that are known in ancient Israel.

No responsible parent allows a baby to crawl around outside where there are deadly snakes! Yet this will not be a concern in the future kingdom of peace. It will be a safe world (see Isaiah 65:25).

III. Saving Son
(MATTHEW 1:21-23)
A. God Is Salvation (v. 21)

21. And she shall bring forth a son, and thou shalt call his name JESUS: for he shall save his people from their sins.

Matthew presents Jesus as the fulfillment of the messianic prophecies of Isaiah and other Old Testament writers. Isaiah's longed-for Messiah arrives when Mary gives birth to *a son.* This young woman and her husband, Joseph, undoubtedly know of Isaiah's promises. But Joseph and Mary's prophetic awareness has a more immediate reference: Joseph is told by an angel that this special son is a result of Mary's miraculous pregnancy.

Jesus is the same name as the Old Testament name *Joshua,* both meaning "the Lord saves." The child, the Messiah, is to be the full personification of God the Savior, the one who will *save his people from their sins.* His mission is not national liberation as an army general, but that of redeeming a world that is lost because of sin.

What Do You Think?

What does the fact that God used obscure people as His instruments for bringing Jesus into the world say about how God may use you in His service?

Talking Points for Your Discussion
- In your church
- In your community
- In your country

B. God Is with Us (vv. 22, 23)

22, 23. Now all this was done, that it might be fulfilled which was spoken of the Lord by the prophet, saying, Behold, a virgin shall be with child, and shall bring forth a son, and they shall call his name Emmanuel, which being interpreted is, God with us.

Matthew takes the many prophetic words of Isaiah and condenses them by quoting Isaiah 7:14. Baby Jesus fulfills Isaiah's words before preaching one sermon or performing one miracle. He does so because His mother does not become pregnant through normal human means. She, a virgin, is the vessel for a miraculous conception through the power of the Holy Spirit (Matthew 1:18). This is the "sign" that Isaiah had foreseen (Isaiah 7:14). This is not a random, unexplained event. It is an unmistakable act of God, a sign that God is present with His people.

In this, Jesus fulfills the intent of the prophetic name *Emmanuel.* Hebrew names usually have a distinct meaning, and many of these names have a religious component. Any Old Testament name ending in *el* has something to do with God. In this case, the name *Emmanuel* literally means, "God is with us" (compare Isaiah 8:8). The virgin birth is a sign of God's provision for His people.

Visual for
Lesson 3

Point to this visual as you introduce the discussion question associated with Matthew 1:23.

> *What Do You Think?*
> How does the reality of "God with us" affect your daily living? What changes do you need to make?
> *Talking Points for Your Discussion*
> - Fear of the Lord (Jeremiah 5:22)
> - Awareness of His awareness (Psalm 139:1-16)
> - Reflecting His presence to others (2 Corinthians 3:18)

❧ *"GOD HATES US ALL"* ❧

The caption above is the title of an album released on September 11, 2001, by the "thrash metal" band *Slayer.* Production problems delayed the release until that fateful day. Ironically, the lyrics in one of the album's songs asked a question that many others raised following the events of 9/11: Why does God allow terrorist attacks and other bad things to happen?

This kind of question is, of course, nothing new. It is asked in the pages of the Bible itself. Bible students recognize this as the basic question asked in the book of Job. See also Judges 6:13.

God's response is to say, in effect, "Here's what I am doing about it: I'm coming to live among you, to save you, to show you my love." All that happened in the birth, ministry, death, resurrection, and ascension of His Son. Those who conclude that "God hates us all" are missing the most important thing.   —C. R. B.

Conclusion
A. He Is Our Peace

Paul presents the accomplishment of Jesus on the cross as going beyond Isaiah's description of the coming *Prince of Peace.* Jesus is more than the bringer of peace. Paul says, "He is our peace" (Ephesians 2:14). Paul goes on to say that Jesus has "broken down" the wall that divides Jew from Gentile, and at the same time, Jesus' work on the cross has reconciled both groups to God (2:16). All of this is an act of "making peace" (2:15).

In the Christmas season, we often see cards wishing for "peace on earth" (see Luke 2:14). Christians understand that this is more than a disbanding of earthly armies. It is the promise of reconciliation between God and humans beings, which makes possible the reconciliation of all men and women. He is our Peace, the Prince of Peace, Jesus Christ our Lord.

B. Prayer

Mighty God, we thank You for the peace You bring to our lives through Your gracious forgiveness. We look forward to the day when all will be subject to Your Son, our glorious Prince of Peace. It is in His name we pray, amen.

C. Thought to Remember
Our king is the eternal Prince of Peace.

INVOLVEMENT LEARNING

Some of the activities below are also found in the helpful student book, Adult Bible Class.
Don't forget to download the free reproducible page from www.standardlesson.com to enhance your lesson!

Into the Lesson

Download the reproducible page and distribute copies of it. Have students complete the Prophecies About Jesus activity. Note: it may take too much time to complete both parts of this two-part puzzle in class. If your time is limited, distribute only one of the two parts. Distribute the other part at the end of class for learners to complete at home.

Into the Word

Prepare a handout titled *The Ruler of God's Kingdom.* Create four columns on it: the leftmost column will contain the headings listed below; the middle-left column will have the heading *Worldly Kingdoms,* but will be blank; the middle-right column will be labeled *Messianic Kingdom,* but will be blank; the rightmost column will have the questions noted below.

Put the following headings down the leftmost column. Space them apart widely:

I. PEACEFUL PRINCE (Isaiah 9:6, 7)
II. BLESSED BRANCH (Isaiah 11:1-8)
III. SAVING SON (Matthew 1:21-23)

Put the following questions in the rightmost column. Align them with the headings in the leftmost column as indicated.

Across from heading I: What exceptional leadership qualities would God's ruler have? What is distinctive about the Messiah's government? What will it be like to live in the Messiah's peaceful kingdom? How do your answers compare and contrast with what we see in worldly kingdoms?

Across from heading II: Why is the lineage of the Messiah important? (See Jeremiah 23:5.) From whom will the Messiah get His wisdom? What qualities reveal the Messiah's spiritual maturity? What kind of a judge will the Messiah be? What is it about the Messiah's domain that will make it peaceful? How do your answers compare and contrast with what we see in worldly kingdoms?

Across from heading III: What does the Messiah provide that is far superior to human rulers? What does that mean to you personally? Why is Isaiah's prophecy of a virgin birth so impressive? What does the virgin birth tell us about the Messiah's nature? What promise is implied in the name *Emmanuel?* How do your answers compare and contrast with what we see in worldly kingdoms?

Form small groups to answer the questions, saving the "compare and contrast" questions until last. Larger classes can form extra groups and duplicate the assignments. Have the groups share their conclusions.

Into Life

Use the following statements and questions to lead a discussion of the benefits of being part of the Messiah's kingdom. *Option:* make handouts of these statements for small-group discussions, but do not include the possible responses.

1. "Some of the aspects of the Messiah's kingdom are yet to occur. Can you name some of these?" *(Possible responses: direct governance by the Messiah, eternity in God's presence, changes in the animal kingdom, the judgment of the wicked.)*

2. "Many of the benefits of being a part of Jesus' kingdom are available to us right now. What are some of them?" *(Possible responses: We have a king who is a Wonderful Counsellor, a mighty God, an everlasting Father, and the Prince of Peace. He has saved us from our sins. He makes His Spirit available to us so that we can benefit from His wisdom and counsel. We can have confidence in Jesus as the Messiah because of fulfilled prophecy.)*

3. "Which of these benefits, either present or future, means the most to you? Why? How will it make a difference in your life this week?"

Allow time for whole-class or small-group discussion. Close with a prayer that praises God for the Messiah and His kingdom, thanking Him that you can be part of it.

GOD IS WITH US

BACKGROUND SCRIPTURE: Isaiah 43
PRINTED TEXT: Isaiah 43:1-7, 10-12

ISAIAH 43:1-7, 10-12

1 But now thus saith the LORD that created thee, O Jacob, and he that formed thee, O Israel, Fear not: for I have redeemed thee, I have called thee by thy name; thou art mine.

2 When thou passest through the waters, I will be with thee; and through the rivers, they shall not overflow thee: when thou walkest through the fire, thou shalt not be burned; neither shall the flame kindle upon thee.

3 For I am the LORD thy God, the Holy One of Israel, thy Saviour: I gave Egypt for thy ransom, Ethiopia and Seba for thee.

4 Since thou wast precious in my sight, thou hast been honourable, and I have loved thee: therefore will I give men for thee, and people for thy life.

5 Fear not: for I am with thee: I will bring thy seed from the east, and gather thee from the west;

6 I will say to the north, Give up; and to the south, Keep not back: bring my sons from far, and my daughters from the ends of the earth;

7 Even every one that is called by my name: for I have created him for my glory, I have formed him; yea, I have made him.

. . . .

10 Ye are my witnesses, saith the LORD, and my servant whom I have chosen; that ye may know and believe me, and understand that I am he: before me there was no God formed, neither shall there be after me.

11 I, even I, am the LORD; and beside me there is no saviour.

12 I have declared, and have saved, and I have shewed, when there was no strange god among you: therefore ye are my witnesses, saith the LORD, that I am God.

KEY VERSE

When thou passest through the waters, I will be with thee; and through the rivers, they shall not overflow thee. —**Isaiah 43:2**

ASSURING HOPE

Unit 1: Comfort for God's People
LESSONS 1–5

LESSON AIMS

After participating in this lesson, each student will be able to:

1. Summarize the Lord's promise of protection to Israel.

2. Explain the modern relevance of the promise of protection and "ransom."

3. Tell how God has protected him or her in a spiritually dangerous situation.

LESSON OUTLINE

Introduction

A. Strange Gods

Has anyone not noticed the wide variety of religious beliefs these days? In cities large and small, there are synagogues, mosques, temples, tabernacles, chapels, churches, and other houses of worship. There is an ocean of Web sites to explain the belief systems of everything from atheism to voodoo. Religious TV shows feature outrageous "holy" men and women. The spirituality section in commercial bookstores is crammed with volumes on New Age religion, humanism, and witchcraft right alongside the Bibles.

This is not a new state of affairs, however. Ancient Israel was surrounded by nations with strange religions. They practiced such things as idol worship, temple prostitution, and human sacrifice. The Israelites allowed these practices to infiltrate their own religious life (2 Kings 17:17; Isaiah 44:17; Hosea 4:14). Yet the people of Israel had a heritage of worshiping and serving the one true God, the only God. Any other so-called "god" was false, and to worship a false god was futile (see Romans 1:21-23).

The Bible sometimes calls these "strange gods" (Deuteronomy 32:16; see Psalm 81:9). If we have placed our faith in the Lord, the one true God, this idea of strange gods has more than one connotation. Some of these fictitious gods are strange in the sense of being just plain weird, like the elephant or monkey gods of the Hindus. Some are strange in that they are unimaginable to us. What kind of god would demand the sacrifice of a son or daughter in order to be appeased? They are also strange or foreign in that they seem to be "distant" in more than one sense. They are alien and frightening in their imperfection and demands. These are not deities that we want to be like or whose image we would be pleased to bear.

Isaiah was deeply concerned that his people understand that there is only one God. All other claims of gods are false and dangerous. Things haven't changed. Despite the appearance of competition among religions in our world, there is still only one God. There is no one besides Him (Isaiah 45:6). This is not because He is the greatest of the gods, but because He is the only God. Any other god proposed to us is strange!

B. Lesson Background

An important theme in the second half of Isaiah is that the people of Israel are to be God's witnesses to the other nations of the earth (Isaiah 45:20, 21; 48:20; etc.). This was not *witness* in the sense of "evangelism," but that of "testimony." Such a witness proclaims eyewitness observation or experience (Isaiah 43:10, today's text).

The concept of using a witness to verify legal claims is very ancient, and the integrity of witnesses is the foundation of all legal systems (compare Exodus 20:16). The wisdom tradition of Israel saw the honest witness as "faithful" in contrast with the false witness (see Proverbs 14:5). The people of the Bible were very aware of the great damage a false witness could bring (see Proverbs 25:18).

The nation of Israel had many occasions in its history to be a witness of and to the power of God. They had seen the plagues inflicted on Egypt to force Pharaoh to release them. They had walked through the miraculously parted Red Sea to escape the Egyptian army. They had seen the glorious mountain of the Lord where they received the law; that peak had the appearance of a mountain on fire (Exodus 19:18). They had seen the collapse of the walls of Jericho without a human hand having touched them.

These mighty acts of the Lord made the Israelites witnesses for their God to all other nations. The law required two or three witnesses to convict someone of a crime (see Deuteronomy 19:15; compare John 8:17). In Israel, God had a whole nation of witnesses.

I. God's Redeeming Love
(ISAIAH 43:1-4)
A. Named and Claimed (v. 1)

1. But now thus saith the LORD that created thee, O Jacob, and he that formed thee, O Israel, Fear not: for I have redeemed thee, I have called thee by thy name; thou art mine.

Isaiah's words at the beginning of this chapter remind Israel of the Genesis creation story. There

Visual for Lesson 4

Point to this visual as you ask, "How do secular and Christian uses of the word *redeemed* differ?"

God "created the heavens and the earth" (Genesis 1:1) and "formed man" from "the dust of the ground" (2:7). But then sin entered the picture, and God needed to redeem His creation. A key part of His plan is to regain possession of Israel. This is a reference to God's deliverance of Israel from Egyptian bondage (see Exodus 6:6). In this act, God created a new nation for His purposes (see Deuteronomy 4:34).

Isaiah portrays an intimate, personal relationship between Israel and the Lord, for the nation is called by name. This personal aspect is made even more resolute by God's declaration *thou art mine*. Such a relationship is exceedingly rare in the ancient world, where the gods of the nations are portrayed as fickle, terrifying deities. In Israel's case, the nation is not commanded to cower in fear, but to *fear not*.

B. Selected and Protected (v. 2)

2. When thou passest through the waters, I will be with thee; and through the rivers, they shall not overflow thee: when thou walkest through the fire, thou shalt not be burned; neither shall the flame kindle upon thee.

The words *will, shall,* etc. show God's promises for the future. The references to *the waters* and *the rivers* surely remind the people of how God led them in the past with regard to the crossings of the Red Sea (compare Nehemiah 9:11) and the original crossing of the Jordan River as the people of Israel entered the promised land (see Joshua 1:11). The reference to protection from fire does not seem to have a specific antecedent in the history of Israel. It is a general picture of trials that they have suffered. This is similar to our talking about "feeling the heat" in certain situations (compare 1 Peter 4:12).

God's promises to Israel do not end with selection, with being designated as His people. God promises to stand by them and protect them. We are reminded of the promise of Paul that nothing is able to separate us from the love of God (Romans 8:38, 39). We too may be determined to "not fear" (Hebrews 13:6), for we are assured of God's protecting hand in our lives.

> *What Do You Think?*
> What are some specific ways that you have experienced God's protecting hand? How is your faith affected in times when God seems to be absent?
> *Talking Points for Your Discussion*
> - In natural disasters (Isaiah 4:6; Psalm 46:2)
> - When attacked by Satan (2 Thessalonians 3:3)
> - In times of uncertainty (Isaiah 41:10)
> - In times of martrydom (Jeremiah 26:20-23; Acts 7:54-60; 12:1, 2)

❧ *FIRE-WALKING* ❧

Every year at the festival of Saints Constantine and Helen, Greek villagers near Thessaloniki walk across a bed of hot coals. Participants believe they are taken hold of by "the saints" as they fall into a trance; this allegedly enables them to walk over the coals without harm.

One legend dates the ritual back to the thirteenth century, when the church of St. Constantine caught fire. Villagers are said to have heard screams coming from the interior, where the icons were calling for help. So people ran into the building and rescued the icons, escaping with no damage to themselves or the icons. Thus the annual commemoration by walking on hot coals.

It is more likely, however, that the ritual has a pagan origin, with a Christian interpretation attached to it later. This accords with testimonies of pagan fire-walkers who practice similar rituals elsewhere. In India and Fiji, the practice is connected with an annual full-moon festival and includes worship of "little gods"—guardian spirits.

Obviously, Isaiah was neither encouraging such a practice nor promising safety to those engaged in it. The metaphor of salvation from or through fire speaks of God's spiritual protection. Those who love God undergo physical trials like everyone else. But God's grace is always present to help us deal with such circumstances.   —C. R. B.

C. Ransomed and Esteemed (vv. 3, 4)

3. For I am the LORD thy God, the Holy One of Israel, thy Saviour: I gave Egypt for thy ransom, Ethiopia and Seba for thee.

God does not need to justify His claim on Israel, but four aspects of God's relationship with the nation are presented. First, the people are reminded that this is *the Lord* speaking, a use of God's divine name that was revealed to Moses at the burning bush (Exodus 3:14, 15).

In addition, God is *the Holy One of Israel,* a favorite designation of Isaiah for God, used about 25 times in the book. This designation emphasizes both the solidarity of God with the nation as well as the separation that God's holiness entails (see Isaiah 12:6). Israel is a people of imperfect holiness, and no one knows this better than the prophet himself (see 6:5). It is a wonderful paradox that the perfectly holy God dwells in the midst of sinful humanity, a paradox that finds ultimate expression in the incarnation of God's Son.

God is also presented as Israel's savior. This title has an active sense here, for God is the one who is saving Israel in the present as He has in the past. This is expanded by the fourth aspect: God as the one who has given a ransom for Israel. This is closely related to the concept of atonement, a price paid for redemption.

In this setting, the sacrificial ransom was the three nations of Egypt, Ethiopia, and Seba. Egypt is the nation of the lower (northern) Nile River valley, while Ethiopia (Cush) is of the upper (southern) region. We do not know where Seba is. But the Bible records a son of the original Cush named

Seba (Genesis 10:7; compare Psalm 72:10), so this is likely a reference to the same people-group.

The imagery of *ransom . . . for thee* reminds us of the devastation God brought on Egypt in the process of freeing the Israelites during the days of Moses. The people of Israel are to remember that God's act of choosing them was not without cost to other nations, nations also loved by God.

4. Since thou wast precious in my sight, thou hast been honorable, and I have loved thee: therefore will I give men for thee, and people for thy life.

Although he is ministering many hundreds of years before the advent of the Messiah, Isaiah gives a remarkable picture of sacrificial, atoning death. God is telling Israel that others died so that they might live. This is the essence of the Christian understanding of the death of Jesus (see 1 Thessalonians 5:10). We too are precious in God's eyes.

> **What Do You Think?**
> How should the fact that God considers His people precious affect the way you live?
> *Talking Points for Your Discussion*
> - Concerning your view of yourself
> - Concerning your view of fellow Christians
> - Concerning your view of unbelievers

II. God's Glorious Gathering
(Isaiah 43:5-7)
A. Calmed by His Presence (v. 5a)

5a. Fear not: for I am with thee.

One of the great promises of the Bible is that we are not alone in our struggles. When we look for help, we do not always expect someone else to solve our problems. Sometimes we just need another person to walk alongside us in our pain. We can face and endure great tribulations if we know that someone is with us (Psalm 23:4). Perhaps the greatest fear in this regard is that God might abandon us (compare 2 Chronicles 15:2).

Isaiah's message reassures Israel that the coming troubles are not a sign of God's abandonment. David cries out when he feels that God has forsaken him (Psalm 22:1); yet in this same psalm David realizes that he is not abandoned (22:24).

Jesus promises that He will always be with His followers (Matthew 28:20). As with Israel, our struggles and trials are not a sign of God's rejection.

B. Collected by His Calling (vv. 5b, 6)

5b, 6. I will bring thy seed from the east, and gather thee from the west: I will say to the north, Give up; and to the south, Keep not back: bring my sons from far, and my daughters from the ends of the earth.

Isaiah sees a future time when a scattered Israel will be gathered. This is a two-pronged prophecy, of future dispersing followed by restoration. We may see at least a partial fulfillment of this word in the return from the Babylonian exile (Ezra 1:2).

The larger picture, however, is of a gathering of God's people in a glorious unity. Hundreds of years after Isaiah, Jesus will speak of a time when the heirs of Abraham, Isaac, and Jacob will be joined at the table by people from all over the world (Matthew 8:11). Isaiah sees a new people of God determined not by their lineage and genealogy, but by the call of God to the table of faith.

> **What Do You Think?**
> Since God will call people from the ends of the earth to Him, how should we react toward other peoples and nations?
> *Talking Points for Your Discussion*
> - Our reaction to ethnic labels
> - Our reaction to news of atrocities
> - Our plan to take the gospel to other nations

❧ *A Joyful Get-Together* ❧

For some folks, family reunions are celebrations of pleasant—often hilarious—family memories. Others look at reunions as ordeals to be endured; if one *must* go, it is something to escape from at the earliest possible moment.

Much of the aggravation of reunions can be alleviated by good planning. There are Web sites that promise help in arranging every detail, from location to food to lodging to activities—all so you can have the "perfect" family reunion. Help is available both for those willing to hire professionals and for do-it-yourselfers.

The great reunion of which Isaiah spoke is still in the future—it is the eventual gathering of all of God's family in harmony and unity. Perhaps we'll be surprised to see some "cousins" there we didn't expect to see; they may equally be surprised to see us! In any case, that reunion won't dwell on our past, which is forgiven in Christ. It will be a never-ending gathering that looks to eternity future.   —C. R. B.

C. Created for His Glory (v. 7)

7. Even every one that is called by my name: for I have created him for my glory, I have formed him; yea, I have made him.

This future gathering is not for the advancement and prestige of Israel, but for God's glory. Isaiah returns to the earlier language of creation, of a people formed and made (compare Isaiah 43:1, above). The existence of the gathered people of God is a manifestation of God's overall plan for humanity's redemption. We should always be mindful that we exist for God's glory, not the other way around.

III. God's Saving Presence
(ISAIAH 43:10-12)
A. The One and Only (v. 10)

10. Ye are my witnesses, saith the LORD, and my servant whom I have chosen: that ye may know and believe me, and understand that I am he: before me there was no God formed, neither shall there be after me.

When the nations are gathered per Isaiah 43:9 (not in today's text), the testimony of witnesses will be heard. The greatest witnesses will be those who have experienced the miraculous in their lives. They have true spiritual sight and hearing (contrast 43:8, not in today's text). Isaiah prophesies that there are many who are willing to hear their testimony (again, 43:9). Truths about existence, the answer to questions of human purpose and destiny, are vital!

God tells His people that this role of witnesses is given to them. They must give testimony to the reality of the one true God, uncreated and eternal. God was not formed, in striking contrast with the

forming of the first man (Genesis 2:7) and of the nation of Israel (Isaiah 43:1, 7, above).

B. The Sole Savior (v. 11)

11. I, even I, am the LORD; and beside me there is no saviour.

The modern phenomenon of shopping for a religion that one likes is debunked here. To see any given religion as a choice among many valid options is ridiculous. There is only one God, not a competing stable of gods. This God is the *I am,* the Lord. There are no other viable options. Therefore, any attempt to look elsewhere for salvation from the human condition is futile. The God of Israel is the only Savior.

When we integrate these exclusive claims of God as the sole Savior with Isaiah's promises of a coming Messiah, we begin to understand the great significance of the birth of Jesus. He is the God-intended and God-provided Savior of humanity. There are no other options that have a promise of salvation, for He alone is "the way" (John 14:6). There is no pathway to salvation other than God's chosen Messiah, Jesus our Lord (Acts 4:12).

C. The Witnessed Lord (v. 12)

12. I have declared, and have saved, and I have shewed, when there was no strange god among you: therefore ye are my witnesses, saith the LORD, that I am God.

Isaiah ends this section by calling the people of Israel back to their heritage, back to a time before Israel became like the other nations that worship strange (false) gods (see Ezekiel 20:32). History reveals that Israel's unfaithfulness takes a terrible toll, for her witness is compromised. Past unfaithfulness does not eliminate the possibility of future faithfulness, however.

God Is with Us

Like Israel, many of us suffer periods in our lives where we fall away and take our eyes off the glory of God. We too are called to return to the time in our faith when there was no competition in our lives from strange gods. We can remember the simple declaration of the Lord: *I am God*.

What Do You Think?

How do you respond to the salvation you have in Christ?

Talking Points for Your Discussion

- In service (Romans 12:1; Ephesians 2:10)
- In worship (Hebrews 10:25)
- In priorities (Matthew 23:23, 24)
- In doctrine (Titus 1:9)

Conclusion

A. Continuing Theme: Witness

Isaiah's theme of *witness* is continued in the New Testament, where the risen Jesus charges His disciples to be His "witnesses" to all the people of the earth (Acts 1:8). In this, believers are following Jesus himself, for He is presented as the ultimate "faithful witness" to the power and holiness of God (see Revelation 1:5). But unlike ancient Israel, our witness should have the result of evangelism (Matthew 28:19, 20). In this way, Christian believers are the new nation of witnesses of the power of God to unbelievers.

Our faith should lead us to testify to the mighty works of God, particularly to the power of the resurrection of Jesus (see Romans 1:4). God does not leave this task to us alone, for He gives us His Spirit as a witness to our status as His children (Romans 8:16). This is the "Spirit of truth" that adds His witness to our own (John 15:26; see 1 John 5:20).

B. Continuing Theme: Only One God

Our consumer society has given us many choices when it comes to products we purchase. I recently did a quick count of the different varieties of soda pop for sale in the supermarket next door, counting nearly 100. We are spoiled by this dizzying array, and sometimes we are paralyzed by too many choices. We are like the proverbial don-key that was placed between two feedboxes and starved to death while trying to decide which one he should eat from.

Some like to think that there are many choices in matters of faith as well. We want to worship, but we want a god who fits our lifestyle and preferences. So we put ourselves up as the judge of many gods, and thereby place God in the dock (that is C. S. Lewis's British term for "witness stand"). We choose a church as we would choose a new car.

Isaiah's insistence that this is mad still speaks today. There is only one God, whether we believe this or not. Our faith or lack of it does not change the reality. God's eternality, power, and singularity do not depend on our acceptance. Similarly, God's ongoing presence in the world is not contingent on our recognition of that fact. God declares that there is no other God. God promises that He is with us. He is our Savior, the only deliverer from the mess we have made of our lives.

C. Prayer

Heavenly Father, we pray to You to save and protect us as You have promised. We pray to You, O God of all nations, never to withdraw Your comforting presence from us, even if we walk through the darkest valley of death. May You find us worthy and useful as Your witnesses to a world that denies Your loving concern. We pray these things in the name of Jesus, our Savior. Amen.

D. Thought to Remember

Be a witness of the only God.

HOW TO SAY IT

Deuteronomy	Due-ter-*ahn*-uh-me.
Egypt	*Ee*-jipt.
Egyptian	Ee-*jip*-shun.
Ethiopia	E-thee-*o*-pee-uh (*th* as in *thin*).
Hebrews	*Hee*-brews.
Isaiah	Eye-*zay*-uh.
Jericho	*Jair*-ih-co.
Jordan	*Jor*-dun.
Nehemiah	*Nee*-huh-**my**-uh.
Pharaoh	*Fair*-o or *Fay*-roe.
Seba	*See*-buh.

INVOLVEMENT LEARNING

Some of the activities below are also found in the helpful student book, Adult Bible Class.
Don't forget to download the free reproducible page from www.standardlesson.com to enhance your lesson!

Into the Lesson

Early in the week, arrange for an acquaintance to make a brief appearance in your class. Have the person dress in an outlandish fashion, mixing a variety of clothing styles, colors, and accessories. He or she is to enter the room at the beginning of class and do three specific things of your choosing (examples: sneezing, doing jumping jacks, and juggling two fruits). The person's time in the room should be about 30 seconds.

After the person leaves, distribute paper and pencils. Tell your class that you want to see how good they are at being witnesses. Ask questions such as: "What color were his/her eyes? What was the second thing he/she did? What kind of shoes was he/she wearing?" Then say, "God told the nation of Israel He wanted them to be witnesses for Him of all the things He had done for them. Let's see what some of them were."

Alternative: Download the reproducible page and make copies of the God Our Savior activity. Divide your class into small teams and have them work together to complete the exercise. Give one point to each team that comes up with something no other team has for each letter in the word *deliverance.* Possible answers include Despair, Evil, Loneliness, Iniquity, Vices, Eternal condemnation, Rejection, Addiction, Not loved, Captivity, Eating disorder. Then say, "God delivered the Israelites from many things. Let's see what some of them were."

Into the Word

Brainstorm: Say, "Before we read today's text, let's see how many things we can think of that the Lord did for the Israelites." Have someone write answers on the board as they are called out. *Possible responses:* God chose them to be His people, delivered them from the death angel, brought them out of slavery, sustained them in the wilderness, parted the Red Sea and Jordan River, gave them the Law, rescued them from their enemies, brought them out of captivity.

Next have someone read Isaiah 43:1-7, 10-12 aloud. Encourage learners to listen for all the things that God says He has done and will do for the Israelites.

Matching: Create a handout that lists the following couplets that summarize the verses from today's text. Have learners work in pairs to match the rhyme with the corresponding verse. A. "When the water's too deep to pass through, I will be there to rescue you." B. "You have the honor of being called by my name; now live so you will never bring me shame." C. "From the farthest west to the rising sun, I bring you back to be as one." D. "You can look low and you can look high, but there's no one else to save you by and by!" E. "I paid the price to set you free. Now, dear ones, you belong to me." F. "There never has been and never will be a god who is remotely like me." G. "I am the Holy One, who tells no lies; I ransomed you from Pharaoh and those other guys." H. "To the ends of the earth I will roam, in order to bring your loved ones home." I. "Swear to tell what's true: I am the God who rescued you." J. "Because you're so precious to me, I traded others to set you free."

Ask for volunteers to share conclusions, which may vary because of similarities among verses. *[Suggested answers: A, v. 2; B, v. 7; C, v. 5; D, v. 11; E, v. 1; F, v. 10; G, v. 3; H, v. 6; I, v. 12; J, v. 4.]*

Into Life

Distribute copies of the activity About to Go Under? Having a Trial by Fire? from the reproducible page. Say, "Let's apply God's love in Isaiah 43:2 to ourselves." Give learners a few minutes to work on the activity's images. Encourage them to write out Isaiah 43:2 longhand. Suggest that they take the paper with them as a reminder this week to trust God for help.

God Is with Us

GOD IS OUR REDEEMER

BACKGROUND SCRIPTURE: Isaiah 44
PRINTED TEXT: Isaiah 44:21-28

ISAIAH 44:21-28

21 Remember these, O Jacob and Israel; for thou art my servant: I have formed thee; thou art my servant: O Israel, thou shalt not be forgotten of me.

22 I have blotted out, as a thick cloud, thy transgressions, and, as a cloud, thy sins: return unto me; for I have redeemed thee.

23 Sing, O ye heavens; for the LORD hath done it: shout, ye lower parts of the earth: break forth into singing, ye mountains, O forest, and every tree therein: for the LORD hath redeemed Jacob, and glorified himself in Israel.

24 Thus saith the LORD, thy Redeemer, and he that formed thee from the womb, I am the LORD that maketh all things; that stretcheth forth the heavens alone; that spreadeth abroad the earth by myself;

25 That frustrateth the tokens of the liars, and maketh diviners mad; that turneth wise men backward, and maketh their knowledge foolish;

26 That confirmeth the word of his servant, and performeth the counsel of his messengers; that saith to Jerusalem, Thou shalt be inhabited; and to the cities of Judah, Ye shall

be built, and I will raise up the decayed places thereof:

27 That saith to the deep, Be dry, and I will dry up thy rivers:

28 That saith of Cyrus, He is my shepherd, and shall perform all my pleasure: even saying to Jerusalem, Thou shalt be built; and to the temple, Thy foundation shall be laid.

KEY VERSE

I have blotted out, as a thick cloud, thy transgressions, and, as a cloud, thy sins: return unto me; for I have redeemed thee. —**Isaiah 44:22**

ASSURING HOPE

Unit 1: Comfort for God's People

LESSONS 1–5

LESSON AIMS

After participating in this lesson, each student will be able to:

1. Summarize God's promise to the future (from Isaiah's perspective) exiles who were about to return to Jerusalem.

2. Tell how God's forgiveness leads to restoration.

3. Tell how God has restored his or her brokenness on a personal level.

LESSON OUTLINE

Introduction

A. I've Been Forgotten

A common, nagging fear is that we have forgotten something important. We use pocket calendars, computer schedulers, and cell phone beeps to tell us what our next appointment or event will be. Even with all this technology, we still forget things. We distrust our memories. Did I turn the stove off? Have I mailed that bill? When is my friend coming to visit? What was the name of that new person I met at church?

Perhaps a deeper fear, though, is that *we ourselves will be forgotten.* I once visited a very elderly woman in a care facility who told me that no friends or family ever came to see her. "I've been forgotten," she said sadly. What a depressing feeling! We want to be remembered and remembered well. Yet our world is increasingly impersonal and fragmented. We remember the names of celebrities, but forget the names of our nieces and nephews. Families often are separated, with members living in different cities. Travel is difficult. Time is scarce. To remember each other takes effort.

A wonderful characteristic of God is that He does not forget us. It is beyond our comprehension how God manages this, with billions of people populating the earth. How can He remember each one? But He does, and He spreads His blessings to each of us from the inexhaustible source of His love. Today's lesson concerns how circumstances might have caused the people of Israel to think they were forgotten.

B. Lesson Background

A unique feature of the religion of ancient Israel was their belief in a singular God; this outlook is called *monotheism.* While this orientation is found throughout the Old Testament, Isaiah's writings are among the clearest and most uncompromising in this regard. Isaiah demands that the people of Israel understand that their God, the Lord, is also the God who controls the destiny of their enemies. It is erroneous to think that international conflicts are paralleled by heavenly conflicts between rival deities. This is not the case. There is only one God over all the nations.

God Is Our Redeemer

Even so, most people in the ancient world understood the heavenly realm to be populated by a multitude of gods. There was a god or goddess in control of each of the important natural processes of the world. These included a weather god, an ocean god, a sun god, a moon god, and many others. Ancient myths told the stories of the conflicts between these gods and how such fights affected the realm of humans. These people were correct in their intuition that there was a reality beyond the perception of human senses, but incorrect in supposing a division of labor and power in the supernatural world. They were especially wrong in believing that each nation had its own set of gods that was loyal to that nation alone.

By contrast, several times in Isaiah we find something like a census of deities in Heaven that always tallies up to exactly one. Isaiah pictures God standing in Heaven alone, unique and unchallenged in His supremacy. The census count is fixed at *one* eternally. The Lord alone is uncreated, and all the other inhabitants of Heaven and earth are created by Him. God says, "There is none like me" (Isaiah 46:9). He is the "God of the whole earth" (54:5).

This one-God orientation is important as we try to understand Isaiah's prophecies about the restoration of Jerusalem. The prophet speaks of Cyrus, who is a future (from Isaiah's perspective) monarch of the Persians. He will allow the people of Israel to return to Jerusalem and rebuild their temple. History calls him *Cyrus the Great* in recognition of his military and political skills. Yet even this person, undoubtedly the most powerful man on earth in his day, was subject to the plans and control of the Lord God of Israel. The Lord is the only God, so it could be no other way.

It may trouble us that God would use a pagan ruler, an unbeliever, to accomplish His purposes. (It also troubled the prophet Habakkuk!) It makes more sense if we recognize that there is only one God, and this one true God is the Almighty for all men and women. Pagan religions have gone off the tracks horribly in trying to understand the world of the gods. God, however, has no issue in understanding that He is God alone, and everyone is subject to Him.

I. Not Forgotten
(ISAIAH 44:21-23)
A. Creator Recalls (v. 21)

21. Remember these, O Jacob and Israel; for thou art my servant: I have formed thee; thou art my servant: O Israel, thou shalt not be forgotten of me.

The opening verse of this section is presented in a poetic structure that walks into the topic with three steps, presents the main point, and then retraces the three steps as it walks back out. The first step in is the command for the people to *remember*. The second step is the presentation of their historic, collective names of *Jacob and Israel;* putting it this way is akin to saying "women and ladies"—the doubled nouns in each case refer to a single group. The third step is to recall that the nation is designated as the Lord's *servant*. We then see the central, climactic statement of this verse: *I have formed thee.*

Isaiah then "backs out" by using another reference to servant followed by a restatement of the people's name, *O Israel*. The third, final step out gives a slight twist on the initial step, however, by presenting the reverse side of remember. Instead of being called to remember, we are told that God promises not to forget.

This structure is powerful. It brackets the main point with the urgency of the memory of Israel and of Israel's God. The people must remember that God remembers something. What? Why? That is the main point: *I have formed thee.* The

HOW TO SAY IT

Babylon	*Bab*-uh-lun.
Bar Kochba	Bahr Kokh-*bah*.
Cyrus	*Sigh*-russ.
Euphrates	You-*fray*-teez.
Habakkuk	Huh-*back*-kuk.
Hadrian	*Hay*-dree-un.
Herod	*Hair*-ud.
Herodotus	Heh-*rod*-uh-tus.
Melchizedek	Mel-*kiz*-eh-dek.
Persian	*Per*-zhuhn.
Zerubbabel	Zeh-*rub*-uh-bul.

Lord is the Creator of the nation, a people created for His purposes. The nation is not a toy cast aside after a period of play. The nation is not a garment given to a charity when no longer wanted. God is Israel's maker and master; that nation is His creation and His servant.

❧ GOOD AND BAD FORGETFULNESS ❧

Amnesia makes for a good plot element in movies and TV shows. A typical use of this plot device is to present a character who wakes up somewhere strange and can't remember how he got there or even who he is. The show holds the audience's attention by presenting interesting clues that help the character begin to remember things piece by piece. All this can make for fascinating viewing, but we sure hope it never happens to us!

Sadly, it *has* happened to us: we forget that we are created in the image of God. That's the worst kind of amnesia. God asks us to remember that He is our Creator and Savior, facts the human race finds all too easy to forget.

However, for those who will turn to the Lord, there is a good side of forgetfulness: "I will be merciful to their unrighteousness, and their sins and their iniquities will I remember no more" (Hebrews 8:12, quoting Jeremiah 31:34). May we ever thank God for His marvelous decision to remember our sins no longer!   —C. R. B.

B. Redeemer Forgives (v. 22)

22. I have blotted out, as a thick cloud, thy transgressions, and, as a cloud, thy sins: return unto me; for I have redeemed thee.

Isaiah now looks forward to a time of restoration for Israel. Although this is in the future for Isaiah, it has a sense of timelessness for any reader.

God calls the people to return, and He assures the nation that the cause of separation has been repaired. This break in relationship is caused by Israel's ongoing unfaithfulness. The Old Testament sees this as a breaking of the covenant with the Lord; such covenant-breaking will be punished harshly (see Leviticus 26:15, 16).

At the time Isaiah writes, Israel is yet to be punished for the unfaithfulness that results in the destruction of the temple and deportation in 586 BC. After this corrective discipline, the Lord will be ready to restore. The biggest barrier to overcome, however, will be the need for God to forgive transgressions and sins. This He will do, for the sins will be blotted out; so certain is this that it is spoken of as already accomplished: *I have blotted out.* Isaiah describes this as being drenched by a heavy fog, like a descending cloud that covers everything with God's mercy and forgiveness.

Israel deserves no credit for this restoration. It is not as if Isaiah is saying, "God has considered your offer and agrees to your terms." This is a unilateral restoration, *I have redeemed*, says the Lord. All is ready for them to return.

C. World Sings (v. 23)

23. Sing, O ye heavens; for the LORD hath done it: shout, ye lower parts of the earth: break forth into singing, ye mountains, O forest, and every tree therein: for the LORD hath redeemed Jacob, and glorified himself in Israel.

This promised restoration is the cause of universal elation. There is rejoicing above the earth (the *heavens*) and below the earth (the *lower parts*). In between are the colossal geographical features of the earth: the *mountains* and the *forest*. Thus this is cosmic celebration. We are reminded that creation itself is affected by the grace and mercy of God. Jesus says during His triumphal entry that if the crowds be silenced, then the rocks themselves will shout out (Luke 19:40). Similarly, Paul pictured an expectant creation, waiting for the consummation of God's plans (Romans 8:19).

The cause of this singing is much more than the fate of a small nation. It is the recognition that God glorifies himself in the redemption of Israel. God shows His power, love, and commitment to

God Is Our Redeemer

redeeming His people. This does not serve to bring glory and acclaim to Israel, but to the Lord.

What Do You Think?

Other than during Sunday morning worship, when do you feel like breaking out in songs of praise to the Lord?

Talking Points for Your Discussion

- Times of victory (Exodus 15:1, 21; Judges 5)
- Times of difficulty (Psalm 59:16)

II. Not Deserted
(Isaiah 44:24-28)
A. Creation Continues (v. 24)

24. Thus saith the Lord, thy Redeemer, and he that formed thee from the womb, I am the Lord that maketh all things; that stretcheth forth the heavens alone; that spreadeth abroad the earth by myself.

Lest the people question the Lord's capacity or intention in redeeming them, Israel is reminded of God's credentials as it affects her situation. He is the one who *maketh all things.* This is colorfully pictured as stretching out the heavens like a tent or pavilion (compare Psalm 18:11) and spreading out the earth like a carpet (compare Psalm 136:6). The earth is the habitation of humans, our world as prepared by God alone. We neither assisted nor advised in this project, a point that is hammered home to the questioning Job (Job 38:4).

What Do You Think?

What are some appropriate ways to respond to the fact that the Lord has not only created you, but also has recreated you in Christ?

Talking Points for Your Discussion

- Isaiah 64:8
- 1 Corinthians 4:1, 2
- Colossians 1:11-14
- James 4:7

This is not all in the distant past, however, for God's creative work is ongoing. It is acknowledged that God *formed thee from the womb.* The creation of the nation of Israel was a work of God. Individually, each child is a new work of God and a sign

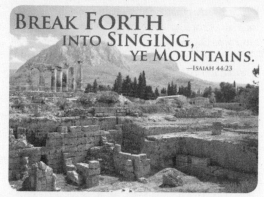

BREAK FORTH
INTO SINGING,
YE MOUNTAINS.
—Isaiah 44:23

Visual for Lesson 5. Point to this visual as you ask the discussion question that is associated with verse 23.

of His continuing creative powers over the earth. The universe as pictured by Isaiah is not static and fixed, but dynamic and changing according to God's plans.

B. People Confounded (v. 25)

25. That frustrateth the tokens of the liars, and maketh diviners mad; that turneth wise men backward, and maketh their knowledge foolish.

Isaiah also pictures a scenario in which God confounds the most clever and confident of all human beings. The *tokens of the liars* are the omens and signs claimed to be miraculous by false prophets. These signs are used to bolster their claims to having supernatural insight. Isaiah says that even their safest predictions (such as, "It will rain tomorrow") may fall flat if God wants to thwart them. The Lord is in control of the signs, not the lying prophets. This is similar to the promise to make *diviners mad* (crazy). They will never get any of their predictions correct if God chooses to have them fail. Their advice will be faulty, for they have no true view of the future unless God grants it.

Another group that is targeted is the learned professional *wise men* of society. They are confident in their accumulated systems of knowledge, but Isaiah knows that these systems will collapse if God acts contrary to their expectations (1 Corinthians 1:19, 20, 27; 3:19, 20). God is not subject to human rules and expectations, even from the wisest of us. Human knowledge and intelligence is small compared with the power and wisdom of God (see Daniel 2:20).

What Do You Think?

In what ways have you seen God frustrate and make foolish the ways of this world?

Talking Points for Your Discussion
- In answered prayers
- In religious debates
- In the growth of a church

C. Promises Performed (v. 26)

26. That confirmeth the word of his servant, and performeth the counsel of his messengers; that saith to Jerusalem, Thou shalt be inhabited; and to the cities of Judah, Ye shall be built, and I will raise up the decayed places thereof.

The haunting picture of desolate Jerusalem that we sense here is found often in Isaiah's words (example: Isaiah 6:11-13). The Creator of the world and of the nation will become the re-Creator in Israel's future.

Despite our advanced technology and construction techniques, we still see pictures of homes and businesses destroyed by hurricanes, floods, and tornadoes. The forces of nature are beyond our control, but nothing is beyond God's control. There is no destruction that God cannot rebuild. There is no decay that cannot be reversed by the power of the Lord. God created and God is able to re-create. This is true for nations, for people groups, and for individuals. While Isaiah is talking about a rebuilt Jerusalem, God can rebuild any life, no matter how broken or desolate.

D. Nature Listens (v. 27)

27. That saith to the deep, Be dry, and I will dry up thy rivers.

In a short verse, Isaiah expresses the truly unimaginable: a word from the Lord can dry up all the water of the earth. The mighty rivers will be waterless. Even more astounding, the oceans can be dried up at a word from God. It is estimated that the oceans of our planet contain more than 300 million cubic miles of water!

Isaiah echoes the creative style of God as found in Genesis 1. There, God is not pictured as a craftsman in a workshop, but as a potentate who gives orders. He speaks, and creation is accomplished. The process of creation is "and God said" (Genesis 1:3). God spoke the oceans into existence (1:9, 10), and He is able to speak them out of existence.

What Do You Think?

What was a time when you saw God work something in a person's life that was as startling as one of His works with the forces of nature?

Talking Points for Your Discussion
- In the life of a believer
- In the life of an unbeliever

❧ POWER OVER NATURE ❧

Glaciers once covered much of North America. The ice gradually receded as the climate changed, leaving the rich farmland of the Midwest—the "breadbasket" of North America—as a contribution to life as we know it today. Another contribution was the formation of the Great Lakes, the largest reservoir of fresh water in the world.

A totally different result of the retreat of the ice shield can be found in east-central Washington state. As the ice melted, the water flowed toward the Pacific Ocean over a 400-foot waterfall that stretched 3.5 miles from one side to the other. (By comparison, Niagara Falls drops only 170 feet.) The demise of the glacial shield resulted in the waterfall's river drying up. What is left of that great waterfall is now the aptly named *Dry Falls.*

God leaves evidence of His power over nature in both the pages of Scripture and in geological features. Those who don't believe the Bible should take a trip to Dry Falls!   —C. R. B.

E. Jerusalem Reborn (v. 28)

28. That saith of Cyrus, He is my shepherd, and shall perform all my pleasure: even saying to Jerusalem, Thou shalt be built; and to the temple, Thy foundation shall be laid.

An amazing prophetic detail is given in this final verse of today's text: the name of the human king who will be God's instrument for accomplishing the promised restoration. He is *Cyrus, the great Persian conqueror*. In 539 BC, the armies of Cyrus will capture the supposedly impregnable city of Babylon. Herodotus, the Greek historian, records that they do this by diverting the Euphrates River, which runs through the city (see Daniel 5:30). According to Herodotus, this allows the Persian army to walk through the once-deep water, reduced to thigh-high level. This tactic may be in mind in Isaiah's statement about the Lord's ability to "dry up . . . rivers" (v. 27, above).

In conquering Babylon, Cyrus will inherit the large population of Jewish people deported from Palestine after the destruction of Jerusalem. Most will be second- and third-generation descendants of the original deportees. But many still will long to return to their holy city and rebuild the temple. This desire will be granted by Cyrus (Ezra 1:1-3).

Isaiah understands this to be much more than a political maneuver by a powerful king who is yet to be born. Rather, this will be by God for God's own righteous purposes (see Isaiah 45:13). In this manner, Isaiah can even speak of Cyrus as being "anointed" by God (45:1). Thus Cyrus is a shadow of the ultimate messianic deliverer yet to come: Jesus. God is the Lord of all, the great and the small, the powerful and the weak. Isaiah pushes the vision of the Lord far beyond any national god to the true position of the King of kings, the Lord of the universe (compare Daniel 2:47).

Conclusion

A. New Jerusalem

Jerusalem may have more recorded history attached to it than any city on earth. We encounter the city initially in the Bible through its mysterious priest-king Melchizedek. He is the "king of Salem," a reference to the city's earliest name (Genesis 14:18). It was conquered by King David to become his capital around 1000 BC. It was the site of the temple of the Lord, built by Solomon in the tenth century BC.

This temple was rebuilt by Zerubbabel in the sixth century BC and lavishly expanded by Herod the Great. Jerusalem was where the Lord Jesus was crucified, buried, and raised from the dead. The temple was destroyed by the Romans in AD 70, and the city itself was destroyed by the Romans during the Bar Kochba Revolt in AD 135. At this time, the Roman Emperor Hadrian placed a ban on Jews entering the city. This ban was in effect until the fourth century. Modern Jerusalem continues to be a focal point of regional unrest.

As important as Jerusalem's history is, the New Testament authors look beyond the earthly city of Jerusalem to a new and greater city for the future. Jerusalem's spiritual role had been as the city of the temple. The temple was the house of the Lord. It was seen as the place where God and people met, "the connecting place" if you will.

The book of Revelation pictures a new Jerusalem (Revelation 21:2). It comes down from Heaven fully built, without need for restoration. It is glorious, to be sure, but its architectural wonder is a minor feature compared with the new reality it represents. By coming down, it obliterates the separation between Heaven and earth. "The tabernacle of God is with men, and he will dwell with them" (Revelation 21:3).

This is not simply a vision of the distant future. Paul pictures the people of God collectively as a temple fit together to be God's dwelling place (Ephesians 2:21, 22). God dwells among us now. He is not far away (Acts 17:27). As He restored ancient Jerusalem, He is able to restore our broken and desolate lives. God's pattern of restoring in the history of ancient Israel is repeated daily and individually among those who trust in Him. He will never forget us. He will never abandon us. He has redeemed us through the blood of His Son, and He will make us whole.

B. Prayer

God, our restorer, may You bring healing to our lives as we trust in You. May You bring us assurance that You have not forgotten us and that You will never desert us. May we be like the mountains and the forest that sing Your praises as You restore us to yourself. We pray these things in the name of Your Son, Jesus, our Savior. Amen.

C. Thought to Remember

God continually renews us.

INVOLVEMENT LEARNING

Some of the activities below are also found in the helpful student book, Adult Bible Class.
Don't forget to download the free reproducible page from www.standardlesson.com to enhance your lesson!

Into the Lesson

Distribute index cards. Ask your learners to write down one prediction of something they think will happen in 2011; have them sign their names on the cards. This can be either a personal, a local, or a national prediction.

Ask for volunteers to share what they have written. Then collect the cards and promise to return them at the end of the year. Say, "How confident are you that this prediction will come true?" After responses, make a transition by saying, "In today's text, Isaiah makes a prediction about a person not yet born who would allow Jerusalem to be rebuilt, even though it had not yet been destroyed. Let's see exactly what Isaiah has to say."

Into the Word

Form your learners into small study-teams or study pairs. Give each team or pair one of the following assignments. (Make duplicate assignments if your class is large enough to have more than three teams or pairs.) Provide a hymnal or chorus book for group A; provide poster board and markers for group B.

Group A: WHAT GOD WILL DO. Read Isaiah 44:21-28. Then focus on verses 21-23 to answer the following questions. 1. What is it that God wants the people to remember? 2. Even though the Israelites will go into captivity because of their sins, what does God promise to do for them? 3. Who is to sing praises to the Lord? 4. For what reason are they to praise Him? 5. What would be an appropriate hymn or chorus that praises God for what He has done? Use the hymnal or chorus book to select one.

Group B: WHY THEY CAN TRUST GOD. Read Isaiah 44:21-28. Then focus on verses 24, 25 to answer the following questions. 1. How involved is God in each person's life? Why would this make us trust Him? 2. To what extent was God involved in creation? 3. What actions does God take against liars, fortune tellers, and "wise" people? 4. Why do these verses give us confidence in God's ability to help us? 5. What are some reasons to trust God to help us? Put those reasons on the poster board.

Group C: HOW GOD WILL HELP. Read Isaiah 44:21-28. Then focus on verses 26-28 to answer the following questions. 1. How does God help His servants who speak for Him? 2. In what specific ways will God restore Judah after the people return from captivity? 3. How does Isaiah describe God's power over nature? 4. How will God use a future leader to help His people? 5. What verbs demonstrate how God will help the people? Write a responsive reading where part of your group asks "How will God help?" with the rest replying with short statements about God's actions.

Allow time for group A to lead the class in singing the song it picked, group B to show its poster, and group C to perform the responsive reading.

Into Life

Option 1. Download the reproducible page and distribute copies of the activity titled Help for the Hurting. As learners remain in their groups, assign one of the three people described in the activity to each group. After several minutes, have each group read aloud the situation and give responses.

Option 2. Before class, prepare index cards by tearing a small piece from each one. Distribute one torn card to each learner. Ask them to write on the card an area of life in which they experienced "brokenness" (examples: anger control, addiction, abuse, immorality, bankruptcy).

Pass around masking tape so your learners can repair their torn cards. Suggest they write a prayer of praise to God for helping to mend the brokenness, restoring them to wholeness. Stress that God can make us new and gives us a fresh start. Ask if there is anyone willing to share his or her story with the class. Close with a prayer of thanks to God for redemption.

God Is Our Redeemer

SALVATION FOR GOD'S PEOPLE

BACKGROUND SCRIPTURE: **Isaiah 45**

PRINTED TEXT: **Isaiah 45:14-25**

ISAIAH 45:14-25

14 Thus saith the Lord, The labour of Egypt, and merchandise of Ethiopia and of the Sabeans, men of stature, shall come over unto thee, and they shall be thine: they shall come after thee; in chains they shall come over, and they shall fall down unto thee, they shall make supplication unto thee, saying, Surely God is in thee; and there is none else, there is no God.

15 Verily thou art a God that hidest thyself, O God of Israel, the Saviour.

16 They shall be ashamed, and also confounded, all of them: they shall go to confusion together that are makers of idols.

17 But Israel shall be saved in the LORD with an everlasting salvation: ye shall not be ashamed nor confounded world without end.

18 For thus saith the LORD that created the heavens; God himself that formed the earth and made it; he hath established it, he created it not in vain, he formed it to be inhabited: I am the LORD, and there is none else.

19 I have not spoken in secret, in a dark place of the earth: I said not unto the seed of Jacob, Seek ye me in vain: I the LORD speak righteousness, I declare things that are right.

20 Assemble yourselves and come; draw near together, ye that are escaped of the nations: they have no knowledge that set up the wood of their graven image, and pray unto a god that cannot save.

21 Tell ye, and bring them near; yea, let them take counsel together: who hath declared this from ancient time? who hath told it from that time? have not I the LORD? and there is no God else beside me; a just God and a Saviour; there is none beside me.

22 Look unto me, and be ye saved, all the ends of the earth: for I am God, and there is none else.

23 I have sworn by myself, the word is gone out of my mouth in righteousness, and shall not return, That unto me every knee shall bow, every tongue shall swear.

24 Surely shall one say, In the LORD have I righteousness and strength: even to him shall men come; and all that are incensed against him shall be ashamed.

25 In the LORD shall all the seed of Israel be justified, and shall glory.

KEY VERSE

Look unto me, and be ye saved, all the ends of the earth: for I am God, and there is none else.

—Isaiah 45:22

ASSURING HOPE

Unit 2: A Future for God's People
LESSONS 6–9

LESSON AIMS

After participating in this lesson, each student will be able to:

1. Tell how Isaiah describes the one true God.

2. Explain why it is important for people in idolatrous eras—both ancient and modern—to believe in God.

3. Write a prayer that praises God for His singular nature.

LESSON OUTLINE

Introduction
  A. The Vindication of Job
  B. Lesson Background
 I. God Vindicates Israel (ISAIAH 45:14-17)
  A. Nations' Acknowledgement (v. 14)
    Wealth for Whom? from Whom?
  B. Nations Shamed (vv. 15-17)
 II. God Withstands Scrutiny (ISAIAH 45: 18-21)
  A. In Doing and Being (v. 18)
  B. In Declaring and Predicting (vv. 19-21)
 III. God Offers Salvation (ISAIAH 45:22-25)
  A. Bowing (vv. 22, 23)
  B. Justification (vv. 24, 25)
    Angry with God?
Conclusion
  A. The Vindication of Christ
  B. Prayer
  C. Thought to Remember

Introduction
A. The Vindication of Job

The story of Job is well known. Job was a likable man who treated family, friends, and strangers with compassion and dignity. Yet Job's world fell apart because of circumstances beyond his control. Death claimed his family, catastrophe destroyed his possessions, and disease inflicted his body. But despite all this, he refused to break faith with God.

Job's "friends" determined that he must have earned his terrible lot. He must have grown prideful in his wealth and neglected the needs of those less fortunate. One after another, his companions dragged his name through the mud. Not truly knowing what God was up to, they assumed that they could judge Job according to the terrible fate that had befallen him.

The reader knows, of course, that God was allowing Satan to test Job. We know that Job's name was tarnished through no fault of his own. Deep inside we long for Job's vindication as we read the account. We long for his name to be restored and for his accusers to be put in their place.

In the sixth century BC, Israel longed for its own vindication (compare Psalm 137). But there was an important difference between Job and the Israelites: Job did not deserve to be punished, but Israel did. Thus God allowed Babylon to sack Jerusalem and exile many people. But in the process the Babylonians and others went too far and dragged the name of Israel and Israel's God through the mud. Those whose wickedness exceeded that of Israel appeared to thrive.

So Israel awaited vindication. The people longed for God to restore them and give the nations the judgment they deserved. In today's passage, Isaiah anticipates this very restoration. Our confidence today is in the God who vows to vindicate the name of Jesus and His people.

B. Lesson Background

The sections of the book of Isaiah appear to address different time periods. Chapters 1–39 clearly discuss events that took place during Isaiah's lifetime in the eighth century BC. God spoke

Salvation for God's People

through Isaiah in this section to warn the Israelites that if they did not repent of their sin then God would use foreign nations to punish them.

Chapters 40–66, however, assume that foreign nations already have come and punished Israel. The concern of this section is to comfort a nation that has been beaten down. This section reassured the Israelites that God had not abandoned them. He planned to restore them and use them as His vehicle of blessing to the nations. In short, God's purpose for Israel would not fail.

Babylon's sack of Jerusalem in 586 BC (compare 2 Kings 25) was an event that was jarring beyond description. The temple was destroyed and the kingship was lost, with both commoners and prominent leaders taken into exile. In short, Israel's world was turned upside down, and the people were driven to desperation. For this reason, God commissioned the prophet Isaiah in anticipation of the time when the punishment for their sins would be complete (Isaiah 40:1, 2).

This comfort takes several forms over the chapters leading up to today's passage: Israel is told that God is coming to save her (Isaiah 40:9-11); God is sovereign over the nations (40:15-24); Israel is God's chosen servant (41:8-10); God is uniquely divine (44:6-8); the idols of the nations are nothing (44:9-20); Jerusalem has a bright future (44:24-28); and God will use the Persian ruler Cyrus as His tool to release the Jews from exile

HOW TO SAY IT

Assyria	Uh-*sear*-ee-uh.
Assyrians	Uh-*sear*-e-unz.
Babylon	*Bab*-uh-lun.
Babylonian	Bab-ih-*low*-nee-un.
Cambyses	Kam-*bye*-seez.
Cyrus	*Sigh*-russ.
Egypt	*Ee*-jipt.
Elie Wiesel	*Ee*-lie *Vee*-suhl.
Ethiopia	E-thee-*o*-pee-uh (*th* as in *thin*).
Israelite	*Iz*-ray-el-ite.
Persian	*Per*-zhuhn.
Sabeans	Suh-*be*-unz.
Seba	*See*-buh.
Somalia	So-*mah*-lee-yuh.

and rebuild Jerusalem (45:1-13). Today's passage follows immediately after this statement of Cyrus's commission.

I. God Vindicates Israel
(ISAIAH 45:14-17)
A. Nations' Acknowledgement (v. 14)

14. Thus saith the LORD, The labour of Egypt, and merchandise of Ethiopia and of the Sabeans, men of stature, shall come over unto thee, and they shall be thine: they shall come after thee; in chains they shall come over, and they shall fall down unto thee, they shall make supplication unto thee, saying, Surely God is in thee; and there is none else, there is no God.

The countries of Egypt, Ethiopia, and Seba (which is the country of the Sabeans) are located in close proximity to one another in northeast Africa (compare Genesis 10:7; Psalm 72:10; Isaiah 43:3). On the surface, this appears to be a straightforward statement that the inhabitants of this area and their wealth will be handed over to Israel on that great day when God restores His people. Those non-Israelites then will confess Israel's God to be the one true God. We wonder, however, why only this limited geographical area is mentioned. Considering the wider historical and literary contexts will give us greater depth of understanding.

We begin by acknowledging that this passage builds on God's calling of Cyrus to deliver Israel (Isaiah 45:1, 13). In so doing, verses 14-17 contrast Israel's future fate with the fate of those who live in northeast Africa. We see the subjugation of that area in verse 14, and we see the salvation of Israel in verse 17 (considered further below). Both begin to happen at the hand of the Persian leader Cyrus. It is he who sets the Jewish exiles free in 539 BC and begins to support their rebuilding efforts.

In 525 BC, the Persian ruler Cambyses, son of Cyrus, becomes the first ruler from the East to defeat Egypt soundly. After Egypt's defeat at the Battle of Pelusium that year, the Egyptians relinquish their material goods, becoming subservient to the Persians for nearly 200 years. This may explain why only a limited geographical area is mentioned.

Having said this, however, it is still entirely possible and even likely that this passage has a larger implication. Even after release from exile, Judah will be a weak nation under the thumb of foreign domination. This passage is God's encouragement that this situation will not always be the case. God promises to restore His people. God's people know that this cannot happen because of their own strength, but because God glorifies himself by using a weak nation to do great things on behalf of all nations.

Historical hindsight reveals to us God's plan in all its clarity: it is through Israel that Messiah comes, for "salvation is of the Jews" (John 4:22). The prediction *they shall fall down unto thee, they shall make supplication unto thee, saying, Surely God is in thee; and there is none else, there is no God* is echoed in Revelation 3:9.

> **What Do You Think?**
> How does God work to bring nations to a knowledge of Him today?
> *Talking Points for Your Discussion*
> - Things God does when nations consciously reject Him
> - Things God does when nations are indifferent to Him
> - Things God is doing in our nation today

❧ WEALTH FOR WHOM? FROM WHOM? ❧

It has been decades since the east African nation of Somalia has had a properly functioning government. Since the colonial powers left, Somalia often has experienced civil war or war with its neighbors. Displacement and starvation resulted.

Many thought that the world was not paying enough attention to these problems. But a new page was turned when Somali pirates started hijacking ships in the Gulf of Aden for ransom. In November 2008, the pirates seized their most impressive prize: a Saudi oil supertanker, for which the pirates demanded $25 million in ransom. Many nations began to ramp up their efforts to protect the shipping lanes.

The wealth of other nations had not been coming to Somalia, so the pirates went about seizing it. In different forms—whether through Ponzi schemes, bank robbery, or bribery of government officials—that is the way of the world. How different it is with God! All wealth belongs to Him. All nations belong to Him. God's actions with regard to those two areas should be an issue of trust and praise on our part.

—C. R. B.

B. Nations Shamed (vv. 15-17)

15. Verily thou art a God that hidest thyself, O God of Israel, the Saviour.

Who could imagine that the God of the universe would carry out His purposes through a lowly nation like Israel? Who could have anticipated that God would use a pagan ruler like Cyrus to begin carrying out these purposes? No one.

God's thoughts are unsearchable (Isaiah 40:28); His ways are higher (55:9). When God wills to hide himself and His purposes, there is nothing we can do to access them. Were it not for God's gracious decision to reveal himself and His will to us through His spoken, written, and incarnate Word, we would still be in the dark. Because God has revealed himself to His people, Israel, they know (or should know) Him not only as God their Creator but also as God their Savior. When God is seen clearly, He is seen as the God who saves.

16. They shall be ashamed, and also confounded, all of them: they shall go to confusion together that are makers of idols.

Though God has revealed himself to Israel, He has not yet done so to the nations (except through nature, which is available to all; see Psalm 19:1; Romans 1:20). So the nations seek God in their own ways. In the confusion caused by their ignorance, they craft gods with their own hands. Yet when God reveals himself to them, these idols will be seen for their worthlessness. The nations who hoped in them *shall be ashamed.*

17. But Israel shall be saved in the LORD with an everlasting salvation: ye shall not be ashamed nor confounded world without end.

Things are much different, however, for the Israelites. They may not be the most powerful nation. They may, in fact, be the nation that suffers the most abuse, ridicule, and shame. But Israel is God's people chosen to usher in the Messiah.

Salvation for God's People

Though they walk with heads bowed into Babylonian exile, they will march out with heads held high (Psalm 126). God is their salvation and will vindicate them.

II. God Withstands Scrutiny
(ISAIAH 45:18-21)
A. In Doing and Being (v. 18)

18. For thus saith the LORD that created the heavens; God himself that formed the earth and made it; he hath established it, he created it not in vain, he formed it to be inhabited: I am the LORD; and there is none else.

Israel's future is not to be grounded in self-achievement, but in divine promise. The God who created the heavens and earth is the guarantor. God has an impeccable, unmatched track record of accomplishments. He created the world with a purpose that will not fail. He formed it deliberately in order to fill it with vegetation, animals, and thriving civilizations. Though human sin introduced chaos into God's good creation, God has willed to bring order to this chaos through His people Israel. His will for Israel is to be done.

B. In Declaring and Predicting (vv. 19-21)

19. I have not spoken in secret, in a dark place of the earth: I said not unto the seed of Jacob, Seek ye me in vain: I the LORD speak righteousness, I declare things that are right.

Though God is hidden from human scrutiny (v. 15, above), when He speaks to His people He does so with unmistakable clarity. God spoke forthrightly to Abraham, Isaac, and Jacob, setting them apart as witnesses to His purposes in world history. Yet God is also clear that should the offspring of these men forsake God's ways, then He will punish them by sending them into exile (Deuteronomy 28:15-68). So it is not because of the power of Assyria and Babylon that Israel finds herself beaten, bruised, and exiled.

God means it when He promises the Israelites that He will bless both them and all nations through them (Genesis 12:1-3; Exodus 19:5, 6). What He declares is true and right and will come to pass without fail. Israel does not follow God in vain. Though God appears to leave them behind, they must remember His prior promise to restore them (Deuteronomy 30:1-10).

20. Assemble yourselves and come; draw near together, ye that are escaped of the nations: they have no knowledge that set up the wood of their graven image, and pray unto a god that cannot save.

God summons refugees from scattered Israel as His witnesses. The Babylonians take many Israelites to Babylon, but the Israelites actually are scattered in multiple directions. Some are dispersed throughout the nations by the Assyrians (compare 2 Kings 17:6); others flee to Egypt (25:26).

God further reminds His people that these nations to which they are scattered are fountains of misinformation. God reminds them of this because the Israelites are and will be tempted to believe the lies of these nations. It may appear that the foreigners who claim that Israel's God is powerless to save them are correct (Isaiah 36:18-20). But the foreigners are duped into thinking that false gods are not only real but more powerful than Israel's God. This is why God reminds the Israelites in Isaiah 44:12-20 that idols are made of the same trees that people use as fuel to cook their food.

21. Tell ye, and bring them near; yea, let them take counsel together: who hath declared this from ancient time? who hath told it from that time? have not I the LORD? and there is no God else beside me; a just God and a Saviour; there is none beside me.

To demonstrate that He alone is divine, God points to the fact that He alone predicts the outcome of events in world history. It was God who told the northern kingdom of Israel that the Assyrians would defeat them if they did not repent; the Assyrians did their job in 722 BC. It was God who said that the southern kingdom of Judah would fall to Babylon if she did not learn from the mistakes of the northern kingdom of Israel; that fall happens in 586 BC. So now, God calls on the people to believe Him as He announces His intent to restore Israel and use Cyrus as His instrument.

God has a proven track record of announcing things to come and bringing them to pass. No idol can do that. Only Israel's God has done this, and only Israel has witnessed His prophetic words come true.

What Do You Think?
Considering God's proven record of fulfilled prophecy, what are some of the Bible's most exciting predictions about your future as a believer?
Talking Points for Your Discussion
- In this life (Mark 10:29, 30; Galatians 5:22-24; 1 Peter 1:8, 9)
- In the life to come (Mark 10:29, 30; John 14:2, 3; Romans 8:18)

III. God Offers Salvation
(ISAIAH 45:22-25)
A. Bowing (vv. 22, 23)

22. Look unto me, and be ye saved, all the ends of the earth: for I am God, and there is none else.

God has made His case and has offered irrefutable evidence. Now it is time for a response. In this light, He invites *the ends of the earth* to look to Him for salvation. It is not clear exactly who *the ends of the earth* are in this verse. God could be talking about the Jewish refugees from the nations in verse 20 (compare Isaiah 11:12), or He could be talking about the nations themselves in their totality. God goes on to say in verse 23 (next) that every knee will bow, which lends support to the idea that it is all nations. But then in verse 25 the focus is back on Israel.

Regardless of who exactly is being addressed in this verse, we can affirm that the one true God is the source of salvation for the entire world. Furthermore, God does not seek to save Israel from its captivity only for Israel's sake. Rather, He rescues Israel so He may continue His mission to use Israel as His vehicle of blessing to the entire world. As Christians, we affirm that people everywhere must turn to God's Son alone for salvation.

What Do You Think?
In addition to supporting or being an overseas missionary, what are some ways to take God's message of salvation to the ends of the earth?
Talking Points for Your Discussion
- Person-to-person methods
- Technological methods
- Prayer techniques

23. I have sworn by myself, the word is gone out of my mouth in righteousness, and shall not return, That unto me every knee shall bow, every tongue shall swear.

The prediction that *every knee shall bow, every tongue shall swear* is echoed in Philippians 2:10, 11. A consistent theme of Isaiah is that God is Ruler over all nations. Though it appears that God loses the battle against the Babylonian gods—since His people seem to have lost out to Babylon—every knee will bow to the true God and every tongue will confess His sovereignty.

This is not the same as saying that every person will be saved. Rather, every person will acknowledge the one true Lord either voluntarily or involuntarily. Thus the Israelites can be confident that God's promise to save and restore them will come to pass. This is the same confidence Christians have. (Paul quotes this passage in Romans 14:11.)

B. Justification (vv. 24, 25)

24. Surely shall one say, In the LORD have I righteousness and strength: even to him shall men come; and all that are incensed against him shall be ashamed.

People divide themselves into two camps: (1) those who find *righteousness and strength* in God and (2) those who resist God's reign only to find shame. Though every knee will bow, some will bow in shame while others will bow in joyful submission. So God entreats His people to find their strength in Him and not to be counted among those who end up ashamed.

❧ *ANGRY WITH GOD?* ❧

Elie Wiesel, winner of the 1986 Nobel Peace Prize, spent many months in Nazi death camps. Recounting the horrors, he writes in his book *Night,* "Never shall I forget that night, the first night in camp, which has turned my life into one long night. . . . Never shall I forget those moments which murdered my God and my soul, and turned my dreams to dust."

During those agonizing days, Wiesel and millions of others were subjected to barbaric cruelties. He recalls being among many prisoners who were forced to watch the hanging of three people. Wiesel recalls hearing someone behind him ask, "Where is God now?" Wiesel heard his own voice answer within him, "Where is He? Here He is—He is hanging here on this gallows."

The ancient Israelites went through several episodes of oppression by foreign powers. During such times, they wondered where God was (example: Judges 6:13). The answer of Scripture must be heard: God is righteous, and ultimately we shall see and understand that truth. "All that are incensed against him shall be ashamed." —C. R. B.

25. In the LORD shall all the seed of Israel be justified, and shall glory.

God is confident of Israel's response. The church is justified before Christ, who is the ultimate *seed of Israel* (Galatians 3:16-29). Though God's people of any given era may seem to be at the bottom of the world's rankings, they will be vindicated by the one and only true God. This is (or should be)

Visual for
Lesson 6

Point to this visual as you ask, "How do the words *salvation* and *justification* relate to each other?"

extremely encouraging to Jews ravaged by Babylon. It remains the source of hope for Christians who suffer deprivation in our own day.

Conclusion
A. The Vindication of Christ

Christians continue to suffer under oppression they've done nothing to deserve. May we learn this lesson from Israel's history: as long as we fix our hope on the only one who is able to save, we will be vindicated. May we remember our Savior Jesus, who also appeared to have been forsaken by God (Matthew 27:46). He suffered a cruel death and had His name dragged through the mud of crucifixion with criminals. But God raised Him from the dead and seated Him at the right hand of the Father. There Jesus awaits the day when every knee will bow and every tongue will confess that He is Lord (Philippians 2:5-11).

B. Prayer

Lord God, You alone are powerful to save. You have proven yourself time and again in Scripture, in world history, and in our lives. Keep our heads turned straight toward You, in whom alone we have hope, through Jesus Christ. Amen.

C. Thought to Remember

God and only God saves.

INVOLVEMENT LEARNING

Some of the activities below are also found in the helpful student book, Adult Bible Class.
Don't forget to download the free reproducible page from www.standardlesson.com to enhance your lesson!

Into the Lesson

Have a learner give a dramatic reading of the fall of Jerusalem as described in 2 Kings 24:18–25:21. This will establish the tone of the dire and depressing situation of God's people that is the (future) backdrop to today's text from Isaiah.

Following the reading, ask, "Without looking back at the text, what were the elements of God's prescribed punishment for the people's persistent sin?" List responses on the board.

Comment: "Isaiah writes for a people who will be totally devastated. Their sense of identity, both political and spiritual, will be compromised severely. They will need God's reassurance that He has not forsaken them. Thus, Isaiah can deliver the hope of today's words, a reinforcement of the promises we have studied the last two weeks."

Into the Word

Ask, "What is it you want to happen when you feel as if nothing is good about your circumstances?" Expect such responses as, "I want to be reassured that everything will get better," "I want to have the company of those who care about me," and "I want someone to tell me what to do." Write answers on the board.

If no one suggests it, ask, "Would you want to be reminded that God is present, that He is the all-powerful God of grace and mercy?" Note that that is Isaiah's encouraging word in the situation of today's text. *Option:* Before or after you ask the opening question, you may wish to ask, "What is it you do *not* want to hear when you feel as if nothing is good about your circumstances?" Jot answers on the board and discuss.

Next, distribute handouts with the following list of descriptions and activities of God (the verse numbers in parentheses should not be included on the handouts): truthful *(v. 19)*; directs history *(v. 14)*; Creator *(v. 18)*; has expectations *(v. 22)*; singular *(v. 18)*; above time *(v. 21)*; invites *(v. 22)*;

Redeemer *(vv. 17, 22)*; self-revealer *(v. 19)*; punishing *(v. 24)*; vindicates *(v. 24)*.

Then say, "Find in today's text an affirmation of the description or activity of God as reflected in each entry of this list. Write a verse number or numbers by each."

This activity can be done in study teams or pairs. Discuss results as a class; expect some variety in the responses. You may wish to put other attributes on the list according to today's text. *Alternative:* Download the reproducible page and use the activity The God Who instead. The descriptions on this exercise are somewhat different from those above, and you may prefer to use it instead. Under either arrangement, be sure to discuss why the descriptions of God were important to Israel's situation.

Into Life

Use a period of directed prayer to conclude your session. Indicate to the class that you will give them several prayer stimulus statements based on today's text, and that you will allow a brief period of time for silent prayer after each statement.

Create your own stimulus statements or use these: (1) Because God has revealed himself to be who He is, we have no cause for fear; praise Him for His attributes. (2) Even our enemies can become servants of God; pray for opportunities to share the gospel with them. (3) All who are in Christ will be found righteous in Him; thank God for that fact. (4) Distress and pain are temporary, but salvation is everlasting; pray for a spiritual understanding of time and eternity. (5) When Christ appears, we will be like Him, according to 1 John 3:2; thank Him for our hope of glory.

As students depart, distribute copies of the stimulus statements and copies of The God Who Hears and Answers Prayers activity from the reproducible page. Encourage your learners to use these in their devotional times during the week ahead.

REASSURANCE FOR GOD'S PEOPLE

BACKGROUND SCRIPTURE: Isaiah 48
PRINTED TEXT: Isaiah 48:12-22

ISAIAH 48:12-22

12 Hearken unto me, O Jacob and Israel, my called; I am he; I am the first, I also am the last.

13 Mine hand also hath laid the foundation of the earth, and my right hand hath spanned the heavens: when I call unto them, they stand up together.

14 All ye, assemble yourselves, and hear; which among them hath declared these things? The LORD hath loved him: he will do his pleasure on Babylon, and his arm shall be on the Chaldeans.

15 I, even I, have spoken; yea, I have called him: I have brought him, and he shall make his way prosperous.

16 Come ye near unto me, hear ye this; I have not spoken in secret from the beginning; from the time that it was, there am I: and now the Lord GOD, and his Spirit, hath sent me.

17 Thus saith the Lord, thy Redeemer, the Holy One of Israel; I am the Lord thy God which teacheth thee to profit, which leadeth thee by the way that thou shouldest go.

18 O that thou hadst hearkened to my commandments! then had thy peace been as a river, and thy righteousness as the waves of the sea:

19 Thy seed also had been as the sand, and the offspring of thy bowels like the gravel thereof; his name should not have been cut off nor destroyed from before me.

20 Go ye forth of Babylon, flee ye from the Chaldeans, with a voice of singing declare ye, tell this, utter it even to the end of the earth; say ye, The Lord hath redeemed his servant Jacob.

21 And they thirsted not when he led them through the deserts: he caused the waters to flow out of the rock for them: he clave the rock also, and the waters gushed out.

22 There is no peace, saith the Lord, unto the wicked.

KEY VERSE

Go ye forth of Babylon, flee ye from the Chaldeans, with a voice of singing declare ye, tell this, utter it even to the end of the earth; say ye, The LORD hath redeemed his servant Jacob. —**Isaiah 48:20**

ASSURING HOPE

Unit 2: A Future for God's People
LESSONS 6–9

LESSON AIMS

After participating in this lesson, each student will be able to:

1. List the names and descriptions that the Lord applies to himself in today's text.

2. Explain the relevance of the names and descriptions of the Lord for people today.

3. Express a resolve to serve God in a specific manner in light of having been freed from spiritual captivity.

LESSON OUTLINE

Introduction

A. What Might Have Been

Past failures can be paralyzing. Some who have made poor educational and career choices are now crushed under the weight of unfulfilling jobs. Some who rushed quickly into marriage struggle to maintain healthy relationships and keep promises. Others who neglected spending time with their children now regret the quality of the relationships that have resulted. Christians and non-Christians alike are plagued with regrets about the past. Sometimes we wish we could do it all over again. We wonder "what might have been" if only we had made better choices.

The Israelites found themselves in a similar situation. They had a bright future when God called them out of slavery in Egypt. With His promise to be with them and to prosper their every step, they were poised to flourish. Yet they violated their side of the covenant and traded success for failure.

It was tempting for them to give up altogether (see the book of Lamentations). But God would not allow them to do that. In today's Scripture, He both reminds the Israelites of what might have been and beckons them to the new future that still could be. In so doing, God also reminds us that our worst failures need not be the last word for our lives. Though we cannot change the past, God can guide our future.

B. Lesson Background

As we noted last week, the Babylonians had taken full control of the southern kingdom of the Israelites, called Judah, by 586 BC. That was about 136 years after Assyria had done the same to the northern kingdom, called Israel. In 586 BC, the temple was destroyed, its vessels were confiscated, and many people were deported to Babylon.

God had foretold that this would happen if the Israelites did not repent of their sin. Yet it was still difficult for the people to process what was happening to them. They were devastated. The book of Lamentations captures the sense of desperation that overcame God's people at this time.

Last week we saw God promise to vindicate Israel in the eyes of the nations. This week He encourages Israel not to dwell on her past failures. God is ready to move forward. Those who wish to go forward with Him had to get on board.

I. Plan
(ISAIAH 48:12-16)

A. Hear Him Who Creates (vv. 12, 13)

12. Hearken unto me, O Jacob and Israel, my called; I am he; I am the first, I also am the last.

In verses 12-16, God calls His people three times to come to attention and hear what He has to tell them. Each time His call appeals to a different aspect of His own character and track record. We would think that God certainly needs no introduction! But the Israelites have shown by their actions that they have forgotten just who it is who calls them to service. In the verse before us, God reminds His people that He is everlasting. He always has been and always will be. Before the world, humanity, and Israel existed—God was.

Those unfamiliar with the nature of Hebrew poetry might be confused as to the exact recipients of this divine address. At first glance, God appears to be summoning two groups in this verse: *Jacob and Israel*. But God is, in fact, calling only one people-group. This is because of the distinguishing feature of Hebrew poetry known as *parallelism*. Parallelism means that the author repeats the same concept using different words. In this verse, then, God is summoning His people who descended from the patriarch Jacob, people who now go by the name of Israel.

13. Mine hand also hath laid the foundation of the earth, and my right hand hath spanned the heavens: when I call unto them, they stand up together.

Even though He should not have to do so, God reminds His people that He who calls them is also He who created the heavens and the earth. It is to the Israelites' shame that God has to remind them of this. Though the Israelites know this on an intellectual level, their actions have not matched their knowledge.

As God calls Israel to listen, He reminds the people that the created order stands at attention when He calls to it. The heavens and the earth immediately recognize and respect the divine call, yet His chosen people are slow to respond.

Are we any different? We have intellectual knowledge that God is the Creator. But our actions can contradict this "head knowledge." That happens when we fret about the bills coming in, when we presume that we don't have time to gather with God's people for worship, and when we rationalize our sinful choices. We too need to be reminded that our Creator possesses all the resources that we need, gives us plenty of time to be faithful to Him, and shows us how to live properly.

What Do You Think?

How should our awareness of God as Creator affect the way we relate to Him personally and conduct ourselves generally?

Talking Points for Your Discussion

- What we say (Ecclesiastes 5:2)
- How we trust (2 Peter 1:3)
- Things we do (1 John 2:3)

B. Hear Him Who Chooses (vv. 14, 15)

14. All ye, assemble yourselves, and hear; which among them hath declared these things? The LORD hath loved him: he will do his pleasure on Babylon, and his arm shall be on the Chaldeans.

This verse requires a bit of digging to figure out who or what is being discussed. Exactly who or what does the phrase *which among them* point to? The context implies a reference to idols. Thus the answer to the question *which among them hath declared these things?* is obvious: none of them (compare Jeremiah 10:5). Only God can declare the things we have just read in verse 13.

The one whom *the Lord hath loved* is Cyrus, since he is the Persian ruler who overthrows *Babylon* and sends the Jewish people home from exile to rebuild Jerusalem (compare Ezra 1:2-8). Though Cyrus is not mentioned by name in this passage, he is named specifically in Isaiah 44:28; 45:1. Cyrus is still in view here in 48:14.

We should not think that God "loves" Cyrus more than God loves the pagan kings of, say,

Babylon or Greece. We learn in Daniel 7 and 8 that, from God's perspective, the rulers of these nations (including Persia) are like beasts. Rather, the term *love* sometimes simply means that God has chosen for His purposes one particular person or nation rather than another one (compare Malachi 1:2, 3; Romans 9:13).

The main point of this verse, however, is that God demonstrates His sovereignty by foretelling that Cyrus will be His instrument of judgment on the Babylonians. Again we see parallelism, since the Chaldeans are the people who inhabit Babylon. So this verse does not depict God using Cyrus against two different groups of people, but against one single group.

15. I, even I, have spoken; yea, I have called him: I have brought him, and he shall make his way prosperous.

This verse, using good Hebrew repetition, reinforces the point made above. Since God declares that He will use Cyrus, king of Persia, for His purposes, Israel can rest assured that this will happen. This is good news for Israel.

Cyrus, who is not yet born as Isaiah prophesies, will have no special affection for Israel. He will not know that God is prospering him in order to judge Babylon and begin restoring Israel. Cyrus merely will choose what he sees as a good foreign policy: he gains the loyalty of vassal nations by sending their leaders back home and supporting their rebuilding projects. Cyrus will be happy as long as these vassals pay him the tribute he requires.

HOW TO SAY IT

Assyria	Uh-*sear*-ee-uh.
Babylon	*Bab*-uh-lun.
Babylonians	Bab-ih-*low*-nee-unz.
Chaldeans	Kal-*dee*-unz.
Cyrus	*Sigh*-russ.
Israel	*Iz*-ray-el.
Lamentations	Lam-en-*tay*-shunz.
Miriam	*Meer*-ee-um.
Moses	*Mo*-zes or *Mo*-zez.
patriarchs	*pay*-tree-arks.
Persian	*Per*-zhuhn.
Yahweh *(Hebrew)*	*Yah*-weh.

When God is finished using Cyrus for His purposes, then God's special favor will be lifted. Then He will use Greece to judge Persia, just as He used Persia to judge Babylon (Daniel 8). Israel is unique in that God's love for His chosen people does not come and go.

❊ GOD'S WORK IN HISTORY ❊

"When, in the course of human events, it becomes necessary for one people to dissolve the political bonds which have connected them with another, and to assume among the powers of the earth, the separate and equal station to which the laws of nature and of nature's God entitle them, a decent respect to the opinions of mankind requires that they should declare the causes which impel them to the separation. We hold these truths to be self-evident, that all men are created equal, that they are endowed by their Creator with certain unalienable rights, that among these are life, liberty and the pursuit of happiness."

At some point in their education, most Americans have read those powerful words from the U. S. Declaration of Independence. Written in 1776, the document set forth the philosophical—yes, even the spiritual—basis for the founding of America. References to self-evident truths about the Creator, the laws of nature and of nature's God have a biblical ring to them.

Not only do the forces of nature obey God's voice, so do the currents of history, as today's text reminds us. While still allowing human beings to exert their own will, God controls the circumstances that provide opportunity for us to bring about the plans He has for the redemption of the world. Are you in tune with those currents of history?　　　　　　　　　　　　—C. R. B.

C. Hear Him Who Commissions (v. 16)

16. Come ye near unto me, hear ye this; I have not spoken in secret from the beginning; from the time that it was, there am I: and now the Lord GOD, and his Spirit, hath sent me.

God wraps up His summons by reminding the Israelites that He has been forthright about His purposes since the beginning. He predicts Israel's fall to Babylon, and He predicts the rise of Cyrus

　Reassurance for God's People

and eventual fall of Babylon. God has kept Israel in the loop concerning His plans for the nations. The Israelites are therefore His witnesses. God reminds them of His past word in hopes that they will stand at attention and heed the new word that He has for them now.

We also read here about the prophet's own commission. Cyrus is not the only one sent. The prophet himself is sent by God's Spirit. With all the speaking God does throughout this book, Isaiah's voice can be overlooked. We should not forget that the original audience does not hear God speak directly to them, but hears God speaking to them through the prophet by God's Spirit.

II. Reaction
(Isaiah 48:17-19)
A. God Leads (v. 17)

17. Thus saith the LORD, thy Redeemer, the Holy One of Israel; I am the LORD thy God which teacheth thee to profit, which leadeth thee by the way that thou shouldest go.

God introduces himself here in a threefold manner that points back to His deliverance of the Israelites from Egypt. First, He introduces himself as *LORD*, which all-capitalized means *Yahweh*; this is the personal name that God revealed to Moses on the mountain. Second, God introduces himself as *Redeemer*, the one who redeemed the people from slavery in Egypt. Third, He repeats that He is *the Holy One of Israel*, a phrase used 31 times in the Old Testament, 25 of which occur in Isaiah.

Furthermore, God is the one who gave His law through Moses to teach the people the right way to live. In God's role as leader, He guided the Israelites through the wilderness and into the promised land. God reminds the people that He is the God of the exodus from Egypt because He intends in their own day to launch a new exodus from Babylon, some nine centuries after the first one.

B. Israel Rejects (v. 18)

18. O that thou hadst hearkened to my commandments! then had thy peace been as a river, and thy righteousness as the waves of the sea.

But the Israelites of the Egyptian exodus did not obey God. In rejecting His commandments, they rejected the means God was using to show them abundant life and use them as a witness to the nations. If Israel had ordered her life according to God's law, the people would have experienced peace, they would have exemplified righteousness, and they would have provided the nations a glimpse of God's wonderful intentions. They would have been blessed by God and would have become a blessing to all nations.

C. Israel Suffers (v. 19)

19. Thy seed also had been as the sand, and the offspring of thy bowels like the gravel thereof; his name should not have been cut off nor destroyed from before me.

Peace . . . as a river.
ISAIAH 48:18

Visual for Lesson 7

Point to this visual as you ask, "In what ways have you experienced God's "peace . . . as a river"?

God continues to enumerate the blessings He would have poured out on Israel. A blessing echoed here is the promise to the patriarchs that their descendents would be like the sands of the seashore (Genesis 22:17; 32:12).

Yet this promise has not come to fruition. What might have been is not reality. The Israelites reject the way of life God intends for them. Instead, they choose the ways of the nations around them. In refusing God's way, they have rejected God's strategy for blessing all nations. The nations are supposed to see God's wisdom manifested in Israel and be drawn to it (Deuteronomy 4:5-8).

To reject God's way is thus to reject God's mission. God cannot accept this, so He destroys the Israelites' sinful ways. He cuts the nation down to size in order to begin anew, to remake the Israelites into a people willing to carry out His plan.

What Do You Think?
What lessons has God taught you from your experiences of disobedience?
Talking Points for Your Discussion
- Blessings that were lost
- Ministry opportunities gained
- Changed attitude toward others who stumble

God's intention has not changed. God sends Jesus to instruct people, to atone for our sins, and to send us out with Holy Spirit power in order to carry out our mission. God uses Christians to show the world what He intends for all. The church is called to be a sign, foretaste, and herald of God's kingdom. As Jesus teaches us, if we are not salty salt and bright light, we become useless for God's purposes (Matthew 5:13-16) and will relive the rejection that Israel experienced.

III. God's Hope for Israel
(Isaiah 48:20-22)
A. New Commission (v. 20)
20. Go ye forth of Babylon, flee ye from the Chaldeans, with a voice of singing declare ye, tell this, utter it even to the end of the earth; say ye, The Lord hath redeemed his servant Jacob.

After being reminded of what could have been, the Israelites can fall into deep depression. There is a danger of merely wallowing in self-pity. But God doesn't rub our noses in our failure only to increase our misery. Nor does He pretend the past never happened. Rather, He meets us where we are now and helps us begin anew, while accepting the reality of what has gone before.

What Do You Think?
How do we "move on" from past failure?
Talking Points for Your Discussion
- The danger of equating "moving on" with "sweeping things under the rug"
- The distinction between failures that do and do not involve sin
- The grief process

For Israel, a new beginning will mean a new exodus. God will send the Israelites forth singing from Babylon. As Moses and Miriam sang of God's great deliverance from Egypt (Exodus 15), these new refugees are called to sing of God's redemption of Jacob (compare Psalm 126). They had been slaves in Egypt; they will be captives in Babylon. But God does not forsake them. He frees them from bondage so they may proclaim *to the end of the earth* that God is their Redeemer.

This theme of freedom from captivity is so important to Jesus that He presents His own ministry as a fulfillment of Isaiah 61:1, 2, which speaks of Israel's deliverance from Babylon (Luke 4:17-21). Christians must continue to sing this song of God's mighty deliverance!

B. Past Provision (v. 21)
21. And they thirsted not when he led them through the deserts: he caused the waters to flow out of the rock for them: he clave the rock also, and the waters gushed out.

Though the captive Israelites will certainly welcome God's deliverance from Babylon, they will also entertain doubts. How will they be able to survive their homeward journey of 1,000 miles? How will they be able to rebuild after arriving? Like Israel's refugees of old, some undoubtedly will prefer the familiarity of captivity in Babylon

Reassurance for God's People

to the many unknowns of the journey home (Exodus 14:11, 12; Numbers 11:5).

Yet the God who created the heavens and earth has plenty of resources to provide for His people. So He reminds them again of their ancestors who left Egypt. God provided not only water as this verse notes (Exodus 17:6), but also manna (Exodus 16:14, 15) and quail (Numbers 11:31). God has unlimited resources, and He desires to meet His people's every need.

❧ THE PAST REMEMBERED ❧

In the autumn of 2005, several men set out from the Pacific coast of Mexico to fish for sharks. Their boat became disabled, and they began drifting westward. They were not rescued until nine months later, thousands of miles across the ocean, near the Marshall Islands. The survivors stayed alive by drinking rainwater and eating raw fish and birds. They told of reading the Bible and praying to be rescued during those long months.

It would seem that the fishermen experienced a providential answer to their prayers in the provision of fresh water and food. The main question now is whether or not the fishermen will credit God with their survival as the years pass.

In today's text, Isaiah reminds Israel of their ancestors' ordeal in the desert, during which time God provided water and food. But facts of history are not enough in and of themselves; the people needed to *remember* and *meditate on* those facts. We humans have certain failings in that area, don't we?
—C. R. B.

C. Final Thought (v. 22)

22. There is no peace, saith the LORD, unto the wicked.

To recall God's miraculous provision of water for the Israelites is also to recall the people's perpetual complaints. Despite all that God did for them, they grumbled and complained. Not only did they grumble about water and food (example: Numbers 11:4-6), they had feared that they couldn't take the promised land (13:26–14:4).

Wicked rebellion is always a breath away. So God reminds the Israelites that His offer of a new start is not for the wicked; it is only for those who accept His grace in faith. The Israelites have a choice to make. Though God offers them new life, Israel may still choose death.

> *What Do You Think?*
> In what ways do God's people experience peace that the wicked do not? How do we account for the fact that some nonbelievers seem carefree while some Christians seem to be always in a state of crisis?
> *Talking Points for Your Discussion*
> - External appearance versus inner reality (Psalms 32:3-5; 73)
> - Temporary pleasures versus real peace (Hebrews 11:25)

Conclusion
A. What Will Be

Past failures were not the final word for the Israelites. After the Babylonian captivity, many returned to Jerusalem to rebuild. Life was not easy. It took several Persian emperors and Jewish leaders plus 10 decades of time before Jerusalem, its temple, and the walls were rebuilt.

Indeed, the mills of God grind slowly from an earthly perspective. So it is tempting to lose hope. Christians continue to suffer—sometimes because of personal unfaithfulness, sometimes because of the unfaithfulness of others.

Yet we are to keep focused on the hope that is before us (Philippians 3:13, 14). Sometimes God delivers us *from* the trials that befall us, sometimes He delivers us *through* them. May Christians always be those who push forward to that which will most certainly be, not being held back by what might have been.

B. Prayer

Gracious God, we thank You for new starts. Though our failures overwhelm us, Your creative power bursts through. Increase our faith so we may see Your power for what it is and draw on that power to move forward. In Jesus' name, amen.

C. Thought to Remember

Embrace what now may be.

INVOLVEMENT LEARNING

Some of the activities below are also found in the helpful student book, Adult Bible Class.
Don't forget to download the free reproducible page from www.standardlesson.com to enhance your lesson!

Into the Lesson

Set up six large cards onto which you have written the letters *I F O N L Y,* one letter per card, in that exact order. Conceal the letters from your learners. As class begins, reveal the first letter *(I)* and the last letter *(Y).* Say, "The first letter stands for *Israel.* The last letter stands for *Yahweh,* that is, God. Notice that there is much keeping the two apart."

Ask the class to identify Israel's sins, making sure that idolatry is mentioned. Then reveal the other letters to show the phrase *if only.* Note that verse 18 of today's text reveals the great *if only* that haunts all people: "O that thou hadst hearkened." Comment, "Isaiah says Israel's reaction to that great 'if only' will be either peace or no peace." Have a learner read verse 18 and then verse 22. Then display the four phrases *Know Christ, Know Peace. No Christ, No Peace.* Ask learners where they have seen this (bumper stickers, etc.).

Into the Word

Distribute envelopes containing the following letters printed on two-inch squares of paper, one letter per square: W A R A N D P E A C E. Each learner should receive one envelope. Shuffle the letters before you put them in the envelopes. Say, "Open your envelope and arrange the letters in it to make the three-word title of a famous book and a key theme of today's text." Once one learner has solved the puzzle—give clues as necessary—ask everyone to arrange their letters to read *WAR AND PEACE.*

Point out once again the peace-phrase in verse 18; draw attention again to verse 22. Comment "There is a war for our souls, but there is peace for those who listen to the Lord. Look at today's text for the *war and peace* theme. Where do you see it? Look at the text and jot down *W* for *war* or *P* for *peace* for each verse, based on the images brought to mind." Allow a few minutes to do so.

Then go through each verse and ask, "W or P?" Allow learners to explain their choices. Although you will have differences of opinion, here are two sample explanations: *P* for verse 12, because God's continuing existence bespeaks the peace of stability and strength; *W* for verse 14, because God speaks of subduing Babylon.

Say, "The God who reveals himself in today's text is quite capable of making war on His enemies. He is quite ready to provide peace for those who trust and obey Him. Let's make a quick list of His acts and attributes that Isaiah identifies, so that we can see both possibilities in Him, both war and peace." Let the class make the list. It is certain to include such elements as His eternal nature (v. 12), His power (v. 13), His utter superiority (v. 14), His trustworthy promises (vv. 14, 15, etc.), His wisdom in what is the way for people to go (v. 17), and His plans for His people (v. 20).

Alternative: Instead of structuring the lesson around the theme of war and peace, use an approach that focuses on the text's imperatives. To do so, download the reproducible page and have learners work on the Simple Imperatives activity individually. Discuss results first in small groups then as a whole class.

Into Life

Download the reproducible page and distribute copies of the Redemption Proclamation activity from it. Discuss your learners' choices.

As learners depart, give each a construction-paper chain of six links (loops), each of which is six inches by one inch. Say, "Let this chain represent the spiritual captivity we have all experienced. Each day in the week ahead, break a link and write on it a freedom resolution you feel in Christ. For example, you could write: 'I thank You, God, for delivering me from the anxieties of earthly living, knowing my eternal purpose. I will worry less and think of eternity more.'"

Reassurance for God's People

LIGHT FOR THE GENTILES

BACKGROUND SCRIPTURE: Isaiah 49:1-7
PRINTED TEXT: Isaiah 49:1-7

ISAIAH 49:1-7

1 Listen, O isles, unto me; and hearken, ye people, from far; The LORD hath called me from the womb; from the bowels of my mother hath he made mention of my name.

2 And he hath made my mouth like a sharp sword; in the shadow of his hand hath he hid me, and made me a polished shaft; in his quiver hath he hid me;

3 And said unto me, Thou art my servant, O Israel, in whom I will be glorified.

4 Then I said, I have labored in vain, I have spent my strength for nought, and in vain: yet surely my judgment is with the LORD, and my work with my God.

5 And now, saith the LORD that formed me from the womb to be his servant, to bring Jacob again to him, Though Israel be not gathered, yet shall I be glorious in the eyes of the LORD, and my God shall be my strength.

6 And he said, It is a light thing that thou shouldest be my servant to raise up the tribes of Jacob, and to restore the preserved of Israel: I will also give thee for a light to the Gentiles, that thou mayest be my salvation unto the end of the earth.

7 Thus saith the LORD, the Redeemer of Israel, and his Holy One, to him whom man despiseth, to him whom the nation abhorreth, to a servant of rulers, Kings shall see and arise, princes also shall worship, because of the LORD that is faithful, and the Holy One of Israel, and he shall choose thee.

KEY VERSE

I will . . . give thee for a light to the Gentiles, that thou mayest be my salvation unto the end of the earth.
—Isaiah 49:6

Assuring Hope

LESSON AIMS

After participating in this lesson, each student will be able to:

1. Describe the mission of God's servant in Isaiah 49.

2. Compare the mission of God's servant with the mission of the church.

3. Express his or her own personal mission statement in terms of this passage.

LESSON OUTLINE

Introduction

A. Pay It Forward

The expression *pay it forward* originally was a financial phrase. A benevolent creditor would sometimes allow a debtor to discharge a debt by paying the owed sum "forward" to someone else who needed help rather than "back" to the creditor. Catherine Ryan Hyde titled a novel after this expression. Widespread attention came when the novel evolved into a motion picture in 2000.

In this film, a boy accepts his teacher's challenge to develop and implement a plan to change the world. The boy's plan was simple. He would do something for three people who could not do that thing for themselves. If each of them, in turn, did the same for three additional people, who did the same for three more people and so forth, then this would trigger an avalanche of good deeds that would eventually bring healing to the world.

This movie struck such a cord because many believe that those who routinely receive blessings should become people who extend such blessings to others. Yet it is important to note what it takes to make such a process work: it takes people who are willing (1) to extend kindness without being repaid and (2) to challenge the recipients of the kindness to go and do likewise. That second part is where the process would break down in our day, I suspect. There are many givers in our world and perhaps even more takers, but few seem to be willing to challenge others to be giving people. In today's lesson we learn that Israel's God has not only chosen Israel to be the recipient of His special favor, but that He also expected them to direct that favor toward others in turn.

B. Lesson Background

Today's passage in Isaiah 49, like chapters 45 and 48 from the two past weeks, is addressed to the Israelites after they have been beaten and bruised by the Babylonians. We remind ourselves, however, that the Babylonian captivity won't even begin until at least 95 years after Isaiah writes.

When that captivity occurs, the people are beaten down not only physically but psychologically, as the book of Lamentations makes clear (also Psalm 137). It was obvious to everyone that Babylon was the stronger nation. It dwarfed Judah numerically, militarily, and territorially. Up to the point of today's lesson, God had assured the Israelites that He had not abandoned them, that He had not been defeated by Babylon's gods, and that He intended to restore them. In chapter 49, we hear partially from Israel's perspective and partially from God's perspective.

One challenge to understanding today's passage is that Isaiah 49 is one of four chapters containing the so-called "Servant Songs" of that book. (The other songs are in chapters 42, 52, and 53.) What these songs have in common is that they all talk about the activity of a particular servant of God.

The thing that is challenging about the Servant Songs is that it is not always clear who the servant is in each passage. Sometimes the reference clearly is to Israel. Sometimes the reference clearly is to an individual person. Identifying the servant is further complicated by the fact that Christians see Jesus as the ultimate fulfillment of many of these passages. Yet this fact does not make the interpretive mystery go away.

Here is not the place to discuss in detail all the possible interpretations of these passages or to try to solve the mystery fully. Below I suggest one way to understand today's passage while acknowledging that there are other possible interpretations.

I. Servant Is Chosen
(ISAIAH 49:1-4)
A. Divine Favor (vv. 1, 2)

1. Listen, O isles, unto me; and hearken, ye people, from far; The LORD hath called me from the womb; from the bowels of my mother hath he made mention of my name.

The voice speaking in this verse is not revealed until verse 3, below. Until we get to verse 3, the only identification we have are eight instances of *me* and *my* (four here in v. 1 and four in v. 2). But in verse 3 it becomes clear that the servant of the Lord is Israel. That is the one saying *listen* in the verse at hand. Israel is portrayed as being called by God by name before birth. The illustration of this is that of a preborn child in a mother's womb.

Abraham	*Ay*-bruh-ham.
Assyria	Uh-*sear*-ee-uh.
Babylon	*Bab*-uh-lun.
Babylonian	Bab-ih-*low*-nee-un.
Barnabas	*Bar*-nuh-bus.
Cyrus	*Sigh*-russ.
Darius	Duh-*rye*-us.
Gentiles	*Jen*-tiles.
Isaiah	Eye-*zay*-uh.
Lamentations	Lam-en-*tay*-shunz.
Messiah	Meh-*sigh*-uh.

Here Israel is claiming what God has already said of Israel in Isaiah 44:2, 24. David and Jeremiah make similar claims (see Psalm 22:9, 10; Jeremiah 1:5). Their shared conviction is that they are not afterthoughts in God's plan. God chooses them from their inception. He has a purpose for them, and that purpose will not fail.

> *What Do You Think?*
> If God makes plans for people and nations "from the womb," how do you resist the idea that "since everything is prearranged, I do not need to make any effort"?
> *Talking Points for Your Discussion*
> - General versus detailed plans
> - God's sovereignty in relation to human free will (Luke 13:34; John 7:17; 1 Peter 1:2; etc.)
> - Things God causes versus things God allows

The identities of those being addressed in this verse are not as clear as that of the speaker. The islands being summoned here are not specified. But it is not important to identify exact geographical locations as much as what they represent.

Throughout Isaiah, the coastal people serve as outsiders and witnesses to what God is doing. Like Israel, these are relatively weak and small nations that have been subjugated by larger empires such as Assyria and Babylon. Sometimes they are portrayed as those who are waiting in hope for God's salvation (Isaiah 51:5). Sometimes they are depicted as enemies of God (59:18). Still other times, they represent those who live on distant shores who have neither heard of God nor seen His glory (66:19). The fact that Isaiah 49:1 emphasizes the distance of these people from Israel (*from far*) indicates that the latter is probably the case.

2. And he hath made my mouth like a sharp sword; in the shadow of his hand hath he hid me, and made me a polished shaft; in his quiver hath he hid me.

Two concepts are communicated in this verse. First is the refined nature of Israel as God's instrument. Though the images of a *sharp sword* and *polished shaft* (arrow) can indicate that God plans to use Israel as a weapon of judgment against the nations, that interpretation is not likely. There is no sense in the surrounding passages that God uses Israel to punish Babylon or any other nation. Rather, it is the *mouth* of Israel that is likened to a weapon. Israel has a message to proclaim on God's behalf. Israel is His witness. Israel needs to testify as to what God has proclaimed long ago and is now doing (Isaiah 43:10, 12; 44:8).

The other concept emphasized is Israel's hiddenness. It is not apparent to other nations that the Israelites are as special as they think they are. Israel appears to be insignificant. So Israel informs the nations that Israel has been in God's safekeeping all along, "laying low" until just the right time when God propels the nation back to significance.

B. Divine Endorsement (vv. 3, 4)

3. And said unto me, Thou art my servant, O Israel, in whom I will be glorified.

Israel now cites God as her witness. Israel is not spinning tales as to her own significance. Israel has been told so by God himself.

Furthermore, God indicates why He has called Israel: God is working in world history to bring himself glory. God certainly has not chosen Israel because the Israelites are special in and of themselves. Nor does He choose them in such a way as to draw attention to their own national greatness. It is always about God and His purposes.

❧ WHEN WE JUST DON'T GET IT ❧

Often we get so wrapped up in our own little world that our own desires and wishes become the driving force of what we do. We fail to understand that each action has larger consequences. This was demonstrated in a major league baseball game in 1976 involving Earl Weaver, manager of the Baltimore Orioles, and Reggie Jackson, one of Weaver's best players.

Jackson could read pitchers well enough that he often could steal second base safely. He was good at it. But one time he did this against the wishes of Weaver, who became angry with Jackson for stealing the base, even though he was safe at second.

The problem was that with Jackson on second base, first base was left open. As a result, the next batter, a power hitter, was walked intentionally. The batter after him was not a good hitter against this particular pitcher, so Weaver had to bring in a pinch hitter, depleting the roster. This put the team in a weaker position at the end of the game, which the Orioles lost. Reggie Jackson was interested in stealing a base; Earl Weaver wanted to win a game.

Something similar happens when we fail to do that which is best for the team (the church) and our manager (God) in our quest for pleasing self. Often it seems that "we just don't get it" that our task is to do all that we do to the glory of God, not for the promotion of self.   —A. E. A.

4. Then I said, I have laboured in vain, I have spent my strength for nought, and in vain: yet surely my judgment is with the LORD, and my work with my God.

Though Israel recognizes her special calling by God, she also confesses that her response to this call has been less than successful. A brief reminder of Israel's track record illustrates this fact. Israel's founding father, Abraham, left his old home behind to gain a new homeland in the promised land. He spent most of his life wandering. His grandchildren went into Egypt to survive a famine. They found themselves there for 400 years, ending up in slavery.

When God finally delivered the Israelites from slavery and brought them into the promised land, they struggled to control the territory. Because of disobedience, the Israelites were battered by the nations around them. The moments of independence and prosperity that the Israelites enjoyed always seemed temporary. And now (from Isaiah's forward-looking perspective) they find themselves in Babylonian exile. Whatever gains they have made until then seem to be lost completely.

Yet Israel is not without hope. The God who called them from the womb still lives and still reigns on high. Israel's secure hope remains in Him.

What Do You Think?

What helped you overcome discouragement at a time when you felt your efforts for the Lord were in vain?

Talking Points for Your Discussion

- Is discouragement a sin? (Numbers 11:14; 1 Kings 19:14; 2 Corinthians 1:8)
- Sources of spiritual encouragement

II. Servant Is Commissioned
(ISAIAH 49:5, 6)
A. Restoring Israel (v. 5)

5. And now, saith the LORD that formed me from the womb to be his servant, to bring Jacob again to him, Though Israel be not gathered, yet shall I be glorious in the eyes of the LORD, and my God shall be my strength.

This verse appears to follow smoothly from the previous one. However, the identity of the *servant* seems to change, since the servant now is predicted *to bring Jacob again* to the Lord. (Just so we don't get confused, we need to remember that *Jacob* and *Israel* are parallel designations for the same people; see the comments on Isaiah 48:12 in Lesson 7.)

Previously, God had said that Israel was His servant (v. 3); now God goes on to say more. In verses 1-3, *me* was Israel, so now we might expect *me* to continue to refer to Israel. Yet the servant in this verse seems to be independent of Israel as a nation. It is this servant's honorable task to bring Jacob/Israel to God—something the people of Jacob/Israel cannot do for themselves.

For this reason, some scholars suggest that the servant in this verse is a Persian ruler, either Cyrus or Darius. Both will be instrumental in God's restoration of Israel many years after Isaiah writes. It also can be argued that Isaiah himself or some other Jewish prophet is the servant in this verse.

Perhaps through their prophetic ministry God is realigning Jacob/Israel with His purposes.

For a solution, I suggest that we read this verse in light of verse 6 (next). Before we move on, however, we remind ourselves that true restoration is about more than the political freedom that foreign emperors can offer. It is about conformity to God's will, without which Israel has no meaningful future.

What Do You Think?

In practical terms, how can God be our strength today, both individually and as a church?

Talking Points for Your Discussion

- Confidence in the ultimate outcome (Philippians 1:19)
- God's strength versus ours (Zechariah 4:6)
- Strength in prayer versus strength in action (Exodus 14:15)
- Our idea of "how much we can handle" (2 Corinthians 4:8, 9; Philippians 4:13)

B. Reaching Gentiles (v. 6)

6. And he said, It is a light thing that thou shouldest be my servant to raise up the tribes of Jacob, and to restore the preserved of Israel: I will also give thee for a light to the Gentiles, that thou mayest be my salvation unto the end of the earth.

The servant of verse 5, whoever he is, will be instrumental in bringing *a light to the Gentiles.* The same was said of the servant in Isaiah 42:6. This helps only slightly, since 42:6 is equally ambiguous about the identity of this servant. Yet if one reads this passage in the context of Isaiah 41:8-10 and 42:19-24, both of which identify the servant as Israel, then it seems likely that this servant is also Israel. Yet how can Israel be God's servant to restore Israel?

One solution is found in the concept of *a remnant.* Though remnant language has not been used in this section, it plays a significant role in Isaiah 10:20-34 and 37:31, 32. The remnant is a faithful group of Israelites whom God says He will use to carry out His purposes for Israel. So the servant in this passage can be that faithful part of Israel that God chooses to restore all of Israel.

Visual for Lesson 8. Point to this visual as you ask, "What are some ways to be a light?" This can be a brainstorming session for small groups.

This proposal is not significantly different from claiming that the servant is a faithful prophet whom God will use to restore Israel. However, the remnant idea does have the advantage of explaining how this servant can become a light to the Gentiles. No individual prophet functions in this way (Jonah is something of an exception in a very limited way). Yet we know that as history moves forward it was precisely through a faithful remnant of Israel, the followers of Israel's Messiah, that God's salvation eventually reaches the Gentiles.

The ultimate role of God's servant is not to restore Israel to the promised land. God's ultimate goal is to use His people Israel to be a blessing to all nations as God originally promised to Abraham (Genesis 12:1-3). God restores Israel so Israel may be God's city on a hill, a royal priesthood, and a holy nation (Exodus 19:5, 6).

Israel loses sight of her mission throughout her long and trying history. When the Israelites are in the promised land, they want to be a nation like the nations. They want to have a king like the nations, a standing army like the nations, and a capital city with a religious shrine just like the nations (1 Samuel 8:5, 19, 20). "Becoming important" became Israel's obsession. When God calls His servant to restore Israel, God's goal is not to make Israel what Israel mistakenly tries to make herself. Rather, He calls Israel back to her original mission. He calls Israel to be apart from the nations in order to be a light to the nations.

The fulfillment of this passage does not begin to happen in earnest until the time of Christ. Holding the baby Jesus in his arms, Simeon prophesies that the child is both the glory of Israel and a light to the Gentiles (Luke 2:25-33). Bringing the light of Christ to the Gentiles is an important task of the first-century church, as evident in the ministries of Paul and Barnabas. They understand their mission in light of this passage in Isaiah (Acts 13:46-48). So today's church should never think that her ultimate task is to gather weekly and conduct worship services. Rather, we gather weekly so God can shape us in such gatherings to continue His mission of shining the gospel light. Like ancient Israel, the church does not exist for her own sake, but for the sake of the world.

> *What Do You Think?*
> In what ways might God's vision for our church be different from our own vision? Why is it important to ask this question?
> *Talking Points for Your Discussion*
> - Thinking locally versus thinking globally
> - "Making disciples" versus "filling seats"

❧ LIGHT MAKES A DIFFERENCE ❧

I thought I had the car windows cleaned. I had spent quite a bit of time with window cleaner and paper towels trying to eliminate every streak. They looked really clean. Then that evening I went for a drive. As cars were coming toward me, their headlights hit my windshield, and that window I thought was streak-free was really badly streaked. When I returned home, I had to pull out the cleaning supplies and start all over.

As Christians we are called to be lights in the world. It is our job to make a difference in the world by shining as lights. When the light of our lives strikes the lives of those of this world, the difference should be evident. The light of Jesus that we shine should reveal the streaks, the imperfections, the sin. Paul states: "For ye were sometimes darkness, but now are ye light in the Lord. . . . Proving what is acceptable unto the Lord. And have no fellowship with the unfruitful works of darkness, but rather reprove them" (Ephesians 5:8,

10, 11). When those in darkness see the difference between their lives and the lives of those who shine as lights for the Lord, they should desire to be clean. But no one can clean himself or herself from sin. That is where we do more than just shine; we also tell about the light of the world who can make them clean.
—A. E. A.

III. Servant Is Exalted
(ISAIAH 49:7)
A. Whom to Whom (v. 7a)

7a. Thus saith the LORD, the Redeemer of Israel, and his Holy One, to him whom man despiseth, to him whom the nation abhorreth, to a servant of rulers.

The Lord speaks yet again about His people Israel. He grants that Israel is despised, even abhorred by the nations. He grants that Israel is forced to serve foreign rulers in humiliation and disgrace. But this is not Israel's final lot.

What Do You Think?
Should we conclude that we are not being effective witnesses if we have not experienced the world's abhorrence? Why, or why not?

Talking Points for Your Discussion
- Obligation of a good reputation (1 Timothy 3:7)
- Prediction that hatred will come (Luke 21:17)
- Honor by ungodly authorities (Daniel 5:29)
- Danger of worldly accolades (Luke 6:26)

B. Reaction and Reason (v. 7b)

7b. Kings shall see and arise, princes also shall worship, because of the LORD that is faithful, and the Holy One of Israel, and he shall choose thee.

Israel will no longer live in shame if she takes seriously her mission: allowing God to gather His people and then send them out as His light to the Gentiles. Kings and princes will pay respect when that happens. Yet it will not happen because Israel is powerful or wise; it will happen because God is faithful. The Holy One will not deny himself, and so He will not fail to accomplish what He wills to accomplish through Israel.

Christ is the ultimate fulfillment of the Servant Songs. Thus Christians share in the exaltation we see here. Though it is Christ who is exalted and sits at the Father's right hand, we have been raised with Him (Ephesians 2:6). For a brief time, Jesus was abhorred, spat upon, and beaten. There was no crown without a cross for Jesus, and so it is with us. Like Israel and Israel's Messiah, the servant church must bear her cross (Luke 14:27).

Conclusion
A. For the World

It must have been great news to the Israelites that their time of punishment would draw to an end. After decades of suffering and humiliation, they received a new lease on life. But with that new lease on life came a reminder of a larger purpose. We may compare this with a 30-year-old person who has lived selfishly for most of life before coming to the Lord. When Jesus delivers him or her from self-centeredness and grants forgiveness, it is tempting for the person to focus almost exclusively on being grateful to Jesus. The person may even meet weekly with fellow believers to express gratitude for God's deliverance. But to do only this is too small a thing for God's people.

God does not set apart a people for himself merely to have them praise Him for setting them apart. He set us apart so we may join His mission of proclaiming His reign to the entire world (Matthew 28:19, 20). What God requires is for us to be His hands and feet on this earth, to grant a dying world a life-giving glimpse of His eternal reign. To neglect this task is to neglect our reason to be. The church, like ancient Israel, exists for the world.

B. Prayer

Lord God, we thank You for giving us a mission that is bigger than ourselves. Help us be a people who live in such a way that the children of this world may catch a glimpse of the light of Your Son. We pray in His name, amen.

C. Thought to Remember

It is too small a thing to be nothing more than recipients of God's salvation.

INVOLVEMENT LEARNING

Some of the activities below are also found in the helpful student book, Adult Bible Class.
Don't forget to download the free reproducible page from www.standardlesson.com to enhance your lesson!

Into the Lesson

Collect in advance one each of the following: small radio, large seed (pumpkin, etc.), lightbulb, bar of soap, a match, charcoal briquette (in a clear sandwich bag), and a smoke alarm. Have these on display as learners arrive.

Begin class by asking, "What do all of these objects have in common?" You will receive a variety of answers, such as "All are found typically around the house," "Each has a specific purpose and use," "Each does something worthwhile when activated." The idea that you want to elicit (or reveal, if necessary) is "Each has a capability that needs to be activated in some manner. Each needs to be 'put to work.'"

Continue: "Today's text reveals a servant of God who has a purpose that extends well beyond self, awaiting the stimulus and occasion to benefit others."

Into the Word

Give each learner a blank, adhesive name tag. Say, "Write your name near the top of your tag. Beneath it write 'Servant of God.' Put the name tag on." Allow time to do so. Then say, "I want us to look at today's short text in two ways: first, as to how the truths relate to the servant of God who was Israel, and second, how those same truths relate to us individually as servants of God."

Read aloud the seven verses of today's text. After you read each verse, verbalize the statement below that applies to the verse in question. After you make each statement, ask, "How does this statement apply to ancient Israel? How does it apply to you, if at all?"

Verse 1: (1) The nations of the world have something important to learn from me. (2) In a real sense, God has had plans for me since I was conceived. (3) God knows my name.

Verse 2: (1) God has given me a message that cuts to the marrow of the soul. (2) I am protected in the very hand of God. (3) God has given me opportunity to "sharpen" myself for His service.

Verse 3: (1) He has called me His servant. (2) My purpose is to bring glory to Him.

Verse 4: (1) To all appearances, my life was wasted up to a certain point. (2) In spite of my failures, God still values me and will use me.

Verse 5: (1) I have a restoring purpose. (2) The only thing that brings me glory is being His.

Verse 6: (1) I have a purpose bigger than myself. (2) In a world darkened by sin, I am to reflect the light of God.

Verse 7: (1) Even though God is ignored, I still need to tell those who have rejected Him that they can repent. (2) God, who is both holy and faithful, has chosen me in spite of myself.

Option: Download the reproducible page and distribute copies of the Called from the Womb activity. Have learners discuss their answers in small groups.

Into Life

Ask the class to define the term *missionary*. Ask them also to characterize, in general terms, the Christian missionaries they know. In the responses, listen for the concept of a person who is so committed to a body of truth that he or she chooses a certain lifestyle of service in order to teach that body of content.

Next, ask the class to help you write a "mission statement for a missionary." It should include the elements above, but it can include others, such as willingness to sacrifice certain earthly comforts. Challenge the class to keep the statement brief. Then distribute copies of the Mission Statement activity from the reproducible page and have learners complete it.

Ask learners to compare and contrast the results. Ask, "Should these statements match? Why, or why not?" You can decide whether you want open comments or simple internal reflection.

WOUNDED FOR OUR TRANSGRESSIONS

BACKGROUND SCRIPTURE: Isaiah 53

PRINTED TEXT: Isaiah 53:1-12

ISAIAH 53:1-12

1 Who hath believed our report? and to whom is the arm of the LORD revealed?

2 For he shall grow up before him as a tender plant, and as a root out of a dry ground: he hath no form nor comeliness; and when we shall see him, there is no beauty that we should desire him.

3 He is despised and rejected of men; a man of sorrows, and acquainted with grief: and we hid as it were our faces from him; he was despised, and we esteemed him not.

4 Surely he hath borne our griefs, and carried our sorrows: yet we did esteem him stricken, smitten of God, and afflicted.

5 But he was wounded for our transgressions, he was bruised for our iniquities: the chastisement of our peace was upon him; and with his stripes we are healed.

6 All we like sheep have gone astray; we have turned every one to his own way; and the LORD hath laid on him the iniquity of us all.

7 He was oppressed, and he was afflicted, yet he opened not his mouth: he is brought as a lamb to the slaughter, and as a sheep before her shearers is dumb, so he openeth not his mouth.

8 He was taken from prison and from judgment: and who shall declare his generation? for he was cut off out of the land of the living: for the transgression of my people was he stricken.

9 And he made his grave with the wicked, and with the rich in his death; because he had done no violence, neither was any deceit in his mouth.

10 Yet it pleased the LORD to bruise him; he hath put him to grief: when thou shalt make his soul an offering for sin, he shall see his seed, he shall prolong his days, and the pleasure of the LORD shall prosper in his hand.

11 He shall see of the travail of his soul, and shall be satisfied: by his knowledge shall my righteous servant justify many; for he shall bear their iniquities.

12 Therefore will I divide him a portion with the great, and he shall divide the spoil with the strong; because he hath poured out his soul unto death: and he was numbered with the transgressors; and he bare the sin of many, and made intercession for the transgressors.

KEY VERSE

He was wounded for our transgressions, he was bruised for our iniquities: the chastisement of our peace was upon him; and with his stripes we are healed. —**Isaiah 53:5**

ASSURING HOPE

Unit 2: A Future for God's People
LESSONS 6–9

LESSON AIMS

After participating in this lesson, each student will be able to:

1. Recount the mission and outcome of the suffering servant in Isaiah 53.

2. Identify the six places in the New Testament where portions of today's text are quoted.

3. Describe one way that his or her life is not currently patterned after the submission of Jesus and make a plan for change.

LESSON OUTLINE

Introduction
    A. Superman
    B. Lesson Background
I. Servant's Appearance (ISAIAH 53:1-3)
    A. Reported and Revealed (v. 1)
    B. Humble and Unattractive (vv. 2, 3)
II. Servant's Suffering (ISAIAH 53:4-9)
    A. Grief, Sorrow, Affliction (vv. 4-6)
        Take a Bullet?
    B. Oppression, Slaughter, Burial (vv. 7-9)
III. Servant's Reward (ISAIAH 53:10-12)
    A. God Wills (v. 10)
        Restored
    B. God Exalts (vv. 11, 12)
Conclusion
    A. Servant People
    B. Prayer
    C. Thought to Remember

Introduction

A. Superman

We live in a world that needs a savior. Countless lives are broken, beaten, and confused. We need someone to intervene—someone to expose the lies that dominate our lives and to set us on the right course.

In the late nineteenth century, the atheistic philosopher Friedrich Nietzsche identified just the sort of savior he thought this world needed. His idealized savior was a man, but certainly no ordinary man. Nietzsche's description of a value-creating being translates somewhat loosely into English as "superman." Nietzsche's vision of such an individual was that of a man who rejects any notion that God or any other being outside the world should be the source of values to govern the world. Nietzsche suggested instead that this superman would trust his own intuitive sense of good and evil.

This superman's sense of right and wrong would be rooted in what helps him succeed and prevents him from failing. Since the superman observes that everything in this world is in a constant state of flux, he acknowledges that all that exists now, including his current value system, must be overcome by what comes next. To keep current, this superman must reinvent himself continually in order to become stronger. Thus, according to Nietzsche, what this world needs is a being who draws on his own internal resources to master the practice of overcoming his former self.

If the brightest minds of our day were to design the savior they think this world needs, it might not look much different from Nietzsche's. It might still be an individual who spurns tradition and is accountable to no one but himself or herself. Or perhaps it would look like one of the countless conflicted heroes of the comic books.

After her decimation by Babylon, Israel also needed a savior. Israel needed someone who could meet them where they were, overcome their sin, and set them on the right course. Today's passage reveals God's promise to send them the hero they needed. But the hero they received was nothing like anyone expected.

Wounded for Our Transgressions

B. Lesson Background

Isaiah 53 addresses the same historical context that was addressed in the last three lessons: God comforted His people Israel, who were oppressed by the Babylonians (although that oppression was many decades in the future as Isaiah wrote). The people were calling into question God's sovereignty and their own future. Yet today's passage also takes place in a wider biblical context that is important to its proper understanding.

This particular "Servant Song," which begins in 52:13, is quoted multiple times in the New Testament as a description of Jesus' ministry, death, and burial (examples: Matthew 8:17; Luke 22:37; 1 Peter 2:22). Perhaps the most well-known passage that connects Jesus with the servant of today's passage is Acts 8:26-35, in which Philip evangelized the Ethiopian eunuch.

The eunuch was reading from an Isaiah scroll and was confused by the verses we now identify as Isaiah 53:7, 8. That is the passage that describes the suffering servant as a sheep being led to slaughter. Philip immediately identified the servant as Jesus and explained the gospel. Today we will discuss this passage in its context and highlight how it points beyond events of the sixth century BC toward the work of Christ.

The last three verses of Isaiah 52, which directly precede today's text, discuss how God's servant is to be exalted despite the reaction of the startled nations. The nations were taken aback by the servant's arrival because they didn't see it coming. It wasn't revealed to them as it was to Israel. Yet all nations will indeed have to reckon with this startling servant.

I. Servant's Appearance
(ISAIAH 53:1-3)
A. Reported and Revealed (v. 1)

1. Who hath believed our report? and to whom is the arm of the LORD revealed?

This verse serves as a transition to the next part of the Servant Song. It is Israel to whom this unexpected message is revealed. It is Israel who is called to believe this scandalous report of the Lord's power (see John 12:37, 38; Romans 10:16).

B. Humble and Unattractive (vv. 2, 3)

2. For he shall grow up before him as a tender plant, and as a root out of a dry ground: he hath no form nor comeliness; and when we shall see him, there is no beauty that we should desire him.

The servant whom God chooses to accomplish His purposes for Israel is, at first blush, entirely unimpressive. He looks like a feeble plant growing in bad soil. He does not appear to be a "superman" in any sense of the word. On the surface, there is nothing appealing or attractive about Him.

As the Ethiopian eunuch does in Acts 8:34, scholars puzzle over the identity of this servant. Some identify him as the nation of Israel, as a subgroup within Israel, as an Israelite prophet like Jeremiah, or as an Israelite governor such as Zerubbabel. Others identify the servant as Darius I, who becomes the Persian king in about 522 BC. Still others claim that the servant is the future Messiah, and so this passage is not fulfilled until the coming of Christ.

According to what follows, either (1) only the last or (2) a combination of the first and last of these views is likely. Either Isaiah is anticipating Jesus only, or Isaiah is discussing God's choice to use lowly Israelites as His instrument of blessing to the nations with these Israelites being led by their lowly Messiah, Jesus. But even if the immediate referent is a particular Israelite or group of Israelites, the ultimate referent must be Jesus, as the New Testament makes clear.

> **What Do You Think?**
> What causes us to overlook people who have great spiritual depth? What will happen when we solve this problem?
> *Talking Points for Your Discussion*
> - Life situation (James 2:2-5)
> - Outward appearance (1 Samuel 16:7)
> - Ethnic or cultural bias (John 4:9; 8:48; Acts 6:1)

3. He is despised and rejected of men; a man of sorrows, and acquainted with grief: and we hid as it were our faces from him; he was despised, and we esteemed him not.

This verse continues the theme of the servant's uncomely appearance by emphasizing how the servant is received. He is rejected, despised, shunned, and ill-esteemed. He is a man deeply grieved.

The fact that God elects to use a servant like this to accomplish His purposes serves as a warning to those who judge people by external appearances. A consistent theme in Scripture is that God often prefers to use those who appear least likely to succeed (example: 1 Samuel 16:7). As a professor at a Christian college, I am reminded yearly that the students with the best grades do not necessarily become the ministers who thrive in the churches. In an age when image is vital, Christians must discipline themselves to retain God's perspective. If not, the world's values are likely to creep into our thoughts and actions.

> **What Do You Think?**
>
> What are some ways we do not esteem Christ as much as we should? How do we correct this problem?
>
> *Talking Points for Your Discussion*
> - How we treat His Word (John 14:15)
> - How we treat others (1 John 4:20)
> - Prayer time spent in praise compared with prayer time spent making requests

II. Servant's Suffering
(ISAIAH 53:4-9)
A. Grief, Sorrow, Affliction (vv. 4-6)

4. Surely he hath borne our griefs, and carried our sorrows: yet we did esteem him stricken, smitten of God, and afflicted.

According to this verse, God's people are to recognize God's hand at work: it is God himself who strikes the servant. The servant somehow carries the burden of the people into His suffering. He does not suffer as a solitary individual, but as a representative of God's people.

As Christians, we are reminded of Hebrews 4:15. Jesus is a high priest who can sympathize with our weakness. In becoming flesh, He bears our humanity and identifies with our weakness. Christians see in Jesus a model for ministry: believers seeking to win the lost should find concrete ways to identify with the lost and meet them where they are. Until we walk in people's shoes, they seldom care about our faith in Jesus.

Jesus' suffering is not only a means to satisfy God's justice, it is also a model for how love conquers evil. It shows Christians how to break through the hard shell of resistance that surrounds people trapped in a life of sin. Jesus does not bear the sufferings of humanity only at the cross, but also throughout His ministry (Matthew 8:16, 17).

5. But he was wounded for our transgressions, he was bruised for our iniquities: the chastisement of our peace was upon him; and with his stripes we are healed.

We are taught further that the servant's identification with God's people has saving consequences. The servant bears not only the sorrows of the people, but also their sins *(transgressions)*. Here it is clear that the servant's suffering is not for wrongs He has done, but for what others have done. Moreover, it is effective: healing and peace result from the servant's suffering.

❧ TAKE A BULLET? ❧

A phrase sometimes used to show one's devotion to another is, "I would take a bullet for that person." The meaning is that if the object of one's love or loyalty were in a life-threatening situation, then the subject would risk life and limb—even to the point of standing in the way of an oncoming bullet—for the sake of the other.

HOW TO SAY IT

Arimathaea	Air-uh-muh-*thee*-uh (*th* as in *thin*).
Babylon	*Bab*-uh-lun.
Babylonian	Bab-ih-*low*-nee-un.
Cyrus	*Sigh*-russ.
Darius	Duh-*rye*-us.
Ethiopian	E-thee-*o*-pee-un (*th* as in *thin*).
eunuch	*you*-nick.
Friedrich Nietzsche	*Free*-drick *Nee*-chuh.
Jeremiah	Jair-uh-*my*-uh.
Messiah	Meh-*sigh*-uh.
Zerubbabel	Zeh-*rub*-uh-bul.

There have been examples throughout history of those who have willingly "taken a bullet," both literally and figuratively, for someone else. A parent who stands between her child and a vicious dog is an example. A policeman who dies in the cause of protecting the citizenry of his town is another. An arm of the U.S. Secret Service is tasked to protect the president no matter what. When asked how it felt knowing he may have to take a bullet, one agent said, "It comes with the job. It's an honor to protect the president. End of discussion."

The ultimate example of sacrificial concern, though, is Jesus Christ. God "made him to be sin for us, who knew no sin; that we might be made the righteousness of God in him" (2 Corinthians 5:21). In an ironic twist, the very author of life lays down His own life. How should we respond to such a one? —A. E. A.

6. All we like sheep have gone astray; we have turned every one to his own way; and the LORD hath laid on him the iniquity of us all.

Now we are told why the servant has to suffer: the servant suffers because God's people act like wandering sheep. Since they refuse to obey the shepherd, the shepherd has to break their cycle of rebellion. Isaiah 40:2 tells us that Israel pays for its sin in full as a result of the Babylonian exile. But that payment is not enough to change the course of sinful human history permanently. Wandering will resume. It too will need to be punished. So God in His sovereign will sends the servant to suffer. God breaks the endless cycle of sin and punishment by introducing something surely unexpected: the innocent sufferer.

We are not given a full-blown theory of atonement in this verse. We are not told here how the suffering of an innocent person can cover the sins of the guilty. No comparison is made to the sacrifices of animals in Israel's law. Romans 3:21-26 and Hebrews 7–10 tell us how and why Jesus' death covers all human sin. But in the verse before us we are told little more than this is God's idea. Out of love and grace, God takes the initiative and makes a way for His people to avoid the endless cycle of guilt and punishment. That is the point of this passage, and we need to be careful not to

miss this point. Understanding the mechanics of how this solution works comes later.

> **What Do You Think?**
> What can we do to have the mind of Christ toward the scattered sheep?
> *Talking Points for Your Discussion*
> - Christ's view (Matthew 9:36)
> - Our obligation (John 21:17)
> - Urgency (Matthew 18:12, 13)

B. Oppression, Slaughter, Burial (vv. 7-9)

7. He was oppressed, and he was afflicted, yet he opened not his mouth: he is brought as a lamb to the slaughter, and as a sheep before her shearers is dumb, so he openeth not his mouth.

The servant does not go kicking and screaming into the suffering. Aware of God's plan and fully submissive to the will of God, the servant accepts His fate without a fight. This passage compares such submission to a speechless lamb before it is butchered.

> **What Do You Think?**
> Under what circumstances, if any, should we "fight for our rights" rather than face injustice with silence as Jesus did? Why?
> *Talking Points for Your Discussion*
> - Our general attitude (Luke 9:23; 14:27; 1 Peter 4:1, 14, 16)
> - Accepting what we deserve (Luke 23:41; 1 Peter 2:20a)
> - Benefits of "defending our rights" (Acts 16:35-40; 22:25)

8. He was taken from prison and from judgment: and who shall declare his generation? for he was cut off out of the land of the living: for the transgression of my people was he stricken.

We are told more of the severity of the servant's lot. The question *who shall declare his generation?* indicates that the servant has no descendants. Combined with *he was cut off out of the land of the living,* this indicates a premature death. He not only suffers but also dies for the sin of the people. Jesus submits to His executioners and refuses to

Visual for Lesson 9. Use this chart to extend your discussion of today's text by comparing Isaiah's predictions with New Testament fulfillment.

put up a fight. Jesus is arrested, judged, and killed at a young age.

9. And he made his grave with the wicked, and with the rich in his death; because he had done no violence, neither was any deceit in his mouth.

Jesus fulfills this passage in two ways. First, Jesus is an innocent man who is tried and convicted like a criminal. He is hung between two thieves as if He were one of them. He neither commits violence nor deceives others for financial gain. Despite His innocence, the servant dies like a common criminal.

Second, Jesus is buried in the grave of a rich man. Matthew 27:57-60 demonstrates that Jesus' burial in the grave of Joseph of Arimathaea fulfills this prophecy.

III. Servant's Reward
(ISAIAH 53:10-12)
A. God Wills (v. 10)

10. Yet it pleased the LORD to bruise him; he hath put him to grief: when thou shalt make his soul an offering for sin, he shall see his seed, he shall prolong his days, and the pleasure of the LORD shall prosper in his hand.

This verse begins by restating the Lord's desire to subject the servant to grief in order to atone for sin. But then an important transition takes place. The servant—who does not have offspring, whose days are cut short, and who experiences sorrow—undergoes a reversal of fortune. He sees His offspring *(seed)*, lives longer *(shall prolong his days)*, and prospers in the Lord. Though it first appears as if the Lord simply "uses up" this innocent servant on behalf of the guilty, ultimately the Lord vindicates the servant. Death is not the final word, but the beginning of a new era of prosperity.

The pattern represented in this verse is captured nicely in Philippians 2:6-11. There Paul notes how Jesus lowered himself, became obedient to the point of death, and was exalted on high. Jesus therefore fulfills this prophecy. Jesus' offspring are not biological descendants of course, but are disciples throughout the earth (Galatians 3:26–4:7).

❧ RESTORED ❧

Restoring antique automobiles or old furniture is big business. Finding that old, abandoned car or that forgotten piece of furniture is, for restorationists, like finding a gold mine. A great amount of time, money, and effort is put into restoring such things to their original condition.

For others, restoration is a more personal task, such as dieting to try to return to a trimmer look. Surgery to remove wrinkles is another example. Again, time, money, and painstaking effort are required. But many find the results worthwhile.

Jesus was beaten, bruised, and disfigured in His physical body. Spiritually, He took the sins of the world upon himself. He temporarily gave up His place with the Father in Heaven. But God took this one and restored Him to that rightful place. Jesus was brought back to His "original condition," and He now intercedes for us at the right hand of the Father. All this results in our own restoration, as the death-curse of sin is reversed. How can we possibly go back to our old ways? —A. E. A.

B. God Exalts (vv. 11, 12)

11, 12. He shall see of the travail of his soul, and shall be satisfied: by his knowledge shall my righteous servant justify many; for he shall bear their iniquities. Therefore will I divide him a portion with the great, and he shall divide the spoil with the strong; because he hath poured out his soul unto death: and he

was numbered with the transgressors; and he bare the sin of many, and made intercession for the transgressors.

The final two verses of our passage echo verse 10 but add greater detail. They restate that the servant suffers to the point of death on behalf of the guilty. He bears their sin and is numbered among sinners. In doing so, He intercedes on their behalf and satisfies God's plan to reconcile them.

A description of the servant's final exaltation is offered anew. He is counted among the great ones and divides the spoils that accompany greatness, although it is not clear exactly what the spoils are. The imagery is meant to convey the restoration of the innocent servant who gives His all so that the guilty may be reconciled to God.

What Do You Think?

In what ways do you honor Jesus for what He has done?

Talking Points for Your Discussion

- Method and content of your prayers
- Frequency of attending corporate worship
- The way you spend money
- The way you prepare for worship

Conclusion

A. Servant People

For the past four weeks we have studied how God intervened to deliver Israel from Babylonian captivity. We have seen that the Israelites were captive not only to a foreign nation but also to the sin that filled their lives and brought about their punishment. God was faithful to deliver His people from both physical and spiritual bondage.

What is important to note as we wrap up our study of Isaiah is the means God used to liberate His people. The Babylonians had mocked both God and His people, dragging their names through the mud. The Israelites responded by doubting God's power, thinking themselves to be forgotten. Many Israelites undoubtedly embraced the alternative power and religion of Babylon.

God could have responded to these offenses in various ways. He could have imposed His way of thinking on Israel and the nations supernaturally.

He could have assembled the heavenly hosts and established His reign with brute force. He could have raised a great warrior-king in Israel to crush Babylon and assert Israel's superiority.

Yet God didn't use any of these strategies. Instead, He told Israel that idol worship was wrong as He used arguments that could be accepted or rejected freely. He claimed that His sovereignty was attested in how He brought His predictions to fruition. God used the foreigner Cyrus to execute judgment against Babylon without overriding Cyrus's own agenda. Finally, He used a gentle servant-leader to form a people to bear witness to His power of reconciliation and new life.

In calling both unfaithful Israel and the faithful servant by the same name—*servant*—God held before Israel a picture of what He aspired that nation to be. This is evident in what God did next with His people: He returned the Israelites to their land without the perks that were supposed to accompany great nations, and He instructed them to wait for the faithful servant to arrive. That would be a servant who would lead them to greatness as God defined greatness.

When that servant arrived in the person of Jesus, He taught God's people that if they were to be His light to the nations, then they would have to follow His path of suffering service. He taught them that such service would be a demonstration of God's power and the proper posture of His people in the world. God's strategy has not changed. Christians and churches in our own day must take seriously the servant posture to which God calls us.

B. Prayer

Lord God, we thank You for not giving up on us. Though Your people have deserved punishment upon punishment, You spare us the final judgment we deserve. Through the cross of Your Son, Jesus, You have broken the power of sin. For this we thank You and praise You. In the name of Jesus, we pray. Amen.

C. Thought to Remember

Give your life for the servant of God
who gave His life for you.

INVOLVEMENT LEARNING

Some of the activities below are also found in the helpful student book, Adult Bible Class.
Don't forget to download the free reproducible page from www.standardlesson.com to enhance your lesson!

Into the Lesson

Distribute copies of the following agree/disagree quiz entitled "The Good Leader." 1. The good leader will defend himself/herself eloquently when criticized. 2. The good leader is usually taller and more attractive in appearance. 3. The good leader will typically be honored in death with a grand funeral and a memorable grave site. 4. The good leader gives off a "blessed-by-God" aura. 5. The good leader receives acclamation and praise. 6. The good leader has true empathy with those in his or her charge. 7. The good leader shares bountifully in the profits and benefits of the endeavor being led. 8. The good leader is known by the company he or she keeps.

Let learners respond freely, and then say, "Today's text is about a good leader. But He is a good leader who might elicit different responses from you relative to the preceding statements. Let's take a look."

Into the Word

Say, "Let's look at today's text to see what we can find related to Jesus as God's good leader."

Option 1: Have one of your good oral readers read today's text, with this substitution: the reader will say "the good leader" each time the word *he* starts a thought; these occur in verses 2 (twice), 3 (twice), 4, 5 (twice), 7 (four times), 8 (twice), 9 (twice), 10 (twice), 11 (twice), 12 (three or four times).

After the reading, ask, "What do you see that seems to be like and unlike the characteristics we've just looked at in our quiz?" Your class will see a variety of similarities and differences as the discussion ensues. Allow free response, but here are two examples: (1) whereas most good leaders eloquently defend themselves when accused, God's good leader remains silent (Mark 14:61), (2) Jesus did not come in a physical body that was naturally attractive according to worldly standards; His appearance probably was simply ordinary.

Option 2: Download the reproducible page and distribute copies of the Expectations and Reality activity. Have learners complete it in small groups or study pairs. Discuss the results. Ask, "What did you find most surprising from your study?"

After completing either option above, distribute work sheets for the following matching items that you have prepared in advance. Include the directions as noted, but do not include the answers, which are given in bracketed italics.

Directions: "Look at today's text verse by verse (column A) and choose the New Testament text that most closely relates (column B). Some are specifically noted as being a fulfillment of prophetic revelation." *Left Column:* A. Isaiah 53:1; B. Isaiah 53:3; C. Isaiah 53:4; D. Isaiah 53:5; E. Isaiah 53:6; F. Isaiah 53:7; G. Isaiah 53:9; H. Isaiah 53:11; I. Isaiah 53:12. *Right Column:* Matthew 8:17 *[C]*; Mark 9:12 *[B]*; Luke 22:37 *[I]*; Acts 8:32 *[F]*; Romans 5:19 *[H]*; Romans 10:16 *[A]*; 1 Peter 2:22 *[G]*; 1 Peter 2:24b *[D]*; 1 Peter 2:25 *[E]*.

Verify the choices your learners make. Be sure to comment on the marvelous precision of the prophetic nature of these truths.

Into Life

Give a small yellow cardboard triangle (three inches or so to a side) to each learner. Provide these directions: "Turn the triangle so it points downward, as a yield sign. Put a large *M* right in the middle. Consider that to stand for *ME*. Then flip the triangle over and put a lowercase *s*. Consider that to represent yourself as a servant that submits to God's will. Look at your triangle once each day in the coming week to decide if 'it's all about ME' or if it's about yielding yourself to God as a submitted servant."

If time permits, have your learners work on the Bookends activity from the downloadable reproducible page. Otherwise, distribute this as take-home work.

JESUS IS THE
MESSIAH

BACKGROUND SCRIPTURE: Mark 8:27–9:1
PRINTED TEXT: Mark 8:27–9:1

MARK 8:27-38

27 And Jesus went out, and his disciples, into the towns of Caesarea Philippi: and by the way he asked his disciples, saying unto them, Whom do men say that I am?

28 And they answered, John the Baptist: but some say, Elias; and others, One of the prophets.

29 And he saith unto them, But whom say ye that I am? And Peter answereth and saith unto him, Thou art the Christ.

30 And he charged them that they should tell no man of him.

31 And he began to teach them, that the Son of man must suffer many things, and be rejected of the elders, and of the chief priests, and scribes, and be killed, and after three days rise again.

32 And he spake that saying openly. And Peter took him, and began to rebuke him.

33 But when he had turned about and looked on his disciples, he rebuked Peter, saying, Get thee behind me, Satan: for thou savourest not the things that be of God, but the things that be of men.

34 And when he had called the people unto him with his disciples also, he said unto them, Whosoever will come after me, let him deny himself, and take up his cross, and follow me.

35 For whosoever will save his life shall lose it; but whosoever shall lose his life for my sake and the gospel's, the same shall save it.

36 For what shall it profit a man, if he shall gain the whole world, and lose his own soul?

37 Or what shall a man give in exchange for his soul?

38 Whosoever therefore shall be ashamed of me and of my words, in this adulterous and sinful generation; of him also shall the Son of man be ashamed, when he cometh in the glory of his Father with the holy angels.

MARK 9:1

1 And he said unto them, Verily I say unto you, That there be some of them that stand here, which shall not taste of death, till they have seen the kingdom of God come with power.

KEY VERSE

[Jesus] saith unto them, But whom say ye that I am? And Peter answereth and saith unto him, Thou art the Christ. —**Mark 8:29**

ASSURING HOPE

Introduction

A. Crunch Time

Crunch time is a familiar phrase for athletes. For a basketball player, it is the final seconds in a close game. For the marathon runner, it is late in the race when he or she "hits the wall" and has to find the strength to continue. For the baseball player it is the final inning of the game with two out and the bases loaded; for both the pitcher and the batter, it is crunch time.

Many moments in our lives can qualify as crunch time. The minister's question "Do you take this woman to be your bride?" creates that kind of time. When a woman is ready to deliver a child, it is that kind of time. When soldiers brace to defend their homeland, when firefighters race into a burning building, when parents have to confront a wayward teen, it is crunch time. Crunch time comes whenever we face an all-important moment of truth.

For Peter and the other disciples in this lesson, one crunch time came at Caesarea Philippi when Jesus challenged them to answer a question. It was time to make a decision, for someone to dare to answer. When Jesus asked His disciples, "But whom say ye that I am?" Simon Peter rose to the occasion and spoke with conviction.

B. Lesson Background

From the very beginning of Jesus' ministry, it was clear that He had come to fulfill the prophecies of Isaiah. John the Baptist prepared the way for Him, just as Isaiah 40:3 had predicted (see Mark 1:2, 3). Jesus announced His purpose at His home synagogue in Nazareth, saying, "The Spirit of the Lord is upon me, because he hath anointed me to preach the gospel to the poor." After quoting Isaiah 61:1, Jesus announced, "This day is this scripture fulfilled in your ears" (Luke 4:21).

Through the following years of His ministry, Jesus demonstrated time and again that He was sent from Heaven to fulfill everything Isaiah and the other prophets had said. As the Messiah, Jesus came to bring salvation and reassurance to God's people, the Jews. In addition, He came to bring light to the Gentiles and bring them into the community of God's people. The most difficult prophecy of Isaiah, however, was that the Messiah would be the suffering servant, who would give His life to bear the sins of all people (Isaiah 53, last week's lesson). Well into the third year of His ministry, Jesus was ready to test the disciples' understanding of His identity and His mission.

I. Decisive Question
(Mark 8:27-30)
A. What Do Others Say? (vv. 27, 28)

27a. And Jesus went out, and his disciples, into the towns of Caesarea Philippi.

Since the feeding of the 5,000 a few months earlier (Mark 6:30-44), Jesus has been largely avoiding both Judea and Galilee. Without the constant distraction of either excessive excitement or annoying opposition, Jesus can spend time preparing His disciples for what is to come. Now they are visiting the towns in the area of Caesarea Philippi, a location nearly 30 miles north and slightly east of the Sea of Galilee, overlooking the northern end of the Jordan River valley.

In this era, many towns are named *Caesarea*, in honor of the emperor of Rome. A larger and more important Caesarea, for instance, is Caesarea Maritima ("Caesarea by the Sea"), which is on the Mediterranean coastline. The town in the area where Jesus and His disciples gather has the additional name *Philippi*, in honor of Philip II (also known as Philip the Tetrarch).

27b. And by the way he asked his disciples, saying unto them, Whom do men say that I am?

In the context of what could be called a leadership retreat (at least until we see the crowd of Mark 8:34, below), Jesus opens the conversation with a question: *Whom do men say that I am?* "Who Jesus is" is a fundamental issue that everyone—especially the disciples themselves—must face. Where does Jesus come from? What is His purpose? The answer to these questions will determine what we do in response to Him.

28. And they answered, John the Baptist: but some say, Elias; and others, One of the prophets.

The disciples answer factually, reporting the various opinions and rumors that are circulating about Jesus. The ideas center around a return to life by a great man of God. Some people think He is John the Baptist, who is already dead by this point, having been beheaded by King Herod (Mark 6:14-29). Others suppose Jesus to be Elias (Elijah); that man also had been God's spokesman, willing to speak out against a king (see 1 Kings 21). The same was true of other great prophets of old.

It is striking that these ideas all presuppose a resurrection of someone who has died. It is also striking that all these ideas assume that Jesus is someone who will prepare for the Messiah, but not that He is the Messiah himself. John the Baptist came to prepare the way (Mark 1:2-4); his identity is bound up with Elijah, who was to be sent before the great day of the Lord (Malachi 4:5; Matthew 17:10-13); the other prophets predicted a variety of things about the coming Messiah. But these were all just men; Jesus is something more.

> *What Do You Think?*
> What are some ways that people today answer Jesus' question, "Who do you say that I am?"
> *Talking Points for Your Discussion*
> - Answers that are similar to the first-century responses
> - Answers that are different from the first-century responses
> - John 12:34

B. What Do You Say? (v. 29)

29a. And he saith unto them, But whom say ye that I am?

Now the question becomes pointed and personal: *But whom say ye that I am?* Have the disciples resolved in their own minds the issue of Jesus' identity? We are about to find out!

❧ *Popular Opinion or . . . ?* ❧

"Run it up the flagpole and see who salutes it" is an old adage familiar to many. The meaning is that you want to find out what people think about an issue before making a final decision. Politicians use opinion polls to find out "which way the wind is blowing" on an issue before taking a stand.

The church is not immune to this way of thinking. People naturally have opinions on how a church should carry out its mission. That is not necessarily bad in and of itself, and wise leaders are good listeners. But danger looms when popular opinions about the Bible are allowed to hold sway over the facts of the Bible.

People today hold many opinions about Jesus. He is regarded as a myth, a misguided fool, and everything in between. But opinions aren't facts, and the church dare not present to the world the Jesus that the world wants or thinks Him to be. The fact is, Jesus is who He claimed to be: the Son of God. In a world filled with opinions about Jesus, it is imperative that Christians hold to the facts of who Jesus really is. —A. E. A.

29b. And Peter answereth and saith unto him, Thou art the Christ.

We can imagine the disciples hanging back, each waiting for someone else to take the lead in answering Jesus' question. Peter is the one who does so: *Thou art the Christ.* (The parallel account of Matthew 16:16 notes that Peter also says "the Son of the living God.") All the hopes of Israel, the destiny of humanity, and the eternal plan of God hang on this man Jesus.

Christ is a Greek word, and its Hebrew equivalent is *Messiah.* They both mean "the anointed one" (compare John 1:41; 4:25). Most of the first-century Jews think this person will be a political figure, a nationalistic king. They assume that He is to sit on the earthly throne of David and rule over an earthly empire. But Jesus will be a leader on God's terms (compare John 6:15).

C. What Not to Say (v. 30)

30. And he charged them that they should tell no man of him.

Even though Peter has confessed a wonderful truth, Jesus commands the disciples to tell no one. Jesus has given similar prohibitions on several previous occasions (see Mark 1:44; 5:43; 8:26; 9:9). Likewise, the demons are forbidden to reveal Jesus' identity (1:25; 3:12).

The need for secrecy seems to be connected with the expectations of the people. When they hear about Jesus' miracles, they overwhelm Him with the sick, the crippled, and the blind (see Mark 1:45). They cannot see that His miracles are pointing beyond present physical needs; these miracles are His credentials as the one who has come from God. When they think about Jesus' identity as possible Messiah, they clamor for Him to establish a kingdom independent from Rome (see John 6:15; Acts 1:6). There will be time later to proclaim to all the world that Jesus is the Christ, but that time is not yet.

II. Predicted Pain
(Mark 8:31-33)
A. Jesus' Suffering (v. 31)

31. And he began to teach them, that the Son of man must suffer many things, and be rejected of the elders, and of the chief priests, and scribes, and be killed, and after three days rise again.

From this point Jesus begins to teach His disciples a painful truth: *the Son of man must suffer many things.* The term *Son of man* is Jesus' favorite self-designation. It is found dozens of times in the Gospels, almost always on the lips of Jesus himself (a rare exception is John 12:34). The title has messianic overtones (see Daniel 7:13, 14), but it also emphasizes Jesus' human side (see Matthew 8:20).

The suffering that Jesus is to undergo will involve rejection by the elders. These are the older

Jesus is . . .

Coming King

HOLY ONE

RISEN LORD

Incarnate Word

Savior

True God

Visual for Lesson 10

Point to this visual as you ask, "How many other titles and descriptions of Jesus can you name?"

Jesus Is the Messiah

and (supposedly) wiser leaders of the Jews. The chief priests and scribes, the respected religious leaders, also will refuse to accept Him. These three groups make up the Sanhedrin, which is the ruling body of the Jews (compare Mark 11:27; also see Isaiah 53:3; John 1:11).

Undoubtedly, the hardest thing of all for the disciples to accept is the prediction that Jesus must be killed. Will not His death destroy all their hopes for the messianic age? How can He reign on David's throne if He is dead? But Jesus' final words provide the answer: *and after three days rise again*. But the disciples are unable to understand or absorb this answer, as the next verse shows.

B. Peter's Protest (v. 32)

32a. And he spake that saying openly.

The fact that Jesus speaks openly reveals a major turning point. Up to this point, Jesus has spoken of His death in figures of speech and allusions (John 2:19; 3:14).

32b. And Peter took him, and began to rebuke him.

Peter rebels as he hears about the coming death. Such a thing is intolerable, unacceptable, unthinkable! So Peter takes Jesus aside and begins to rebuke Him. Peter has clearly forgotten his place: it is not his job to tell Jesus what to do, but to obey Him. The prediction of the Son of Man's sufferings to come will be repeated in Mark 9:30-32 and 10:32-34, where the disciples will again find it impossible to accept. But these things must happen (v. 31, above); this is the Father's will.

C. Jesus' Rebuke (v. 33)

33. But when he had turned about and looked on his disciples, he rebuked Peter, saying, Get thee behind me, Satan: for thou savourest not the things that be of God, but the things that be of men.

The other disciples likely share Peter's opposition to what Jesus has said. That's probably why Jesus turns and looks at them. Jesus rebukes Peter in front of them all. Knowing that Peter's way of thinking stands between Him and the cross, Jesus says, in effect, "Get out of my way! Don't think you can stop me!"

Shockingly, Jesus then addresses Peter as *Satan*. But this is an appropriate designation for at least two reasons. First, the word *satan* refers to an enemy; this is seen in 1 Samuel 29:4, where the Hebrew word is translated "adversary." If Peter stands in the way of Jesus completing His mission, then Peter is indeed an enemy. Second, Peter is repeating a temptation of the devil in the wilderness by suggesting that Jesus does not really need to allow himself to be harmed in order to carry out His mission (Matthew 4:5, 6).

III. Demanding Challenge
(MARK 8:34–9:1)

A. Requirements of Discipleship (vv. 34, 35)

34. And when he had called the people unto him with his disciples also, he said unto them, Whosoever will come after me, let him deny himself, and take up his cross, and follow me.

HOW TO SAY IT

Caesarea Maritima	Sess-uh-*ree*-uh Mar-uh-*tee*-muh.
Caesarea Philippi	Sess-uh-*ree*-uh Fih-*lip*-pie or *Fil*-ih-pie.
Judas Iscariot	*Joo*-dus Iss-*care*-ee-ut.
Judea	Joo-*dee*-uh.
Messiah	Meh-*sigh*-uh.
messianic	mess-ee-*an*-ick.
Nazareth	*Naz*-uh-reth.
Sanhedrin	*San*-huh-drun or San-*heed*-run.
synagogue	*sin*-uh-gog.
Tetrach	*Teh*-trark or *Tee*-trark.

Jesus uses the fact of His pending death to teach the demands of discipleship. The demands apply to everyone, as seen by the fact that Jesus now calls *the people unto him with his disciples also.* All who decide to follow Him must be ready to make the ultimate sacrifice: they must deny themselves. It is not merely that they must renounce sinful ways or indulgent luxuries; they must renounce the very right to control their own lives. Thus should every follower *take up his cross.*

❧ GIVE UP OR GIVE IN? ❧

Each year on Good Friday in the Philippines, some people go through what is called a *devotional crucifixion.* This involves allowing themselves to be nailed to a cross as a reenactment of the crucifixion of Jesus. They do so for various reasons, usually as an appeal to God to answer a prayer.

But this is not what Jesus meant when He called on people to take up their crosses. He was, instead, asking for a complete denial of self, no matter what the cost. The word picture of this command can be found in the Roman practice of forcing a criminal to carry his own cross to the crucifixion site.

The model of giving one's self is the life of Jesus. He did this physically when He carried His cross, as far as He was able, to His crucifixion. Dare we do less in a spiritual sense?   —A. E. A.

35. For whosoever will save his life shall lose it; but whosoever shall lose his life for my sake and the gospel's, the same shall save it.

Again Jesus speaks of choices. One person might decide to do everything possible to save his or her own life, to claim the right to live life as desired. But like the rich fool Jesus warned about, such a person will one day leave it all behind and go empty-handed to judgment (see Luke 12:16-21).

The wise disciple therefore is willing to lose his or her life for Jesus' sake and for the cause of the gospel. Such a person is willing to surrender life, realizing that that is the only way ultimately to save it. This means having a willingness to forfeit material life in return for the bounty of Heaven. This means being willing to lose social standing in order to stand with the people of God. It means being willing to lose one's physical life in exchange for eternal life. It means being willing to surrender one's very soul to the safety of Jesus' hands.

> **What Do You Think?**
> What are some things you have done to "lose your life" for Christ? What more can you do?
> *Talking Points for Your Discussion*
> - Issues of thinking
> - Issues of behaving
> - Issues of speaking

B. Logic of Discipleship (vv. 36, 37)

36. For what shall it profit a man, if he shall gain the whole world, and lose his own soul?

Jesus asks His followers to think clearly about this life in relation to the next. Imagine that someone could *gain the whole world,* win the whole game of life, and "die with the most toys" (as the saying goes). Even if such a far-fetched dream became reality, what would be the profit if such a person loses his or her eternal soul in the process?

The word *soul* can refer to a person's life on earth, as in the Greek of Matthew 6:25 and most other New Testament uses. Or it can refer to a person's eternal soul, as in Revelation 6:9. Both ideas fit well in this teaching of Jesus.

37. Or what shall a man give in exchange for his soul?

Jesus carries the logic of His argument further. When a person looks at life and eternal destiny, what can be given in exchange for it? What possible price would be high enough for a good bargain for one's soul? Or if such a person should realize that his or her soul has been lost, what can possibly be given to get it back?

> **What Do You Think?**
> What are some things that people seem willing to give in exchange for their souls? What has to happen for them to realize their foolishness?
> *Talking Points for Your Discussion*
> - Matthew 6:24
> - Matthew 26:14-16
> - Mark 10:17-31
> - Luke 12:13-21

C. Urgency of Discipleship (vv. 38; 9:1)

38. Whosoever therefore shall be ashamed of me and of my words in this adulterous and sinful generation; of him also shall the Son of man be ashamed, when he cometh in the glory of his Father with the holy angels.

People who prefer the approval of *this adulterous and sinful generation* rather than Jesus' approval are unfit to be called disciples. *Adultery* and other words associated with sexual immorality often are used in the Bible to refer figuratively to idolatry (example: Ezekiel 23:37). To be ashamed of Jesus implies that a person is proud of something else instead. Whatever that is, it is an idol.

Jesus' return will be in the glory of the Father, which the faithful will share (Colossians 3:4). Jesus' will return in the company of *the holy angels,* with whom the faithful will share eternity (Revelation 7:9-12). In light of all this, how can anyone in any earthly generation be ashamed of Jesus?

What Do You Think?
What are some ways to identify ourselves clearly as followers of Christ?
Talking Points for Your Discussion
- Ways that are similar to how first-century Christians could have done it
- Ways that were not available to first-century Christians

9:1. And he said unto them, Verily I say unto you, That there be some of them that stand here, which shall not taste of death, till they have seen the kingdom of God come with power.

Verily I say unto you is a phrase Jesus uses dozens of times in the Gospels to introduce a particularly important truth. Now He announces to His disciples that some of them will live to see the coming of the kingdom of God.

This is a difficult prediction to interpret, and there are several proposals. We should start by establishing what it does *not* mean: Jesus is not predicting that His return will occur during the disciples' lifetimes. What Jesus may be referring to, rather, is that the church, which He has just promised that He will build (see the parallel at Matthew 16:18), will come soon.

Amazing things will happen when the church is established on the Day of Pentecost! Judas Iscariot will die before that day. The other apostles will see the long-awaited *kingdom of God come with power,* just as Jesus promised (see Acts 1:6-8; 2:42).

Another theory is that *the kingdom of God come with power* refers to the way Christ's spiritual reign from Heaven manifests itself after the resurrection. Many important things happen after Jesus' ascension: the number of disciples multiplies rapidly, the disciples perform various miracles, the Gentiles are included, etc. All of these can be seen as ways that the kingdom comes with power.

Conclusion

A. What Kind of Messiah?

People in the first century can be criticized fairly for wanting a Messiah on their own terms. They were more interested in His miracles than in His message. They were eager for Him to overthrow Rome, but they did not necessarily want Him to rule in their hearts.

But what kind of Messiah do *we* expect Jesus to be? Do we expect that He provide health and wealth? Do we think He should be the "heavenly genie" that grants all our wishes? Let us learn from Peter's experience that we do not dictate to Jesus. He is God's Messiah, on God's terms.

B. What Kind of Disciple?

A true disciple does not ask, "Am I happy with Jesus?" Instead, he or she asks, "Is my Lord happy with me?" True discipleship has its costs, but it also has unimaginable rewards. Therefore the true disciple will echo Peter, "You are the Christ—and You are my Lord."

C. Prayer

Father, we thank You for sending Your own Son to be the Messiah who would give His life for us. Help us to be faithful disciples. May we never be ashamed to take our stand with Jesus and the truth of the gospel. We pray in His name, Amen.

D. Thought to Remember

Take up your cross today.

INVOLVEMENT LEARNING

Some of the activities below are also found in the helpful student book, Adult Bible Class.
Don't forget to download the free reproducible page from www.standardlesson.com to enhance your lesson!

Into the Lesson

Give each learner an envelope containing a cross cut into eight pieces as shown below:

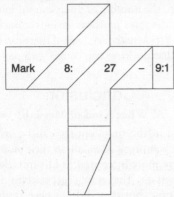

Make sure the paper you use for these has a clearly indicated "correct" side (lightly patterned, etc.), so pieces are not reversed. On the pieces of the cross's crossbar, learners will find the reference for today's study text, which will be the basic clue for assembly.

Once learners finish, ask, "What key truth about the cross is found in today's text?" The answer is in Jesus' words in verse 34b.

Produce a small container of olive oil. Ask, "Now what does this oil have to do with the cross we just assembled?" The answer expected is that we associate the cross with King Jesus, and kings in biblical times typically were anointed to their positions with olive oil. Say, "The *Christ* or *Messiah*, both meaning 'Anointed One,' was to have a position of power, but He would be put to death on a Roman cross. So the oil and the cross are ideal symbols of Jesus as Messiah."

Then ask a reader to return to last week's text and read aloud Isaiah 53:3-5, 7-10a. Say, "No Christian can miss the prophecy of the Messiah's cruel rejection and death when looking at it after the fact. But today's text shows a great misunderstanding of that reality."

Into the Word

Say, "Today's text offers a series of questions and answers. So perhaps we can examine the text with a series of questions and answers as well."

Then ask the following questions. After the simple factual answers are given, push deeper by asking, "Why is this fact important?" 1. Where was Jesus on the occasion of the events in the text? *(v. 27)* 2. Who did the people think Jesus might be? *(v. 28)* 3. What did Jesus instruct about revealing His true identity? *(v. 30 and commentary)* 4. When Jesus spoke plainly about what the near future held for Him, what sort of reaction did He get? *(v. 32b)* 5. What was the basic error in Peter's thinking? *(commentary on v. 33)* 6. What sort of reactions do you suppose resulted when Jesus spoke of taking up a cross? *(vv. 34, 35)* 7. How did Jesus' comments on the value of one's soul relate to His correction of Peter's thinking? *(vv. 33b, 36, 37)* 8. In what ways was Jesus' audience showing shame regarding Jesus and His words? *(v. 38)* 11. What do you understand to be the fulfillment of Jesus' prophecy that some there on that day would see His kingdom come in power? *(commentary on 9:1)*

Into Life

Ask, "What might the media and the general population think and/or say when politicians wear (or do not wear) a piece of jewelry or clothing that is in some way 'patriotic'?" Allow brief responses, but do not allow the discussion to become political.

Then ask, "What are some ways to bear (not simply wear!) the cross as the image of the Messiah's sacrifice? What should a follower of Christ expect others to notice and say as a result?" Allow responses, but highlight the positive elements, such as occasions for witnessing. Download the reproducible page and distribute its two activities as take-home work.

Jesus Is the Messiah

JESUS IS
GOD'S SON

BACKGROUND SCRIPTURE: Mark 9:2-13
PRINTED TEXT: Mark 9:2-13

MARK 9:2-13

2 And after six days Jesus taketh with him Peter, and James, and John, and leadeth them up into an high mountain apart by themselves: and he was transfigured before them.

3 And his raiment became shining, exceeding white as snow; so as no fuller on earth can white them.

4 And there appeared unto them Elias with Moses: and they were talking with Jesus.

5 And Peter answered and said to Jesus, Master, it is good for us to be here: and let us make three tabernacles; one for thee, and one for Moses, and one for Elias.

6 For he wist not what to say; for they were sore afraid.

7 And there was a cloud that overshadowed them: and a voice came out of the cloud, saying, This is my beloved Son: hear him.

8 And suddenly, when they had looked round about, they saw no man any more, save Jesus only with themselves.

9 And as they came down from the mountain, he charged them that they should tell no man what things they had seen, till the Son of man were risen from the dead.

10 And they kept that saying with themselves, questioning one with another what the rising from the dead should mean.

11 And they asked him, saying, Why say the scribes that Elias must first come?

12 And he answered and told them, Elias verily cometh first, and restoreth all things; and how it is written of the Son of man, that he must suffer many things, and be set at nought.

13 But I say unto you, That Elias is indeed come, and they have done unto him whatsoever they listed, as it is written of him.

KEY VERSE

There was a cloud that overshadowed them: and a voice came out of the cloud, saying, This is my beloved Son: hear him. —**Mark 9:7**

ASSURING HOPE

Unit 2: The Fulfillment of God's Promise

LESSONS 10–13

LESSON AIMS

After participating in this lesson, each student will be able to:

1. Retell in detail the story of the transfiguration of Jesus.

2. Compare and contrast the disciples' points of confusion with modern confusion about Jesus and His work.

3. Express a commitment to focus on Jesus and to "hear . . . him" above all the competing voices.

LESSON OUTLINE

Introduction

A. Metamorphosis

A striped caterpillar climbs to a precarious perch on a tree limb, clumsily hangs down, and begins to spin a cocoon (more precisely, a chrysalis) about itself. In only a few days what was once a mere caterpillar begins to break free from the cocoon. Fragile wings unfurl and harden as the caterpillar transforms into a beautiful Monarch butterfly. The Greek name for "transformation" comes directly into English as our word *metamorphosis*.

On a high mountain north of Galilee, Jesus experienced a metamorphosis before the startled eyes of three disciples. We call this experience His *transfiguration,* but literally in the original language it is *metamorphosis.* This was a spectacular change of His visible form. What happened there was different from a butterfly's metamorphosis, however, in two important ways. First, when Jesus' appearance changed into shining glory, it was an unveiling of what had been His true nature all along. Second, this revelation of His glory was temporary, because Jesus changed back to His earthly appearance rather quickly.

For just this brief moment the mantle of flesh was transformed, and Jesus was seen in the majesty that was rightly His. But then the shining glory left Him so that He might resume His journey toward the cross. (Parallels to today's text are Matthew 17:1-13 and Luke 9:28-36.)

B. Lesson Background

The transfiguration follows about a week after Peter's confession of Jesus as "the Christ" (Matthew 16:16). Following that confession, Jesus voiced certain promises, including the fact that He would rise from the dead (Mark 8:31). He promised that He would build His church on a rock and that that church would never be defeated (Matthew 16:18). He promised that the Son of Man would someday come in the glory of the Father (Mark 8:38). Following these breathtaking promises, Jesus took His "inner circle" of three disciples to a mountaintop where He gave them proof that such promises would be kept. The proof was a glimpse of His true glory.

Jesus Is God's Son

Jesus also made certain demands following Peter's confession. He demanded that Peter not try to revise the plans of God (Mark 8:32, 33). He demanded that all who chose to follow Him had to give up the rights to their own lives, take up their crosses, and follow Him (Mark 8:34). He demanded that His disciples not be ashamed of Him, even though their belief was at odds with that of their own generation (Mark 8:38).

Because these demands of discipleship are so challenging, Jesus also needed to give evidence to these first leaders of the church that whatever price they paid would be worth it. The ultimate evidence in that regard was the resurrection. Preliminary to that event was the evidence of the transfiguration.

I. Transfiguration
(MARK 9:2, 3)
A. Setting (v. 2)

2. And after six days Jesus taketh with him Peter, and James, and John, and leadeth them up into an high mountain apart by themselves: and he was transfigured before them.

Peter, James, and John are sometimes known as the "inner three" or "inner circle" of the apostles in that they witness things the others do not (compare Mark 5:37; 14:33). Perhaps these special experiences are necessary for Peter because he will preach the first gospel sermon (Acts 2:14-40); for James because he will die as the first apostolic martyr (Acts 12:1, 2); and for John because he will

HOW TO SAY IT

chrysalis	*kri*-suh-lus.
Elias	Ee-*lye*-us.
Elijah	Ee-*lye*-juh.
Galilee	*Gal*-uh-lee.
Hermon	*Her*-mun.
Herodias	Heh-*roe*-dee-us.
Jezebel	*Jez*-uh-bel.
Malachi	*Mal*-uh-kye.
Messiah	Meh-*sigh*-uh.
metamorphosis	*met*-tuh-**mor**-fuh-suss.
Tabor	*Tay*-ber.

live on to speak and write to the church for virtually the rest of the first century.

The time frame *after six days* refers to Peter's confession and the events surrounding it. They climb a high mountain, which is not named. The site traditionally proposed is Mount Tabor in Galilee (compare Joshua 19:22). But it is difficult to think of this mountain as "high," since its summit is just over 1,800 feet above sea level. A more likely site is Mount Hermon. It is near Caesarea Philippi (Mark 8:27) and is over 9,000 feet high.

Jesus' change of form is a visible transformation. The true glory of Jesus is presented in a manner that the apostles can see with their own eyes. It is not a vision or a dream.

B. Sight (v. 3)

3. And his raiment became shining, exceeding white as snow; so as no fuller on earth can white them.

The outward manifestation of Jesus' transformation is described in straightforward terms. His clothing becomes whiter and brighter than anything the three apostles have ever seen. A *fuller* is someone who bleaches clothing. Jesus' garments are as white as the snow on the mountaintops (compare Daniel 7:9). The parallel accounts add descriptions of how the appearance of Jesus' face is altered (see Matthew 17:2; Luke 9:29). It must be such a spectacular sight that human words can scarcely describe it (compare Revelation 1:13-16).

II. Historic Visitors
(MARK 9:4-8)
A. Heroes' Appearance (v. 4)

4. And there appeared unto them Elias with Moses: and they were talking with Jesus.

While the apostles are trying to grasp the meaning of Jesus' amazing transfiguration, two renowned figures from Israel's history appear. One is Elias (Elijah), Israel's great prophet of the ninth century BC. Moses, the second named, is Israel's great lawgiver of the fifteenth century BC.

As speculation, some students propose that these two represent "the law" (in the person of Moses) and "the prophets" (in the person of Elias) coming to pay homage to the long-awaited Messiah. Both Moses and Elias participated in great acts of revelation on mountains (Exodus 3:1; 19:20; 1 Kings 18:19-46; 19:11-13). Another great revelatory event on a mountain is under way.

Moses and Elias are *talking with Jesus,* and Luke 9:31 adds that they are talking about His forthcoming departure. These three know the plan of God and the mission of Jesus. They know what awaits Him in Jerusalem.

B. Peter's Suggestion (vv. 5, 6)

5. And Peter answered and said to Jesus, Master, it is good for us to be here: and let us make three tabernacles; one for thee, and one for Moses, and one for Elias.

Peter, rarely at a loss for words, apparently blurts out the first thoughts that come to his mind: *it is good for us to be here.* In proposing to build *three tabernacles* or tents, he probably has in mind those that are built every year at the Feast of Tabernacles (Leviticus 23:42). Does Peter think that Moses and Elias (Elijah) plan to stay awhile?

No doubt Peter means well and only wants to help. But Peter's knee-jerk plan puts Jesus on the same level with Moses and Elias. To be put on a par with Moses and Elias would be a great honor for anyone but Jesus. But the point of the transfiguration is that Jesus has a divine glory that is far above the rank of the greatest of humans.

What Do You Think?

What are some impulsive things that Christians do today? What techniques can we use to restrain knee-jerk impulses?

Talking Points for Your Discussion
- When on an emotional or spiritual "high"
- When at an emotional or spiritual "low"

---

6. For he wist not what to say; for they were sore afraid.

Peter speaks, even though he has no idea what to say. He and James and John are too terrified to think straight. Moses and Elias (Elijah) have been dead for many centuries, and yet here they are talking with Jesus. And while the apostles have seen Jesus as a great teacher and miracle worker,

they have not seen anything like this display of majestic splendor.

The disciples' fear is parallel to that of the shepherds who heard the angel's announcement of the birth of Jesus and were surrounded by the glory of God (see Luke 2:9). The disciples are afraid because this is an event they cannot comprehend.

C. God's Pronouncement (vv. 7, 8)

7. And there was a cloud that overshadowed them: and a voice came out of the cloud, saying, This is my beloved Son: hear him.

Now the point of this dramatic scene becomes clearer as the visual imagery is accompanied by words spoken by God himself. This voice was heard before, when Jesus was baptized in the Jordan River. Then as now, God identifies Jesus as His Son (compare Mark 1:11).

The depiction of the cloud on this mountaintop reminds us of the cloud on Mount Sinai (see Exodus 19:9). It is a depiction of God's presence. Notice that in Mark 1:11 (and the parallels Matthew 3:17 and Luke 3:22), God's voice comes from "heaven." But here God's voice comes *out of the cloud.* If that means that God is more immediately present than He was at Jesus' baptism, then the purpose of the cloud may be to protect the disciples from gazing on what is too sacred for them to see. No one can see God and live (Exodus 33:20). Even so, the disciples are allowed to see the sacred glory of the Son.

The voice from the cloud identifies Jesus and commands the disciples to *hear him.* Both words carry important meaning. When God tells them to hear, it means they should not repeat the recent mistake of opposing what Jesus says (Matthew 16:22; Mark 8:32). They are to pay attention and accept Jesus' words, whether they like them or not. When Jesus speaks, they are to listen!

The second word in the phrase *hear him* sharply separates Jesus from Moses and Elias (Elijah). Moses spoke the word of God in his day, as did Elias. The people were expected to listen to and to heed those two spiritual giants. But now it is not Moses with his laws nor Elias with his prophecies through whom God speaks. It is Jesus who speaks for God.

❧ WANTING TO LISTEN ❧

Last night I made my five-year-old son take a break from playing his computer game. He had reached a new level and was getting frustrated because he didn't know how to get through the more complex challenges.

After he had a tearful time out, I thought he was ready to hear an explanation of why he needed to take a break. But he was so sure he was not going to like what I had to say, it was all I could do to get him to sit still and listen. Finally, I had to hold him down and say forcefully, "*Alex,* listen to me! I'm going to let you play if you will just listen!" Perhaps if we took the time to listen to what God has to say, we would better understand His loving purposes. We may even discover that what He has to say is not as "bad" as we expect.

Maybe there are times we have not consulted God about a decision because we were afraid He would say *no,* when all along He wanted to give us an enthusiastic *yes!* In other cases, maybe His answer would have been, "Yes, but not yet. You'll enjoy it more if you wait," or perhaps, "I have something better in mind. You're going to love this!" Listen to God today. You may be surprised at what He has to say. —A. W.

8. And suddenly, when they had looked round about, they saw no man any more, save Jesus only with themselves.

The sudden disappearance of Moses and Elias (Elijah) intensifies the words of God concerning His Son. No longer will Moses speak for God, because the old covenant is about to be replaced (see Mark 14:24; Colossians 2:14). No longer will

the people need to read the words of Elias and the prophets to anticipate the coming of the Messiah because the one who fulfills all those prophecies is here. From now on, the disciples must listen to Jesus! He is God's final message and the messenger to the human race (see Hebrews 1:1, 2).

Moses and Elias attest to Jesus' greatness, but He does not need their assistance. Their job was to prepare for His coming, and they did their job well. But now Jesus is here. Therefore, Moses and Elias are removed from the scene.

III. Results
(MARK 9:9-13)
A. Son of Man Will Rise (vv. 9, 10)

9. And as they came down from the mountain, he charged them that they should tell no man what things they had seen, till the Son of man were risen from the dead.

This demand for secrecy is the same that was heard the previous week (see Mark 8:29, 30). Even so, we sympathize with how hard it must be for Peter, James, and John to pretend that nothing out of the ordinary has happened! The need for secrecy is bound up with the danger of having incomplete information. At this point, it would be easy to draw wrong conclusions about what Jesus comes to do.

The need for secrecy, however, will last only until the Son of Man has risen from the dead. Just

Visual for Lesson 11. Use this visual to start a discussion about the things that distract us from listening to Jesus.

as His identity as Messiah is inseparably linked with His upcoming death (Mark 8:29-31), the glory of His transfiguration is inseparably linked to His subsequent resurrection. He will die, but the tomb will not be able to hold Him. God will not leave the Son of Man—His own Son—in the grave. This is the key point Peter will stress when he freely proclaims the risen Lord on the Day of Pentecost (see Acts 2:29-36).

What Do You Think?

Under what circumstances is secrecy a good idea in the church? When is it not a good idea?

Talking Points for Your Discussion
- Matthew 18:15-17
- Acts 23:22
- 1 Timothy 5:19
- Issues involving preliminary, unfinalized plans

10. And they kept that saying with themselves, questioning one with another what the rising from the dead should mean.

As they make the long journey back down the mountain, Peter, James, and John have opportunity to talk among themselves. They keep pondering this saying of Jesus. What can He possibly mean by *rising from the dead*?

Jesus has, in fact, already clearly told them that He will be killed and will rise again (Mark 8:31). He will tell them again as they pass through Galilee (9:31); when they hear these words that third time and cannot understand them, they will be afraid to ask Jesus to explain (9:32). Jesus will tell them a fourth time as they approach Jerusalem (10:34). But the disciples still will not be able to accept the clear meaning of Jesus' words (see Luke 18:32-34, which is parallel to Mark 10:34).

❧ UNBELIEVABLE! ❧

A professor I know makes an astonishing offer to his students every semester: he announces that the best work will receive an *A* even if it does not meet the requirements, since he grades exams strictly on a comparative basis. This means that if each student turned in a sheet of paper with only his or her name on it, then the professor would have no choice but to give everyone a 100, because all the papers would be equal in quality!

For years, students did not take him literally. Recently, however, that professor finally had a group of students take him seriously. The unbelievable came true: the entire class received a 100 simply for writing their names!

Though Jesus often spoke in parables, He intended His words to be taken literally when He spoke of His death and resurrection. The disciples had a hard time with this whole concept. Many today still struggle with the idea of Christ's resurrection. But the resurrection is the core of the gospel (1 Corinthians 15). Do we really believe that God acted in this marvelous way and that Christ's resurrection guarantees our own? —A. W.

B. Elias Has Come (vv. 11-13)

11. And they asked him, saying, Why say the scribes that Elias must first come?

The disciples have just seen Elias (Elijah) with Moses, and this triggers a connection for them. While they are afraid to ask about Jesus' death and resurrection, they have the courage to ask about Elias. Why do the scribes say that Elias must come before the Messiah comes?

The reason that the scribes say this is that the prophet Malachi said the same thing some 400 years earlier. The closing words of the Old Testament promise that God will send Elias the prophet before the coming of the Day of the Lord (see Malachi 4:5, 6). Therefore the disciples wonder: Does the appearance of Elias on the mountaintop mean that the Day of the Lord is at hand?

What Do You Think?

When is it healthy to inquire about the timing of Jesus' plans, and when is it unhealthy?

Talking Points for Your Discussion
- Mark 13:4
- Acts 1:6, 7
- Revelation 6:10

12. And he answered and told them, Elias verily cometh first, and restoreth all things; and how it is written of the Son of man, that he must suffer many things, and be set at nought.

In reply, Jesus confirms that it is necessary for Elias to come in advance of the Messiah. Elias is to restore the hearts of the fathers to their children in that preparatory work (Malachi 3:1; 4:6). But even when *all things* are restored in that sense, it does not mean that everything will be smooth and easy for the Messiah. It will still be necessary for *the Son of man* to *suffer many things*. The Messiah will *be set at nought*, snubbed by the very people He comes to save. The disciples must realize what lies ahead.

13. But I say unto you, That Elias is indeed come, and they have done unto him whatsoever they listed, as it is written of him.

Jesus carries His explanation further. In fact, Elias (Elijah) has already come—in the person of John the Baptist. Jesus has already explained this earlier in Matthew 11:11-14, but apparently His words have not sunk in as the parallel Matthew 17:13 reveals. John the Baptist, who came in the spirit and forcefulness of Elias, is the one who fulfills the centuries-old prophecy of Malachi.

The similarities of John and Elias have been noted often. Both were bold prophets who defied kings and called the nation to repentance. Both had a strange appearance, lived in the wilds, and ate unusual food. Both endured the wrath of an evil woman and her influence on the king.

The vicious words of Jezebel that threatened Elias with death were not fulfilled (1 Kings 19:2). Instead, Elias rode victoriously to Heaven in a chariot of fire (2 Kings 2:11), with Jezebel meeting an inglorious end (2 Kings 9:30-37). John, for his part, was beheaded at the request of the evil Herodias (see Mark 6:17-28). Thus John suffered the fate proclaimed for Elias. Jesus will suffer death as well as He submits to the will of God.

> **What Do You Think?**
> How should we respond when Christians are persecuted and even martyred for Christ?
> *Talking Points for Your Discussion*
> ▪ Acts 8:1b, 4
> ▪ Acts 12:5
> ▪ Acts 16:37; 22:25
> ▪ 1 Peter 4:12-19

Conclusion
A. They Never Forgot

The disciples who were present at the transfiguration never forgot their mountaintop experience. They saw the Lord in His true glory, and it changed their lives forever. Peter wrote of this many years later when he recalled the experiences "when we were with him in the holy mount" (2 Peter 1:18). Peter was forever changed by what he saw.

Near the end of the first century, John could look ahead to a future day of glory. With eager confidence he wrote, "We know that, when he shall appear, we shall be like him; for we shall see him as he is" (1 John 3:2). He knew that everything is changed when seeing the Lord as He really is.

B. We Must Always Remember

Through the disciples' testimony we can watch with spiritual eyes as the Lord is transformed into His true glory. We can remember that we serve a Lord whose glory and power far transcend everything on earth.

Jesus' metamorphoses on the mount of transfiguration and from the empty tomb reveal His power to bring about our own metamorphosis. Jesus demonstrated that He has the power to change us into what we can never be on our own. As we surrender ourselves to His authority, we are "transformed by the renewing" of our minds (Romans 12:2), and we are changed degree by degree into the glory of His image (see 2 Corinthians 3:18).

Jesus has the power to change us "in a moment, in the twinkling of an eye" (see 1 Corinthians 15:52). When Jesus returns, He will change our lowly bodies to be like "his glorious body" (Philippians 3:21). "We shall be like him; for we shall see him as he is" (1 John 3:2).

C. Prayer

Father, we praise You and we praise Christ Jesus our Lord in all His glory and splendor. Help us to proclaim Your majesty in all the world. In Jesus' name we pray, amen.

D. Thought to Remember

One day we will see Jesus in all His glory.

INVOLVEMENT LEARNING

Some of the activities below are also found in the helpful student book, Adult Bible Class.
Don't forget to download the free reproducible page from www.standardlesson.com to enhance your lesson!

Into the Lesson

Display blanks in the following arrangement:

— — — — — —

— —

— — — — — — — — —

Ask the class to take turns suggesting letters you can use to fill in the blanks, in the manner of the television game show *Wheel of Fortune;* however, vowels can be guessed like any other letter. Tell them the category is "a common how-we-know-things expression." The truth you want to reveal is *Seeing Is Believing.*

Once identified, say, "In today's text, God provides visual evidence of truths He revealed through Jesus to the disciples a week earlier, in last week's lesson. The transfiguration in today's study is a powerful visual demonstration of the divine nature and glory of Jesus."

Option: Download the reproducible page and place copies of the Mountaintop Experiences activity from it in chairs for learners to work on as they arrive.

Into the Word

Give each learner a blank sheet of paper and ask them to create three columns headed *Moses, Elijah,* and *Jesus.* Say, "I am going to read a series of statements. As I do, put the statement number under its proper column heading. Some statements may go under more than one heading." The statements below include the answers and biblical references in italics, but do not include those as you read the statements to the class.

1. This servant of God went into Heaven in a spectacular way. *[Elijah, 2 Kings 2:1, 11, 12; Jesus, Acts 1:9-11]* 2. This servant of God was a precursor of John the Baptist. *[Elijah, Matthew 11:11-14]* 3. This servant of God once had a change in facial appearance from being in the presence of God. *[Moses, Exodus 34:29; Jesus, Luke 9:29]* 4. This servant of God confronted a powerful political ruler

with God's word. *[Moses, Exodus 5:1, etc.; Elijah, 1 Kings 18; Jesus, Matthew 27:11]* 5. This servant of God had a time of trial while alone in a wilderness. *[Moses, Exodus 3:1–4:17; Elijah, 1 Kings 19:1-14; Jesus, Matthew 4:1-11]* 6. This servant of God indicated to His followers that He would rise from the dead *[Jesus, Mark 9:9]* 7. This servant of God was not allowed to finish the task originally assigned to him *[Moses, Deuteronomy 34:1-8]* 8. This servant of God was the one who superseded the others in every way. *[Jesus, Mark 9:8; Hebrews 1:1-3]*

Let the group reveal their choices; as they do, refer to the text references given. However, do not simply move through the list in a mechanical way. Rather, make sure to use the questions as entry points to discuss appropriate aspects of today's study text. For example, questions 7 and 8 should be used to introduce the lesson commentary on Mark 9:8.

Into Life

Give each learner an image of a radio or stereo unit. Have this line repeated seven times underneath the image:

I have heard the voice of _____,
but Jesus says _____.

Say, "A quick scroll of a radio dial reveals many voices. These voices are designed to inform and enlighten (newscasters), to stir emotions and opinions (talk-show hosts), to entertain and elate (musicians). The listener chooses." Then ask your learners to fill in the blanks. To stimulate thinking, suggest this example: "I have heard the voice of materialism, but Jesus says my life does not consist of things!" Suggest they ponder the statement each day in the week ahead, noting "voices" they hear and Jesus' teaching to the contrary.

Alternative: Download the reproducible page and use the Metamorphosis activity instead of the above.

JESUS CAME TO SERVE

BACKGROUND SCRIPTURE: Mark 10:35-45

PRINTED TEXT: Mark 10:35-45

MARK 10:35-45

35 And James and John, the sons of Zebedee, come unto him, saying, Master, we would that thou shouldest do for us whatsoever we shall desire.

36 And he said unto them, What would ye that I should do for you?

37 They said unto him, Grant unto us that we may sit, one on thy right hand, and the other on thy left hand, in thy glory.

38 But Jesus said unto them, Ye know not what ye ask: can ye drink of the cup that I

drink of? and be baptized with the baptism that I am baptized with?

39 And they said unto him, We can. And Jesus said unto them, Ye shall indeed drink of the cup that I drink of; and with the baptism that I am baptized withal shall ye be baptized:

40 But to sit on my right hand and on my left hand is not mine to give; but it shall be given to them for whom it is prepared.

41 And when the ten heard it, they began to be much displeased with James and John.

42 But Jesus called them to him, and saith unto them, Ye know that they which are accounted to rule over the Gentiles exercise lordship over them; and their great ones exercise authority upon them.

43 But so shall it not be among you: but whosoever will be great among you, shall be your minister:

44 And whosoever of you will be the chiefest, shall be servant of all.

45 For even the Son of man came not to be ministered unto, but to minister, and to give his life a ransom for many.

KEY VERSE

Even the Son of man came not to be ministered unto, but to minister, and to give his life a ransom for many. —**Mark 10:45**

ASSURING HOPE

LESSON AIMS

After participating in this lesson, each student will be able to:

1. Relate the account of James and John's request for chief seats and the ensuing discussion of "greatness."

2. Compare the quest for esteem evident in James and John with that of our own time.

3. State at least one specific way he or she can serve others in the coming week.

LESSON OUTLINE

Introduction

A. God's Mount Rushmore

Few sights around the world are more impressive than the Mount Rushmore National Memorial in South Dakota. The famous images of American Presidents George Washington, Thomas Jefferson, Abraham Lincoln, and Theodore Roosevelt comprise the world's largest sculpture. The 60-foot tall figures were intended to represent the ideals of American democracy by honoring four of the country's greatest leaders.

By contrast, what would God sculpt to represent His ideals for His people? What is the impressive image that God would provide to remind us of what He wants us to be? Whose image would He carve into His iconic mountain?

Today's Scripture passage could be characterized as God's Mount Rushmore. In it we learn the quality essential to greatness from God's point of view. In it we learn who has supremely demonstrated that quality and why above all things we are to make that quality of His our own.

B. Lesson Background

Since the decisive day in Caesarea Philippi when Peter said to Jesus, "Thou art the Christ" (Mark 8:29; Lesson 10), Jesus spoke to His disciples openly and directly about His pending death (8:31; 9:31). Yet the disciples failed to understand Him (9:32), and Peter even argued with Him (8:32). Clearly it was not easy to understand how the Christ—the promised "anointed one" sent by God—could possibly suffer such a fate.

The disciples, like us, were accustomed to the idea that great people are those who can exercise power over others, who can command others to do their bidding to benefit those who have the power and give the orders. For them, the hated Roman conquerors represented the greatness of power, and the disciples desired that their pagan overlords would be overthrown by an even mightier power. Like us, the disciples struggled to imagine any other way that a person can be great, whether that person is the Christ or anyone else.

By contrast, Jesus challenged them to think very differently. Those who want to save their lives must lose them (Mark 8:35). Those who belong to God's kingdom must become like little children (9:37; 10:15). It is impossible for those who rely on their own resources to enter God's kingdom (10:24, 25). Being "first," Jesus told His disciples, consisted of serving others—being "last" in ordinary terms (9:35).

In today's passage, Jesus brings these ideas together for His disciples. He will tell them again what it means to be great in God's kingdom. More particularly, He will tell them why in God's kingdom greatness is defined in a way that seems upside down. (Matthew 20:20-28 is parallel.)

I. Jesus Speaks to Two
(Mark 10:35-40)
A. Bold Request (vv. 35-37)

35. And James and John, the sons of Zebedee, come unto him, saying, Master, we would that thou shouldest do for us whatsoever we shall desire.

Our text begins with a conversation between Jesus and James and John. The latter two are brothers who have followed Jesus since they left their fishing business on the Sea of Galilee (Mark 1:19, 20). While their personal inquiry sparks the conversation, the issue is not theirs alone. Their request reflects the mind-set of all the disciples.

These two fishermen have left everything behind to follow Jesus. As a result, they have been witnesses to His miracles and students of His teaching. They themselves worked miracles and proclaimed God's Word when Jesus sent them out to preach with the others (Mark 6:7, 12, 13). Certainly they are convinced that Jesus has the power to do anything and that they stand strongly enough in His favor to ask for anything.

Nevertheless, the request sounds audacious. They address Jesus respectfully and submissively as *Master*. But they betray that submissiveness in asking Jesus to do whatever they want. On the mountain of transfiguration, where both were present a few months earlier, the voice from the cloud ordered them to listen to Jesus (Mark 9:7, Lesson 11). But here they seem more intent on telling Him what they want than on listening.

Adding to the irony is the fact that the request to *do for us whatsoever we shall desire* comes right on the heels of another death prediction by Jesus (Mark 10:32-34). These two disciples—and probably the others as well—clearly are clueless regarding what is about to happen in Jerusalem!

> **What Do You Think?**
> What do your requests to Jesus say about what you think is most important?
> *Talking Points for Your Discussion*
> - Matthew 5:44
> - Luke 12:13, 14
> - John 15:7
> - 2 Thessalonians 1:11
> - 1 Timothy 3:1, 2
> - James 5:16

36. And he said unto them, What would ye that I should do for you?

Jesus' reply is gracious and open. He says nothing to call out James and John's presumption. Although He is indeed their master, He is willing to consider their request. He does not exercise His prerogative to refuse them immediately.

37. They said unto him, Grant unto us that we may sit, one on thy right hand, and the other on thy left hand, in thy glory.

James and John ask for something very significant! Like Peter, they now believe that Jesus is "the Christ," God's promised king. They believe that Jesus will be enthroned in the position of supreme power. Perhaps when He arrives in Jerusalem, they think, or perhaps at some other time, Jesus will assume His rightful place of kingly authority and will begin to rule over His people.

James and John, like the other disciples, did not understand Jesus when He warned them about His pending death. They apparently do not expect Him to die, arise, ascend, and be enthroned in Heaven. They anticipate an enthronement on earth. Jesus is for them largely a king like other kings, simply more righteous and more powerful, destined to rule the entire world with godly justice.

By asking to sit on either side of Jesus when He is enthroned, James and John desire the most prominent positions (except for Jesus' own position) in

Jesus' kingdom. They want to share in the power and prestige that they expect will be His.

B. Probing Response (vv. 38-40)

38. But Jesus said unto them, Ye know not what ye ask: can ye drink of the cup that I drink of? and be baptized with the baptism that I am baptized with?

Jesus' response to James and John offers a correction to their understanding. Just as the disciples have misunderstood Jesus' warnings about His death, so now James and John do not understand the nature of their own request.

On an earlier occasion when Jesus spoke to His disciples about His forthcoming death, He said that following Him meant taking up a cross and losing one's life (Mark 8:34-37). Here Jesus asks whether the disciples can drink of that same cup or receive that same baptism.

We can infer from Jesus' earlier teaching that He uses these terms to speak about His death on the cross. That is all the more likely when we notice that on the eve of His death Jesus will use a cup as a symbol of the giving of His blood (Mark 14:23, 24) and ask that God take "this cup" from Him (14:36). In Luke 12:50, Jesus also speaks of a baptism that He must undergo, also apparently a reference to His death.

So Jesus challenges the two to understand what they previously have not. If James and John truly want to share in Jesus' glory, they must share in His suffering as well. They need to understand and accept His cup and His baptism to understand what true glory is.

HOW TO SAY IT

Caesarea Philippi	Sess-uh-*ree*-uh Fih-*lip*-pie or *Fil*-ih-pie.
claustrophobia	klos-truh-*foe*-bee-uh.
Galilee	*Gal*-uh-lee.
Gentiles	*Jen*-tiles.
iconic	eye-*kahn*-ick.
pagan	*pay*-gun.
patriarch	*pay*-tree-ark
Serbia	*Sir*-bee-uh.
Zebedee	*Zeb*-eh-dee.

39a. And they said unto him, We can.

James and John respond in a way that indicates that they once again do not understand Jesus' point. Their enthusiasm to share Jesus' cup and baptism does not reflect the solemnity of one who faces the prospect of death.

39b. And Jesus said unto them, Ye shall indeed drink of the cup that I drink of; and with the baptism that I am baptized withal shall ye be baptized.

For all the disciples, their present lack of understanding is not the end of the story. When confronted with Jesus' arrest and death, they will flee (Mark 14:50). Yet when Jesus is raised from the dead, they will be invited back into fellowship with Him (16:7). When they witness the fateful events of Jesus' death and resurrection, they will be able to understand who He is as God's king and what He has accomplished on the cross. Then they can know what it means to share in His suffering and in His glory.

❧ BE CAREFUL WHAT YOU ASK FOR ❧

I've always had a touch of claustrophobia. My heart still pounds a little faster when I remember crawling under our family's mobile home as a boy to retrieve my sister's runaway guinea pig.

As an adult I decided it was time to conquer this fear, so I asked one of my friends to take me caving with him. Truly, I didn't know what I was in for! He's skinnier than I am, so I struggled to drag myself through crawl spaces he slithered through with ease. Once I lost my balance and almost tumbled into a crevasse. Halfway through the experience, I realized my energy was almost gone (as was that of our dimming flashlights). It was my childhood nightmare multiplied many times over!

That experience reminds me that there are times we should be profoundly grateful when we *don't* get what we ask for! What grief has God saved us from by giving a firm and wise *no* to some of our most reckless desires! —A. W.

40. But to sit on my right hand and on my left hand is not mine to give; but it shall be given to them for whom it is prepared.

For now, however, James and John still do not really understand. So Jesus continues to speak to them in a way that is memorable but difficult, like a riddle that they can solve only after His resurrection. Jesus speaks obliquely about those who will sit at His right and left. These places have been prepared by God (Matthew 20:23). Interestingly, the next time that we read of someone at Jesus' right and left in Mark's Gospel is when Jesus is crucified between two thieves (Mark 15:27)!

> **What Do You Think?**
> How do we distinguish between the preparations that are God's job and the preparations that are our job?
> *Talking Points for Your Discussion*
> ▪ Ephesians 2:10; 4:11, 12
> ▪ 2 Timothy 2:21; 3:16, 17; 4:2
> ▪ 1 Peter 1:13-16

II. Jesus Speaks to Twelve
(MARK 10:41-45)
A. World-style Response (v. 41)

41. And when the ten heard it, they began to be much displeased with James and John.

We might read this verse and think that the other disciples are upset because they realize that the request of James and John is inappropriate. But every member of the Twelve probably shares the same perspective, which is not surprising when we consider human nature. The others are upset because they also want prominence and glory when Jesus assumes His throne. In the next verse, Jesus responds to the fundamental misunderstanding that they all share.

> **What Do You Think?**
> What are some things that can result in conflict between Christians? How do we get to the point where we can resolve such issues in a healthy way, and not just sweep them under the rug?
> *Talking Points for Your Discussion*
> ▪ Minor issues (Philippians 4:2)
> ▪ Major issues (Acts 15:36-41)

B. Pagan-style Greatness (v. 42)

42. But Jesus called them to him, and saith unto them, Ye know that they which are accounted to rule over the Gentiles exercise lordship over them; and their great ones exercise authority upon them.

Jesus begins His response by reminding the disciples of the behavior of the Gentiles. As He speaks about those who are regarded as rulers, the disciples certainly think of the Roman imperial government. For their entire lifetimes, the disciples have known what it is to be ruled by a foreign empire. They undoubtedly resent the taxes they pay, the violence their people experience, and the indignities they suffer because of Roman rule. The way that the Romans rule is hateful to the disciples and their fellow countrymen.

But it is noteworthy that Jesus does not refer to the Romans directly but to Gentiles, that is, to people who do not belong to the nation of Israel. For the disciples and other Jewish people of the time, this term does not signify just those who belong to another nation, but those who do not know God or belong to God's people. To say *Gentile* is to say *pagan,* one who is ignorant of God.

Thus Jesus is stating flatly that the desire to exercise power over others is characteristic of people who do not know God. It is at the core of experiences that the disciples deeply resent, and with good reason. Yet desire for this kind of power is what the disciples are displaying now. They show that they aspire to be like people who do not know God and who do the very things that they despise.

C. Jesus-style Greatness (vv. 43-45)

43. But so shall it not be among you: but whosoever will be great among you, shall be your minister.

Jesus now draws the contrast. His disciples are not to be like the pagans, whose rule they resent. They will pursue greatness on entirely different terms. Greatness for followers of Jesus will not consist of the exercise of power, but of being a servant to others.

The *King James Version* translates Jesus' key term with the English word *minister.* While in today's

English we associate that term with a preacher in a church, or perhaps with a leader of a government department in a parliamentary system, the term is used here to mean "servant." It translates a word in the original language text that is used for ordinary household servants, people whose duty it is to tend to the needs of others.

Being a servant in Jesus' time is no exalted matter, just as it is not in virtually every human culture. Being a servant means giving of one's time and effort day after day to supply what others require. Such a position has no glamour or status, and it does not pay very well either! It is not a position to which people aspire. But Jesus says that those who are great in His kingdom, the kind of people who sit at his right and left when He is enthroned, are those who will live that very kind of life.

> **What Do You Think?**
> What type of person do you find difficult to serve? How do you grow spiritually in that situation?
> *Talking Points for Your Discussion*
> - Difficulties traceable to personality differences
> - Difficulties traceable to worldview differences
> - Difficulties traceable to conflicting cultural norms

44. And whosoever of you will be the chiefest, shall be servant of all.

This verse uses parallelism to restate the point of the previous verse, but it adds intensity. In the previous verse Jesus speaks of one who is great; here He intensifies the statement by speaking of one who is first *(chiefest).*

In the previous verse, Jesus used *minister,* which is the equivalent of the modern English word servant. Now in the *King James Version* we read the word *servant,* but it translates a word in the original language that refers to a slave. Jesus has heightened His language, ascribing first place not just to one who serves for pay, but to the lowliest person in the disciples' world: a bond slave.

Jesus intends to leave no doubt. He is stating emphatically that compared with the pagan point of view, His kingdom is upside down. The last person anyone sees as being in first place is a slave, someone who has no rights or power, but lives entirely to serve other people.

> **What Do You Think?**
> How can we become servants to all without allowing people to treat us as doormats?
> *Talking Points for Your Discussion*
> - The example of Jesus (John 2:15; etc.)
> - The example of Paul (Acts 16:37; etc.)
> - "Being a servant" vs. "being servile"

❧ HUMILITY ❧

On a mission trip to Serbia recently, I had the opportunity to share a meal with a group of Orthodox priests. I didn't know what to expect. After all, a few short years ago my country was bombing theirs to force the Serbian government to change its oppressive policies. Furthermore, some differences in doctrine between my understanding of Christianity and theirs seemed insurmountable.

Intimidated by such thoughts, I found myself seated by an elderly monk named Brother David. With long gray beard, skullcap, and dark robes, he looked to me like an Old Testament patriarch. Yet what truly moved me was his humility—his downcast eyes, gentle smile, soft and cautious answers to doctrinal questions, and even holding my coat as I prepared to leave. Only later would I learn that he was a close friend and advisor to the Patriarch of the Serbian Orthodox church, the most important religious leader in the country.

There are many people who are close to the centers of power, and most of them will be soon forgotten. However, in the simple actions of gracious speech, smiling, and holding my coat, a humble monk set an example I will tell my children and grandchildren about. What example of humility do you project?　　　　　　　　　—A. W.

45. For even the Son of man came not to be ministered unto, but to minister, and to give his life a ransom for many.

Jesus now explains why this upside-down kingdom is the way it is. In Jesus' kingdom, being least and serving others is greatness because that is exactly what Jesus himself does.

As He does so often, Jesus refers to himself as *the Son of man*. It appears that He uses this expression to remind His disciples of a figure in the vision of Daniel 7 who is called "one like the Son of man" (Daniel 7:13). This one receives power from God and overcomes the beastly kingdoms of Daniel's vision, establishing God's never-ending reign over the earth.

So the Son of Man should rightly be a powerful being. And indeed He is: Jesus is unashamed to claim power and authority for himself as the Son of Man. But here He is turning the tables. Jesus says that He does not exercise His power as do the pagans, or even as the disciples aspire to exercise power. He does not come to be served, *to be ministered unto*. No, the powerful king to whom God gives all authority comes to serve others.

Jesus does that serving in a distinct way. Throughout His ministry, we see Jesus acting on behalf of others: healing the sick, casting out evil spirits, providing food for the hungry, delivering His disciples from danger. But the central, defining act of service comes near the end of the story, as Jesus dies on the cross.

Jesus has spoken clearly about His death ever since Peter first affirmed that Jesus is the Christ (Mark 8:29). Here Jesus states why He is determined to go to His death: it is to provide a ransom. While we probably associate that term with a payment to kidnappers, in Jesus' time it is used mostly for a payment made to give freedom to a slave. So Jesus pictures His death as something that will liberate captive people.

Their captivity, of course, is the guilt of rebellion against God. Jesus will give His life as a payment to give the rebels freedom. By dying, Jesus will take on himself the punishment that those rebels deserve. His one life will provide a substitutionary payment for the many who are sinners.

Jesus focuses His life on this one mission: to give His life for the sake of undeserving people. His purpose is to serve others, at the greatest imaginable cost and despite our unworthiness. Since this is what the almighty Son of Man does, then this is what true greatness consists of. Because God sends His Son to serve at the cost of His life, we too must serve others sacrificially.

EVEN AS THE
SON OF MAN . . .

Visual for
Lesson 12

Point to this visual as you ask, "Is this the kind of service Jesus had in mind? Why, or why not?"

Conclusion
A. The Model Servant

Everything around us seems to encourage us to seek power and position. Whether we look at school, jobs, family, friends, or media, all seem to tell us that taking first place, having authority, wealth, and status should be our ambition. If we are honest with ourselves, we will admit that we are happy to listen to that message and follow it.

Everything around us sends us toward power and position except one thing: the cross of Christ. The gospel turns worldly values upside down. We have been served by the greatest one. He served us even to the point of giving His life for us in death. That great truth compels us to reassess our lives and our ambitions. When we serve others as Jesus did, we will discover what life is to be about.

B. Prayer

Lord Jesus, we admit that we love to take first place. Please teach us again that You are the God who entered our world as a servant. Teach us the joy of serving others as You served us. In Christ's name we pray. Amen.

C. Thought to Remember

"You can't live a perfect day without doing something for someone who will never be able to repay you" (John Wooden).

INVOLVEMENT LEARNING

Some of the activities below are also found in the helpful student book, Adult Bible Class.
Don't forget to download the free reproducible page from www.standardlesson.com to enhance your lesson!

Into the Lesson

Download the reproducible page and distribute copies of the Mount Rushmore activity from it. Have your learners work on this in small groups of three or four.

Discuss results as a class. Note to the class the identification that is most common; ask why they think that is so. Ask learners to state their criteria for their choices. Compare and contrast the various criteria the groups used.

Into the Word

Have one of your better oral readers read today's text aloud. Then say, "Now let's try an exercise in immediate free association. I am going to put some words and phrases on the board. When you see them, say the first thing that pops into your mind with regard to the text you just heard."

Write, in advance, the following onto strips of poster board for easy handling and display: *arrogance, immaturity, tough demands, foolish answer, disappointment, group disruption, conflict resolution, bad examples, expectations of greatness, best example, exact opposite, fighting words, leadership quality,* and others of your choosing, based on your text study.

Affix the strips to the board one at a time, allowing time for responses. Jot the responses on the board. When finished, ask, "Now tell me where you would apply these phrases to the ideas of today's text."

Though learners may be able to make a case for other choices, here are some possibilities: *arrogance:* request of James and John (v. 37); *immaturity:* the brothers' thinking more highly of themselves than justified, a childish perspective; *tough demands:* Jesus' questioning whether the brothers can follow in His footsteps (v. 38); *foolish answer:* the brothers' naïve confidence (v. 39); *disappointment:* they were not assured of getting what they wanted (v. 40); *group disruption:* the "2

vs. 10" split in the disciples' unity (v. 41); *conflict resolution:* the peacemaker Jesus assembled His disciples for corrective teaching (vv. 42, 43); *bad examples:* the typical, tyrannical way that government officials operate (v. 42); *expectation of greatness:* differing viewpoints (v. 43); *best example:* the Son of Man's example (v. 45); *exact opposite:* two extremes of roles (vv. 43-45); *fighting words:* "I'm better!" (v. 37); *leadership quality:* the attitude and act of serving others (vv. 43-45).

This activity will allow a close look at the text and encourage learner thought; the phrases themselves may help learners see themes and grand truths. Encourage your learners to compare and contrast the disciples' misunderstandings about greatness with the attitudes of contemporary leaders and would-be leaders.

Into Life

Give each learner a circular piece of poster board that is 1½" in diameter. Prepare these in advance to have a coin-like appearance. On one side have the word *PRIVILEGED;* on the other side have the word *PRODUCTIVE.*

As you turn one of the "coins" in your fingers, say, "The follower of Christ is privileged. Yet the lifestyle of the follower of Christ is not that of idle privilege, but one of productivity. In our lives of service, we know that "God is able to make all grace abound toward you; that ye, always having all sufficiency in all things, may abound to every good work" (2 Corinthians 9:8). Keep this 'coin' handy this week as a reminder that God grants you the privilege of being His child and that He also grants you the opportunity to serve, to abound in good works."

Option. If time allows, download the reproducible page and have learners complete the Fighting Over Chairs activity individually. Discuss results as a class. This can be a take-home exercise if your time is short.

JESUS IS COMING AGAIN

BACKGROUND SCRIPTURE: **Mark 13**
PRINTED TEXT: **Mark 13:14-27, 31**

MARK 13:14-27, 31

14 But when ye shall see the abomination of desolation, spoken of by Daniel the prophet, standing where it ought not, (let him that readeth understand,) then let them that be in Judaea flee to the mountains:

15 And let him that is on the housetop not go down into the house, neither enter therein, to take any thing out of his house:

16 And let him that is in the field not turn back again for to take up his garment.

17 But woe to them that are with child, and to them that give suck in those days!

18 And pray ye that your flight be not in the winter.

19 For in those days shall be affliction, such as was not from the beginning of the creation which God created unto this time, neither shall be.

20 And except that the Lord had shortened those days, no flesh should be saved: but for the elect's sake, whom he hath chosen, he hath shortened the days.

21 And then if any man shall say to you, Lo, here is Christ; or, lo, he is there; believe him not:

22 For false Christs and false prophets shall rise, and shall show signs and wonders, to seduce, if it were possible, even the elect.

23 But take ye heed: behold, I have foretold you all things.

24 But in those days, after that tribulation, the sun shall be darkened, and the moon shall not give her light,

25 And the stars of heaven shall fall, and the powers that are in heaven shall be shaken.

26 And then shall they see the Son of man coming in the clouds with great power and glory.

27 And then shall he send his angels, and shall gather together his elect from the four winds, from the uttermost part of the earth to the uttermost part of heaven.

. . . .

31 Heaven and earth shall pass away: but my words shall not pass away.

KEY VERSE

Then shall they see the Son of man coming in the clouds with great power and glory. —**Mark 13:26**

ASSURING HOPE

Unit 2: The Fulfillment of God's Promise

LESSONS 10–13

LESSON AIMS

After participating in this lesson, each student will be able to:

1. Summarize the lesson text's warnings and promises in light of their context.

2. Distinguish between literal and figurative language in today's text.

3. Tell one way his or her life is different because of a belief in Jesus' imminent return.

LESSON OUTLINE

Introduction

A. Who's in Charge Here?

Most of us probably have had this experience. We walk into a store or an office, and we see chaos. Surrounded by clutter, people are ignoring their responsibilities. As far as real work is concerned, nothing is being accomplished. We came expecting to receive service, but instead we are ignored.

What do we do in such a situation? We probably ask, "Who's in charge here?" We want to speak to anyone with responsibility to keep order and get things done. When we see mayhem, we assign blame to the person in charge.

That experience can have a wider focus. At any point in history, we can find chaos. Injustice, violence, and evil can be found in every era. An honest look at the world can lead us to ask, "Who's in charge here?" especially when we ourselves are the ones experiencing injustice, violence, and evil. We honestly wonder whether a good God is genuinely in charge. If the world is a mess, God would appear to be at fault.

That issue is at the center of today's text. Peter had confessed Jesus to be "the Christ" (Mark 8:29), God's promised king who would overthrow evil and establish a kingdom of justice and peace. Peter was right in his confession: Jesus is indeed the Christ (Messiah). But the disciples' expectation about God's king and His kingdom needed some modifying. The king would establish God's kingdom of justice and peace, but not in the way they anticipated.

A. Lesson Background

Today's text is part of a long discourse that Jesus gave to His disciples in the week leading up to His crucifixion and resurrection. In the days preceding, Jesus was acclaimed by the crowds as God's king (Mark 11:9, 10). He took action against those doing business in the temple courts (11:15-19). And He gave a vivid picture of the religious leaders' rejection of Him and of the judgment that God would bring on them in response (12:1-12).

In this setting, Jesus told His disciples that they could expect the magnificent temple structure to be destroyed (Mark 13:2). Expecting that Jesus was about to assert himself as God's king, the disciples likely believed that the destruction of the temple would mean that God would immediately replace it with a greater temple that would fulfill His promises (Isaiah 56:7). Surely the destruction of the temple must mean that God's glorious reign was about to be revealed in full!

But instead of speaking about glory, Jesus warned about difficulty and hardship. In the paragraphs just preceding today's text, Jesus cautioned His disciples to expect more of what they had experienced in the past: wars, earthquakes, famines, and persecution (Mark 13:3-13). Yet in the midst of all that, they could remain confident that God would be with them and would be victorious (13:26, 27). (Parallels to today's text are Matthew 24:15-31; Luke 21:20-28.)

I. Warning of the Coming Siege
(MARK 13:14-20)

A. Practical Steps (vv. 14-16)

14. But when ye shall see the abomination of desolation, spoken of by Daniel the prophet, standing where it ought not, (let him that readeth understand,) then let them that be in Judaea flee to the mountains.

In this middle section of Jesus' speech to His disciples, He delivers some sayings that are difficult for modern readers to understand. However, the point is clear for His disciples, even if it is not what they expect. Jesus describes a terrible siege

HOW TO SAY IT

Amos	*Ay*-mus.
Anastasia	Eh-nuh-*stay*-shuh.
Antiochus	An-*tie*-oh-kus.
Bolsheviks	*Bowl*-shuh-viks.
Czar	Zar.
Epiphanes	Ih-*piff*-a-neez.
Hosea	Ho-*zay*-uh.
Judaea	Joo-*dee*-uh.
Messiah	Meh-*sigh*-uh.
paganism	*pay*-guh-nih-zum.
Thessalonians	*Thess*-uh-*lo*-nee-unz
	(*th* as in *thin*).

that will stop worship in the temple and threaten the lives of everyone trapped by it. The event will challenge the disciples' faith, but Jesus assures them that He will enable them to overcome.

In this description, Jesus offers an expression that may be obscure to us but is very familiar to His disciples: *the abomination of desolation.* The concept occurs in Daniel 9:27; 11:31; 12:11, each time referring to something that stops the offering of sacrifices in the temple.

Most interpreters of Daniel understand that the prophet uses this expression to describe a time about 200 years before Jesus' ministry. That was when Israel was ruled by the Greek emperor Antiochus IV Epiphanes. Antiochus had attempted to outlaw the practice of Israel's religion in his territories, and he had erected an idol in the Jerusalem temple to supplant the worship of Israel's God with paganism. What Jesus is saying to His disciples, then, is that something like Antiochus will appear again, something that will once again bring a terrible end to sacrifice in the temple.

> **What Do You Think?**
> What personal "abominations" hinder you from worshiping God? How do you overcome these?
> *Talking Points for Your Discussion*
> - Work-related issues
> - Family-related issues
> - Hobbies

The temptation under such circumstances is to make a stand and fight. But Jesus tells His followers to do the exact opposite. They must not fight, but flee. God's purpose will not be accomplished by their offering resistance to these events. But He can protect them if they heed the warning and leave the city for the safety of the mountains.

15. And let him that is on the housetop not go down into the house, neither enter therein, to take any thing out of his house.

The most urgent need for a person facing an impending siege is to leave the city. Once the siege has begun, those inside the city are trapped.

So Jesus stresses the urgency by warning that nothing should interfere with immediate flight.

Houses in the Israel of Jesus' time generally have flat roofs that serve rather like a patio and can be reached by a stairway built against an outside wall. Pausing to go inside the house after going down the steps will take only a moment. But the situation is too dangerous for even a moment's delay.

> **What Do You Think?**
> If you had only two minutes to get out of your home before it collapsed, what would you take with you, besides family members? What does your answer say about what you value?
>
> **Talking Points for Your Discussion**
> - Things related to Christianity
> - Things unrelated to Christianity

16. And let him that is in the field not turn back again for to take up his garment.

This verse reinforces the point made by the previous one: fleeing the siege is of the utmost urgency. If a worker in a field has laid aside a certain garment, he or she should not even take a few steps to retrieve it before fleeing.

B. Severe Hardship (vv. 17-19)

17. But woe to them that are with child, and to them that give suck in those days!

The reason that flight must be quick is now clear: the horrors of the siege will be enormous. In the world of the Bible, the terrible hardships of warfare are often emphasized by focusing on the suffering of pregnant women and mothers of young children (2 Kings 6:24-29; 15:16; Hosea 13:16; Amos 1:13). Obviously not among the soldiers who fight, these mothers are innocent victims of the warfare surrounding them (compare Luke 23:29).

18. And pray ye that your flight be not in the winter.

Jesus again emphasizes the great hardships of the coming siege. Winter in Israel is the rainy season, when mud makes roads impassable. The disciples should look to God to provide them with favorable conditions for their escape.

19. For in those days shall be affliction, such as was not from the beginning of the creation which God created unto this time, neither shall be.

Jesus brings to a climax His description of the suffering that the siege will bring. For those who experience it, it will be more terrible than anything that they have known or heard of in the past or can imagine in the future. Destroying their familiar and sacred surroundings and threatening the lives of everyone around them, the siege will seem to put all of life in peril. Jesus' disciples must not dismiss the threat that this event will bring. They must be ready to respond as He instructs, or they will face the full force of the attacking army.

> **What Do You Think?**
> Thinking of spiritual affliction or temptation, how do we know when to flee and when to stay put to fight it out?
>
> **Talking Points for Your Discussion**
> - Fleeing: 1 Corinthians 6:18; 10:14; 1 Timothy 6:9-11
> - Fighting it out: Acts 17:16, 17; Galatians 2:1-5

❧ DUCK AND COVER ❧

Those who lived through the Cold War may remember the public safety films of the 1950s. One of the most naïve of these instructed schoolchildren to "duck and cover" under desks in the event of a nuclear attack. If only it were that simple!

The Jews in Jeremiah's day pursued a defense plan that was just as absurd. The people eventually were to observe an enemy army approaching the city. The prophet warned them not to trust "in lying words, saying, The temple of the Lord, The temple of the Lord, The temple of the Lord" (Jeremiah 7:4). The mere presence of the temple would not be a good-luck charm to stave off disaster, neither in Jeremiah's day nor in the first century AD.

When it comes to the Final Judgment, many people today are pursuing "defense" plans that are equally absurd. "I'm basically a good person" and "God won't judge me for this, since He's the one who made me this way" are just two examples. But these will not work. Though the lost will try to "duck and cover" in mountain caves, they will not be able to escape discovery and judgment

(Revelation 6:15-17). How much better to invite God's grace to fall on us now than to have His wrath fall on us later! —A. W.

C. Promised Protection (v. 20)

20. And except that the Lord had shortened those days, no flesh should be saved: but for the elect's sake, whom he hath chosen, he hath shortened the days.

Jesus' words in verse 19 echo those of Daniel 12:1; coupled with Daniel's warning is a promise that God will faithfully deliver His people from the threat. Jesus makes the same point here. The coming siege of Jerusalem will be awful. But for Jesus' followers, the siege's awfulness will underline God's power and faithfulness. God will act as only He can to spare His people the full force of the siege's destruction.

The term *elect* is important in this verse. The word means "chosen" and is used in the Old Testament to refer to Israel as God's chosen people (Isaiah 45:4). Here Jesus uses it to identify His followers as the chosen people of God. As such, they can rely on God's provision in all circumstances, even the most extreme imaginable.

For His people, God has *shortened the days* of the upcoming disaster. Clearly, only God can control the events of history in a way that can be described as shortening the days. The full measure of His divine power will be at work to protect His people in their time of trouble.

Jesus has now made clear to His disciples what they will face in the forthcoming siege of Jerusalem. It will come not merely because of human action, but because God allows it. It will bring all the horrors associated with siege warfare. Safety will be found only by those who heed the warning to flee. Even those who flee will face enormous hardship. But despite the grave threat, God will protect and deliver His people.

History tells us that a Roman army lays siege to Jerusalem some 40 years after Jesus warns His disciples. The Romans do this to end a Jewish rebellion against the Roman Empire. After brutal fighting and slow starvation, the Jewish rebels are overcome. The Romans break through the walls of Jerusalem and destroy the city and its temple.

That Jesus warns of this event in advance, even telling His disciples not to resist but to flee, provides enormous assurance. Despite the seeming chaos, Jesus is indeed in control of history and is providing for His people.

II. Warning of False Messiahs
(Mark 13:21-23)

A. Appeals to Ignore (vv. 21, 22)

21. And then if any man shall say to you, Lo, here is Christ; or, lo, he is there; believe him not.

During the coming hardships, Jesus' followers can easily believe that He is not in control of events. The crisis can induce them to look elsewhere for God's deliverer.

So Jesus warns the disciples beforehand of the temptation to follow another. Others will claim to have found the Messiah leading a political movement, commanding a military rebellion, or preaching a novel message. Jesus' disciples must ignore them. Instead, His followers are to endure hardship with confident faith that Jesus will protect and deliver them just as He promises.

22. For false Christs and false prophets shall rise, and shall show signs and wonders, to seduce, if it were possible, even the elect.

That such false Christs will appear is sure. Their claims will be convincing—to a point. They will demonstrate the kinds of powerful acts that readily persuade people that these people exercise God's power. But such appeals are unconvincing for those who know Jesus. True disciples are committed to Him as God's true king. Knowing that He warns them of imposters, they stand firm. Maintaining their commitment marks them as God's true people—*the elect*, or chosen.

> *What Do You Think?*
> What false Christs and false prophets vie for people's attention today? What do they promise? What tactics do they use?
> *Talking Points for Your Discussion*
> - Putting hope in people (politicians, etc.)
> - Putting hope in things (the lottery, etc.)
> - Putting hope in philosophies (humanism, etc.)

Point to this visual as you ask, "How should the
certainty of Jesus' return cause us to live?"

❧ DELUDED THINKING ❧

The Bolsheviks murdered the last Czar of Russia and his family in 1918. But rumors persisted that one or more of the children may have survived. One of the best-known rumors involves Anna Anderson, who claimed in 1920 to be Anastasia, one of the Czar's daughters. (Interestingly, that name is the Greek word for "resurrection.") Even after DNA testing proved that Anna was not related to the royal family, many people clung to the hope that she really was Anastasia.

One of the reasons for this hope was a belief that the survival of one of the royal children might lead to an eventual restoration of the glory days of the Russian monarchy. Thus Anna served as a kind of "messiah figure" for royalists. The problem in the logic is that of first envisioning a desired end result, then finding evidence—however flimsy—that will hopefully lead to or bring about that desired end.

It is not likely that we will hear someone on the street say literally "I am the Christ" or "I am the Messiah." Yet some charismatic leaders (both religious and secular) seem all too eager to allow themselves to be seen as messiah figures if it will further their ends. It's hard to figure out who is worse, the messiah figure or the followers of that figure who delude themselves. Make sure that you are neither. There is only one Christ, only one Messiah.
—A. W.

B. Assurance of Christ's Control (v. 23)

23. But take ye heed: behold, I have foretold you all things.

This verse brings to a close Jesus' warnings about the hardships that His followers will face. Jesus has demonstrated His sovereignty by announcing these things beforehand—with the vital assurance that He will protect His followers through everything. Far from showing Jesus to be out of control, such events underline His supreme rule. So His disciples can renew their confidence when they have such experiences, knowing that Jesus has warned them beforehand.

Again, it is worth noting how events in history unfold. During the Roman siege of Jerusalem, various factions arise claiming that one person or another is God's Messiah. Jesus' warnings cannot prove truer!

III. Promise of Christ's Victory
(MARK 13:24-27, 31)
A. Foundations Shaken (vv. 24, 25)

24. But in those days, after that tribulation, the sun shall be darkened, and the moon shall not give her light.

Jesus now gives a promise that more than offsets the hardships that He just described. *Tribulation,* a word that simply means "trouble" or "pressure," is not the end of the story. The evil and suffering that characterize this present age will be eliminated as God transforms His creation so that His righteousness is utterly supreme.

When the prophets of the Old Testament promised God's victory, they sometimes described the transformation of the heavenly bodies. Those great objects seem to be unchanging. Among the pagans, they are worshiped. But when God establishes the fullness of His rule, He will bring such a change that even those things that seem most stable and powerful will be transformed. God will be supreme, as things in which people have placed their confidence will be gone.

Jesus' words echo the prophets'. Isaiah 13:10 speaks of the darkening of the sun and moon. For Isaiah, that meant judgment against everything that stood in opposition to God. Jesus' expression points to the same idea: God will be supreme over all. (See also Ezekiel 32:7, 8; Joel 2:10, 31; 3:15.)

25. And the stars of heaven shall fall, and the powers that are in heaven shall be shaken.

Jesus continues with more imagery from the prophets. Isaiah 34:4 speaks of the falling of stars, again as an image of judgment and the establishing of God's reign. The phrase *the powers that are in heaven* suggests spiritual forces that are worshiped by pagans who associate them with the twinkling lights of the night sky. Again, God will establish His rule and defeat everything that opposes Him.

B. Son of Man Appears (v. 26)

26. And then shall they see the Son of man coming in the clouds with great power and glory.

Throughout the Gospels, Jesus refers to himself with the phrase *Son of man*. He seems to have chosen this expression to connect himself with the prophetic vision of Daniel 7. In that passage, the prophet has a vision of four terrible beasts, representing four kingdoms (Daniel 7:3-12). But then a human figure appears, "one like the Son of man," who establishes God's righteous rule (7:13, 14).

That is the very image that Jesus employs here. What transforms this present, evil age into the righteous rule of God is Jesus himself. He promises to return with divine glory to deliver His people and defeat His enemies. As Jesus' followers endure the hardships that He has described earlier, they can look forward to His coming to declare His glory and establish God's rule over all.

C. God's People Gathered (v. 27)

27. And then shall he send his angels, and shall gather together his elect from the four winds, from the uttermost part of the earth to the uttermost part of heaven.

Jesus' coming in glory means rescue and blessing for His people. Though they are scattered through suffering and persecution, He will faithfully gather them to be with Him, no matter where they are. As the apostle Paul affirms, even death cannot keep Christ from gathering His people, for He comes both for the dead and the living (1 Thessalonians 4:12-18).

D. Jesus' Words Certified (v. 31)

31. Heaven and earth shall pass away: but my words shall not pass away.

When surrounded by trouble and evil, we cannot easily see anything else. Jesus assures His followers that His words are true despite what they see. Though wickedness and injustice may seem to have the upper hand, Jesus will reign supreme. His promises are surer than anything we know.

> *What Do You Think?*
> How should the eternally enduring promises of God affect the way you live life daily?
> *Talking Points for Your Discussion*
> - Regarding short-term decisions
> - Regarding long-term decisions

Conclusion
A. The Lord Will Deliver

Centuries of history give us certain advantages over Jesus' disciples. As we read His words, we know how accurately He spoke. Wars, famines, and earthquakes have continued in every era. False Messiahs try to turn believers from their faith. Jerusalem indeed was destroyed by the Romans. Jesus was right about all of that.

But just like Jesus' disciples, we daily confront a world filled with evil. We find ourselves victims of that evil. We are tempted to give in to despair. Like the disciples, we need the assurance that God does not abandon His people. Whatever trouble we face, we are not forsaken. The Lord can deliver us just as He did them. And when He returns, He returns for us. He will reign supreme, and His people will be the beneficiaries.

B. Prayer

Lord Jesus, give us endurance as we face hardships. Give us confident hope for Your promised return. Give us trust in Your provision always. We pray in Jesus' name. Amen!

C. Thought to Remember

"For our light affliction, which is but for a moment, worketh for us a far more exceeding and eternal weight of glory" (2 Corinthians 4:17).

INVOLVEMENT LEARNING

Some of the activities below are also found in the helpful student book, Adult Bible Class.
Don't forget to download the free reproducible page from www.standardlesson.com to enhance your lesson!

Into the Lesson

Enter the classroom wearing a sandwich board, similar to the ones worn by sidewalk prophets that are common in comic strips. (Tape two poster boards together at the top, with strips of cloth three inches wide and fifteen inches long. That way you can slip the two over your head.) On the front, have in bold letters the phrase *The End Is Near!* On the back, have the question *Are You Ready?* After a few smiles and laughs, say, "This warning is a realistic one, both for today's study text and at any point in history."

Affix on a wall a rectangle of yarn or twine that is about four feet high by eight feet wide. Point to the rectangle and say, "It was stone blocks perhaps of about this size that caught the attention of Jesus' disciples as they walked in Jerusalem." Have a reader read Mark 13:1, 2 for the specific occasion that elicited Jesus' teaching regarding things to come.

Into the Word

Prepare handouts of the following paraphrase of the first verses of today's text. Use the heading *How Bad Is It Going to Get?* This is intended as an antiphonal (back-and-forth) reading by two groups, as noted below. (If you prefer, you can use two individual readers.)

Group 1: "As Jesus said, 'It is going to be bad!'" *Group 2:* "How bad is it going to get?"

Group 1: "You will see the ungodliness wreaking havoc." *Group 2:* "What should we do?"

Group 1: "Everyone should flee!" *Group 2:* "What if we are resting atop our houses?"

Group 1: "Don't even go inside to take anything with you. There is no time." *Group 2:* "But what if we are out working in the fields?"

Group 1: "You don't even have time to grab your outer garment. Run!" *Group 2:* "But what about expectant mothers and those with nursing children?"

Group 1: "Woe to those who are unable to flee in haste." *Group 2:* "If it comes in the cold, rainy months, we'll need extra clothes."

Group 1: "Pray that this ruin comes in the dry season." *Group 2:* "How bad is it going to get?"

Group 1: "Worse than it's ever been. Worse than you can expect to see again ever." *Group 2:* "Surely the Lord will save us!"

Group 1: "He will but shorten the days of anguish for the sake of His dearly beloved." *Group 2:* "Surely a Savior will rise up!"

Group 1: "Many will claim to be God's Anointed. Don't listen." *Group 2:* "It can't get any worse, can it?"

Group 1: "The sun will darken. The moon will hide itself. The stars will fall from the skies. The heavens will shudder." *Group 2:* "Where is the Son of Man when we need Him?"

Group 1: "You will see the Son of Man. You will see Him come in glory and power. You will see His angels come to rescue you." *Group 2:* "Wow! How good can it get?"

Direct your class's attention to Mark 13:14-27. Ask how they see the reading above as comparing and contrasting. Then have your groups read these closing lines (to parallel verse 31): *Group 2:* "How bad is it going to get?" *Group 1:* "Heaven and earth will all pass away!" *Group 2:* "How good is it going to get?" *Group 1:* "The words of God's Son will never pass away!"

Option: Download the reproducible page and distribute copies of the activity Signs of His Coming. Have learners work in pairs to complete it. Discuss the results as a class

Into Life

Download the reproducible page and distribute copies of the Solid Stone Walls activity. Have learners work on this in pairs or small groups. If your time is short, this can be a take-home exercise.

Jesus Is Coming Again

WE WORSHIP
GOD

Special Features

Lessons
Unit 1: A Guide for Leaders

Unit 2: Reasons for Praise

Unit 3: John's Vision of Worship

QUARTERLY QUIZ

Use these questions as a pretest or as a review. The answers are on page iv of This Quarter in the Word.

Lesson 1

1. Paul describes the lifting of "holy hands" as an act of prayer. T/F. *1 Timothy 2:8*

2. Paul advises women to adorn themselves with good _____. *1 Timothy 2:9, 10*

Lesson 2

1. A bishop (elder) in a church should have an aptitude toward what? (business management, teaching, music?) *1 Timothy 3:2*

2. Church leaders should be able to affirm the mystery of the Christian faith with a pure _____. *1 Timothy 3:9*

Lesson 3

1. Timothy was told not to let others despise him just because he was very old. T/F. *1 Timothy 4:12*

2. Timothy received a spiritual gift through a laying on of hands. T/F. *1 Timothy 4:14*

Lesson 4

1. A church member who refuses to provide for his own family is worse than whom? (an infidel, a Roman, a Gentile?) *1 Timothy 5:8*

2. Elders who rule well are worthy of double _____. *1 Timothy 5:17*

Lesson 5

1. Paul endured his many hardships for the sake of whom? (the elect, the angels, the Egyptians?) *2 Timothy 2:10*

2. The great error of Hymenaeus and Philetus was in teaching that the _____ had already taken place. *2 Timothy 2:17, 18*

Lesson 6

1. One way to build ourselves up in the faith is to pray in the _____ _____. *Jude 20*

2. We save others by pulling them out of what (the River of Death, quicksand, the fire?) *Jude 23*

Lesson 7

1. When Jesus rode into Jerusalem, the crowds cut down tree branches. T/F. *Mark 11:8*

2. Where did Jesus spend the night after His triumphal entry? *Mark 11:11*

Lesson 8

1. When Jesus' tomb was opened, the guards held their ground. T/F. *Matthew 28:4*

2. The disciples went back to Galilee as Jesus instructed. T/F. *Matthew 28:16*

Lesson 9

1. For Jesus to be equal with God was a form of robbery. T/F. *Philippians 2:6*

2. Jesus took upon himself the form of a what? (soldier, servant, angel?) *Philippians 2:7*

Lesson 10

1. John was invited into Heaven by a voice that sounded like a _____. *Revelation 4:1*

2. One of the four beasts near the heavenly throne was like an eagle. T/F. *Revelation 4:7*

Lesson 11

1. The robes worn by the multitudes in Heaven are what color? (white, red, gold?) *Revelation 7:9*

2. The multitudes in Heaven have come through great _____. *Revelation 7:14*

Lesson 12

1. The new earth that John sees has a vast, mighty sea. T/F. *Revelation 21:1*

2. To enter the city, your name must be written in the Lamb's book of _____. *Revelation 21:27*

Lesson 13

1. John shows us that angels should be worshiped in Heaven. T/F. *Revelation 22:8, 9*

2. The Spirit and the _____ say, "Come." *Revelation 22:17*

QUARTER AT A GLANCE

by Mark S. Krause

WORSHIP MEANS different things to different people. For example, some associate worship only with the time of congregational singing that takes place during a church gathering. But what about the other things we do on Sunday morning? Is the public reading of Scripture considered worship? Is the preaching of God's Word an act of worship? Some Christians might be surprised to learn what the Bible has to say about proper worship.

There are three primary questions concerning worship that should be answered:

> *Whom do we worship?*
> *How do we worship?*
> *Why do we worship?*

Many of our understandings of worship are taken from the Old Testament, specifically from the book of Psalms. This quarter's lessons look at the New Testament to give us a more focused understanding of worship that is distinctively Christian.

Unit 1: A Guide for Leaders

Paul gave Timothy instructions to guide his role as the primary leader of the church of ancient Ephesus. Many of these instructions are related to the church's worship. For example, Lesson 1 looks at prayer as an act of worship. Lesson 4 addresses the church's ministry of benevolence for widows, spoken of in 1 Timothy 5:4 as a way to show piety. In other words, acts of kindness for others are acts of worship too. If we listen to these texts, we will find some answers to the *how* question.

Unit 2: Reasons for Praise

The lessons of Unit 2 are drawn from various books of the New Testament and help us with the *why* and *whom* issues of worship. A common thread in these lessons is that we worship God for the gracious mercy He has extended to us in the work and person of His Son, Jesus Christ. This is dramatically portrayed in Lesson 7, which looks at one of the most glorious examples of worship: the triumphal entry.

We find more help with the *whom* question in Lesson 9. There we will see the so-called "Christ Hymn" of Philippians 2 speaking of acts of worship given to the risen Lord: our kneeling in submission and confessing the lordship of Jesus. It provides powerful language to reinforce the properness and necessity of giving worship to the one whom God has "highly exalted."

Unit 3: John's Vision of Worship

This unit's lessons are taken from the New Testament's great book of worship, Revelation. These lessons provide answers for all three questions of *whom, how,* and *why.*

Lessons 10 and 11, coming from earlier chapters of Revelation, will take us to scenes of worship found in the throne room of Heaven. We will see that Heaven is a place of continuous worship and praise. Worship involves all the residents of that glorious realm.

Lessons 12 and 13 look at worship from the other end of the book of Revelation, as worship occurs in the New Jerusalem. There we are given

> *Heaven is a place of continuous worship.*

a powerful example of improper worship when the author, John, falls on his face to worship the angel who has shown him the secrets of Heaven. This is unacceptable, and the angel forbids and rejects John's act, reminding him, "Worship God" (Revelation 22:9). These selections from Revelation are a fitting conclusion to the quarter's look at the rich tapestry of Christian worship found in the New Testament.

by Kenny Boles

ROME RULED the known world of the first century AD, the setting of the New Testament. Rome's marvelous stone roads connected the far-flung cities of the empire. Her navy and merchant ships roamed the Mediterranean Sea. This "physical openness" allowed different cultural, philosophical, and religious ideas to flow across borders rather freely.

Old Religious Practices

Each locality in the Roman Empire was likely to have its own preferred deity. See, for example, Acts 14:13 and 19:27. By the time of the New Testament, however, the gods of Rome were losing sway in the hearts of the people. Philosophers had taught the people to doubt; experience had taught them to despair. The people still served the classical gods, but with little enthusiasm. The worship of the emperor as divine grew cold and lifeless after the death of Nero in AD 68.

Practically speaking, the citizens of the empire worshiped their money more than their gods. The worship of idols was primarily an attempt to use the gods for their own purposes, rather than giving themselves to serve the gods.

Religious Competition

Into this vacuum of lifeless religion came new religions with new gods. The cult of Cybele, a fertility goddess in Asia Minor, had followers who emasculated themselves in a frenzy of devotion. The cult of Dionysius spread religious frenzy and wine-induced ecstasy all over Italy. From Egypt came the worship of Isis, the goddess of motherhood and fertility. Devotees of Mithras met in caves to share sacred meals and to initiate converts with the blood of a sacred bull.

These religions emphasized the "mystery" of secret knowledge and rituals. Because of the confusion that arose out of competing religions, Rome created an official list of "licit" religions. Any new, illicit religion faced opposition from the government and eventual extermination.

Jewish Faith and Worship

The Jews by contrast worshiped their God without any idols or images to represent Him. In spite of this unusual practice, by the first century AD Rome had accepted Judaism as a "licit" religion. Jews everywhere could worship their invisible God freely. Some Romans even had a grudging admiration for the one-God outlook of the Jews, in contrast with their own cluttered pantheon.

But living in cities throughout the empire, far from the Jerusalem temple, the priests, and the sacrifices, Jews were forced to ask themselves, "What rituals and acts of worship can we observe in order to maintain our distinctiveness?" Their answer: the practice of circumcision, the keeping of the Sabbath, and the eating of kosher food. These could be practiced wherever Jews lived, with local synagogues as focal points. The transition from temple to synagogue became permanent everywhere when Jerusalem and the temple were destroyed in AD 70.

Christian Faith and Worship

Worship in synagogues became a model for the earliest church. But there was a problem: the Romans eventually came to realize that Christianity was not a minor variation of Judaism, but a new religion. Thus Christianity was illicit and subject to elimination. While the Jews could build synagogues as places to practice their "licit" religion, Christians did not erect any houses of worship for at least 200 years. Christians worshiped more privately than publicly, sometimes even secretly, to avoid persecution.

Today we are familiar with Christianity's struggles regarding what worship "should" be and how to do it. Perhaps some reflection on the earliest struggles to worship will help!

THIS QUARTER IN THE WORD

Answers to the Quarterly Quiz on page 226

Lesson 1—1. true 2. deeds. Lesson 2—1. teaching. 2. conscience. Lesson 3—1. false. 2. true. Lesson 4—1. an infidel. 2. honor. Lesson 5—1. the elect. 2. resurrection. Lesson 6—1. Holy Ghost. 2. the fire. Lesson 7—1. true. 2. Bethany. Lesson 8—1. false. 2. true. Lesson 9—1. false. 2. servant. Lesson 10—1. trumpet. 2. true. Lesson 11—1. white. 2. tribulation. Lesson 12—1. false. 2. life. Lesson 13—1. false. 2. bride.

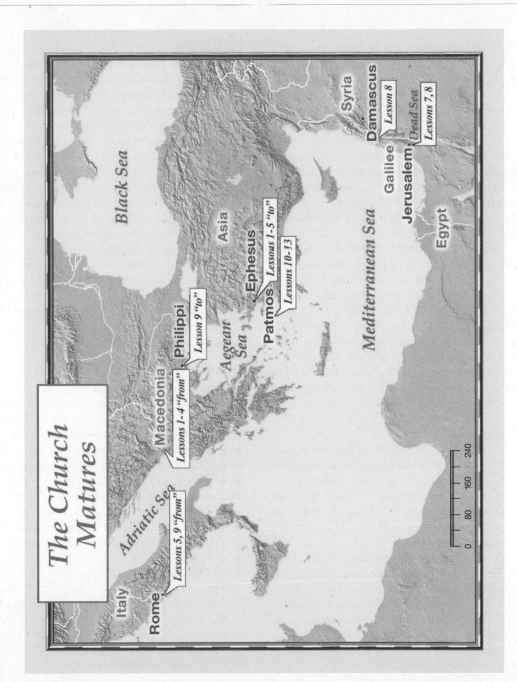

The Church Matures

Black Sea

Italy

Rome
Lessons 5, 9 "from"

Adriatic Sea

Macedonia

Philippi
Lesson 9 "to"

Lessons 1-4 "from"

Aegean Sea

Asia

Ephesus

Patmos
Lessons 1-5 "to"
Lessons 10-13

Mediterranean Sea

Syria

Damascus
Lesson 8

Dead Sea
Lessons 7, 8

Galilee

Jerusalem

Egypt

Nile

0 80 160 240

BIBLE ALIVE!

Teacher Tips by James Riley Estep, Jr.

MANY DO NOT SEE the Bible as being relevant for today. Christians disagree. We affirm the continuing relevancy of the Bible for at least two reasons. First, Scripture is authored ultimately by the eternal God. While the Bible was indeed penned by men, they were not the ultimate authors (2 Timothy 3:16; 2 Peter 1:21). Second, the Bible addresses unchanging human needs and nature. Regardless of advances in science, we still struggle to meet basic needs, to overcome evil, to find redemption, etc. A stroll through the book of Ecclesiastes demonstrates such struggles are not new.

However, many folks ignore the Bible not because of some profound philosophical or historical argument against it. Rather, they don't listen to it because it simply *seems* irrelevant given the way that it is taught. Have we taken a Word that is described as "quick, and powerful" (Hebrews 4:12) and treated it as if we were dissecting a frog in science class? The Bible is not outdated, but our teaching methods may be! Let's examine three ways to make the Bible come alive in our teaching: illustrate, participate, and express.

Illustrate

When you are teaching, make sure to use *illustrations*, both verbal and visual, to demonstrate the reality of Scripture and its relevance for today. Each lesson in this commentary contains at least two verbal illustrations to help you do this. Jesus himself was the master of the verbal illustration; think of His parables.

Visually, you can show pictures or even videos of the geography of the Holy Land. You can use GoogleEarth for this if your classroom has Internet access. The *Adult Resources* packet available for each quarter's lessons in this commentary is a kit of visuals that will help you illustrate. It includes a CD that provides visual resources digitally, including PowerPoint™ presentations.

Participate

Having your students participate in the biblical narrative means helping them engage in the activity of that narrative. For example, you can have your learners try making bricks both with and without straw if the lesson is on Exodus 5:6-18 (brick recipes are on the Internet). This will add a tactile element to the narrative, helping your learners sense the text in a way beyond hearing.

"Acting it out" thus requires the learners to place themselves into the narrative. Beyond merely asking, "How would you have felt if you were them?" acting-it-out asks learners to wrestle with choices in a hands-on way. Notice the difference: you're not asking them just to think *about* the biblical text, but to place themselves *inside* it. This helps the learner realize that Bible characters were real people facing real-life situations. There are limits, of course. For example, having your learners make their bricks out in the hot sun is not recommended!

Express

Finally, your learners can encounter the living Word as you help them express it through their lives. For example, you can ask the learner to personalize a psalm, describing their family in light of a passage on community. You also could hold a "mock" elders' meeting in which participants grapple with how to ensure that a widow in the church has her daily needs met (use fictitious names) in line with 1 Timothy 5 (Lesson 4). The learning activities included with each lesson will help your learners express the text in their lives.

It's Relevant!

Will your learners experience the Word of God merely as an academic discussion, to be left behind as they get back to "real life"? Or will they experience the Word as "quick, and powerful, and sharper than any twoedged sword" (Hebrews 4:12)? *Illustrate, participate, express!*

WORSHIP
GUIDELINES

BACKGROUND SCRIPTURE: 1 Timothy 2
PRINTED TEXT: 1 Timothy 2

1 TIMOTHY 2

1 I exhort therefore, that, first of all, supplications, prayers, intercessions, and giving of thanks, be made for all men;

2 For kings, and for all that are in authority; that we may lead a quiet and peaceable life in all godliness and honesty.

3 For this is good and acceptable in the sight of God our Saviour;

4 Who will have all men to be saved, and to come unto the knowledge of the truth.

5 For there is one God, and one mediator between God and men, the man Christ Jesus;

6 Who gave himself a ransom for all, to be testified in due time.

7 Whereunto I am ordained a preacher, and an apostle, (I speak the truth in Christ, and lie not;) a teacher of the Gentiles in faith and verity.

8 I will therefore that men pray every where, lifting up holy hands, without wrath and doubting.

9 In like manner also, that women adorn themselves in modest apparel, with shamefacedness and sobriety; not with broided hair, or gold, or pearls, or costly array;

10 But (which becometh women professing godliness) with good works.

11 Let the woman learn in silence with all subjection.

12 But I suffer not a woman to teach, nor to usurp authority over the man, but to be in silence.

13 For Adam was first formed, then Eve.

14 And Adam was not deceived, but the woman being deceived was in the transgression.

15 Notwithstanding she shall be saved in childbearing, if they continue in faith and charity and holiness with sobriety.

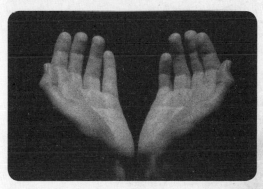

KEY VERSE

There is one God, and one mediator between God and men, the man Christ Jesus. —**1 Timothy 2:5**

WE WORSHIP GOD

Unit 1: A Guide for Leaders

LESSONS 1–4

LESSON AIMS

After participating in this lesson, each student will be able to:

1. Tell what instructions Paul gave for the church where Timothy was, both for the church as a whole and for specific groups within the church.

2. Explain how the instructions reflect the will of God as expressed in the gospel.

3. Identify one thing that hinders implementing Paul's instructions in his or her life and make a plan to remove it.

LESSON OUTLINE

Introduction

A. Family Resemblance

Look at a family portrait and what do you notice? Usually we see ways that the family members resemble each other. Today's text reminds us of the Christian family resemblance. Followers of Jesus are part of God's family. Their membership in that family should be reflected in the way that they live. The resemblance should be most obvious when the family is gathered together, as we do for worship.

What makes us members of God's family is God's saving message, the good news of Jesus. The family resemblance means putting that message into practice. That is what today's text will tell us to do.

B. Lesson Background

The books of 1 Timothy, 2 Timothy, and Titus are known as the *Pastoral Epistles*. These are letters that the apostle Paul wrote to two of his younger associates in ministry. The letters provided those church leaders instructions on dealing with the problems that arose day to day in their churches. Probably written near the end of Paul's ministry, the letters reflect the challenges of leading the church in a sinful world.

Paul wrote 1 Timothy to his son in the faith Timothy, who began working with Paul during Paul's second missionary journey (Acts 16:1-3). About 13 years after that journey began, Paul wrote this letter as Timothy was ministering in Ephesus (1 Timothy 1:3). Paul had taken the gospel to that city on his third missionary journey (Acts 19).

The church faced the challenge of life in a large city that was dominated by a popular pagan religious cult. We recall that the city of Ephesus was home to the great pagan Temple of Artemis (Diana), one of the seven wonders of the ancient world. Paul's actions in Ephesus threatened some of Diana's devotees, and a riot resulted (Acts 19:23-41). But every church, no matter its setting, faces the difficulty of its members living and working together in ways that reflect the new life in Christ instead of the life of sin. All those issues are reflected in this letter.

I. Instructions for the Church
(1 Timothy 2:1-7)

A. Christians' Prayers (vv. 1, 2)

1. I exhort therefore, that, first of all, supplications, prayers, intercessions, and giving of thanks, be made for all men.

Having warned against false teaching and having offered thanks to God for His saving mercy in chapter 1, Paul now begins his instructions to the church about its life together. The false teachers might insist that an elite class has special privileges before God. But Paul insists otherwise, since prayers are to be offered on behalf of everyone. Those who know God through Jesus Christ will offer prayers not just for themselves or a few others.

To emphasize this point, Paul uses several different words for prayer. *Supplications* are prayers that ask God for a blessing or help of some kind. *Intercessions* translates a word that indicates a request offered to a superior, a picture of the believer addressing almighty God. *Giving of thanks* refers to the other side of prayer: expressing gratitude to God for help and blessings received. In the middle of the list is the general term *prayers,* which can stand for every kind of communication with God. The combination of terms gives extraordinary emphasis to this command to pray.

2. For kings, and for all that are in authority; that we may lead a quiet and peaceable life in all godliness and honesty.

Although prayers are to be offered "for all men" (v. 1), some people have such power and influence that they become the particular objects of prayer. In Paul's setting, the designation *kings* definitely includes the Roman emperor, probably the infamous Nero at the time of writing. Paul includes others having political and military power as he writes of *all that are in authority.*

In Paul and Timothy's time, people offer prayers and sacrifices to the emperor himself as if he were a god. The people also commonly offer prayers or sacrifices in asking that powerful figures be granted long lives and increased power or wisdom. Paul's instruction is differently focused, as the gospel demands: Christians are to pray that the powerful will rule in such a way that Chris-

tians can live according to God's will. When Christians are free to worship God and share the gospel in peace, God's will is accomplished.

> *What Do You Think?*
> What are some specific things for which Christians can pray regarding world leaders?
> *Talking Points for Your Discussion*
> - Areas that have a direct impact on Christianity
> - Areas that have an indirect impact on Christianity

❧ *Prejudice or Prayer?* ❧

Abraham Lincoln is widely regarded as one of the greatest—if not *the* greatest—American president. Many believe his Emancipation Proclamation to be one of the outstanding expressions of democratic principles.

But Lincoln was roundly criticized in his time. He was demonized for not announcing the end of slavery earlier. He was charged with overstepping the president's constitutional powers. He was blamed personally when the fortunes of war turned against the Union army. Even today, various Web sites and books seek to destroy what they call "the Lincoln myth."

We are all too familiar with this tendency to defame our leaders. Regardless of party, modern presidents are subjected to vicious criticism, often by Christians. One wonders how much more effectively our leaders might govern if Christians were to follow the instructions of the apostle Paul! Do our political leanings ever inhibit us from fulfilling our Christian obligation to pray for those in authority over us?   —C. R. B.

HOW TO SAY IT

Artemis	*Ar*-teh-miss.
Ephesus	*Ef*-uh-sus.
Ezekiel	Ee-*zeek*-ee-ul or Ee-*zeek*-yul.
Galatians	Guh-*lay*-shunz.
Gentiles	*Jen*-tiles.
Nero	*Nee*-row.
Philippians	Fih-*lip*-ee-unz.
Titus	*Ty*-tus.

B. God's Will (vv. 3, 4)

3. For this is good and acceptable in the sight of God our Saviour.

Above all, God's desire is to save humankind. The term *savior* is often used by Roman officials to celebrate their own accomplishments. Paul's point is that God is the true Savior.

4. Who will have all men to be saved, and to come unto the knowledge of the truth.

Now Paul makes utterly clear where the church's focus belongs. God's primary plan is not just to fulfill our desires or even to give us peaceful lives. Rather, it is to bring salvation to every person (compare Ezekiel 18:23; 2 Peter 3:9). The church's prayers for all people, especially for rulers, are ultimately prayers that God will enable the church to share the good news with everyone.

C. Gospel's Core (vv. 5-7)

5. For there is one God, and one mediator between God and men, the man Christ Jesus.

In a world with many rulers and many gods, it is easy to imagine many paths to a good life. But Paul now explains why there can be only one way of salvation. The verse begins with a statement echoing the famous confession of Israel in Deuteronomy 6:4. To that Paul adds another line of confession: that there is *one mediator . . . Christ*. The term *mediator* indicates a person who acts as a go-between with others, bringing harmony and reconciliation where there has been hostility.

What Do You Think?

How have you responded to those who have wrong beliefs regarding how we gain access to God? What improvements can you make?

Talking Points for Your Discussion

- Dialogue vs. demonization (1 Peter 3:15)
- Find common ground (Acts 17:22-27)
- Use your network of fellow Christians to help you (1 Thessalonians 3:2)

---

6. Who gave himself a ransom for all, to be testified in due time.

Christ became the one and only mediator through His death on the cross, which provided the payment that brought freedom—the *ransom*—to sinners (compare Mark 10:45). He gave himself willingly as a sacrificial offering that satisfies God's wrath against sin and so makes peace between God and sinners who have rebelled against Him (Romans 3:21-26).

The phrase *testified in due time* emphasizes that salvation through Christ is to be announced to all people. That is God's plan. That "due time" is now, Paul implies. Now is the time to unite in prayer that the church can fulfill God's will to make the truth of Christ known to all.

7. Whereunto I am ordained a preacher, and an apostle, (I speak the truth in Christ, and lie not;) a teacher of the Gentiles in faith and verity.

Paul combines three terms to emphasize his own role in sharing the good news. He is a *preacher,* a word that is used in Paul's time for heralds who make official announcements for rulers. An *apostle* is the authorized messenger of an important personage. And as a *teacher of the Gentiles,* Paul carries the good news to those previously excluded from God's people (Acts 9:15; Galatians 2:7, 8).

Paul's life shows the urgency of sharing God's good news with everyone. There can be nothing more important than making that truth known.

II. Instructions for Men
(1 Timothy 2:8)
A. To Do (v. 8a)

8a. I will therefore that men pray every where, lifting up holy hands.

Paul's instructions to men continue his emphasis on the church gathered for prayer. What he says flows directly from the central truths just emphasized. If there is one God and one way of salvation and if God's way of salvation is for all people, then that salvation should draw people together in unity and harmony. That reality must be expressed when the church gathers for worship.

The lifting up of hands in worship and prayer is an ancient practice as well as a modern one. But Paul's point is not primarily about what we do with our hands when we pray. It is, rather, that genuine prayer should be characterized by personal holiness.

B. Not To Do (v. 8b)

8b. Without wrath and doubting.

There is no wrath in a unified church. Christ took God's wrath upon himself at the cross. Thus how can church members possibly justify wrath against one another? The word *doubting* in the antique language of the *King James Version* translates a word that probably signifies "disputing" or "arguing" in this context. Again, this is at odds with the church's unified faith in God's salvation.

Paul probably singles out the men (v. 8a) for this instruction because of specific circumstances in the Ephesian church. But such unity is obviously vital for all believers, men and women.

> **What Do You Think?**
> What does Paul's prohibition against disputing imply regarding the way we respond to fellow believers when a difference of opinion arises?
> *Talking Points for Your Discussion*
> - Matters of faith (doctrinal differences)
> - Matters of expediency (method differences)

❧ FIRST THINGS FIRST ❧

Atheists currently are having a field day criticizing religion. Richard Dawkins, in *The God Delusion*, blames religion for most of the world's ills. Christopher Hitchens, in *God is not Great: How Religion Poisons Everything*, claims that religion is "violent, irrational, intolerant, allied to racism, tribalism, and bigotry, invested in ignorance and hostile to free inquiry, contemptuous of women and coercive toward children."

During a panel discussion, Hitchens was asked to imagine himself alone in an unfamiliar city at night. Would he feel safer or less safe if he were approached by strangers who were coming from a prayer meeting? Hitchens answered by listing cities such as Belfast, Beirut, and Bethlehem, where a prayer meeting might not be evidence of his safety. Admittedly, the "holy hands" of which Paul speaks have not been much in evidence at times.

Using intellectual arguments to defeat atheism is important. But unless Christianity demonstrates its "holy hands" to the world, such arguments will be hollow and unconvincing. Do love and unity characterize our churches?   —C. R. B.

Visual for Lesson 1. *Keep this map posted for the entire quarter to help your learners maintain a geographical perspective.*

III. Instructions for Women
(1 TIMOTHY 2:9-15)
A. Godly Modesty (vv. 9, 10)

9. In like manner also, that women adorn themselves in modest apparel, with shamefacedness and sobriety; not with broided hair, or gold, or pearls, or costly array.

Ephesus in Paul's day has a significant number of wealthy residents. We can expect that some members of the church are among them. People typically enjoy displaying their wealth; doing so gives a sense of prestige and power. But for those who know the good news of the gospel, such displays are inappropriate.

So Paul gives specific instruction to women: they are not to make a show of their wealth with elaborate hairstyles (*broided* means "braided"), jewelry, or clothing (compare 1 Peter 3:3-5). To do so is inconsistent with the humility of Jesus. Instead the women are to demonstrate modest discretion (stressed further by the word *shamefacedness*) and wise self-control. Such virtues are the genuine fruit of a life touched by God's salvation.

As we think about the application of these words to the present, we need to keep the underlying principle in mind. What is ostentatious or immodest in one culture may not be so in another. The question we should ask ourselves is whether our appearance communicates the unselfish humility that flows from knowing Jesus.

10. But (which becometh women professing godliness) with good works.

Modest appearance is just the start. For Christians, real adornment consists of serving others in response to Christ's having served us. These instructions are probably a response to elitism. God's salvation does not make some people better than others. Rather, it compels all to serve one another in humility (compare 1 Peter 5:5).

B. Respectful Demeanor (vv. 11, 12)

11. Let the woman learn in silence with all subjection.

The gospel has an uplifting, liberating effect. For women in Paul's time, the good news means that women and men are equals before God (Galatians 3:28). In a culture in which women are often treated as personal property, the difference is enormous!

But this new standing can be misunderstood. Newfound equality can be distorted. Some of the women in the Ephesian church may have begun to act in ways that show disrespect to men. In the culture of the time, a woman who speaks excessively or authoritatively in a public assembly is commonly seen as bringing shame on the men in the group, especially those of her own family.

When the church gathers, there is to be order (1 Corinthians 14:40). This orderly behavior is to include silence on the part of women (see also 1 Corinthians 14:33b-35). However, this is not to be taken as commanding "absolute silence," since Paul talks about women praying and prophesying in 1 Corinthians 11:5. We also note that the word translated *silence* here is related to the term rendered "peaceable" in verse 2. These observations point to a need for a respectful demeanor.

We can make similar observations about the term *subjection.* As Paul uses it here, it does not mean that women mindlessly follow orders, but that they willingly defer to male leadership. Christ willingly gave His life for the sake of others (1 Timothy 2:6, above), so Christians willingly put others first (Philippians 2:3).

12. But I suffer not a woman to teach, nor to usurp authority over the man, but to be in silence.

Paul's instructions regarding women have become a matter of controversy. Opinions vary widely about what boundaries he lays out for gender roles in the church's life. We cannot settle every question about this passage in the space available here, but we can come to a strong understanding of its original meaning.

This verse continues the instructions of the previous one. Verses 11 and 12 together lead us to believe that there is a problem regarding gender roles in the Ephesian church that Paul needs to address. Specifically, the issue before us includes the teaching function. What Paul appears to forbid is not women teaching as such, but women teaching men in an authoritative way. A woman teaching men authoritatively will bring shame on the men in the assembly. Instead, women should seek peace and order through their behavior, reflected again with *silence,* the word in verses 2 and 11 that indicates orderly peace. Paul certainly expected and encouraged women to be active with the Word of God. Specifically, he instructs that the women who are more mature should become mentors in the faith for younger women (Titus 2:3-5). Thus both women and men are to learn and share the gospel message in biblically appropriate ways.

Christian women and men should be sensitive to the dynamics of their culture as they interact with each other. Both should remember that they are equals before the Lord (but equality in status is not the same as saying that men and women have identical roles in the church; see below). Both should remember that their concern as followers of Christ is to be for the good of others. The larger context of the Pastoral Epistles reminds us that men will best be mentored in the gospel by other men, and women by other women.

Worship Guidelines

C. Biblical Example (vv. 13-15)

13. For Adam was first formed, then Eve.

This is a key verse in establishing the basis of Paul's argument to this point. What Paul says is not optional based on cultural practice. Rather, it is mandatory because of the order of creation. If certain people in the Ephesian church believe that equality in Christ means that they no longer need to be concerned about gender roles, Paul's instructions provide a direct correction.

God's creation of the first woman followed His creation of the first man. God created the woman to be a fitting partner for the man (Genesis 2:18; compare 1 Corinthians 11:8, 9). As man and woman, and as husband and wife, they are equal. But by creating the husband first, God invested in him the solemn responsibility of leadership.

Christian women must therefore not interpret their equality in the gospel as overturning that foundational relationship. Their concern for God's will is to make them supportive of the leadership role of their husbands (again, see 1 Corinthians 14:33b-35). The verse before us establishes that the boundaries of the role distinctions between men and women, whatever those boundaries may be, are to be found in the order of creation, not in shifting cultural mores.

14. And Adam was not deceived, but the woman being deceived was in the transgression.

The illustration continues with the story of temptation and sin found in Genesis 3. The serpent's temptation was aimed at the woman; she was the one who first believed the serpent's lie. Of course, her husband joined her in the act, so both were blameworthy. If the women of the Ephesian church have come to believe that they are somehow invulnerable to temptation, the story of Eve warns them otherwise (compare 2 Corinthians 11:3).

15a. Notwithstanding she shall be saved in childbearing.

It might seem that Paul is stating that women can have forgiveness of sin only if they bear children. But such a concept is foreign to his teaching that faith in Christ brings salvation (Romans 5:1; Galatians 2:16; Ephesians 2:8-10). Rather, Paul's point appears to be that a woman should persevere in her salvation by continuing to embrace her role as a woman. *Childbearing* is mentioned not because all Christian women must bear children, but as an example of a woman's distinct role.

> **What Do You Think?**
> How do you deal with Scriptures that are hard to understand?
> *Talking Points for Your Discussion*
> - Philippians 4:9
> - 2 Peter 1:12
> - 2 Peter 3:15, 16

15b. If they continue in faith and charity and holiness with sobriety.

Paul mentions key virtues for women to embrace. Such virtues are not evident if anyone, male or female, acts with pride and selfishness.

Conclusion

A. Whom Do You Resemble?

Paul paints a picture of a gathered church as God's family. As God's family, the church should obviously resemble the family's head. We have been saved by Christ, who gave His life for unworthy sinners. If our worship displays modesty, humility, and concern for others instead of ourselves, it shows the family resemblance. If not, we resemble something—or someone—else.

B. Prayer

O God, make us less concerned with ourselves, our rights, and our preferences when we gather. Teach us to pursue what You have called us to do. In the name of Jesus, who became a man to serve us, amen!

C. Thought to Remember

Take your place in the family portrait.

VISUALS FOR THESE LESSONS

The visual pictured in each lesson (example: page 237) is a small reproduction of a large, full-color poster included in the *Adult Resources* packet for the Spring Quarter. That packet also contains the very useful *Presentation Helps* on a CD for teacher use. Order No. 020039211 from your supplier.

INVOLVEMENT LEARNING

Into the Lesson

Bring to class five to eight books with titles that begin with *How to.* You can find such books in a public library, or you can simply put on books labels with fake titles such as *How to Do Almost Everything in Less Time* and *How to Kiss an Elephant.*

Introduce the books and ask, "Which of these titles sounds most useful to you?" Let learners comment, and then pull out a book on which you have added the title *How to Worship* in big letters. Ask, "How about this one? Would it be helpful?" This is your lead in for today's lesson.

Into the Word

Divide your class into three groups. Give each group one of the following discussion-direction statements. If you have a large class, create more groups and double up the assignments. (Caution: Delete discussion questions that you think will result in overly negative, critical responses.)

Group One: Look at the text and pick one verse that best summarizes the truth that elicits worship. How do our worship assemblies best emphasize that truth? How can we be more effective?"

Group Two: In today's text, the initial emphasis (v. 1) and later emphasis (v. 8) is on prayer. What elements of Paul's directives do we do best with? Which needs the most improvement?

Group Three: Verses 9-15 of today's text feature directives about women's responsibilities and roles. What in those verses most confuses you? What do you see as being strictly first-century cultural elements? What are the permanent elements of those directions? What criteria do we use to distinguish between cultural and permanent elements?

Allow about eight minutes for deliberations. Give each group four minutes to report its conclusions. Do not allow reactions until all three groups have reported.

Returning to Group One's comments, ask the class to look at 1 Timothy 1:15, 17 (not in today's text). Read those verses aloud and comment, "We worship because God is worthy. We worship because Christ Jesus has redeemed us. We see the same truths emphasized in 1 Timothy 2:3-5. Where and how can we do better?"

For Group Two's comments, note, "Paul's words on prayer include truths about content, purpose, attitude, and frequency. What more can we say about prayer?" *Option:* Download the reproducible page and use the Hands and Prayer exercise at this point.

For Group Three's comments, say (if your class includes women), "Women first. How do you react to the Spirit's words?" After responses, ask, "How are Paul's thoughts on submission and silence not a sign of inferiority? What difference does that make?" (Caution: The discussion here has the potential of becoming very lively, even heated; make sure you are thoroughly familiar with the observations in the lesson commentary on this issue.) Continue: "How does simple, non-showy apparel reflect a desire to direct attention away from self and toward God?"

Wrap up the discussion by noting that next week's study from 1 Timothy 3 will address the leadership role and responsibility of men in the church. Ask, "Is Paul as demanding of men as he is here of women? We'll look forward to and see that next time."

Option: Download the reproducible page and use the Principles of Worship exercise as your wrap up of this section instead of the above.

Into Life

Display the following question: *How do I see my worship changing as a result of our study of 1 Timothy 2?* You can have learners discuss this question as a whole class, in small groups, or in pairs.

Download the reproducible page and distribute copies of the Whom to Please exercise as students depart.

LEADERSHIP
QUALITIES

BACKGROUND SCRIPTURE: **1 Timothy 3**
PRINTED TEXT: **1 Timothy 3**

1 TIMOTHY 3

1 This is a true saying, if a man desire the office of a bishop, he desireth a good work.

2 A bishop then must be blameless, the husband of one wife, vigilant, sober, of good behaviour, given to hospitality, apt to teach;

3 Not given to wine, no striker, not greedy of filthy lucre; but patient, not a brawler, not covetous;

4 One that ruleth well his own house, having his children in subjection with all gravity;

5 (For if a man know not how to rule his own house, how shall he take care of the church of God?)

6 Not a novice, lest being lifted up with pride he fall into the condemnation of the devil.

7 Moreover he must have a good report of them which are without; lest he fall into reproach and the snare of the devil.

8 Likewise must the deacons be grave, not doubletongued, not given to much wine, not greedy of filthy lucre;

9 Holding the mystery of the faith in a pure conscience.

10 And let these also first be proved; then let them use the office of a deacon, being found blameless.

11 Even so must their wives be grave, not slanderers, sober, faithful in all things.

12 Let the deacons be the husbands of one wife, ruling their children and their own houses well.

13 For they that have used the office of a deacon well purchase to themselves a good degree, and great boldness in the faith which is in Christ Jesus.

14 These things write I unto thee, hoping to come unto thee shortly:

15 But if I tarry long, that thou mayest know how thou oughtest to behave thyself in the house of God, which is the church of the living God, the pillar and ground of the truth.

16 And without controversy great is the mystery of godliness: God was manifest in the flesh, justified in the Spirit, seen of angels, preached unto the Gentiles, believed on in the world, received up into glory.

KEY VERSE

Holding the mystery of the faith in a pure conscience. —1 Timothy 3:9

WE WORSHIP GOD

Unit 1: A Guide for Leaders

LESSONS 1–4

LESSON AIMS

After participating in this lesson, each student will be able to:

1. Enumerate the key qualities for church leaders as described in the text.

2. Tell how each quality is important to leading a congregation today.

3. Commit to develop in one's own life the qualities needed by church leaders.

LESSON OUTLINE

Introduction

A. The Leadership Industry

Billions of dollars are spent every year in the quest for good leadership. People buy books, attend seminars, pay for consultations, and earn degrees—all to make themselves better leaders. Meanwhile, businesses, schools, governments, nonprofit agencies, and churches spend countless hours and dollars to find or train effective leaders. At election time, candidates spend fortunes promoting their leadership skills while voters complain about the lack of true leaders.

We are surrounded by a leadership industry. What is gained by all this effort? Most would say that good leadership is still not common. We have been disappointed too many times by our leaders. We have probably been especially disappointed by our own leadership failures.

Where can we turn for a better perspective? Does Scripture tell us the secret to leadership? The answer to that question is *no*—and *yes*. If we think that there is a scriptural "magic formula" that will create leaders, we will be disappointed. But if we want to know what God calls leaders to be, our text for today can give us a clear picture.

B. Lesson Background

The books of 1 Timothy, 2 Timothy, and Titus, were written by Paul to give his associates in ministry direction in strengthening the church. Timothy was working with the church of Ephesus, where a form of false teaching had damaged the church (compare 1 Timothy 1:3; 4:1-3; and 6:20, 21). That teaching threatened the core of the gospel: that all people are sinners, all equally in need of God's grace through Jesus Christ. Sound leadership was imperative in such a circumstance. So in 1 Timothy 3, Paul instructed Timothy on the kind of leaders the church needed.

We might expect that Paul would advise Timothy on the actions that leaders should take: how they can evaluate the past, assess the present, and make sound plans for the future. But Paul focuses first not on what leaders *do*, but on who they *are*. Paul gives not an action plan for leaders, but a portrait of character.

Leadership Qualities

In this light, today's passage provides lists of qualities that church leaders need to possess. Such lists were common in Paul's time. They were not intended to be complete, point-by-point checklists. Rather, they suggested a full picture of the needed qualities. (Some students prefer the stronger word *qualifications,* the implication being that failure to meet any one item of the list disqualifies a candidate from the leadership position in question.)

We can compare the items on these lists to brush strokes in a fine oil painting. If we examine each brush stroke, we can precisely identify its length and color. But to understand it fully, we need to see how it fits into the context of the picture as a whole. So it is with Paul's list of leadership qualities. We should identify each term carefully. But to understand them as Paul intended, we need to see how each quality fits with the others.

I. Ideal Elders
(1 Timothy 3:1-7)
A. Their Task (v. 1)

1. This is a true saying, if a man desire the office of a bishop, he desireth a good work.

The term *bishop* may be confusing. Today, the title *bishop* has come to refer to a person who has authority over many congregations in a church hierarchy. But the term that Paul uses applies to leaders in all kinds of settings in his day. In the church, it is used interchangeably with the term translated "elders" in Titus 1:5 (compare 1:7). We see the terms brought together in Acts 20:17, 28 and 1 Peter 5:1-4: those who are elders—those with spiritual maturity—provide oversight for the church, like a shepherd caring for a flock.

Leadership in the church is a difficult, often thankless, duty. This is all the more so when facing a challenge like the false teaching in the Ephesian

church. So Paul affirms that leading the church is a noble task. Leaders are not a spiritual elite, but they fulfill a duty that all should honor.

B. Their Character (vv. 2, 3)

2. A bishop then must be blameless, the husband of one wife, vigilant, sober, of good behaviour, given to hospitality, apt to teach.

What Paul emphasizes is not organizational models or leadership duties, but the leaders' character. Those who lead the church toward maturity in Christ need to be people who are themselves growing toward that maturity. Their lives need to reflect the character of Christ himself. Thus the description of the ideal church leader begins with characteristics of genuine godliness.

The list begins with the idea of being *blameless.* This term does not demand complete sinlessness; otherwise, no one could ever lead the church (compare 1 Timothy 1:15). Rather, it suggests someone whose life reflects obvious qualities of godliness.

> *What Do You Think?*
> Why is not "judgmental" to try to recognize blamelessness or godliness in a potential leader?
> *Talking Points for Your Discussion*
> - 2 Corinthians 11:2
> - Philippians 2:14, 15
> - 1 Timothy 6:6
> - 2 Peter 3:13, 14

The phrase *husband of one wife* is literally "a man of one woman." Many have tried to determine whether this phrase indicates a specific marital situation. For example, does it refer to a man who is married only once and is still married to his first wife? Such attempts do not succeed in explaining the phrase in its original context, however. In this setting, it probably indicates a character trait: a man who is faithful in marriage, who is chaste in relationships with the opposite sex. Such discipline is not only obedient to God's will, it also reflects God's own faithfulness to His people.

To be *vigilant, sober, of good behaviour* continues the portrait of mature godliness. Individually, the

HOW TO SAY IT

Blagojevich	Bluh-*goy*-uh-vich.
Corinthians	Ko-*rin*-thee-unz (*th* as in *thin*).
Ephesus	*Ef*-uh-sus.
Titus	*Ty*-tus.

terms indicate someone who is restrained and controlled, someone who leads an orderly life. Such wisdom and discipline reflect a life delivered from rebellion against God, now submitted to God, doing His will and imitating His character.

To be *given to hospitality* indicates a person who is generous in caring for and encouraging others (compare Titus 1:8; 1 Peter 4:9). Hospitality is vital in the first-century church (compare 3 John 8; contrast 2 John 10). But hospitality also reflects God's own actions: He grants us a home in the world and welcomes us into His family.

To be *apt to teach* indicates that teaching is always a key function of the church leader. But in the context of this letter, the emphasis is probably less on the ability to give an interesting lesson and more on sound understanding of the gospel. For the church to stand unified against false teaching, it needs leaders who understand thoroughly and accurately the saving message. The leader needs to know what genuine spiritual maturity is in order to be able to lead others to that maturity.

3. Not given to wine, no striker, not greedy of filthy lucre; but patient, not a brawler, not covetous.

Many of the positive descriptions of verse 2 now have contrasting, negative descriptions. This is something like the dark colors of a painting that make the bright colors stand out all the more.

Not given to wine obviously indicates shunning intoxication (compare Proverbs 20:1). To be "vigilant, sober, of good behaviour," which we just read, depends at least on disciplined moderation with alcohol, if not complete abstention. The Christian is not to be controlled by alcohol or other substances, but by God's Spirit (Ephesians 5:18).

No striker indicates the person who refuses aggressive conflict, whether physical or verbal. Those who have been reconciled to God by the death of Jesus live by God's peace. That quality is underlined with the terms *patient* and *not a brawler*. Christ did not resist those who sought to kill Him, and we are compelled to meet aggression with the same kind of gentleness.

Not greedy of filthy lucre and *not covetous* speak to a leader's attitude toward possessions (Matthew 6:19-21; 1 Timothy 6:6-10).

From time to time, we see the spectacle of a politician who is charged with misusing the powers of office. One such incident followed the U. S. presidential election of 2008. With the election of Barack Obama to that office came the need to fill his vacated seat in the U. S. Senate. Illinois Governor Rod Blagojevich had the responsibility to make that appointment.

In the process, however, the governor was charged with trying to sell the office to the highest bidder! On January 29, 2009, the Illinois state senate voted 59–0 to remove the governor from office. The evidence that the governor was "greedy of filthy lucre" was overwhelming.

Added to the governor's disgrace was embarrassment to the state of Illinois—the land of "Honest Abe" Lincoln. The ripples of a political scandal extend far beyond the disgraced politician himself or herself. And so it is with church leaders. May we choose them wisely.

—C. R. B.

C. Their Households (vv. 4, 5)

4. One that ruleth well his own house, having his children in subjection with all gravity.

The focus shifts from personal qualities to a place where those qualities can be demonstrated: the home. The term *ruleth* does not necessarily indicate autocratic, dictatorial rule. It was often used for diligent concern, the "rule" of a godly father, not that of a tyrant.

Good leadership in the home is demonstrated in the lives of those whom the parent nurtures: the children. The emphasis here is that the children's lives demonstrate orderliness (as in vv. 2, 3). Because these qualities are the consequence of faith in the gospel, we can assume that the leader nurtures his children in the that faith (Titus 1:6).

What Do You Think?
What cultural signs of being "a good father" are different today from those of, say, 20 years ago? Why is this question important?
Talking Points for Your Discussion
- Deuteronomy 6:6-9
- Ephesians 6:4

5. (For if a man know not how to rule his own house, how shall he take care of the church of God?)

It is interesting that Paul points to the home, not some other sphere like business or the military, as the testing ground for leadership qualities. A wider perspective reminds us, however, that even the most diligent Christian parents do not always succeed in transmitting faith in their children. Paul himself was not successful in leading everyone to lasting faith (1 Timothy 1:19, 20; 2 Timothy 4:10). Jesus warned that not all seed falls on good soil (Matthew 13:18-23).

Paul's instructions assume that church leaders will be taken from among household leaders, that is, fathers. Does this mean that only fathers can lead the church? To answer that, we should keep the analogy of a painting in mind: the description here is less a checklist than a total portrait that emerges from collective brush strokes. The home is a very useful place in which to see godly character demonstrated, but it is not the only place that tests and proves such character (see v. 7, below).

D. Their Maturity (v. 6)

6. Not a novice, lest being lifted up with pride he fall into the condemnation of the devil.

The portrait is rounded off with a warning that the leader's character needs to be tested and proven. The term *novice* indicates one who is newly planted in the faith. That expression reminds us of Jesus' parable of the sower, which warns that seed that sprouts in bad soil will not grow to maturity (Matthew 13:5, 6, 20, 21). Not all who begin in the faith will persist.

Investing too much leadership responsibility in a believer who is relatively new to the faith may promote the kind of pride that threatens reliance on God. Pride seems to have been the devil's own original sin, challenging the authority of God himself. Therefore, those who yield to pride place themselves in danger of the condemnation that the devil himself will receive.

How long must someone be a Christian in order to be *not a novice*? Paul gives no specific standard. Again, he paints a picture rather than supplying a checklist.

E. Their Reputation (v. 7)

7. Moreover he must have a good report of them which are without; lest he fall into reproach and the snare of the devil.

The description ends as it began in verse 2: the leader needs a good reputation in the community *(them which are without)*. To be ambassadors of the gospel to the world, they must be respected by the world (see 2 Corinthians 8:21). Those who fall (or jump) into *the snare of the devil* (compare Genesis 3) do not exhibit the qualities in Paul's portrait. Their reputation betrays a character out of line with God's salvation.

II. Ideal Deacons
(I Timothy 3:8-13)
A. Their Character (vv. 8-10)

8. Likewise must the deacons be grave, not doubletongued, not given to much wine, not greedy of filthy lucre.

Attention now shifts to deacons. The term *deacon* translates a word that commonly means "servant." Of course, all Christians are called to live as servants (Mark 10:42-45). But the first-century church recognizes some of its members as servants in a special sense. They perhaps take responsibility for specific areas of church ministry, as in Acts 6:1-6 (although the word *deacon* is not used there).

As with the discussion in verses 1-7 above, Paul's focus on the deacons is not so much on what they *do*, but the kind of people they *are*. Like the elders, deacons must reflect the transforming power of the gospel. They are to be distinguished by their serious behavior, their honesty, their self-control, and their reliance on God's provision. *Filthy lucre* refers to profit gained by shady means.

What Do You Think?

How do we address greediness in a leader? How does greediness affect a leader?

Talking Points for Your Discussion

- Regarding misuse of power (1 Kings 21)
- Regarding who is favored (Psalm 10:3)
- Regarding family life (Proverbs 15:27)
- Regarding deceitfulness (Jeremiah 8:10)

---

9. Holding the mystery of the faith in a pure conscience.

The deacon's life must stand on the firm foundation of the faith. The phrase *the mystery of the faith* emphasizes that although God's plan of salvation was once unknown, God has revealed it in the gospel. The false teachers in Ephesus, the city of Timothy's church, probably teach a mystery hidden to all but a few. Paul insists that the gospel is a mystery revealed that anyone can receive by faith. This is a follow-up discussion of the mystery of Christ that Paul previously wrote in a letter to the church in Ephesus (Ephesians 1:9; 3:2-6).

To hold that mystery *in a pure conscience,* one must put the gospel into practice. Deacons need not only understand the good news, but live it.

10. And let these also first be proved; then let them use the office of a deacon, being found blameless.

Like those discussed in verses 1-7, deacons need character that has been demonstrated over time, with observable actions. They must live lives that are not subject to common criticism because of obvious inconsistencies.

B. Their Wives (v. 11)

11. Even so must their wives be grave, not slanderers, sober, faithful in all things.

This verse presents a translation issue. The word translated *wives* here also commonly means "women," as we discussed regarding verse 2. In

"HOLDING THE MYSTERY OF THE FAITH IN A PURE CONSCIENCE."

Visual for Lesson 2. *As you study verse 9, point to this visual and ask, "What is a practical way to hold the mystery of the faith in a pure conscience?"*

its original language, the text does not specify the word *their,* which is inserted in many English translations to make sense of the text. So is Paul talking about "deacons' wives" or "women in general"? The first of these two possibilities makes the most sense, given what Paul has just said in verse 10. To shift from discussing "a deacon" in verse 10 to "women in general" in verse 11 then back to "the deacons" in verse 12 would be quite jarring. Even so, the challenge to be *grave, not slanderers, sober, faithful in all things* should apply to everyone, shouldn't it?

Once again, the qualities listed reflect the previous list: honorable behavior, gentle speech, self-control and moderation, consistent devotion. As in verses 1-7, the same transformed character needs to shine through.

C. Their Households (v. 12)

12. Let the deacons be the husbands of one wife, ruling their children and their own houses well.

Paul's instructions here mirror what he says in verses 2 and 3. Thus the same comments apply.

D. Their Service (v. 13)

13. For they that have used the office of a deacon well purchase to themselves a good degree, and great boldness in the faith which is in Christ Jesus.

Deacons have a vital work! By serving, they obtain a good standing, the meaning of *purchase to themselves a good degree.* The Ephesian false teachers teach that secret knowledge gives a person high rank. Paul's response stands in contrast: faithful service is what makes for spiritual standing. As Jesus taught, the greatest of all will be the servant of all (Mark 10:43-45).

What Do You Think?
What are some things that faithful service purchases? Which do you think is most valuable?
Talking Points for Your Discussion
- Proverbs 22:1
- Matthew 6:1-4
- Colossians 3:22-24

Leadership Qualities

III. Ideal Church

(1 Timothy 3:14-16)

A. Nature (vv. 14, 15)

14. These things write I unto thee, hoping to come unto thee shortly.

Paul writes to assist churches in his absence. But he always seeks to be present with the churches whenever he can. As a leader of leaders, he remains personally engaged.

15. But if I tarry long, that thou mayest know how thou oughtest to behave thyself in the house of God, which is the church of the living God, the pillar and ground of the truth.

The church exists by God's saving truth to share that truth. Therefore, it must live consistently by that truth, starting with the leaders but including all its members. This is not the first time Paul has discussed issues of behavior regarding the church at Ephesus (see Ephesians 5:15-20).

What Do You Think?

What steps can you take to make sure you behave properly as part of "the house of God"?

Talking Points for Your Discussion
- Behavior toward fellow believers
- Behavior toward nonbelievers

B. Mystery (v. 16)

16. And without controversy great is the mystery of godliness: God was manifest in the flesh, justified in the Spirit, seen of angels, preached unto the Gentiles, believed on in the world, received up into glory.

This verse may quote from an early Christian hymn that summarizes the gospel. God's mystery is not a secret, as the false teachers argue, but is something very public: that in Jesus, God himself entered the world, rose and ascended after dying for our sins, and makes himself known to all through the preaching of the gospel until He returns. The hymn makes these points line by line.

The truth of this message changes everything. We must live as Christ lived, to serve others. That message determines the character of the church's leaders and members. This chapter thus closes with a reminder of the central truth of the gospel. The qualities of Christian leadership are determined not by "what works" in worldly terms, but by the core gospel message.

❧ ALL THE CLUES WE NEED ❧

Mystery stories are the favorite reading material of many. The reason for their popularity is that a good mystery will keep the reader guessing almost to the very last page. In 1949, there was a spin-off of the genre in a board game called *Clue©*.

When the game begins, three cards that name the murderer, the weapon, and the location are placed in an envelope. The number of characters, weapons, and rooms create hundreds of possible solutions. Many people love the challenge of figuring out the mystery of the fatal combination.

However, the "mystery of godliness" isn't really a game of wits. After all, no one was able to figured out ahead of time the method God would use to reveal himself as a human to bring us salvation. But now all the "clues" that make it possible for us to know the answer are revealed in Christ. These clues are available to everyone. —C. R. B.

Conclusion

A. Becoming Christlike

If we are surrounded by interest in leadership, we are also surrounded by frustration with leadership. People are inclined to find fault with those who lead. Sadly, the church is infamous for criticizing her leaders. If the church is not doing well, we do not want our share of the responsibility, so we pin the blame on others. Today's passage forbids us from doing that. The qualities for the church's leaders belong in the lives of all Christians (see Ephesians 5:3, 4, 18, etc.). If the church is not yet what it should be, the solution is not to blame leaders. It is to become better Christ-followers.

B. Prayer

Lord, make us, Your church, conformed to Jesus' image. We pray in His name, amen.

C. Thought to Remember

Reflect the Lord's character.

INVOLVEMENT LEARNING

Some of the activities below are also found in the helpful student book, Adult Bible Class.
Don't forget to download the free reproducible page from www.standardlesson.com to enhance your lesson!

Into the Lesson

Distribute handouts of the following list of words. The first letters should be capitalized and bold, as shown: **A**vailable, **D**octrinally sound, **E**ager, **E**xperienced, **H**ospitable, **I**ntegrity personified, **L**oyal, **P**atient, **R**espected, **S**ensible. Say, "This is a list of qualities for those who lead the church. Please prioritize the list by ranking the entries from 1 (least significant) to 10 (most significant).

After learners complete the task, say, "I am now going to give another listing." Put the same words on display atop one another, so that the first letters are aligned top-to-bottom in this sequence: Loyal, Eager, Available, Doctrinally sound, Experienced, Respected, Sensible, Hospitable, Integrity personified, Patient. (You may wish to have these on card-stock strips for quickness of handling.) Learners no doubt will notice the first letters spell the word *LEADERSHIP* in your arrangement.

Option: Expand this segment by downloading the reproducible page and distributing copies of the Bad Leaders exercise. Discuss conclusions.

Into the Word

Say, "In today's text of 1 Timothy 3, Paul writes the Spirit's requirements for the church's two primary leadership roles: elders (bishops) and deacons." Ask the class to read through that text silently and consider the 10 qualities in the preceding list, trying to identify verses that relate.

After a few minutes, have learners suggest their choices. Then ask, "What qualities in the text do you see that are missing from this list?" Suggestions may include marital status, self-control, moderation in habits, gentleness, generosity, honesty, and nature of family life. Let the class respond freely.

Display a popular book about leadership, such as *The 21 Irrefutable Laws of Leadership* by John C. Maxwell. Invite a class member to review the book beforehand and come prepared to summa-

rize the "secrets" the author offers. This will allow you to compare and contrast the suggestions of the author with the attributes the Holy Spirit emphasizes through the pen of the apostle Paul.

Bring the discussion to a conclusion by pointing to 1 Timothy 3:16. Say, "Here Paul summarizes the basic truths of the gospel and of Christ. Some suggest that this may be an early Christian hymn." Help your learners memorize that verse. If you have a musically talented class member, recruit him or her to develop a simple tune by which the words (even if slightly adapted) can be sung.

Provide each learner with a set of six index cards, each printed with one of the phrases/lines from 1 Timothy 3:16, beginning with "God was manifest." Suggest that in the week ahead learners occasionally shuffle the six and then see if they can rearrange them in the proper order; doing this enough times will fix the "hymn" firmly in mind. Point out the logical sequence of the ideas: from incarnation to ascension and glorification.

Into Life

Say, "At one time, elementary school students received a 'conduct' grade on their report cards. Paul says he writes so his readers will know how to conduct themselves, expressed simply as 'how one ought to behave' in the *King James Version*."

Give each learner a four-block strip of paper that is printed with the letters A, B, C, D, one per block. Give this direction: "Use this 'grading strip' as your Bible bookmark for this week. Look at it each day during your time of private Bible study. Evaluate your 'conduct' for the day (or the preceding one), as you ponder God's requirements for the leaders of His church. Repent of any problem areas, and ask God's grace for forgiveness and His strength for a better day to follow."

Download the reproducible page and distribute copies of the Reading a Good Mystery activity as take-home work.

LEADERSHIP
PRIORITIES

BACKGROUND SCRIPTURE: 1 Timothy 4:6-16

PRINTED TEXT: 1 Timothy 4:6-16

1 TIMOTHY 4:6-16

6 If thou put the brethren in remembrance of these things, thou shalt be a good minister of Jesus Christ, nourished up in the words of faith and of good doctrine, whereunto thou hast attained.

7 But refuse profane and old wives' fables, and exercise thyself rather unto godliness.

8 For bodily exercise profiteth little: but godliness is profitable unto all things, having promise of the life that now is, and of that which is to come.

9 This is a faithful saying and worthy of all acceptation.

10 For therefore we both labour and suffer reproach, because we trust in the living God, who is the Saviour of all men, specially of those that believe.

11 These things command and teach.

12 Let no man despise thy youth; but be thou an example of the believers, in word, in conversation, in charity, in spirit, in faith, in purity.

13 Till I come, give attendance to reading, to exhortation, to doctrine.

14 Neglect not the gift that is in thee, which was given thee by prophecy, with the laying on of the hands of the presbytery.

15 Meditate upon these things; give thyself wholly to them; that thy profiting may appear to all.

16 Take heed unto thyself, and unto the doctrine; continue in them: for in doing this thou shalt both save thyself, and them that hear thee.

KEY VERSE

Take heed unto thyself, and unto the doctrine; continue in them: for in doing this thou shalt both save thyself, and them that hear thee. —1 Timothy 4:16

WE WORSHIP GOD

Unit 1: A Guide for Leaders

LESSONS 1–4

LESSON AIMS

After participating in this lesson, each student will be able to:

1. List the activities and attitudes Paul tells Timothy to be diligent about in his ministry.

2. Explain the roles of teaching and personal example in the development of godliness in the church.

3. Suggest a scale by which he or she can measure personal progress in the areas Paul addresses.

LESSON OUTLINE

Introduction

A. Aiming at Nothing

There is an old story about a man who passed by a curious looking barn. On the side of the barn were painted several targets, each with an arrow exactly in the center of the bull's-eye. The man saw the farmer standing nearby and remarked, "Someone must be a very good archer, to have hit all those bull's-eyes." The farmer replied, "Well, not really. My son shoots those arrows in the barn and then paints a target around each of them, wherever they strike."

Many people live that way. They aim at no special target in life; they simply accept whatever happens. They aim at nothing, they hit it every time, and pretend that what they end up with is just fine.

Followers of Jesus cannot afford to live aimless lives. Our Lord became a man and died for us to achieve a goal: to make us His forgiven people, now and forever. His goal is now our goal. Having received salvation in Christ, we should want our lives to reflect that salvation, to be conformed to His will. And we should want others to enjoy the same kind of life.

B. Lesson Background

The background for today's lesson is the same as that of our two previous lessons, thus that information need not be repeated here. One item that can receive additional attention, however, is the presence of the so-called *mystery religions* in the area around Ephesus, the city where Timothy ministered. Such religions taught that one can have an exalted spiritual status by learning secret knowledge and observing special rules about abstaining from certain foods and from marriage. Apparently, some of this thinking had infected the church at Ephesus.

In response, Paul discussed the revealed nature of the Christian "mystery" extensively in his letter to the Ephesians (see Ephesians 1:9; 3:2-11; 5:32; 6:19). Further, Paul specifically gave Timothy instructions to pass on to that church regarding how to live together and choose leaders in ways that reflect the true gospel of Jesus Christ.

In the passage just prior to today's text, Paul warned that the kind of false teaching the church confronted was exactly characteristic of "the latter times." From the perspective of the gospel, such times began with the resurrection of Jesus. So the struggle with false teaching was serious. It represents the battle of the end times.

That description of false teaching raises questions. What should the church's leaders do to counter such teaching? What strategy should leaders employ in this battle? The answer is to focus our aim on the right target and understand the right means of hitting that target.

I. Target of Leadership: Godliness

(1 TIMOTHY 4:6-10)

A. Through Keeping the Truth (vv. 6, 7)

6. If thou put the brethren in remembrance of these things, thou shalt be a good minister of Jesus Christ, nourished up in the words of faith and of good doctrine, whereunto thou hast attained.

Part of Timothy's task as a leader is to remind the church of what Paul has said in the previous section (*these things,* referring to 1 Timothy 4:1-5). God's blessing is not to be found by avoiding certain foods or abstaining from marriage or in any other practice that is unrelated to the good news of Jesus (compare Colossians 2:20-23). Timothy's aim is to direct his people back to the truth and away from such teaching.

The Greek word behind the term *minister* in this verse simply signifies "servant." (Interestingly, this same Greek word was translated as "deacon" in last week's lesson.) As one who leads the church, Timothy is no less and no more than a servant of Christ. Being Christ's servant means first of all being devoted to training oneself in the true gospel teaching. Paul's encouragement is for Timothy to maintain constant devotion to it.

7. But refuse profane and old wives' fables, and exercise thyself rather unto godliness.

Compared with the good news of Jesus, what the false teachers offer is utterly worthless and ridiculous. The fact that their stories are *profane*

means that they are devoid of anything connected with God.

Old wives' fables are literally "myths associated with old women." That phrase is used in Paul's time to express the complete worthlessness of a story or idea. Of course, everyone knows that men as well as women can circulate such falsehoods, as can the young as well as the old. These myths perhaps seek to embellish the stories of the Old Testament to promote the false teachers' concepts (compare 1 Timothy 1:4; Titus 1:14).

A person who gives attention to such myths will necessarily give less attention to the right objective: true godliness. The term *godliness* means the kind of life that shows proper respect for God. Timothy should pursue godliness as an athlete pursues fitness through exercise. Sports and physical fitness are an interest in Paul's culture just as they are in ours (compare 1 Corinthians 9:24). The comparison stresses that godliness, like athletic fitness, increases with diligent practice.

> *What Do You Think?*
> What are some ways a Christian can train for godliness? How does this compare with things we do for our bodies?
> *Talking Points for Your Discussion*
> - Spiritual vs. physical diet
> - Spiritual vs. physical exercise
> - Spiritual vs. physical behavior
> - Spiritual vs. physical bad habits

B. Through Diligent Practice (vv. 8-10)

8. For bodily exercise profiteth little: but godliness is profitable unto all things, having promise of the life that now is, and of that which is to come.

Paul's words about physical exercise here are not entirely negative. He affirms that physical exercise brings some (a *little*) benefit. He does not tell us to ignore our bodies as if they are unimportant; that approach belongs more to the false teachers (again, 1 Timothy 4:3-5). For Paul, the body is good because it is created by God.

But in the bigger picture, physical exercise is of limited value, relatively speaking. Exercise,

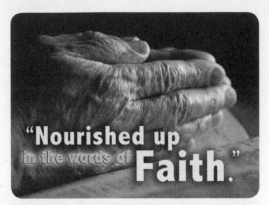

"Nourished up in the words of Faith."

Visual for Lesson 3. *Turn this statement into a question as you discuss verse 6: "How can you better nourish yourself in the words of faith?"*

nutrition, and rest promote longer, healthier lives, but no one can stop the process of aging that ultimately leads to death. On the other hand, genuine godliness is beneficial both in the present and in eternity. The godly life yields peace, harmony, and contentment that is not to be found by any other means. And unlike physical health, spiritual health lasts forever. Death cannot interrupt it.

9. This is a faithful saying and worthy of all acceptation.

In 1 and 2 Timothy and Titus, Paul labels a number of statements as *faithful* or true (1 Timothy 1:15; 2 Timothy 2:11; Titus 3:8). These seem to be memorable statements that encapsulate key truths. These statements need to be considered carefully and remembered well. So Paul applies that label to his previous statement about the benefits of exercising toward godliness. There can be nothing more important than pursuing what is best in life: genuine spiritual maturity.

10. For therefore we both labour and suffer reproach, because we trust in the living God, who is the Saviour of all men, specially of those that believe.

Because godliness is the greatest good one can pursue, it is worth pursuing no matter the difficulties. Thus Paul uses terms that emphasize the effort that godliness deserves.

Why should anyone pursue such a difficult task? Paul gives the reason: who God is and what He has done. The phrase *the living God* stresses that the Christian's trust is in the true God who is active in the world, not in idols that have no reality. This true God has done something extraordinary for us: He gave himself for the sake of all people, so He is the Savior of all. But for that salvation to be effective, the sinner must accept it. Therefore, God is more particularly the Savior of *those that believe.* If the true God has done this great thing, what in life can be more important than responding to what He has done?

> **What Do You Think?**
> In what ways have you or those you know suffered reproach for the cause of Christ? What has been the result?
> *Talking Points for Your Discussion*
> ▪ Verbal abuse
> ▪ Financial hardship
> ▪ Physical abuse
> ▪ Discrimination

As Paul develops his instructions on godliness, he stresses two parallel ideas: (1) Christian leaders need to lead others to true godliness, (2) but to do so, leaders must themselves single-mindedly pursue godliness. How does the Christian leader lead others toward godliness? That question is the focus of the second section of the text.

❧ SEEKING SUPERIOR PERFORMANCE ❧

Alex Rodriguez, or "A-Rod," was one of professional baseball's heroes for several years. That all changed for many fans in early 2009, when he admitted having taken steroids while playing for the Texas Rangers in 2001–2003. A-Rod is a three-time American League Most Valuable Player, but admission of the use of performance enhancing drugs sullied his reputation. He said the $252 million contract he had with the Rangers caused him to take the drugs so he could "prove to everyone that I was worth being [called] one of the greatest players of all time."

Major League Baseball was lax in those years about the use of such drugs. Evidence suggests many other players were enhancing their performance just as Rodriguez was. It was all in an attempt to get an edge.

There are no shortcuts to spiritual growth. Clever political moves, etc., to work oneself up in a church hierarchy are just that. Superior spiritual performance comes, as Paul says, by laboring and suffering in our spiritual training.　　—C. R. B.

II. Means of Leadership: Teaching
(1 TIMOTHY 4:11-16)
A. Authority (v. 11)
11. These things command and teach.

What Paul has just discussed is important for all in the church, both leaders and followers. The message needs to be understood with the mind and embraced by the will. So Paul tells Timothy both to teach it and to command it.

This brief instruction mirrors the way Paul writes to Timothy in the entire passage. These verses contain a remarkably high number of direct commands. But woven into those commands are phrases pointing to the central truths of the gospel. Rightly understood, the good news of Jesus is a matter for the head and the heart, always leading to action.

B. Example (v. 12)
12. Let no man despise thy youth; but be thou an example of the believers, in word, in conversation, in charity, in spirit, in faith, in purity.

The gospel is a hard message to receive (John 6:60-66). Those who lead others to grow in the gospel face all kinds of objections. Here Paul anticipates one that Timothy may face. While we do not know exactly how old Timothy is when Paul writes, clearly he is young enough to be considered less than fully credible by some people.

Paul's instruction is not that Timothy should argue or assert power to overcome the perception of his youthfulness. Rather, Paul challenges Timothy to become a more outstanding example of Christian maturity. His example should cover the whole range of life. *Word* indicates his speech. *Conversation* in the *King James Version* is not a term for speech, but for the general manner of one's life. *Charity* is love, the virtue that drives all Christian behavior, our response to God's love

demonstrated in the cross. *Faith* likewise undergirds all of Christian living, expressing trust in the God who has saved us. *Purity* indicates devotion to God as one who belongs entirely to Him and lives with pure motives.

Paul's term for *example* is strong, indicating something that actively molds and shapes the lives of others. Timothy's life as a Christian leader is to be so compelling that others will be actively challenged to pursue the kind of life that he lives. By leading such a life, Timothy can overcome the reservations that some have about his youth (compare Titus 2:15).

> *What Do You Think?*
> What are some things young people can do to earn the respect of those who are older?
> *Talking Points for Your Discussion*
> - Concerning traditions
> - Concerning hurts
> - Concerning apprehensions

C. Word (v. 13)
13. Till I come, give attendance to reading, to exhortation, to doctrine.

Having stressed teaching with authority in verse 11 and teaching by example in verse 12, Paul now addresses the importance of teaching by word. This verse combines three terms to describe such teaching. *Reading* refers to the verbalizing of Scripture publicly. Because books in the ancient world are scarce and expensive, private reading is unusual. Instead, books are read out loud to groups of people. Among first-century Christians, that means primarily reading from the Old Testament Scriptures. By the time that Paul writes to Timothy, it probably also means reading from earlier letters of Paul and perhaps even one or more of the Gospels.

That reading is to be combined with *exhortation,* which indicates verbal encouragement to right actions. The message read from the Scriptures always demands life-change. Timothy must encourage the church to act on the implications of the scriptural message.

The word *doctrine* may sound difficult and forbidding, but it simply means "teaching."

Teaching based on the Scriptures will stand in sharp contrast with the speculative teaching of the false teachers. Sound teaching is based on the gospel message, not on fanciful stories claiming secret knowledge (v. 7, above). Scriptural teaching always points the way to the godly life that Paul describes.

This combination of scriptural reading with encouragement and teaching based on it is very familiar to us. It represents the kind of teaching and preaching that continues in the church today, the very thing you are doing right now in your class. Teaching the biblical message and encouraging people to live by it are absolutely central to Christian leadership.

❧ WHAT UNDERGIRDS SOUND DOCTRINE ❧

For much of history, the idea of *revealed truth* held sway: truth is revealed by God. Today, *postmodernism* is king. This mind-set includes the idea that truth is personal to each individual.

One result of postmodernism is the denial that Christianity has any greater claim to truth than any other religion. As bad as that viewpoint is, things get even worse when Christians themselves begin to believe it. When that happens, the result is, among other things, support within the church for various sinful lifestyles. Those who still seek biblical faithfulness can end up being compared with the misguided souls who created witch hunts in the past.

Paul's advice to Timothy is timeless: adherence to sound doctrine (which points to the existence of absolute truth) is the foundation of good leadership. Although the specific issues may change over time, the church is always to be concerned with casting absolute truth against falsehood. We may thank God that the day of witch hunts is long past. But a proper concern for the truth of Scripture never goes out of date.   —C. R. B.

HOW TO SAY IT

Colossians	Kuh-*losh*-unz.
Corinthians	Ko-*rin*-thee-unz (*th* as in *thin*).
Ephesians	Ee-*fee*-zhunz.
Ephesus	*Ef*-uh-sus.

D. Gift (v. 14)

14. Neglect not the gift that is in thee, which was given thee by prophecy, with the laying on of the hands of the presbytery.

God is at work in Timothy's life to empower him as a leader. All Christians have received the Holy Spirit (Acts 2:38) and have been given gifts by the Holy Spirit for service (Romans 12:4-8; 1 Corinthians 12:4-11; Ephesians 4:11-13). Paul reminds Timothy of his own giftedness so that he will remember the importance of the service to which his gifts call him.

The fact that Timothy's gift was given *by prophecy* may mean that certain prophets in the church received a message from God promising that Timothy would serve as a leader when Timothy became a Christian and received the Holy Spirit. Or it may mean that later in Timothy's life he is recognized as having gifts for leadership because of prophetic messages. In either case, Timothy should remember that God actively directs him to his leadership ministry and empowers him to accomplish it.

Laying on of the hands in the Bible is a posture taken in prayer. By placing hands on another person, those who pray are asking God to give that person a particular blessing. It may be done to appoint a person to do a particular task (Acts 6:6; 8:17; 2 Timothy 1:6). The one praying asks God to enable the person to accomplish the task. In Timothy's case it was the presbytery—that is, the church's leadership—who had offered this prayer for his blessing. Unless Timothy received more than one laying on of hands, 2 Timothy 1:6 indicates that Paul participated in this. The verse before us describes something close to what Christians mean by "ordination" today. We note in passing that the word *presbytery* is rooted in the word translated "elder(s)" in 1 Timothy 5:17, 19, etc.

With this solemn background, Timothy has a vivid reminder of the importance of his ministry. God is behind it from beginning to end. Timothy's ministry demands the most diligent attention.

We should recognize how much we have in common with Timothy. We may not be "ordained" or have had hands laid on us. But as Christians we are all gifted by the Spirit for service. Like Timothy, we have a solemn duty to remember and carry out.

> **What Do You Think?**
> How does a recognition of the spiritual gifts you have from God affect you?
>
> *Talking Points for Your Discussion*
> - Regarding service toward church unity (Romans 12:4, 5; 1 Corinthians 12:4-7)
> - Regarding serving others (Romans 12:6-8; 1 Peter 4:10)
> - Regarding the gifts that others possess (1 Corinthians 12:21)

> **What Do You Think?**
> What are some specific steps you can take to assure that you will continue to grow in spiritual maturity?
>
> *Talking Points for Your Discussion*
> - Internet usage
> - Television watching
> - Devotional time

E. Persistence (vv. 15, 16)

15. Meditate upon these things; give thyself wholly to them; that thy profiting may appear to all.

As a Christian leader, Timothy's constant pre-occupation needs to be the priority of a godly life and faithful teaching. The term translated *meditate* can mean "think about constantly" or "put something into practice constantly." Either way, the point is clear. The same idea is in the phrase *give thyself wholly to them,* which more literally is simply "be in them." Timothy is to see his call to leadership as his very life, the center of all that he does.

By living this way, others will see Timothy's own growth in godliness and will be challenged by it. *Profiting* refers to "making progress." As Timothy grows in Christlikeness, those around him will feel his influence deeply.

16. Take heed unto thyself, and unto the doctrine; continue in them: for in doing this thou shalt both save thyself, and them that hear thee.

This verse brings the themes of this passage to a fitting summary. Timothy's first attention needs to be on his own life: he must grow continually toward godly maturity. With that, he must attend to his teaching, both knowing what he must teach—the gospel and its implications—and being active in doing the teaching. These should be his constant preoccupations, the priority of his life, not just as a leader of people, but as a follower of Christ.

Close attention to these matters will *both save thyself, and them that hear thee.* Timothy will stand

Conclusion
A. What Leadership Is All About

It has been said that leading by example is not just the best way to lead, it is the only way. When the church fulfills the will of God, it is always led by those who reflect the saving gospel. They know the destination to which God has called His people, and they are moving toward that destination while they encourage others to join them.

Some of us know that we are leaders in the church. We have accepted responsibilities that involve teaching, guiding, and directing others to grow in God's Word and work. In this passage we can hear God's call to be deliberate and diligent in pursuing godliness.

Some of us think that we are not leaders. But in fact, every Christian has the position and the power to lead in some regard. You may be the only available example of a Christ-follower to some family, friends, and coworkers.

The Christian faith does not have ranks. Every Christian is a sinner saved by grace, a pilgrim on the way to a destination. Living out that truth is what Christian leadership is all about.

B. Prayer

Great God, we ask You to lead us to true godliness, being more like You. As You have saved us, we ask You to empower us to lead others to the same salvation. In the name of Jesus who died to save us, amen.

C. Thought to Remember

Pursue spiritual maturity.

INVOLVEMENT LEARNING

Some of the activities below are also found in the helpful student book, Adult Bible Class.
Don't forget to download the free reproducible page from www.standardlesson.com to enhance your lesson!

Into the Lesson

Create a handout of the following matching exercise. Put copies in chairs for students to work on as they arrive. Give your handout the title "Survey of Bad Doctrines." Print the text of 1 Timothy 1:3 at the top. Include these instructions: "Look at the following texts in 1 Timothy and match them to the bad doctrine suggested on the right."

Left-hand column: A. 1:15; B. 1:17; C. 2:4; D. 2:5; E. 3:16; F. 4:3; G. 4:8; H. 6:6; I. 6:14.

Right-hand column:

1. There is no God, but if He does exist He is limited in some way.

2. There are various ways to come to God, all equally valid.

3. Marriage is best avoided if one wants to be holy.

4. Getting rich is what really matters.

5. Jesus is not going to come again.

6. A sound mind in a sound body is the highest good.

7. Jesus did not actually come in the flesh.

8. There is no such thing as absolute truth, especially in regard to proper behavior.

9. Sin is not real; it is a term that labels what some consider to be bad choices.

Suggested answers: A-9; B-1; C-8; D-2; E-7; F-3; G-6; H-4; I-5.

Discuss the results. Say, "Paul is warning Timothy of the strong temptations to accept error as truth as he describes the godly leader's role in today's text from 1 Timothy 4."

Into the Word

Recruit a volunteer to wear around his or her neck a sign that reads *BAD LEADER*. Your volunteer will read the following statements, pausing after each one. Each statement will be a preface to the whole class joining in to read one or two verses of today's text from 1 Timothy 4 after each comment by the bad leader (BL), as noted.

BL: Let people believe what they want. They can figure things out on their own. *Class reads verse 6.*

BL: What I like to study is the discoveries of the ancient mystical thinkers. *Class reads verse 7.*

BL: Working out at the gym takes most of my spare time. I'm going to keep myself healthy and strong so I'll live to be a hundred! *Class reads verse 8.*

BL: I'm not aware of anything that everybody has to know and accept. *Class reads verses 9, 10.*

BL: I like to make suggestions, not offer commands. *Class reads verse 11.*

BL: I can't be anybody's role model. *Class reads verse 12.*

BL: People can just read the Bible quietly in their own homes. They don't need to hear from me. *Class reads verse 13.*

BL: I don't think of myself as being "gifted" in any sense. *Class reads verse 14.*

BL: I'll get around to studying the Bible when I have time. *Class reads verses 15, 16.*

The antithetical statements of the bad leader will allow you to highlight the faulty thinking of many. *Option:* If time allows, download the reproducible page and distribute copies of the These Things activity; have your learners work on this in small groups. Discuss results.

Into Life

Download the reproducible page and distribute copies of the No Pain, No Gain exercise. Have students work on this either as a whole class, in small groups, or in pairs.

Prepare in advance handouts that have seven "bow and arrow" targets, one for each day of the week ahead. Put the word *godliness* in the bull's-eye of each. Distribute these as students depart. Say, "Post your targets in a place where you will see them early each day as a reminder that your target for the day is godliness."

COMPASSIONATE
SERVICE

BACKGROUND SCRIPTURE: **1 Timothy 5:1-22**
PRINTED TEXT: **1 Timothy 5:1-8, 17-22**

1 TIMOTHY 5:1-8, 17-22

1 Rebuke not an elder, but intreat him as a father; and the younger men as brethren;

2 The elder women as mothers; the younger as sisters, with all purity.

3 Honour widows that are widows indeed.

4 But if any widow have children or nephews, let them learn first to shew piety at home, and to requite their parents: for that is good and acceptable before God.

5 Now she that is a widow indeed, and desolate, trusteth in God, and continueth in supplications and prayers night and day.

6 But she that liveth in pleasure is dead while she liveth.

7 And these things give in charge, that they may be blameless.

8 But if any provide not for his own, and specially for those of his own house, he hath denied the faith, and is worse than an infidel.

. . . .

17 Let the elders that rule well be counted worthy of double honour, especially they who labour in the word and doctrine.

18 For the scripture saith, thou shalt not muzzle the ox that treadeth out the corn. And, The labourer is worthy of his reward.

19 Against an elder receive not an accusation, but before two or three witnesses.

20 Them that sin rebuke before all, that others also may fear.

21 I charge thee before God, and the Lord Jesus Christ, and the elect angels, that thou observe these things without preferring one before another, doing nothing by partiality.

22 Lay hands suddenly on no man, neither be partaker of other men's sins: keep thyself pure.

KEY VERSE

If any provide not for his own, and specially for those of his own house, he hath denied the faith, and is worse than an infidel. —1 Timothy 5:8

WE WORSHIP GOD

Unit 1: A Guide for Leaders

LESSONS 1–4

LESSON AIMS

After participating in this lesson, each student will be able to:

1. Summarize Paul's instructions for how Timothy should relate to various groups of people in the church.

2. Discuss how to apply Paul's instructions on providing assistance in light of the existence of governmental aid programs today.

3. Work with others to develop a plan by which the church can provide compassionate assistance to those in need—especially where governmental assistance is unavailable.

LESSON OUTLINE

Introduction

A. Learning a "Love Language"

A married person may struggle to express love for his or her spouse in ways that the spouse understands. As a solution, counselors who follow Gary Chapman's philosophy may encourage such a person to learn the spouse's "love language." How does the wife or husband understand best that love is being expressed? Is it by spending time together? by helping with common household tasks? by listening carefully? by offering encouragement?

Any of those actions can express genuine love. But to communicate love effectively, the husband or wife needs to understand and do what best connects with the spouse's own needs. The husband needs to choose the actions that speak his wife's "love language" and vice versa.

The church faces a similar challenge: effectively communicating God's love in a sinful world. God's love in the cross needs to be demonstrated in ways that speak love to the world. The world may not easily understand that its essential need is for forgiveness, but it can often understand practical acts of compassion that are grounded in the gospel.

The instructions in this text have to do with that love language of practical compassion. When the church sees a need, it must express the love of God in ways that meet that need.

But because the world remains sinful, that task is never easy. People who are the objects of compassion can make a sham of the church's love. Leaders who are infected with sin can use their position to serve themselves. To be effective, the church must reckon with those grim realities. Today's text gives instruction on those matters as well.

B. Lesson Background

Today's text continues Paul's instruction to his young associate Timothy, who worked with the church in the great city of Ephesus. The background is the same as that of the first three lessons in this series, so that need not be repeated here.

But today's text requires us to grapple with certain challenges that Timothy faced that have not yet been addressed in this series. One such challenge was that of economic disparity. Like any city, Ephesus had people who were rich and poor, powerful and vulnerable. Among the most vulnerable were widows, a major subject of today's lesson. Men held the rights to most property, and women had few opportunities to support themselves. Consequently, women who lost their husbands could find themselves destitute.

Leadership is a great challenge in such settings (compare Acts 6:1). Leaders have difficult, time-consuming work. Sadly, leaders can also exploit their power for selfish ends. The text also deals with these issues, so that the church's compassionate witness can remain pure and clear.

I. How to Treat Fellow Believers
(1 Timothy 5:1-8)
A. Men and Women (vv. 1, 2)

1. Rebuke not an elder, but intreat him as a father; and the younger men as brethren.

The term *elder* can take two distinct senses: "older man" and "church leader." Here it clearly has the first meaning, as it contrasts with "younger men" in the second part of the verse, as well as older and younger women in verse 2 (below).

The term *rebuke* suggests the image of striking or punishing with words. The young leader should not try to overcome his youth with unrestrained aggression. To do so is inconsistent with the good news: God has not treated sinners in that way.

Instead of a harsh verbal attack, Paul instructs Timothy to *intreat him as a father,* which indicates positive, loving encouragement. Just as a respectful son will not attack his father, so should the young leader treat older men, even when they need guidance. Leviticus 19:32 reveals that the need for such respect is not a new thing.

Likewise, *younger men* should also be encouraged as family members, like brothers. Even with those who are his age or younger, Timothy should not lead aggressively, but compassionately.

❧ *That Troubling Younger Generation* ❧

"I see no hope for the future of our people if they are dependent on the frivolous youth of today, for certainly all youth are reckless beyond words. When I was a boy, we were taught to be discreet and respectful of elders, but the present youth are exceedingly [disrespectful] and impatient of restraint." This quote is attributed to the Greek poet Hesiod, who lived about 700 BC. Some of us may be thinking, "Hesiod hadn't seen anything!"

Each generation tends to dismiss its own youthful foibles as harmless "kid stuff" and to see in the current younger generation the evidence of civilization's downfall. What seems especially to rankle "oldsters" is behavior that is disrespectful toward age.

Respect is a two-way street. The young Timothy (1 Timothy 4:12) is to show respect to those both older and younger than he. In so doing, he will set an example for those two age-groups to do the same with each other. So can we. —C. R. B.

2. The elder women as mothers; the younger as sisters, with all purity.

The instruction continues with corresponding advice about older and younger women. Here Paul adds the additional phrase *with all purity.* Male church leaders operate in dangerous territory in their relationships with women in the church. The power of leadership can be used by unscrupulous leaders to take sexual advantage of women easily. This truth has been demonstrated far too often in many sad cases. Timothy's actions toward women, younger and older, must reflect pure motives. Leaders must be careful to live blamelessly, giving no just cause for criticism (1 Timothy 3:2).

> **What Do You Think?**
> How do you treat members of your Christian family with purity?
> *Talking Points for Your Discussion*
> - In your thoughts about them
> - In your actions toward them
> - In your conversation with them
> - In your conversations about them

B. Widows (vv. 3-6)

3. Honour widows that are widows indeed.

To be *widows indeed* means to have genuine needs that cannot be met through family, as the following verses will show. To give support to such needy folk is part of the church's expression of God's love, so Paul endorses it with a firm command here (compare Acts 6:1-6).

4. But if any widow have children or nephews, let them learn first to show piety at home, and to requite their parents: for that is good and acceptable before God.

When a widow has family members, they are to provide her care, as is the custom in the culture of the time. The word *nephews* in the *King James Version* translates a term that means "descendants," here indicating grandchildren.

For family members to care for a widow is to *show piety,* or genuine godliness. This is not just a social convention. Honoring the God of the gospel means expressing generous compassion in practical ways. Thus, caring for a needy widow is acceptable to God because it is an action modeled on God's loving actions toward us.

God is not the only one honored by such actions. So are the parents and grandparents who are cared for. *To requite* them literally means "to pay them back." Of course, nothing can fully pay back a parent, any more than a follower of Christ can pay back God for His grace. But by caring for the needy widow, the children and grandchildren honor parents and grandparents by imitating God's generosity.

> **What Do You Think?**
> How can Christians resist cultural and social pressures to shift elder-care responsibilities entirely to the government?
> *Talking Points for Your Discussion*
> - Living in a "long-distance culture"
> - A "me first" spirit

5. Now she that is a widow indeed, and desolate, trusteth in God, and continueth in supplications and prayers night and day.

Paul's description of the true widow focuses on what her economic state can mean for her spiritual condition. People of faith who are in physical need come to a vivid realization: they have nowhere to turn but to God alone.

This verse specifies the widow who is *desolate,* that is, one who is without family to support her. Such a person turns to God in trust. That trust is

expressed in constant *supplications and prayers* in asking God for help.

This instruction makes sense when we realize that the church's support of widows is not just of a material nature, but of spiritual benefit as well. By supporting the needy widow, the church becomes the means by which God answers the widow's prayers. Her trust in God is vindicated by the church's actions. By contrast, for the church to support a widow who has other means of support is not so much an answer to prayer as it is a means of enabling her selfishness or that of her relatives.

> **What Do You Think?**
> How might God use you to answer the prayers of one who is "a widow indeed"?
> *Talking Points for Your Discussion*
> - In meeting physical needs
> - In meeting financial needs
> - In meeting emotional needs
> - In meeting spiritual needs

6. But she that liveth in pleasure is dead while she liveth.

In contrast with the prayerful, needy widow of verses 3-5 is one who lives *in pleasure,* which refers to luxury. Paul has warned already about the dangers of wealth (1 Timothy 2:9), and he will do so again (6:6-10). A luxurious, wealthy lifestyle encourages us to the false notion that we have everything that we need.

Such a life, Paul says, is no life at all. It does not reflect what God gives His people through Christ's resurrection, a life that comes through His free gift. For the church to extend support to a widow who has the means to live luxuriously is to undermine her relationship with God, subsidizing death instead of life.

C. Family (vv. 7, 8)

7. And these things give in charge, that they may be blameless.

Timothy is to make Paul's instructions *(these things)* clear to everyone. In regard to widows' support, everyone must understand what the church does (and does not do) and why. The reason is that all *may be blameless,* above common criticism. Paul's

Compassionate Service

concern is not merely that money is not wasted. Rather, the support of widows must encourage growth in godliness for them and their families.

This is practical compassion. It begins by meeting obvious material needs. It aims not just at providing those necessities, however, but also in leading people to know the true God better and follow His Son more closely.

8. But if any provide not for his own, and specially for those of his own house, he hath denied the faith, and is worse than an infidel.

Paul again stresses the responsibility of relatives to care for family members. By a noble custom of the time, observed even by pagans, families care for widowed relatives. A Christian who refuses this duty, thinking that the church will pick up the slack, thus acts worse than even *an infidel*. To ignore needs in one's own family is to deny the Christian faith, which is grounded on the generous love and grace of God.

This verse helps us understand the boundaries of the practical instruction both in this section and in verses 9-16, which continue the discussion about widows. Paul is criticizing believers who refuse to care for widowed relatives. Because women in Paul's time are expected to adhere to the religion of their husbands and families, the church probably knows some Christian widows who have been shunned by their pagan families for becoming Christian. Such widows are truly "alone" in the sense that Paul describes in verse 5, and so become fitting recipients of church support.

In the verses that follow that are not in today's text, Paul gives more specific instructions about caring for widows. The specifics are related to the situation of the Ephesian church. But all reflect a concern to encourage widows and their families

HOW TO SAY IT

Corinthians	Ko-*rin*-thee-unz (*th* as in *thin*).
Ephesian	Ee-*fee*-zhun.
Ephesus	*Ef*-uh-sus.
Hesiod	Hee-*see*-ud.
infidel	in-fuh-dell.
Leviticus	Leh-*vit*-ih-kus.
Philippians	Fih-*lip*-ee-unz.

Compassion & Respect for ALL.

Visual for Lesson 4. *Start a discussion by turning this statement into a question: "How can we show compassion and respect for _____?*

toward faithful, godly behavior, as well as providing for physical needs. Jesus had harsh words for those who used clever logic to avoid supporting their parents (Mark 7:9-13).

II. How to Treat Church Leaders
(1 TIMOTHY 5:17-20)
A. Elders' Reward (vv. 17, 18)

17. Let the elders that rule well be counted worthy of double honour, especially they who labour in the word and doctrine.

After his discussion of widows' support, Paul's attention turns to the issue of church leaders. Unlike the elders of verse 1, *the elders* here are church leaders, as the description of their ministry indicates. The honor to which Paul refers is tangible monetary support, as in verse 3, above. So Paul's point is that the church should provide monetary support for effective elders. The phrase *double honour* suggests generous support. Most particularly, that support should be directed to those who teach God's Word, the foundational function of church leadership.

The church's monetary support of its leaders is a controversial matter in Paul's time, just as it is now. Dishonest religious teachers are everywhere in Paul's world. People offering religious teaching are infamous for seeking out wealthy patrons who will enable them to live luxuriously, only to leave town quickly when others became suspicious.

Paul himself therefore refused to receive payment from the churches where he ministered, wanting to demonstrate the graciousness of the gospel by his own generosity. But as Paul refused that support, he affirmed that he and others had a right to expect it (1 Corinthians 9:1-15).

Yet Paul willingly received monetary gifts from Christians who wanted to support his ministry (Philippians 4:10-19). The purpose of that support was not so much to pay Paul back for his work, but to free him to preach and teach the gospel full time, without his having to give time and effort to making a living at tentmaking (Acts 18:1-3).

That perspective helps us understand these instructions. The church does not pay its leaders merely to compensate them for their work. But by providing generous support, we free the church leader to be devoted entirely to ministry.

> **What Do You Think?**
> What factors need to be addressed in considering financial support for church leaders?
> *Talking Points for Your Discussion*
> - In the economy in general
> - In the church in particular
> - Regarding standards of living
> - In avoiding the appearance of evil

18a. For the scripture saith, thou shalt not muzzle the ox that treadeth out the corn.

As he does in 1 Corinthians 9:9, which is also a discussion of support for church leaders, Paul quotes from Deuteronomy 25:4 to demonstrate his point. The command there is to Israel's farmers: when their oxen are tied to the threshing floor and walk around on the grain to separate the kernels from the stalks and hulls, the oxen are to be free to eat whatever they want. Paul's point is that if God cares that the hard-working oxen be fed, surely He cares more that the hard-working church leader be fed!

18b. And, The labourer is worthy of his reward.

Paul does not leave the matter just with the comparison with oxen. His argument matches Jesus' instructions to His disciples (see Matthew

10:10; Luke 10:7). Jesus' point is that God will care for the disciples through the gifts received from those to whom they preach. So for the Ephesian church leaders, God's care comes through the church's generosity with those who share God's Word.

B. Elders' Correction (vv. 19, 20)

19. Against an elder receive not an accusation, but before two or three witnesses.

Even church leaders can act corruptly. Their power may seem small, but sinful humans can use even a little power for selfish ends. Paul therefore reminds Timothy that church leaders may be accused of wrongdoing.

Of course, the accusation itself may be dishonestly self-seeking or simply mistaken. Paul applies the standard found in the law of Israel: multiple witnesses are needed to confirm the truth of an accusation (Deuteronomy 17:6; 19:15). That implies not just a minimum number of witnesses, but a credible case confirmed by investigation (compare 2 Corinthians 13:1).

20. Them that sin rebuke before all, that others also may fear.

The chapter began with the instruction not to give a harsh rebuke to an older man (v. 1). Now Paul points to an exception: the church leader who sins. Paul's expression indicates habitual sin. The rebuke that Paul commands is the end of the process that Jesus lays out in Matthew 18:15-17.

The point of the rebuke is twofold. One, of course, is to provoke the sinner to repent. The other Paul indicates in this verse: to warn others of the consequences of sin. Notorious sin among the church's leaders is destructive. But the outcome can be redemptive when the church handles the sin with practical compassion.

III. What Outlook to Have
(1 TIMOTHY 5:21, 22)
A. No Favoritism (v. 21)

21. I charge thee before God, and the Lord Jesus Christ, and the elect angels, that thou observe these things without preferring one before another, doing nothing by partiality.

Compassionate Service

Timothy must exercise his own leadership authority with purity. Paul emphasizes this command by reminding Timothy that God, Christ, and God's angels are witnesses. As an accusation against an elder should have multiple witnesses, so Timothy is reminded that this command comes with multiple witnesses. The specific command is to show no favoritism or prejudice. If God's love is for all people without partiality, then the church's leaders are to act consistently with that impartial love (compare Acts 10:34, 35).

> **What Do You Think?**
> What are some steps you can take to keep from showing favoritism?
> *Talking Points for Your Discussion*
> - Mark 9:35
> - Philippians 2:3, 4
> - James 2:1-4

❧ WAS IT FAVORITISM BACKFIRING? ❧

Robert H. Schuller began his ministry in Southern California in 1955. Today, most are familiar with the magnificent Crystal Cathedral, which is the primary fixture of Schuller's church and broadcast ministry. Schuller handed over the reigns of ministry to his son, Robert A. Schuller, in 2006. Some were concerned at the time that this was favoritism. But in any case, it all came undone less than three years later when the father fired the son over differences in vision regarding the ministry.

Similar problems have erupted in other ministries when the son of the founder-father became the chosen successor. For example, Richard Roberts, son of Oral Roberts, resigned in 2007 as president and CEO of Oral Roberts University under a cloud of ethical and legal questions.

Paul's advice to Timothy to demonstrate impartiality is sound counsel! What guardrails are in place at your church to prevent favoritism from rearing its ugly head?   —C. R. B.

B. No Haste (v. 22a)

22a. Lay hands suddenly on no man.

The laying on of hands is a posture of prayer, as we discussed in the lesson involving 1 Timothy 4:14. The warning is to avoid designating individuals as leaders too quickly, without careful evaluation. Those given the trust of leadership must have demonstrated the character to lead in a godly manner. Practical compassion demands that prospective leaders be carefully evaluated, both for the sake of the leadership candidate and those led.

C. No Impurity (v. 22b)

22b. Neither be partaker of other men's sins: keep thyself pure.

But Timothy should be just as careful for himself. He should mind the company he keeps, not sharing in the evil in others' lives. He must remain pure. This charge applies not just to his relationships with members of the opposite sex (v. 2, above), but to right motives and actions in all respects.

Conclusion
A. The Language of God's Love

How can the church demonstrate the love of God to a sinful, loveless world? The answer in our text is clear enough: church members demonstrate God's love in the way they interact. Church members are to be known for their love and respect for each other, not by the petty arguments and jealousies that seem all too common.

The church demonstrates God's love with practical generosity for those in need. Our concern is not just the physical need, but also growth in faith and godliness. Just as the first-century church cared for needy widows, we can work together to care for those who are vulnerable.

To accomplish this ministry of practical compassion requires that the church have dedicated leaders whose lives reflect God's love with growing purity. They know the language that speaks God's love to the world that needs to hear it.

B. Prayer

O God, the challenges and needs of our world are great. Make us, Your church, the instruments of Your love for the world. In Jesus' name, amen.

C. Thought to Remember

Pure religion includes compassion (James 1:27).

INVOLVEMENT LEARNING

Some of the activities below are also found in the helpful student book, Adult Bible Class.
Don't forget to download the free reproducible page from www.standardlesson.com to enhance your lesson!

Into the Lesson

Recruit one male and one female learner to voice the following comments. They will do so as they walk back and forth in front of your class, as if they were simply strolling down the street and crossing paths with other people. Ask the actors to use facial and hand gestures appropriately and dramatically. Feel free to adjust these comments to fit the nature of your class.

1. "Hey, old geezer, you're too slow to be walking, let alone driving!" 2. "Look at that old grandma's outfit, straight from the 1970s." 3. "You there, kid, you're as ugly as a mashed toad!" 4. "Hey, you pretty young thing, I could teach you a few things about love!" 5. "Don't you think we're paying our preacher too much?" 6. "Since that lady's husband died, she's gone around looking dowdier by the month." 7. "Did you hear what I heard about Jim Smith, who pretends to be an elder at our church?" 8. "Oh, those Davises, don't they live over in that old run-down part of town in one of those old run-down houses?" 9. "I know Joe Johnson is new to the church. But I think he'd make an ideal teacher for our high school class. He's handsome, athletic, and a good talker."

When your actors complete the comments, ask, "Do you ever hear such remarks? Today's text of Paul's instructions to Timothy reminds us that such ungodly approaches to human relationships are nothing new. Let's take a look."

Into the Word

Give each learner a copy of the following list. Say, "I want you to write a name by each entry on this list, the name of someone in our congregation; do not repeat a name, but you may skip entries if you need to." 1. older man; 2. younger man; 3. older woman; 4. younger woman; 5. a widow with no family nearby; 6. a widow with relatives close by; 7. someone who provides well for his or her family; 8. an elder you respect for ser-

vice to your church; 9. someone who serves your church and should be paid (or paid more) for that service; 10. someone who best exemplifies impartiality in life and behavior.

Allow a few minutes for learners to complete their lists. Then ask individuals to read aloud these verses and verse segments from 1 Timothy 5: verse 1a; verse 1b; verse 2a; verse 2b; verses 3 and 5; verse 4; verse 8; verse 17; verse 18; verse 21. After each is read, say, "Now beside the name you have written for _____ [fill in "older man," etc., from the list], make a note as to Paul's directive for Christian relationship."

Alternative: Download the reproducible page and use the Righteous Relationships activity instead of the above (this can be an Into Life exercise if you prefer).

Going through the list with your class will allow for commentary, explanation, and group discussion. Wrap up by saying, "If you were going to summarize or characterize in one word all of the relationship principles Paul gives, what would that one word be?" Let learners suggest freely. Expect responses such as *respect, love, compassion,* and *grace.* Ask how these summaries relate to the Golden Rule (Luke 6:31) and to Jesus' response to the question regarding the greatest commandment (Matthew 22:37-39).

Into Life

Discuss a possible project of group assistance to someone on the learners' lists. This can include, for example, a service project of home maintenance for a widow in need or a one-time "thank you" gift to a person who volunteers more than most do. Suggest that each learner make a personal list later with an intent to honor or support one person fitting each category in today's text.

Download the reproducible page and distribute copies of the Purity Possibility activity as take-home work as your learners depart.

Compassionate Service

REMEMBER
JESUS CHRIST

BACKGROUND SCRIPTURE: **2 Timothy 2**
PRINTED TEXT: **2 Timothy 2:8-19**

2 TIMOTHY 2:8-19

8 Remember that Jesus Christ of the seed of David was raised from the dead according to my gospel:

9 Wherein I suffer trouble, as an evil doer, even unto bonds; but the word of God is not bound.

10 Therefore I endure all things for the elect's sakes, that they may also obtain the salvation which is in Christ Jesus with eternal glory.

11 It is a faithful saying: For if we be dead with him, we shall also live with him:

12 If we suffer, we shall also reign with him: if we deny him, he also will deny us:

13 If we believe not, yet he abideth faithful: he cannot deny himself.

14 Of these things put them in remembrance, charging them before the Lord that they strive not about words to no profit, but to the subverting of the hearers.

15 Study to shew thyself approved unto God, a workman that needeth not to be ashamed, rightly dividing the word of truth.

16 But shun profane and vain babblings: for they will increase unto more ungodliness.

17 And their word will eat as doth a canker: of whom is Hymenaeus and Philetus;

18 Who concerning the truth have erred, saying that the resurrection is past already; and overthrow the faith of some.

19 Nevertheless the foundation of God standeth sure, having this seal, The Lord knoweth them that are his. And, let every one that nameth the name of Christ depart from iniquity.

KEY VERSE

Study to shew thyself approved unto God, a workman that needeth not to be ashamed, rightly dividing the word of truth. —**2 Timothy 2:15**

WE WORSHIP GOD

Unit 2: Reasons for Praise
LESSONS 5–9

LESSON AIMS

After participating in this lesson, each student will be able to:

1. List what Paul tells Timothy to remember and to remind others of.

2. Compare and contrast contemporary false teachings with the ungodly teaching about which Paul warned Timothy.

3. Make a list of some important passages of Scripture and commit them to memory.

LESSON OUTLINE

Introduction

A. Hymns, Ancient and Modern

The great reformer Martin Luther (1483–1546) revolutionized how music was used in church worship. Before Luther, the medieval mass was sung by the choir in the chancel (the raised part of the sanctuary). The people standing in the nave (the lower part of the sanctuary) were not active participants. The service was done in Latin, and the congregants could not understand most of this ceremony. They were expected to be mute spectators.

Luther rewrote the procedures to allow for active participation of the congregation through the singing of liturgy and hymns. He believed that the highest purpose of music was to be used as a form of worship. In the preface to his hymnal of 1524, Luther wrote, "I would like to see all the arts, especially music, used in the service of him who gave and made them."

J. S. Bach (1685–1750) later brought Luther's ideals to glorious fruition. Although Bach is now celebrated for compositions such as his *Brandenburg Concertos,* he was first and foremost a church musician. He believed both in using music as a vehicle to worship God and in the inclusion of the gathered believers in this musical praise.

Luther, Bach, and many others have contributed to the glorious musical heritage of the church. For this we should be grateful. This heritage traces its origins to the Bible itself, for Scripture has always been the primary source for the music of God's people. Today's lesson includes an early Christian hymn. Studying it lets us see how the doctrine of the church was incorporated into its music, something still being done today.

B. Lesson Background

The New Testament offers us two letters to Timothy, a beloved protégé of Paul. Our previous four lessons are drawn from 1 Timothy. The Lesson Background noted in those four studies applies here, and thus need not be repeated. However, the lesson at hand moves us to 2 Timothy. This takes us forward in time about two years; thus there is a bit of additional background to consider.

Remember Jesus Christ

Second Timothy probably is Paul's final letter. The great apostle wrote from Rome, where he had been imprisoned for preaching the gospel (2 Timothy 2:8, 9, part of today's text). He did not expect to be released, but had prepared himself for death (4:6). Timothy was in Ephesus (4:12), ministering to a church that was very dear to Paul's heart. Paul wanted very much for Timothy to come to Rome so that he might see him one last time (4:21).

We do not know whether Timothy made it in time, and Paul was unsure that this would happen when he wrote the letter. It is not surprising, therefore, to find that the letter is a mix of encouragement and doctrinal reminders.

There is a certain poignancy in this letter that is equal to, if not greater than, that of any other book of the Bible. Paul expected death, but he had no regrets. He remembered those things that were most precious to him: his Lord, his messages, and his friends. History tells us that Paul was martyred during the latter days of Nero's reign, probably in AD 67. This letter may have been written just a few days before Paul's death.

I. Remember the Core Message
(2 TIMOTHY 2:8-13)
A. Resurrection (v. 8)

8. Remember that Jesus Christ of the seed of David was raised from the dead according to my gospel.

Although Paul has been ministering with Gentiles for some 30 years, he still remembers the Jewish heritage he shares with Timothy (Acts 16:3). Their Lord is not just referred to as *Jesus Christ*, but also as *the seed of David*, the great king of Israel's history (see Romans 1:3). To be in the lineage of David is a requirement for Jesus to be the Jewish Messiah (Christ), the anointed one of God. Paul never separates Jesus' messiahship from His Jewishness, and neither should we. At times, the Bible sees the phrase *seed of David* as emblematic for the entire nation of Israel at its best (see Jeremiah 33:22).

The next detail that Paul mentions, that Jesus *was raised from the dead*, is also vital. This claim can be made for no other king, including David

himself (see Acts 2:29). Paul is clear and emphatic: the resurrection is the core, the foundation, the essential nonnegotiable of his gospel (compare 1 Corinthians 15).

B. Suffering (vv. 9, 10)

9. Wherein I suffer trouble, as an evil doer, even unto bonds; but the word of God is not bound.

It is difficult for us to know or even imagine what Paul experiences while imprisoned in Rome *(unto bonds)*. We often see artistic representations of this that show him in a clean, airy house, chained to a nice big table, with an attentive and respectful Roman soldier guarding him. These pictures may feature Luke nearby, ready to attend to Paul's needs.

This may have been the case for the first Roman imprisonment (Acts 28:16, 30). While writing 2 Timothy, however, the more likely scenario is that Paul is in a dungeon-like prison cell—dark, damp, cold, and vermin-ridden. There probably is no table or chair, and Paul may be chained to a wall. Visitors may be permitted, but most of his time probably is spent alone.

It is likely that the letter of 2 Timothy is not written down by the apostle himself, but is given orally to Luke (see 2 Timothy 4:11), who writes it out and sends it to Timothy. For Paul to say that he is suffering as an evildoer deserves to suffer does not mean that he actually is a criminal. Rather, the idea is that there is nothing in his treatment to differentiate him from the murderers, thieves, and other criminals in his jail.

Paul contrasts this confinement with the power of the gospel. For him, *the word of God is not bound*. This is one of the most inspiring phrases

HOW TO SAY IT

Gentiles	*Jen*-tiles.
Hymenaeus	Hi-meh-*nee*-us.
medieval	muh-*dee*-vul.
Messiah	Meh-*sigh*-uh.
Philetus	Fuh-*lee*-tus.
protégé	*pro*-tuh-zhay.
Titus	*Ty*-tus.

to be found in any of Paul's letters. Although Paul may be restrained physically, his message cannot be. This is not because Paul personally empowers his words, but because he preaches the Word of God. God's Word embodies a spiritual power that no human can crush (see 1 Thessalonians 1:5).

The theme of Paul's ministry is the power of the gospel to save and change lives (Romans 1:16; 1 Corinthians 1:17, 18). The prison sufferings are hard on this old man, but they do nothing to dampen his confidence in the power of the Christian message: Jesus has died for our sins and has been raised from the dead by the Father.

10. Therefore I endure all things for the elect's sakes, that they may also obtain the salvation which is in Christ Jesus with eternal glory.

Paul's passion for souls is on full display. This is the man who is willing to be cursed if his fellow Israelites can be saved (Romans 9:3). If Paul's hardships result in salvation for others, then he is a willing sufferer. His outlook takes the long view: enduring hardship in this life will be rewarded by spending eternity with Christ Jesus in eternal glory (compare Colossians 1:24-29).

Those who have been saved are referred to as *the elect* in the New Testament (example: Titus 1:1). To become one of the elect involves being called, being chosen, and being faithful (Revelation 17:14). Jesus draws everyone to himself (John 12:32), although this drawing can be resisted (Acts 7:51). We are chosen to inherit eternal life as a result of our faithful, free-will response to the call of the gospel. As Paul sits in a prison, he is sustained and uplifted by memories of those many persons who have found salvation because of his evangelizing efforts.

What Do You Think?

In what ways are Christians suffering today so that others might be saved? How is that suffering similar to and different from Paul's suffering?

Talking Points for Your Discussion

- Financial sacrifices
- Physical restrictions
- Emotional abuse

C. Saying (vv. 11-13)

11a. It is a faithful saying.

By introducing the next part of his letter as *a faithful saying,* Paul means more than "this is something I want you to remember." It is more like, "recall this saying, a word we have shared many times." What follows are likely the words from an early hymn, a worship tradition of the church written by Paul or someone else. The tight, logical construction of the saying that follows is a powerful way to express the faith of the faithful.

The early church made use of hymns found in the Old Testament, particularly the Psalms (see Ephesians 5:19; Colossians 3:16). But these are limited in their expression of the full message of the gospel: the divinity of Christ, the power of His resurrection, the forgiveness of sins. For these ideas, the first-century church needs new expressions of the faith. Paul's example here of a faithful saying is one that has established itself by widespread and frequent usage in the congregations.

11b, 12a. For if we be dead with him, we shall also live with him: if we suffer, we shall also reign with him.

The faithful saying Paul quotes in verses 11b-13 has four *if/then* statements. (Although the word *then* is not explicitly included, the concept is there nonetheless.) Each gives a possible condition and follows it by giving the results of that condition.

The first two statements, here in verses 11b, 12a, reflect the authentic nature of Christianity. They both set forth aspects of the faith that are sacrificial in practice. We are called to die to self (compare Romans 6:3; Galatians 2:20) and to suffer for Christ (see 2 Timothy 1:8).

What Do You Think?

In what specific ways do you still need to "die to self"? What prevents you from yielding in these areas?

Talking Points for Your Discussion

- Areas of thought
- Areas of habit
- Priorities in spending time

The promises that accompany these hardships more than make up for our sacrifices, however.

Remember Jesus Christ

We are assured that our dying to self will be followed by living with Christ (see Romans 6:4), and that our suffering will result in reigning with Christ in glory. If we remember that the church of Paul's day experiences a high degree of persecution and suffering, we realize that these promises must be of great comfort.

12b, 13a. If we deny him, he also will deny us: if we believe not, yet he abideth faithful.

The next two *if/then* statements describe false faith, inauthentic Christianity. They picture the possibility of the twin dangers of denying Christ and not believing in Him. We are told that these will result in the offender's being denied by Christ himself (compare Matthew 10:32, 33).

13b. He cannot deny himself.

The hymn bases the conclusion of verses 12b, 13a on the faithfulness of Christ himself, for He is the one who *cannot deny himself*. His promises are always sure, whether they be positive or negative in their outcome.

We can imagine that the first four statements follow the same musical pattern. The tag line at the end, *he cannot deny himself*, then might follow a different musical pattern to wrap things up.

II. Remember the Central Ministry
(2 TIMOTHY 2:14-19)

A. Persistent Reminding (v. 14)

14. Of these things put them in remembrance, charging them before the Lord that they strive not about words to no profit, but to the subverting of the hearers.

Paul's themes of the centrality of the resurrection and the faithfulness of Christ are to be held up to Timothy's congregation on a repeated basis. Once is never enough for the gospel, for we need to hear it over and over.

In bringing the focus back to the gospel, Paul broaches another topic: verbal battles taking place within the congregation. There is nothing to be gained in hearing constant arguments about things that don't really matter. Not only is it a pointless waste of time, it also has the negative effect of subverting the hearers. Experience shows

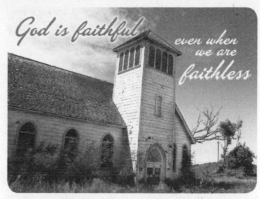

Visual for Lesson 5. *Start a discussion by pointing to this visual as you ask, "What is your reaction when you see a shuttered church building?"*

that church fights are rarely about important doctrines, although that does happen sometimes (compare 1 Timothy 6:3-5). More often, church members squabble because of personality conflicts and a vying for control. To this, Timothy must say, "Stop! You are tearing our church apart!"

> *What Do You Think?*
> What can be done to prevent the negative consequences of quarreling in the church?
> *Talking Points for Your Discussion*
> - How we pray
> - How we confront privately
> - How we confront publicly
> - Our job vs. the Holy Spirit's job

B. Studious Working (v. 15)

15. Study to shew thyself approved unto God, a workman that needeth not to be ashamed, rightly dividing the word of truth.

If the bickering is about doctrine, the first step to ending it is to have a minister who is well-grounded in the Scriptures personally. This kind of person can pilot the congregation's ship through threatening doctrinal reefs. This person will be recognized as *rightly dividing the word of truth* (compare 2 Timothy 3:16). The verb *study* implies "diligence." The word of truth is quite deep at points. Patient diligence is required to plumb those depths.

We saw in two lessons previously Paul's stress to Timothy that Timothy's youth need not be an obstacle to his authority as long as he proves that he is reliable and lives a life that is above reproach (1 Timothy 4:12). Even as a young minister, Timothy should be capable of putting an end to unprofitable quarrelling (4:6).

❧ WHEN INTUITION OVERRIDES FACT ❧

Several years ago, a television reporter was present at the outdoor graduation ceremonies of one of the Ivy League universities. The day was hot, and the faculty and graduates were sweltering as they stood in the sun in their academic gowns. The reporter asked several people—students and faculty—why they thought the weather is hotter in summer than in winter.

Several answered that it is because the earth is closer to the sun in summer. Of course, that is not correct. The truth, rather, is that it is the tilt of the earth's axis that accounts for heat and cold of the seasons. The humor is found in the fact that those giving the wrong answer were all associated with a prestigious institution of higher education—they should have known the answer!

Sometimes we speak of things being true when our intuition tells us to do so. We end up looking foolish when our intuition is proved wrong. No one is immune from this danger. Even the smartest people can come up with intuitive—but incorrect—answers to questions about what the Bible teaches. That is why diligence in study is called for. Only through diligent study will we be able to handle the word of truth correctly. —C. R. B.

C. Dangerous Teaching (vv. 16-18)

16, 17a. But shun profane and vain babblings: for they will increase unto more ungodliness. And their word will eat as doth a canker.

Paul uses strong language to condemn the unprofitable speech. To be *profane* means to dishonor God. The idea of *vain babblings* is "empty talk." Some folks ramble on and on about things they shouldn't (1 Timothy 4:7; Titus 3:9). Such speech can be disastrous in its effects. It leads to deeper ungodliness by trivializing important aspects of the church's teaching. This happens as less important things—even downright wrong things—are allowed to take priority.

Such babblings will *eat as . . . a canker,* a most unpleasant image. The reference here is not to something like a canker sore, in terms of the small lesions that people get on the lips or gums. Rather, the image is that of gangrene. This is the condition of flesh rotting away on a living person. Gangrene is malodorous and hideous. It is deadly if not stopped.

17b, 18. Of whom is Hymenaeus and Philetus; who concerning the truth have erred, saying that the resurrection is past already; and overthrow the faith of some.

Paul moves beyond generalities to give Timothy two concrete examples of the dangers of the problem being described: *Hymenaeus and Philetus.* These are two apostate teachers of Paul's day, who may have been associates of Paul and Timothy at one time (see 1 Timothy 1:20). Their error is summarized as *saying that the resurrection is past already,* with the result that some hearers are despondent and have lost their faith.

We can only imagine why these two have come up with such a distortion of the faith. This is not a denial of Christ's own resurrection. Rather, it is a claim that the general resurrection of the believing dead is past, and it has been missed. We can speculate that Hymenaeus and Philetus may be like teachers of the modern era who set dates for the return of Christ. When those dates come and go with no apparent change, there is often an attempt to spiritualize the events, saying that things happened "invisibly" or "secretly." To deny the future resurrection by saying it is past is to knock out one of the pillars of the faith. This cannot be allowed to pass without challenge.

❧ No Laughing Matter ❧

Setting dates for the return of Christ and the resurrection of the dead has a long history. When the predictions prove false, the false prophets come up with "explanations," often to start over again with a new prediction. Ironically, some folks in Paul's day were saying that the resurrection of the dead had *already* occurred.

We may be tempted merely to laugh off such declarations as the work of crackpots. But Paul notices that some Christians had lost their faith as a result of the doctrinal error that Hymenaeus and Philetus had put forth. That's no laughing matter.

There is plenty of doctrinal error "out there." We may not be able to do much about it, and often it is not wise to try. Far more important is the doctrinal error that is "in here"—inside our own church. Such error must be dealt with, not laughed off. Eternal destinies are at stake.   —C. R. B.

D. Foundation Standing (v. 19)

19. Nevertheless the foundation of God standeth sure, having this seal, The Lord knoweth them that are his. And, let every one that nameth the name of Christ depart from iniquity.

The final exhortation is the most valuable of all. We can and should strive for unity and doctrinal purity, but human efforts alone will always fall short of the goal. We must remember that in the end it is God himself who guards His church. Paul gives a vivid word picture for this: a foundational cornerstone with a seal inscribed on it.

The seal has two lines of words. First, *the Lord knoweth them that are his* (compare John 10:14; 1 Corinthians 8:3). Second, *let every one that nameth the name of Christ depart from iniquity*

(compare Proverbs 16:6). God knows whose heart is true, who has faith (Numbers 16:5). He does not need our help in keeping track of others. Our job is personal in forsaking sinful ways.

Like the "faithful saying" above, these two lines are probably tried and true sayings of the church. We rest secure in the knowledge that God knows us as His children. But we are called to action by this knowledge—the action of fleeing from the ungodliness that is foreign to a child of God.

Conclusion

A. Making Doctrine Memorable

We use many techniques to help us remember things. I used to put a rubber band around my wrist to help me remember that I needed to stop by the grocery store on my way home from work. For years, I used an electronic personal digital assistant (PDA) to beep when I had an upcoming appointment. I have had successes and failures with such techniques.

How do we remember the great, comforting doctrines of the faith? One way that is ancient yet still viable is to place core teachings in verse. Even more effective for some is to combine these verses with song. See if you can complete the following lines of well-known hymns: "For still our ancient foe, . . ." (a doctrinal reminder of Satan's purpose); "I once was lost but now . . ." (a doctrinal statement about the regenerative power of salvation); "And sinners plunged beneath the flood lose . . ." (an expression of the doctrine of the atonement).

See, you may have memorized more than you realize! Let us never grow tired of filling our minds and hearts with Scripture and the great truths of the Christian faith. They will be a resource of strength in time of need.

B. Prayer

Father, we are blessed by the mighty truths of the gospel. May we be faithful as we treasure these truths and pass them on to the next generation of believers. We pray in Jesus' name, amen.

C. Thought to Remember

The gospel is our sure foundation for living.

INVOLVEMENT LEARNING

Some of the activities below are also found in the helpful student book, Adult Bible Class.
Don't forget to download the free reproducible page from www.standardlesson.com to enhance your lesson!

Into The Lesson

Before class begins, draw a three-column chart on the board; column headings are *Song Line, Completed Song Line,* and *Doctrinal Teaching.* List under the first column the following lines from Christian songs: 1. But that thy blood . . . ; 2. For still our ancient foe . . . ; 3. Mercy, there was great, and . . . ; 4. From the water lifted me, now . . . ; 5. Jesus loves me, this I know; for . . . ; 6. The church's one foundation . . . ; 7. All is calm, all is bright. Round yon . . .

Ask learners to complete the lines and list the doctrines highlighted. (*Option:* Put the above on handouts for individual or small-group completion.) Feel free to substitute songs that are familiar to your class. The song completions and associated doctrines are 1. was shed for me [atonement]; 2. doth seek to work us woe [Satan's purpose]; 3. grace was free [grace]; 4. safe am I [assurance]; 5. the Bible tells me so [the centrality of Scripture]; 6. is Jesus Christ her Lord [the church]; 7. virgin, mother and child [the virgin birth].

Say, "Music and poetry are powerful tools for teaching. Such tools were used in Old Testament times. Paul uses these tools to teach core values and behavior for authentic Christian living."

Into the Word

Summarize the Lesson Background. Then distribute a handout titled "Tips for a Healthy Church." On it have two columns with the headings *Remember This* and *Do This.* Ask learners to work in pairs. The pairs will read verses 8-10 and 14-19 from today's text and list the appropriate actions under each heading. Inform your learners that they will consider the other verses a bit later.

After a few minutes, discuss conclusions. The *Remember This* column list should include "Jesus was raised from the dead"; "Jesus was the seed of David"; "God's Word is not restricted"; "God's foundation is unshakable"; and "God knows who are His." The list in the *Do This* column should include "endure challenges"; "be diligent for God's approval"; "don't be ashamed"; "use the word of truth properly"; "avoid worthless talk"; and "reject sinfulness."

Review the lists, asking why each item is important. Also, use the lesson commentary to explain the concepts in verse 19 regarding God's foundation and the Lord's knowledge of those who are His.

The lower part of the handout should have the following three-column activity. Title the activity "If/Then." The columns will be headed *If, Then,* and *Illustrate/Explain.* Using the lesson commentary, introduce verses 11-13 as "faithful sayings." Then ask learners to complete the columns quickly. As your learners work, write the first two columns on the board. After your learners finish, ask them to tell what they wrote in the *Illustrate/ Explain* column. You may need to use the lesson commentary to explain verse 13b.

Alternative: Download the reproducible page and use the Grasping the Core Message activity instead of the above.

Into Life

Ask the class to work in four teams to create a worship service on the theme *Living Authentic Christianity.* The service will be based on the "faithful sayings" of verses 11-13. Of course, the remaining verses of the printed text may also be used to develop the theme.

Give each team a marker and poster board to list plans for the service. Team 1 will select the music. Team 2 will develop a drama to help capture the interest in the theme. Team 3 will select appropriate Scripture readings (other than today's text) and develop a Communion theme. Team 4 will develop the sermon outline. Allow teams to report.

Alternative: Use the My Worship Song exercise from the reproducible page instead of the above.

Remember Jesus Christ

REMEMBER THE WARNINGS

BACKGROUND SCRIPTURE: Jude 17-25

PRINTED TEXT: Jude 17-25

JUDE 17-25

17 But, beloved, remember ye the words which were spoken before of the apostles of our Lord Jesus Christ;

18 How that they told you there should be mockers in the last time, who should walk after their own ungodly lusts.

19 These be they who separate themselves, sensual, having not the Spirit.

20 But ye, beloved, building up yourselves on your most holy faith, praying in the Holy Ghost,

21 Keep yourselves in the love of God, looking for the mercy of our Lord Jesus Christ unto eternal life.

22 And of some have compassion, making a difference:

23 And others save with fear, pulling them out of the fire; hating even the garment spotted by the flesh.

24 Now unto him that is able to keep you from falling, and to present you faultless before the presence of his glory with exceeding joy,

25 To the only wise God our Saviour, be glory and majesty, dominion and power, both now and ever. Amen.

KEY VERSES

Now unto him that is able to keep you from falling, and to present you faultless before the presence of his glory with exceeding joy, to the only wise God our Saviour, be glory and majesty, dominion and power, both now and ever. Amen. —**Jude 24, 25**

WE WORSHIP GOD

Unit 2: Reasons for Praise
LESSONS 5–9

LESSON AIMS

After participating in this lesson, each student will be able to:

1. Summarize what Jude says the apostles foretold.

2. Contrast the people whose coming the apostles foretold with the kind of people Jude urges his readers to be.

3. List three practical ways to show mercy to a doubter.

LESSON OUTLINE

Introduction

A. Preventing Falls

When my daughter was just learning to walk, I had her with me at my church one afternoon. We were out in the hall, and I was talking with a church member just before leaving for the day. I suddenly noticed that my little daughter had toddled down the hall, out of my sight. I knew that there was a flight of stairs around the corner. After I retrieved her, my friend said, "I have never seen you move so fast!" My reply: "That's my *daughter,* man!" I had saved her from a tumble, perhaps a deadly fall.

The last half of the book of Jude, our text for this week, is concerned with saving Christian brothers and sisters from a fall from their faith. How fast do we move in these cases? How much do we care? While we trust in God for our salvation, Jude issues a call that we can hear today: let us do all we can to save our beloved fellow believers from a disastrous fall. And let us trust God for our salvation, no matter what danger threatens us.

B. Lesson Background

Jude wrote his letter over 1,900 years ago to encourage his readers to put up a fight for the faith. Jude understood that this battle has very high stakes, since his readers faced a struggle for the future of authentic, apostolic Christianity.

Jude himself was a brother of James (Jude 1) and a half-brother of Jesus. Although Jesus' brothers were not believers during His lifetime (Mark 3:21; John 7:5), they became believers after His resurrection (Acts 15). The name *Jude* is the same as "Judas," "Juda," or "Judah"—the distinction being minor variations in spelling (see Matthew 13:55; Mark 6:3). When we see the name *Judas* in this context, we are not talking about Judas Iscariot, of course.

We know little else about Jude the man or his church. We don't know what kind of building Jude's church met in. We don't even know for sure where it was located (perhaps in Jerusalem). Jude's congregation may have met in a larger home that one of the members provided for Sunday worship gatherings. Possibly, it was a Jewish synagogue building that had been converted to a church.

Wherever it was that Jude's congregation met, we can be pretty sure that the facility was modest. No stained glass windows. No red carpet. No choir robes. No heated baptistery. No organ. No wood carvings. No bell tower.

The details of the meeting place have not been preserved for us, but the nature of Jude's church survives in his letter. His church understood that it was the people and the relationships that made up a worshiping community—the bride of Christ, the redeemed people of the Lord. Jude's congregation knew that the church was to be a refuge from the world, a place were members loved and accepted one another without pretence or regard to status. Their identity as Christians depended on these facts. But there was a threat.

> **What Do You Think?**
> Is our church known for providing refuge and loving acceptance? Why, or why not?
> *Talking Points for Your Discussion*
> - Refuge that leads to involvement
> - Loving acceptance that leads to growth
> - 1 Thessalonians 5:11, 14

I. Saving from False Ones
(Jude 17-19)
A. Warning Reminder (vv. 17, 18)

17. But, beloved, remember ye the words which were spoken before of the apostles of our Lord Jesus Christ.

HOW TO SAY IT

Amos	*Ay*-mus.
Corinthians	Ko-*rin*-thee-unz (*th* as in *thin*).
Galatians	Guh-*lay*-shunz.
Jerusalem	Juh-*roo*-suh-lem.
Judas Iscariot	*Joo*-dus Iss-*care*-ee-ut.
Philippians	Fih-*lip*-ee-unz.
synagogue	*sin*-uh-gog.
Thessalonians	*Thess*-uh-*lo*-nee-unz (*th* as in *thin*).
Zechariah	*Zek*-uh-*rye*-uh.

Jude begins to offer a cure for the problem he has been discussing up to this point. That problem is the presence of dangerous, unrepentant, false teachers who have come into the fellowship. These are pretenders, not contenders (Jude 3). Jude has already said that in the end this is God's issue, and we cannot completely solve the dilemma of charlatans in the church (Jude 14, 15). Yet this is no excuse for a lack of diligence. That diligence must include remembering *the words which were spoken before of the apostles of our Lord Jesus Christ* (compare 2 Peter 3:2).

18. How that they told you there should be mockers in the last time, who should walk after their own ungodly lusts.

Mocking involves ridicule. Mocking may include imitation of speech or mannerisms in a way designed to embarrass the one being mocked. It is an intentionally cruel, cynical act (compare Genesis 21:9).

One of the shameful details of Jesus' trials and crucifixion is the mocking He endured from the Roman soldiers (Matthew 27:29), from Herod (Luke 23:11), and from the Jewish leaders (Mark 15:31). The mockers of Jude's day are ridiculing the serious and faithful teachers of the church. This is shown by an immoral lifestyle, an indulgence in ungodly lusts.

While it might seem that these false teachers mock with impunity, we should remember Paul's promise that "God is not mocked" (Galatians 6:7). Mockers, scoffers, and ridiculers are a scourge of the church, and a sign of the last time, the final era of human history (compare 2 Peter 3:3).

> **What Do You Think?**
> In what ways is Jesus Christ being mocked today?
> *Talking Points for Your Discussion*
> - By believers who should know better
> - By unbelievers

B. Spiritual Charlatans (v. 19)

19. These be they who separate themselves, sensual, having not the Spirit.

The core problem with these false teachers is that they are not authentic Christians, for they do not have the presence of the Holy Spirit in their lives (see Romans 8:9). To be sensual means that satisfying various worldly appetites is their primary purpose in life. They are controlled by the human appetites for money, sex, power, fame, etc.

Jude also warns that the false nature of these charlatans may be seen in the divisions they cause within the church. The word translated *separate* referred originally to the drawing of boundary lines. It is used here to characterize those who want to be exclusive, not inclusive, in an ungodly way. They put unbiblical restrictions on fellowship by saying, "Follow my ideas or get out." They want to limit the ministry and fellowship of the church according to their own preferences, saying, "We don't want your kind of people in our church" (compare 3 John 9, 10).

Christ prayed that His disciples might "be one," revealing His desire that the church be united, not divided (John 17:21). When someone splits the church, this intended unity is sinfully destroyed. It makes sense, then, that such church-dividers are out of tune spiritually with God's will, living only to gratify their own agendas and desires.

II. Saving with Fear
(JUDE 20-23)
A. Building in Prayer (v. 20)

20. But ye, beloved, building up yourselves on your most holy faith, praying in the Holy Ghost.

Jude now turns his attention away from the false brothers to focus on those who are listening attentively to his message, the true believers. He urges them to continue building up their lives of faith (compare Colossians 2:7; 1 Thessalonians 5:11). This process of personal reformation has three aspects as presented by Jude in this verse and the next.

First, they are to continue *praying in the Holy Ghost*. The marvelous promise of Romans 8:26 is that we don't have to be perfect in prayer. The Holy Spirit, sent to us by our Savior and Lord, Jesus Christ, helps us pray as we ought. He is our advocate, our counselor, our comforter. But this happens only if we let Him.

Most of us don't pray in the Holy Spirit very well on a crowded bus or while we are in freeway traffic. It is hard to do so while we are watching TV. It takes time, time alone with God or with a prayer partner or two. Hint: prayer should involve not only talking to God, but also being still before God as we allow the Holy Spirit to convict, change, and comfort us (compare Psalms 37:7; 46:10; 131:2).

What Do You Think?
How can you do better at praying in the Holy Spirit?
Talking Points for Your Discussion
- Time
- Place
- Frequency
- Nature of your prayers

B. Looking for Mercy (v. 21)

21. Keep yourselves in the love of God, looking for the mercy of our Lord Jesus Christ unto eternal life.

The second aspect in the process of personal reformation is for Jude's readers to keep themselves *in the love of God*. They do this while *looking for the mercy of our Lord Jesus Christ*.

At first glance, these may seem to be curious expressions, but they are not hard to understand. The meaning is that we accept the love of God, and we love Him back. We never take the love of God for granted. We do not abuse it. We do not neglect it. George Matheson (1824–1906) wrote about it this way:

> O Love that wilt not let me go,
> I rest my weary soul in Thee;
> I give Thee back the life I owe,
> That in Thine ocean depths its flow—
> May richer, fuller be.

If we are to continue building our faith, we must keep ourselves immersed in the love of God.

Third, we are called to anticipate *eternal life*. This, of course, is the bottom line, our ultimate fallback position. No matter how bad life gets, we have an assurance of salvation through our Lord

Jesus Christ, and no one can take this away from us. As Paul proclaimed, nothing can separate us from the love of God (Romans 8:35-39). The false teachers can blather away selfishly. The false brothers can mock and ridicule attempts to be faithful and holy. But no one can take away God's gift of eternal life.

C. Pulling from Fire (vv. 22, 23)

22. And of some have compassion, making a difference.

Jude exhorts his congregation to love the indecisive ones back into fellowship. We have no way to compel anyone to attend our church. We cannot do it! Any church that exists by Christ's ideal is a voluntary organization.

People are drawn away from the church for many reasons. They may sit on the fence for many years, with occasional attendance or participation. How do we get them to return? How do we bring them back?

The most important thing is that they must feel loved. They must feel wanted and accepted. The church must be a place where they can join with other brothers and sisters who are struggling, just like us, day by day, to find the way to live in a manner pleasing to God.

23. And others save with fear, pulling them out of the fire; hating even the garment spotted by the flesh.

Those who are falling away can be restored. Thus Jude calls his readers to become spiritual firefighters, rescuing those who have broken fellowship. We are called to be *pulling them out of the fire,* saving their eternal lives. God himself is a spiritual firefighter (see Amos 4:11; Zechariah 3:2), and so must we be.

No Christian should be indifferent when a brother or sister drifts away from the church and abandons the faith. We cannot compel such a person to repent and return to the faith, of course. But our hearts must not be so cold and uncaring that we merely allow the backslider to go his or her own way (see Galatians 6:1, 2). We should not be complacent when people don *the garment spotted by the flesh* as they resume an immoral and ungodly lifestyle.

❧ HAVING THE RIGHT TRAINING ❧

Imagine that you are among the first to arrive at the scene of a plane crash. The wreckage is ablaze, and passengers are trapped inside. What would you do? It comes down to two things: your training and your equipment.

The Aircraft Rescue and Fire Fighting facility in Duluth, Minnesota, teaches professional firefighters what to do. The facility has a Boeing 757 simulator fitted with nozzles that shoot propane-gas flames and artificial smoke in and around the plane, all controlled by computers. Trainees must extinguish the fire within two and one-half minutes to pass the test. That brief time is all that survivors of a fiery plane crash typically have to get out alive.

Do you view your church as a Spiritual Rescue and Fire Fighting facility? Jude tells us of our responsibility to save those in danger. We have the equipment we need (the Bible). But do we have the training? Professional firefighters undergo special training that enables them to perform their life-saving task. What kind of training do you think is necessary for the more important task of spiritual rescue?
—C. R. B.

III. Saving from a Fall
(JUDE 24, 25)

A. Presented Faultless (v. 24)

24. Now unto him that is able to keep you from falling, and to present you faultless before the presence of his glory with exceeding joy.

Jude ends his letter with a prayer. It has been called both a *benediction* ("word of blessing") and a *doxology* ("word of praise"). Whichever term we use, we should see the marvelous way it celebrates our relationship with God through Jesus Christ.

He will Keep You from Falling

Visual for Lesson 6

Point to this visual as you ask, "What are some ways that God has kept you from falling?"

Jude directs a confident heart to God as the one who can keep us from falling. The phrasing carries the idea of tripping, of stumbling badly. However dangerous this may be physically as we walk on the sidewalk, it is far more tragic spiritually if we fall in our Christian walk. Yet we all have had a time in our Christian lives when we fell, when we stumbled spiritually and felt like we could not get up and go on. Jude's confidence is that God is able to keep us from falling in the first place. He explains this in three ways.

First, God will *present you faultless*. The idea of *faultless* means that we are without blemish (compare Jude 23). That is not talking about skin problems, as if God will finally clear up our acne. It means, rather, that we no longer have the stain of sin on our souls (Philippians 1:10; 1 Thessalonians 5:23).

Second, we are allowed into the *presence of his glory*. We are in the presence of a Holy God, and we do not burn up because of our sin. Our God-given faultlessness permits us to endure God's glory. Through the work of Christ, the glory of God is no longer unapproachable for us (see Colossians 1:22; 1 Timothy 6:16).

Third, we are to be overwhelmed with *joy*. We stand spiritually before the judgment throne of God, in the very presence of the Almighty, the Creator of the universe, and we do so free from the stain of sin! We do not need to cower and hide.

We do not need to cover our shame with fig leaves (Genesis 3:7). We stand in the unhindered presence of the Lord, filled with a joy provided by the Holy Spirit.

❧ *EASE OF FALLING SYNDROME* ❧

Bungee jumpers, skydivers, and amusement park thrill-seekers seem to take delight in experiencing the sensation of falling. The rest of us typically fall because of inattention, obstacles in our path, or a physical condition that affects our equilibrium.

Some folks in the latter category are said to have "ease of falling syndrome." Take, for example, the case of a man admitted to the hospital after three days of falling backward and to his right when he tried to sit, stand, or walk. As he fell, he could make none of the bodily adjustments we normally employ to recover from being off balance. Doctors eventually discovered a massive "bleed" deep in his brain. The man's falling symptoms disappeared immediately after the surgery that drained the blood.

Spiritually speaking, all of us are susceptible to "ease of falling syndrome." However, there is hope: God can—and wants to—provide us with the stability that will keep us from falling. Will you accept His help, or will you try to handle everything on your own?　　　—C. R. B.

B. Power Forever (v. 25)

25. To the only wise God our Saviour, be glory and majesty, dominion and power, both now and ever. Amen.

How is God able to keep us from falling? Jude presents six ways.

First, God is our Savior; He can save us through Jesus Christ our Lord (see 1 Corinthians 1:18).

Second, He is able to save by His glory. The glory of God has the sense of overwhelming brilliance, of powerful, blinding light. We glorify God (see Psalm 66:2; Matthew 5:16), but we do not add to His glory by doing so. God is already complete in His glorious power (compare Exodus 15:6, 7).

The third factor is God's majesty. This is a strong word based on the root from which we get our prefix *mega-*. We might say that God's majesty is His "mega-ness." God is the biggest, and there is no close second. There is no contest with God when it comes to majesty.

Fourth, God preserves us because of His dominion. This is the same root word from which we get the biblical term *Almighty* (see Revelation 1:8). The term gives a word picture of controlling something by having it within one's grasp. I have power over that which I hold in my hand. There can be no limits on God's grasp. He is always in control.

Fifth, we are presented faultless because of God's power. This is a term derived from the political sphere and is used to refer to the authority of a king or a government official. God's power is not political, however. There are no checks and balances with God. There is no palace intrigue, no office politics. There are no powerful senators or special interests. There are no referenda to determine the will of the people. There are no influential pollsters or newspaper columnists to sway God one way or the other. God's authority is both absolute and perfect in its execution. It is never capricious or misused. It is always just and righteous.

Sixth, God empowers us because of His eternality, *both now and ever*. God is not pressed for time, not limited by days or years. God is the one "which is, and which was, and which is to come" (Revelation 1:4).

Conclusion

A. Win Forever

Pete Carroll has made *win forever* the motto of his University of Southern California football team. While this becomes trite with overuse, it is truly inspiring when we pause to think about it. Can we "win forever"? Yes, but only through the power of God, the one who is able to keep us from falling. We have all eaten of the fruit of sin. Some of us may have done so heavily this very week, as if sin were an all-you-can-eat buffet. Do not despair. God can keep you from falling. You can win forever.

Others have struggled mightily with persistent sin issues, trying and failing, hoping and then having hopes dashed. We might feel as if we have tried God's patience to the limit, that our quota of forgiveness and grace is long since exhausted. Do not despair. God can keep you from falling, and you can win forever.

We all have periods in life when God seems distant. These are times when our prayers seem ineffective and useless. We feel that God is so far away that He is unreachable. Perhaps we feel like praying the so-called Agnostic's Prayer: "O God, if there is a God, save my soul, if I have a soul."

Sometimes it seems like our prayer life is trapped in an area where the cell-phone coverage is very spotty. Our conversations with God break up and are cut off. "Thou hast covered thyself with a cloud, that our prayer should not pass through" (Lamentations 3:44). We cannot hear what God is saying to us, and we doubt whether He is hearing what we say to Him. We are tempted to despair. But do not despair, for He can keep you from falling. If we trust in Him, we can truly win forever.

Our God is not only the God who picks us up and restores us to himself, He is also the God who will never abandon us. He will never go back on His promise to have us stand before His glorious presence, faultless and filled with joy.

B. Prayer

Father, may we first give our praise and thanks to the one who snatched us from the fire of judgment: Jesus Christ, our Savior. Then may we follow His example in being unwilling to have any of His sheep wander away. May we make our church a place where love flows, where there is genuine concern for each member of our fellowship. We pray these things in the name of our Savior, amen.

C. Thought to Remember

Seek out those who are falling away.

INVOLVEMENT LEARNING

Some of the activities below are also found in the helpful student book, Adult Bible Class.
Don't forget to download the free reproducible page from www.standardlesson.com to enhance your lesson!

Into the Lesson

Option #1. Tell the class you will be asking them to tell stories of tragic or near tragic falls. While they are thinking, tell one from your own experience or relate the story printed in the lesson commentary's Introduction. After three or four stories, transition to Bible study by saying, "The most tragic of falls is falling away from God. Today's study will give tips on how to prevent that."

Option #2. Play a word-association game. Tell the class to write down the first thing that comes to mind when you say these three words: *falling, ungodly,* and *mockers*. Ask for responses. Then say the next three words: *faith, mercy,* and *faultless*. Ask for responses. Transition to Bible study by saying, "Jude uses the first group of words to heighten our senses to people who might draw us away from God. As such, many of the responses were negative and fearful. The second group consists of words that Jude uses to encourage us to remain faithful to the Lord. Responses thus were more positive and hopeful."

Into the Word

Summarize the Lesson Background. Structure your comments to lead into "an interview with Jude." Early in the week, give one of your learners a copy of the questions below and a photocopy of today's lesson commentary so he can come prepared. A first-century costume is desirable.

After reading today's printed text with the class, say, "We're going to allow Jude to help us understand his encouragements and teachings. Here he is; please welcome *Jude*." (Allow for a smattering of applause.)

Interview questions: 1. Jude, you warn us about people who would mock or scoff at us. What do you mean by the word *mock*? 2. You mention how mockers or scoffers may separate or divide the church. Tell us more about the risks of this type of behavior. 3. You share tips on how to build our-

selves up in the faith. One of the tips is to pray in the Holy Spirit. What do you mean by that? 4. Another encouragement you give is to keep ourselves in the love of God. Exactly how do we do that? 5. It is apparent in your writings that you have no doubt that people who have fallen away can be restored. Explain your encouragements to use compassion or mercy to aid in their restoration. 6. The kind of prayer you use to close your letter we often call *a benediction*. Why is your benediction important for us?

Thank "Jude" for appearing and consenting to an interview. *Alternative:* Instead of the above interview, download the reproducible page and have your learners form small groups to complete the two exercises on it. Discuss results.

Into Life

Pose these discussion questions either to the class as a whole or to small groups: 1. Without necessarily thinking of anyone in particular, what are some practical ways that we may fulfill Jude's passion for helping those who have fallen away? 2. What does Jude's letter teach you about preserving in your own relationship with God?

Commitment Activity #1. Give each learner an index card. Say, "Write down the name of one person who has slipped away from the Lord. What will you do this week to encourage that person to renew his or her relationship with the Lord?" Suggest that the contact be as personal as possible (examples: phone call, face-to-face visit); impersonal methods such as e-mail should be avoided.

Commitment Activity #2. Give each learner a handout on which to write a personal prayer of benediction. This prayer should have overtones of that individual's personal spiritual walk. The handout will have these starters on it:

To Him who is able . . .
To Him who has . . .
Be . . .

PRAISE THE LORD

BACKGROUND SCRIPTURE: Mark 11:1-11
PRINTED TEXT: Mark 11:1-11

MARK 11:1-11

1 And when they came nigh to Jerusalem, unto Bethphage and Bethany, at the mount of Olives, he sendeth forth two of his disciples,

2 And saith unto them, Go your way into the village over against you: and as soon as ye be entered into it, ye shall find a colt tied, whereon never man sat; loose him, and bring him.

3 And if any man say unto you, Why do ye this? say ye that the Lord hath need of him; and straightway he will send him hither.

4 And they went their way, and found the colt tied by the door without in a place where two ways met; and they loose him.

5 And certain of them that stood there said unto them, What do ye, loosing the colt?

6 And they said unto them even as Jesus had commanded: and they let them go.

7 And they brought the colt to Jesus, and cast their garments on him; and he sat upon him.

8 And many spread their garments in the way: and others cut down branches off the trees, and strawed them in the way.

9 And they that went before, and they that followed, cried, saying, Hosanna; Blessed is he that cometh in the name of the Lord:

10 Blessed be the kingdom of our father David, that cometh in the name of the Lord: Hosanna in the highest.

11 And Jesus entered into Jerusalem, and into the temple: and when he had looked round about upon all things, and now the eventide was come, he went out unto Bethany with the twelve.

KEY VERSE

They that went before, and they that followed, cried, saying, Hosanna; Blessed is he that cometh in the name of the Lord. —**Mark 11:9**

WE WORSHIP GOD

Unit 2: Reasons for Praise

LESSONS 5–9

LESSON AIMS

After participating in this lesson, each student will be able to:

1. List the sequence of events that constituted the triumphal entry.

2. List some contexts in which spontaneous praise is especially appropriate.

3. Implement a seven-day devotional reading plan that will prepare his or her heart for resurrection Sunday.

LESSON OUTLINE

Introduction
  A. Palm Trees
  B. Lesson Background
 I. Preparation for Praise (MARK 11:1-8)
  A. Understanding the Need (vv. 1-3)
    "Why?"
  B. Gathering the Resources (vv. 4-6)
  C. Spreading the Praise Table (vv. 7, 8)
II. Outpouring of Praise (MARK 11:9-11)
  A. Hosanna in the Highest (vv. 9, 10)
    Jesus Through Filters
  B. Entering the Temple (v. 11)
Conclusion
  A. Praise Explosion
  B. Prayer
  C. Thought to Remember

Introduction

A. Palm Trees

I live in Los Angeles, which must rank near the top of palm-tree cities for the United States. Palm trees are everywhere! And they are lovely. They have an unmistakable look: trunks of varying height and thickness, crowned with clusters of large, drooping leaves.

Properly speaking, palm trees have no branches, just leaves or fronds at the top. They present a particularly beautiful silhouette when profiled against a darkening sunset sky at the close of the day.

Palm Sunday gets its name from this tree, cultivated since ancient times. Historical sources indicate that the date palm tree was widespread in the Jordan River valley and Galilee and may have been common in Jerusalem (see Psalm 92:12).

These trees were neglected and cut down after the Roman devastation of Palestine that culminated with the destruction of Jerusalem in AD 70. This tree is portrayed on Roman coins issued to

celebrate the imperial victory. One popular species, called *the Judean date palm,* was thought to have become extinct by the end of the second century.

In a remarkable recovery effort, scientists in Israel managed to germinate a 2,000-year-old seed from a Judean date palm in 2005. The resulting tree, nicknamed *Methuselah,* is currently growing under controlled conditions. It was about five feet tall in 2008. If successful, this holds the prospect of letting us see the same type of palm fronds that were spread before Jesus on that great day when the multitude shouted, "Hosanna in the highest!"

B. Lesson Background

The Sunday before Jesus' arrest and crucifixion is traditionally called Palm Sunday. Sunday had no religious significance for the ancient Jews. Their description for the day was simply "the first day of the week" (see Acts 20:7), meaning the first day of the workweek after the Sabbath day.

The events of the week leading up to the death and resurrection of Jesus are set in the context of a Jewish holiday time that celebrated both the week-long Feast of Unleavened Bread and the daylong Passover (see Leviticus 23:5). Both festivals were derived from the events of the exodus of Israel from slavery in Egypt. Passover marked the deliverance from the death of the firstborn, the final plague (see Exodus 12:12, 13). Unleavened bread commemorated the hasty meal the Israelites were to eat just before they fled from Egypt (see 12:8).

In Jesus' time, Passover was considered to be a pilgrimage festival. That meant that all Jewish men were expected to celebrate it in Jerusalem, if possible. For Jews living in distant cities (like Rome), this pilgrimage might be a once-in-a-lifetime event, carefully planned, executed, and treasured for the rest of one's life. Jews living in Palestine often were able to attend this festival each year, taking time off after the spring harvest to do so.

I. Preparation for Praise
(MARK 11:1-8)
A. Understanding the Need (vv. 1-3)

1a. And when they came nigh to Jerusalem, unto Bethphage and Bethany, at the mount of Olives.

Up to this point, Jesus and His disciples have operated primarily in Galilee, about 60 miles

HOW TO SAY IT

Aramaic	*Air*-uh-*may*-ik.
Bethany	*Beth*-uh-nee.
Bethphage	*Beth*-fuh-gee.
Galileans	Gal-uh-*lee*-unz.
Galilee	*Gal*-uh-lee.
Jerusalem	Juh-*roo*-suh-lem.
Maccabees	*Mack*-uh-bees.
Messiah	Meh-*sigh*-uh.
Methuselah	Muh-*thoo*-zuh-luh (*th* as in *thin*).
Samaria	Suh-*mare*-ee-uh.

north of Jerusalem. Now, thousands of the Jews head south to be near the temple for the Passover Feast (compare John 6:4, 5). The usual route, around Samaria, makes the trip closer to 100 miles (compare John 4:9).

Jesus and His disciples use Bethany as their base of operations while in the Jerusalem area (see Mark 11:11). This village is tucked behind the Mount of Olives, a couple of miles from the gates of Jerusalem. The city and all the surrounding villages are crowded with pilgrims at this time, and they make use of lodgings wherever they can find them. Bethany is the home of Mary, Martha, and Lazarus. Jesus has stayed at their house before (John 11:1). Mark mentions that Jesus visits the home of Simon the leper in Bethany, but we do not know the connection between this man and Jesus' other friends (see Mark 14:3).

With village names in ancient Israel, the prefix *beth* means "house of . . ." For example, Bethlehem means "house of bread," Bethel means "house of God," Bethany means "house of dates," and Bethphage means "house of figs." Combined with the mention of the Mount of Olives, we are reminded of the agricultural centers that are near the temple. The two villages mentioned are not large, probably a few hundred residents in each. It is possible that these two towns are so close that they have, in effect, become one general settlement.

1b, 2. He sendeth forth two of his disciples, and saith unto them, Go your way into the village over against you: and as soon as ye be entered into it, ye shall find a colt tied, whereon never man sat; loose him, and bring him.

We do not know which disciples are sent on this mission (contrast Luke 22:8), but it must seem curious to them. The colt they are to find is further described as "a young ass" (donkey) in John 12:14. We are not intended to visualize a baby donkey that is small and frail, but a full-grown animal ready to be used. The significance of the detail *whereon never man sat* is that this animal has not yet been broken for riding.

These directions may be an example of Jesus' supernatural knowledge and authority. But the directions may also reflect a prearranged situation, since the colt will be found tied, possibly indicating it has been retrieved from a stable or pasture and prepared for an expected service. Jesus likely has many friends who have been awed and gratified by His bringing Lazarus, their fellow villager, back from the dead (John 11:17-45).

3. And if any man say unto you, Why do ye this? say ye that the Lord hath need of him; and straightway he will send him hither.

That the use of the donkey probably is prearranged is indicated by the instructions Jesus gives to the two disciples. They need only mention the authority of the Lord (Jesus), and the owners will release the colt to them without objection or security. Jesus' authority alone is sufficient.

❧ "Why?" ❧

"Why do I have to go to bed now?" is a typical question a child asks. When the logical answer "You have to get up early for school" doesn't settle the matter, parents are tempted to retreat to the position of authority: "Because I said so!" Parents come to realize quickly that logical answers often do not suffice when a child asks "why?" In many cases, the child merely wants to argue.

Jesus had a lot of experience in dealing with "why" questions (examples: Matthew 13:10; 15:2; Luke 5:30; John 14:22). He made a practice of giving logical, coherent answers. Jesus anticipated that the "why" question might arise as He sent His disciples for the donkey on which He was to ride. His answer in this case rested on His authority: "The Lord hath need of him." There was no argument.

We still love to ask "why," don't we? We may do so when we begin to realize that the Lord is leading us, either through Scripture or through conscience, to serve Him in a certain way. In many cases, the simple answer to our "why" is, "Because the Lord needs us to do it." The level of our spiritual maturity will be seen in the way we respond to that simple truth.   —C. R. B.

B. Gathering the Resources (vv. 4-6)

4. And they went their way, and found the colt tied by the door without in a place where two ways met; and they loose him.

The two disciples find things just as Jesus has predicted. Mark has a detail that is not included in the other Gospel accounts: the house is where two roads meet. Again, this shows the perfect plan of Jesus. If the animal were farther away, then the men would have had to make a decision as to which of the two ways they should follow to get there. Instead, the picture we get is that the animal is in plain sight and ready to be used.

> **What Do You Think?**
> When was a time that the Lord made His will clear to you and you obeyed? What was the result?
> **Talking Points for Your Discussion**
> - Walking in the Spirit
> - Choosing whether or not to obey
> - Walking by faith, not by sight

5. And certain of them that stood there said unto them, What do ye, loosing the colt?

Not surprisingly, the action the two disciples take to untie the animal is challenged. This indicates that the two are not personally known to the owners.

6. And they said unto them even as Jesus had commanded: and they let them go.

There is no problem, however, and the challengers yield the animal to the two disciples. The disciples do more than just throw out the name of Jesus, though. The phrase *said unto them even as Jesus had commanded* indicates that the disciples assert that Jesus needs this animal (v. 3, above). The disciples are not serving themselves or taking advantage of their close relationship with the Master. They are gathering resources to be used for Jesus' purposes, and right now He needs a donkey to ride.

> **What Do You Think?**
> How do we release things for the Lord's use without allowing others to take advantage of us?
> **Talking Points for Your Discussion**
> - Dealing with "guilt trips" that others put on us
> - Discerning the Lord's will
> - Acting in another's best interest
> - Dealing with feelings of selfishness

Praise the Lord

C. Spreading the Praise Table (vv. 7, 8)

7. And they brought the colt to Jesus, and cast their garments on him; and he sat upon him.

The young donkey is not saddled, and it may not even have a bridle. Perhaps it is simply led by a rope around its neck. The disciples do not allow Jesus to ride bareback, which would be undignified. They use their outer cloaks to make an impromptu pad upon which the Lord can sit.

8. And many spread their garments in the way: and others cut down branches off the trees, and strawed them in the way.

Another use is found for the surplus garments: they are spread on the road between Bethany/Bethphage and Jerusalem. This is a well-traveled road, but it is not paved. Thus it consists of hard-packed dirt.

The crowd is wearing their pilgrimage finery, for the people are on their way to the holy city. These might be white cloaks, making the covered roadway a brilliant path in the bright sun (compare 2 Kings 9:13). The scene is enhanced by cutting branches from the nearby trees. John identifies these as palm branches (John 12:13), and they are added to the roadway.

Although none of the Gospels say that the crowd waves the palm branches, it is likely that they do. Palm fronds are used in this way to signify praise (see Revelation 7:9). We know that they were used in the triumphal procession of Simon Maccabee when he entered the citadel of Jerusalem in about 141 BC (see the nonbiblical 1 Maccabees 13:51; compare 2 Maccabees 10:7). It is natural to desire to do something physical when we praise, whether that is to raise our hands, sway our bodies, lift our voices, or wave a palm branch. Praise is more than a warm feeling in the heart. It needs to be expressed.

> **What Do You Think?**
> What physical expressions of worship are common at our church, if any? How are allowances made for differences of expression?
> *Talking Points for Your Discussion*
> - Example of worship leaders
> - Cultural background of the congregation

BLESSED IS HE!

Visual for Lesson 7

Point to this visual as you introduce the discussion question that is associated with verse 9b.

II. Outpouring of Praise
(Mark 11:9-11)

A. Hosanna in the Highest (vv. 9, 10)

9a. And they that went before, and they that followed, cried, saying.

Mark's picture is of Jesus and His disciples in the middle of a very large procession of pilgrims into the holy city. Something like this parade of pilgrims into Jerusalem during Passover time has been experienced for hundreds of years. It is a time of joy, excitement, and expectation. This year, however, things are different. There is a thrill in the air, and the focus of it is Jesus.

This large crowd is shouting praises in a riotous unity. Many are Galileans, and they likely have heard Jesus teach, seen Him heal, and eaten of the multiplied loaves beside the sea. This is their local hero coming to the temple, acclaimed as Messiah.

9b. Hosanna; Blessed is he that cometh in the name of the Lord.

The cry of the crowds is taken from Psalm 118. That psalm gives the story of a procession of triumphant warriors returning to Jerusalem and its temple. It is, perhaps, the army of King David himself. The psalm pictures the leader demanding entrance (Psalm 118:19, 20), which is granted (118:21). It also has the famous cornerstone prophecy (118:22, 23), applied by Jesus to himself later in this same week (Mark 12:10, 11).

The climactic point of the psalm is when the worshipers turn to God in praise and supplication, crying, "Save now, I beseech thee, O Lord!" (Psalm 118:25). Mark records that the crowd that is acclaiming Jesus cries out much the same thing. Mark, however, chooses not to translate the phrase and gives it to us in the original Aramaic: *Hosanna.*

The crowd includes another phrase taken from Psalm 118: *Blessed is he that cometh in the name of the Lord* (compare 118:26). This stamps the ministry of Jesus with a spiritual, religious purpose rather than a political one. Jesus does not need a legion of followers wearing body armor and carrying deadly weapons as He advances toward Jerusalem. He is coming as God's man for God's purposes.

What Do You Think?

How well does our church do in focusing the praise and attention on Jesus? What elements can disrupt that focus?

Talking Points for Your Discussion
- Authentic praise vs. inauthentic performance
- Personal preferences
- Heartfelt vs. habitual

---

10. Blessed be the kingdom of our father David, that cometh in the name of the Lord: Hosanna in the highest.

The third part of the crowd's cry probably has mixed meanings, however. They acknowledge Jesus as the heir of David (compare Mark 10:47). This is a statement of belief in Jesus as the chosen one, the Messiah, the Christ of God (see Mark 1:1). The mixed feelings of the crowd have to do with their understanding of what the role of the Messiah is to be. Although Jesus has no army, there are some who want Him to assume David's throne, to become the rightful king in Jerusalem (see John 6:15). This new king is to be their deliverer, one who will restore the fortunes of Israel and drive the hated Romans from their land (see Acts 1:6).

But this is neither Jesus' mission nor His intention. He is sent to ransom captive Israel from its sins (Mark 10:45), not from bondage to the Romans.

During the turbulent 1960s and early 1970s, a protest movement that advocated "liberating" the possessions of others gathered momentum. Whatever imbalance seemed unjust to the protesters (such as one person's possession of a luxury item) was "made right" by theft or destruction. An extreme example was the actions of the so-called Symbionese Liberation Army.

This outlook involved seeing things through a specific worldview filter of anarchism. Since Jesus was being touted by some in the 1960s as "the first hippie," then advocates of this worldview could see His "liberation" of the donkey (Mark 11:1-6) as justification for modern acts of theft.

The danger is obvious: if we're not careful, we may end up making Jesus anything we want Him to be depending on the filters through which we choose to view Him. The crowd of Jesus' triumphal entry saw Him as a deliverer of a certain type. As a result, the crowd shouted *Hosanna!* But a short time later, at least some of these same people probably were in the crowd that shouted *Crucify!* (15:13, 14). How quickly our filters can change!
—C. R. B.

B. Entering the Temple (v. 11)

11. And Jesus entered into Jerusalem, and into the temple: and when he had looked round about upon all things, and now the eventide was come, he went out unto Bethany with the twelve.

The magnificence of the temple in Jesus' day is known throughout the world. It is actually a complex of buildings with a central sanctuary, broad courtyards, and huge porticos (walkways covered with a roof supported by columns) around the perimeter. There is nothing approaching the temple's grandeur in Jesus' home area, Galilee.

Some think that Mark presents Jesus almost as a tourist here—someone sightseeing in the big city and gawking at the main attraction, the temple. Under this mistaken impression, He is the country boy who will purchase a T-shirt and some postcards at a souvenir stand. This misunderstands the text, however. Jesus has been to Jerusalem before and has seen the temple many times (see Luke

2:41). Jesus is about 33 years old at the time of the triumphal entry of today's lesson. If we consider the likelihood that He also observes the Feast of Tabernacles in Jerusalem each autumn (see John 7:1-10), this means He has visited the temple dozens of times just to observe these festivals.

Thus this irreverent interpretation of Mark's portrayal of Jesus is unnecessary. He is not a first-time observer of the temple, but a last-time observer, considering the week as a whole. Jesus has many memories and attachments to this holy place. He can remember His loving mother, Mary, providing His temple clothes to don after He had taken His ritual cleansing bath. He can surely remember holding the hand of His father, Joseph, the first time He ascended the temple steps. Although Jesus is critical of the management of the temple (Mark 11:15-19), He also knows that this is a site where many sincere and pious Jews come to meet their God. There are abuses, but not all is fakery in this place (example: Mark 12:41-44).

What Do You Think?

Have you ever taken a pilgrimage to a place that held memories of spiritual significance to you? How did this help you spiritually?

Talking Points for Your Discussion

- Gratitude for blessings received
- Increased desire to bless others
- Expectation of future blessings

Jesus knows even more than the fact that this will be His last Passover visit to the temple (see Mark 10:33, 34). He also knows that the days of the temple itself are numbered. His divine foreknowledge allows Him to know that there will be a day when "there shall not be left one stone upon another" (Mark 13:2). This is fulfilled when the Romans destroy the temple in AD 70.

Mark concludes this section with a simple note that Jesus and the 12 return to Bethany for the night. The momentous week has begun, the week that changes history forever. The acclaimed Son of David will soon die on a cross. But He will rise again in less than a week, and things will not be the same ever again.

Conclusion

A. Praise Explosion

When I was a boy of age 6, I was finally deemed old enough to wear a suit to church for Easter Sunday. This was not a new outfit, having been passed down from my older brother. But it was new to me, and I was intrigued by the potential of looking all grown up when I went to church.

That morning my unruly hair was brushed, then plastered with some goop. My hands and nails were clean, my teeth were brushed. I was ready to don the suit. This included a couple of things I was not accustomed to, though. I had to wear a white dress shirt and a clip-on tie. I also had a leather belt to hold up the pants, which were too big.

What I remember the most about this was the difficulty I had in keeping the shirt tucked in. I would push it into my pants on one side only to find it flapping out on the other. I would tuck in the front and realize I had a tail sticking out in the back. This was mainly because the shirt, also a hand-me-down, was a couple of sizes too big.

Sometimes I think praise is like that. It is too big to keep tucked in. It wants to come out, to be expressed and enjoyed. We are made to be creatures of praise for our Creator. To deny praise is foolishly to deny our central being. Palm Sunday is a story about this desire to praise (Luke 19:40). The circumstances were right. There was a large crowd of people who had come a great distance with worship in their hearts. They had a great praise literature in the psalms of their heritage. And then they had the proper object of praise to spur them to celebrate: Jesus, the Messiah, the very Son of God.

B. Prayer

Holy God, we praise You. We praise You with our hearts, with our minds, with our lives. May a day like Palm Sunday spur us to even higher levels of praise. Hosanna! Glory to You in the highest. May Your name be praised forever. We pray in Jesus' name, amen.

C. Thought to Remember

Praise Jesus!

INVOLVEMENT LEARNING

Some of the activities below are also found in the helpful student book, Adult Bible Class.
Don't forget to download the free reproducible page from www.standardlesson.com to enhance your lesson!

Into the Lesson

Option #1, Worship Memories: Mount several poster boards on walls before class members arrive. Each poster board should have the phrase *Memories of Worship* written at the top. As learners enter the classroom, ask each to recall an especially significant moment of worship or praise in his or her life. Distribute markers for learners to jot the occasion of that memory on one of the poster boards. (Make sure the paper is thick enough so the ink doesn't bleed through onto the wall.) Next, ask each class member to do a "neighbor nudge," sharing the details of the event he or she noted on the poster with a person sitting nearby.

Option #2, Worship Definitions: Ask the class to define *worship*. Jot ideas on the board. Come prepared with a dictionary definition of worship to compare and contrast. Challenge the class to distinguish between *worship* and *expressions of worship*. Leave the ideas displayed on the board throughout the lesson.

Say, "Worship and praise moments may happen in different settings and may be expressed in different ways. Today, we'll enjoy one of the significant memories of worship that has lingered in the minds of many people through the centuries."

Into the Word

Read today's printed text to the class. Then divide the class into groups of two to four. Give each group a written assignment, a piece of poster board, a marker, and copies of the lesson commentary on verses noted in the assignment. Class size may dictate the need to adjust group sizes. Also, download the reproducible page and distribute copies of the Learning About Worship activity. Say, "When you finish your group assignment, take a few minutes to jot your thoughts with regard to learning about worship."

P&P Group. Review the attached information from the Lesson Background about the Passover

and pilgrimages. One group member should be prepared to share your discoveries with the class.

B&A Group. Read the lesson commentary and clarify for the class (1) the significance of the prefix *Beth-* in village names (v. 1), and (2) the importance of the "accessories" of the colt (vv. 2-6), the garments (vv. 7, 8a), and the branches (v. 8b).

P&W Group. Read the lesson commentary notes on verses 9-11 and tell the class the significance of these praise and worship words chosen from Psalm 118.

M&T Group. Read the commentary notes on verse 11. Then share with the class the information about Jesus' memories of His times spent in the temple. You may use your "sanctified imagination" to suggest possibilities.

Allow groups to report discoveries and conclusions. Discuss learners' conclusions regarding the Learning About Worship exercise. Follow up with these discussion questions: 1. What lessons, ideas, or motivations for worship do you discover by reading of the event in today's text? 2. What are some special memories of worship that you experienced in a group setting?

Into Life

Conclude the lesson by allowing the class to worship through creative writing of a prayer. Put the following sentence starters on a handout or on the board:

Holy God, I praise You with _____ and _____.
Lord, I praise You for _____ and _____.
When I read how people praised You when Your Son entered Jerusalem, I am spurred to _____.
Hosanna! Glory to You in the highest. May Your name _____. Amen.

Allow class members to read their prayers aloud as time allows. Download the reproducible page and distribute copies of the Personal Expressions of Worship activity as take-home work.

Praise the Lord

GO AND TELL

BACKGROUND SCRIPTURE: **Matthew 28**

PRINTED TEXT: **Matthew 28**

MATTHEW 28

1 In the end of the sabbath, as it began to dawn toward the first day of the week, came Mary Magdalene and the other Mary to see the sepulchre.

2 And, behold, there was a great earthquake: for the angel of the Lord descended from heaven, and came and rolled back the stone from the door, and sat upon it.

3 His countenance was like lightning, and his raiment white as snow:

4 And for fear of him the keepers did shake, and became as dead men.

5 And the angel answered and said unto the women, Fear not ye: for I know that ye seek Jesus, which was crucified.

6 He is not here: for he is risen, as he said. Come, see the place where the Lord lay.

7 And go quickly, and tell his disciples that he is risen from the dead; and, behold, he goeth before you into Galilee; there shall ye see him: lo, I have told you.

8 And they departed quickly from the sepulchre with fear and great joy; and did run to bring his disciples word.

9 And as they went to tell his disciples, behold, Jesus met them, saying, All hail. And they came and held him by the feet, and worshipped him.

10 Then said Jesus unto them, Be not afraid: go tell my brethren that they go into Galilee, and there shall they see me.

11 Now when they were going, behold, some of the watch came into the city, and shewed unto the chief priests all the things that were done.

12 And when they were assembled with the elders, and had taken counsel, they gave large money unto the soldiers,

13 Saying, Say ye, His disciples came by night, and stole him away while we slept.

14 And if this come to the governor's ears, we will persuade him, and secure you.

15 So they took the money, and did as they were taught: and this saying is commonly reported among the Jews until this day.

16 Then the eleven disciples went away into Galilee, into a mountain where Jesus had appointed them.

17 And when they saw him, they worshipped him: but some doubted.

18 And Jesus came and spake unto them, saying, All power is given unto me in heaven and in earth.

19 Go ye therefore, and teach all nations, baptizing them in the name of the Father, and of the Son, and of the Holy Ghost:

20 Teaching them to observe all things whatsoever I have commanded you: and, lo, I am with you always, even unto the end of the world. Amen.

KEY VERSE

As they went to tell his disciples, behold, Jesus met them, saying, All hail. And they came and held him by the feet, and worshipped him. —**Matthew 28:9**

WE WORSHIP GOD

Unit 2: Reasons for Praise

LESSONS 5–9

LESSON AIMS

After participating in this lesson, each student will be able to:

1. List some key events that happened between the discovery of the empty tomb and Jesus' giving of the Great Commission.

2. Explain the connection between the resurrection and the Great Commission.

3. Write a prayer of gratitude that thanks God for Jesus' constant presence.

LESSON OUTLINE

Introduction

A. False Reporting

Not long ago, we received a disturbing letter from the gas company. They had determined that several thousand houses, including ours, were equipped with gas meters that were calibrated incorrectly at the factory. The result was that the meters had been giving false readings for years. The utility's claim was that they had lost millions of dollars over an estimated six years of false data. The company's solution was to add a small surcharge on our bill to be paid out over two years.

Many people had been affected by this inaccuracy. It had gone uncorrected for years. When it was discovered, those informed were incredulous (like us) and chose not to believe the truth at first. I would guess that some of our more stubborn neighbors still refuse to accept this claim, choosing to fight a losing battle against the gas company even though the evidence is clear.

The existence of solid evidence should cause us to think certain ways, but that doesn't always happen. For example, there was no denying the emptiness of Jesus' tomb, so some made up a lie that His body had been stolen by His disciples. Their lie is still circulated today. It has contributed to the disbelief of uncounted millions.

We are blessed to know that the Christian faith is not based on a false report. We have a faith based on truth confirmed by witnesses who did not lie (Proverbs 14:5). They reported an incredible yet true event, and no amount of lying can change their testimony.

B. Lesson Background

All four Gospels tell the story of the empty tomb. Each account has unique details. For example, Matthew is our only source of information concerning the action by the Jewish leaders to seal and guard the tomb (Matthew 27:62-66). But the fact of the empty tomb is attested by all four Gospel authors. It is a fact assumed by the other books of the New Testament (example: Acts 13:29-31).

Skeptics through the centuries have put forth many theories to explain (or, rather, explain away) the tomb's emptiness. But there is no credible alternative explanation to that of resurrection: a dead body came back to life and exited the tomb, leaving it empty. There is no scientific explanation for this. It cannot be reproduced in a laboratory. But it is a fact. Jesus' resurrection holds the promise that we too will be raised to dwell with Him forever (1 Corinthians 15:23).

I. Women Witnesses
(MATTHEW 28:1-10)
A. Dawn Visit (v. 1)

1. In the end of the sabbath, as it began to dawn toward the first day of the week, came Mary Magdalene and the other Mary to see the sepulchre.

The Gospels record the actions of a small group of devoted women disciples who return to the tomb of Jesus after the Sabbath. They intend to do a more fitting job of honoring His body with spices and oil. This return is necessitated by the hurried burial of Jesus on Friday afternoon. The haste was caused by the need to finish the burial work before sundown, for that marked the beginning of the Jewish Sabbath, when no work is allowed (see Exodus 20:10; Luke 23:54-56; John 19:42). So the soonest the women are permitted to do their work after Jesus' burial on Friday is Sunday, *the first day of the week* (also Mark 16:1, 2; Luke 24:1; John 20:1).

In Jewish reckoning, the old day ends and the new day begins at sundown. Theoretically, then, Mary Magdalene and her friends could have come to finish their work after sundown on the Sabbath. But these women do not live in a world of outdoor streetlights or night-vision goggles. Artificial lighting is limited to small lamps, candles, and handheld torches. This makes it impractical to revisit the tomb until dawn on Sunday morning.

We can assume that the women arrive at the tomb sometime before 7 AM, as the sky is still gaining its full light. Matthew gives the impression that Mary Magdalene is the leader of group (see Matthew 27:61). *The other Mary* is identified in the parallel of Mark 16:1 and Luke 24:10 as "the mother of James." If we combine Matthew 13:55; 27:56; Mark 15:40, 47, this Mary may be the mother of Jesus, but this is not certain.

> *What Do You Think?*
> How does the determination and courage of the women serve as an example to you?
> *Talking Points for Your Discussion*
> - In witnessing
> - In reverence
> - In making sacrifices

B. Angelic Earth-Shaker (vv. 2-4)

2. And, behold, there was a great earthquake: for the angel of the Lord descended from heaven, and came and rolled back the stone from the door, and sat upon it.

Matthew also records that an earthquake occurs at the moment of Jesus' death (Matthew 27:51). These two quakes are more than natural and coincidental shifts in the earth's tectonic plates. These are supernatural temblors, a sign of the activity and presence of God (compare Isaiah 29:6).

The mention of *the door* and *the stone* indicates that the tomb has been carved out of a rocky hillside (Matthew 27:57, 60). The opening is sealed by rolling a large stone in front of the entrance. Fancier tombs have stones carved specifically for their location, stones that are placed in channels to make the rolling easier.

If we estimate that this stone is 3 feet in diameter and 1 foot thick, that calculates to a volume of about 7 cubic feet. Limestone weighs about 170 lbs. per cubic foot, so a sealer stone of this size

HOW TO SAY IT

Galileans	Gal-uh-*lee*-unz.
Magdalene	*Mag*-duh-leen or Mag-duh-*lee*-nee.
Pentecost	*Pent*-ih-kost.
Pharisees	*Fair*-ih-sees.
Pilate	*Pie*-lut.
Sadducees	*Sad*-you-sees.
Sanhedrin	San-huh-drun or San-*heed*-run.
sepulchre	*sep*-ul-kur.

weighs about 1,200 lbs. If this stone is 4 feet in diameter (a more likely size), it weighs well over a ton. Such a stone is too heavy for the women to roll away, and they know it (Mark 16:3). *The angel of the Lord* has no difficulty with this task, however. He rolls the stone away and sits on it as if waiting for the women to come.

3, 4. His countenance was like lightning, and his raiment white as snow: and for fear of him the keepers did shake, and became as dead men.

The appearance of the angel is supernaturally brilliant, particularly overwhelming in the semi-light of early dawn. It is reminiscent of the appearance of Jesus at the Transfiguration (Matthew 17:2), a glimpse of the glory of God.

The keepers are the soldiers sent by Pilate and the Jewish leaders (Matthew 27:65). They had sealed the tomb, probably using hot wax and an official signet ring (27:66). After fainting from fear, the soldiers presumably revive later to find the angel gone and the tomb open and empty, so they run away and report back (28:11, below).

C. Astounding Announcement (vv. 5-7)

5. And the angel answered and said unto the women, Fear not ye: for I know that ye seek Jesus, which was crucified.

As at the Transfiguration (Matthew 17:7), the witnesses are told not to be afraid, a command repeated shortly by Jesus himself (28:10, below). They have nothing to fear from the *angel,* for he knows exactly why they have come to the tomb. In looking for the crucified Jesus, the women are looking for a dead Jesus, whose corpse they can anoint with oil and rub with spices.

6. He is not here: for he is risen, as he said. Come, see the place where the Lord lay.

Can we really understand how dumbfounded the women are when they hear these words? Jesus was dead, but now He is not. The women's quest for a dead Christ is now pointless. To prove his point, the angel invites the women to come and see that the tomb is now empty. The women had seen a dead body lain in this rock-hewn grave (Matthew 27:60, 61). Now they are invited to be the first witnesses to the body's absence, the initial evidence that Christ is risen from the dead.

Oley Speaks (1874–1948) was a songwriter. His first job was as a railway clerk, but he had some musical talent so he moved to New York City, hoping to hit the big time. He took music lessons, becoming a successful singer. He appeared in recitals and oratorios. He also composed songs for a classical repertoire. He was the Director of the American Society of Composers, Authors, and Publishers from 1924 to 1943. Perhaps Speaks' most successful composition was his 1907 song "On the Road to Mandalay," borrowed from Rudyard Kipling's poem. It sold over a million copies.

Speaks also wrote several religious-classical songs. These are rather "starched" by today's standards, but were widely popular in the mid–twentieth century. My favorite is one I have not heard for quite a while. But I still get chills whenever I think of "In the End of the Sabbath," a word-for-word musical rendition of Matthew 28:1-6 in the *King James Version*. With dramatic force supported by strong musical chords, it builds to the climax: "He is not here, for He is risen." Does this fact move you? If not, why not?   —J. B. N.

7. And go quickly, and tell his disciples that he is risen from the dead; and, behold, he goeth before you into Galilee; there shall ye see him: lo, I have told you.

After the women are invited to come and see, they are commanded to go and tell. This news is too big, too important to keep secret. Jesus' disciples and these women are all Galileans. The phrases *he goeth before you into Galilee; there shall ye see him* echo Jesus' promise of Matthew 26:32; Mark 14:28.

D. Joyous Encounter (vv. 8-10)

8. And they departed quickly from the sepulchre with fear and great joy; and did run to bring his disciples word.

This awesome experience terrifies the women at the same time it gives them great joy. It is no wonder that they run to tell the disciples (also John 20:2). Mark puts this in even stronger terms, saying they "fled" from the tomb (Mark 16:8). They have urgent news; it must be delivered immediately.

9. And as they went to tell his disciples, behold, Jesus met them, saying, All hail. And they came and held him by the feet, and worshipped him.

The women's surprises are not finished. We are told nothing about Jesus' appearance, but we can see that they recognize Him. Their worshipful response is understandable. To grasp Jesus by His feet means that they are on their knees.

10. Then said Jesus unto them, Be not afraid: go tell my brethren that they go into Galilee, and there shall they see me.

Jesus understands their joy and their terror, so He repeats the comforting words of the angel: *Be not afraid.* He also repeats the angel's instructions for the disciples: *go into Galilee.* Naturally, these Galilean pilgrims plan to return home to Galilee after the conclusion of the Passover celebration. Now there is an additional importance to their return trip, for they are promised that they will see Jesus back there. Even so, the trip back to Galilee does not begin for several days (John 20:26).

II. False Witnesses
(MATTHEW 28:11-15)
A. Priests Are Informed (v. 11)

11. Now when they were going, behold, some of the watch came into the city, and shewed unto the chief priests all the things that were done.

Visual for Lesson 8

As you discuss verses 6 and 7, point to this visual and ask, "How do these four verbs apply to us?"

Matthew turns from the joyous story of reunion to a dismal tale of deception. *Shewed* has the sense of "reported." *The watch* is the unit of soldiers of Matthew 27:66, having been stationed at the tomb to keep the body in it. They failed.

B. Plot Is Devised (vv. 12-14)

12. And when they were assembled with the elders, and had taken counsel, they gave large money unto the soldiers.

This is a meeting of the Jewish high council, the Sanhedrin (compare Matthew 27:1). The chief priests of verse 11 are Sadducees, while the elders are Pharisees. They have thought to this point that their successful plot to kill Jesus would end their "problem," but now another problem has developed. As they did with Judas Iscariot (Matthew 26:15), they use money as the "solution."

13, 14. Saying, Say ye, His disciples came by night, and stole him away while we slept. And if this come to the governor's ears, we will persuade him, and secure you.

Any reservations the soldiers may have are allayed when the Sanhedrin promises to protect them. Sleeping on guard duty is a serious offense. The word *persuade* leaves the idea that the Jewish leaders will bribe Pilate too, if necessary.

It should be remembered that there is no dispute about the tomb's being empty. The evidence that there is a supernatural explanation is strong, given that the soldiers have witnessed the angel and the earthquake. But to admit this evidence would be to make the Sanhedrin's plot against Jesus a terrible mistake, an offense against God. One lie leads to another, and the guilt is compounded.

> **What Do You Think?**
>
> Why do people refuse to change their belief when overwhelming evidence says they should?
>
> *Talking Points for Your Discussion*
> - Psalm 10:4
> - John 11:48
> - Romans 1:28-31

C. Lie Is Spread (v. 15)

15. So they took the money, and did as they were taught: and this saying is commonly reported among the Jews until this day.

For the Sadducees, the denial of Jesus' resurrection is necessary because they deny any possibility of resurrection (see Acts 23:8). While the Pharisees do believe in resurrection, they cannot imagine Jesus as being raised by God, thus having His claims vindicated. The first-century Christians understand that the resurrection of Christ is foundational to their faith (1 Corinthians 15:14). Matthew's reference shows that this stubborn refusal to accept the resurrection becomes a standard position of the majority of Jews as he writes (*until this day*), perhaps 30 years or so after the resurrection.

❧ THEY TOOK THE MONEY ❧

My older daughter was about two and a half years old when I began teaching at a Bible college. She became friends with the daughter of the minister where we worshiped. It so happened that the dean of the Bible college also attended that church.

Not too long after we moved there, there was a church potluck dinner. My daughter and her little friend were sitting at a table eating quietly when the dean came over. He tried to get acquainted, but my daughter was rather reserved and shy. She glanced up at him once, but then ignored him.

He then placed a nickel on the table and said, "If I give you a nickel, will you talk to me?" She ignored him. He replaced the nickel with a dime.

She would not even look at him. He replaced the dime with a quarter. He said, "Your daddy is a friend of mine." My daughter then took the quarter and said quietly, "But you're no friend of mine." She then ignored him.

This anecdote has always amused me with its innocent simplicity. Indeed, she took the money. But there's a big difference between what she did at her innocent age and what the adult soldiers did. Their action involved no innocent simplicity. The falsehood they helped perpetuate has eternal consequences. Don't fall for it.   —J. B. N.

III. Worldwide Witnesses
(MATTHEW 28:16-20)

A. Worshiping and Doubting (vv. 16, 17)

16. Then the eleven disciples went away into Galilee, into a mountain where Jesus had appointed them.

The remaining disciples, depleted in number because of the suicide of Judas (Matthew 27:5), eventually depart for home as instructed. The mountain they ascend is perhaps one of the rocky hills surrounding the Sea of Galilee. This is a place they have been before. Some associate this meeting with the time of Jesus' ascension, but Matthew does not say this. See instead Luke 24:50, 51, which makes clear that the ascension happens in Judea.

17. And when they saw him, they worshipped him: but some doubted.

The fact that the disciples worship means they fall prostrate on the ground, the physical position of submission. Matthew mentions that some doubt, giving us the impression that some of the 11 are not completely convinced that Jesus is indeed raised. This may indicate that something is obscuring an obvious identification. Their initial view of Jesus may be of a cloaked figure (compare Luke 24:15, 16). Luke tells us that some who see the resurrected Jesus believe Him to be a ghost or apparition of some kind (Luke 24:37).

Though Matthew mentions only the 11 disciples, some students believe this is the occasion noted in 1 Corinthians 15:6 when more than 500 brethren see the risen Jesus. This is a different way to explain the context in which some are doubtful.

B. Going and Teaching (vv. 18-20)

18. And Jesus came and spake unto them, saying, All power is given unto me in heaven and in earth.

This verse begins Matthew's final words for Jesus. This verse and the next two serve as the "marching orders" for His disciples. The words still ring true today, for the task outlined by Jesus is not yet complete. Jesus begins His speech by establishing His authority with the broadest claim He has ever made. Without any qualifications, He asserts that He has been given all power in both earth and Heaven. We are reminded of the great heavenly throne room scene in Revelation when the Lamb (representing Jesus) is accorded eternal power on the same level as God (Revelation 5:13).

19, 20a. Go ye therefore, and teach all nations, baptizing them in the name of the Father, and of the Son, and of the Holy Ghost: teaching them to observe all things whatsoever I have commanded you.

These verses are often referred to as the Great Commission, the missionary imperative of the church. The commission is based on two commands. First, the disciples of Jesus are to *go*—to proceed from the mountain out into the world until they have touched all nations (compare Acts 1:8). Second, they are to *teach*. The word used for teach means "to disciple," that is, to cause those whom they meet to become followers of Jesus.

This discipling process has two parts. It begins with baptizing. The significance of baptism becomes clearer on the Day of Pentecost. At that time, Peter will proclaim baptism as a proper response to those who yield their lives to Jesus (see Acts 2:38, 41). Jesus' instructions show that Christian baptism is accompanied by a confessed belief in the Father, Son, and Holy Ghost. Such a confession demands a recognition of the full divinity of Jesus and thus acknowledges Him as Lord.

The second aspect of discipling is to train the baptized in the teachings and commands of Jesus. In including this, Matthew is directing the reader back to his own book, for it serves as an invaluable repository of the teachings of Jesus. To be Jesus' follower means we take up the cross and follow Jesus no matter what the cost (Matthew 10:38; 16:24).

20b. And, lo, I am with you always, even unto the end of the world. Amen.

The last part of Jesus' speech serves to reassure the disciples that His resurrection is not a temporary situation. Even if He leaves them physically (which He will do at the ascension), He will never abandon them spiritually (see Matthew 18:20).

Jesus' presence is guaranteed in this way until *the end of the world*, meaning until He returns. This promise of presence both reassures the disciples and empowers them in their designated task of being witnesses to all the world for Jesus.

Conclusion

A. Discipling the Nations

The Joshua Project tracks the progress of the gospel among the known people groups of the world (see www.joshuaproject.net). This project estimates that about 40 percent of the world's population exists in people groups that do not have a viable Christian witness. What this means is that the need for cross-cultural missionaries has not diminished. Unreached people cannot come to faith in Jesus unless someone strategically and intentionally goes to them and teaches them about the risen Lord, Jesus Christ. Our task is clear!

B. Prayer

Lord Jesus, Ruler of Heaven and earth, give us a passion for lost souls. May we help to fulfill Your Great Commission as we go wherever You send us. May we never forget Your comforting and sustaining presence. We pray in Jesus' name, amen.

C. Thought to Remember

Go and tell that Jesus is risen.

INVOLVEMENT LEARNING

Some of the activities below are also found in the helpful student book, Adult Bible Class.
Don't forget to download the free reproducible page from www.standardlesson.com to enhance your lesson!

Into the Lesson

Prepare a handout with the heading *Easter Traditions*. Include these instructions: "On this page, jot down descriptions of activities, songs, and/or decorations that are a part of Easter traditions. Your answers may include both religious and secular traditions." Place handouts in chairs for learners to begin working on as they arrive.

Begin class by asking learners to share their lists; jot responses on the board. Then ask learners to tell you if each activity, song, or decoration listed is rooted in fantasy or in real, historical events. Write the letter *F* (fantasy) or *R* (reality) next to items listed on the board.

Make the transition to Bible study by saying, "A big part of dealing with the commemoration of Jesus' resurrection is separating fantasy from reality. Unfortunately, there are many people in our world who would list the resurrection of Jesus from the dead as *fantasy*. Today, we'll look at the event and some of the issues surrounding it."

Into the Word

Read today's printed text aloud. Then assign the following questions to five study teams or pairs. Give each group a piece of poster board, marker, and a photocopy of the appropriate page(s) from the lesson commentary. (*Alternative:* You can modify these assignments to be discussion questions for the entire class).

Error Group: Review the Lesson Background and imagine some theories that people might use to "explain away" the empty tomb. Give a reason why each theory is untenable.

Evidence Group: List hints or evidences in today's text (and other gospel accounts) that the resurrection of Jesus actually happened.

Connections Group: Today's text (v. 2) and Matthew 27:51 speak of two earthquakes. Discuss why you think God used earthquakes at Jesus' death and resurrection. Isaiah 29:6 may offer clues. Also,

what do you see is the connection between the resurrection and the Great Commission? Further, why would the denial of the resurrection of Jesus be especially important to the Sadducees?

Steps Group: Examine Matthew 28:19, 20. List and describe the steps Jesus outlines for an effective discipling process.

Blessings Group: Create a list of the blessings that come to today's world through the resurrection of Jesus. Circle what you believe to be the most significant blessing.

Allow each group to share its conclusions with the class as a whole.

Into Life

Select one or more of the following options, based on the nature of your class and the time available.

Option #1. Ask, "Why can the butterfly be a symbol of new life?" (Expected response: it transforms from being a caterpillar.) Distribute handouts of the outline of a butterfly. Include 2 Corinthians 5:17 as a caption. Suggest that learners place their butterfly on their bathroom mirrors for the week ahead as a daily reminder of their new life in Christ.

Option #2. Display the closing promise from today's printed text. Explain that one of the attributes of God is His *omnipresence* (ability to be everywhere at once). Ask learners to write a prayer that praises God for this attribute. The prayer should express why God's omnipresence is comforting. Ask for volunteers to read their prayers.

Option #3. Download the reproducible page and distribute copies of the An Action Text exercise. Have learners work on this either as a class or in small groups.

Option #4. Download the reproducible page and distribute copies of the Promises from an Empty Tomb exercise. Have learners work on this either as a class or in small groups.

Go and Tell

BE LIKE JESUS

BACKGROUND SCRIPTURE: Philippians 2:1-11

PRINTED TEXT: Philippians 2:1-11

Harmony of Mind

PHILIPPIANS 2:1-11

1 If there be therefore any consolation in Christ, if any comfort of love, if any fellowship of the Spirit, if any bowels and mercies,

2 Fulfil ye my joy, that ye be likeminded, having the same love, being of one accord, of one mind.

3 Let nothing be done through strife or vainglory; but in lowliness of mind let each esteem other better than themselves.

4 Look not every man on his own things, but every man also on the things of others.

5 Let this mind be in you, which was also in Christ Jesus:

6 Who, being in the form of God, thought it not robbery to be equal with God:

7 But made himself of no reputation, and took upon him the form of a servant, and was made in the likeness of men:

8 And being found in fashion as a man, he humbled himself, and became obedient unto death, even the death of the cross.

9 Wherefore God also hath highly exalted him, and given him a name which is above every name:

10 That at the name of Jesus every knee should bow, of things in heaven, and things in earth, and things under the earth;

11 And that every tongue should confess that Jesus Christ is Lord, to the glory of God the Father.

KEY VERSE

Let this mind be in you, which was also in Christ Jesus. —**Philippians 2:5**

WE WORSHIP GOD

Unit 2: Reasons for Praise

LESSONS 5–9

LESSON AIMS

After participating in this lesson, each student will be able to:

1. Describe the humility of Christ and of His followers as presented in Philippians 2.

2. Compare and contrast the humility described in the text with the prevailing attitude of contemporary culture.

3. Identify one problem area in his or her life to correct by following Jesus' example of humility and self-sacrifice.

LESSON OUTLINE

Introduction

A. Good Music

Music is a combination of tone and rhythm. There are many possible combinations. In vocal music, multiple singers singing the same tones with the same rhythm at the same time are said to be singing *in unison*. There is a pleasantness in this sound, with many voices combining into one voice with rich texture. Unison singing is like the rope with many strands, stronger because of its components.

If the singers are singing the same rhythmic pattern with different, yet complementary tones, we call this *harmony*. If singers are singing different, harmonizing notes with different, yet complementary rhythms, we call this *counterpoint;* an example of this is the singing of a round like "Row, Row, Row Your Boat."

Good music may employ unison, harmony, and counterpoint, but it will have a coordinated feel. This overall coordination, overall unity comes from the mind of the composer, who has arranged the variations to make the music interesting and to use the strengths of various types of voices to best effect.

The church is made up of members with differing levels of knowledge, experience, and commitment. But this variety does not mean that the church has to be a tangled mess of dissonance and confusion. Those with different opinions may still exist in harmony. Those with different ministries and avenues of service may still produce a pleasing counterpoint together. When the church speaks in unison on the essentials of faith and practice, it produces a mighty voice that commands attention.

All of this is possible only if the members are attuned to the same composer and reading from the same composition. This composer is Jesus, the Lord of the church and the author of salvation. The composition is His Word.

B. Lesson Background

Paul first visited Philippi about AD 52, while on his second missionary journey. He met several memorable characters as he founded the church in that city (Acts 16:11-40). Lydia, a wealthy merchant woman, was prominent (v. 14). Paul was arrested when he delivered a girl from a demonic spirit, thereby depriving her masters of her services as a moneymaking fortune-teller (vv. 16-18). The city jailer was converted after an earthquake freed Paul and Silas from their bondage (vv. 27-33). Paul and Silas then confronted the city magistrates rather than leave town quietly (vv. 38, 39). It seems there was not a dull moment for Paul in Philippi!

About 10 years later, Paul ended up in Rome under house arrest, awaiting a trial before the emperor (Acts 28). During all this time, he maintained contact with his beloved Philippians via letter and personal messengers. When the Philippians learned of Paul's plight, they sent a trusted member, Epaphroditus, to Rome to minister to Paul (Philippians 2:25; 4:18). The book of the Bible we call *Philippians* is a letter from Paul carried back to the church by this same Epaphroditus. It is an expression of joy and encouragement, even in this dark and difficult time for Paul.

Rome is about 600 miles from Philippi as the crow flies. It would be a short flight by plane today. In Paul's day, however, the journey between the two cities involved both overland travel and voyage by ship. Rather than a 90-minute flight, it may have taken a month or more to go from one city to the other.

Travel within the Roman Empire was relatively safe, but accidents and weather catastrophes were always a threat. We can imagine that Epaphroditus was extra careful in his return, having a mixture of urgency (to deliver this marvelous letter) combined with a sense of caution not to allow his mission to fail. We today are glad he made it safely, or we would not have the privilege of enjoying this treasured book.

I. Realizing Unity
(**PHILIPPIANS 2:1-4**)

A. Harmony of Mind (vv. 1, 2)

1. If there be therefore any consolation in Christ, if any comfort of love, if any fellowship of the Spirit, if any bowels and mercies.

Paul begins this section of his letter with four if-statements. These statements all describe conditions that prevail in a harmonious church. An English translation cannot convey fully the depth of Paul's expression for these four conditions. These *ifs* are not just possibilities or probabilities in Paul's mind. They are certainties. This is almost strong enough for us to replace the *if* of each statement with *since*—*since* there is consolation in Christ, . . . *since* there is comfort of love, . . . *since* there is fellowship of the Spirit, . . . *since* there are bowels and mercies.

The word *consolation* has the sense of giving hope and support to the discouraged and disaffected. We derive comfort from our assurance of the love of Christ; Paul declares in Romans 8:38, 39 that nothing can separate us from this love.

Furthermore, we have fellowship through our interconnected gift of God's Holy Spirit. The Greek word here is *koinonia,* which you may have seen used as the name for a Sunday school class; it carries the idea "sharing in community." When we have fellowship, we do things together. We share meals together and pray together (Acts 2:42). We share the tasks of ministry (2 Corinthians 8:4). Sometimes, we suffer together (Philippians 3:10).

> **What Do You Think?**
> What can be done to help church members connect with one another beyond Sunday morning?
> *Talking Points for Your Discussion*
> - Fellowship opportunities
> - Bible-study opportunities
> - Service projects

The fellowship of the church also gives us *bowels and mercies*. This is an older use of the word *bowels*, based on the idea of "inmost parts," our central being and emotions. The word *mercies* has the sense of compassion and sympathy. Paul is saying that the church is not a hard-edged place where we must all keep a stiff upper lip and never let down our guard. We fellowship with people who care about us as individuals. They weep when we weep. They feel loss when we feel loss (see Philippians 1:7).

2. Fulfil ye my joy, that ye be likeminded, having the same love, being of one accord, of one mind.

Paul has given four conditional *ifs* in verse 1. He now gives the *then* part: the command to fulfill his joy. He does not mean by this any sense of finality, as if he will enter a state of permanent bliss if they do as he asks. He is in a depressing situation while imprisoned in Rome. Although he is able to have a ministry in this place (Acts 28:30, 31; Philippians 1:13), he would rather be in Philippi with his friends and children in the faith. Even at a distance, however, he will receive joy if he knows of their faithfulness.

Paul lists three ways in which the Philippians can give him this joy. They can be *likeminded*, meaning that their minds are focused on the same thing. Second, they can have *the same love*, meaning that their affection and concern for one another is not divided or exclusive: all love and all are loved.

Third, Paul asks that they be *of one accord, of one mind*. We could translate the first idea of this couplet as "souls together," with the idea of interconnected lives. This will be actualized when Paul's readers have one mind. This is the same word used in the first way Paul suggests, *likeminded*. Thus Paul has come full circle in his purposes for the Philippians, emphasizing again the necessity for harmony in purpose and direction in their fellowship.

> *What Do You Think?*
> How harmonious is our church?
> *Talking Points for Your Discussion*
> - Proper criteria for evaluating church harmony
> - Improper criteria for evaluating church harmony

B. Harmony of Action (vv. 3, 4)

3. Let nothing be done through strife or vainglory; but in lowliness of mind let each esteem other better than themselves.

Paul does not separate the church's unified mind-set from its unity in actions. It is a surprising truth that church members that do things together may find more consensus in beliefs and attitudes. Working side-by-side in ministry tends to help us understand and appreciate one another far more than heated debate and censure.

Paul gives two general categories for judging the activities of the church. First, there should be nothing done from the motivations of *strife or vainglory*. Paul has already criticized those who preach out of "contention" (Philippians 1:16), the same word translated *strife* here. This is a word tilted toward the motivation of self-serving actions. Paul's antidote to such selfishness is to act with the best interests of others as paramount—to esteem others better than self (compare Romans 12:10).

❧ Esteeming Others ❧

When I first began teaching at a Christian university, there was a dignified elderly gentleman who also shared the teaching in my department. A native of Kentucky, he was the epitome of southern charm and gentility. He was always cordial and polite. When engaged in conversation, he never interrupted anyone. He was soft-spoken and sincere. We never heard him raise his voice or say an unkind word. He was the embodiment of a refined, dignified gentleman.

He had a habit of always holding the door for others to pass through before himself. In fact our dean once commented, "It is impossible to go through a doorway behind him!" If anyone ever reached the door before him, holding it open for this professor to pass through, he would simply reach around and hold the door open even wider. With a courtly gesture he would say, "Oh, please," and motion the other person through.

On a couple of occasions I had determined that I would outdo him in social graces. I held the door open for him to pass through. When he demurred and motioned for me to go ahead, I stood fast and gently urged him to go through. With a regal bow of his head he would then go through, yielding to my entreaty. He was a dignified gentleman through and through. He took the posture of a servant, esteeming others better than himself. He set an example for me. When was the last time you served as this kind of example for others?

—J. B. N.

Be Like Jesus

4. Look not every man on his own things, but every man also on the things of others.

Paul's second category of action has to do with things that serve the interests of others, not just our own interests. He is not expecting the Philippians to become busybodies, intruding into the activities of others in an unwelcome manner (see 2 Thessalonians 3:11; 1 Timothy 5:13). Rather, he is urging them to act in ways that serve the common good and the good of the individual members. This may be in spiritual matters such as prayer and teaching, but also in physical matters such as food and shelter (also 1 Corinthians 10:24, 33).

II. Recognizing Humility
(PHILIPPIANS 2:5-8)
A. Think Like Jesus (vv. 5, 6)

5. Let this mind be in you, which was also in Christ Jesus.

For Paul, the key to being likeminded (Philippians 2:2, above) is not found in debate that leads to an uneasy compromise. It is not found in a mixing of brightly colored opinions until we arrive at a benign and inoffensive gray. It is, rather, in conforming our thinking to that of our Lord, Jesus Christ. It is to yield our colors to the dazzling purity of Christ Jesus (Matthew 17:2).

What Do You Think?
What have you seen in other Christians that indicates that they have the mind of Christ?
Talking Points for Your Discussion
- Specific methods of service
- Generosity in giving
- Matthew 5:47

❧ THE MIND OF JESUS ❧

When I was in college many years ago, one of the most fascinating books I read was *The Mind of Jesus,* by William Barclay. Barclay (1907–1978) wrote over 80 books, mostly on New Testament topics. His books included a 17-volume Daily Study Bible commentary, which collectively sold over a million copies. The *Mind of Jesus* covers various aspects of Jesus' teachings.

The portion of the book that I remember most is Chapter 15, entitled "The Men against Jesus." There Barclay evaluates the scribes and Pharisees, the Sadducees and priests, and then the people. Each group had its own fears about what Jesus represented, saw Him as a threat, and resisted Him and His message.

But Jesus relentlessly adhered to His commitment to doing the Father's will in spite of the opposition. He did so in all purity and devotion. It is this "mind of Christ" that Paul calls us toward. How do you respond to this call?   —J. B. N.

6. Who, being in the form of God, thought it not robbery to be equal with God.

What is this mind of Christ (compare 1 Corinthians 2:16)? It begins with a recognition of His standing with God the Father. Paul reveals a profound truth when he says that before Jesus came to earth in human form, He existed *in the form of God.* Furthermore, Jesus did not move into this position out of an ambitious climbing of the ladder of Heaven's hierarchy. He has had equality with God all along. The Son's equality with the Father is not based on achievement. It just *was* and *is* (John 17:5). Its truth lies in the depths of the nature of our God as Trinity: Father, Son, and Holy Spirit.

Despite this standing, Christ did not cling to this position with greedy selfishness. He had everything, literally, more than we can imagine, but His attitude of selflessness allowed Him to relinquish this standing in order to save humanity.

HOW TO SAY IT

cacophony	kuh-*kaw*-fuh-nee.
Epaphroditus	Ee-*paf*-ro-*dye*-tus .
Gethsemane	Geth-*sem*-uh-nee (G as in *get*).
Isaiah	Eye-*zay*-uh.
koinonia *(Greek)*	koy-no-*nee*-uh.
Lydia	Lid-ee-uh.
Philippi	Fih-*lip*-pie or *Fil*-ih-pie.
Philippians	Fih-*lip*-ee-unz.
Silas	*Sigh*-luss.
Thessalonians	Thess-uh-*lo*-nee-unz
	(*th* as in *thin*).

B. Act Like Jesus (vv. 7, 8)

7. But made himself of no reputation, and took upon him the form of a servant, and was made in the likeness of men.

The expression *made himself of no reputation* is a startling description of what the incarnation entailed for the Son of God. The literal Greek says that Christ "emptied himself." As Emily Elliott (1836–1897) wrote, "Thou didst leave Thy throne and Thy kingly crown, when Thou camest to earth for me."

This is unfathomable for us, but Paul helps us understand better when he says that Christ assumed the form of a servant. Our modern idea of what a servant does obscures the roughness of this word, which carries the idea of "slave." It is not just that Christ came to serve humankind, but that His incarnation involved the surrender of His freedom, etc. He became a man, with all the limitations that that demanded (John 1:14; Romans 8:3).

> **What Do You Think?**
> In what area of your life do need to relinquish your "rights," humble yourself, and/or sacrificially help others? How does Jesus' example help you do this?
>
> *Talking Points for Your Discussion*
> - The roadblock of an "entitlement" mentality
> - Viewing certain tasks as "beneath us"
> - Maintaining a proper motive

8. And being found in fashion as a man, he humbled himself, and became obedient unto death, even the death of the cross.

We see Jesus' humanity expressed vividly in His prayers in the Garden of Gethsemane on the night of His betrayal. His human nature was horrified by that which awaited Him: a degrading arrest, mocking trials, betrayal by His disciples, brutality from the Roman guards, and the shame and agony of the cross. The time in the garden was a point of decision for Jesus, a potential turning point. We must believe that He had the potential to reject His mission, to walk away from the danger and escape from Jerusalem. But it was for the cross that He had come to earth (see John 12:27).

His spirit of submission was acted out in obedience (compare Hebrews 5:7, 8).

Paul is using this example to encourage the Philippians to act out their faith, even when it is difficult or dangerous. They are obedient when they serve others rather than self. For this, Jesus is the ultimate and perfect example.

III. Resulting Glory
(Philippians 2:9-11)
A. Divine Respect (v. 9)

9. Wherefore God also hath highly exalted him, and given him a name which is above every name.

Paul is not promising the Philippians an automatic payoff for unselfish actions. If that were the case, the actions could not be fully unselfish. However, it is instructive for him to tell the rest of Jesus' story. Jesus did not die a painful and shameful death to be forgotten by God and have His body rot in the grave. Instead, Jesus has been exalted, raised from the dead and glorified in Heaven (Acts 2:33; Hebrews 1:3, 4). Paul signifies this by God's act in granting Jesus *a name which is above every name* (Ephesians 1:21).

What exactly is this name? Paul does not say, but a vision of John reveals this as a title: "King of kings and Lord of lords" (Revelation 19:16). There is no human ruler who supersedes or surpasses Jesus in any way. He is honored by God in an eternal act of respect.

B. Universal Submission (vv. 10, 11)

10. That at the name of Jesus every knee should bow, of things in heaven, and things in earth, and things under the earth.

Paul explains the position of Jesus in describing a scene of universal surrender. To "bow the knee" is an act of submission, of recognition of one's superior and master. It has often been noted that Paul does not say this will be done willingly by all knee-bowers. He looks forward to a day of universal submission to the King of kings, even by the rebellious who reject Jesus (Isaiah 45:23; Romans 14:11). There will be no opting out of bowing to the Lord of lords. For some, this will be an act of joyous worship; for others, it will be a necessary act caused by God's command.

11. And that every tongue should confess that Jesus Christ is Lord, to the glory of God the Father.

The final act of submission will be a verbal acknowledgment of the lordship of the Christ. The one who became a universal servant, whose servanthood made everyone His master, becomes the universal Lord with everyone as His servants. There is no conflict here with the sovereignty of God, for this is done *to the glory of God the Father* (see 1 Corinthians 15:27, 28).

Paul wants the Philippians to know that they are part of this picture. He is not saying that unselfish service on their part will result in exaltation in Heaven as was the case with Jesus. Rather, Paul is saying that we should follow Jesus' example so that we exalt Him as Lord in our own lives.

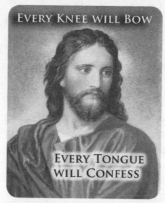

EVERY KNEE WILL BOW

EVERY TONGUE WILL CONFESS

Visual for Lesson 9

Point to this visual as you introduce the discussion question that is associated with verses 10 and 11.

> *What Do You Think?*
> How does the image of every knee bowing and every tongue confessing Jesus as Lord influence your daily walk with Him?
> *Talking Points for Your Discussion*
> - In how you interact with Jesus' enemies
> - In how you interact with fellow believers
> - In how you prioritize your time

Conclusion

A. Coordinated Churches

Some people seem to have a natural ability of coordinated movement. They move smoothly and gracefully, even when there is no particular need to do so. The rest of us often feel uncoordinated. When we hammer a nail, we hit our thumb. When we walk upstairs, we trip on the last one.

Many churches feel uncoordinated too. The members are not on the same page in purpose or action. In fact, they seem to have as many pages as Tolstoy's *War and Peace*. This creates a cacophony of voices, a chaos of activity. The result is that little is accomplished, frustration builds, and leaders burn out.

Paul sensed some of this cross-purpose situation in Philippi. He longed for this beloved church to achieve unity in their fellowship. Ultimately, he knew this would come from looking at Jesus. After all, it is His church, the church of Christ. He died for it, purchasing it with His own blood (1 Corinthians 6:20).

In following Jesus, we find the example of self-sacrifice and concern for others. We find the ongoing pattern of service and love for one another. The church that adopts this mind-set will not only be placing itself under the full lordship of the Lord of lords, it will also find a new sense of "coordinatedness"; its self-imposed clumsiness will disappear. It will also discover the joy of esteeming others and placing their interests first.

B. Prayer

God of all creation, we marvel at the faithful obedience of Your Son, Jesus, who obeyed all the way to the cross. We marvel at His determination to be a servant of all by taking on human form. We marvel at His devotion to do all things for Your glory.

May we find purpose in our lives by following His example. May we find unity in our church by looking at Him rather than ourselves. May we present a joyous harmony in our actions, pleasing to Your ears. We pray this by the name that is exalted above all other names, amen.

C. Thought to Remember

Practice Christ's humility.

INVOLVEMENT LEARNING

Some of the activities below are also found in the helpful student book, Adult Bible Class.
Don't forget to download the free reproducible page from www.standardlesson.com to enhance your lesson!

Into the Lesson

Option #1. Prepare 10 sheets of paper that have the letters of the word *Likeminded* on them, one each. Capitalize the *L* as a clue to the activity. Distribute the sheets of paper to 10 class members, one each. Say, "You hold the letters to the key word for today's study. Work with each other to arrange these 10 letters in the correct order until you discover the hidden word." If your class is smaller than 10, give some learners more than one sheet of paper.

When the answer is discovered, affix the letters in their correct order to the wall with temporary, "safe pull" tape. Make the transition to Bible study by saying, "*Likeminded* is a key word in today's text and in Christian living. We are challenged to have the mind of Christ. Today, we'll discover wonderful tips in how to accomplish this task."

Option #2. Ask learners to work in teams to list lines from Christian hymns and songs that describe characteristics of Jesus. Examples: "What a Friend" and "Jesus Loves Me." List their findings on the board. Make the transition to Bible study by saying, "Christians are called to be like Jesus as much as possible. Today's study will provide practical tips on how to accomplish this task."

Into the Word

Activity #1. Distribute photocopies of today's printed text. Before reading the text with the class, ask them to watch for and underline clues to living a Christlike life. Some will underline as you read; others will need a few extra minutes to finish.

As your learners are completing their underlining, affix two poster boards to the wall. One poster should have the heading *Attitudes, Values, and Actions to Embrace*. The other poster should have the heading *Attitudes, Values, and Actions to Avoid*. Ask two class members to act as "scribes" to record on the poster boards the answers that learners have discovered and underlined.

Activity #2. Have class members work in pairs. Half the pairs are to select a key word from the text that typifies the goal of the passage. The other half of the pairs are to search the text and select a key verse that summarizes the message of the passage. After a few minutes, call for answers. While affirming each answer given, explain that your personal choice for a key word is *likeminded* from verse 2 and the key verse is verse 5. Use the lesson commentary to explain your reasons.

Activity #3. Have learners close their Bibles for a test. Download the reproducible page and distribute copies of the Which Words? activity. Say, "Fill in the words that you think fit in the blanks, then open your Bibles to check your work." Discuss the results.

Into Life

Say, "Paul longed for those in the church at Philippi to enjoy a mind-set and lifestyle that demonstrated the qualities mentioned in today's text." Ask class members to work in small teams or pairs as they make a list of behaviors, values, and activities of your church that demonstrate these healthy qualities. They may write on the back of the handout distributed earlier. Then, ask them to develop a couple of ideas for a way your class can encourage these behaviors to continue. Allow groups to report their observations and ideas.

Say, "Of course, Christlike values, attitudes, and behaviors are encouraged not just for the church as a corporate body. Christlikeness also is a personal goal." Ask each person to look at the qualities that he or she underlined in the text. Ask class members to select and circle one of these attitudes or behaviors they would like to emphasize in their lives for the coming week. *Option:* Download the reproducible page and use the Likeminded Living activity at this point.

Distribute copies of the More Models activity from the reproducible page as take-home work.

PERPETUAL PRAISE

BACKGROUND SCRIPTURE: Revelation 4

PRINTED TEXT: Revelation 4

REVELATION 4

1 After this I looked, and, behold, a door was opened in heaven: and the first voice which I heard was as it were of a trumpet talking with me; which said, Come up hither, and I will shew thee things which must be hereafter.

2 And immediately I was in the spirit: and, behold, a throne was set in heaven, and one sat on the throne.

3 And he that sat was to look upon like a jasper and a sardine stone: and there was a rainbow round about the throne, in sight like unto an emerald.

4 And round about the throne were four and twenty seats: and upon the seats I saw four and twenty elders sitting, clothed in white raiment; and they had on their heads crowns of gold.

5 And out of the throne proceeded lightnings and thunderings and voices: and there were seven lamps of fire burning before the throne, which are the seven Spirits of God.

6 And before the throne there was a sea of glass like unto crystal: and in the midst of the throne, and round about the throne, were four beasts full of eyes before and behind.

7 And the first beast was like a lion, and the second beast like a calf, and the third beast had a face as a man, and the fourth beast was like a flying eagle.

8 And the four beasts had each of them six wings about him; and they were full of eyes within: and they rest not day and night, saying, Holy, holy, holy, Lord God Almighty, which was, and is, and is to come.

9 And when those beasts give glory and honour and thanks to him that sat on the throne, who liveth for ever and ever,

10 The four and twenty elders fall down before him that sat on the throne, and worship him that liveth for ever and ever, and cast their crowns before the throne, saying,

11 Thou art worthy, O Lord, to receive glory and honour and power: for thou hast created all things, and for thy pleasure they are and were created.

KEY VERSE

Immediately I was in the spirit: and, behold, a throne was set in heaven, and one sat on the throne.

—**Revelation 4:2**

WE WORSHIP GOD

Unit 3: John's Vision of Worship
LESSONS 10–13

LESSON AIMS

After participating in this lesson, each student will be able to:

1. List three important features of John's vision of worship.

2. Distinguish between elements of John's vision of worship that can and cannot be implemented in earthly worship services.

3. Write a hymn or poem that can be used in contemporary worship to express a sentiment similar to what is found in the text.

LESSON OUTLINE

Introduction
   A. Symbols and Symbolism
   B. Lesson Background
I. Throne in Heaven (REVELATION 4:1-6a)
   A. John in the Spirit (vv. 1, 2)
   B. Appearance of the Enthroned (v. 3)
   C. Description of the Setting (vv. 4-6a)
      Two Thrones
II. Worship in Heaven (REVELATION 4:6b-11)
   A. Creatures (vv. 6b-9)
   B. Elders (vv. 10, 11)
      Customs
Conclusion
   A. What Moves You to Worship?
   B. Prayer
   C. Thought to Remember

Introduction

A. Symbols and Symbolism

Symbols. The very word calls forth images that define a culture, a country's uniqueness as a nation, its sports teams, its special occasions, etc. Symbols may be used to capture the immense majesty of something.

In the Old Testament, the nation of Israel was accustomed to the use of symbols and symbolism. Consider the use of unleavened bread in Passover celebrations (Exodus 12:39). Consider the 12 stones that marked the crossing of the Jordan River (Joshua 4:1-7). Consider the covenant sign of circumcision (Genesis 17:11). Symbols are intended to "stand for" something in a memorable, visual way.

The danger with symbols and symbolic writing is that misinterpretation is all too easy. Misinterpretation happens when we "read into" the symbols a meaning that is not intended by the original writer. We must use discernment and caution when trying to interpret symbols and symbolic language.

B. Lesson Background

Revelation was written by the apostle John while in exile on the island of Patmos (Revelation 1:9). The dating of the book is somewhere around AD 90–96. The book of Revelation is saturated with symbolism. This makes it one of the most difficult to interpret books of the Bible. Even so, a broad picture is clear: John wanted his readers to know that good will overcome evil in the end. This fact should bring hope to all who are persecuted for their faith.

Our lesson begins just after John finishes his address to the seven churches in chapters 2 and 3. Chapter 4, today's text, opens up a new dimension of the revelation that John experiences.

I. Throne in Heaven
(REVELATION 4:1-6a)
A. John in the Spirit (vv. 1, 2)

1a. After this I looked, and, behold, a door was opened in heaven.

The *after this* transition marks a turning point from chapters 2 and 3, where John addresses the seven churches. Even so, what John is about to experience is a continuation of the vision he began to experience in chapter 1.

Scholars describe John as being in some kind of "ecstatic state," having already been in Heaven, in a sense, when he saw Jesus in 1:12-20. The description of a door to Heaven is symbolic of revelation that is about to take place, as John will be made privy to what is on the other side of the door. Whether John actually goes through the doorway or simply looks through it is not certain.

1b. And the first voice which I heard was as it were of a trumpet talking with me; which said, Come up hither, and I will shew thee things which must be hereafter.

The voice John hears is the same voice that commands him in Revelation 1:19 to write what he witnesses. We draw this conclusion because the voice's nature *of a trumpet* matches 1:10-12. The phrase *shew thee things which must be hereafter* clearly puts the events that John is about to witness into a future context for him.

2a. And immediately I was in the spirit.

We may find it confusing to read that John is *in the spirit*. What does that really mean? We begin by realizing that this is not a new thing for John, since he was "in the Spirit" in Revelation 1:10. This is undoubtedly a supernatural encounter with God. The idea of being "in the Spirit" resonates with John's original audience, since Old Testament prophets wrote in similar terms (compare Ezekiel 8:1-4). John may be telling his readers that he is moving deeper into the Spirit, or he simply may want to emphasize that God is the source of his vision. Both explanations are plausible.

2b. And, behold, a throne was set in heaven, and one sat on the throne.

While in this state, John sees a throne and the one sitting on it. We immediately get a sense that this individual is God. Revelation 4:9, considered below, will remove any doubt. This impression is bolstered by the images depicted in 1 Kings 22:19; Isaiah 6:1; and Ezekiel 1:25-28. The imagery is certainly not new to John's original readers who know their Old Testament!

B. Appearance of the Enthroned (v. 3)

3. And he that sat was to look upon like a jasper and a sardine stone: and there was a rainbow round about the throne, in sight like unto an emerald.

John seems to struggle to describe the sheer majesty of God. Words alone seem insufficient to the task. The imagery John uses to describe the radiance of God is that of precious jewels in all their brilliance.

The rainbow is another symbolic description of something that radiates beauty. The image of God sitting on His throne in Heaven as the centerpiece of all creation, radiating majesty in indescribable beauty, is something that all Christians can understand and embrace. The imagery in Ezekiel 1:26-28 is similar.

C. Description of the Setting (vv. 4-6a)

4a. And round about the throne were four and twenty seats.

It is interesting to note that John describes the place where God sits simply and elegantly as *the throne*. John now notices that there are 24 additional seats that surround that throne. Although we see the word *seats* in English, the Greek word for God's *throne* and these 24 *seats* is the same.

4b. And upon the seats I saw four and twenty elders sitting, clothed in white raiment; and they had on their heads crowns of gold.

HOW TO SAY IT

Armenia	Ar-*me*-nee-yuh.
Augustus Caesar	Aw-*gus*-tus *See*-zer.
cherubim	*chair*-uh-bim.
Corinthians	Ko-*rin*-thee-unz (*th* as in *thin*).
Ezekiel	Ee-*zeek*-ee-ul or Ec-*zeek*-yul.
Herod	*Hair*-ud.
Isaiah	Eye-*zay*-uh.
omniscience	ahm-*nish*-unts.
Patmos	*Pat*-muss.
Pompey	*Pom*-pay.
seraphim	*sair*-uh-fim.
Sinai	*Sigh*-nye or *Sigh*-nay-eye.
Tigranes	Tie-*gran*-us.

Each of the 24 additional thrones is occupied by an elder. There are varied opinions as to who these elders are and/or whom they represent. One interpretation is that the elders represent the ideal church as comprised of the 12 sons of Jacob (Genesis 35:23-26; Exodus 24:4; 28:21) plus the 12 apostles (Matthew 19:28). Others interpret the 24 to represent angels who assist in the divine rule of all creation, but Revelation 7:11 (Lesson 11) seems to indicate that the angels and the elders are not the same.

There are other interpretations, and there is no real consensus as to the correct one. The description of white clothing and crowns of gold is consistent with other descriptions found in Scripture for holiness and royalty (compare Revelation 7:13, 14, next week's lesson).

5a. And out of the throne proceeded lightnings and thunderings and voices.

John deepens his description of God's throne. Lightning and thunder accompanied the presence of God at Mount Sinai (see Exodus 19:16-20; 20:18). Psalm 77:18 describes God's dramatic activity using the terms *thunder* and *lightning*. Early Christians easily recognize the symbols that John uses to describe the majesty of God on the throne.

5b. And there were seven lamps of fire burning before the throne, which are the seven Spirits of God.

The *seven lamps of fire . . . which are the seven Spirits of God* echo Revelation 1:4, where John talks of the "seven Spirits which are before his throne." Scholars differ in their interpretation of these Spirits. Some propose that the 7 Spirits represent the fullness of God's Holy Spirit. Others see a symbol of angelic beings. The number 7 is quite important in the book of Revelation, occurring over 50 times (about 14 percent of all the Bible's uses). Given that the number 7 typically represents "perfection" in Revelation, the interpretation of the 7 Spirits representing the fullness of God's Spirit seems best (compare Zechariah 4:2).

❧ TWO THRONES ❧

Lyman Frank Baum wrote *The Wonderful Wizard of Oz* in 1900. Baum's work has been subjected to various symbolic interpretations. For example, some literary critics have seen Baum's work as a parody of the late nineteenth-century Populist conflict against industrialization and financial monopolies. The Scarecrow (symbolizing Midwestern farmers) and the Tin Man (symbolizing urban industrial workers) form an alliance to achieve what they desire; the yellow brick road (symbolizing the monetary gold standard) leads nowhere.

Others have seen a symbolic message that is hostile to Christianity. When Dorothy and the others finally gain access to the throne room, they are subjected to thunderous noises and flashes of light. When asked for his identity, the Wizard replies with claims of power and greatness—claims that soon prove false.

Regardless of what we do with the symbolism (if anything) in regard to the Wizard of Oz, there is no question about John's record: God sits on His throne, out of which proceed lightnings and thundering. The question that remains is whether or not He sits on the throne of your heart. Does He?

—J. B. N.

6a. And before the throne there was a sea of glass like unto crystal.

John now seems to pull back a little from the throne itself in order to give us a broader view of the throne room of Heaven. The idea of a sea as smooth as glass is an image of peace, serenity, and even the sovereignty of God in His control over nature (compare Psalm 89:8; Mark 4:39). The phrase *like unto crystal* means that the sea is clear. (Think of the phrase "crystal clear.")

> **What Do You Think?**
> Is your life right now more like a crystal sea or like a stormy ocean? Why do you say this?
> *Talking Points for Your Discussion*
> - Minor daily turbulence vs. ongoing, long-term storms
> - "Internal" vs. "external" storms

Ezekiel 1:22-26 offers further insight as to what the sea of glass represents. While Ezekiel does not specifically state that the "firmament" that is the color of "crystal" is a sea with the throne sitting above it, the overall idea seems to connect with John's imagery of *a sea of glass*. If we follow through with Ezekiel's vision of the throne, the nature of Ezekiel's "firmament" and John's "sea of glass" serve to symbolize God's mastery over creation and separateness from it.

II. Worship in Heaven
(REVELATION 4:6b-11)
A. Creatures (vv. 6b-9)

6b. And in the midst of the throne, and round about the throne, were four beasts full of eyes before and behind.

We now move to descriptions of the roles of those who are in the heavenly throne room. As we ponder the symbolism, we remember that John is describing a scene of worship. Indeed, the book of Revelation is the New Testament's book of worship.

The phrase *in the midst of the throne* suggests that the four beasts now in view are in the immediate presence of God. But who are these beasts, and what purpose do they serve? Interpretations vary. But we are probably safe in concluding (1) they are not wild animals and (2) they are not angels, because Revelation 7:11 distinguishes among "all the angels," "the elders," and "the four beasts."

We can see various similarities and differences in the descriptions of the four creatures of Ezekiel 1:5-14 and the four beasts of Revelation 4:6b-8. One important difference is that the beasts described here are *full of eyes before and behind* (also v. 8, below). The result of having so many eyes is that the beasts can observe everything. This can symbolize God's omniscience (His knowledge of all things).

Visual for Lessons 10 & 13. *Point to this visual as you ask, "What most excites you about the prospect of worship in Heaven?"*

7. And the first beast was like a lion, and the second beast like a calf, and the third beast had a face as a man, and the fourth beast was like a flying eagle.

John continues by observing specific features of the four beasts. Only one of the beasts has a human face, while the others are described with characteristics from the animal kingdom.

Again, there are competing interpretations as to the meaning of these symbols. One interpretation views these beasts as representative of general categories of creation: wild animals (*lion*), domesticated animals (*calf*), human beings (*man*), and sky creatures (*eagle*). Another interpretation is that the faces represent various qualities of God. Under this theory, the lion, calf, man, and eagle symbolize God's power, faithfulness, intelligence, and sovereignty, respectively.

8a. And the four beasts had each of them six wings about him; and they were full of eyes within.

The description of the beasts as being *full of eyes* repeats the description of verse 6, above. Further, we now are introduced to the fact that the four beasts have six wings each, as John continues to reach back to Old Testament imagery. The cherubim of Ezekiel 10 are "full of eyes" (v. 12), they have faces of a cherub, man, lion, and eagle (v. 14), but they have four wings rather than six (v. 21). We find six wings attributed to the seraphim of Isaiah 6:2.

What Do You Think?
How is your daily routine affected by knowing that God sees everything?
Talking Points for Your Discussion
- Holy things you are more careful to do and say
- Unholy things you "explain away" by thinking that God doesn't really care

8b. And they rest not day and night, saying, Holy, holy, holy, Lord God Almighty, which was, and is, and is to come.

The hymn that the beasts sing acknowledges the holiness and sovereignty of God. What is important here in verse 8 is the role that the beasts have: they offer continuous praise, which is the sense of *day and night*. The threefold *holy, holy, holy* matches Isaiah 6:3. We can think of these beasts as the worship leaders of Heaven (see v. 9, next).

We may wonder about the reference to *night* when Revelation 21:25 says "there shall be no night there." The context of 21:25 is that of an absence of evil in the New Jerusalem (see Revelation 21:27; compare John 3:19; 1 Thessalonians 5:1-7). We are careful to recognize a flexible use of symbolic language.

> **What Do You Think?**
> How does our worship recognize the holiness of God? How can we do better?
> *Talking Points for Your Discussion*
> ▪ Specific hymns or songs we sing
> ▪ Proper understanding of what holiness is
> ▪ Identifying things that distract us from experiencing the holiness of God

9. And when those beasts give glory and honour and thanks to him that sat on the throne, who liveth for ever and ever.

The "day and night" worship (v. 8b, above) presents itself in distinct ways. The *glory and honour and thanks* the beasts offer find echoes in 1 Corinthians 10:31; 1 Peter 2:17; and Psalm 30:12, respectively. The phrase *him that sat on the throne, who liveth for ever and ever* clearly identifies God and the eternal nature of His presence. Verse 9 serves as a transition to what occurs in verses 10, 11, next.

> **What Do You Think?**
> How well are we doing in giving God "glory, honor, and thanks" in our worship experience?
> *Talking Points for Your Discussion*
> ▪ Roadblocks to giving God glory, honor, thanks
> ▪ Positive markers that we are giving God glory, honor, thanks

B. Elders (vv. 10, 11)

10. The four and twenty elders fall down before him that sat on the throne, and worship him that liveth forever and ever, and cast their crowns before the throne saying.

As the beasts lead in the worship, the elders follow. The imagery of the elders casting their crowns before the throne may startle us to realize that anyone but God would have a crown. But God promises a "crown of life" to the faithful (James 1:12; Revelation 2:10).

❦ CUSTOMS ❦

Rules of social decorum are often the result of old practices. Frequently symbolic, these customs convey meaning to those who are cultured in the social graces.

I recall that when a man was introduced to a woman in the mid-twentieth century, he always took off his hat if he was wearing one. This was a sign of respect. Movies of the American Old West often show a man wearing a cowboy hat doing something similar. He might not remove his hat, but he would touch the front brim with his fingers and give her a nod of greeting to acknowledge her formally.

This custom can be traced back further still. In mid–nineteenth century America, it was customary for a man to raise his hat when passing a lady on the street. The higher he raised his hat, the more respect he demonstrated. Not to raise his hat meant that he didn't acknowledge her as a woman worthy of respect, which in turn was considered a slur at her morals.

Going back further, historical records indicate that Tigranes, the King of Armenia, fell to his knees and cast his crown at Pompey's feet when that Roman general entered the king's territory. This indicated the king's subservience to Rome. When King Herod met Augustus Caesar at Rhodes, Herod too removed his crown. It is this same symbolism that John records. What in your life do you need to cast at the feet of Jesus today to show your allegiance to Him?   —J. B. N.

11. Thou art worthy, O Lord, to receive glory and honour and power: for thou hast created

all things, and for thy pleasure they are and were created.

Like the beasts, the elders acknowledge the holiness and sovereignty of God in recognizing that He deserves *glory and honour and power*. But we now have the added element of God's worthiness for His role as Creator.

Those whom we consider spiritual leaders in the church today readily relinquish their authority before God. Thus it also is in Heaven. As we work our way through all the symbolism of this passage, John's message becomes clear: God is holy and sovereign. He created all living things. For these He deserves our endless praise and worship. Revelation 4 is not only a vivid description of the heavenly throne room, it also teaches us that continual praise and worship is a proper response to who God is.

What Do You Think?

How does our worship bring pleasure (or displeasure) to God?

Talking Points for Your Discussion

- Psalm 147:11
- Proverbs 12:22
- Isaiah 1:11-16

Conclusion

A. What Moves You to Worship?

John used symbols from the Old Testament that many of his readers recognized. The stories of the God of Israel and His relationship with His people were burned deep in the heart of the ancient Jew. These symbols had been passed down through the generations. These symbols moved them to worship.

These symbols should move us to worship as well. But the symbols in John's Revelation are not the only ones that can cause us to do so. Think of a beautiful sunset or full moon, which remind us of God's creative genius. Think of the Lord's Supper, which reminds us of the atoning sacrifice that Jesus made for our sins. Think of the symbolism of death and resurrection that we see in a baptism. The symbols that compel us to worship can help bring us through difficult times.

It is easy to get caught up in trying to interpret precisely the symbols and symbolism of the book of Revelation. People spend lots of time looking for hidden meanings or trying to discover the timeline of Jesus' return. A broader viewpoint is more useful: Revelation is a book of hope for those who persevere in their faith and endure. The late first-century church was persecuted (1 Peter 4:12-19). John himself had been exiled to Patmos. The apostle Paul had been executed by the time John wrote. This new movement called *Christianity* seemed destined to die. Times were tough, Rome seemed to be in charge, and circumstances were bleak. Christians then needed hope, just as we need hope today.

John wants us to understand that *worship is the key*. Worship serves to remind us of who is really in charge.

Our hope is based in the ability and determination of a holy and sovereign God, who will work His plan to conclusion. He is in total control, despite the circumstances we experience. The fact that God "was and is and is to come" is a timeless reminder of this fact.

Each day finds God on His throne, and everything that is happening is out in front of Him where He can keep watch over it. He cannot and will not be blindsided or surprised. Revelation 4 reminds us of this eternal truth. Our proper response is to praise and worship Him who sits on the throne.

B. Prayer

Father, use this passage from Your holy Word to remind us that You reign supreme in sovereignty and holiness. This fact does not change, despite what we may be facing in life.

Help us, Lord, to have the courage and faith to praise and worship You through all seasons of our lives. We thank You for Your enduring love and presence. We eagerly await the day when we can worship directly at your throne in Heaven. In Jesus' name we pray, amen.

C. Thought to Remember

When you have a problem,
begin with worship.

INVOLVEMENT LEARNING

Into the Lesson

Put this coded message on display: VNQCR ZQD HMZCDPTZSD. Put on display also a sheet of brown construction paper you have marked to resemble a simple wooden door. Affix it so that it will swing on "hinges" of tape. Tell the class you are going to reveal the mystery of the code. Swing open the door to reveal an arrow pointing to the right (from viewer's perspective).

If no one catches the clue, say, "Look to the right!" If still no one gets the secret, put a *W* over the *V*. Put an *A* over the *Z* and an *I* over the *H*. Each letter needs to be changed to the next letter to the right in alphabetical sequence (with *Z* reverting to *A*) to solve the riddle: "Words are inadequate"!

Say, "That is what John struggles with as he writes about what he was privileged by God to see." This will introduce two concepts in today's text: the concept of revelation and the image of the door John saw opened into Heaven. Continue: "Since words are inadequate, John uses many figures and symbols to help convey his vision to us. And sometimes even those symbols—such as our right-pointing arrow under the door—need further explanation!"

Alternative: Download the reproducible page and distribute copies of the Doors as Symbols exercise. Have learners begin working on this individually as they arrive. This will introduce the subject of symbolic language.

Into the Word

Give each learner a handout with three doors drawn on it, labeled *Door Number One, Door Number Two,* and *Door Number Three.* Ask learners to "find out what's behind each door" by identifying three important features of John's vision of worship seen in today's text. Give learners time to read the text and make their choices of what to "put behind each door," writing choices directly on the doors.

Have learners share their choices by asking someone to the right or left, "[name], which door do you want?" When the second party responds, the initiator can reveal his or her choice.

Let this continue until all learners have been involved (can be a small group activity). Elements that may be "behind the doors" include "a throne surrounded by thrones," "living creatures with many eyes," "a row of 24 crowns laid before the central throne," etc. This will help each learner see what John saw, and give you an opportunity for offering explanations and commentary.

Into Life

Have an artistic member of your class prepare a drawing of a door of about 3" by 5". Make enough copies for each learner to have one. Copies should be on light brown paper; lamination is desirable. Give each learner a "door" and these directions: "Put this in your Bible right before the book of Revelation. Each time you see it, let it remind you that Revelation is God's open door to Heaven, the open door through which John saw his vision of Heaven, the open door we all anticipate entering with Christ."

Download the reproducible page and distribute copies of the Angels' Song (and Ours) activity. In advance, ask a musically talented member of the class to put it to a simple tune and be prepared to lead the class in singing it.

To promote the idea of making music to praise God, distribute paraphrases of lines of the text and ask learners to suggest a second line to form a simple couplet. For example, you might distribute the line "Before the throne of Heaven, a sea of glass shines clear"; a possible second line your learners might create is "And in that glass reflected I see my Father dear." Ask a musically talented class member to bring a hymnal or songbook that indexes songs by meter; this will allow him or her to suggest tunes for the lyrics very quickly.

Perpetual Praise

THANKFUL WORSHIP

BACKGROUND SCRIPTURE: Revelation 7:9-17

PRINTED TEXT: Revelation 7:9-17

REVELATION 7:9-17

9 After this I beheld, and, lo, a great multitude, which no man could number, of all nations, and kindreds, and people, and tongues, stood before the throne, and before the Lamb, clothed with white robes, and palms in their hands;

10 And cried with a loud voice, saying, Salvation to our God which sitteth upon the throne, and unto the Lamb.

11 And all the angels stood round about the throne, and about the elders and the four beasts, and fell before the throne on their faces, and worshipped God,

12 Saying, Amen: Blessing, and glory, and wisdom, and thanksgiving, and honour, and power, and might, be unto our God for ever and ever. Amen.

13 And one of the elders answered, saying unto me, What are these which are arrayed in white robes? and whence came they?

14 And I said unto him, Sir, thou knowest. And he said to me, These are they which came out of great tribulation, and have washed their robes, and made them white in the blood of the Lamb.

15 Therefore are they before the throne of God, and serve him day and night in his temple: and he that sitteth on the throne shall dwell among them.

16 They shall hunger no more, neither thirst any more; neither shall the sun light on them, nor any heat.

17 For the Lamb which is in the midst of the throne shall feed them, and shall lead them unto living fountains of waters: and God shall wipe away all tears from their eyes.

KEY VERSE

[They] cried with a loud voice, saying, Salvation to our God which sitteth upon the throne, and unto the Lamb. —Revelation 7:10

WE WORSHIP GOD

Unit 3: John's Vision of Worship
LESSONS 10–13

LESSON AIMS

After participating in this lesson, each student will be able to:

1. Summarize the actions and reactions of the great multitude.

2. Explain some of the symbols in the text.

3. Make a plan to incorporate elements of today's text into times of personal worship.

LESSON OUTLINE

Introduction

A. Stain Removal

Have you ever noticed how many products and how-to guides there are that deal with the removal of stains? Typing "stain removal" or "stain remover" into an Internet search engine will yield several hundred thousand hits!

Stains ruin things. Faced with the choice of either replacing the ruined item or attempting to remove the stain, it's almost always more economical to do the latter. Thus stain removal has become big business.

Stain removal is also God's business. Sin causes unholy stains on our souls. Christ gave His life for His church so "That he might present it to himself a glorious church, not having spot, or wrinkle, or any such thing; but that it should be holy and without blemish" (Ephesians 5:27).

God does not treat us as something to be discarded automatically because we bear the stain of sin. He wants to remove the stain, and the cross of Christ is His tool for doing so. The final result of God's stain removal efforts is the subject of today's lesson.

B. Lesson Background

A lot happens between Revelation 4 (last week's lesson) and Revelation 7 (this week's study). Chapter 5 continues the theme of worship in Heaven, even though the opening of the 7 seals of judgment is imminent. The angels, the beasts, and the 24 elders all participate in worship of God. Chapter 6 then describes the opening of the first 6 seals of judgment.

When a seal is broken in Revelation 6, various symbolic things happen. The opening of the first seal is accompanied by the appearance of a white horse, which represents the lust for conquest; a good example of this is the Roman Empire (6:1, 2). The opening of the second seal is accompanied by the appearance of a red horse, which symbolizes war; this is both the ancient and modern plague of humanity (6:3, 4). The opening of the third seal is accompanied by the appearance of a black horse, which stands for famine; this is a usual consequence of war (6:5, 6). The opening of the fourth seal is accompanied by the appearance of a the pale horse, which denotes death; this is the ultimate result of war (6:7, 8).

The opening of the fifth seal (Revelation 6:9-11) is accompanied by a question from the people of God: "How long, O Lord?" (6:10). The answer is that they must wait "for a little season," that is, a little longer (6:11). While they wait, their confidence is found in the way they address God: "O Lord, holy and true" (6:10). When the sixth seal is opened, the events that unfold are such that people attempt to hide from the wrath of God (6:15-17).

The opening of the seventh seal, which introduces God's final judgment on the wicked and unbelieving, is delayed until Revelation 8:1. Thus chapter 7, today's study, functions as an interlude between the opening of the sixth and seventh seals.

As we read of God's stern judgment that manifests itself with the opening of the seven seals, we may wonder, "What about the people of God?" or, as John notes the wicked saying in the last phrase of 6:17, "Who shall be able to stand?" The interlude of chapter 7 provides the answer: it is God's people who can stand!

In the first eight verses of chapter 7, we see that God seals 144,000 of His people to protect them from the tribulations that the first 6 seals inaugurated. The number 144,000 is not to be taken literally, as if Heaven were run by census takers. The number 12, which occurs 35 times in Revelation, is an important number relating to God's people. (See the discussion of the 24 elders in Lesson 10.) The number 144,000, or 12 times 12,000, refers to the ultimate, multiplied people of God. These are pictured as coming from the nation of Israel, but they are not alone.

I. Gathered for Worship
(REVELATION 7:9-12)

A. Identity, Appearance, Praise (vv. 9, 10)

9. After this I beheld, and, lo, a great multitude, which no man could number, of all nations, and kindreds, and people, and tongues, stood before the throne, and before the Lamb, clothed with white robes, and palms in their hands.

The *after this* transition links this passage to Revelation 7:1-8 while signifying a shift in perspective. Instead of God's people standing at the precipice of the great tribulation on earth as seen in Revelation 7:1-8, John sees a vision of people standing before the throne of God. They are victorious in His presence. They are under the eternal care and guidance of the Lamb.

The church has stood firm in its commitment to Jesus, and now it shares in the final victory. For those who must endure tribulation on earth, this message brings hope that God is still in control and will have final judgment over the wicked.

This passage also teaches us that, as we have seen in chapter 4, our response to the one holy God is to praise and worship Him regardless of our circumstances. Whereas John merely "heard the number" of the 144,000 in verse 4, here he sees the multitude of people standing before the throne of God.

We interpret this group of people to represent all believers. This verse is very clear to point out that the *great multitude* includes people of all races, nations, family relationships, and languages. The church, consisting of Jew and Gentile from all the corners of the earth, stands before God. The presence of such an expansive and diverse group of people leads us to believe that the gospel has been preached to the ends of the earth prior to the final judgment (Matthew 28:19, 20).

From the viewpoint of symbolism, the Lamb is Jesus, of course. White robes are symbolic of righteousness (more on this later). The palm fronds remind us of Palm Sunday and Jesus' triumphal entry into Jerusalem (see Lesson 7).

What Do You Think?
In what circumstances are victory celebrations appropriate and inappropriate for Christians? Explain your reasoning.
Talking Points for Your Discussion
- Proverbs 24:17
- Luke 15:32

10. And cried with a loud voice, saying, Salvation to our God, which sitteth upon the throne, and unto the Lamb.

The multitude breaks out in praise and worship of God. There certainly is good reason for the multitude to express gratitude! God has brought them salvation. In defeating Satan and exacting His final judgment on all evil, God successfully works out His plan of salvation. The multitude praises this final victory.

The Palm Sunday cry of "Hosanna" (Mark 11:10; see Lesson 7) means "God, save us!" Understandably, the Jews of Jesus' day were hoping for God's miraculous saving of their nation. The cry *Salvation to our God* is a fulfillment of that Palm Sunday appeal. In Heaven the people of God shout "Salvation!" to celebrate an accomplished fact. They are the multitude of the saved, and the salvation is attributed both to God and to the Lamb.

What Do You Think?

How do we achieve a balance between enthusiastic loudness and contemplative silence in worship? Why is it important to do so?

Talking Points for Your Discussion

- Loudness before God: 2 Samuel 6:14, 15; Nehemiah 12:43; Luke 19:37
- Silence before God: Habakkuk 2:20; Zephaniah 1:7; Revelation 8:1
- Why people disagree over the volume level of worship

❧ *BABEL REVERSED* ❧

One listing claims that there are 6,912 known languages in the world today. To keep this multiplicity somewhat workable, the United Nations establishes only 6 to be "official" for its purposes: Arabic, Chinese, English, French, Russian, and Spanish. Statements made at U.N. meetings in any of these 6 are immediately translated into the other 5 for those in attendance. If someone wishes to address an official U.N. meeting in any other language, the speaker must provide someone who can translate.

This language problem and the rivalries among them is just one of the frustrating results of human pride traceable to the Tower of Babel (Genesis 11:1-9). We don't know which, if any, of the 6,912

languages we will speak in Heaven. But we are assured that when people of all tongues are before the throne of God, they will all shout out their praises to God in the unified language of worship. Does this future fact excite you?   —J. B. N.

B. Angels, Elders, Creatures (vv. 11, 12)

11, 12. And all the angels stood round about the throne, and about the elders and the four beasts, and fell before the throne on their faces, and worshipped God, saying, Amen: Blessing, and glory, and wisdom, and thanksgiving, and honour, and power, and might, be unto our God for ever and ever. Amen.

As the multitude praises and worships God, the angels, elders, and four beasts join in. We discussed these beings in our lesson on Revelation 4. As before, they assume a prostrate posture of worship.

The doubled *Amen* (literally, "it is true") signifies their agreement with what the multitude says in verse 10. The two amens serve as bookends for the beautiful sevenfold worship chant of *blessing . . . glory . . . wisdom . . . thanksgiving . . . honour . . . power . . . might* (see also Revelation 5:12).

What Do You Think?

What role does (or should) the word *Amen* play in our worship?

Talking Points for Your Discussion

- Deuteronomy 27:14-26
- Romans 1:25; 9:5; 11:36
- Avoiding a rote use of this word

II. Reasons for Worship
(REVELATION 7:13-17)
A. Who and Whence (vv. 13-15)

13. And one of the elders answered, saying unto me, What are these which are arrayed in white robes? and whence came they?

John is now approached by *one of the elders,* who inquires about the identity and origin of the multitude. We may find it odd that the question of the identity of the multitude is posed from an elder to John rather than the other way around. There is nothing within the passage to indicate

Thankful Worship

that John has any knowledge about the multitude beyond what he has witnessed thus far.

Perhaps John is confused by what he sees, so the elder is merely starting a conversation to clear things up for John. If so, what we have is a rhetorical technique of question and subsequent answer (next verse) by the one who poses the question. This is not the first time that an elder has spoken to John (see Revelation 5:5).

14a. And I said unto him, Sir, thou knowest. And he said to me, These are they which came out of great tribulation.

The fact that the elder identifies the multitude as those who have come *out of great tribulation* raises certain questions: Does "came out of" mean that they were martyred during that tribulation, or does it mean they lived through it? Is there reference here to a single, massive tribulation (as in "the" great tribulation), or is this a reference to the various "great" troubles that come and go as history unfolds?

Opinions vary, but the important thing is that the people have remained faithful. They have not surrendered their faith in Christ. They have not permitted themselves to worship false gods nor have they allowed unbelief to creep into their lives. John's message is one of hope to those who either go through or die during trials and tribulation: you will be in God's presence afterward.

What Do You Think?

What "tribulations" today are most likely to draw people away from Christ? Which are you most susceptible to?

Talking Points for Your Discussion
- Stresses: job, health, financial, family, etc. issues
- Temptations: sexual, material, etc. issues

14b. And have washed their robes, and made them white in the blood of the Lamb.

The last half of verse 14 paints a vivid image that we see repeated numerous times in the New Testament: our sins are washed away, cleansed *in the blood of the Lamb* (Acts 20:28; Romans 5:9; 1 Corinthians 6:11; 2 Peter 1:9; Hebrews 9:22; Revelation 12:11). The Lamb, of course, is Jesus

Christ. The result of faithfulness is the privilege of being able to stand spotless in God's presence (see the next verse).

❧ REWARDED ❧

We have all heard that "beauty is in the eye of the beholder," and it may be that *great tribulation* is in the experience of the subject. Many people have claimed to have undergone great persecution, but we have to wonder how much of it is brought on by their own personality quirks. Some people claim persecution when actually they are abused not because of their faith, but because other people simply can't tolerate their abrasive personalities. We all know people who simply are obnoxious, nosy, bossy pests.

Even so, genuine persecution has existed and does exist. Many Christians in the centuries of the early church lost their lives because they refused to participate in the worship of the traditional gods of pagan Rome. In his *Ecclesiastical History,* Eusebius tells many of their stories.

There is Blandina, the slave girl who was verbally tormented, then forced to sit in a red-hot chair, and finally gored to death by a wild bull. Sebastian was shot full of arrows. The Forty Martyrs of Sebaste were stripped naked and forced to stand on a frozen lake until they succumbed. Polycarp was burned at the stake. Even before John wrote the Revelation, Peter and Paul had been executed in Rome—Peter crucified upside down, and Paul beheaded. Thousands of others faced similar threats and executions.

But John says that those who come out of great tribulation wear white robes (the sign of purity) because they have been washed in the blood of the

HOW TO SAY IT

Babel	*Bay*-bul.
Blandina	Blan-*dee*-nuh.
Ecclesiastical	Ih-klee-zee-*as*-tih-kul.
Eusebius	You-*see*-be-us.
Hebrews	*Hee*-brews.
Polycarp	Paw-lee-*karp*.
Sebaste	Seh-*bas*-tee.
Sebastian	Suh-bah-*styahn*.

lamb. They have withstood the temptations and now stand around the throne of God singing His praises. Those who experience tribulation today can expect the same reward. —J. B. N.

15. Therefore are they before the throne of God, and serve him day and night in his temple: and he that sitteth on the throne shall dwell among them.

The word *therefore* indicates transition as John shifts from identifying the multitude and their status to describing what the people do in the presence of God. God has protected the faithful through all their difficulties. His plan of salvation has come to fruition.

Thus the people praise and *serve him day and night in his temple*. God protects them with His immediate presence. Because He now dwells among them, the people have direct access to Him at all times. (See also the discussion of *day and night* in Lesson 10 with regard to Revelation 4:8; 21:25.)

B. What and Why (vv. 16, 17)

16, 17. They shall hunger no more, neither thirst any more; neither shall the sun light on them, nor any heat. For the Lamb which is in the midst of the throne shall feed them, and shall lead them unto living fountains of waters: and God shall wipe away all tears from their eyes.

Visual for Lesson 11. *Point to this visual as you ask, "Which of these seven worship-words is most powerful to you? Why?"*

These two verses are among the most comforting that we find in Revelation. They give us a glimpse of what the future holds for the multitude in the consummated kingdom of God.

But this is not just a picture of future bliss. Much of this is a spiritual image of our lives today. We are sheltered by our Savior. We suffer no eternal damage from the natural world. We live with the comfort of God in our lives. We do indeed suffer the daily sorrows of life, but God overcomes these.

We now live lives of protection and purpose. At the center of the throne is the Lamb, and the Lamb is the center of our lives (compare Isaiah 49:10). Our purpose is to trust, obey, and follow Him (John 21:22). Jesus bids us follow Him today and every day (Matthew 16:24).

We thus die to self and rejoice in our service to Him (1 Corinthians 15:31). The reference to the absence of tears in Heaven echoes Isaiah 25:8: "He will swallow up death in victory; and the Lord God will wipe away tears from off all faces; and the rebuke of his people shall he take away from off all the earth: for the Lord hath spoken it."

> **What Do You Think?**
> What sorrow do you most look forward to God removing from your life?
> *Talking Points for Your Discussion*
> - Loss of loved ones (2 Samuel 18:33; Luke 8:52; etc.)
> - Loss of familiar surroundings (Jeremiah 9:19; etc.)
> - Injustice (Malachi 3:5; etc.)

The Bible offers us many images of God and Jesus as our shepherd. A trustworthy shepherd feeds and waters the flock, an image that resonates here as well. Isaiah 49:10, 13 is marvelous: "They shall not hunger nor thirst; neither shall the heat nor sun smite them: for he that hath mercy on them shall lead them, even by the springs of water shall he guide them. . . . Sing, O heavens; and be joyful, O earth; and break forth into singing, O mountains: for the Lord hath comforted his people, and will have mercy upon his afflicted." Psalm 23 is perhaps the best known reference to God as the shepherd who leads His people through times of trouble, provides for their needs, and comforts them. To John's first-century audience, the idea of being in the eternal presence of God and being cared for by Him as a shepherd clearly brings about tremendous hope for the future.

❧ *Eternal Comfort* ❧

My wife and I raised two daughters; more recently we have become grandparents. We have seen many tears in the process. Sometimes these were shed by the children, sometimes by the parents. Sometimes one of our girls would cry after falling off a tricycle. Sometimes there were tears when a high-school friend snubbed her and said extremely unkind things. Such is normal for teenagers, but the tears came anyway.

We parents have wept over their pain and disillusionment. Sometimes we have cried because we broke promises made to each other. We have cried when death has claimed family members or friends. We have cried over economic loss and times of hospitalization. But in all such instances we have wrapped our arms around each other and provided tissues to wipe away the tears.

I know that God is a far better parent than I ever was. So it is no stretch for me to think of God not just wiping tears from our eyes, but also holding us closely in His arms and telling us it will be all right. That's Heaven.   —J. B. N.

Conclusion

A. Praising God at All Times

Why do we praise God? That's an important question. Alongside it, we should also ask *When do we praise God?*

The two questions actually are interrelated. The *why* question can be answered only in the context of answering the *when* question. It is easy to praise God when things are good in our lives, but it is a different matter when the storms of life arrive. When times are great, God is so good! When times are tough, when we are being hammered everywhere we turn, then it's tempting to think that maybe God is not the God who is faithful. But God is always faithful. Thus we praise God

continually, regardless of our circumstances or the season of life we find ourselves in.

If we are honest with ourselves, then we will admit that our reasons for praising or not praising God often are linked to our circumstances. Often our focus is on ourselves, on our own limited outlook, and not on the nature and character of God. We may become tempted to compromise our faith when it seems that God is not listening and the prayer door to Heaven is bolted shut. We may question whether the Christian life is worth the cost when we find ourselves unemployed, persecuted for our belief in Christ, or suffering through a family breakup. Although the first century was a different time from cultural, political, and economic standpoints, at our core we are not much different from John's original audience. Human nature doesn't change.

Our study of Revelation 4 (Lesson 10) taught us that we worship God because of His holiness and His sovereignty; Revelation 7:9-19 further teaches us that we find hope that God will lead us in victory through our trials. Thus we continually praise and worship Him regardless of our circumstances.

Romans 8:28 tells us that God will work all things for the good of those who love Him and are called to His purpose. The key is that we have a choice in how we respond when life goes awry. Believers are not immune to storms in life. Will we choose to face these times with God and His promises by our side?

B. Prayer

Father, use today's passage from Your Word to remind us that You are there to guide, comfort, and provide for us even in—or especially in—the midst of the trials and storms of life. We need to be reminded that we are to praise and worship You at all times and in all circumstances.

We pray, Lord, that You would empower us to lift our arms and voices to You at all times. We thank You for Your enduring love and presence. In Jesus' name we pray, amen.

C. Thought to Remember

Praise God no matter what.

INVOLVEMENT LEARNING

Some of the activities below are also found in the helpful student book, Adult Bible Class.
Don't forget to download the free reproducible page from www.standardlesson.com to enhance your lesson!

Into the Lesson

Have the text of Revelation 6:17 on display as your class assembles. Distribute to six learners as they arrive one small envelope each, closed with a golden seal (easy to find in an office supply store). Have the following phrases on cards in the six envelopes, one per envelope: *card 1:* the sound of thunder and a mighty warrior on a white horse; *card 2:* a fiery red horse with a rider who stirs up devastating wars; *card 3:* a rider on a black horse carrying the scales of judgment; *card 4:* a pale horse with Death as its rider, followed closely by Hades; *card 5:* martyred Christians crying for justice; *card 6:* a great earthquake, with the sun turning black, the moon blood red, and the stars falling from heaven.

Have the envelopes numbered appropriately. Ask the holders to break open the envelopes and read the cards in sequence. Then note the verse you have on display. Say, "Who can stand . . . when the final judgment comes? That is what John is about to find out. And there is a seventh seal, unbroken as we come to today's text in Revelation 7."

Have a white robe, such as a baptismal gown, hanging conspicuously in your learning space. You can refer to it at the discussion of verses 9 and 14, if no one calls attention to it earlier.

Into the Word

Give each learner a sheet with the two words THANKFUL WORSHIP printed vertically down the middle. Say, "Write an idea and a verse number by at least 10 of these letters. What you write should identify something that motivates you to 'thankful worship,' the theme of today's study. Create your list as an acrostic."

To get your learners started, suggest this strategy: "Look at the revealed truths of this text and complete this statement: 'I will give God thankful worship because ___.'" Allow learners time and the freedom of their own choices, but here is a sample acrostic for the words and the text: I will be *T*earless (v. 17); I will be *H*olding palm leaves to celebrate the victory of the Lamb (v. 9); *A*ngels will be ever present (v. 11); there will be *N*o more tribulation (v. 14); *K*nowledge will replace ignorance (vv. 13-15); *F*reedom from discomfort will be eternal (v. 16); salvation is *U*niversal for those who choose Christ (v. 9); we will be *L*ed by the Lamb (v. 17); the *W*ater of life will be freely available (v. 17); *O*verwhelming numbers are there (v. 9); I will be *R*obed in white, purified by the Lamb's blood (vv. 9, 14); *S*alvation belongs to God, and only He can provide it (v. 10); *H*unger will be no more, for God will provide all we need (v. 16); *I* will be there (v. 9); the *P*resence of God is certain (v. 15).

As entries are discussed, encourage learners to add the other choices of other class members to their own lists.

Ask the class to repeat Psalm 23:1 in unison. Then ask "What is there in Revelation 7 that supports the confident expression of the truth we just read?" Point to verses 15-17 for elements of the "no wants" of which the psalmist speaks. Use Psalm 23:1 to stress that the images and promises of Revelation 7 are not new. To establish this point further, download the reproducible page and distribute copies of the That Seems Familiar activity for learners to complete.

Into Life

Download the reproducible page and distribute copies of the In the Multitude exercise. Have learners complete this as a whole class (if your class is small) or in small groups (if your class is large).

Conclude: "A good practice for the Christian is to repeat the benediction of Revelation 7:12 both as the day begins and as the day ends. Another spiritual discipline you can use for the week ahead is to meditate on one element of that benediction each day." Download the reproducible page and distribute as learners depart copies of the An "Amen Sandwich" exercise to help them do this.

NEW ORDER OF THINGS

BACKGROUND SCRIPTURE: **Revelation 21**
PRINTED TEXT: **Revelation 21:1-8, 22-27**

REVELATION 21:1-8, 22-27

1 And I saw a new heaven and a new earth: for the first heaven and the first earth were passed away; and there was no more sea.

2 And I John saw the holy city, new Jerusalem, coming down from God out of heaven, prepared as a bride adorned for her husband.

3 And I heard a great voice out of heaven saying, Behold, the tabernacle of God is with men, and he will dwell with them, and they shall be his people, and God himself shall be with them, and be their God.

4 And God shall wipe away all tears from their eyes; and there shall be no more death, neither sorrow, nor crying, neither shall there be any more pain: for the former things are passed away.

5 And he that sat upon the throne said, Behold, I make all things new. And he said unto me, Write: for these words are true and faithful.

6 And he said unto me, It is done. I am Alpha and Omega, the beginning and the end. I will give unto him that is athirst of the fountain of the water of life freely.

7 He that overcometh shall inherit all things; and I will be his God, and he shall be my son.

8 But the fearful, and unbelieving, and the abominable, and murderers, and whoremongers, and sorcerers, and idolaters, and all liars, shall have their part in the lake which burneth with fire and brimstone: which is the second death.

. . . .

22 And I saw no temple therein: for the Lord God Almighty and the Lamb are the temple of it.

23 And the city had no need of the sun, neither of the moon, to shine in it: for the glory of God did lighten it, and the Lamb is the light thereof.

24 And the nations of them which are saved shall walk in the light of it: and the kings of the earth do bring their glory and honour into it.

25 And the gates of it shall not be shut at all by day: for there shall be no night there.

26 And they shall bring the glory and honour of the nations into it.

27 And there shall in no wise enter into it any thing that defileth, neither whatsoever worketh abomination, or maketh a lie: but they which are written in the Lamb's book of life.

KEY VERSE

He that sat upon the throne said, Behold, I make all things new. —**Revelation 21:5**

WE WORSHIP GOD

Unit 3: John's Vision of Worship

LESSONS 10–13

LESSON AIMS

After participating in this lesson, each student will be able to:

1. Describe the new Jerusalem.

2. Explain some of the symbolism incorporated into the description of the new Jerusalem.

3. State one way that he or she will align personal behavior with the new order of things to come.

LESSON OUTLINE

Introduction

A. "If I Ruled the World"

"If I Ruled the World" was a song made famous in America in the early 1960s by Tony Bennett. The lyrics opine that "if I ruled the world" things would be very different. Every day would be springtime, and every person would be singing a new song. There would be beauty, happiness, and sunshine everywhere. How much better everything would be "if I ruled the world"!

On the negative side, ideas like this are a criticism of God. If there is a God, why doesn't He make the world better? If God is good, why does His world have wars, famines, earthquakes, and floods? Why is there sickness, pain, and death? If only we could be God for a little while, we are tempted to think, we could make everything so much better.

On the positive side, such ideas sound like they come straight out of the book of Revelation. In the new order of things, when the new Heaven and the new earth are finally what God really wants them to be, everything *will* be much better. Everyone *will* sing a new song (Revelation 5:9; 14:3). Joy and happiness *will* be in our hearts, because God will have wiped away every tear and banished every sorrow and pain. Instead of singing sappy songs about how we would rule the world, we would do well to pray all the more fervently, "Thy kingdom come, Thy will be done in earth, as it is in heaven" (Matthew 6:10).

B. Lesson Background

In John's great vision, events march toward a final showdown between good and evil. John foresees the day when God's kingdom wins the final triumph (Revelation 19). Everyone will stand before God's throne to be judged. The devil, the beast, and the false prophet—as well as death and Hades and all those whose names are not in the book of life—are thrown into the lake of fire and brimstone (Revelation 20).

So the slate of evil is wiped clean. The curse of the fallen world is lifted. As the smoke of battle clears from chapters 19 and 20, John sees a glorious new vista. In the new world, God's people will be blessed with a new order of things. It will be a final paradise where everything is the way God wants it to be. All the sorrows, all the sufferings, all the persecutions are over. The drama of human history reaches its final act—and God gives victory to His people.

I. City of God
(REVELATION 21:1-3)
A. New World (vv. 1, 2)

1. And I saw a new heaven and a new earth: for the first heaven and the first earth were passed away; and there was no more sea.

"In the beginning God created the heaven and the earth" (Genesis 1:1). What God created was good. But the original creation became corrupted by sin, and it fell into decay and death. So God promised that one day He would create "new heavens and a new earth: and the former shall not be remembered" (Isaiah 65:17). Living in exile on the island of Patmos (Revelation 1:9), John is privileged to get a glimpse of what all that will look like. Other apostles write of this coming glory as well (see Romans 8:19-22; 2 Peter 3:12, 13).

Thus John's vision of *a new heaven and a new earth* isn't a new idea, but it bears repeating. The raging seas, which are in ancient times a symbol of mortal danger and untamed chaos, will be no more. Everything that went wrong with creation will be cleansed, renewed, replaced.

What Do You Think?
Using your "sanctified imagination," what are some things that will be absent from the new heaven and earth?
Talking Points for Your Discussion
- Things that tempt
- Things that threaten
- Things that frighten

---

2. And I John saw the holy city, new Jerusalem, coming down from God out of heaven, prepared as a bride adorned for her husband.

When Isaiah prophesied that God would make new heavens and a new earth, he also said that God would "create Jerusalem a rejoicing, and her people a joy" (Isaiah 65:18). Now John sees the holy city made new. The focal city of God's people throughout most of the Old Testament becomes our own heavenly dwelling.

Jerusalem is not only the capital city of the ancient Jew, it is also the birthplace of the church (Acts 2). The *new Jerusalem*, then, becomes a fitting symbol of the future home of all God's people. The faithful Jews of the Mosaic covenant before Christ will be joined by the faithful Christians of the new covenant of Jesus Christ.

God's people, from every age, are seen collectively as *a bride adorned for her husband.* Israel of old had this promise: "Thou shalt be called Hephzibah [my delight is in her], and thy land Beulah [married]: for the Lord delighteth in thee, and thy land shall be married" (Isaiah 62:4). Similarly, the church has been told that just as husbands are to love their wives, Christ loved the church and sanctified it so "that he might present it to himself a glorious church, not having spot, or wrinkle, or any such thing" (Ephesians 5:25-27). In the world to come, God's faithful community will cry, "Alleluia: . . . the marriage of the Lamb is come, and his wife hath made herself ready" (Revelation 19:6, 7; compare 21:9).

B. New Resident (v. 3)

3. And I heard a great voice out of heaven saying, Behold, the tabernacle of God is with men, and he will dwell with them, and they shall be his people, and God himself shall be with them, and be their God.

The most spectacular thing about Heaven will not be the angels or the beauty or the carefree bliss. It will be the personal presence of Almighty God himself. John states the fact three times: God's *tabernacle* (or "dwelling place") *is with men;* He *will dwell with them;* and God himself will *be with them.*

In the days of Moses, the people of Israel had a foretaste of living in God's presence. They were instructed by God to erect a beautiful tent called a *tabernacle,* with a separate chamber called "the most holy place" (see Exodus 26). In at least a symbolic sense, the glory of God filled that earliest temple (Exodus 40:34, 35).

In the time of Jesus Christ, the disciples got an even better foretaste of living in God's presence. As the apostle John wrote, "And the Word was made flesh, and dwelt among us, (and we beheld his glory, the glory as of the only begotten of the Father,) full of grace and truth" (John 1:14). Jesus also told His disciples, "He that hath seen me hath seen the Father" (John 14:9). In the final chapter of salvation history, the Father himself will dwell with His people. All the earlier promises and fore-shadowings will have been fulfilled.

> ### What Do You Think?
> Practically speaking, how do you experience God living among His people today?
> *Talking Points for Your Discussion*
> - In comfort
> - In teaching
> - In daily provisions
> - In peace

❧ To Be with Them ❧

One of the great figures of Russian literature is Leo Tolstoy (1828–1910). Born into the Russian aristocracy, Tolstoy was favored with wealth virtually his entire life. A dissolute young man, his early diaries reflect his turmoil as he tried to understand life and his place in it. He could become extremely introspective and cynical, qualities that appeared strongly in his novels. His two major works, *War and Peace* and *Anna Karenina*, speak to his struggles.

Tolstoy experienced deep religious feelings. He ultimately decided that the peasants on his estate lived lives that were happier than his, despite their poverty and grinding toil. In 1884 he abandoned his wealth to his family and went to live as a celibate peasant. He ate only what he could grow, and he gave up tobacco and alcohol. He tried to live among his people as one of them, but he failed. His wife had to provide him food, or he would have starved.

God lived among His people in His Son, and it was not a failure. And in the new Jerusalem, God will again dwell with His people. That won't be a failure either. —J. B. N.

II. Gifts of God
(Revelation 21:4-8)
A. No More Tears (vv. 4, 5)

4. And God shall wipe away all tears from their eyes; and there shall be no more death, neither sorrow, nor crying, neither shall there be any more pain: for the former things are passed away.

Earth has often been called "the vale of tears," and not without good reason. All people have their share of sorrow and suffering; everyone experiences pain; no human family is immune to death. But God is going to change all that.

The penalty of death, brought onto the human race by Adam and Eve, will be removed (see Genesis 2:17; 3:19). Living forever will be a joy, because all the negative things of the old life will be stripped away. The *sorrow* of funerals and failures will be gone. The *crying* of frustration and disappointment will no longer be heard. Never again will the *pain* of illness, injury, or heartache be felt. All the old order of things will have *passed away*.

❧ No More Death ❧

In a letter to a French correspondent in 1789, Benjamin Franklin observed that "In this world, nothing is certain but death and taxes." Death is certainly a reality, and the more aged I become, the more experience with it I achieve. Death has claimed both of my parents as well as an older brother and other family members. My wife has lost both of her parents as well as an older sister. I am not complaining; my experience is typical of people my age.

It is not just death, however. Advancing age also often brings with it declining health. Although I believe I am currently in relatively good shape (given my age!), I have had two rounds of angioplasty. My wife's knees do not work as well as they used to. Other friends have experienced arthritis, Alzheimer's, Parkinson's Disease, macular degeneration, hearing loss, etc. When Robert Browning said, "Grow old along with me! The best is yet to be," he lied. He was only 52 when he wrote that in 1864. Old age, decreasing physical ability, and death are sad facts of life.

But we have the assurance that eventually death will be no more. When John Donne (1572–1631) wrote "Death Be Not Proud," he ended it with "Death, thou shalt die." Indeed! —J. B. N.

5. And he that sat upon the throne said, Behold, I make all things new. And he said unto me, Write: for these words are true and faithful.

God, who sat on the throne of judgment just a few verses earlier (Revelation 20:11), now speaks directly to John. He begins with the word *Behold,* as if to say, "Pay special attention right here!" The wonderful news is not that God merely is going to make new things; rather, He is going to make *all things new.* Creation will reboot, so to speak, and begin with a new, clean slate. The fact that God affirms His word to be *true and faithful* means that He does not hesitate, as if to waffle on whether He really means it or not. He does not equivocate or leave himself a loophole. It will happen.

> *What Do You Think?*
> What are some things that you are especially looking forward to being made new? Why?
> *Talking Points for Your Discussion*
> - Physical issues
> - Spiritual issues
> - Relationship issues

B. No More Thirst (v. 6)

6. And he said unto me, It is done. I am Alpha and Omega, the beginning and the end. I will give unto him that is athirst of the fountain of the water of life freely.

When God declares that something will happen, it is a done deal. Everything begins and ends with Him, since He is *Alpha and Omega* (the first and last letters of the Greek alphabet). Just as John records in a similar statement at the beginning of his book, God is the one "which is, and which was, and which is to come, the Almighty" (Revelation 1:8).

God promises to meet our needs. This is not a new promise (see Psalm 36:8, 9). The distractions of a fallen world tempt people to forsake God as "the fountain of living water" in favor of "broken cisterns, that can hold no water" (Jeremiah 2:13).

C. No More Lack (v. 7)

7. He that overcometh shall inherit all things; and I will be his God, and he shall be my son.

Several times the book of Revelation promises blessings to those who overcome. In each of the letters to the seven churches of Asia, there is a specific promise in this regard (Revelation 2:7, 11, 17, 26; 3:5, 12, 21). Whenever we are weary of the struggle, we should consider the ultimate outcome of the victory: we *inherit all things.* What better status can one have than to be declared God's child (compare 2 Samuel 7:14)?

> *What Do You Think?*
> How is the idea of being an heir of God a comfort to you in your daily struggles?
> *Talking Points for Your Discussion*
> - Galatians 3:26–4:7
> - Ephesians 1:13, 14

D. No More Evil (v. 8)

8. But the fearful, and unbelieving, and the abominable, and murderers, and whoremongers, and sorcerers, and idolaters, and all liars, shall have their part in the lake which burneth with fire and brimstone: which is the second death.

Not everyone will get to enjoy the blessings of Heaven. Some have been too fearful and unbelieving to trust God. They have disobeyed His commands, becoming abominable and guilty of a variety of grave sins. The list of sins we see here is repeated in Revelation 22:15 (next week's lesson). It is not a new list (compare Matthew 15:19; 1 Corinthians 6:9, 10; etc.).

The lake that burns *with fire and brimstone* is the lake of "everlasting fire" that Jesus says is prepared "for the devil and his angels" (Matthew 25:41; compare Revelation 20:10). God is not willing for anyone to perish (2 Peter 3:9). But those who insist on following Satan will also follow him to his destiny. While the first death separates a person from all those he or she loves on earth, the second death separates a person from God himself.

III. Glory of God

(REVELATION 21:22-27)

A. God Is the Temple (v. 22)

22. And I saw no temple therein: for the Lord God Almighty and the Lamb are the temple of it.

At first glance, we may find it odd that John sees no physical temple in the new Jerusalem. Upon reflection, however, we can understand why a physical temple is not needed in Heaven, for no additional sacrifices for sin must be made. Moreover, the old temple actually kept people away from God in a certain sense. Only the high priest could enter the most holy place (the "Holy of Holies"); only the priests could enter the holy place; Jewish men were restricted to the courtyard of the men; Jewish women were restricted to the courtyard of the women; and all Gentiles were restricted to an outer courtyard.

But in Heaven there are no such restrictions; the Father and the Lamb are immediately accessible to redeemed people. That is the significance of the fact that *the Lord God Almighty and the Lamb are the temple of it.* All barriers associated with the old temple are gone.

B. God Is the Sun (v. 23)

23. And the city had no need of the sun, neither of the moon, to shine in it: for the glory of God did lighten it, and the Lamb is the light thereof.

At various points in history, humans have been allowed to experience the illumination of the glory of the Lord. Think of Mount Sinai (Exodus 24:17), the beginning of the priestly ministry (Leviticus 9:23, 24), the dedication of the temple (2 Chronicles 7:1-3), the appearance of angels to shepherds (Luke 2:9). But those were temporary manifestations—they came and went. The situation in the new Jerusalem, however, will be permanent (compare Isaiah 60:19, 20).

C. God Is the Holy King (vv. 24-27)

24. And the nations of them which are saved shall walk in the light of it: and the kings of the earth do bring their glory and honour into it.

Earlier in this book, John saw people of every nation and tongue standing before the throne, praising the God of Heaven (Revelation 7:9, previous lesson). Now he sees these people in terms of being *the nations of them which are saved.* When combined with the acknowledgment that even *the kings of the earth* will be there, we see the ancient prophecy of Isaiah reaching fulfillment: "The Gentiles shall come to thy light, and kings to the brightness of thy rising" (Isaiah 60:3).

25. And the gates of it shall not be shut at all by day: for there shall be no night there.

Ancient cities are known for their walls and their gates. The gates are shut at various times for various reasons (example: Nehemiah 13:19). But unlike the gates of ancient cities, the gates of the capital city of Heaven will never be shut. This will fulfill the prophecy of Isaiah 60:11.

In addition, there will be no night. It is in the darkness of night, after all, when evil people tend to do their evil deeds (Isaiah 29:15; John 3:19). The darkness of night inhibits productive work (John 9:4). People stumble in darkness (John 11:10). Those are the kinds of things that Heaven does not need!

26. And they shall bring the glory and honour of the nations into it.

Just as the psalmist predicted centuries before, the day will come when "all kings shall fall down before him: all nations shall serve him" (Psalm 72:11). The "him" in that verse refers to "the king's son" of 72:1. Perhaps the psalmist saw no further than application to Solomon, son of King David. But God has something much broader in mind.

HOW TO SAY IT

Alpha	*Al*-fa.
Beulah	*Bew*-luh.
Hephzibah	*Hef*-zih-bah.
Mosaic	Mo-*zay*-ik.
Nehemiah	*Nee*-huh-**my**-uh
Omega	O-*may*-guh or O-*mee*-guh.
Patmos	*Pat*-muss.
Sinai	*Sigh*-nye or *Sigh*-nay-eye.
tabernacle	**tah**-burr-**na**-kul.
whoremongers	*hor*-mon-gers (g as in get).

At this point in John's great vision, the wicked have already been cast into the lake of fire (Revelation 21:8), and only the nations of those who are saved are present (21:24). Therefore, Heaven will not be defiled. Only those whose names are written in the Lamb's book of life will enter. These people have been washed in the blood of the Lamb (7:14), and their names are in His book (20:12, 15).

27. And there shall in no wise enter into it any thing that defileth, neither whatsoever worketh abomination, or maketh a lie: but they which are written in the Lamb's book of life.

The New Jerusalem features nothing unholy. All things there are pure as God and redeemed humanity live together (Isaiah 52:1). The Lamb has made such conditions possible. There is complete separation from the wicked. Those whose names *are written in the Lamb's book of life* (compare Philippians 4:3) gain the promise of Revelation 21:7: "He that overcometh shall inherit all things."

> *What Do You Think?*
> Do you ever fear that you will be excluded from Heaven? Why, or why not?
> *Talking Points for Your Discussion*
> ▪ Defeating a "trying hard, never sure" mind-set
> ▪ Evaluating recurring sin
> ▪ Examining anew the promise of eternal life

Conclusion

A. The Way We Were (and Are)

John's first-century world was a place of brutality. As much as one-third of the population of the Roman Empire was in slavery. Perceived threats, such as the new Christian religion, were confronted with force. Much of the wealth was in the hands of a few; most of the people lived hand-to-mouth in poverty. Disease and famine were frequent; no one could hold back death for long.

As Ecclesiastes 1:4-9 reminds us, generations come and generations go, but things don't really change all that much. There is nothing new under the sun. Slavery still exists in many places; we still live in a world of fragile peace; disease and famine still take the lives of millions every year. Even with all the advances in medical technology, many

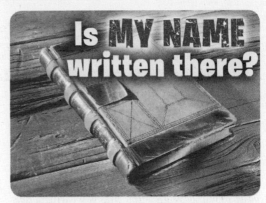

Visual for Lesson 12. *Point to this visual as you lead your class in singing the famous hymn "Is My Name Written There?"*

never reach the age of 70 of Psalm 90:10. The way we were is the way we still are, and that is why we long for the new order of things.

B. The Way God Is

But things are going to change! The way our world is now is going to change into the way God wants it to be. He promises an everlasting kingdom. Everything wrong with the old fallen world will be fixed; every pain and sorrow will go away. In God's world, there will be no sickness, no tears, no death.

This wonderful new order of things is much like the original order of things, the way things were before sin entered the picture. God, who does not change (Malachi 3:6; James 1:17), has always wanted to provide a paradise of bliss for His people. Thus, the story of paradise lost is finally the story of paradise regained. Everything that God ever wanted for us—everything God ever promised to us—will at last be realized in Heaven.

C. Prayer

Our Father in Heaven, we thank You for our eternal home in Heaven. Forgive us for too often becoming friends of this present world. Help us to lift our vision and catch a glimpse of the glory that awaits us. In Jesus' name, amen.

D. Thought to Remember

Be one of God's people!

INVOLVEMENT LEARNING

Some of the activities below are also found in the helpful student book, Adult Bible Class.
Don't forget to download the free reproducible page from www.standardlesson.com to enhance your lesson!

Into the Lesson

Download the reproducible page and put copies of the Making New from Old exercise in chairs. Learners can work on this as they arrive.

Introduce an unnamed "visiting prophet" who has been given a glimpse of things to come. At your signal, have an actor, who is wearing a simple eye mask, walk in and present the following short monologue:

"Seeing images of death and destruction is not pleasant. Line after line, page after page, God gave me a revelation of just such horror. Delivering that message is even less pleasant. No one wants to hear bad news. Yet, God's servant must speak the things he sees and hears, bad . . . and good.

"Thankfully, I was also given good news to follow the bad. God says, 'Behold, I create new heavens and a new earth: and the former shall not be remembered, nor come into mind. But be ye glad and rejoice for ever in that which I create: for, behold, I create Jerusalem a rejoicing, and her people a joy. And I will rejoice in Jerusalem, and joy in my people: and the voice of weeping shall be no more heard in her, nor the voice of crying.'"

When your "prophet" finishes, he should leave the room. Immediately ask, "Who was that masked prophet?" Someone will no doubt say, "John." But at that answer, say, "Not so!" Identify your prophet as Isaiah and note that his message of new heavens and a new earth is recorded in Isaiah 65:17-19. You may wish to have that read once again. Say, "All along, God has intended to replace the old and corrupted with the new and glorious. Today's text is His final picture of that marvelous, cataclysmic change."

Into the Word

Give each learner a badge or ID sticker with the following on it: *U or O?* Do not make an initial explanation. Request volunteers to read aloud the following verses: Revelation 2:7; 2:11; 2:17; 2:26; 3:5; 3:12; 3:21. After all are read, ask, "Now that you've heard those verses, read verse 7 of today's text and tell me what one of the letters on the label you have stands for." The answer is for the *O* is some form of the word *overcome*.

Once that word is identified, ask, "What then is the opposite of being an overcomer? Clue: starts with *U*." The word you want is *undergoer*. Once someone figures that out, say, "Read verse 8 of today's text and tell me why *undergoer* is a good opposite for *overcomer*."

Allow responses; you're looking for a reply that notes that those who are not cleansed by the blood of the Lamb undergo the horrors of God's wrath, judgment, and punishment. They "go under"! Comment that the book of Revelation is God's picture of the time He will say to the saved, "Come on over, overcomers!" and to the lost, "Go under, you who must undergo my wrath and justice!"

Ask the class to examine the remaining verses of the text to answer the question, "What do God's overcomers receive?" Encourage your learners to look at the entirety of today's text for answers. This can be a small-group exercise. Their discoveries should include elements such as (1) the beauty of a new heaven and earth, (2) the very presence of God, (3) freedom from the tears of pain and sorrow, (4) freedom from deterioration and death, (5) no more unmet physical needs, (6) the absence of all sinners that shame and threaten, (7) no more need for a physical temple for worship, (8) no more darkness, with its threats and unknowns, (9) the freedom of open gates, and (10) the surrounding presence of those whose motives are pure.

Into Life

Download the reproducible page and distribute copies of the If I Ruled the World exercise. Learners can complete this in small groups or study pairs. If time is running short, this can be a take-home exercise.

New Order of Things

WATER OF LIFE

BACKGROUND SCRIPTURE: Revelation 22
PRINTED TEXT: Revelation 22:1-9, 13-17

REVELATION 22:1-9, 13-17

1 And he shewed me a pure river of water of life, clear as crystal, proceeding out of the throne of God and of the Lamb.

2 In the midst of the street of it, and on either side of the river, was there the tree of life, which bare twelve manner of fruits, and yielded her fruit every month: and the leaves of the tree were for the healing of the nations.

3 And there shall be no more curse: but the throne of God and of the Lamb shall be in it; and his servants shall serve him:

4 And they shall see his face; and his name shall be in their foreheads.

5 And there shall be no night there; and they need no candle, neither light of the sun; for the Lord God giveth them light: and they shall reign for ever and ever.

6 And he said unto me, These sayings are faithful and true: and the Lord God of the holy prophets sent his angel to shew unto his servants the things which must shortly be done.

7 Behold, I come quickly: blessed is he that keepeth the sayings of the prophecy of this book.

8 And I John saw these things, and heard them. And when I had heard and seen, I fell down to worship before the feet of the angel which shewed me these things.

9 Then saith he unto me, See thou do it not: for I am thy fellowservant, and of thy brethren the prophets, and of them which keep the sayings of this book: worship God.

. . . .

13 I am Alpha and Omega, the beginning and the end, the first and the last.

14 Blessed are they that do his commandments, that they may have right to the tree of life, and may enter in through the gates into the city.

15 For without are dogs, and sorcerers, and whoremongers, and murderers, and idolaters, and whosoever loveth and maketh a lie.

16 I Jesus have sent mine angel to testify unto you these things in the churches. I am the root and the offspring of David, and the bright and morning star.

17 And the Spirit and the bride say, Come. And let him that heareth say, Come. And let him that is athirst come. And whosoever will, let him take the water of life freely.

KEY VERSES

[The angel] shewed me a pure river of water of life, clear as crystal, proceeding out of the throne of God and of the Lamb. In the midst of the street of it, and on either side of the river, was there the tree of life.

—**Revelation 22:1, 2**

WE WORSHIP GOD

Unit 3: John's Vision of Worship
LESSONS 10–13

LESSON AIMS

After participating in this lesson, each student will be able to:

1. List several characteristics of the city and the residents of Heaven.

2. Compare and contrast the list of those excluded from Heaven with characteristics of modern society.

3. Express his or her own reasons for wanting to answer the invitation of the Spirit and the bride to "Come!"

LESSON OUTLINE

Introduction

A. Where There's Water, There's Life

When scientists sent probes to the surface of Mars, they eagerly anticipated finding the answer to an old question: Is there water—and life—on Mars? They thought that maybe if there were ice hidden under the rocks, then there might be some evidence of microscopic life. Their line of thought was based on this earthly observation: where there's water, there's life.

It is true that life on earth depends on water. Even desert creatures have to have some water—the water that was lovingly provided by the Creator. We cannot imagine life existing without it. Therefore, it is fitting that God should provide "a pure river of water of life" to sustain the inhabitants of Heaven. The abundance of this life-giving water, flowing like a river from the throne of God, means that it is a plentiful supply that will never run out. For this water—for this life—God is to be forever worshiped and praised.

B. Lesson Background

Today's lesson is from the final chapter of the great Revelation that was given to John in his exile on the island of Patmos (Revelation 1:9). It is the victorious culmination of all the scenes of struggle that preceded. Beyond the great judgment scene of chapter 20, God's people come to enjoy the new Heaven and new earth of chapter 21 (Lesson 12). The final chapter shows God providing the water of life and the tree of life—everything necessary to sustain eternal life for His people. The curse is lifted; paradise is regained.

Perhaps it is also appropriate as part of the Lesson Background to review the biblical truth that God's people will have bodies in Heaven, bodies that will drink the water of life and eat from the tree of life. The New Testament is emphatic that the dead in Christ shall rise from the dead just as Jesus did (1 Thessalonians 4:14-16), that they will have a new kind of body (1 Corinthians 15:35-54), and that this body will be fashioned to be like Christ's glorious body (Philippians 3:21). It will be just as Job knew so long ago: after his body has been destroyed, "Yet in my flesh shall I see God:

whom I shall see for myself, and mine eyes shall behold, and not another" (Job 19:26, 27).

I. What John Sees
(REVELATION 22:1-5)
A. Water of Life (v. 1)

1. And he shewed me a pure river of water of life, clear as crystal, proceeding out of the throne of God and of the Lamb.

The angel who began showing John the wonders of the heavenly Jerusalem (Revelation 21:9-14) now continues the tour. The river the prophets had longingly foreseen will finally come into being (see Ezekiel 47:1-12; Joel 3:18; Zechariah 14:8). Father and Son—the source of the pure water of life—are pleased to share it with us.

❧ NOTHING PURER ❧

Bible images can affect people in different ways, depending on their life situations. For instance, John's imagery of abundant pure water brings to mind a contrasting image of the house in the Midwest where I grew up. That house lacked modern plumbing. The only semblance of plumbing we had was one cold-water tap, in the kitchen.

We lived in an unincorporated area outside a major city, and the city did not provide any services, including city water. So each house had its own well. Fortunately the water table was high, so access to water wasn't a problem. But the water quality wasn't the best. We kept a half-gallon glass jug in the refrigerator to have cold water. Over time, the sides of the jug became orange because of the water's high iron content. When we finally got an inside bathroom and a water heater, we could turn on the hot-water tap and smell the odor of metal in the water.

Those who have never had to put up with low-quality water might have a harder time relating to John's image of pure water. But when the time comes, we will all be grateful for how pure that heavenly water will be. It will be God's "water of life"—water like no other!   —J. B. N.

B. Tree of Life (v. 2)

2. In the midst of the street of it, and on either side of the river, was there the tree of life, which bare twelve manner of fruits, and yielded her fruit every month: and the leaves of the tree were for the healing of the nations.

The great boulevard in the center of the city will have a river flowing down the middle of it. Like a beautiful parkway, the river will have *the tree of life* planted on each side (apparently there are at least two such trees). This tree of life, originally available in the Garden of Eden, was forfeited by Adam and Eve (Genesis 3:22-24). In the new Jerusalem, it will be free to all once more.

Unlike ordinary fruit trees, however, this tree will produce different kinds of fruit. And the harvest is monthly, not yearly like ordinary trees. God not only provides abundantly, but also in great variety! The tree of life will ensure good health, with its leaves for the *healing of the nations* (see Ezekiel 47:12). The word *sickness* does not occur anywhere in John's Revelation, because this healing from the tree of life prevents it.

C. Presence of God (vv. 3-5)

3. And there shall be no more curse: but the throne of God and of the Lamb shall be in it; and his servants shall serve him.

With one short statement, John erases the sin-scourge of human history: *there shall be no more curse.* The fallen world, infested with thorns (Genesis 3:18) and in bondage to decay and corruption (Romans 8:21), will be redeemed. The human race will be released from the afflictions of pain, sorrow, and death (Genesis 3:16-19). All the consequences of sin will be removed.

HOW TO SAY IT

Alpha	*Al*-fa.
Babylon	*Bab*-uh-lun.
Beatitudes	Bee-*a*-tuh-toods (*a* as in *mat*).
Cornelius	Cor-*neel*-yus.
Ezekiel	Ee-*zeek*-ee-ul or Ee-*zeek*-yul.
Messiah	Meh-*sigh*-uh.
Omega	O-*may*-guh or O-*mee*-guh.
Patmos	*Pat*-muss.
whoremongers	*hor*-mon-gers (g as in get).
Zechariah	Zek-uh-*rye*-uh.

The greatest penalty was that Adam and Eve forfeited fellowship with God. But in Heaven, we will enjoy the unlimited presence of God once more. The *throne of God,* indicating His personal presence, will be in the city. Sharing the throne and the glory will be *the Lamb,* the Messiah who was slain for the sins of the world (see John 1:36; 1 Peter 1:19).

Cartoons depict people in Heaven sitting around on clouds strumming harps. But life in Heaven will not be an aimless existence. Just as God gave Adam a job to do in taking care of the garden (Genesis 2:15), in Heaven the saints of God will serve Him.

4. And they shall see his face; and his name shall be in their foreheads.

John wrote "no man hath seen God at any time" (John 1:18). Even Moses, "whom the Lord knew face to face" (Deuteronomy 34:10), was not allowed to see God directly (Exodus 33:20). But Jesus said, "Blessed are the pure in heart: for they shall see God" (Matthew 5:8). The redeemed in Heaven *shall see his face.*

What Do You Think?
Do you look forward to seeing the face of God? Why, or why not?
Talking Points for Your Discussion
- Causes of fearful apprehension
- Causes of joyful anticipation

The stamping of God's name on the foreheads of the saints carries with it important implications. Earlier in John's vision, the saints with God's seal on their foreheads are sheltered from the hurt that falls on earth and sea (Revelation 7:3). Later, these saints take their stand with the Lamb on Mount Zion, and they are identified by having His Father's name written on their foreheads (14:1). Now, in this final view of heavenly bliss, God's people proudly display their allegiance to God and membership in His community: His name is on their foreheads (compare 3:12).

5. And there shall be no night there; and they need no candle, neither light of the sun; for the Lord God giveth them light: and they shall reign for ever and ever.

The contrast of light with darkness is used both literally and figuratively in the Bible. In a literal sense, the citizens of the heavenly Jerusalem will not need sunlight, nor will they need a candle or any other source of artificial light. The Lord God himself will give them all the light they need (compare Isaiah 60:19, 20; Zechariah 14:7; Revelation 21:23, 25).

The figurative sense likely is intended as well, as we recall that Jesus rescues the saints from the "power of darkness" (Colossians 1:13) and calls us to walk in the light instead of the darkness (John 8:12; 1 John 1:5, 6). Those who "are not of the night, nor of darkness" (1 Thessalonians 5:5) will bask in the eternal light of a sin-free Heaven.

This is the context in which we, the saints, will reign with God forever and ever. We will drink from the river of the water of life; we will be nourished by the fruit; we will be healed by the leaves of the tree of life; we will walk in the light of God's own glory; we will reign in the designated area of God's own dominion.

II. What John Hears
(REVELATION 22:6-9, 13-17)
A. Recognize God's Truth (v. 6)

6. And he said unto me, These sayings are faithful and true: and the Lord God of the holy prophets sent his angel to shew unto his servants the things which must shortly be done.

Just as before, the angel assures John that everything he is telling him is *faithful and true* (see Revelation 19:9; 21:5). All the scenes of Heaven that John is seeing are accurate and real. Heaven is not a state of mind; Heaven is a place (John 14:2). The streets of gold, the river of crystal-clear water, the tree of life, reigning with God forever—it is all true!

The Lord God of Heaven is the same God who spoke through *the holy prophets* in the Old Testament. They predicted the coming of the Messiah, the new covenant, and even some of the scenes of Heaven (see 1 Peter 1:10-12). They spoke of the glory that is to come, and now John is allowed to see that glory. What was seen in the distant future by the holy prophets is drawing closer.

From God's perspective it even can be said that it all must *shortly be done* (compare Revelation 1:1).

B. Keep God's Truth (v. 7)

7. Behold, I come quickly: blessed is he that keepeth the sayings of the prophecy of this book.

Jesus now speaks directly for himself, rather than through the angel. (The angel will speak again in verse 9; Jesus will speak again in verse 13.) The good news is that Jesus will *come quickly*. Those who suppose that He is slow in returning should remember that God's timing is not the same as our timing, and that God delays the second coming to give people time to repent (2 Peter 3:8, 9).

There are seven beatitudes, or sayings about those who are blessed, in the book of Revelation (here and 1:3; 14:13; 16:15; 19:9; 20:6; 22:14). The blessing in this verse is promised to the person who keeps *the sayings of the prophecy of this book*. To "keep" the sayings of this book doesn't mean just to obey them, but also to preserve them without addition or subtraction (Revelation 22:19). The one who keeps the sayings learns the lesson about loyalty to God rather than Babylon (Revelation 17–19).

C. Worship God in Truth (vv. 8, 9)

8. And I John saw these things, and heard them. And when I had heard and seen, I fell down to worship before the feet of the angel which shewed me these things.

John is emphatic in his statement that he himself actually sees and hears the things that he writes. Then, overwhelmed by all that he has heard and seen, John falls down to worship at the feet of the heavenly messenger just as he tried to do earlier (Revelation 19:10). But angels are not to be worshiped (Colossians 2:18). Neither human nor angel should accept the glory that belongs to God (see Acts 12:21-23).

9. Then saith he unto me, See thou do it not: for I am thy fellowservant, and of thy brethren the prophets, and of them which keep the sayings of this book: worship God.

Just as Peter had to forbid Cornelius from worshiping him (Acts 10:25, 26; compare 14:11-18), the angel says to John *See thou do it not*. The angel is not worthy of worship. He is simply a fellow servant with John and the holy prophets who have foreseen these things. The angel is also a fellow servant of all believers who will *keep the sayings of this book*. All creatures great and small, angelic and human, have one ultimate task: *worship God*.

D. Alpha and Omega (v. 13)

13. I am Alpha and Omega, the beginning and the end, the first and the last.

When we recall that *Alpha and Omega* are the first and last letters of the Greek alphabet, we realize that the three couplets we see here are different ways of saying the same thing. Again, the speaker is Jesus (as He will identify himself in v. 16, below). Jesus was with the Father from the

Visual for Lessons 10 & 13. *Point to this visual as you ask, "In what ways will our worship in Heaven be the same and different from our worship now?"*

beginning (John 1:1), and He will exercise judgment at the end (John 5:22). From the first to the last, the Son is joined in authority and power with the Father.

Jesus should therefore be the beginning and the end of every believer's life. He should be our first thought in the morning and our last thought at night. We should make Him our shepherd from earliest childhood, our Savior to the last of our days. In that way we can honor Him as our own Alpha and Omega.

❧ NO OTHER ALPHA ❧

We owe a great deal to the Greek language, not the least of which is our alphabet. In fact, the word *alphabet* itself consists of the names of the first two letters of the Greek alphabet—*alpha* and *beta*. Many of the letters in the Greek alphabet transfer directly into English.

The first letter of the Greek alphabet finds many uses in English. We refer to dominant creatures as *alpha males* and *alpha females*. The field of physics speaks of *alpha particles, alpha rays,* etc. In astronomy, the *alpha star* is often the brightest star in a constellation. The first chapter of a collegiate Greek-letter society is called *the alpha chapter.*

But the most important use of the word *alpha* is in reference to Jesus. He is the dominant one; He is the brightest one; He is the first one. Is there another alpha in your life that you have allowed to displace Him?   —J. B. N.

E. Insiders and Outsiders (vv. 14, 15)

14. Blessed are they that do his commandments, that they may have right to the tree of life, and may enter in through the gates into the city.

This *blessed are they* is the last of the seven beatitudes in Revelation (see discussion in v. 7, above). Two specific rights are given to those who are blessed to belong to God. First, they have the privilege of eating from *the tree of life,* a privilege that was taken away from Adam and Eve (Genesis 3:22, 23). Second, they have free access *through the gates into the city.* Only citizens have unlimited right to enter a city, and faithful disciples will be the citizens of Heaven.

We should note in passing the thought *do his commandments, that they may have right to the tree of life* does not indicate the possibility of salvation by law-keeping. We are saved by grace, not by works (Ephesians 2:8, 9). Our works of obedience naturally result from our love for Jesus (John 14:15; 15:10; Ephesians 2:10; 2 John 6; etc.).

15. For without are dogs, and sorcerers, and whoremongers, and murderers, and idolaters, and whosoever loveth and maketh a lie.

Unworthy people, referred to as *dogs* (as in Philippians 3:2), are denied access to Heaven. They have practiced all manner of evil. The kinds of sinners listed are representative of all who will be separated from God in His holiness.

To understand fully what it means to be *without* (that is, outside the city), we turn back to Revelation 21:8 (last week's lesson). There we find the same list of sins as pertaining to those who will spend eternity in "the lake which burneth with fire and brimstone." Jesus described such people as being "cast out into outer darkness: there shall be weeping and gnashing of teeth" (Matthew 8:12; compare 1 Corinthians 6:9, 10).

F. Identity and Invitation (vv. 16, 17)

16. I Jesus have sent mine angel to testify unto you these things in the churches. I am the root and the offspring of David, and the bright and morning star.

Jesus himself opens the way so that no one will need to be left outside. It is He who sends His angel to testify to John the messages for the churches. As *the root and the offspring of David* (see also Isaiah 11:1, 10; Revelation 5:5), Jesus is the Messiah who brings salvation to all nations. He is the "Star out of Jacob" of Numbers 24:17. He is the *bright and morning star* that comes as God's light dawns on His people (2 Peter 1:19; Revelation 2:28). The "true Light, which lighteth every man" (John 1:9) will be the eternal light of Heaven.

17. And the Spirit and the bride say, Come. And let him that heareth say, Come. And let him that is athirst come. And whosoever will, let him take the water of life freely.

So the invitation is extended. The Spirit of Christ (as the Spirit is named in Romans 8:9) and the bride of Christ (identified as the church in Ephesians 5:25-27, 32) together say, *Come.* This invitation is to be repeated by everyone who hears the reading of this book; they should carry the invitation to everyone: *Come.* The invitation should echo in the heart of everyone thirsty for the living water: *Come.* This invitation is open for *whosoever will,* that is, for whoever wants the water of life that God offers. It is available freely and abundantly to everyone who desires to have it.

> *What Do You Think?*
> How well is your church doing at extending the invitation to come?
> *Talking Points for Your Discussion*
> - Across neighborhood boundaries
> - Across cultural boundaries

There is a blessing in the Beatitudes promised for those who "hunger and thirst" for righteousness: they will be filled (Matthew 5:6). This scene in Heaven is the ultimate fulfillment of that promise. Those who thirst for the blessings of God—and even more, for the presence of God—will have the abundant satisfaction of their hearts' desires.

Conclusion
A. A Return to Eden?

When we think of Heaven, it is only natural, perhaps, to focus our attention on the abundance of the blessings that await us there. The water of life, necessary to sustain us, will flow like a river from the throne of God. The tree of life, provided for our sustenance, will bear a new crop monthly. The incredible wealth, depicted as jewels, pearls, and streets of gold, dazzles our imagination.

The paradise of Eden is not lost forever. It will be recovered—and more! Heaven is not just a recovery. It is the final perfection of what humanity enjoyed in the beginning. God still wants to bless us with abundant life. Jesus will fulfill His promise that He will give us life more abundantly (John 10:10). When John saw a glimpse of all that awaits the faithful, He could only say, "Even so, come, Lord Jesus" (Revelation 22:20).

B. A Return to God

The best thing about Heaven, however, will be immediate access to God. The full fellowship of Eden will be regained when God lives personally among His people (Revelation 21:3), when Jesus returns to take us to be with Him (John 14:3).

Jesus prayed on the night before His death that people would believe in Him and thereby have fellowship with God (John 17:20-24). We begin to experience this kind of fellowship with God when we walk according to His commands (1 John 1:3, 5, 6). We also begin to experience fellowship with the divine in the presence of the Holy Spirit (Ephesians 1:13, 14; Philippians 2:1). The full abundance of fellowship with God, however, will come only in Heaven.

At last we will be able to see the God whom we love and worship. At last we will be able to fulfill the very purpose of our own creation. At last our souls will be at rest, when we finally have returned home to God.

C. Prayer

Heavenly Father, we thank You for this glimpse into the glories of Heaven that await us. May we thirst to partake of the river of the water of life and hunger for the fruit of the tree of life. Let us long to be forever in Your presence. With John we say, "Come, Lord Jesus!" In His name we pray, amen.

D. Thought to Remember

The final outcome will be worth it.

INVOLVEMENT LEARNING

Some of the activities below are also found in the helpful student book, Adult Bible Class.
Don't forget to download the free reproducible page from www.standardlesson.com to enhance your lesson!

Into the Lesson

As learners arrive, hand them each a half sheet of paper with one of the following six headings, so that an approximately equal number have each: *Great Cities on Great Rivers; Kinds of Fruit; Sources of Light; Types of Sinners; Designations/Names Given to Jesus; People Who Received a Message from an Angel.* Have these instructions printed on each handout: "Take three minutes to make a brainstorm list of what the heading calls for."

Allow learners to share their lists aloud, at least one of each category as you call for it. Say, "Today's text includes all these categories. The great city on a great river is the heavenly New Jerusalem. The variety of fruits come from the tree of life. God will be the only needed source of light. Jesus names the types of sinners who will be left outside Heaven. He calls himself, once more, the Alpha and Omega among other titles and designations He is given in the book of Revelation, and John is God's last biblical recipient of an angel's message. We will see them all in our study."

Into the Word

Have your learners flip over their sheets for the following activity. Say, "I want you to read through today's text and then write five things that will be in Heaven, and then write five things that will not. You may select specific words from the text or concepts implied by the words. I will give you an example for each, but you cannot use either for your list: one thing in Heaven, *river*; one thing not in Heaven, *unforgiven sinners.*"

Allow five to eight minutes for their work. Then choose one of these two ways for learners to show their lists to others: (1) have everyone stand, circulate, and exchange their lists silently with one another until you ask all to be seated, or (2) let learners pass their sheets around the room in a designated direction until they have seen most or all. (You will have to be the "courier" of the lists

between learners seated on the ends or from the front of your group to the back.)

At the end, ask, "What were the words you saw most often?" Allow answers. Then ask, "What were the words you saw only once or twice?" Allow answers. Ask, "What words did you see, if any, that you would like explanations for?" Allow inquiries and explanations. Both for the common and the uncommon words, you may wish to ask why those ideas appeared in the frequency they did; discuss the emphases in the collective lists and the issue of what is most significant about the scene of Heaven in today's text.

These lists and ensuing discussions will allow a good observation of the characteristics of the heavenly city and the residents of that city. You can have learners sort their words into those two categories: words about the city and words about the inhabitants.

Option: Download the reproducible page and use the Sounds Familiar activity to compare and contrast the ones left outside the gate of Heaven (v. 15) with high visibility sinners today.

Into Life

Recruit a proficient computer user to prepare in advance the following in the form of an invitation. Front: a line drawing of a stream running by a tree in full leaf with fruit. Inside: "The Spirit and the bride say 'Come!' R.S.V.P." Include a response card with the notation to be filled in: "It is my great desire to come, because _____."

Distribute one copy to each learner. Suggest that learners ponder their reasons for wanting to be a part of that great multitude who will one day stand at the feet of the enthroned Lamb, the one who has been slain for them.

Download the reproducible page and distribute copies of the Return to Eden exercise. This can be either a small-group exercise or a take-home activity, depending on available time.

GOD INSTRUCTS
HIS PEOPLE

Special Features

Lessons

Unit 1: God's People Learn from Prosperity

Unit 2: Listening for God in Changing Times

Unit 3: A Case Study in Community

QUARTERLY QUIZ

Use these questions as a pretest or as a review. The answers are on page iv of This Quarter in the Word.

Lesson 1

1. Who or what hardened the hearts of Israel's enemies? (Israel, the Lord, drought?) *Joshua 11:20*

2. Under Joshua the land had no rest from war. T/F. *Joshua 11:23*

Lesson 2

1. God commanded Joshua to be strong and very _____. *Joshua 1:7*

2. The Israelites left behind some of the women and children on the east of the Jordan. T/F. *Johsua 1:14*

Lesson 3

1. Rahab hid the Israelite spies in a root cellar. T/F. *Joshua 2:6*

2. How did the people in and around Jericho feel about Israel? (fearful, defiant, amused?) *Joshua 2:24*

Lesson 4

1. What animal horn was used to make trumpets? (ox, rhino, ram?) *Joshua 6:4*

2. The Israelites were allowed to keep the silver of Jericho for themselves. T/F. *Joshua 6:19*

Lesson 5

1. Achan hid in his _____ the devoted things he stole. *Joshua 7:22*

2. Achan's remains were burned after he was stoned. T/F. *Joshua 7:25*

Lesson 6

1. After Joshua, the Lord raised up _____ to save the people. *Judges 2:16*

2. In the time of the judges, corruption became worse and worse. T/F. *Judges 2:19*

Lesson 7

1. How is the King of Moab described? (tall, left-handed, fat?) *Judges 3:17*

2. After killing the king of Moab, Ehud left his weapon behind. T/F. *Judges 3:22*

Lesson 8

1. The Lord declared that Gideon had too few men to fight the Midianites. T/F. *Judges 7:2*

2. What reward did Gideon ask of the Israelites? (earrings, the kingship, nothing?) *Judges 8:24*

Lesson 9

1. God told the Israelites to go cry out to the gods they had chosen. T/F. *Judges 10:14*

2. How many Ammonite towns did Jephthah destroy? (2, 20, 200?) *Judges 11:33*

Lesson 10

1. What people-group was Israel's main enemy at the time of Samson? *Judges 13:1*

2. Samson's mother was instructed not to drink wine. T/F. *Judges 13:4*

Lesson 11

1. Naomi begged her daughters-in-law not to abandon her. T/F. *Ruth 1:8, 11*

2. The daughter-in-law of Naomi who returned to Moab was named _____. *Ruth 1:14*

Lesson 12

1. Boaz said that Ruth had taken refuge under God's what? (wings, hands, eyes?) *Ruth 2:12*

2. During the harvest mealtime, Ruth didn't get enough to eat. T/F. *Ruth 2:14*

Lesson 13

1. Where in the town did Boaz conduct his legal transaction regarding Ruth? (forum, market, gate?) *Ruth 4:1*

2. The kinsman who was ahead of Boaz at first refused to buy the land. T/F. *Ruth:4:4*

3. Ruth was the widow of whom? (Elimelech, Mahlon, Joshua?) *Ruth 4:10*

QUARTER AT A GLANCE

by Walter D. Zorn

God's people are to live in community. This is not a new expectation, as our texts from Joshua, Judges, and Ruth make clear. These books help us learn the biblical concept of "corporateness" as they offer both positive and negative examples.

Community Courage and Faith

God's promise of land to Israel was very ancient (Genesis 12:1-3). That promise was fulfilled under the leadership of Joshua. Trusting God's promises takes courage! It took courage for two spies to go into Jericho to scout the defenses. It took courage for Rahab to hide and protect those spies. Rahab had decided to "switch communities," so to speak, and that decision undoubtedly required a lot of faith and soul-searching. All three of those individuals were acting with a larger view to community.

The subsequent fall of Jericho was clearly God's doing, since marching around a city, blowing trumpets, and shouting can hardly be considered military maneuvers. The people learned that obedience to God brought victory, but that lesson could be learned only by exercising faith and courage. Rahab even became part of the lineage of Jesus!

Community Sin and Disaster

Sadly, the Israelites had to learn the hard way that the disobedience of one could bring disaster on many. They could not defeat the small village of Ai because of the disobedience of one man: Achan. His sin of keeping the "accursed thing" prevented the *entire* nation from continuing victory. Not until Achan and his *entire* family were executed could Israel move forward to fulfill her destiny. Achan was a man who took his eye off the good of the community. The result was community disaster as the Lord withdrew His blessing.

If the disobedience of one could bring such a disaster, what would be the result of the disobedience of the community as a whole? That is the subject of the book of Judges. With Joshua and the conquering generation gone, Israel was influenced by the pagan culture surrounding her. She decided to listen to that culture rather than to God.

The result was the notorious "sin cycle" of the book of Judges: disobedience, wrath of God, oppression by enemies, distress and outcry, deliverance by a judge, peace during the lifetime of the judge, and then repeated disobedience. This cycle repeated itself several times during the period of the judges (about 1373 to 1043 BC).

> **Trusting God's promises takes courage!**

But courage and faith were not completely lacking during this period. Ehud was the most aggressive judge: he assassinated the Moabite king, Eglon. On the other hand, Gideon was the most reluctant judge, deciding to seek several "signs" of God's presence before going into battle. Jephthah was a fearless warrior. Manoah and his wife were not judges, but they exercised faith in heeding God's instructions for raising the judge Samson.

Community Generosity and Blessing

The conclusion to this quarter's lessons comes from the book of Ruth, set during the period of the judges. Following personal tragedy, Ruth, a Moabitess, decided to cast her lot with her mother-in-law, Naomi, and the Israelite people—another example of "switching communities." This choice and a good work ethic led to unexpected blessings, and Ruth ended up in the lineage of Jesus.

Who would have thought that the community of Christ would be preceded by people such as a prostitute (Rahab) and a Moabitess (Ruth)? Yet Galatians 3:28–4:7 says that we too are in the lineage of Christ. Is that any less surprising?

by Lloyd M. Pelfrey

THE ISRAELITE conquest of Canaan seemed to occur with relative ease. But what about the other leading nations of that era—the Hittites, Assyria, Mitanni, etc.—didn't they care about what was going on? Were they not concerned that the land bridge between them and Egypt was being occupied by invaders?

Nations to the East

These questions have several answers. The first one is straightforward: God arranged the historical events of these nations so that they were not really interested with the founding of the new nation of Israel. For the most part, they had internal interests that kept them occupied, or they were declining in their influence.

In addition, there were several groups of people on the move at the time. Such groups were not considered threatening as they moved from place to place, often in search of pasture for their flocks. Israel was not considered a nation by others. It had no territory previously, and these former slaves had simply wandered from place to place for four decades. They were not thought to be a threat.

Egypt

Egypt controlled Canaan during the 40 years that the Israelites were in the wilderness. This was accomplished by the Pharaoh who had experienced the 10 plagues; he took vengeance on others to offset his defeats by the God of Israel.

This had the effect of creating in the promised land a subdued, unorganized people who did not provide strong resistance to the invasion by Israel. The people of the land of Canaan finally formed two coalitions to defend themselves against Israel: a southern group (Joshua 10) and a northern group (Joshua 11), but Israel defeated them easily.

The Pharaoh of Egypt at the time was more concerned with his personal luxury than military actions. He wanted peace, not war. There was therefore no resistance to Israel by Egypt during Joshua's conquests. Egypt was in decline.

The Seven Nations of Canaan

The "seven nations of Canaan" of Deuteronomy 7:1 are described as being stronger than Israel. The Hittites, one of the -ite nations listed there, made a technological breakthrough about 1400 BC, roughly the time of Joshua's conquest, when they developed iron-working. Iron was superior to bronze for weapons. Israel would not have this technology until the time of King David, some 400 years later (compare 1 Samuel 13:19-22).

But success for God's people didn't depend on having the best weapons. Once a dominant force in the area, the Hittites had retreated toward their own region at the time of Joshua's conquest. Despite being stronger than Israel, the Hittites were no longer a superpower. God was working to help His people. Thus did Israel take "all the land of the Hittites" (Joshua 1:4).

The other peoples of Canaan had formed city-states. Each city had its own king, and each king ruled his little domain (see the listing of 31 kings in Joshua 12:9-24). The concern of each king was protecting his city, not helping others. Mutual cooperation (as in Joshua 11:5) was more of an afterthought. Even the name *Jebusites* shows that that group was city-oriented, for the Jebusites were primarily the people who lived in or near Jebus (that is, Jerusalem; 1 Chronicles 11:4).

The God Who Was and Is Different

Religiously, one Pharaoh of Egypt attempted to have a type of monotheism, but this was rejected by his successors. Each god was thought to have distinctive powers, but only within his sphere of influence. The God of Israel was and is different. He is Lord of Heaven and earth, and He is always working to accomplish His purposes.

THIS QUARTER IN THE WORD

Mon, May 30	Hope in God's Promises	Acts 26:1-7
Tue, May 31	God's Promises to Israel	Romans 9:1-5
Wed, June 1	Children of the Promise	Romans 9:6-12
Thu, June 2	Children of the Living God	Romans 9:22-26
Fri, June 3	Since We Have These Promises	2 Corinthians 6:14–7:1
Sat, June 4	Abound in Hope	Romans 15:7-13
Sun, June 5	God's Promises to Moses Fulfilled	Joshua 1:1-6; 11:16-23
Mon, June 6	God's Commandments Given	Deuteronomy 5:28-33
Tue, June 7	Listen and Learn	Deuteronomy 31:7-13
Wed, June 8	Treasure God's Word	Psalm 119:9-16
Thu, June 9	Walk in God's Ways	1 Kings 2:1-4
Fri, June 10	As Long as He Sought God	2 Chronicles 26:1-5
Sat, June 11	Teach Me, O Lord	Psalm 119:33-40
Sun, June 12	The Key to Success	Joshua 1:7-18
Mon, June 13	The Promises of God	2 Corinthians 1:16-20
Tue, June 14	God's Promises Kept	Joshua 21:43–22:6
Wed, June 15	Rahab's Confession of God	Joshua 2:10-14
Thu, June 16	Rahab's Pact with the Spies	Joshua 2:17-21
Fri, June 17	Rahab's Help Rewarded	Joshua 6:22-25
Sat, June 18	Rahab and Her Works	James 2:18-25
Sun, June 19	Rahab's Protection of the Spies	Joshua 2:2-9, 15, 16, 22-24

Mon, Aug. 15	Sharing Bread with the Poor	Proverbs 22:1-9
Tue, Aug. 16	Provision for the Poor	Leviticus 19:1-10
Wed, Aug. 17	Generosity in the Kingdom	Matthew 20:1-15
Thu, Aug. 18	Sharing Equally	1 Samuel 30:21-25
Fri, Aug. 19	Ready to Share	1 Timothy 6:11-19
Sat, Aug. 20	Taking Initiative	Ruth 2:1-7
Sun, Aug. 21	A Kind Benefactor	Ruth 2:8-18
Mon, Aug. 22	Pray for the Faith Community	Philippians 1:3-11
Tue, Aug. 23	The Blameless Walk	Psalm 15
Wed, Aug. 24	Integrity of Heart	1 Kings 9:1-5
Thu, Aug. 25	Walking in Integrity	Psalm 26:1-11
Fri, Aug. 26	Integrity Provides Security	Proverbs 10:6-11
Sat, Aug. 27	Persisting in Integrity	Job 2:1-9
Sun, Aug. 28	Helping the Right Way	Ruth 4:1-10

Answers to the Quarterly Quiz on page 338

Answers to the Quarterly Quiz on page 338

Lesson 1—1. the Lord. 2. false. **Lesson 2**—1. courageous. 2. true. **Lesson 3**—1. false. 2. fearful. **Lesson 4**—1. ram. 2. false. **Lesson 5**—1. tent. 2. true. **Lesson 6**—1. judges. 2. true. **Lesson 7**—1. fat. 2. true. **Lesson 8**—1. false. 2. earrings. **Lesson 9**—1. true. 2. 20. **Lesson 10**—1. Philistines. 2. true. **Lesson 11**—1. false. 2. Orpah. **Lesson 12**—1. wings. 2. true. **Lesson 13**—1. gate. 2. false. 3. Mahlon.

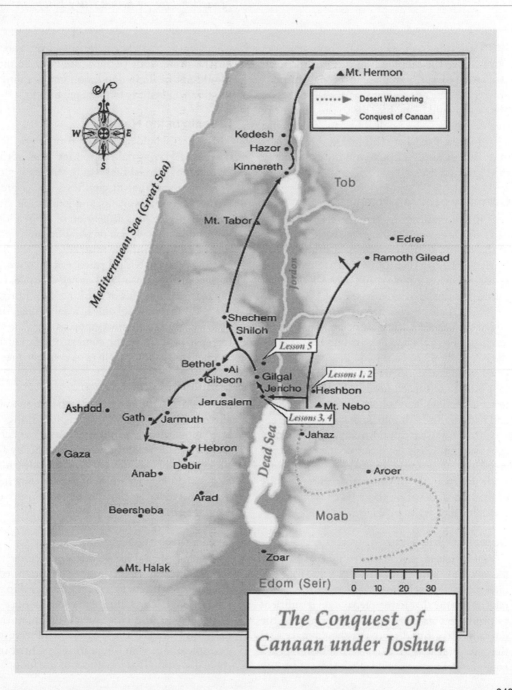

Mt. Hermon

Desert Wandering
Conquest of Canaan

Kedesh
Hazor
Kinnereth

Tob

Mediterranean Sea (Great Sea)

Mt. Tabor

Edrei
Ramoth Gilead

Jordan

Shechem
Shiloh

Lesson 5

Bethel
Ai
Gibeon
Gilgal
Jericho
Lessons 1, 2
Heshbon

Ashdod
Jerusalem
Mt. Nebo

Gath
Jarmuth
Lessons 3, 4

Jahaz

Gaza
Hebron
Debir

Aroer

Anab

Dead Sea

Arad

Beersheba

Moab

Mt. Halak

Zoar

Edom (Seir)

0   10   20   30

The Conquest of Canaan under Joshua

YOUR SPIRITUAL LIFE

Teacher Tips by James Riley Estep, Jr.

EVER HEARD the axiom, "The pew rarely rises above the pulpit"? It means that the spiritual maturity of those in a congregation is unlikely to be greater than that of their preacher. The same could be said for the spiritual maturity levels of those in an adult Bible study class with regard to their teacher. This means that teachers must be constantly in tune with the condition of their spiritual lives.

Overview of Three Domains

Spiritual maturity (or lack thereof!) manifests itself in three ways: Christian worldview (life of the mind), Christian experience (heart), and Christian service (hands). We may refer to these as the *cognitive, affective,* and *active* domains of spiritual maturity, respectively.

We see these three reflected in Scripture. It is said of one of the Old Testament's most recognized teachers, "For Ezra had prepared his heart to seek the law of the Lord, and to do it, and to teach in Israel statutes and judgments" (Ezra 7:10). Notice that Ezra didn't teach until he had prepared his heart (affective), had sought the law (cognitive), and had put his faith into practice (active).

This model has found many contemporary expressions in Christian literature and within congregations. We grow in spiritual maturity through study (sharpening our Christian intellect, our life of the mind), devotion (heart), and service (putting faith into active practice).

Domain of the Mind

Bible teachers have to study in preparing their lessons. This study, of course, aids the teacher's own spiritual development. However, it is a mistake to assume that lesson preparation is sufficient to promote your own spiritual maturity in the domain of the mind. Teachers should make sure they are *being* taught. Self-study of Scripture is a good thing, but you should also be part of a group where you are the student, learning from another. Furthermore, your personal study of Scripture should not be limited to lesson preparation, but should include study for personal benefit.

Domain of the Heart

Teachers should also have a regular practice of devotion. "Having daily devotions" does not simply refer to personal Bible study. Rather, it means practicing spiritual disciplines such as prayer, fasting, personal worship, and journaling. Some teachers neglect this dimension of their spiritual lives, substituting lesson preparation time for personal devotion. This is a mistake.

Having an established practice of devotion, perhaps by using a devotional or prayer guide, helps the teacher center his or her inner life (heart) on God. This happens not only in a daily "quiet time" of devotions, but also in a group setting. The sharing that happens in the context of relationships can benefit the spiritual lives of everyone present.

Domain of Service

Yes, teaching is your service, and being a teacher aids in the promotion of your spiritual life. But how about also committing yourself to acts of service outside of your teaching role? Many adult Bible study classes not only gather to learn, but also schedule opportunities for their class members to serve in the church and community on a regular basis.

Dual Concern

Teachers should have a dual concern for their spiritual life. Primarily, we are to be concerned for our own growing and deepening relationship with God through Jesus Christ. However, we must also be concerned with how our spiritual maturity is modeled to others. The teacher should serve as an example of one who is maturing in Christ in all three domains. That too is part of teaching.

GOD KEEPS
HIS PROMISES

BACKGROUND SCRIPTURE: Joshua 1:1-6; 11:1–12:24
PRINTED TEXT: Joshua 1:1-6; 11:16-23

JOSHUA 1:1-6

1 Now after the death of Moses the servant of the LORD it came to pass, that the LORD spake unto Joshua the son of Nun, Moses' minister, saying,

2 Moses my servant is dead; now therefore arise, go over this Jordan, thou, and all this people, unto the land which I do give to them, even to the children of Israel.

3 Every place that the sole of your foot shall tread upon, that have I given unto you, as I said unto Moses.

4 From the wilderness and this Lebanon even unto the great river, the river Euphrates, all the land of the Hittites, and unto the great sea toward the going down of the sun, shall be your coast.

5 There shall not any man be able to stand before thee all the days of thy life: as I was with Moses, so I will be with thee: I will not fail thee, nor forsake thee.

6 Be strong and of a good courage: for unto this people shalt thou divide for an inheritance the land, which I sware unto their fathers to give them.

JOSHUA 11:16-23

16 So Joshua took all that land, the hills, and all the south country, and all the land of Goshen, and the valley, and the plain, and the mountain of Israel, and the valley of the same;

17 Even from the mount Halak, that goeth up to Seir, even unto Baalgad in the valley of Lebanon under mount Hermon: and all their kings he took, and smote them, and slew them.

18 Joshua made war a long time with all those kings.

19 There was not a city that made peace with the children of Israel, save the Hivites the inhabitants of Gibeon: all other they took in battle.

20 For it was of the LORD to harden their hearts, that they should come against Israel in battle, that he might destroy them utterly, and that they might have no favour, but that he might destroy them, as the LORD commanded Moses.

21 And at that time came Joshua, and cut off the Anakims from the mountains, from Hebron, from Debir, from Anab, and from all the mountains of Judah, and from all the mountains of Israel: Joshua destroyed them utterly with their cities.

22 There was none of the Anakims left in the land of the children of Israel: only in Gaza, in Gath, and in Ashdod, there remained.

23 So Joshua took the whole land, according to all that the LORD said unto Moses; and Joshua gave it for an inheritance unto Israel according to their divisions by their tribes. And the land rested from war.

KEY VERSE

As the LORD commanded Moses his servant, so did Moses command Joshua, and so did Joshua; he left nothing undone of all that the LORD commanded Moses. —**Joshua 11:15**

GOD INSTRUCTS HIS PEOPLE

Unit 1: God's People Learn from Prosperity

LESSONS 1–5

LESSON AIMS

After participating in this lesson, each student will be able to:

1. Tell how God kept His promise to give the land of Canaan to the Israelites.

2. Explain why personal responsibility and action may be required to receive something promised.

3. Commit to one action to take in order to receive something God has promised.

LESSON OUTLINE

Introduction
  A. Promises and Piecrusts
  B. Lesson Background
  I. Commission (JOSHUA 1:1-6)
  A. Exhortation to Joshua (vv. 1, 2)
    Bringing Change
  B. Extent of the Land (vv. 3, 4)
  C. Encouragement to Joshua (vv. 5, 6)
 II. Mission (JOSHUA 11:16-23)
  A. Places Conquered (vv. 16, 17)
    Manifest Destiny?
  B. Peoples Conquered (vv. 18-22)
  C. Promises Reviewed (v. 23)
Conclusion
  A. Keeping Promises
  B. Prayer
  C. Thought to Remember

Introduction

A. Promises and Piecrusts

Is it true that promises, like piecrusts, are made to be broken? That statement has been traced back to 1681, when a British periodical criticized a certain individual by claiming, "He makes no more of breaking Acts of Parliaments, than if they were like Promises and Pie-crust, made to be broken."

Things haven't changed much in 430 years! Politicians running for office are still accused of making promises they cannot keep. Many politicians make promises with all good intentions of keeping them. Some people, sadly, make promises with *no* intention of keeping them. An automobile dealer relates the story of an individual who made the down payment on a car and drove away. He disappeared and could not be found. The world would be much different if people simply kept their promises. Think of what the world would be like if there were no more "piecrust promises"!

B. Lesson Background

God sometimes makes promises that He does not wish to keep. An excellent example is the occasion of Jonah's dramatic announcement to the people of Nineveh that it would be destroyed in 40 days. It was not destroyed at that time, and Jesus provided the explanation: the people of Nineveh genuinely repented when they heard Jonah's message (Matthew 12:41). One conclusion is that God makes at least two types of promises: absolute and conditional.

An example of an absolute promise is God's decision to grant the land of Canaan to Abram's descendants (Genesis 12:7). The promise was repeated (15:18; 17:8), and significant information was added (15:13). The promise that was first given to Abram was also given to his son Isaac (26:3), and then to Isaac's son Jacob (35:12). Joseph, one of Jacob's sons, had confidence in that promise (50:24, 25). The Lord's promise about Canaan was repeated when He challenged Moses to lead the Hebrews from slavery to the land "flowing with milk and honey" (Exodus 3:8; compare Leviticus 20:24; Numbers 13:27; Deuteronomy 31:20).

God Keeps His Promises

As the book of Joshua begins, the Israelites were camped in the plains of Moab at the edge of Canaan, across the Jordan River from Jericho (Numbers 22:1). It had been 40 years since they left Egypt. They had been camped in Moab for as long as 8 or 9 months. Their presence in the area was considered a threat to Balak, the king of Moab (Numbers 22–24). Balak sent for Balaam, a highly regarded prophet, to come and curse the Israelites. The memorable incident of his donkey's talking to him occurred during Balaam's sojourn to Moab (Numbers 22:23-35). Balaam, however, blessed Israel instead of cursing this new nation.

Subsequent events included a war with the Midianites (Numbers 25:16-18), accounts of a second military census (Numbers 26), and the commissioning of Joshua to succeed Moses (27:1-23). Two and one-half tribes made a request to Moses to remain in the territory east of the Jordan, and this was granted (32:33). Moses gave three farewell addresses in the book of Deuteronomy before his death. This was followed by a 30-day period of mourning (Deuteronomy 34:8).

This lengthy review is intended to show that God had a plan for His people. Much time had elapsed since those promises were first given, including the 40 years since the exodus from Egypt. Moses was dead, and Joshua was waiting for instructions from the Lord. God's promise was about to be fulfilled.

I. Commission

(Joshua 1:1-6)

Deuteronomy 34:8 reveals that a period of 30 days elapses between the death of Moses and the opening of today's text. This is a time of mourning. It is also a transition period for a new generation of leadership to assume its responsibilities. Israel is a nation that has no homeland, but that is about to change.

A. Exhortation to Joshua (vv. 1, 2)

1. Now after the death of Moses the servant of the Lord it came to pass, that the Lord spake unto Joshua the son of Nun, Moses' minister, saying.

Joshua is the leader. He has served as Moses' assistant the past 40 years. Very early in the wilderness wanderings, Joshua was thrust into the role of military leader (Exodus 17:8-13). This happened even before the Israelites reached Mount Sinai. Joshua was with Moses when Moses ascended the mount to receive the Law (24:13; 32:15-19), and Joshua probably saw Moses shatter the stone tablets of the commandments (32:19).

> **What Do You Think?**
> How should we honor a servant of God who has died? What mistakes should we avoid in doing so?
> **Talking Points for Your Discussion**
> ▪ Regarding continued teaching of his or her life lessons
> ▪ Regarding continued support for his or her priorities
> ▪ Regarding expectations of the next servant to fill the deceased's shoes

This is the first of several times that God speaks to Joshua. It is of interest that Joshua's name means "the Lord is salvation" or "salvation is of the Lord." When the Hebrew Old Testament is translated into the Greek version known as the Septuagint in about 250 BC, the name *Joshua* is translated into the name that we know as *Jesus*. Entering a land of promise is associated with both individuals.

2. Moses my servant is dead; now therefore arise, go over this Jordan, thou, and all this people, unto the land which I do give to them, even to the children of Israel.

God is ready for His people to begin the conquest of Canaan. The year is about 1407 BC. This means it has been almost 700 years since God first promised the land to Abram's (Abraham's) descendants (Genesis 12:7). God fulfills His promises, but the time period seems unusually long for today's "instant gratification" generation. The apostle Peter reminds us, however, that one day with the Lord is as a thousand years, and a thousand years as one day (2 Peter 3:6-10). God is not in a hurry. He also has promised a judgment when the earth will be burned, and that is still pending.

Visual for
Lesson 1

Keep this map posted for Lessons 1–5 to help your learners have a geographical perspective.

The command of God about crossing the Jordan River may cause Joshua to wonder about God's timing. Such a crossing would be relatively simple at the end of the dry season, when the Jordan is a quiet stream. Now, however, it is the end of the rainy season, in March (Joshua 4:19). The rains and melting snows mean that the Jordan is in flood stage (3:15; 4:18). Yet God will make the crossing possible, and this miracle will validate Joshua as the leader.

❧ *Bringing Change* ❧

New leadership often brings with it hope for change. Voters may express hope that new leadership will show "the way out of the wilderness." The "wilderness" in modern situations is always figurative in nature; by contrast, the wilderness in ancient Israel's situation was quite literal! The problem with a figurative wilderness is that the nature of the wilderness is in the eye of the beholder, and public opinion about it can shift.

God's perspective is not based on anything so fickle as public longing for (or resistance to) change. God's plan for Israel had two goals. The first was to bring that nation out of a literal wilderness into the promised land. The second was to use Israel to usher in the Messiah, in order to deliver the nations from the figurative wilderness of sin. God is still bringing about this spiritual change. In what ways are you helping bring it about?

—C. R. B.

B. Extent of the Land (vv. 3, 4)

3. Every place that the sole of your foot shall tread upon, that have I given unto you, as I said unto Moses.

Joshua receives God's assurance that he will continue to be successful as a military leader for Israel. The land does not yet belong to Israel, but to receive such a promise from God is almost the same as possessing it. There will be battles ahead, but the victory belongs to the Lord and His people.

4. From the wilderness and this Lebanon even unto the great river, the river Euphrates, all the land of the Hittites, and unto the great sea toward the going down of the sun, shall be your coast.

The description of the extent of the region to be conquered agrees with what had been stated previously (see Genesis 15:18-21; Exodus 23:31; Deuteronomy 1:7, 8). The land area is given from the south *(the wilderness)* to the northwest where the mountains of Lebanon are located. On the northeast and east is the Euphrates River, often referred to simply as "the river" (Exodus 23:31) or "the flood" (Joshua 24:14, 15). All the northern areas are summarized in the phrase *all the land of the Hittites*. These people earlier controlled the eastern region of what is now Turkey. At the time of Joshua they are no longer a dominant force, but their influence is still recognized. The western boundary *the great sea* refers to the Mediterranean Sea.

HOW TO SAY IT

Ai	*Ay*-eye.
Anakims	*An*-a-kims.
Baalgad	*Bay*-ul-gad (gad with a short "a" as in bad)
Canaan	*Kay*-nun.
Euphrates	You-*fray*-teez.
Jeroboam	Jair-uh-*boe*-um.
Midianites	*Mid*-ee-un-ites.
Philistine	Fuh-*liss*-teen or *Fill*-us-teen.
Seir	*See*-ir.
Septuagint	Sep-*too*-ih-jent.
Sinai	*Sigh*-nye or *Sigh*-nay-eye.
Uzziah	Uh-*zye*-uh.

God Keeps His Promises

Israel will not conquer all the land in the days of Joshua. Pockets of resistance are left for the individual tribes to mop up, but they will not follow through. The Israelites will quit before they are finished. The fulfillment does come, however, in the times of David and Solomon, when the entire area yields to Israelite control. The same areas are again controlled by Israel and Judah in the days of Jeroboam II (northern kingdom of Israel) and Uzziah (southern kingdom of Judah) in about 760 BC.

C. Encouragement to Joshua (vv. 5, 6)

5. There shall not any man be able to stand before thee all the days of thy life: as I was with Moses, so I will be with thee: I will not fail thee, nor forsake thee.

Commands and promises are mingled. When God issues commands, they are followed frequently by supporting information that gives assurance. Joshua has already experienced the fact that obedience to God's commands brings the desired blessings. The Israelites captured 60 cities in the region east of the Sea of Galilee during the last days of Moses (Deuteronomy 3:4). Israel did not suffer any casualties in a previous battle with the Midianites (Numbers 31:49), and that fact is quite startling. God blesses obedience.

Now, however, Moses is dead. Thus Joshua needs to receive the special assurance that the Lord will be with him as He *was with Moses.* This affirmation is strengthened by the phrases that immediately follow.

> **What Do You Think?**
> When was a time you felt a special need to know that you were not forsaken by God? How did you grow spiritually in that time?
> *Talking Points for Your Discussion*
> - Health crisis
> - Family crisis
> - Financial crisis
> - Church crisis

6. Be strong and of a good courage: for unto this people shalt thou divide for an inheritance the land, which I sware unto their fathers to give them.

Before Moses died, he twice commanded Joshua to be courageous in the task (Deuteronomy 31:7, 23). The Lord himself tells Joshua three times to be courageous in Joshua 1:6, 7, 9. The dictionaries have several definitions of *courage.* A summary of them would be "the quality of mind that enables one to meet danger and difficulties with firmness or valor, perhaps with the casting aside of fear." The exhortation to Joshua is followed by a promise: that he will live so as to be able to allocate portions of the land of Canaan among the tribes of Israel.

> **What Do You Think?**
> When you are prone to fear, what promises of God give you courage?
> *Talking Points for Your Discussion*
> - Deuteronomy 31:6
> - 2 Chronicles 32:7
> - Psalm 23
> - Psalm 118:6
> - Matthew 28:20

II. Mission

(Joshua 11:16-23)

Much happens between chapters 1 and 11. This includes the glorious victory at Jericho (chapter 6) and the defeat at Ai (chapter 7). Ai ultimately falls (chapter 8), but then the Israelites allow themselves to be deceived by the Gibeonites (chapter 9). Following that, Joshua defeats many kings (chapters 10, 11), the results of which are summarized next.

A. Places Conquered (vv. 16, 17)

16. So Joshua took all that land, the hills, and all the south country, and all the land of Goshen, and the valley, and the plain, and the mountain of Israel, and the valley of the same.

The conquered territories are described in topographical terms. This summary makes it sound so simple. But the ones who participate in the travels and the battles can testify of the toils and weariness they experience.

17. Even from the mount Halak, that goeth up to Seir, even unto Baalgad in the valley of Lebanon under mount Hermon: and all their kings he took, and smote them, and slew them.

Verse 17 describes the same territory, and precise geographical locations are now given. Mount Halak is in the far south or southeast as one goes toward Seir (or Edom). Baalgad is located in the far north, near Mount Hermon.

A third method of describing the success of the Israelites is to refer to the kings that are defeated. A complete list of the places where such kings reign is found in Joshua 12. The last verse of that chapter says that there are 31 such kings.

What Do You Think?

What spiritual "territory" is the Lord leading you to conquer today?

Talking Points for Your Discussion

- An area of sin
- An area of faith
- An area of relationships
- An area of ministry

❧ MANIFEST DESTINY? ❧

When settlers from the Old World arrived on the east coast of what we now call the United States, they saw a seemingly limitless continent stretching westward. To many, that continent was just asking to be conquered. History reminds us that this meant displacing a large indigenous population that was ill-prepared to defend itself against the newcomers.

As settlers surged westward, a sense of *manifest destiny* developed. The phrase asserted that America had a divine call (a destiny) that was obvious (plainly manifest) to conquer the whole continent. That phrase first appeared in the media in 1839. John Gast's famous 1872 painting *American Progress* captured the spirit of the movement. The painting features "Columbia," an angelic being personifying the United States, floating westward. In so doing, she is bringing settlers behind her along with the symbols of civilization.

Discussing the rightness or wrongness of the claim to *manifest destiny* can lead to heated discussions. But there was to be no debate about ancient Israel's destiny. God himself was the one who identified for Joshua the territory that was to be Israel's. Even so, it is a mistake to think of God's reign in terms of geographical boundaries at any time in history (compare John 18:36). His kingdom encompasses the globe. The Christian's *manifest destiny* is to expand that kingdom in the human heart (Matthew 18:19, 20).   —C. R. B.

B. Peoples Conquered (vv. 18-22)

18. Joshua made war a long time with all those kings.

Joshua was one of the two "good" spies sent into Canaan years before; the other was Caleb (Numbers 14:6-9). It is Caleb who provides the information that defines the *long time* of this conquest period: it is six years, according to his statement in Joshua 14:7-12.

That passage notes that Caleb was 40 years old when he went to spy out the land, and that he is 85 when he makes his request to receive the area of Hebron as his inheritance. The sending of the original 12 spies occurred slightly over a year after Israel had left Egypt, so Caleb was 39 at the time of the exodus. The 40 years in the wilderness puts him at 79 at the end of that period. He is 85, so it is 6 years later. To read the account in the book of Joshua can leave the impression that the battles take place in one summer, but that is not the case.

The conquest began with a central thrust into the land, when Jericho and Ai were captured and burned. That was followed by a southern campaign and then a northern campaign.

19. There was not a city that made peace with the children of Israel, save the Hivites the inhabitants of Gibeon: all other they took in battle.

This is a reference to the events of Joshua 9. Messengers from four Hivite cities (9:17) deceive the Israelites by pretending to be from a distant region, and they are able to make a covenant of peace with Israel. Gibeon is the leading city of the Hivites. It is this covenant that precipitates "the battle of the long day," beginning when a southern coalition attacks Gibeon (Joshua 10).

20. For it was of the LORD to harden their hearts, that they should come against Israel in battle, that he might destroy them utterly, and that they might have no favour, but that he might destroy them, as the LORD commanded Moses.

God Keeps His Promises

The spies that Joshua had sent to Jericho brought back the report of the peoples' fear (Joshua 2:24). The inhabitants are, however, fighting for their homes and their lives, and it is *of the Lord* that they resist the invasion. God had stated to Abram (Abraham) that the iniquity of these peoples was not yet complete or full (Genesis 15:16), but now it is. Archaeological findings show that the peoples of Canaan are grossly immoral. God's justice demands that judgment be realized on them. Judgment day has come!

21, 22. And at that time came Joshua, and cut off the Anakims from the mountains, from Hebron, from Debir, from Anab, and from all the mountains of Judah, and from all the mountains of Israel: Joshua destroyed them utterly with their cities. There was none of the Anakims left in the land of the children of Israel: only in Gaza, in Gath, and in Ashdod, there remained.

The Anakims deserve special attention, for it is they who gave the "grasshopper complex" to the Israelites when the 12 spies investigated the land (Numbers 13:33). The faith of Joshua and Caleb at that time is now fully justified, for Israel destroys them. The only exceptions are the few who escape to the Philistine towns noted here. Gaza is still in the news today. Ashdod is one of the largest cities in modern Israel.

> **What Do You Think?**
> What leadership qualities did Joshua possess that are worth emulating today?
> *Talking Points for Your Discussion*
> - Exodus 24:13
> - Numbers 14:6-8
> - Joshua 23, 24

C. Promises Reviewed (v. 23)

23. So Joshua took the whole land, according to all that the LORD said unto Moses; and Joshua gave it for an inheritance unto Israel according to their divisions by their tribes. And the land rested from war.

The military operation against Canaan is successful. The Lord keeps His promises, and Joshua takes *the whole land* of Canaan with His help.

The promises made to Abraham, Isaac, Jacob, and Moses have come to fruition. This new nation under God has its own land, the land of Israel.

Conclusion
A. Keeping Promises

It is important for people to keep their word, but some promises seem to have a higher priority. One such is the oath of induction into the military. To break this oath is to invite scorn and a dishonorable discharge.

The vows of marriage also should invite resoluteness, but they have often become like piecrust—made to be broken. Clearly, secular society is viewing marriage vows with less seriousness than in days gone by. Do we treat our new covenant with Jesus with all the seriousness it deserves?

Becoming a Christian should be considered a lifelong commitment of the highest priority. Jesus is to be the center of a person's life in all the decisions that are made. Each first day of the week serves as a reminder of God's love, and there are tugs of the heart to go to the assembly with fellow believers. To be a disciple of Jesus is to seek first His kingdom in every aspect of life. God keeps His promises. Do we?

B. Prayer

Almighty God, thank You for this time of study that reminds me of promises I have made to You and to others. Today I vow to do my best to honor You by fulfilling my commitments in such a way that others know I belong to You. In Jesus' name, amen.

C. Thought to Remember
Claiming Jesus as Lord
is not to be a piecrust promise.

VISUALS FOR THESE LESSONS

The visual pictured in each lesson (example: page 348) is a small reproduction of a large, full-color poster included in the *Adult Resources* packet for the Summer Quarter. That packet also contains the very useful *Presentation Helps* on a CD for teacher use. Order No. 020049211 from your supplier.

INVOLVEMENT LEARNING

Some of the activities below are also found in the helpful student book, Adult Bible Class.
Don't forget to download the free reproducible page from www.standardlesson.com to enhance your lesson!

Into the Lesson

Download the reproducible page and place copies of The Ancient Promise activity in chairs. Learners can work on it as they arrive. Then say, "God made a very important promise to all these people. Today's lesson will show us how He kept it."

Into the Word

Option #1. Prepare the following activity titled "Would Joshua Say That?" and have your students work together in small groups to complete it. Say, "Read the following quotes and compare them to the verse indicated from Joshua 1 or 11. Then write in *Yes* or *No* to indicate whether or not Joshua might have said it."

1. "Why me? I have no leadership experience." *(1:1; also see Exodus 17:8-13);* 2. "It's up to me to take this land for the Israelites." *(1:2);* 3. "Whatever property we step on, God will give it to us." *(1:3);* 4. "God says our boundaries will extend from Lebanon to the Euphrates through Hittite country to the Great Sea." *(1:4);* 5. "I'd better watch my back or someone will try to take over as leader." *(1:5);* 6. "I'm so glad God is going to be with me the same way He was with Moses." *(1:5);* 7. "I know God will understand if I'm a little fearful and weak in the knees." *(1:6);* 8. "With God's help we took the entire land!" *(11:16);* 9. "We conquered their kings and kept them as captives." *(11:17);* 10. "I wish we could have conquered the Hivites, but they were too tough for us!" *(11:19).*

"Yes" answers: 3, 4, 6, 8; "No" answers: 1, 2, 5, 7, 9, 10.

Option #2. On the board write the following headings: *What Were God's Promises to Joshua (Joshua 1:1-6)? What Were God's Requirements of Joshua (Joshua 1:1-6)?* and *What Were God's Fulfilled Promises (Joshua 11:16-23)?* Depending on the size of your class, you may either work through the text together to find the answers or assign columns to small groups to work on. Encourage

your learners to come up with as many answers as possible.

Suggested answers include the following: 1. God would give the land to the Israelites, including every place where they set their foot; no one would be able to stand up against Joshua all his life; God would be with Joshua as He was with Moses. 2. Joshua would take over Moses' job as leader of the Israelites, lead them in crossing the Jordan River, conquer the territory, trust God to support his leadership and be with him all the way, and be strong and courageous. 3. God enabled Joshua and the people to take the entire land, to capture and kill all their kings, to harden the peoples' hearts to wage war so he could destroy them completely, to distribute the inheritance to the various tribes, and to give them rest from war.

Follow up with these questions, either to small groups or to the class as a whole: "How did God's promises to Joshua give him encouragement for the job he was given?" "To what extent did God keep His promises to Joshua?" "What did Joshua need to do on his part to be sure that God could keep His promises?" For the latter, be sure to include ideas such as Joshua had to believe God's promises, accept his assignment, and be strong and courageous in completing it.

Into Life

On the board write the following promises: "I will support and defend the constitution of my country against all enemies . . . So help me God." "I promise to love and cherish you till death do us part." "I accept Jesus as my Lord and Savior and surrender my life to His will." Have your students pair off and discuss these promises. Ask, "What conditions, if any, accompany these? Which do you need to do a better job of keeping during the coming week?" Encourage prayer for one another.

Distribute copies of Promises with Provisos from the reproducible page as take-home work.

God Keeps His Promises

GOD EXPECTS OBEDIENCE

BACKGROUND SCRIPTURE: Joshua 1
PRINTED TEXT: Joshua 1:7-18

JOSHUA 1:7-18

7 Only be thou strong and very courageous, that thou mayest observe to do according to all the law, which Moses my servant commanded thee: turn not from it to the right hand or to the left, that thou mayest prosper withersoever thou goest.

8 This book of the law shall not depart out of thy mouth; but thou shalt meditate therein day and night, that thou mayest observe to do according to all that is written therein: for then thou shalt make thy way prosperous, and then thou shalt have good success.

9 Have not I commanded thee? Be strong and of a good courage; be not afraid, neither be thou dismayed: for the LORD thy God is with thee whithersoever thou goest.

10 Then Joshua commanded the officers of the people, saying,

11 Pass through the host, and command the people, saying, Prepare you victuals; for within three days ye shall pass over this Jordan, to go in to possess the land, which the LORD your God giveth you to possess it.

12 And to the Reubenites, and to the Gadites, and to half the tribe of Manasseh, spake Joshua, saying,

13 Remember the word which Moses the servant of the LORD commanded you, saying, The LORD your God hath given you rest, and hath given you this land.

14 Your wives, your little ones, and your cattle, shall remain in the land which Moses gave you on this side Jordan; but ye shall pass before your brethren armed, all the mighty men of valour, and help them;

15 Until the LORD have given your brethren rest, as he hath given you, and they also have possessed the land which the LORD your God giveth them: then ye shall return unto the land of your possession, and enjoy it, which Moses the LORD's servant gave you on this side Jordan toward the sunrising.

16 And they answered Joshua, saying, All that thou commandest us we will do, and whithersoever thou sendest us, we will go.

17 According as we hearkened unto Moses in all things, so will we hearken unto thee: only the LORD thy God be with thee, as he was with Moses.

18 Whosoever he be that doth rebel against thy commandment, and will not hearken unto thy words in all that thou commandest him, he shall be put to death: only be strong and of a good courage.

KEY VERSE

Be thou strong and very courageous, that thou mayest observe to do according to all the law, which Moses my servant commanded thee: turn not from it to the right hand or to the left, that thou mayest prosper whithersoever thou goest. —**Joshua 1:7**

GOD INSTRUCTS HIS PEOPLE

Unit 1: God's People Learn from Prosperity

LESSONS 1–5

LESSON AIMS

After participating in this lesson, each student will be able to:

1. Summarize God's expectation and the people's response.

2. Compare and contrast God's expectations of the ancient Israelites with His expectations of Christians today.

3. Confess one area where he or she is not meeting God's expectations and make a plan for change.

LESSON OUTLINE

Introduction

A. Boot Camp

The phrase *boot camp* is associated with the first weeks of training in a branch of the military. One purpose of boot camp is to condition trainees to respond with immediate obedience to legal commands. It is absolutely essential that legal orders be obeyed without argument. A father is said to have asked his son what he learned in boot camp, and the son replied that he had learned what the word *now* means!

Being a follower of Jesus also has expectations of obedience. Jesus says that the person who loves Him will obey what He commands (John 14:15). In the latter part of the Great Commission, Jesus states that disciples are to be taught to obey everything that He commands (Matthew 28:20). Peter affirms that the Holy Spirit is given to those who obey Him (Acts 5:32). Paul states that Jesus will punish those who do not obey Him (2 Thessalonians 1:8). Even "the apostle of love," John, writes that love is perfected by keeping or obeying the word of Christ (1 John 2:4, 5).

Perhaps it would be a good idea to have a boot camp for new Christians—just to help them realize that there are important obligations in living for Christ. The training might even include the meaning of the word *now*!

B. Lesson Background

The previous lesson developed, in part, Joshua 1:1-6. Today's lesson considers the remaining verses of Joshua 1, thus the historical background for this lesson is the same as that of last week. Therefore a different emphasis is given to help the student understand the mind-set of the Israelites as they prepared to enter Canaan.

The Israelites had been in Egypt for 430 years (Exodus 12:40, 41). During that time, the favored family of Jacob ended up becoming a slave nation, with all that pertains to that status. They endured severe hardships under Egypt's taskmasters.

As the Israelites left Egypt, this new nation under God experienced freedom from servitude. History demonstrates that with freedom can come a tendency to abuse it, as some people come to think that they may do as they wish, without restraint. Israel had witnessed mighty miracles and the plagues on the Egyptians, and it had the leadership of Moses. These factors should have combined to produce a grateful, obedient people. Instead they become experts in defiance and disobedience. They are accused of rebelling 10 times—perhaps a figure of speech meaning "many times" (Numbers 14:22).

The Israelites who left Egypt did not go directly to the land that God promised to Abraham, Isaac, and Jacob. Instead they had a stopover at Mount Sinai, the place where Moses had witnessed the burning bush. That was where God had promised that He would bring the Israelites to worship (Exodus 3:12). While there, they received the law and constructed the tabernacle as the center of their worship (Exodus 19–27).

Early in the second year after leaving Egypt, the Israelites departed from Sinai and moved toward the southern edge of Canaan (Numbers 10:11, 12). Moses then sent 12 spies into the land. They were gone 40 days (13:25), a number that became very significant. Ten of the spies demonstrated a lack of trust in God to lead them successfully to conquer Canaan, and the people sided with them.

The result was punishment by God. First, they had to spend 40 years in the wilderness, a year for each day the spies were gone (Numbers 14:34). Second, out of the 603,550 men of war, only Joshua and Caleb, the 2 "good" spies, lived to enter Canaan (1:46; 2:32; 14:30). This means that an average of about 43 men died each day for the

remaining 38 years of the 40-year sentence (Deuteronomy 2:14). Every death served as a reminder of the disobedience of the first generation.

One sarcastic maxim is that *the only thing you learn from history is that no one learns from history.* Each generation seems determined to make its own mistakes. The second generation in Israel, however, was different. When it came time to advance into Canaan under Joshua, the men of war pledged their support. Their commitment was different from that of the previous generation.

I. Lord's Commands
(Joshua 1:7-9)
A. Courage and Obedience (v. 7)

7a. Only be thou strong and very courageous, that thou mayest observe to do according to all the law, which Moses my servant commanded thee.

One verse in last week's study is very similar to the exhortation we see here. Joshua is charged in Joshua 1:6 to be strong and courageous, and a reason is given: that he may divide among the people the land of Canaan that the Lord promised to the patriarchs. A similar charge is given in the first verse of today's lesson, but this time the word *very* is added. An additional factor expressed to Joshua in this verse is that he is to keep *all the law* that Moses had written down as the constitution of Israel. Joshua is not simply to read the law. He is to obey the ordinances that the Lord prescribes.

The word given as *law* is the Hebrew word *torah.* The word primarily means "instruction," and it often refers to the recognized set of instructions that includes the first five books of the Bible. Those five sometimes are called *the Pentateuch.*

7b. Turn not from it to the right hand or to the left, that thou mayest prosper whithersoever thou goest.

For Joshua to keep what is written means following a straight path in that regard. He must not turn *from it to the right hand or to the left.* The practices and promises of other religious groups may be very enticing, but Joshua must be determined not to go with them. His is not to be a smorgasbord belief system—some of this and a

HOW TO SAY IT

Abraham	*Ay*-bruh-ham.
Canaan	*Kay*-nun.
Egypt	*Ee*-jipt.
Gadites	*Gad*-ites.
Isaac	*Eye*-zuk.
Manasseh	Muh-*nass*-uh.
Moab	*Mo*-ab.
Moses	*Mo*-zes or *Mo*-zez.
Pentateuch	*Pen*-ta-teuk.
Reubenites	*Roo*-ben-ites.
torah *(Hebrew)*	*tor*-uh.

little of that. He cannot swerve in any direction so as to taste what looks appealing. As Joshua considers this requirement, perhaps he thinks of Deuteronomy 28:14.

What Do You Think?
What biblical principle of obedience do you most struggle with? Why?
Talking Points for Your Discussion
- Regarding priorities: Acts 4:19; 5:29
- Regarding religious rituals: 1 Samuel 15:22
- Regarding the extent of obedience: Joshua 11:15; Luke 2:39

B. Meditation and Obedience (v. 8)

8. This book of the law shall not depart out of thy mouth; but thou shalt meditate therein day and night, that thou mayest observe to do according to all that is written therein: for then thou shalt make thy way prosperous, and then thou shalt have good success.

The caution *shall not depart out of thy mouth* sounds somewhat strange at first—as if Joshua should not share the law verbally with others. But Joshua is to keep it in his mouth in order to be able to do three things: reflect on it, obey it, and enjoy the blessings that come from this obedience. The principle of Deuteronomy 6:6-9 must also be considered: Joshua and all who know the law are to teach it to others.

It is intriguing that Joshua is to *meditate . . . day and night* on the law. We make decisions throughout each waking moment of the day, but first those decisions must be evaluated and compared with what God has instructed His people to do. This thought parallels what is given in Deuteronomy 6:7—any hour of the day or night is a good time to teach children or anyone else about God's ways.

Meditating on God's Word continuously is an important theme of Psalm 119 (see 119:15, 23, 48, 78, 97, 99, 148). Such a concept with regard to God's Word contrasts vividly with the current culture in which biblical wisdom is neither known nor understood. Many people today are biblically illiterate, and God's law has never been in their mouths or hearts.

What Do You Think?
What areas of meditation do you find to be most beneficial spiritually?
Talking Points for Your Discussion
- Psalm 1:2; 119:48
- Psalm 63:6; 104:33, 34
- Psalm 143:5
- Philippians 4:8

❧ PERFECT LAW, PERFECT SYSTEM ❧

Chief Judge Judy Hardcastle banned Judge Elizabeth Halverson from a courthouse in Las Vegas in May 2007. Halverson allegedly had allowed her two private bodyguards to bypass security checks, thus jeopardizing security. Things escalated as charges and countercharges flew back and forth.

Eventually, the Nevada Commission on Judicial Discipline permanently removed Judge Halverson from the bench in November 2008 after a disciplinary hearing. The commission found her guilty of sleeping during legal proceedings, having improper contact with jurors, treating her staff members like servants, and acting unethically in making statements to the press.

Whether the commission acted correctly or incorrectly toward Judge Halverson, cases such as this demonstrate that human legal systems need checks and balances to prevent abuse by those who create and administer the law. Not so with God's legal system. He is the perfectly just steward of His perfectly just law. Only good things can result when one meditates on that law as God instructed Joshua to do. —C. R. B.

C. Courage and God's Presence (v. 9)

9. Have not I commanded thee? Be strong and of a good courage; be not afraid, neither be thou dismayed: for the LORD thy God is with thee whithersoever thou goest.

The Lord begins with a question that should remove all doubt about the outcome. If God gives the command, then why is there any hesitation? In this case, God intends for the results to be what He has planned for centuries: to give this land to Abram (Abraham) and his descendants (Genesis 12:7). God's ultimate purpose is to send the Messiah into the world at the appointed time, and what Joshua is doing is part of that plan.

This is the third time in this chapter that God challenges Joshua to *be strong* as he assumes his leadership role. Moses had given the same challenge when he commissioned Joshua as his successor (Deuteronomy 31:7, 23). We wonder if Joshua is hesitant in view of his having led Israel's army for 40 years and after the recent military successes on the east side of the Jordan. Joshua previously enjoyed the support and wisdom of Moses, but that has changed. He is on his own—with the promises of God as his blessed assurance.

> **What Do You Think?**
> Under what circumstances are you most afraid to move forward for God? How do you overcome your fear?
> *Talking Points for Your Discussion*
> - Lacking confidence in promises: Genesis 28:15; Matthew 28:20
> - Feelings of exhaustion: 1 Kings 19:4
> - Fearing the enemy: Deuteronomy 20:1
> - Uncertainty about pending trials: Isaiah 43:2
> - Feeling alone: Matthew 18:20

II. Joshua's Commands
(JOSHUA 1:10-15)
A. To the Officers (vv. 10, 11)

10. Then Joshua commanded the officers of the people, saying.

Joshua's preparatory commands to *the officers of the people* demonstrate his trust in God. Joshua shows that he is ready to begin the invasion of Canaan. The procedure described indicates that the people are organized: a command from Joshua quickly moves through the officers to everyone. We see the tribal organization in Numbers 26. We see a military organization with a chain of command in Numbers 31:14, 48, 52-54; Deuteronomy 1:15.

11. Pass through the host, and command the people, saying, Prepare you victuals; for within three days ye shall pass over this Jordan, to go in to possess the land, which the LORD your God giveth you to possess it.

The initial commands are for the people to make preparations to move away from what has almost become their home in the plains of Moab. All their equipment, livestock, and food for the journey must be prepared. The fact that the time period is given as *three days* surely makes for interesting conversations. The people are not going to wait until late summer to cross the Jordan River, at the end of the dry season. That would be sensible, but God has a better plan.

Joshua 4:19 states that the crossing takes place on the tenth day of the first month. It is therefore late March or early April, meaning that the Jordan is at flood stage (4:18). It will take a miracle for the thousands of elderly and small children to make their way across the flooding Jordan. But a miracle is exactly what God intends to provide, for this will confirm Joshua as God's approved leader.

> **What Do You Think?**
> What are some areas in which God is challenging you to act on by faith right now?
> *Talking Points for Your Discussion*
> - In your church
> - In your family
> - At work

B. To the Transjordan Tribes (vv. 12-15)

12, 13. And to the Reubenites, and to the Gadites, and to half the tribe of Manasseh, spake Joshua, saying, Remember the word which Moses the servant of the LORD commanded you, saying, The LORD your God hath given you rest, and hath given you this land.

Numbers 32 relates the decision to allow the two and one-half tribes mentioned here to settle on the east side of the Jordan River. That is the context of the instructions that Joshua is about to deliver.

14, 15. Your wives, your little ones, and your cattle, shall remain in the land which Moses gave you on this side Jordan; but ye shall pass before your brethren armed, all the mighty men of valour, and help them; until the LORD have given your brethren rest, as he hath given you, and they also have possessed the land which

the LORD your God giveth them: then ye shall return unto the land of your possession, and enjoy it, which Moses the LORD's servant gave you on this side Jordan toward the sunrising.

As Joshua addresses the members of these eastern, transjordan tribes, he reminds them that they made a commitment to help the other tribes possess the land of Canaan. It was on this condition that Moses had granted permission to these tribes to settle permanently in the territory that is east of the Jordan (Numbers 32:32, 33). Thus the expectations stated here are nothing new. The fact that the family members who are not included in the men of war are to remain behind is not a new provision either (see 32:26).

Some students think that the 40,000 of Joshua 4:13 is the sum total of the invasion force, not just the total of the 2½ tribes mentioned here. But 40,000 is less than 7 percent of the 601,730 of Numbers 26:51. Thus it is more reasonable to see the 40,000 as applying only to the 2½ tribes.

Even so, the second census of armed men in Numbers 26 gives a total number of military-age men for these 2½ tribes as 110,580 (adding 43,730 for Reuben, 40,500 for Gad, and half of Manasseh's 52,700, or 26,350). Since 40,000 is only about 36 percent of 110,580, what does *all the mighty men of valour* really mean? How can 36 percent be considered "all"?

The solution may be found in Numbers 32:27. That passage says that "thy servants will pass over, every man armed for war, . . . to battle." Thus the "all" of Numbers 32:21 and Joshua 1:14 might refer only to "all those" of the 2½ tribes who have the full complement of necessary armaments, which is the 40,000. Stated differently, although 40,000 is not even close to being "absolutely all" of the men who are of military age of these 2½ tribes per Numbers 26, it could indeed be "absolutely all" of the men who have the proper equipment for battle.

We noted in last week's lesson that the conquest period lasts 6 years. It is interesting to speculate about whether the same 40,000 soldiers from the eastern tribes remain on campaign for the entire 6 years. We don't know if a rotation policy is in place like we see in military deployments today. Soldiers are frequently gone for years in ancient times.

III. Tribes' Commitments
(JOSHUA 1:16-18)
A. Obedience Promised (vv. 16, 17)

16. And they answered Joshua, saying, All that thou commandest us we will do, and whithersoever thou sendest us, we will go.

Opinions differ concerning the identity of the speakers that answer Joshua. The immediate context indicates that they are representatives of the two and one-half eastern (transjordan) tribes. The minority view is that the representatives from all the tribes are involved in this affirmation, for they are addressed in verses 10, 11. It is safe to assume that the affirmations are held by everyone.

The factor of determined obedience permeates the answer to Joshua. This generation has endured 40 years in the wilderness because of the disobedience and complaining of their parents and grandparents. They know that actions have consequences, and this new generation does not intend to repeat the mistakes made by their ancestors.

17. According as we hearkened unto Moses in all things, so will we hearken unto thee: only the LORD thy God be with thee, as he was with Moses.

The commitment is accompanied by a spoken blessing: an earnest desire that the Lord be with Joshua *as he was with Moses*. The armed men range in age from 20 to about 60. The lower number of this age range is established by Numbers 1:3; 26:2; etc. No soldier is older than about 60 except Joshua and Caleb (14:28-35). This generation has accepted the fact that God worked through Moses to do what was humanly impossible. Thus these soldiers are confident that their obedience will assure that God's presence will be with Joshua as well.

What Do You Think?
What are some areas in which our church needs to obey the will of God? What will it take to get us moving in that regard?
Talking Points for Your Discussion
- In an area of trust
- In an area of submission
- In an area of sacrifice

God Expects Obedience

Two thousand years of church history demonstrates a certain cycle: church practice and/or doctrine will begin to move along a path that some find objectionable; then voices will cry out that "it's time to get back to basics," "back to the foundations," etc. So a movement will start for that to happen. Then the cycle will begin anew.

There are many examples. One can be found within the Roman Catholic Church of the latter part of the twentieth century. That faith perspective went through a modernization of its liturgy that left some adherents longing for the old ways that called for a stricter regimen. One such was Thomas Monaghan, founder of Domino's Pizza. He decided to create a community where traditional Roman Catholic values would be honored. So in 2002 he started building the town of Ave Maria, Florida, where that would happen. We wonder what the result will be 100 years from now! Will some claim that the town's faith practices have become deficient, in need of renewal?

As the Israelites prepared to enter the promised land, they took vows to keep the historic faith of Israel. The challenge for godly people throughout history has been to demonstrate determined obedience to God's will while facing the pressures of contemporary life. And so it still is. —C. R. B.

B. Support Pledged (v. 18)

18a. Whosoever he be that doth rebel against thy commandment, and will not hearken unto thy words in all that thou commandest him, he shall be put to death.

These determined statements are not just idle words. They are backed by a resoluteness based on experiences. The people will not allow grumbling and disobedience to infect and influence others; they promise to *put to death* anyone whose actions smack of rebellion—a serious commitment!

18b. Only be strong and of a good courage.

For the fourth time in this chapter, Joshua receives an exhortation about being *strong*. The three others were expressed by the Lord; this one comes from the soldiers. Thus does Joshua assume the leadership role for which the Lord has prepared him through the previous 40 years.

BE STRONG AND COURAGEOUS
— JOSHUA 1:7, 9, 18

Visual for Lesson 2. *Point to this visual as you ask the discussion question that is associated with Joshua 1:9.*

Conclusion

A. The Importance of Obedience

Any structured society must have obedience to its governing precepts. Without that, anarchy will result. The concept of obedience is best learned early. Parents may use a variety of methods to enforce what is said. Each child is different, and the good parent will recognize the differences and guide each child accordingly. If a child does not learn to obey, he or she may develop disrespect for all who are in authority—teachers, employers, law enforcement officers, and even God.

Some parents abdicate this responsibility. Perhaps they hope the child-care workers or the public schools will come to the rescue. Those who work in these areas are to be admired for the good things they accomplish, but learning to obey should begin early—in the home. The Israelites learned that disobedience brought tragedy. Obedience was vital for them; it still is for us.

B. Prayer

Almighty God, with Your help, I promise to go where You want me to go, to say what You want me to say, and to be what You want me to be. In Jesus' name, amen.

C. Thought to Remember

Jesus wants to be your Savior,
but He must first be your Lord.

INVOLVEMENT LEARNING

Some of the activities below are also found in the helpful student book, Adult Bible Class.
Don't forget to download the free reproducible page from www.standardlesson.com to enhance your lesson!

Into the Lesson

Download the reproducible page and distribute copies of the Mother Says . . . activity. Have students pair off and discuss the questions. Ask for volunteers to share some of their mother's sayings. Then say, "Our parents gave us rules for our safety, to keep the household running smoothly, etc. In all cases, our parents expected to be obeyed. In today's lesson, God gave Joshua and the Israelites some very specific instructions, and He expected to be obeyed. Let's see how they responded."

Into the Word

Before class, ask five people to read the Scripture text from Joshua 1 aloud. You will need one person each to read the words of God (vv. 7-9) and Joshua (vv. 11, 13-15), two people to read in unison the words of the Israelites to Joshua (vv. 16b-18), and a narrator to read the remaining words (vv. 10, 12, 16a). Encourage a dramatic reading.

Distribute the interview assignments below, one for each of three small groups; if your class is large enough for more than three groups, distribute duplicate assignments. Say, "Read today's text and use it to prepare your interview. Select two people to do the interview and one person to be interviewed, as indicated. You may use the questions or come up with some of your own." Provide each group with the lesson commentary related to the people in their interview: Joshua, vv. 7-15; an Israelite, vv. 10, 11, 16-18; a Reubenite, vv. 12-18.

Interview #1: Joshua. 1. How did God's expectation of courage help you do the job He gave you? 2. How did being familiar with Moses' law help you? 3. What did you do to become familiar with it? 4. What specific instructions did you give the officers? 5. Why was it so important for the eastern tribes to help the rest of the Israelites? 6. Were you pleased with the response you received? How so?

Interview #2: An Israelite. 1. What instructions did you receive from the officers? 2. What did you

do to prepare? 3. How did it feel to know that you were finally going in to possess the land? 4. Did you believe it was really going to happen? 5. How serious were you and the rest of the people about obeying God this time?

Interview #3: A Reubenite. 1. Why did you decide to settle on the east side of the Jordan (see Numbers 32:1-5)? 2. What deal had you made with Moses in order to settle there? (32:16-19) 3. How long were you committed to helping the other Israelites conquer the land? 4. How did you respond when Joshua reminded you of your promise? 5. What encouraging words did you say to him?

Allow time for each group to present its interview. If you have more than one group doing the same interview, have each one present only some of the questions.

Into Life

Create the following handout titled *What Does God Expect?* Use these headings over two columns: "God's Expectations for Joshua & the Israelites" and "God's Expectations for Us." In the left-hand column make the following rows: 1. Be strong and very courageous (v. 7); 2. Obey Moses' law (v. 7); 3. Meditate on God's Word (v. 8); 4. Live right (v. 8); 5. Don't fear (v. 9); 6. Prepare for the journey ahead (v. 11); 7. Help your fellow Israelites (vv. 13-15); 8. Obey or die (v. 18). In the right-hand column, write the following references: 1. Philippians 4:13; 2. Mark 12:30, 31; 3. 2 Timothy 2:15; 4. Matthew 6:33; 5. Matthew 5:11, 12; 6. 1 Peter 4:7; 7. Galatians 6:1, 2; 8. Romans 6:23.

Include these instructions: "Compare God's expectations then and now. How are they similar? How are they different?" Have the class form small groups; assign two to four rows for each group to look up the Scriptures and discuss the questions. Allow groups to share their conclusions. Distribute copies of the Staying on Track activity from the reproducible page as a take-home exercise.

God Expects Obedience

GOD PROTECTS HIS PEOPLE

BACKGROUND SCRIPTURE: Joshua 2
PRINTED TEXT: Joshua 2:2-9, 15, 16, 22-24

JOSHUA 2:2-9, 15, 16, 22-24

2 And it was told the king of Jericho, saying, Behold, there came men in hither tonight of the children of Israel to search out the country.

3 And the king of Jericho sent unto Rahab, saying, Bring forth the men that are come to thee, which are entered into thine house: for they be come to search out all the country.

4 And the woman took the two men, and hid them, and said thus, There came men unto me, but I wist not whence they were:

5 And it came to pass about the time of shutting of the gate, when it was dark, that the men went out: whither the men went I wot not: pursue after them quickly; for ye shall overtake them.

6 But she had brought them up to the roof of the house, and hid them with the stalks of flax, which she had laid in order upon the roof.

7 And the men pursued after them the way to Jordan unto the fords: and as soon as they which pursued after them were gone out, they shut the gate.

8 And before they were laid down, she came up unto them upon the roof;

9 And she said unto the men, I know that the LORD hath given you the land, and that your terror is fallen upon us, and that all the inhabitants of the land faint because of you.

· ·

15 Then she let them down by a cord through the window: for her house was upon the town wall, and she dwelt upon the wall.

16 And she said unto them, Get you to the mountain, lest the pursuers meet you; and hide yourselves there three days, until the pursuers be returned: and afterward may ye go your way.

· ·

22 And they went, and came unto the mountain, and abode there three days, until the pursuers were returned: and the pursuers sought them throughout all the way, but found them not.

23 So the two men returned, and descended from the mountain, and passed over, and came to Joshua the son of Nun, and told him all things that befell them:

24 And they said unto Joshua, Truly the LORD hath delivered into our hands all the land; for even all the inhabitants of the country do faint because of us.

KEY VERSE

[The spies] said unto Joshua, Truly the LORD hath delivered into our hands all the land; for even all the inhabitants of the country do faint because of us. —**Joshua 2:24**

GOD INSTRUCTS HIS PEOPLE

Unit 1: God's People Learn from Prosperity

LESSONS 1–5

LESSON AIMS

After participating in this lesson, each student will be able to:

1. Retell the story of the spies in Jericho and how Rahab protected them.

2. Compare and contrast the actions of Rahab with those of believers in hostile environments today.

3. Pray for believers who live in areas dominated by those who oppose the gospel.

LESSON OUTLINE

Introduction

A. Providential Protection

The chief of an American Indian tribe traveled many miles to see George Washington, the man he described as the "favorite of Heaven." The year was 1770, and the chief's assessment was based on the famous battle near the Monongahela River that took place on July 9, 1755, during the French and Indian War. Approximately 1,400 troops under British General Edward Braddock were a few miles from Fort Duquesne (modern Pittsburgh). They had crossed the river and were going up a ravine when an ambush force of French and Indians attacked. The battle lasted two hours. When it was over, the British had suffered more than 50 percent casualties. The casualties included every officer on horseback except one—a 23-year-old lieutenant colonel named George Washington.

The chief gave an account of the battle from his perspective. The British soldiers in red uniforms were easy targets for the French and the Indians from their places in trees, behind rocks, or other safe cover. As the battle progressed, the chief ordered his men to concentrate their fire on Washington, the only officer who was still on horseback. His horse was shot from under him twice, and both times he changed to horses from fallen officers. These were good marksmen, and they could not understand why the officer was not even wounded. The chief then did something strange: he ordered his men to stop firing, for he concluded that this man was under a "special protection of the Great Spirit."

After the battle, Washington examined a strange tear in a sleeve of his coat, discovering that it had been made by a bullet. He found three other holes in his coat. Bullets had gone through his coat, but the force of the bullets was spent, and they did not reach his body. Washington wrote that it was by the "all-powerful dispensations of Providence" that he had been protected.

This account is thrilling, but it also raises questions. First, what is *providence* in such situations? It may be defined as ordinary happenings over a period of time in which the total impact is to fulfill God's purpose in a remarkable way. No miracles are involved in acts of providence, for natural laws are not set aside by the supernatural. Acts of providence are sometimes called miracles, but there are differences that must be recognized.

The current lesson is about some "haps" of history that are recorded in Joshua 2. Things just happened, but they worked to bring about God's protection for key individuals who helped bring about the fulfillment of promises that God had made in prior centuries. The final effects are still in process today through Jesus Christ.

B. Lesson Background

Joshua 2:1 is the verse between the previous study and this one. Its basic content is that Joshua sent two men as spies to see the land and Jericho, and that they lodged in the house of a prostitute named Rahab. The verse deserves additional attention before beginning the commentary on the selected verses for today.

Rahab. Her occupation as a prostitute gives concern to many. As far back as Josephus (a first-century Jewish writer), attempts have been made to say that she was simply an innkeeper. That probably was one of the services that she offered. Two New Testament passages confirm that she was a prostitute: Hebrew 11:31 praises her for her faith, while James 2:25 states that she was justified by her works of receiving the spies and then sending them out another way (out the window on the wall, which was illegal in some ancient cities). Matthew 1:5 tells us that she was the mother of Boaz, the person who married Ruth in the book of Ruth. Rahab is therefore in the lineage of the Messiah.

The spies may have gone to Rahab's place because (1) strangers going to her home would be normal, (2) the location of her home on the wall could facilitate an emergency escape, and (3) the Lord led them there because she was an astute individual who was developing a faith in the God of Israel.

The timing. The careful student will recall that Joshua had said that Israel would cross the Jordan in three days (Joshua 1:11). Rahab instructed the spies to hide for three days after they left her house, and they followed her advice (2:16, 22). This could make Joshua's statement seem erro-

neous. Scholars have suggested various ways to resolve the problem. Let us offer two of those proposals here. *Proposal #1:* The events in Joshua 2 are a "meanwhile, back at the ranch" situation; it is possible to translate the primary verb of Joshua 2:1 to say that Joshua *had* sent the spies earlier. *Proposal #2:* Two of the three-day periods mentioned in the early chapters of Joshua (1:11; 3:2) may be combined, thus being the same period of time; the day to move the nation from a large base camp to the edge of the Jordan does not count.

The spies. According to Joshua 6:23, the spies were "young." The fact that the Jordan was in flood stage (Joshua 3:15; 4:18) dictated that the strength of young men was necessary to attempt a crossing. They probably went upstream to a ford and made their way across. Some students suggest that after crossing the Jordan the spies (1) made their way to the west in order to approach Jericho from the opposite side, (2) wore garments that did not reflect Israelite attire, and (3) pretended to be merchants with wares to sell.

There are 2 spies this time, compared with the 12 spies who came into the land some 39 years before (Numbers 13). Previously, it was the Lord who commanded that the spies be sent; this time it seemed to be Joshua's decision. Perhaps he had learned that you can have too many spies and opinions, but he still wanted to know more about Jericho, its fortifications, and its people.

I. Reactions to the Spies
(Joshua 2:2, 3)
A. Reporting to the King (v. 2)

2. And it was told the king of Jericho, saying, Behold, there came men in hither tonight of the children of Israel to search out the country.

We proposed in the Lesson Background some ways the spies may try to conceal their presence. But any efforts of deception are in vain. The people of Jericho are on the alert, and the spies are detected. At this time Canaan is composed of city-states, and each leading city has a king. The presence of the spies is reported to him.

The Jericho of the Old Testament is on a mound of eight to nine acres, about six or seven miles from

Visual for Lesson 3. *Use this question as a lead-in to a discussion that compares and contrasts the trust of Rahab with that of the spies and your learners.*

the Jordan River. The city has a double wall and is well fortified. The people of Jericho have had an adequate amount of time to make necessary improvements to their defenses. The people of the city are fully aware that the Israelites are just on the other side of the Jordan River (Joshua 2:9-11). Travelers undoubtedly have told the city residents that the Israelite objective is to conquer Canaan.

What Do You Think?

In what sense are Christians called "to search out the country" today? How do we do this?

Talking Points for Your Discussion

- Understanding culture: 1 Chronicles 12:32
- Recognizing evil: Amos 5:13
- Knowing whom to pray for and not pray for: Jeremiah 7:16; 11:14; 14:11; Matthew 5:44

B. Request by the King (v. 3)

3. And the king of Jericho sent unto Rahab, saying, Bring forth the men that are come to thee, which are entered into thine house: for they be come to search out all the country.

The king of Jericho takes quick action. The message the king's men bring is intended to create concern or fright in Rahab's mind about the men who have entered her house. It is interesting that the king's men do not just burst in and search her home. Perhaps their deference indicates a certain respect for personal or property rights.

II. Deceiving the Delegation
(Joshua 2:4-7)

A. Statements of Deception (vv. 4, 5)

4, 5. And the woman took the two men, and hid them, and said thus, There came men unto me, but I wist not whence they were: and it came to pass about the time of shutting of the gate, when it was dark, that the men went out: whither the men went I wot not: pursue after them quickly; for ye shall overtake them.

What prompts Rahab to hide the spies? Joshua 2:9, which we will consider below, provides a clue. The text before us suggests that Rahab has already hidden the spies by the time the king's men arrive. Perhaps someone has rushed to tell her that the king's men are coming, or she may have seen their approach from her elevated residence on the wall.

When the king's men arrive, Rahab begins with a statement of truth: *There came men unto me.* The remainder of what she says, however, is a fabrication that is intended to deceive the king's representatives. Her final comment is to the effect that any pursuit should be done without delay. This is a clever way of expressing a false concern. It is designed to prompt the king's men to hurry from her house.

Rahab's deliberate deception causes many Christians some hesitation, since lying is a sin (Exodus 20:16). Is it ever "right" to tell a lie? Rahab's deception is treated in various ways. Some have excused her because she is part of a culture that is so corrupt that God has passed judgment on it to destroy it. When promising the land to Abraham hundreds of years before, the Lord said that "the iniquity of the Amorites is not yet full" (Genesis 15:16); now, however, it is time for judgment to begin.

The words of Rahab are sometimes explained by noting that this is a military matter, and deception is frequently used in time of war. Camouflage apparel is standard in the military. Joshua himself will use the ambush method in the second attack on Ai (Joshua 8), and that involves deception. He will have his forces pretend to flee in order to draw the defenders of Ai away from the city. Then the ambush group can rush in and burn the city.

God Protects His People

The bottom-line result in any case is that Rahab's deception results in the spies being spared. God will judge such matters with justice, mercy, and grace.

> **What Do You Think?**
> How do you come to grips with Rahab's lie in light of Psalm 5:6 and Proverbs 12:22?
> *Talking Points for Your Discussion*
> - The issue of motive
> - The issue of "ends justifying the means"
> - The issue of situation ethics
> - The issue of "lesser of two evils"

B. Acts of Deception (vv. 6, 7)

6. But she had brought them up to the roof of the house, and hid them with the stalks of flax, which she had laid in order upon the roof.

In many cultures, the roof of a dwelling is a place to enjoy evening breezes and to dry agricultural products. In this case, we see the roof being used to dry flax. The stalks, each about three or four feet long, are soaked in water for several weeks before being dried in the sun. The dried strips are then stacked to await later use for making linen.

7. And the men pursued after them the way to Jordan unto the fords: and as soon as they which pursued after them were gone out, they shut the gate.

The king's men have confidence in Rahab's statements, so they quickly begin the futile chase to capture the spies. A ford of the Jordan River is a likely destination to attempt an escape crossing, so the pursuers head in that direction.

As soon as the pursuers leave the city, the gate is shut in case the spies are hiding somewhere inside

HOW TO SAY IT

Ai	*Ay*-eye.
Duquesne	Due-*cane*.
Habakkuk	Huh-*back*-kuk.
Jericho	*Jair*-ih-co.
Josephus	Jo-*see*-fus.
Monongahela	Muh-non-guh-*hee*-luh.
Rahab	*Ray*-hab.

the city. This is a prudent decision, but the circumstances are in place for the spies to escape another way.

> **What Do You Think?**
> How do we resist chasing falsehood?
> *Talking Points for Your Discussion*
> - Myths and urban legends (compare 1 Timothy 4:7)
> - "The newer the truer" (compare 2 Timothy 4:3)
> - Outright deceit (compare 2 Timothy 3:13)

III. Rahab's Faith
(Joshua 2:8, 9, 15, 16)

A. In Her Confession (vv. 8, 9)

8, 9. And before they were laid down, she came up unto them upon the roof; and she said unto the men, I know that the LORD hath given you the land, and that your terror is fallen upon us, and that all the inhabitants of the land faint because of you.

Rahab appears to be very resourceful, and this is respected by the Israelite spies. They know that she could have revealed their presence. They seem ready to rest for the night before implementing a plan of action. She goes to them on the roof and makes two affirmations that say much about her.

First, she has concluded that the Lord is giving Canaan to Israel. It is amazing that she uses the special name of God (Yahweh) in her remarks. She has heard of the conquests that Israel has made in recent months (compare Numbers 21, 31; Deuteronomy 3:6; etc.). She now believes in the God of Israel.

Second, Rahab reveals that the people of Canaan are terrified. Attitude is important in any type of conflict, whether it is in sports or military action. The Canaanites' fearfulness gives the Israelites a distinct advantage for the task ahead (see Joshua 5:1, etc.).

> ❧ **PERCEIVING THE FUTURE** ❧
>
> "Blessed are those who can foresee the tides of history" is *not* one of the Beatitudes! However, those who have that sense of where things are going can make a significant difference.

Henry Ford (1863–1947) was one such individual. He saw the automotive assembly line as the way to put the world on wheels—so he did. Another person with an accurate vision of the future, although lesser known, was Michael J. Cullen (1884–1936). He saw the possibilities inherent in offering customers a wide range of grocery products in large quantities. The empty garage in Queens, New York, where Cullen opened his business became the model of the modern successor to his idea: the supermarket. Both men accurately perceived the currents of history and launched their ideas to coincide.

Rahab was certainly aware that "terror is fallen upon us, and that all the inhabitants of the land faint" because of the pending Israelite invasion. She was no different from any of her countrymen in that regard. But she had the faith and foresight to see that the future lay with the Israelites and the God who was directing them. Her faith led her to take an action that could have resulted in being condemned for treason. But the greater risk was opposing God. So she wisely chose to become a part of the changes she saw coming. Wise people still seek to see where God is leading and align themselves with His movements in history.

—C. R. B.

B. In Her Counsel (vv. 15, 16)

15. Then she let them down by a cord through the window: for her house was upon the town wall, and she dwelt upon the wall.

We do not know how much time passes before the spies make their exit from Rahab's house. Perhaps they leave very early the next morning in order to have daylight as they travel.

The method of escape is to go *through the window* from Rahab's house, which is high above the ground—perhaps 40 feet or more. There may be as much as 15 feet between the walls themselves. This event has similarities to Saul's escape from Damascus, when he was lowered in a basket (Acts 9:25).

Later, a scarlet thread is used to mark Rahab's house for protection (Joshua 2:18). Sometimes it is claimed that this is what she uses to help the spies descend the wall. The words are entirely different, however, so the two items are not the same.

16. And she said unto them, Get you to the mountain, lest the pursuers meet you; and hide yourselves there three days, until the pursuers be returned: and afterward may ye go your way.

There is a very hilly region with caves just west and north of Jericho. That is probably the place where the spies hide for three days. It is of interest that tradition says Christ's wilderness temptation happens in the same area (Matthew 4:1-11).

IV. Canaan's Fear
(Joshua 2:22-24)
A. Spies' Return (vv. 22, 23)

22. And they went, and came unto the mountain, and abode there three days, until the pursuers were returned: and the pursuers sought them throughout all the way, but found them not.

The spies follow Rahab's guidelines. We wonder if Joshua has set a timetable for his men. If their return is later than he has suggested, he naturally will be concerned about what has happened to them.

23. So the two men returned, and descended from the mountain, and passed over, and came to Joshua the son of Nun, and told him all things that befell them.

The spies survive their time in hiding and make their way to cross the Jordan in order to reach Joshua. We assume that Joshua listens with great interest as they tell him of the events of the past few days. Joshua 2:17-21 (not in today's text) states the conditions with which Rahab must comply in order for her and her family members to be spared. It is important that this information be passed to key leaders. God is protecting His people, both the spies and Rahab.

B. Spies' Report (v. 24)

24. And they said unto Joshua, Truly the LORD hath delivered into our hands all the land; for even all the inhabitants of the country do faint because of us.

The attitude of the spies is that of confidence. This confidence contrasts sharply with the attitude of the residents of Jericho, who are extremely fearful. This information provides encouragement to the Israelites, and especially to Joshua. This report is a marked contrast with the majority report of the spies in Numbers 13:25-33!

❧ A MATTER OF PERSPECTIVE ❧

Attention "chocoholics": Imagine yourself with a limitless supply of chocolate. Would that be heaven-on-earth to you? Now consider the story of Darmin Garcia, who was working at the Debelis Corporation in Kenosha, Wisconsin. That company supplies the ingredients that go into making the chocolate confections we love so much. In August 2006, Garcia was pushing chocolate into a vat. The chocolate got stuck, suddenly gave way, and Garcia slid into the vat. For two hours, his coworkers, police, and firefighters tried to get him out of the 110-degree vat, but the chocolate was so thick it was like quicksand.

Finally, a large quantity of cocoa butter was mixed in, which thinned the solution enough so Garcia could be pulled to safety. After his rescue, he said, "It was in my hair, in my ears, my mouth, everywhere." It makes you wonder if he'll ever eat chocolate again!

The Hebrew spies reported with wonder at the way God was delivering the Canaanites into Israel's hands. Yet they could also see that the Canaanites had a different perspective: fear. How we interpret the events in our lives is highly dependent on whether we are with God or against Him. It's a bit like our attitude toward chocolate: there's a big difference between savoring it and drowning in it!

—C. R. B.

Conclusion

A. Those Unanswerable Questions

The introductory comments about a remarkable event in George Washington's early career stimulate other questions. Why were some troops killed and some spared? That question has no definitive answer. Could God have spared all of them? To ask this question is to answer it: He could have! Habakkuk was told that the just shall live by faith, regardless of what happens. Paul repeats this (Romans 1:17). It is not always essential to understand, but it is always necessary to trust God.

What about headlines that tell of Christians who are killed by religious extremists, or the Christian couple brutally murdered in their home, or Christian aid workers who are raped and murdered, or the fact that (according to tradition) all the apostles but John suffered death as martyrs?

The Bible does not give explanations for such questions. We may only evaluate the situations and then give opinions. First, there is nothing wrong with waking up in Heaven. Second, it does seem that in some circumstances God moves to bring about His desired results by preserving some lives but not others at specific points in history. Third, it is observed that the levels of faith for the people involved differ and may not be the determining factor. Even so, may we all have the faith of Rahab!

B. Prayer

Almighty God, thank You for these examples of faith that will make it easier to handle tough decisions in critical circumstances. In Jesus' name we pray, amen.

C. Thought to Remember

It is not essential to understand,
but it is necessary to trust God.

INVOLVEMENT LEARNING

Some of the activities below are also found in the helpful student book, Adult Bible Class.
Don't forget to download the free reproducible page from www.standardlesson.com to enhance your lesson!

Into the Lesson

Before class, write the following scrambled words vertically on the board: *ATES TEBL, HEDILS, THOWDACG, RAMAL, MAILYRIT, AEDIMRS, CLIPEO.* If possible, keep the words covered. Have students form small groups of three or four. Tell them they are to unscramble the words on the board and try to discover what they all have in common. The first group to figure out the common idea should call it out, even if they haven't solved all the words. Allow groups to keep working until most of them have unscrambled the words. The unscrambled words are *SEAT BELT, SHIELD, WATCHDOG, ALARM, MILITARY, SIDEARM,* and *POLICE,* and the common idea is *protection.*

Congratulate the winning team. Then say, "While human beings have come up with some good ways to protect themselves, no one can protect us like God can. Today's text is about a very interesting way that God protected Joshua's two spies so they could take Joshua the information he needed."

Into the Word

Option #1. Download the reproducible page and distribute copies of the Not Quite Right activity. Have students work in pairs or small groups to complete it. The changes to be made are as follows:

Verse 2, Some Israelites came *tonight*

Verse 3, The king *sent a message* to Rahab

Verse 4, but I *had no idea where they were from*

Verse 5, I *don't know which way* they went

Verse 6, stalks of *flax*

Verse 7, *fords* of the Jordan

Verse 8, *Before* the spies lay down

Verse 9, we're falling down from *fear*

Verse 15, a cord of rope *through a window*

Verse 16, hide there *three* days

Verse 22, looked *everywhere* for them

Verse 23, told Joshua *everything*

Verse 24, *all* of the people are scared to death.

Option #2. Before class ask two good readers to practice presenting the lesson text from Joshua 2. One will read the words spoken by Rahab, and the other will read everything else. Before they begin to read, divide your class into two groups and have each group select a spokesperson. Tell both teams to listen closely to the story of Rahab and the spies so they can help retell it.

After the two readers have finished, tell the spokespeople that their teams can help prompt them as they are telling the story. Let them know that as one of them is telling the story, you will say *Switch!* and the other one has to take over. Be sure to say *Switch!* three to five times so both sides have several turns.

Into Life

Earlier in the week, search the Internet to identify areas where it's dangerous to take a stand for Christianity. Lead your class in a discussion of Rahab's actions by asking the following questions: 1. Why did Rahab help the spies? 2. What was she risking by helping them? 3. What did she hope to gain by helping them? 4. How did it work out for her? *(Read Joshua 6:22, 23; Matthew 1:5, 6.)* Following that discussion, note that there are many believers around the world who live in countries hostile to their belief. Present the results of your Internet search. Then ask, "How are these situations similar to that of Rahab?" and "How are these situations different from that of Rahab?"

Distribute copies of the Prayer for Those in Danger activity from the reproducible page. Ask students to share other stories of where Christians are in danger for their faith. Spend time praying for those Christians as a class or in small groups. Either give learners time to write out such a prayer or ask for volunteers to pray for suffering Christians around the world, or both.

God Protects His People

GOD GIVES VICTORY

BACKGROUND SCRIPTURE: Joshua 5:13–6:27

PRINTED TEXT: Joshua 6:2-4, 12-20

JOSHUA 6:2-4, 12-20

2 And the LORD said unto Joshua, See, I have given into thine hand Jericho, and the king thereof, and the mighty men of valour.

3 And ye shall compass the city, all ye men of war, and go round about the city once. Thus shalt thou do six days.

4 And seven priests shall bear before the ark seven trumpets of rams' horns: and the seventh day ye shall compass the city seven times, and the priests shall blow with the trumpets.

. . . .

12 And Joshua rose early in the morning, and the priests took up the ark of the LORD.

13 And seven priests bearing seven trumpets of rams' horns before the ark of the LORD went on continually, and blew with the trumpets: and the armed men went before them; but the rereward came after the ark of the LORD, the priests going on, and blowing with the trumpets.

14 And the second day they compassed the city once, and returned into the camp: so they did six days.

15 And it came to pass on the seventh day, that they rose early about the dawning of the day, and compassed the city after the same manner seven times: only on that day they compassed the city seven times.

16 And it came to pass at the seventh time, when the priests blew with the trumpets, Joshua said unto the people, Shout; for the LORD hath given you the city.

17 And the city shall be accursed, even it, and all that are therein, to the LORD: only Rahab the harlot shall live, she and all that are with her in the house, because she hid the messengers that we sent.

18 And ye, in any wise keep yourselves from the accursed thing, lest ye make yourselves accursed, when ye take of the accursed thing, and make the camp of Israel a curse, and trouble it.

19 But all the silver, and gold, and vessels of brass and iron, are consecrated unto the LORD: they shall come into the treasury of the LORD.

20 So the people shouted when the priests blew with the trumpets: and it came to pass, when the people heard the sound of the trumpet, and the people shouted with a great shout, that the wall fell down flat, so that the people went up into the city, every man straight before him, and they took the city.

KEY VERSE

It came to pass at the seventh time, when the priests blew with the trumpets, Joshua said unto the people, Shout; for the LORD hath given you the city. —**Joshua 6:16**

GOD INSTRUCTS HIS PEOPLE

Unit 1: God's People Learn from Prosperity

LESSONS 1–5

LESSON AIMS

After participating in this lesson, each student will be able to:

1. Describe the Lord's unusual strategy for the capture of Jericho.

2. Give instances of people who have triumphed in unusual ways in physical and spiritual battles.

3. Write a prayer for a spiritual problem that cannot be defeated without the Lord's help.

LESSON OUTLINE

Introduction

A. Victory in "Complete Surrender"

Chariots of Fire is the title of a 1981 movie. The film is a tribute to Eric Liddell (1902–1945), the "Flying Scotsman," who won two medals in the 1924 Olympic games held in Paris: the gold medal in a 400-meter race and a bronze medal in a 200-meter race.

The film vividly shows Liddell's commitment to his faith in that he would not participate in events on Sunday. He had learned about the timing for such events several months before, but the film portrays him as acquiring this information just as he was boarding the ship to go with the team to France. His prior knowledge gave him a chance to train for the 400-meter competition instead of his specialty, the 100-meter event. He was not expected to do well, but he set a world record with a time of 47.6 seconds.

Liddell was born to missionary parents in northern China. A year after the 1924 games and after graduating from college, he returned as a missionary and teacher to the country of his birth. He was interred in a Japanese prison camp during World War II, where he was assigned to be a math teacher and a supervisor for a sports program. A brain tumor eventually caused his death while in captivity. His last words were reported to be, "It's complete surrender." Complete surrender to God's will is always the route to victory for God's people, whether marching around ancient Jericho or confronting a modern evil.

B. Lesson Background

Following the events of last week's lesson, the nation of Israel moved to the edge of the Jordan River and waited three days for further instructions. The people were commanded to sanctify themselves, for their quest was to be spiritual as well as physical. The people were instructed to stay at least 3,000 feet (2,000 cubits) from the ark (Joshua 3:4). It is suggested that this showed respect for God's presence in their midst, and it allowed more people to witness the coming miracle. The Lord spoke to Joshua and said that Joshua would be magnified through what was about to happen (3:7).

As the feet of the priests touched the edge of the Jordan, the waters retreated to the town of Adam (Joshua 3:15, 16), about 16 miles north of the mouth of the Dead Sea. Thus a very wide area became available to use. Some of the older Israelites had experienced the crossing of the Red Sea in their youth, and they should have had no hesitation about moving forward.

This is one of the great miracles of the Old Testament, but some have tried to minimize it by finding natural explanations. It is true that the flow of the Jordan has been stopped temporarily several times when cliff banks fell into the water in upstream locations. Those instances do not account for what we see in the text: the timing when the waters receded, the timing when the waters returned, and the fact that the Israelites crossed on dry ground (Joshua 3:17).

The Lord instructed Joshua to build a memorial for this event at the new campsite west of the Jordan, a place that would be called Gilgal. Twelve stones from the riverbed formed the altar (Joshua 4:1-3). Joshua then took the initiative in having a second memorial (4:9). When future generations would ask about the memorials, they were to be told what the Lord did for His people (vv. 6, 7).

The rite of circumcision had not been observed during the wilderness wanderings (Joshua 5:5). So Joshua instructed the people to renew this aspect of their covenant relationship with the Lord (5:2-9). The word *Gilgal* is from a verb that means "to roll," so a noun form of the word was given to this site where this distinctive shortcoming was rolled away (5:9).

According to the instructions given by Moses 40 years before, the Passover was observed on the

HOW TO SAY IT

Bethel	*Beth*-ul.
Gilgal	*Gil*-gal (G as in *get*).
Goliath	Go-*lye*-uth.
Jahaziel	Juh-*hay*-zuh-el.
Jehoshaphat	Jeh-*hosh*-uh-fat.
Jericho	*Jair*-ih-co.
rabbis	*rab*-eyes.
Yahweh *(Hebrew)*	*Yah*-weh.

fourteenth day of the first month (Exodus 12; Joshua 5:10). The manna ceased on the next day (Joshua 5:12). Thus all the cooks in Israel had to improvise new recipes.

I. Joshua's Visitor
(JOSHUA 6:2-4)

Joshua, a spy himself some 39 years before, is scouting the city of Jericho on his own (Joshua 5:13). Suddenly he realizes he is not alone. A "man" is opposite him with a drawn sword. Joshua asks the man to identify himself, and the man says that he is the captain of the Lord's host—probably the angelic host. Joshua responds by falling on his face to the ground. The man's presence makes the ground holy, so Joshua is instructed to remove his sandals (Joshua 5:13-15).

A. Assurances for Joshua (v. 2)

2. And the LORD said unto Joshua, See, I have given into thine hand Jericho, and the king thereof, and the mighty men of valour.

The term used to refer to this "man" (Joshua 5:13) changes; now he is *the Lord*. The word *Lord* is in capital letters in most versions to indicate that it is the sacred name of God—Yahweh.

The assuring message for Joshua is that he will be completely victorious over Jericho. The city seems to be better fortified than the walled cities that were conquered on the eastern side of the Jordan (see Deuteronomy 3:4, 5), so this is an encouraging statement. Archaeology has shown that the lower wall of Jericho is of large stones, and there is a mud brick wall on top of the stone portion. The total height is 40 feet or more. Jericho is a strategic site that guards the entrance to Canaan from the east. The city is over 800 feet below sea level, making it the lowest city on earth.

B. Actions to Take (vv. 3, 4)

3. And ye shall compass the city, all ye men of war, and go round about the city once. Thus shalt thou do six days.

The Lord's military strategy for Joshua's army is much different from what the old soldier is probably anticipating. Nothing is said about battering rams, scaling ladders, or other weapons. The first part of the plan involves a circling of the city each day for six days. Obviously, the people are to stay far enough away to avoid arrows or sling stones. It will take about 45 minutes for one such circuit.

What Do You Think?
How does waging spiritual warfare for God differ from the way the world wages war? How do you resist being persuaded by the world's ways in this regard?

Talking Points for Your Discussion
- Regarding weapons used: 2 Corinthians 10:4
- Regarding nature of the enemy: Ephesians 6:12
- Regarding end result: 2 Timothy 4:7, 8

4. And seven priests shall bear before the ark seven trumpets of rams' horns: and the seventh day ye shall compass the city seven times, and the priests shall blow with the trumpets.

The instructions continue by making this to be more than a military operation: it is also a spiritual undertaking, involving the ark and seven priests carrying rams' horns. Horns of this type are used for both religious and military purposes (compare Exodus 19:13; Leviticus 25:9; 1 Samuel 13:3).

II. Six Days

(Joshua 6:12-14)

Verses 5-11 (not in today's text) cite procedural instructions—first from the Lord to Joshua (v. 5), then from Joshua to the people (v. 6). Then comes the order to move out (v. 7). As we arrive at the next section in today's text, the Israelites are about to begin the second of the seven trips around Jericho.

A. Preparations to March (v. 12)

12. And Joshua rose early in the morning, and the priests took up the ark of the Lord.

Joshua is a person who acts promptly. Both here and in Joshua 3:1 he is depicted as a person who rises early. As the priests take *up the ark of the Lord,* we may safely assume that the men of war who are to participate in the daily march also are ready to take their places.

What Do You Think?
What things cause you to respond more slowly to God's commands than you should? How do you overcome this problem?

Talking Points for Your Discussion
- Desire for worldly things (Mark 10:22)
- Desire to be liked (Matthew 10:22)
- Fear (Matthew 25:24, 25)
- Laziness (Hebrews 6:12)

B. Order of March (v. 13)

13. And seven priests bearing seven trumpets of rams' horns before the ark of the Lord went on continually, and blew with the trumpets: and the armed men went before them; but the rereward came after the ark of the Lord, the priests going on, and blowing with the trumpets.

The order of march is not one of the details given by the heavenly messenger, but it may be included in what is said. The result is this: *armed men* as a vanguard, *seven priests* with *seven trumpets,* the ark of the covenant carried by the other priests mentioned in verse 12, and more armed men to protect the rear (see also Joshua 6:9).

The total number of soldiers available to Joshua according to Numbers 26:51 is 601,730. Some soldiers undoubtedly stay on the east side of the Jordan River to guard the possessions and families in that area (Numbers 32; see also analysis of Joshua 1:12-15 in Lesson 2). Joshua probably deploys only a portion of the remainder.

There are two types of sounds that accompany the encircling of the city: trumpets and marching feet. The footwear of the marchers does not make much noise. The sound of the trumpets is the dominant factor. The Israelites are not to utter a word throughout the march. If there are taunts from the walls, there is to be no answer (Joshua 6:10).

C. Method of March (v. 14)

14. And the second day they compassed the city once, and returned into the camp: so they did six days.

The strange procedure is to be followed each day for a total of six days. At the end of each day's march of a single circuit around the city, the men return to camp. We can only wonder what the inhabitants of Jericho think of this strange ritual. Perhaps they think that these actions are intended to put some type of spell on them. Or perhaps they think this is the beginning of a lengthy siege.

❧ NO DECEIT NEEDED ❧

In the days leading up to the Allied invasion of France on June 6, 1944, Allied forces conducted *Operation Fortitude*. This was an exercise in deception, intended to fool the Nazis regarding the time and place of the invasion. It worked.

When Joshua was preparing to conquer Jericho, the tactics God prescribed were considerably different. There was no deception—quite the opposite! For six days, Israel made a show of force by marching around the city. Because of these daily marches, Jericho's king knew the exact composition and location of the opposing force. The only thing he was not aware of was the power of God.

For a pagan king to be unaware of God's power is perhaps understandable. For a Christian to be unaware of God's power is inexcusable! Sometimes Christians use the world's means in pursuing personal goals or the goals of their church. That's tantamount to saying, "I'm not quite sure I can trust God to make such and such happen, so I'm going to try my own method." Will we trust God or rely on our own devices?   —C. R. B.

III. Seventh Day
(JOSHUA 6:15-19)

Which day of march is a Sabbath? As the Israelites approached Mount Sinai after leaving Egypt, the Lord said that no one was to go from his or her place on the Sabbath (Exodus 16:29). The concept of being allowed to travel a limited distance on a Sabbath is still in the future. (A Sabbath day's journey is mentioned in Acts 1:12, but it is not in the Law of Moses; it is added later by rabbis.) An exception is made for the work of the priests in sacrificing animals each Sabbath day, so the capture of Jericho may be viewed as another exception. It is often assumed that the seventh day of marching is a Sabbath, for it is a very special day.

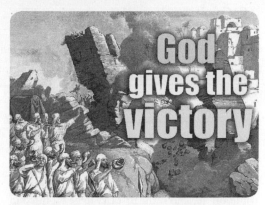

Visual for Lesson 4. *Point to this visual as you ask, "What are some ways that God gives the victory today?"*

A. Rising and Marching (v. 15)

15. And it came to pass on the seventh day, that they rose early about the dawning of the day, and compassed the city after the same manner seven times: only on that day they compassed the city seven times.

The people are following the instructions in Joshua 6:4 exactly. *On the seventh day* it is necessary that the priests and soldiers take their places as soon as there is enough light, for they are to circle Jericho seven times. The march itself will take slightly over five hours, plus the time for each person to make the trip from his camping location. Thus it will be about noon when the seventh circuit is completed. Excessive heat will not be a problem, for it is still spring.

B. Command and Promise (v. 16)

16. And it came to pass at the seventh time, when the priests blew with the trumpets, Joshua said unto the people, Shout; for the LORD hath given you the city.

There is a distinctive blowing of the rams' horns *(trumpets)* during the seventh circuit. Then Joshua gives both a command and a promise! The command is to break the silence (Joshua 6:10) by having everyone shout (6:5). The promise is that the Lord is giving the city to them. The promise of victory provokes an excited compliance with this unusual military strategy of the Lord.

C. Condemnation and Concession (v. 17)

17. And the city shall be accursed, even it, and all that are therein, to the LORD: only Rahab the harlot shall live, she and all that are with her in the house, because she hid the messengers that we sent.

A recognized way to acquire wealth rapidly is by means of the spoils of war—assuming that you live! For the Israelites, the distribution of such plunder is directed by the Lord (see Numbers 31:25-47). However, the spoils of war are treated differently this time: there is to be no distribution. Jericho is the first city to be captured in Canaan, and everything in it is dedicated to God. Thus the city is described as *accursed*. This word often means "to set apart for destruction." In this case, all precious metals are to be given to the treasury of the Lord, and all life is condemned. Joshua makes an exception in order to honor the agreement the spies made with Rahab.

> **What Do You Think?**
> What "types" of people do we sometimes think should not receive God's grace? How might God's viewpoint be different from ours?
> *Talking Points for Your Discussion*
> - Personal enemies (Matthew 5:39; Romans 12:17; 1 Peter 3:9)
> - Those who oppose our teaching (2 Timothy 2:25)
> - Outcasts of society (Mark 1:40, 41)
> - Sinners (John 8:2-11)

Many have expressed concern about the destruction of the inhabitants of Jericho. It must be remembered that the God who creates life also has the right to determine if life will continue. The flood in the time of Noah was a judgment on humanity, and the actions against Jericho and Canaan are similar judgments on corrupt people.

D. Restriction and Reasons (vv. 18, 19)

18. And ye, in any wise keep yourselves from the accursed thing, lest ye make yourselves accursed, when ye take of the accursed thing, and make the camp of Israel a curse, and trouble it.

Joshua emphasizes that the armed men must not do what has been their custom—taking plunder for themselves. If they disobey, then the condemnation on Jericho will be transferred to *the camp of Israel*. The lesson following this one will offer us a vivid illustration of what happens when one person deliberately disobeys God's command.

> **What Do You Think?**
> What are some "accursed things" that God wants you to keep away from? How do you do this?
> *Talking Points for Your Discussion*
> - Being proactive (Proverbs 4:14; Ephesians 6:13; 2 Peter 3:17)
> - Being reactive (Proverbs 1:10; 1 Corinthians 6:18)

19. But all the silver, and gold, and vessels of brass and iron, are consecrated unto the LORD: they shall come into the treasury of the LORD.

Certain metals have always been valuable, and this is certainly true in Joshua's day—about 1400 BC. The mention of iron is especially interesting. This black metal is highly prized, for a sword made from other metals is no match for an iron sword (compare 1 Samuel 13:19-22).

IV. Joshua's Validation
(JOSHUA 6:20)

The final phase of Jericho's destruction is about to begin. Joshua himself knows what is coming next, because the Lord has told him (Joshua 6:5).

A. Command Obeyed (v. 20a)

20a. So the people shouted when the priests blew with the trumpets: and it came to pass, when the people heard the sound of the trumpet, and the people shouted with a great shout, that the wall fell down flat.

It is interesting to speculate on whether the people know what to expect when they shout. Are they simply obeying the command, thinking this is the normal procedure for an attack? We easily imagine that they and the inhabitants of Jericho are startled as the walls began to crumble and fall. The dust and noise are undoubtedly tremendous.

Some have put forth naturalistic explanations to try to "explain away" the miraculous. Some propose that an earthquake occurred at just the right time. Others assert that the vibrations produced by marching feet, the trumpets, and the shouting combine to cause the walls to disintegrate. To believe in a great God for whom nothing is impossible makes much more sense. This agrees with the writer of the book of Hebrews who affirms that it was "by faith" that the walls fell after the people marched for seven days (Hebrews 11:30).

Several archaeological expeditions have been conducted at Jericho over the last 80 years. The conclusions are contradictory, often depending on the preconceived thoughts of the team leaders. Findings from about 1997 uncovered a new section that seems to add confirmation to the biblical account.

B. Capture Completed (v. 20b)

20b. So that the people went up into the city, every man straight before him, and they took the city.

The Hebrews go up and over the piles of rubble, with every person going straight ahead in obedience to the Lord's commands (Joshua 6:5). The victory is complete, and the promises that the Lord made to Joshua (see Joshua 1) come to pass. Joshua's leadership is fully validated.

The final verses of Joshua 6 tell us of the rescue of Rahab and her family. They live outside the camp temporarily (v. 23), and she is still living at the time of the writing of the book (v. 25). Joshua puts a curse on anyone who attempts to rebuild Jericho as a fortified city (v. 26). The curse is fulfilled about 550 years later when Hiel, a man from Bethel, rebuilds the city (see 1 Kings 16:34).

What Do You Think?

What are some battles that God has fought for you in which He has given you victory?

Talking Points for Your Discussion

- In oppositions from others (Psalm 44:5; John 16:33)
- In various challenges of life (Romans 8:35-37)
- In challenges to your faith (1 John 5:4)

A basic computer can be purchased for less than $500. Such a computer has capabilities many, many times greater than an "ancient" one of 15 years ago. The newer computers have the ability to read and write DVDs, connect wirelessly, process digital photos—the list goes on and on. The earlier computers had none of these features, yet their prices were many times greater! But before we smirk too much at the "ancient" computers, remember that today's powerful models exist only because the rudimentary models preceded them.

When the Israelites consummated their victory at Jericho, it seemed like a simple matter: shout and watch the walls fall down. However, that marvel came only because Israel had followed God's rudimentary instructions for each day of the week that led up to the victory. We shouldn't expect to experience God's blessings without paying attention to first things first. He may be testing us to see if we will do so. —C. R. B.

Conclusion

A. The Battle Is the Lord's!

The statement above is David's comment just before he killed Goliath (1 Samuel 17:47). A prophet named Jahaziel made a similar statement to King Jehoshaphat when he was preparing to go into battle (2 Chronicles 20:14, 15). For God's people, victory is not by sword, spear, or stone. Battles are won as they fulfill God's goals.

Reversals often precede victories. But remaining steadfast in difficult times increases spiritual strength. It must always be remembered that victories are not ultimately decided on earth, but in the judgment courts of Heaven, for the battle is the Lord's.

B. Prayer

Almighty God, help me to live victoriously for You today—as an example for others and to show my gratitude for all You have done for me. In Jesus' name, amen.

C. Thought to Remember

"Faith is the victory that overcomes the world!"

INVOLVEMENT LEARNING

Some of the activities below are also found in the helpful student book, Adult Bible Class.
Don't forget to download the free reproducible page from www.standardlesson.com to enhance your lesson!

Into the Lesson

Option #1. Provide to small groups handouts with the following instructions: "Imagine that you are a general in the days before gunpowder, and you are planning to conquer a city guarded by armed men behind a 40-feet-high wall. From the following list, select three items and describe how you would use them to defeat the enemy: *battering rams, scaling ladders, catapults, flaming arrows, siege towers, trumpets, swords, shields."*

Call for reports after five minutes. Determine if anyone selected trumpets as one of the items; ask why or why not. Say, "Trumpets were an essential part of the battle plan that God gave the Israelites to conquer Jericho. Let's see what other unusual things He had them do."

Option #2. Download the reproducible page and place in chairs copies of the God's Battle Plan activity. Students can work on this as they arrive.

Into the Word

Prepare a two-column chart, with one column titled "Ancient Army's Usual Procedure" and the other "God's Unusual Procedure." Write the following items down the left column: 1. Battle plans designed by army leaders; 2. War cries used to terrify enemy; 3. Religious officials not in battle's forefront; 4. Soldiers are entitled to treasure as spoils of war; 5. Promises made to army's opponents not kept; 6. Walled cities defeated after long siege and construction of ramps; 7. The army's leaders take full credit for the victory.

In the right column include the following Scripture references (but **not** the suggested answers, which are in italics): 1. Joshua 6:2-4. *God designed the battle plan.* 2. Joshua 6:10, 13. *All of the people were completely silent; the only sound was the trumpets blowing.* 3. Joshua 6:13-16. *The priests and the ark of the Lord were the central part of the procession.* 4. Joshua 6:17-19. *Everyone was forbidden to keep anything of value from Jericho, since it was dedicated to the Lord.* 5. Joshua 2:12-14; 6:17. *Joshua made sure the promises made to Rahab were kept.* 6. Joshua 6:20. *The walls collapse after the people obey God's instructions to march around the city, blow trumpets, and shout.* 7. Joshua 6:2, 19. *Joshua and the people know that the victory is the Lord's.*

Have students work in small groups to complete the right column. Use the following questions to lead a discussion: "What do you think the Israelites' first reaction was when they heard the plan?" "How do their actions demonstrate a willingness to obey, even when it didn't appear to make sense?" "What effect do you think their actions had on the people of Jericho?" "Did this tactic cause the Israelites to be more willing or less willing to give God the credit for the victory? Why?"

Into Life

Option #1. Say, "I'm going to tell you a true story of how Christians were helped in an unexpected way. *Story:* 'It was a bitter winter in the northeastern U.S., and a Christian family had no money to clothe their two children properly because of the father's long-term unemployment. A friendly neighbor (not a Christian and a former prostitute) brought over a big bag of quality winter clothes, gloves, and boots that her son had outgrown. They were a perfect fit. A few days later a Catholic charity (the family was Protestant) gave them brand new school outfits for each child.'"

Ask learners if they think this was "a God thing." Have them think about times in their lives when God surprised them with the way He helped—ways that seemed like strong walls were knocked down. Offer a prayer of thanksgiving to God for His amazing ability to help us out in ways we do not anticipate.

Option #2. Make copies of the Knocking Down Walls activity from the reproducible page. Have students work on these individually, or distribute as a take-home activity.

GOD RESPONDS TO DISOBEDIENCE

BACKGROUND SCRIPTURE: Joshua 7, 8

PRINTED TEXT: Joshua 7:1, 10-12, 22-26

JOSHUA 7:1, 10-12, 22-26

1 But the children of Israel committed a trespass in the accursed thing: for Achan, the son of Carmi, the son of Zabdi, the son of Zerah, of the tribe of Judah, took of the accursed thing: and the anger of the LORD was kindled against the children of Israel.

. . . .

10 And the LORD said unto Joshua, Get thee up; wherefore liest thou thus upon thy face?

11 Israel hath sinned, and they have also transgressed my covenant which I commanded them: for they have even taken of the accursed thing, and have also stolen, and dissembled also, and they have put it even among their own stuff.

12 Therefore the children of Israel could not stand before their enemies, but turned their backs before their enemies, because they were accursed: neither will I be with you any more, except ye destroy the accursed from among you.

. . . .

22 So Joshua sent messengers, and they ran unto the tent; and, behold, it was hid in his tent, and the silver under it.

23 And they took them out of the midst of the tent, and brought them unto Joshua, and unto all the children of Israel, and laid them out before the LORD.

24 And Joshua, and all Israel with him, took Achan the son of Zerah, and the silver, and the garment, and the wedge of gold, and his sons, and his daughters, and his oxen, and his asses, and his sheep, and his tent, and all that he had: and they brought them unto the valley of Achor.

25 And Joshua said, Why hast thou troubled us? the LORD shall trouble thee this day. And all Israel stoned him with stones, and burned them with fire, after they had stoned them with stones.

26 And they raised over him a great heap of stones unto this day. So the LORD turned from the fierceness of his anger. Wherefore the name of that place was called, The valley of Achor, unto this day.

KEY VERSE

The children of Israel committed a trespass in the accursed thing: for Achan, . . . of the tribe of Judah, took of the accursed thing: and the anger of the LORD was kindled against the children of Israel. —Joshua 7:1

GOD INSTRUCTS HIS PEOPLE

Unit 1: God's People Learn from Prosperity

LESSONS 1–5

LESSON AIMS

After participating in this lesson, each student will be able to:

1. Describe Achan's sin, its seriousness, and its punishment.

2. Cite examples of how disobeying God causes undesirable effects for many.

3. Describe a temptation that he or she struggles with and determine a course of action to live above it.

LESSON OUTLINE

Introduction

A. Responses to Disobedience

It was a family vacation, and the father was driving as the family enjoyed the scenery of the mountains. At one point, the father changed from the secondary road to a tertiary one—that fine line on the map that indicates a road of lesser quality. Just as the car changed roads, a sign confronted them with a warning: *Road Closed.*

In spite of reservations by others in the car, the father went ahead. He remembered having been here before, and he was confident that he could negotiate around any obstacle. The family would be able to enjoy even more spectacular views.

Just before merging back with the first road, they came to a place where a bridge was being replaced. There was no way around. As they returned to the place where they had taken the more scenic route, they were greeted by a message with bold letters on the back of the sign that had been ignored: *We told you so.*

That's humorous, but warnings regarding expected conduct are often viewed as affronts to personal liberty. Authorities are to be challenged or disregarded. Compliance is optional. We think we know better.

Respect for authority should begin in the home. But the homes of today often deliver mixed messages on expectations. The guidelines often change as children are shuffled from the home of one divorced parent to another. Children seem to understand that emotional forces are at work that will make discipline by a nonparent difficult in blended families.

Experts in family life recommend that families develop lists of expectations along with consequences for infractions. For this plan to work, there must be consistency in application. If a person in authority abdicates responsibility, then family dynamics deteriorate. This is a lesson that is clearly evident in the Old Testament.

B. Lesson Background

Our four previous studies have shown that Israel's determined obedience to God produced the successes that the previous generation forfeited

God Responds to Disobedience

because of disobedience. Some of the people experienced the full 40 years of punishment in the wilderness wandering. The evidence accumulated to show that the repeated disobediences and complaining by their ancestors was totally unacceptable behavior to God. The rebellious adults who left Egypt perished in the wilderness.

The farewell address of Moses in the book of Deuteronomy also had a strong effect. Moses' death took place a short time before the book of Joshua begins. In his speeches, Moses vividly contrasted the results for obedience and disobedience, not only for that generation, but also in the future (see Deuteronomy 27 and 28). Over 200 times Moses used the imperatives *hear, do, obey, keep.*

The second generation—that is, the one that followed Joshua's leadership—did well in listening and learning. Many good things happened as a result. The people pledged to obey Joshua. They accepted the news from the two spies sent to Jericho that the inhabitants of Canaan were terrified. The conquest of Jericho was completely successful. Simple obedience to God's unusual battle plans produced a stunning victory. This was the first of three cities in Canaan that the book of Joshua says were burned. The others were Ai (Joshua 8:18, 19) and Hazor (11:11).

From all outward appearances, the conquest of Canaan was going extremely well. But during the assault on Jericho, a deliberate, disobedient, defiant sin entered Israel. What would be the consequences for the nation of Israel, and what could be done about it to make things right again? That topic is the lesson for today.

HOW TO SAY IT

Achan	*Ay*-kan.
Achor	*Ah*-core.
Ai	*Ay*-eye.
Babylon	*Bab*-uh-lun.
Canaan	*Kay*-nun.
Haggai	*Hag*-eye or *Hag*-ay-eye.
Hazor	*Hay*-zor.
Shinar	*Shye*-nar.
Zabdi	*Zab*-dye.
Zimri	*Zim*-rye.

I. Sin of Achan

(JOSHUA 7:1)

The last sentence of Joshua 6 is a positive declaration that the Lord is with Joshua and his fame is in all the land. That's a good thing in terms of putting fear into the enemies. But the problem is that false confidence can develop as God's expectations are viewed as something less than mandatory.

A. Crime Specified (v. 1a)

1a. But the children of Israel committed a trespass in the accursed thing.

The word *but* is ominous: Israel has been perverse or treacherous concerning the special ban on Jericho. The inhabitants, its contents, and the city itself were to be set apart for destruction (Joshua 6:18); *accursed thing* refers to items that are devoted to the Lord by destruction (also 7:11, 12, 13, 15). The exception in the case of Jericho is that all precious metals were to have been given to the treasury of the Lord (6:19). Outwardly, it seems that compliance has been complete. But there is a problem, as we shall see.

B. Culprit Identified (v. 1b)

1b. For Achan, the son of Carmi, the son of Zabdi, the son of Zerah, of the tribe of Judah, took of the accursed thing.

The percentage for compliance with God's commands is exceptionally good. It is better than 99.99 percent, for only one person of the entire Israelite army succumbs to the temptation of violating the ban on Jericho. Yet the sin of one man makes the entire nation guilty of violating a specific, sacred sanction. The man's name is *Achan,* and his ancestry is traced back three generations, and then to *the tribe of Judah.* King David will come from this tribe some 400 years later. But at this moment there is a sin problem, and the sin must be dealt with.

The careful student will notice that the accounts and versions differ on the name of Achan's grandfather. Here it is *Zabdi,* but *Zimri* in 1 Chronicles 2:6. The latter spelling is sometimes transferred to Joshua 7:1 in both ancient and contemporary versions. Some of the Hebrew letters in the two names are similar in form, and this may have caused confusion for ancient scribes.

C. Consequence Stated (v. 1c)

1c. And the anger of the LORD was kindled against the children of Israel.

The sin of Achan has far-reaching effects, for the entire nation is considered guilty. If anyone brings any of the devoted items into the camp, then all Israel is affected by being subject to *the anger of the Lord*. Before we raise the question of the "fairness" of punishing the many for the sin of the one, keep in mind that Joshua gave fair warning that this would happen (Joshua 6:18, previous lesson).

> **What Do You Think?**
> What are some sins today that have a broader effect than on just the one who commits them? What are some of those effects?
> *Talking Points for Your Discussion*
> - In the church
> - In families
> - In business
> - In a nation

II. Summons by the Lord
(JOSHUA 7:10-12)

The intervening verses that are not in today's text (Joshua 7:2-9) tell us that Achan's sin results in the loss of 36 men in the next military encounter: the defeat at Ai. It is easy to imagine that the family members of the dead men ask why, for such losses and defeats are not expected.

Just a few months before this unexpected turn of events, a major operation had been conducted against Midian. It had the amazing result that Israel did not lose any of its men (Numbers 31:49). Now this sudden reversal from victories to a defeat is a shock to Joshua. When things go wrong, there is a tendency to look for someone or something to blame. Joshua's response to the loss is to blame God for the disaster at Ai (Joshua 7:6-9). Joshua tears his clothes and falls to the ground in disbelief. Other leaders join him in this emotional reaction, and then the Lord speaks to Joshua.

A. Command to Joshua (v. 10)

10. And the LORD said unto Joshua, Get thee up; wherefore liest thou thus upon thy face?

The Lord challenges Joshua. This is not a time for prayer. Appropriate action is the only thing that will correct the situation (compare Exodus 14:15). The Lord is preparing Joshua to understand why his forces suffered defeat and what must be done.

B. Crime Described (v. 11)

11. Israel hath sinned, and they have also transgressed my covenant which I commanded them: for they have even taken of the accursed thing, and have also stolen, and dissembled also, and they have put it even among their own stuff.

As stated before, only one person actually trespasses by violating a specific command. But the contagion of sin has the effect that the entire nation shares in the event and becomes guilty. The sin is by one man, but it is viewed as if the entire nation has stolen that which belongs to God.

In December of 520 BC—many centuries after Joshua—the prophet Haggai asks the people of Jerusalem to consult the priests for a ruling. He describes two hypothetical situations. In one scenario, that which is holy touches that which is ordinary; in the second scenario, the reverse happens. The outcome of both situations is that the unholy always corrupts (Haggai 2:11-14), and that is the effect of the sin of Achan. The ritual holiness of the Israelites is defiled. Acceptable worship is voided because of the sin of disobedience. Items that were to be set aside for destruction are in the camp. Thus Israel has lost the power and might that only God can provide.

> **What Do You Think?**
> What are some things we have among our "stuff" that needs to be discarded?
> *Talking Points for Your Discussion*
> - In the area of entertainment
> - In the area of possessions
> - In the area of relationships
> - In the area of attitude

God Responds to Disobedience

C. Consequences for Israel (v. 12)

12. Therefore the children of Israel could not stand before their enemies, but turned their backs before their enemies, because they were accursed: neither will I be with you any more, except ye destroy the accursed from among you.

The explanation by the Lord makes it very clear that the reason for the loss at Ai is that the entire nation is under the special ban that had been pronounced on Jericho. The former military successes were not accomplished by any military or physical superiority on the part of Israel. It was not by might or power, but by the presence of God that they had been successful (see Zechariah 4:6).

There is only one way to secure God's blessing again, and that is to destroy any items in the camp that are under the curse that was on Jericho. At this point, only the guilty party knows who is responsible. We speculate that his emotions surge in several directions: guilt, sorrow, grief, and fear.

❧ CONTAGION OF SIN ❧

Nobody knew about HIV/AIDS in 1970. Today, perhaps two million people die of AIDS annually.

In some African countries, one of every five people is infected. Children who have lost parents to AIDS number in the millions in Africa. In at least two African countries, more than three-quarters of all orphans are AIDS orphans. Many innocent people catch the disease from an infected spouse who has committed adultery and/or lose one or more parents for this reason.

Violations of God's standards have consequences. Sometimes the consequences affect only the guilty party, but often there is a ripple effect as the consequences spread to others. Such is the case with sexually transmitted diseases (such as AIDS), and such was the case with Achan's sin. His sinful behavior resulted in the death of 36 Israelites at Ai. His family (who may have participated in the cover-up) and the nation suffered.

Horror stories abound of churches that fell apart because there was "sin in the camp" of hidden immoral behavior on the part of a church leader. The warning "be sure your sin will find you out" (Numbers 32:23) still applies.   —C. R. B.

Visual for Lesson 5. *Use the startling imagery of this visual to enhance your discussion of the question associated with Joshua 7:11.*

III. Successful Search
(JOSHUA 7:22, 23)

In the intervening verses that are not in today's text, Joshua orders the people to consecrate themselves, for the guilty party is to be identified through a series of drawing lots that will lead to the selection of one man. Joshua's instructions specify that the guilty person and the dedicated items are to be burned. The prescribed procedure is followed, and Achan is identified as the guilty person, whose primary sin is disobedience.

We see a tender side of Joshua depicted in Joshua 7:19. Achan has been identified, Joshua addresses him as "my son," and then asks him to confess. Disobedience has its consequences, and the penalty must be administered, but doing so may produce sorrow.

A. Messengers Sent (v. 22)

22. So Joshua sent messengers, and they ran unto the tent; and, behold, it was hid in his tent, and the silver under it.

In the previous verse, Achan describes the three things he has taken: a coat imported from Shinar (or Babylon), silver that weighs 200 shekels, and a wedge of gold. Joshua's messengers find everything just as Achan describes.

Achan has made the effort to hide these things in his tent by burying them (Joshua 7:21). The fact that Achan has gone to the trouble of hiding the items indicates that he knows that what he has done is wrong. The urgency of the situation is seen in the fact that Joshua's messengers run to Achan's tent.

❧ THE HIDING PLACE ❧

Corrie ten Boom's book *The Hiding Place* is well known among Christians. The "hiding place" was a small building in Haarlem, Netherlands. The family business was in the shop on the first floor, and the family lived in the floors above. The Ten Boom family used the building to provide shelter for Jews and members of the Dutch underground after the Nazis invaded Holland in 1940.

This refuge was an expression of the family's commitment to live for Christ regardless of cost. When the family was betrayed on February 28, 1944, Corrie and her family were arrested. Four died in prison, but Corrie survived to tell the story to the world.

Achan also had a secret hiding place in his home, but what a difference there was! His hiding place concealed sinfully obtained treasure, while that of the Ten Booms hid refugees from sinful predators. But more important than Achan's physical place for hiding his loot was the hiding place in his heart where he harbored a sinful attitude. That's where sin starts. We can get rid of many "things" that detract from our walk with Christ, but unless we turn the hiding place in our heart inside out, those "things" will come back.

—C. R. B.

B. Displayed Items (v. 23)

23. And they took them out of the midst of the tent, and brought them unto Joshua, and unto all the children of Israel, and laid them out before the LORD.

With the stolen items now in Joshua's possession, they are placed *before the Lord* to demonstrate obedience to the divine commands. This procedure becomes an object lesson from which all may learn that the Lord expects obedience. It is possible that others had been tempted to take some of the treasures of Jericho for themselves, but the need to conquer such thoughts now receives a dramatic confirmation.

IV. Sentence for Achan

(JOSHUA 7:24-26)

The time for judgment has arrived.

A. Extent Described (v. 24)

24. And Joshua, and all Israel with him, took Achan the son of Zerah, and the silver, and the garment, and the wedge of gold, and his sons, and his daughters, and his oxen, and his asses, and his sheep, and his tent, and all that he had: and they brought them unto the valley of Achor.

The penalty for possessing the devoted items extends to all of Achan's possessions and family members. One of the laws given by Moses is that children are not to be put to death for the sins of parents and vice versa (Deuteronomy 24:16). We may assume that Achan's sons and daughters know of their father's act—after all, it's hard not to see a large amount of contraband being buried inside one's tent—but do nothing about it. Thus they are subject to judgment as well. Children are conditioned by peer pressure not to snitch. But there are many situations when wrongs must be reported. No mention is made of a wife, so many students assume that she is deceased.

The original command was for the precious metals to go into the treasury of the Lord (Joshua 6:19), but no mention is made of what becomes of the objects that are in Achan's possession. In all probability the original guidelines are followed: the precious metals are given to the treasury of the tabernacle. The significance of the designation *the*

God Responds to Disobedience

valley of Achor, where Achan, his family, and his possessions are taken, is given in verse 26 (below).

B. Execution Completed (v. 25)

25. And Joshua said, Why hast thou troubled us? the LORD shall trouble thee this day. And all Israel stoned him with stones, and burned them with fire, after they had stoned them with stones.

Joshua delivers a stinging rebuke, and the punishment is carried out (compare Exodus 19:13). The execution method is that of stoning. The Mosaic legislation prescribes it more than any other. Burning is added to the procedure, and this tends to parallel what happened to Jericho. The "destruction" of the dedicated items is now complete.

> **What Do You Think?**
> What was a time when God dealt with your sin less harshly than you deserved? How did things turn out?
> *Talking Points for Your Discussion*
> ▪ A time when you acted in ignorance
> ▪ A time when you knew better

C. Event Remembered (v. 26)

26. And they raised over him a great heap of stones unto this day. So the LORD turned from the fierceness of his anger. Wherefore the name of that place was called, The valley of Achor, unto this day.

The first impression is that this is a redundant, unnecessary stoning, but that is not the case. The purpose is to erect a stone memorial as an example to future generations. This is not to be a monument for sin, but for the consequences of sin. This is the third stone memorial in the book of Joshua. The first two were to commemorate the crossing of the Jordan.

A name is given to the location: *The valley of Achor.* The word *Achor* means "trouble" or "troubling," so this becomes "The Valley of Trouble." It is quickly seen that the words *Achan* and *Achor* are similar. The similarity has caused the word *Achar* to be used as Achan's name in a genealogical listing in 1 Chronicles 2:7.

> **What Do You Think?**
> How do you reconcile the anger and judgment of God with His love and mercy? What happens when we emphasize one of those areas to the point where the other is minimized?
> *Talking Points for Your Discussion*
> ▪ Considering the totality of God's nature
> ▪ Considering the ramifications of sin
> ▪ Considering the cross of Christ

Conclusion

A. But God Knew!

The title of this lesson, "God Responds to Disobedience," is true. But frequently there is a period of time between the sin and its punishment. Achan may have thought that the passing of time meant that he had escaped detection, but God knew that the sin had occurred. Sin has its wages.

The sin of David with Bathsheba is another example of a person's thinking that he has masterfully arranged to appear innocent. David created the illusion of being compassionate in marrying the widow of a fallen solider. Instead, David had coveted another man's wife, committed adultery, and arranged for the husband to be killed. What looked like just another military casualty actually was the culmination of sinful actions. God responded to the disobedience, although He waited several months to do so (2 Samuel 11, 12).

A caution must be expressed, however. Some tend to look on all reversals as divine judgments for sin. The example of Job proves that this may not be the case. Sometimes things just happen, and sometimes events will not be understood in this lifetime. Each Christian is to overcome through trust in God, thus being an example to others.

B. Prayer

Almighty God, help me overcome temptation. As I do, I understand that this will strengthen me and be an example to others that they may also live victoriously in Christ. In Jesus' name, amen.

C. Thought to Remember

May your life not be a memorial for sinful acts.

INVOLVEMENT LEARNING

Some of the activities below are also found in the helpful student book, Adult Bible Class.
Don't forget to download the free reproducible page from www.standardlesson.com to enhance your lesson!

Into the Lesson

Download the reproducible page and have students work in pairs to complete the activity One Man's Evil. Discuss answers. Then say, "Today's lesson features a man who, unlike Hitler and Stalin, didn't intend to kill anyone. Nevertheless, his evil resulted in the deaths of others. His name is Achan."

Into the Word

Obtain 10 sheets of construction paper; these should be variously colored, but light enough to write on. Put the following across the tops of the sheets, a single entry on each sheet: 1. (v. 1) God's anger; 2. (vv. 1, 11) The Israelites; 3. (vv. 4, 5) Ai; 4. (v. 5) 36 Men; 5. (v. 6) Joshua and the elders; 6. (v. 9) The Canaanites; 7. (v. 12) God withdraws; 8. (v. 25) Achan; 9. (v. 25) Achan's children; 10. (v. 26) A monument. Have markers and masking tape available for each group.

Ask students to form into small groups of three or four; distribute the sheets among them. For a small class, split the class in half and give each group five sheets. Say, "I'd like you to help me make a display that shows the bad things that happened because of Achan's sin. For each sheet read the verses and write a summary statement on the paper of one of the negative consequences. A word or two are given to get you started."

As your students work, write the words *ACHAN STOLE* in the center of the board; draw a circle around them. When the groups have completed the task, have them read their statements in order and affix them to the wall or the edge of the board. Also have them draw an arrow from *ACHAN STOLE* to their summary statement.

While various answers are possible, here are some possibilities: 1. God's anger burned against Israel; 2. The Israelites were considered guilty; 3. Ai defeated the Israelites; 4. 36 men died; 5. Joshua and the elders despaired; 6. The Canaanites would

hear and be emboldened; 7. God withdraws from Israel; 8. Achan was stoned to death; 9. Achan's children were stoned as well; 10. A monument reminded future generations of Achan's sin. Make the point that one man's sin led to serious consequences for many others.

Into Life

Option #1: Discussion. Use the following questions to lead your class in discussing God's punishment of Achan. "Why was Achan's sin so much worse than 'ordinary' stealing?" "Why was God's punishment on Achan so severe?" "What lesson did the Israelites' defeat by Ai teach them?" "Why was Achan's family included in the punishment?" "What lesson is there for us to learn from this event?"

Distribute index cards and ask learners to think about a personal temptation that could cause great harm to themselves and others if they give in to it. Encourage them to write three steps they will take this week to overcome this temptation with God's help. Suggest that they put the card in a place where they will be able to read it daily in the week ahead.

Option #2: Dialogue. In groups, have students look over the following list of statements. Ask them to select one for which to create a dialogue between this person and a Christian who disagrees with the statement. 1. "Since God is so merciful and loving, I just don't believe He would ever send someone to Hell." 2. "My sins are not nearly as bad as some other people's, including some Christians I know. I think God will let me in to Heaven." 3. "The God of the Old Testament was about judgment and punishment, but Jesus is all about love and forgiveness." Ask for volunteers to either act out the dialogue or share their responses.

Option #3: Blessings List. Distribute copies of One Man's Goodness from the reproducible page for students to use as a take-home activity.

LISTEN TO GOD'S JUDGES

BACKGROUND SCRIPTURE: **Judges 2; 21:25**
PRINTED TEXT: **Judges 2:11-19**

JUDGES 2:11-19

11 And the children of Israel did evil in the sight of the LORD, and served Baalim:

12 And they forsook the LORD God of their fathers, which brought them out of the land of Egypt, and followed other gods, of the gods of the people that were round about them, and bowed themselves unto them, and provoked the LORD to anger.

13 And they forsook the LORD, and served Baal and Ashtaroth.

14 And the anger of the LORD was hot against Israel, and he delivered them into the hands of spoilers that spoiled them, and he sold them into the hands of their enemies round about, so that they could not any longer stand before their enemies.

15 Whithersoever they went out, the hand of the LORD was against them for evil, as the LORD had said, and as the LORD had sworn unto them: and they were greatly distressed.

16 Nevertheless the LORD raised up judges, which delivered them out of the hand of those that spoiled them.

17 And yet they would not hearken unto their judges, but they went a whoring after other gods, and bowed themselves unto them: they turned quickly out of the way which their fathers walked in, obeying the commandments of the LORD; but they did not so.

18 And when the LORD raised them up judges, then the LORD was with the judge, and delivered them out of the hand of their enemies all the days of the judge: for it repented the LORD because of their groanings by reason of them that oppressed them and vexed them.

19 And it came to pass, when the judge was dead, that they returned, and corrupted themselves more than their fathers, in following other gods to serve them, and to bow down unto them; they ceased not from their own doings, nor from their stubborn way.

KEY VERSE

They would not hearken unto their judges, but they went a whoring after other gods, and bowed themselves unto them. —**Judges 2:17**

GOD INSTRUCTS HIS PEOPLE

Unit 2: Listening for God in Changing Times

LESSONS 6–10

LESSON AIMS

After participating in this lesson, each student will be able to:

1. Describe the sin cycle that the people of God experienced during the period of the judges.

2. Compare and contrast the sin cycle of the period of the judges with what can be observed by behavior in contemporary society.

3. Describe a sin cycle in his or her life, and make a plan to break it.

LESSON OUTLINE

Introduction

A. When Times Are Bad

September 11, 2001, is a date that shall live in infamy in the United States of America. The events of that day led to some notable responses from the American public. First of all, there was a tremendous sense of unity and patriotism that arose as flags emerged on every street. Second, President Bush's vow to strike back at the terrorists and their base of operations was applauded by the people as with one voice. The third response was the sudden rise in church worship attendance.

My son, a preacher in Illinois, told me that his church experienced an immediate increase in attendance of about 50 for almost 6 months after 9/11. But after that, attendance slid back to the "normal" numbers. When things are going well, people tend not to worry about spiritual things. But when things go bad, such as on 9/11, people become serious about their spiritual welfare, at least for a while. In the Old Testament period of the judges (about 1373–1043 BC), the people ignored God when things were going well, but in times of trouble they repented and cried out to God for help. God would raise up a judge to provide the help they needed. Then the people would backslide, and a cycle of sin would begin anew.

B. Lesson Background

Judges 2:11-19 (today's text) is best understood in its literary context. We notice that Judges 2:6-9 is somewhat parallel to Joshua 24:29-31, both of which give an account of Joshua's death. Judges begins with the words, "Now after the death of Joshua" (Judges 1:1; compare Joshua 1:1, "Now after the death of Moses"). Judges 1:1–2:5 describes events that happened before Joshua's death, thus interrupting the story line as it moves from the book of Joshua to Judges. Therefore, Judges 2:6-10 is a flashback to Joshua 24, when Joshua assembled the people at Shechem for the nation to enter into a renewal of the covenant.

The lengthy introduction of the book of Judges is thus a historical review that prepares the reader for what happens next. Judges 1:1–2:5 introduces the overall conquest of Canaan in the south, the middle, and the north. But the tribes did not complete the task of driving out the Canaanites (Judges 1:19, 21, 27-36; compare Joshua 13:1-13; 16:10; 17:12, 13, 16-18; 18:2-4). They could have done so, but the Israelites settled into a "good enough" syndrome that fell short of full obedience to God.

Judges 2:1–3:6 serves as a doctrinal introduction to the rest of the book of Judges. First, the angel of the Lord speaks on behalf of Yahweh God, rebuking the Israelites for their disobedience in failing to destroy the Canaanites (compare Genesis 15:16; 48:22; Exodus 3:8, 17; Leviticus 18:28). Instead, the Israelites took only part of the hill country and made accommodations with the Canaanites (Joshua 16:10; Judges 2:2).

The Israelites should have destroyed the idolatrous worship of the Canaanites, but did not. As a consequence, God announced, "I will not drive them out from before you; but they shall be as thorns in your sides, and their gods shall be a snare unto you" (Judges 2:3). The generation that came after Joshua "knew not the Lord, nor yet the works which he had done for Israel" (Judges 2:10).

At this point in the narrative, the biblical writer introduces us to the infamous "sin cycle": apostasy, oppression, cry of distress, deliverance by a judge, period of peace, and then a return to apostasy.

HOW TO SAY IT

Amalekites	*Am*-uh-leh-kites or Uh-*mal*-ih-kites.
Asherah	Uh-*she*-ruh.
Ashtaroth	*Ash*-tuh-rawth.
Astarte	A-*star*-te (first *a* as in *had*).
Baal	*Bay*-ul.
Canaan	*Kay*-nun.
Jephthah	*Jef*-thuh (*th* as in *thin*).
Mesopotamians	*Mes*-uh-puh-***tay***-me-unz.
Midianites	*Mid*-ee-un-ites.
Othniel	*Oth*-ni-el.
Philistines	Fuh-*liss*-teenz or *Fill*-us-teenz.
Shamgar	*Sham*-gar.
syncretism	***sin***-kruh-*tih*-zem.
Tarot	*Ter*-oh.
Yahweh *(Hebrew)*	*Yah*-weh.

Some folks who like alliteration suggest these six phases can be shortened to four with the descriptors *sin, sorrow, supplication, salvation.*

This cycle will be repeated several times in the book of Judges. It becomes the blueprint for the stories of the six major judges (Judges 3–16). Since Judges 1:1–2:5 and 17:1–21:25 do not follow this pattern, the book of Judges can be divided into three parts: (1) the double introductions of Judges 1:1-36 and 2:1–3:6; (2) the six major judges of Judges 3:7–16:31; and (3) the double appendix of Judges 17–18 and 19–21.

Yahweh used the enemy peoples in and around Canaan to "prove Israel, whether they will keep the way of the Lord to walk therein, as their fathers did keep it, or not" (Judges 2:22). While God was testing His people, He was also teaching them about warfare (3:2). The enemies of Israel are listed in Judges 3:3, 5. This is not a complete list, as will be seen. However, instead of fighting these pagan peoples, Israel compromised by intermarrying with them (3:6). Thus begins the story of the six major judges and why Israel had to listen to them.

I. Evil and Apostasy
(JUDGES 2:11-13)
A. Embracing Idolatry (v. 11)

11. And the children of Israel did evil in the sight of the LORD, and served Baalim.

Sadly, this is not the only time the phrase *and the children of Israel did evil in the sight of the Lord* is used (see also Judges 3:7, 12; 4:1; 6:1; 10:6; 13:1). The evil of the generation of Israelites that follows Joshua is that they forget Yahweh God, who delivered their father's generation from Egyptian bondage (2:10). To refuse to remember is a form of rebellion. This means that this generation turns a deaf ear to the beliefs of their parents.

The Israelites turn to the gods of Canaan, crediting those deities as the source of their present prosperity. Thus the people serve and worship the Baalim as well as Yahweh. The word *Baalim* is the Hebrew plural form of *Baal*. Baal is the god of the storm, which means that the people think he provides rain that causes crops to grow. His name can signify "husband," "lord," or "master." The Canaanites look to him for good harvests and, therefore, prosperity. The new generation of Israelites refuses to acknowledge Yahweh as the sole source of all good things. Instead, the Israelites add the worship of whatever Baal is worshiped by the local Canaanite population.

What Do You Think?
What modern gods are Christians tempted to embrace? How do you resist these temptations?
Talking Points for Your Discussion
- The gods of "things"
- The gods of "attitudes"

B. Forsaking God (vv. 12, 13)

12. And they forsook the LORD God of their fathers, which brought them out of the land of Egypt, and followed other gods, of the gods of the people that were round about them, and bowed themselves unto them, and provoked the LORD to anger.

To forsake the Creator is bad enough ("knew not the Lord," Judges 2:10b). But to forsake one's deliverer ("nor yet the works which he had done for Israel," 2:10c) compounds the disobedience. The people had been given fair warning by Joshua (Joshua 23:12, 13; 24:20, 23). That is one of the reasons that God required the total destruction of the Canaanite inhabitants. Baal worship easily snares the Israelites, proving to be "thorns in [their] sides" (Judges 2:3). *The gods of the people that* surround the Israelites are many (1 Kings 11:7; 2 Chronicles 25:20; etc.).

13. And they forsook the LORD, and served Baal and Ashtaroth.

Even before the Israelites entered the promised land, they had indulged in the sordid worship of Baal (Numbers 25). The consequences of such worship were disastrous (25:4, 5, 7-9, 16-18). Baal is worshiped in many places, as the inclusion of the word *Baal* in various names of places testifies (see Exodus 14:2; Numbers 32:38; Joshua 11:17; etc.). In Canaan it seems that every high hill has an idolatrous representation of Baal and Asherah.

Ashtaroth is the Hebrew plural form for *Asherah*, sometimes translated as "grove [of trees]." Astarte is the proper name for this goddess. She is Baal's consort in Canaanite religious mythology, being a goddess of war and fertility.

The annual mating of Baal and Asherah is thought to cause the land and its people to become fertile and therefore prosperous. These two are consistently paired in the Scriptures (see Judges 3:7; 6:25-30; 1 Kings 16:32, 33; 18:19; 2 Kings 17:16). A stone pillar is set up representing the male god, perhaps as part of an altar, within a grove of trees that represents the goddess (see 1 Kings 14:23). A wooden pole in the ground is used to represent the goddess if there is no grove of trees. Human sexual acts are part of the ritual used to entice the gods to do the same with each other in order to bring about the fertility desired. "Sacred prostitution" makes itself known in pagan religions (example: Genesis 38:21).

This kind of "worship" results in what might be called open-air pornography (again, Numbers 25). Such "acts of worship" are part of what makes this evil so enticing.

❧ ECLECTIC SPIRITUALITY ❧

"I'm a very spiritual person." Perhaps you've heard people describe themselves that way. But before we acknowledge them as godly, we ought to ask what they mean by being "spiritual." In the 1970s, an eclectic form of spirituality became popular under the name of *New Age*. It comes at the end of a long line of syncretistic religious practices that goes back to Old Testament times.

A significant number of people accept various *New Age* ideas such as belief in astrology for telling the future, belief that crystals have healing power, and belief that Tarot cards are reliable guides for decision-making. Christians have been known to add these beliefs to their Christianity. Throwing concepts such as reincarnation and karma into the stew seems quite appealing to some.

The Bible speaks out strongly against this kind of mix-and-match spirituality. Old Testament Judaism and New Testament Christianity are specifically exclusive. Attempting to draw power or knowledge from the spirit world is forbidden

(Leviticus 20:27; Deuteronomy 18:11). There are to be no other gods above, below, or alongside the one true God. It's easy to criticize the ancient Israelites for their failings in this regard. But apparently many today haven't been able to overcome their errors. Are you one of them?　　—C. R. B.

II. Oppression and Distress
(JUDGES 2:14, 15)
A. Enemy Pressure (v. 14)

14. And the anger of the LORD was hot against Israel, and he delivered them into the hands of spoilers that spoiled them, and he sold them into the hands of their enemies round about, so that they could not any longer stand before their enemies.

The cycle advances as the Lord delivers the Israelites *into the hands of their enemies round about* (see also Judges 3:8, 12; 4:2; 6:1). There are three primary enemies in this regard. First are those who want to regain land that had been taken by Joshua's generation: the Philistines and the Canaanites. Second are those who are merely plunderers (desert tribes), who are looking for food at harvest time: Midianites and Amalekites. Third are those of the transjordan area who are distantly related to the Israelites from patriarchal times: Edom (from Esau) and Moab and Ammon (from Lot's daughters). Each enemy will rise up in its own time and power to "spoil" the peace of Israel.

In addition to these primary categories of enemies should be included the Mesopotamians (see Judges 3:8). The strongest of all these enemies is the Philistines because of their advanced and exclusive technology in iron (see Joshua 17:16; Judges 1:19; 1 Samuel 13:19-22).

B. Divine Pressure (v. 15)

15. Whithersoever they went out, the hand of the LORD was against them for evil, as the LORD had said, and as the LORD had sworn unto them: and they were greatly distressed.

God causes these enemies to prevail and plunder the Israelites at various times. This is divine distress placed on the people because of their misplaced allegiance. The distress phase of the sin

Keep this map posted to help your learners gain a geographical perspective as you study Judges.

cycle includes cries of agony at other times (Judges 3:9, 15; 4:3; 6:6, 7). We may assume that the same happens here, although not explicitly stated.

> **What Do You Think?**
> What are some methods that the Lord uses (or might use) to correct His wayward people today?
> *Talking Points for Your Discussion*
> ▪ Methods of direct punishment
> ▪ Methods of natural consequences

III. Deliverance and Peace
(JUDGES 2:16-18)
A. Judges Provided (v. 16)

16. Nevertheless the LORD raised up judges, which delivered them out of the hand of those that spoiled them.

Exactly who are these judges? The English word *judge* does not really convey what the word means to ancient Israel. The judges are charismatic military leaders. Their judging function, as we think of that concept today, seems to be secondary (Judges 4:5). Judges are saviors of the people during times of military crisis. Even though God causes great distress among the people, He also shows extravagant grace in the form of military victory and deliverance by Spirit-filled characters.

The judges are colorful characters indeed! Not much is known of Othniel (Judges 3:7-11), but Ehud is a cunning assassin, noted to be left-handed (3:12-30). Deborah predicts that credit would be given to a woman for the ultimate victory over an enemy (4:9). Gideon is a very reluctant hero who fought using psychological warfare (7:16-23). Jephthah, son of a prostitute and hated by his half brothers, makes a rash vow that results in the "sacrifice" of his daughter (11:30-40). Samson is the strangest of them all—a lifetime Nazarite who breaks every vow a Nazarite is supposed to keep (14:8, 9, 17; 16:17-19; compare Numbers 6).

The sin cycle always includes God's provision of a judge, savior, or deliverer (see Judges 3:9, 15; 4:4-7; 6:14; 11:29; 13:24, 25). Each judge represents God's grace to His people. God often chooses to work through the human instrument.

> **What Do You Think?**
> What leadership qualities are most needed when the church faces a crisis?
> *Talking Points for Your Discussion*
> - Qualities of character
> - Qualities of scriptural knowledge
> - Qualities of interpersonal skills

❧ THE POWER OF LEADERSHIP ❧

In early 2000, Peter W. Schramm was deliberating on who should be declared Person of the Century. His conclusion: "If there is any one man responsible for saving the best in our civilization in the twentieth-century, it is Winston Churchill."

Churchill served on the front lines in World War I. Back in England, he was elected to Parliament at age 25 and went on to hold a variety of high government offices. Churchill saw the dangers of Communism and Nazism long before most free world leaders did.

As prime minister, Churchill's eloquent speeches rallied the British people to stand strong against the Nazi onslaught. The Churchill Centre and Museum at the Cabinet War Rooms affirms Churchill's ability to inspire people, his unique strategic insight, his relentless passion, and his imperturbable personality.

The judges whom God raised up to save Israel undoubtedly had some of these same traits, to varying degrees. But the most important thing they had was God's support. God often prefers to work through human weakness, and we definitely see character flaws in the judges! God does not always search for "a Churchill" to lead in His work. Think about what that means: today, God may be searching for *you* to lead.   —C. R. B.

B. Disobedience Continues (v. 17)

17. And yet they would not hearken unto their judges, but they went a whoring after other gods, and bowed themselves unto them: they turned quickly out of the way which their fathers walked in, obeying the commandments of the Lord; but they did not so.

In spite of God's grace expressed through the judges, Israel refuses to listen to them. The people often exhibit a lack of commitment to the covenant with Yahweh God even in the midst of the deliverances. Yahweh is their true "husband" (the meaning of Baal), not the Baals of the Canaanites (see Hosea 2:16, 17).

The word *whoring* is shockingly appropriate for describing Israel's actions. The people bow down before their lovers, the fertility gods of Canaan (compare Jeremiah 3:1-3). The last phrase in the book of Judges is like an exclamation point for this problem: "every man did that which was right in his own eyes," and that was not very right!

> **What Do You Think?**
> How would you counsel parents to help them raise children to follow in their footsteps of faith?
> *Talking Points for Your Discussion*
> - Things to do
> - Things not to do
> - Scriptures that apply

C. Compassion Offered (v. 18)

18. And when the Lord raised them up judges, then the Lord was with the judge, and delivered them out of the hand of their enemies all the days of the judge: for it repented the Lord because of their groanings by reason of them that oppressed them and vexed them.

Listen to God's Judges

God shows compassion by means of the peace that prevails while a particular judge lives. In the sin cycle, sometimes this may be clearly stated for the judges; at other times the characterization of "rest" or "peace" is not specifically stated and may or may not be implied: Othniel, 40 years of rest (Judges 3:11); Ehud, 80 years of rest (3:30); Deborah, 40 years of rest (5:31); Gideon, 40 years of rest (8:28); Tola, 23 years (10:2); Jair, 22 years (10:3); Jephthah, 6 years (12:7); Ibzan, 7 years (12:9); Elon, 10 years (12:11); Abdon, 8 years (12:14); and Samson, 20 years (15:20).

Shamgar is mentioned only briefly (Judges 3:31). Eli and Samuel are also judges, but they are not discussed in the book of Judges. The fact that the Lord lets these cycles go on for more than 300 years shows His patience.

IV. Death and Cycle
(JUDGES 2:19)
A. Corruption (v. 19a)

19a. And it came to pass, when the judge was dead, that they returned, and corrupted themselves more than their fathers.

The story line of the book of Judges is not just that of a repeating cycle of sin, but of a downward spiral. As we read from one judge's story to the next, we get the impression that things are getting worse and worse until the judges themselves show themselves to be less than honorable (Jephthah and Samson in particular). While Judges 17–21 do not follow in chronological order with the rest of the book of Judges, those chapters reveal the extent of corruption that prevails during a time when Israel has no king (see Judges 17:6; 18:1; 19:1; 21:25). Unfortunately, Israel will learn that even having a king will not keep corruption at bay.

What Do You Think?

Why do some people return to sin while others do not? How does this serve as a warning for you?

Talking Points for Your Discussion
- When times are good
- When times are bad

B. Persistence (v. 19b)

19b. In following other gods to serve them, and to bow down unto them; they ceased not from their own doings, nor from their stubborn way.

It is very difficult to break the sin cycle. From the time of Moses (about 1440 BC) until the Babylonian exile (586 BC), Israel is not able to resist the allure of idolatry. Not until after the exile and reforms of Ezra and Nehemiah do God's people break this cycle. It takes the loss of land, kingdom, and temple before the people finally listen to God's Word and acknowledge that He means what He says (see Deuteronomy 28:15-69; 30:15-20).

Conclusion
A. Breaking the Sin Cycle

God's people even today are never far away from combining Christianity with worldly things; this is the evil of syncretism. The current time—the postmodern era—is marked by a lack of belief in absolutes. The result, among other things, is an easy spirituality and an "it's all good" religious pluralism. Modern culture has become highly idolatrous, and God's judgment can bring such a culture down at any time.

The sin cycle of our day is just as difficult to break as it was in ancient Israel's. Sin and evil always lead to God's judgment and the oppression of the sinner, although God in His grace might delay that judgment for quite some time. God's ultimate response to the sin cycle was to send Jesus as the deliverer. If we listen to Him, we can break the cycle. Those who do not listen to Him will continue down the road to destruction.

B. Prayer

O God, our Father, forgive our idolatrous ways when we lust after materialism, depend on our military power, and boast of our position among the nations. Teach us to heed the lessons of history with regard to the consequences of obedience and disobedience. In Jesus' name, amen.

C. Thought to Remember

Break the cycle of sin by listening to Jesus.

INVOLVEMENT LEARNING

Some of the activities below are also found in the helpful student book, Adult Bible Class.
Don't forget to download the free reproducible page from www.standardlesson.com to enhance your lesson!

Into the Lesson

Put the following sentences with letter blanks on display:

The Book of Judges is a

S ___ ___   S ___ ___

S ___ ___ ___ ___.

Say, "I'm going to give you a series of letters in alphabetical order. Decide where you think each letter should go to make a true statement regarding the studies we are going to do for the next five weeks in the Book of Judges."

Give the following letters one at a time, pausing for learner discussion and decisions after each: A, D, I, N O, R, T, Y. The desired statement is *The Book of Judges is a Sad Sin Story.* You may note that the letters fit in the sequence given except for the letter T.

Into the Word

Give each learner a handout with this heading: *The Repetitious Outline of the Book of Judges.* Include this list of major points, spaced down the sheet:

> I. The Israelites . . .
>
> II. God . . .
>
> III. God . . .
>
> IV. The Israelites . . .

Ask learners to read the text and fill in the four major parts of the outline—the four oft-repeated "turning points" in the book of Judges and in today's text. Allow a few minutes for work, then call for results. Although individual wording may differ, the primary ideas are: I. The Israelites do evil in God's sight; II. God becomes angry and delivers them to enemies; III. God relents and provides a deliverer; IV. The Israelites fall (or jump) back into sin.

Once you agree on a sampling, say, "Now I want you to develop the outline. Put an *A* and a *B* line under each main point, and examine the text for those subordinate ideas." Allow a few minutes, then call for answers. Here are possibilities: I.A. The people serve idols; I.B. The people's disobedience angers God; II.A. God's holy anger leads Him to allow enemies to dominate His people; II.B. God takes away His protection of the people; III.A. God sees their anguish and sends them a savior; III.B. With God's help, the deliverer successfully fights against the enemies of Israel; IV.A. The people listen to the deliverer for a time; IV.B. The people return to the sins of the past and add even more.

As learners work on the above, do not allow them to see the outline provided with the lesson. After they finish their sub points, have learners compare and contrast their results with the outline provided with the lesson.

Alternative: Download the reproducible page and distribute copies of the activity What Did They Do? instead. This activity offers a way to accomplish the above without using a formal outline with main points and sub points.

Into Life

Distribute copies of the Get Away and Don't Go Back! activity from the reproducible page. This activity calls for learners to ponder several "mottoes" to help them stay away from sin, and you can use this activity in various ways. *Option #1:* Have learners (individually, in study pairs, or in small groups) rank-order these seven mottoes from 1 (most helpful) to 7 (least helpful). Discuss reasons. *Option #2:* Ask learners to voice the passage of Scripture that most helps them resist sin; then ask learners to select the motto that most closely resembles that passage. Discuss reasons. *Option #3:* Create a handout of a matching exercise by breaking each motto into two segments—the first segments to go into the left-hand column, the second segments (mixed up) to go into the right-hand column. Have learners work in study pairs or in small groups to create the best matches.

USE GOD'S
STRENGTH

BACKGROUND SCRIPTURE: Judges 3:7-31; 21:25
PRINTED TEXT: Judges 3:15-25, 29, 30

JUDGES 3:15-25, 29, 30

15 But when the children of Israel cried unto the LORD, the LORD raised them up a deliverer, Ehud the son of Gera, a Benjamite, a man lefthanded: and by him the children of Israel sent a present unto Eglon the king of Moab.

16 But Ehud made him a dagger which had two edges, of a cubit length; and he did gird it under his raiment upon his right thigh.

17 And he brought the present unto Eglon king of Moab: and Eglon was a very fat man.

18 And when he had made an end to offer the present, he sent away the people that bare the present.

19 But he himself turned again from the quarries that were by Gilgal, and said, I have a secret errand unto thee, O king: who said, Keep silence. And all that stood by him went out from him.

20 And Ehud came unto him; and he was sitting in a summer parlour, which he had for himself alone. And Ehud said, I have a message from God unto thee. And he arose out of his seat.

21 And Ehud put forth his left hand, and took the dagger from his right thigh, and thrust it into his belly:

22 And the haft also went in after the blade; and the fat closed upon the blade, so that he could not draw the dagger out of his belly; and the dirt came out.

23 Then Ehud went forth through the porch, and shut the doors of the parlour upon him, and locked them.

24 When he was gone out, his servants came; and when they saw that, behold, the doors of the parlour were locked, they said, Surely he covereth his feet in his summer chamber.

25 And they tarried till they were ashamed: and, behold, he opened not the doors of the parlour; therefore they took a key, and opened them: and, behold, their lord was fallen down dead on the earth.

. . . .

29 And they slew of Moab at that time about ten thousand men, all lusty, and all men of valour; and there escaped not a man.

30 So Moab was subdued that day under the hand of Israel. And the land had rest fourscore years.

KEY VERSE

When the children of Israel cried unto the LORD, the LORD raised them up a deliverer, Ehud the son of Gera, a Benjamite, a man left-handed. —**Judges 3:15**

GOD INSTRUCTS HIS PEOPLE

Unit 2: Listening for God in Changing Times

LESSONS 6–10

LESSON AIMS

After participating in this lesson, each student will be able to:

1. Summarize the actions of Ehud and the results.

2. Tell why Ehud's success might have seemed unexpected and compare his situation with unlikely heroes today.

3. Describe a way that he or she will be an unexpected source of help to someone in the week ahead.

LESSON OUTLINE

Introduction

A. Asking for Help

My family moved to Michigan from Illinois in 1976. I had been in the located ministry for 13 years, serving as youth minister, preacher, and education director. With these ministry experiences and a graduate degree, I was called to teach at a Bible college. But my wife and I had a twofold problem: we had always lived in parsonages (and thus had no equity in a house), and we were taking a huge cut in salary to move from located ministry to teach in a Bible college.

I remember my broken heart when my wife cried as we searched for housing. We could not afford anything either close to the school or worth living in. We both cried out, "God, if you want us here, help us find a house to buy!" The very next day my wife was hired as secretary for a church planting organization. The part-time salary could make house payments. However, we still needed a down payment for a house. I called my dad, and instantly we had $4,000 for the house we bought. Within a year we were able to pay him back. He refused to accept interest for the year.

We learned early in life that when we are in trouble and need help, we should always call on God. He will respond, often through other people. Even if we are in trouble because of our own mistakes or sins, it is still appropriate to cry to God for help. He will deliver.

B. Lesson Background

Judges 1:1–3:6 forms the lengthy introduction to that book. The brief story of Othniel (3:7-11) introduces the judges per se. The account of Ehud (today's lesson), who served from about 1319 to 1239 BC, follows that of Othniel. Israel was being oppressed by the Moabites; they held the Israelites under tribute.

With help from the Ammonites and Amalekites, King Eglon of Moab attacked and took the "city of palm trees," which was Jericho. That city was probably still in ruins at the time (see Joshua 6:26). It would not be rebuilt until the time of King Ahab (see 1 Kings 16:34), over 300 years after the time of Ehud. Even so, the area had precious resources.

Use God's Strength

It also was a strategic site for control of the southern Jordan Valley area (Judges 3:13).

Thus, Eglon controlled some part of Benjamite territory, as well as Reuben's territory (which was east and south of the Jordan, north of Moab itself). Moab, a near neighbor of Judah and Benjamin, was located just east of the Dead Sea (which today is the southern part of the country of Jordan). The Ammonites were located north and east of Moab, while the Amalekites were seminomads living on the southern fringe of Israel; all were continually bitter enemies of the Israelites who had invaded "their" land (see Genesis 19:37, 38; Exodus 17:8-16; Numbers 13:29; Deuteronomy 25:17-19).

The sin of Israel is emphasized for today's lesson by the double statement in Judges 3:12: "And the children of Israel did evil again in the sight of the Lord: and the Lord strengthened Eglon the king of Moab against Israel, because they had done evil in the sight of the Lord." Thus, God used Moab as His instrument of punishment for His wayward people.

I. Deliverer Given
(JUDGES 3:15-20)
A. Left-handed Man (v. 15)

15. But when the children of Israel cried unto the LORD, the LORD raised them up a deliverer, Ehud the son of Gera, a Benjamite, a man lefthanded: and by him the children of Israel sent a present unto Eglon the king of Moab.

In the previous lesson, we noted the sin cycle of apostasy, oppression, cry of distress, deliverance by a judge, period of peace, and then a return to apostasy. Two points of this cycle are given in the verse before us: *the children of Israel* (perhaps limited to two or three tribes) cry out to God for help, and He responds by giving them *a deliverer*.

It seems that every part of this ancient story has meaning. The name of *Ehud* means "one" or perhaps "majesty." Certainly Ehud is going to accomplish part of his task alone, and in the end it will be a majestic victory. We see irony in the text in the fact that Ehud is a Benjamite, which means "son of the right hand," although Ehud himself is left-handed. Many other Benjamites are left-

handed as well (see Judges 20:16). The Hebrew language does not use the literal term *left-handed,* since the culture considers this condition as a physical defect. Instead, it literally says "restricted as to his right hand." For Ehud, this will be anything but a defect, as we shall see!

Perhaps to overcome a stigma of being left-handed, the Benjamites may have forced themselves to become ambidextrous (see 1 Chronicles 12:2). As a left-hander myself, I can testify to society's dissatisfaction with this so-called defect (in the 1950s) and to my own ambidextrous ability.

> **What Do You Think?**
> What was a time in your life that a seeming disadvantage that you had turned out to be an advantage?
> *Talking Points for Your Discussion*
> - A physical issue
> - A personality issue
> - A family heritage issue

Each year the Israelites are required to pay tribute to King Eglon of Moab. Thus the noun *present* is not a gift freely and gladly given, as we think of such today. This tribute probably takes the form of agricultural produce, with many people required to transport it (Judges 3:18, below).

> **What Do You Think?**
> How do your experiences with the consequences of sin compare and contrast with Israel's oppression for her sin?
> *Talking Points for Your Discussion*
> - In terms of an ongoing cost ("tribute")
> - In terms of subjection to ungodly people
> - In terms of the way you word your prayers

B. Two-edged Sword (v. 16)

16. But Ehud made him a dagger which had two edges, of a cubit length; and he did gird it under his raiment upon his right thigh.

Ehud, who will end up being a lone assassin, makes himself a special weapon. We normally think of a dagger as a kind of knife, but the length noted here means that this is more than a knife. It is a double-edged short sword of about 14 inches (this is probably a "short cubit," which is measured from the elbow to the top knuckle of a closed fist; by contrast, a "full cubit" is about 18 inches). Almost certainly Ehud makes it with no hilt.

With the long flowing robes or outer garment worn in the Middle East, even today, this kind of weapon is hidden easily as Ehud attaches it to *his right thigh*. This is a good place for a left-handed man to conceal a weapon. Few will think of finding a weapon on that side of his body. This action by Ehud tells us that the Israelites are desperate.

> **What Do You Think?**
>
> What do you find most difficult and least difficult when you do something God has called you to do?
>
> *Talking Points for Your Discussion*
> - Developing a plan
> - Putting a plan into practice
> - Asking others for help
> - Thinking big because God is involved

C. Moabite King (vv. 17, 18)

17, 18. And he brought the present unto Eglon king of Moab: and Eglon was a very fat man. And when he had made an end to offer the present, he sent away the people that bare the present.

HOW TO SAY IT

Amalekites	*Am*-uh-leh-kites or Uh-*mal*-ih-kites.
ambidextrous	am-bih-**dek**-strus.
Ammonites	*Am*-un-ites.
Ehud	*Ee*-hud.
Elohim *(Hebrew)*	El-o-*heem.*
euphemism	*you*-fuh-*mih*-zum.
Gilgal	*Gil*-gal (G as in *get*).
Jericho	*Jair*-ih-co.
Moabites	*Mo*-ub-ites.
Othniel	*Oth*-ni-el.
reich	rahyk.
Seirath	Seh-*eye*-rath.
Septuagint	Sep-*too*-ih-jent.
Wiesenthal	*Vee*-zuhn-thal.

Carrying the present (tribute) demanded by *Eglon king of Moab* probably requires many people. Thus Ehud has a large entourage when he arrives in the king's presence. King David will turn things around by requiring Moab to pay tribute to him; but that is over 300 years in the future from this point (2 Samuel 8:2).

The comment regarding King Eglon's obesity is meant as an attack on his person and a ridicule of his lifestyle. He is a "fat cat," feeding on the Israelite's precious food—food that they desperately need and which Eglon apparently doesn't need. The emphasis on the present (tribute), used three times in two short verses, is designed to contrast with the real "present" that Ehud will give to the Moabite king. It is somehow related to the king's fatness. Indeed, this present (tribute) will end up in the king's belly but not by eating!

D. Secret Message (vv. 19, 20)

19. But he himself turned again from the quarries that were by Gilgal, and said, I have a secret errand unto thee, O king: who said, Keep silence. And all that stood by him went out from him.

It is difficult to visualize the geographical movements in the story. However, Gilgal is only about three miles from Jericho. Jericho—or what remains of its ruins—is strategically located to control the southern Jordan Valley and the borders between the competing nations. Based on what we read in verse 20 (below), King Eglon may have built for himself a summer home in the captured territory in which the ruins of Jericho are located.

The phrase *turned again from the quarries that were by Gilgal* is difficult to interpret. The Hebrew phrasing has four possible meanings: (1) "not very close to any recognized divine images," (2) "with carved stones including inscriptions," (3) "standing stones" that are identical to the stones of Joshua 4:20-24, and (4) "quarries." The last of these is the translation of the *King James Version,* which matches that of the Septuagint (which is the Greek version of the Old Testament that came into being before Christ). Whatever they are, the story line uses them as a marker to indicate where Ehud turns away from his porters of the present

Use God's Strength

(tribute) to seek a private audience with the king. In so doing, Ehud plays on Eglon's gullibility and desire for knowledge of the divine.

The phrase *secret errand* refers to a divine oracle. Ancient kings cherish such oracles in their desire to know future events. Thus, King Eglon hushes those in hearing distance and dismisses his servants so that only he will hear the oracle. The irony in this part of the story is that "secret errand" can also be translated "secret thing," which will end up being the hidden sword strapped to Ehud's right leg. King Eglon will soon get the message!

20. And Ehud came unto him; and he was sitting in a summer parlour, which he had for himself alone. And Ehud said, I have a message from God unto thee. And he arose out of his seat.

So far Ehud's plans have worked perfectly. He is now alone in the presence of the king. They are in the king's private *summer parlour,* literally "an upper room of coolness." This is a room built on top of the house or palace. The room is fully equipped with the luxuries for a king, including a toilet (the importance of which the rest of the story will make clear). Such a room has many windows to catch the breezes at the elevated height.

The secret word at issue is *a message from God.* We note that Ehud uses the generic word for God, which is *Elohim*, not the personal name for Israel's God, which is *Yahweh.* This is more acceptable to a pagan king such as Eglon, who interprets this to be "a message from the gods," since Hebrew words ending in *–im* are plural. With great anticipation for an oracle, the obese king struggles to his feet to receive the message. It is unusual for a king to stand before anyone!

II. King Assassinated
(Judges 3:21-25)
A. Hidden Weapon (v. 21)

21. And Ehud put forth his left hand, and took the dagger from his right thigh, and thrust it into his belly.

If the king does not know that Ehud is left-handed, he soon finds out. The unexpected oracle from God is *Die!*

❧ TUNNEL VISION ❧

Tunnel vision is "extreme narrowness of viewpoint." Sometimes tunnel vision results from allowing one's thinking to be so controlled by "the way things are now" that future possibilities cannot be envisioned. Take the field of technology, for example. Participating in a trial telephone conversation between Washington and Philadelphia in 1876, U.S. President Rutherford B. Hayes commented, "That's an amazing invention, but who would ever want to use one of them?" Who, indeed!

King Eglon's thinking definitely was not controlled by "the way things are now." Quite the opposite! He desperately wanted a glimpse of what the future held. But he was so anxious to peer into the future through a secret, divine oracle from Ehud that he unwittingly placed himself in mortal danger. This is a form of tunnel vision that fighter pilots call "target fixation." That's when one becomes so focused on a target that emerging dangers go unnoticed.

Both extremes of tunnel vision can affect the church. We may be so comfortable and focused on "the way we do things now" that we can't see that our church is becoming irrelevant to our community. On the other hand, we may develop such a target fixation to improve things with the latest fad that we fail to grasp the danger of the doctrinal problems that the fad brings along with it. Beware both extremes.　　　　—C. R. B.

B. Impaled Enemy (v. 22)

22. And the haft also went in after the blade; and the fat closed upon the blade, so that he

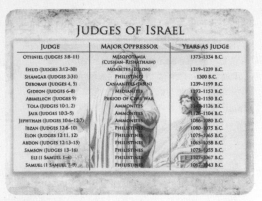

JUDGES OF ISRAEL

JUDGE	MAJOR OPPRESSOR	YEARS AS JUDGE
OTHNIEL (JUDGES 3:8–11)	MESOPOTAMIA (CUSHAN-RISHATHAIM)	1373–1334 B.C.
EHUD (JUDGES 3:12–30)	MOABITES (EGLON)	1319–1239 B.C.
SHAMGAR (JUDGES 3:31)	PHILISTINES	1300 B.C.
DEBORAH (JUDGES 4, 5)	CANAANITES (JABIN)	1239–1199 B.C.
GIDEON (JUDGES 6–8)	MIDIANITES	1192–1152 B.C.
ABIMELECH (JUDGES 9)	PERIOD OF CIVIL WAR	1152–1150 B.C.
TOLA (JUDGES 10:1, 2)	AMMONITES	1149–1126 B.C.
JAIR (JUDGES 10:3–5)	AMMONITES	1126–1104 B.C.
JEPHTHAH (JUDGES 10:6–12:7)	AMMONITES	1086–1080 B.C.
IBZAN (JUDGES 12:8–10)	PHILISTINES	1080–1075 B.C.
ELON (JUDGES 12:11, 12)	PHILISTINES	1075–1065 B.C.
ABDON (JUDGES 12:13–15)	PHILISTINES	1065–1058 B.C.
SAMSON (JUDGES 13–16)	PHILISTINES	1075–1055 B.C.
ELI (1 SAMUEL 1–4)	PHILISTINES	1107–1067 B.C.
SAMUEL (1 SAMUEL 7–9)	PHILISTINES	1067–1043 B.C.

Visual for Lesson 7. *This chart will help your learners keep a chronological perspective as you assist their study of Judges.*

could not draw the dagger out of his belly; and the dirt came out.

As mentioned above, the weapon probably has no crosspiece (hilt) for the handle. It is more likely a straight piece of bronze with two sharp edges, plus a leather wrapping for a handle. The lack of a crosspiece means that Ehud can thrust the entire sword, plus handle, into the king's belly so deeply that Ehud cannot draw the weapon back out.

The reading of *and the dirt came out* is difficult in the Hebrew text. The problem is that the Hebrew word being used occurs only here in the Old Testament. Thus we have no other text for comparison. In any case, the imagery is vivid and gruesome. The picture is that the sword is thrust with such force that it goes all the way through the king's belly, releasing the contents of the intestines.

C. Dramatic Escape (v. 23)

23. Then Ehud went forth through the porch, and shut the doors of the parlour upon him, and locked them.

It's one thing to carry out an assassination; it's another thing entirely to make a successful getaway. As we read of Ehud's escape, we wonder how much of this represents advance planning and how much he is making up as he goes along. Does Ehud have prior familiarity with the king's summer parlor and its porch?

In any case, Ehud somehow manages to lock the doors of the parlor behind him, thus buy-

ing time to make good his escape. Perhaps as he departs Ehud says to the king's servant, "The king is using the toilet, so don't bother him just yet." But this is just speculation. We can envision Ehud walking away slowly to avoid raising suspicion.

D. Shocking Discovery (vv. 24, 25)

24. When he was gone out, his servants came; and when they saw that, behold, the doors of the parlour were locked, they said, Surely he covereth his feet in his summer chamber.

After Ehud leaves, the servants to King Eglon sooner or later attempt to check on him. When they discover that the doors of the parlor are locked, they surmise that he is using his toilet facilities. The phrase *he covereth his feet* is a euphemism for "relieving oneself" or "responding to nature's call" (see 1 Samuel 24:3).

25. And they tarried till they were ashamed: and, behold, he opened not the doors of the parlour; therefore they took a key, and opened them: and, behold, their lord was fallen down dead on the earth.

We easily imagine the servants delaying as they exchange self-conscious looks with one another. This time gap allows Ehud to escape to Seirath, which may be just north of Jericho, in the tribal territory of Ephraim (v. 26, not in today's text). There Ehud will rally his forces against the Moabites.

III. Enemy Defeated
(JUDGES 3:29, 30)
A. Victory Achieved (v. 29)

29. And they slew of Moab at that time about ten thousand men, all lusty, and all men of valour; and there escaped not a man.

Ehud blows a ram's horn to gather the Israelites for battle against the Moabites (v. 27, not in today's text). But the battle is already half won with the enemy king dead. Kings in ancient times embody the nation, especially since the king is the leader of the army. Soldiers often will quit and run away if their king falls in battle. King Ahab has himself propped up all day in his chariot even though mortally wounded (1 Kings 22:35); after the soldiers realize that the king is dead, they flee (22:36).

Use God's Strength

Another demoralizing factor is for an army to sense that it is surrounded, with no fallback position available. Ehud creates this scenario as he captures "the fords of Jordan" (Judges 3:28). These two factors contribute heavily to the annihilation of the 10,000-man army of the Moabites.

What Do You Think?

What was a time when another person's actions opened the door for you to act? How did things turn out?

Talking Points for Your Discussion

- A benevolent act
- A confrontational act
- A courageous act
- A cowardly act

B. Moab Subjugated (v. 30)

30. So Moab was subdued that day under the hand of Israel. And the land had rest fourscore years.

Thus the tables are turned. The Moabites, bereft of both king and army, are subdued. Moab may now have to pay tribute to the Israelites, although the text does not say that. The usual procedure is for a subjugated people to pay some kind of tribute in order to keep their lives and part of their possessions, but the difficulty of that here is that Israel has no central government to accept such tribute. In any case, the Moabites are subjugated for 80 years after having oppressed Israel for 18 (Judges 3:14).

❧ TURNING THE TABLES ❧

Simon Wiesenthal, the famed "Nazi hunter," died in September 2005, at age 96. The Nazis had sought to destroy the Jewish people. But the tables were turned after World War II, and the hunters became the hunted. Wiesenthal helped bring more than 1,100 Nazi war criminals to justice. He had a powerful motive to do so: he and his wife lost 89 family members in the Nazi death camps.

The oppression of Hitler's "thousand-year reich" lasted 12 years. Moab, by comparison, had oppressed Israel for 18 years prior to God's using Ehud to turn the tables. This would not be the last time a startling reversal of fortunes would come

about in the Old Testament. Outside the exploits of the judges, the actions of Queen Esther come to mind most notably.

Wiesenthal helped correct an injustice after it had occurred; Ehud helped correct an injustice while it was occurring; Esther helped prevent an injustice before it occurred. What role is God calling you to serve in today?   —C. R. B.

Conclusion

A. Unusual Help, Moral Question

This is the first story told of the major judges that reveals how God can use human intermediaries to deliver His people in times of great distress. All we need to do is call on Him. A people who had no hope had a chance for a peaceful future because a man at God's call was willing to act.

Assassination usually is considered to be morally wrong. Perhaps it is in most circumstances. But would the assassination of Adolf Hitler have been wrong? A group of conspirators tried doing just that during World War II. Several lost their lives in the failed attempt. But we marvel at their conviction as they tried to rid the world of an evil.

Sadly, history tells us of many misguided assassins. Think of John Wilkes Booth, Lee Harvey Oswald, and James Earl Ray. Although in the case of today's lesson, "the Lord raised them up a deliverer, Ehud" (Judges 3:15), we wonder if Ehud overstepped a moral boundary by becoming an assassin to complete his mission. Sometimes a God-called person does bad things. God called Samson too, but we cannot excuse all of his behavior on that basis. When God calls you to a task, pray that your actions will be above reproach "not only in the sight of the Lord, but also in the sight of men" (2 Corinthians 8:21).

B. Prayer

O Lord, deliver us in these dangerous times. Raise up for us Christian leaders who will act with courage and faith in these times of crisis. We trust You alone for our future. In Jesus' name, amen.

C. Thought to Remember

Always call on God. He will respond.

INVOLVEMENT LEARNING

Some of the activities below are also found in the helpful student book, Adult Bible Class.
Don't forget to download the free reproducible page from www.standardlesson.com to enhance your lesson!

Into the Lesson

As learners arrive, have each go to a display board and sign his or her name with the left hand. Most right-handers will be unsatisfied with the result, but indicate that that quality is irrelevant.

As class begins, draw attention to the signatures and ask, "Can you identify anyone who is a natural left-hander?" Let the class speculate, even if there is none. (Only about 1 in 11 is naturally left-handed.) At the end, announce, "Today's study is about a natural left-hander who turned his difference into a distinct advantage to accomplish God's work."

Into the Word

Ask your learners to recall something in their lives that occurred 18 years ago. Some will be able to specify events, but probably most will not. After responses, note that many of the Israelites who lived at the time of today's lesson would have had no problem remembering one thing in particular that happened 18 years prior: the beginning of the Moabite oppression.

Read Judges 3:12-14. Ask, "What would you be doing in such distressing circumstances?" Someone will respond, "Pray for freedom." When someone does, say, "That's exactly what our text says happened."

Have class members take turns reading verses of today's text aloud. Then give your learners a handout of the following questions to ponder in small groups.

1. Judges 3:12 indicates that because of the people's evil ways, God gave Moab's King Eglon power over Israel. Does God still work this way today? Why, or why not?

2. On what basis should one expect God to deliver him or her from dire circumstances, such as Israel was in?

3. How is it right, if ever, that God's people should pay tribute/taxes to a governing authority they consider to be evil? (Mark 12:13-17; Romans 13:6, 7)

4. Ehud appears to have kept his plan a secret from all the other tribute bearers. When is it right, if ever, to keep secret one's plans to act on behalf of God?

5. What does King Eglon's decision to give a private audience to one of his oppressed subjects say about his character?

6. Judges 3:26-28 indicates that Ehud knew that killing the king was only part of a successful mission. What examples can you cite of missions that began well but were left incomplete, both in the Bible and in modern time? (Israel's conquest of the promised land is just such an example.)

Into Life

Note that Ehud got a hard and dangerous assignment from God. The opportunities to help relieve God's people of various stresses still abound. Ask, "What are some of those stresses you see in our own church family?" You undoubtedly will receive generic answers such as "Some families are struggling financially due to job loss (or medical expenses, etc.)." Then personalize the question by asking, "Who is one of God's people in need that you can help this week? Write the name down, but don't show it to anyone." Suggest that each person plan to surprise someone this week with a provision of help that is unexpected.

Download the reproducible page and use one or both activities to help your learners carry today's study into the coming week. The Chosen by God activity will allow your learners to ponder their own "Ehud assignment" to take on a risky, perhaps undesirable, task. To stress that God's tasks require followers as well as leaders, use the Follow Me! A Call to Arms activity; this will challenge your class to pause to consider what part of "the armor of God" they lack—the part they most need before following a leader into battle.

Use God's Strength

LET GOD RULE

BACKGROUND SCRIPTURE: Judges 6–8; 21:25
PRINTED TEXT: Judges 7:2-4, 13-15; 8:22-26a

JUDGES 7:2-4, 13-15

2 And the LORD said unto Gideon, The people that are with thee are too many for me to give the Midianites into their hands, lest Israel vaunt themselves against me, saying, Mine own hand hath saved me.

3 Now therefore go to, proclaim in the ears of the people, saying, Whosoever is fearful and afraid, let him return and depart early from mount Gilead. And there returned of the people twenty and two thousand; and there remained ten thousand.

4 And the LORD said unto Gideon, The people are yet too many; bring them down unto the water, and I will try them for thee there: and it shall be, that of whom I say unto thee, This shall go with thee, the same shall go with thee; and of whomsoever I say unto thee, This shall not go with thee, the same shall not go.

. . . .

13 And when Gideon was come, behold, there was a man that told a dream unto his fellow, and said, Behold, I dreamed a dream, and, lo, a cake of barley bread tumbled into the host of Midian, and came unto a tent, and smote it that it fell, and overturned it, that the tent lay along.

14 And his fellow answered and said, This is nothing else save the sword of Gideon the son of Joash, a man of Israel: for into his hand hath God delivered Midian, and all the host.

15 And it was so, when Gideon heard the telling of the dream, and the interpretation thereof, that he worshipped, and returned into the host of Israel, and said, Arise; for the LORD hath delivered into your hand the host of Midian.

JUDGES 8:22-26A

22 Then the men of Israel said unto Gideon, Rule thou over us, both thou, and thy son, and thy son's son also: for thou hast delivered us from the hand of Midian.

23 And Gideon said unto them, I will not rule over you, neither shall my son rule over you: the LORD shall rule over you.

24 And Gideon said unto them, I would desire a request of you, that ye would give me every man the earrings of his prey. (For they had golden earrings, because they were Ishmaelites.)

25 And they answered, We will willingly give them. And they spread a garment, and did cast therein every man the earrings of his prey.

26a And the weight of the golden earrings that he requested was a thousand and seven hundred shekels of gold.

KEY VERSE

And it was so, when Gideon heard the telling of the dream, and the interpretation thereof, that he worshipped, and returned into the host of Israel, and said, Arise; for the LORD hath delivered into your hand the host of Midian. —**Judges 7:15**

Unit 2: Listening for God in Changing Times

LESSONS 6–10

LESSON AIMS

After participating in this lesson, each student will be able to:

1. Tell how Gideon becomes an example both of wise and unwise leadership in his victory over the Midianites and the episode of the ephod, respectively.

2. Explain how good leaders can make big mistakes.

3. Pray for church and civic leaders to have godly wisdom and avoid foolish choices.

LESSON OUTLINE

Introduction

A. Testing God's Rule

Is it ever right to test God? The answer depends on our motives and God's invitation to do so. In Malachi 3:10, the Lord invites a test of His ability and willingness to bless. The Lord invited King Ahaz to test God, but that king sinfully refused to do so (Isaiah 7:10-12). On the other hand, the Israelites' testing of God at Meribah is presented in a negative light (Exodus 17:7; Numbers 20:13; Psalm 106:32). Ultimately, however, it was the people themselves who were tested at Meribah (Psalm 81:7). Trying to test God may well end up saying more about us than about Him! Thus it was with Gideon.

B. Lesson Background: Gideon's Reluctance

Like other leaders called by God, Gideon was reluctant. The Mosaic covenant required that there be no testing of God (Deuteronomy 6:16); yet Gideon tested God at least three times.

The first test was just after Gideon was called by the angel of the Lord to save the people (Judges 6:12-14). From the very beginning, Gideon tried to weasel out of his calling (6:7-15). When the Lord insisted that Gideon accept, Gideon asked for "a sign" that this was truly God speaking (6:17). The angel of the Lord complied (6:18-24).

The second test was requested after Gideon was filled with God's Spirit to lead (Judges 6:34). Gideon requested that a fleece of wool be covered with dew in the morning while the ground around it remained dry (6:37). It happened just that way (6:38), but that was not convincing for Gideon! So in his third test, Gideon asked God to reverse the miracle (6:39). God did so (6:40).

God has a sense of humor, indeed, for during all this God described Gideon as a "mighty man of valour" (Judges 6:12). He declared that Gideon would smite the Midianites in "thy might" (6:14). What descriptions for a reluctant warrior! What Gideon should have listened to were these words: "The Lord is with thee," "Have not I sent thee?" and "Surely I will be with thee" (6:12, 14, 16). Fully appreciating the sovereignty and power of God helps us overcome fear and weakness.

C. Lesson Background: Israel's Situation

The sin cycle of the story line of Judges is clearly marked in the account of Gideon (see Judges 6:1). Apostasy led to oppression. This is an indication of God's sovereignty at work in bringing judgment on His sinful people. For seven long years the Midianites, with the aid of Amalekites and the "children of the east" (a nomadic group from the Syrian desert, east of the Jordan River), raided the Israelites at harvesttime in order to take the best of their produce, including livestock (6:3, 4). The Israelites resorted to hiding in caves and assembling fortresses to protect themselves from the multitude of marauders (6:2).

The Midianites, related to God's people through Abraham and Keturah (Genesis 25:2-4), mostly had a history of friendly relations with Israel. Moses married a Midianite woman (Exodus 2:21), although that was about 300 years in the past from the standpoint of today's lesson. The Midianites were probably located south of Palestine and eastward in northern Arabia. Apparently, they were seminomadic at the time of Gideon (Judges 6:5); as antagonists to Israel, see Numbers 22:4-7; Psalm 83:9; Isaiah 10:26.

On the other hand, the Amalekites were always adversaries to Israel (Deuteronomy 25:17-19; 1 Samuel 15:2, 3). They were descendants of Esau (Genesis 36:12), being a nomadic or seminomadic people who lived on the southern fringes of the promised land. Israel first encountered them in the desert trek to Mount Sinai (Exodus 17:8-16).

The "cry of distress" segment of the sin cycle is found in Judges 6:7. But instead of sending a judge immediately, God sent a prophet to remind Israel that it was her fault for the oppression (6:8-10). Eventually, Gideon was called and "the Spirit of the Lord came upon" him (6:34).

I. God's Decision
(JUDGES 7:2-4)

Rather than heaping on more oppression, the angel of the Lord calls Gideon to be God's deliverer. But Gideon is skeptical of God's presence and power (Judges 6:13). Present difficulties often do not give hope for the future.

By this point in our story, Gideon already has sounded the trumpet for battle (Judges 6:34, 35; compare Numbers 10:9). As a result, 32,000 men have gathered from the tribes of Israel. The tribes mentioned in Judges 6:35 are the ones primarily affected by the Midianite oppression. While the Midianites and their allies are encamped in the Valley of Jezreel at Endor (6:33), the Israelites gather at the well of Harod (7:1), about halfway between the Hill of Moreh (to the north) and the foot of Mount Gilboa (to the south).

A. 32,000 to 10,000 (vv. 2, 3)

2. And the LORD said unto Gideon, The people that are with thee are too many for me to give the Midianites into their hands, lest Israel vaunt themselves against me, saying, Mine own hand hath saved me.

In spite of the fact that the enemy has well over 100,000 men (Judges 8:10), God declares that the 32,000 Israelites (7:3, below) are *too many,* lest the Israelite tribes take credit for any victory. This foreordained victory must be interpreted as divinely accomplished, and not by human effort. Otherwise, Israel will never learn to depend on God.

❧ HOOSIERS ❧

The 1986 movie *Hoosiers* is about a team from small-town southern Indiana in 1952 that seemed to come out of nowhere to win the state high

Abimelech	Uh-*bim*-eh-lek.
Amalekites	*Am*-uh-leh-kites
	or Uh-*mal*-ih-kites.
ephod	*ee*-fod.
Ephraimites	*Ee*-fray-im-ites.
Hagar	*Hay*-gar.
Ishmaelites	*Ish*-may-el-ites.
Keturah	Keh-*too*-ruh.
Manasseh	Muh-*nass*-uh.
Meribah	*Mehr*-ih-buh.
Midianites	*Mid*-ee-un-ites.
Mosaic	Mo-*zay*-ik.
Naphtali	*Naf*-tuh-lye.
Zebulun	*Zeb*-you-lun.

school basketball championship. In the movie, the team had only seven players. They were down to four players in one game, so the manager, Ollie MacFarlane, went in.

With the score tied, MacFarlane was fouled in the final seconds. He sank two free throws for the win. But in his interview with a sports writer after the game, he acted as if he were the star. The coach glared at him, but said nothing. Everyone knew his two shots were crucial, but they also knew he was not the star of the game.

Everyone reading this can think of an incident that is similar to the problem above. God is aware of the human tendency to claim credit (compare Daniel 4:30). But God always wants it to be obvious that He is the one who gives the victory. Zechariah 4:6 still applies.　　　　—J. B. N.

3. Now therefore go to, proclaim in the ears of the people, saying, Whosoever is fearful and afraid, let him return and depart early from mount Gilead. And there returned of the people twenty and two thousand; and there remained ten thousand.

According to the Mosaic law, there are several reasons why a man can be exempt from warfare (see Deuteronomy 20:5-8). One of these reasons is recounted here: *Whosoever is fearful and afraid, let him return.* When two-thirds of the army walks away, it must suck the air out of Gideon's lungs! No military leader can fathom this. Usually, it's "the more, the better."

The reference to *mount Gilead* is hard to interpret. Gideon is encamped at Mount Gilboa, at the well of Harod (Judges 7:1). Some suggest that the reference to Gilead is part of an idiom meaning "as a bird flies from Mount Gilead," which would explain the use of Gilead in this context.

B. 10,000 to 300 (v. 4)

4. And the LORD said unto Gideon, The people are yet too many; bring them down unto the water, and I will try them for thee there: and it shall be, that of whom I say unto thee, This shall go with thee, the same shall go with thee; and of whomsoever I say unto thee, This shall not go with thee, the same shall not go.

Just as Gideon tested God, by now three times (see the Lesson Background), so God tests Gideon. Surely Gideon cannot believe that more men have to be sent away! Judges 7:5 (not in today's text) specifies the procedure for determining who shall stay and who shall go, based on differing procedures for drinking water. The result is that only 300 remain. Obviously, you cannot use 300 soldiers to make a conventional frontal assault on an army of over 100,000! Something different will have to happen. God is teaching Gideon to depend upon His power regardless of circumstances.

What Do You Think?

What was a time when you felt challenged to follow a leader whose plan seemed contrary to human wisdom? How did things turn out?

Talking Points for Your Discussion

- Regarding your church's local outreach
- Regarding support of a missionary
- Regarding a church building program

II. Enemy's Dream
(JUDGES 7:13-15)

Gideon has every human reason to fear the task that God is giving him: attack a multitude of Midianites with only 300 men (Judges 7:8). Of course, God knows that Gideon fears his prospects. So God instructs Gideon to take his servant and go to the outskirts of the enemy camp to eavesdrop on the talk of the enemy warriors (7:9-12).

A. Image and Interpretation (vv. 13, 14)

13. And when Gideon was come, behold, there was a man that told a dream unto his fellow, and said, Behold, I dreamed a dream, and, lo, a cake of barley bread tumbled into the host of Midian, and came unto a tent, and smote it that it fell, and overturned it, that the tent lay along.

God gives a specific dream to a specific man. Even the pagans believe that dreams can be a form of divine-to-human communication.

Gideon overhears the telling of the dream. It is regarding *a cake of barley bread* that crushes a Midianite tent. What Gideon thinks about this

Let God Rule

dream is important, of course, but even more important is what the Midianite soldiers think of it (next verse).

> **What Do You Think?**
> How do we distinguish between dreams sent by God and "normal" dreams? Why is it important to do so?
> *Talking Points for Your Discussion*
> - Rarity of God-sent dreams in the Bible
> - Jeremiah 23:25-32
> - Acts 2:17
> - Revelation 22:18, 19

14. And his fellow answered and said, This is nothing else save the sword of Gideon the son of Joash, a man of Israel: for into his hand hath God delivered Midian, and all the host.

God's work in lowering enemy morale is evident, as the dream and its interpretation begin to circulate. Palpable fear is in the hearts of the Midianites before Gideon attacks. We presume that God was also working this way just before the attack on Jericho. The spies who were sent to scout Jericho became aware of low enemy morale in their discussion with Rahab (see Joshua 2:9).

A Midianite warrior interprets the parable correctly. In the dream, the cake of barley bread represents Gideon, who threshed grain in Judges 6:11; the tent represents the nomadic Midianites. Two more remarkable things must be noted. One is that the Midianite knows Gideon's name. The other is that the Midianite knows that God is behind Gideon. To realize that you're fighting against God must be the most demoralizing thing there is! And Gideon is right there within earshot of the enemy soldiers to hear it all.

> **What Do You Think?**
> Besides having God behind it, what did Gideon's battle plan have in its favor? What does this say, if anything, regarding the plans you make?
> *Talking Points for Your Discussion*
> - From a Midianite perspective
> - From an Israelite perspective
> - From Gideon's perspective

B. Worship and Action (v. 15)

15. And it was so, when Gideon heard the telling of the dream, and the interpretation thereof, that he worshipped, and returned into the host of Israel, and said, Arise; for the LORD hath delivered into your hand the host of Midian.

Gideon's response is humble submission to the Lord by worship. After various tests and revelations, Gideon finally is convinced that God will give him the victory. Therefore, Gideon returns to his camp emboldened to act as the leader he is called to be by God. This must give his 300 chosen men confidence as well, strengthening their hands for the task ahead.

Gideon divides his men into three companies. Each man is to carry a trumpet and a torch covered by an empty pitcher (Judges 7:16, not in today's text). At "the beginning of the middle watch" (about 10:00 PM, to maximize confusion in the darkness), Gideon instructs his men to blow their trumpets and reveal the torches by breaking the pitchers (7:19, 20). The combination of the strange noises of crashing vessels, trumpet blasts, and the flickering lights of the torches that surround the camp causes confusion. The Midianites begin to fight each other (7:22). Also, the dream has its effect when the 300 men cry out: "The sword of the Lord, and of Gideon!" (7:20).

> **What Do You Think?**
> What was an experience you had of God producing a great victory through limited resources? How did you grow spiritually through this experience?
> *Talking Points for Your Discussion*
> - In your church
> - In your personal life
> - In your family life
> - At work

III. Battle's Aftermath
(JUDGES 8:22-26a)

Gideon then sends messengers to call his fellow Israelites from the tribes of Manasseh, Naphtali, and Asher. Ephraimites join in to block the escape by the fords of the Jordan (see Judges 7:19-24; compare what the Israelites did in this regard to the Moabites in last week's lesson). The Ephraimites capture and execute two Midianite princes and bring their heads to Gideon. Later, Gideon pursues two kings of Midian, captures them, and executes them promptly (Judges 7:25–8:21; Psalm 83:11). Victory comes to Gideon, but only God can be given the credit!

An interesting thing to note as we make the transition into our final section is that Gideon leads from the front (Judges 7:17). This may be an important factor in the offer that follows.

A. Offer (v. 22)

22. Then the men of Israel said unto Gideon, Rule thou over us, both thou, and thy son, and thy son's son also: for thou hast delivered us from the hand of Midian.

The phrase *men of Israel* probably refers at least to the tribes of Manasseh, Asher, Naphtali, and Zebulun. The Ephraimites are angry with Gideon (Judges 8:1). Even though their resentment subsides (8:2, 3), they still might not be disposed to join the request *rule thou over us, both thou, and thy son, and thy son's son also.*

Gideon is being offered a dynastic kingship. This means that the Israelites do not recognize that the victory is the Lord's. The people view Gideon as a hero, and they want his kind of leadership. Little do they realize what they are asking, for Gideon's son Abimelech will attempt to be king, with disastrous results (see Judges 9).

B. Refusal (v. 23)

23. And Gideon said unto them, I will not rule over you, neither shall my son rule over you: the Lord shall rule over you.

Gideon firmly declines the offer, and rightly so. He himself knows who has really gained the victory over the Midianites. The various tests, the success of psychological warfare at night, and the slaughter of the majority of the enemy are evidence of a divine victory, not a human one. Gideon knows that God rules as king and that He can protect His people in the future.

But in about 140 years, the Israelites will indeed end up with a king. Philistine pressure will prompt the tribes to ask Samuel, the last of the judges, to appoint a king. Samuel will give in reluctantly and anoint Saul as Israel's first king (see 1 Samuel 8:5; 10:1). The people of Israel find it difficult to follow God's rule regardless of circumstances.

> **What Do You Think?**
> How does today's lesson highlight the differences between God's ways and ours?
> *Talking Points for Your Discussion*
> - In the value placed on numbers
> - In the character traits of those chosen
> - In the value of planning strategy
> - In how the aftermath is handled

C. Request (v. 24)

24. And Gideon said unto them, I would desire a request of you, that ye would give me every man the earrings of his prey. (For they had golden earrings, because they were Ishmaelites.)

Even though Gideon refuses a dynastic kingship, he does request that each man give him the golden earrings of the Ishmaelite warriors. The Ishmaelites are traced through Abraham and Hagar (Genesis 16:15). But here the term *Ishmaelites* probably refers to a broader group of nomadic people in the east (see Genesis 37:25-28, where *Ishmaelites* are the same as *Midianites*).

Visual for Lesson 8

Point to this visual as you ask, "How is courage to follow different from courage to lead?"

Let God Rule

D. Plunder (vv. 25, 26a)

25. And they answered, We will willingly give them. And they spread a garment, and did cast therein every man the earrings of his prey.

The tribes involved with Gideon are so relieved to be rid of the Midianite oppression that they willingly reward Gideon with the gold earrings. This is a small price to pay, since the Midianites have been taking crops and livestock from the Israelites for years. Now true prosperity can return to the land.

26a. And the weight of the golden earrings that he requested was a thousand and seven hundred shekels of gold.

The amount of gold is incredible! Depending on the shekel weight, Gideon's take amounts to somewhere between 40 and 75 pounds of gold. Gideon is wealthy overnight. He also obtains other plunder to increase this wealth (see Judges 8:21, 26b).

Sadly, our story does not end well. Gideon takes some of the gold and makes an ephod (Judges 8:27a), the nature of which we are not entirely certain. It may be patterned after the high priest's ephod with much gold ornamentation. Or it may be a pure gold replica of the high-priestly garment. More likely, it is a freestanding image of some kind that easily becomes an idol to worship. The second commandment prohibits the worship of God in any form or image (Exodus 20:4). This is a snare to Israel (see Judges 8:27b). After Gideon's death, the people will return to full idol worship (8:33).

The land has peace for 40 years after deliverance through Gideon (Judges 8:28). Sadly, the sin cycle will continue after Gideon's death (8:33-35).

❧ THE SPOILS OF WAR ❧

It is interesting to note what soldiers consider to be the spoils of war. In the American Civil War, for example, it was common to quantify a victory by the number of regimental battle flags or artillery pieces that were captured. On more than one occasion, a victory was thwarted or delayed when soldiers stopped to secure a captured cannon rather than pursue the demoralized opponents.

But flags and cannons weren't the only things prized for capture in that war. Sometimes the plunder was simply food. On the first day of the Battle of Shiloh, April 6, 1862, the hungry Confederates stopped their morning attack to consume the breakfasts that Union soldiers had just prepared but had abandoned under the Confederate assault. This pause and the resulting disorganization may have cost the Confederates the victory in that battle because of a loss of momentum.

Although some plunder is symbolic while other plunder is practical, either kind can be a distraction. The spoils of war that Gideon ended up with had a terrible result (Judges 8:27). Just as the battle itself belongs to the Lord, so also does the aftermath. Remember to pray about both! —J. B. N.

Conclusion
A. Let God Rule

Some scholars think that Gideon refused the offer of a kingship only out of politeness, but ended up being a ruler anyway. They point to his large harem and 70 sons (Judges 8:30), his use of jewelry and royal clothes, making and using the ephod-oracle, the naming of one of his sons *Abimelech* (meaning "my father a king"; 8:31), etc.

None of these things prove that Gideon was a king. Perhaps what all this *does* show is that Gideon had a difficult time letting God rule. The Israelites as a whole also had a problem letting God rule. After Gideon's death, the Israelites immediately returned to pagan worship (Judges 8:33), revealing that the influence Gideon was able to exert while alive "didn't take."

Let this be a warning to us. God can do marvelous things, but will we seek to "grab the gold" when all is said and done? God chose Gideon to be a leader of a certain type to accomplish a certain task. We do well to go as far as God wants us to go, but no further.

B. Prayer

Our Father, You are our powerful king. Change our weakness into strength, our fearfulness into courage. May we not waver in difficult times. In Jesus' powerful name, amen.

C. Thought to Remember

Follow God's leading as you accept His rule.

INVOLVEMENT LEARNING

Some of the activities below are also found in the helpful student book, Adult Bible Class.
Don't forget to download the free reproducible page from www.standardlesson.com to enhance your lesson!

Into the Lesson

As learners arrive, have the following equations displayed on the board to pique curiosity:

$$135,000 \div 32,000 = 4.2$$
$$135,000 \div 10,000 = 13.5$$
$$135,000 \div 300 = 450$$

Ask the class if these figures look familiar. If no one knows the answer, say, "The 135,000 is the number of troops that opposed Gideon, according to Judges 8:10. The 32,000 is the number of troops Gideon started with, thus his forces were outnumbered by more than 4 to 1 at the outset. When 22,000 went home, the remaining 10,000 were outnumbered by more than 13 to 1. With Gideon's army ultimately whittled down to a mere 300, his forces were outnumbered 450 to 1! Much has been said about the various ways that Gideon tested God. But God was also testing Gideon. Now I am going to test *you!*"

Into the Word

"Letter off" your learners by pointing to them one by one as you say "A, B, C, D" in turn. Each student will be designated with one of the letters. Then say, "I am going to give you a multiple-choice test on today's study. After I give the choices, I will say, 'Will the real answer please stand?'"

Use the following questions or those of your own design. Correct answers are noted in italics. (*Option:* You can either read or not read the lesson text aloud before you begin; choosing not to read the text first will result in a pretest for the lesson ahead.) Ask the "answer" to stand only after all four choices are read.

1. The enemy to be defeated by Gideon was from (A) Gilead, (B) Jerubbaal, (C) Moreh, *(D) Midian.* 2. God was concerned with the number of Gideon's soldiers because there were (A) too few, *(B) too many,* (C) not enough horses, (D) several Egyptians present. 3. The first disqualifier God gave for Gideon's soldiers involved (A) those over four cubits tall, (B) any who were naturally left-handed, *(C) any who were afraid,* (D) any over 50 years of age. 4. In the first downsizing of the army, about how many left? (A) one quarter, (B) one third, (C) one half, *(D) two thirds.* 5. While spying, Gideon overheard an enemy soldier recounting a dream of *(A) a loaf of bread,* (B) heavy rains, (C) birds of prey, (D) lightning. 6. Gideon's immediate reaction to the enemy soldier's dream was (A) disbelief, *(B) worship,* (C) a request for more troops, (D) getting drunk. 7. After winning the battle, Gideon requested *(A) a share of the spoils,* (B) to be made king, (C) a retirement ceremony, (D) a copy of the law.

Follow this test by distributing copies of the Gideon: The Whole Story activity from the reproducible page for completion by small groups. This will allow a broader look at Gideon's service (and failures). Follow by discussing ways in which Gideon is and is not a good role model.

Into Life

Ask, "Who from nonbiblical history can you identify as a good leader who made a serious mistake?" Let several respond. (You may wish to modify this question to keep a political tirade from developing; for example, you could ask about leaders who lived only before the twentieth century.) Then ask, "When should a mistake or sin force a leader to step down?" After some opinions are expressed, distribute copies of the Good Leaders and Bad Mistakes activity from the reproducible page, which you have downloaded. Remind your learners that God sometimes used leaders who made bad mistakes and/or committed sin.

Close with a time of "sentence prayers" for various leaders, to be chosen by the ones praying. Suggest that prayers be that God's grace and forgiveness will be evident to the leader and that the leader will experience God's Spirit as an encouragement to continue boldly, in spite of mistakes.

Let God Rule

RETURN TO
GOD'S WAYS

BACKGROUND SCRIPTURE: Judges 10:6–11:33; 21:25
PRINTED TEXT: Judges 10:10-18; 11:4-6, 32, 33

JUDGES 10:10-18

10 And the children of Israel cried unto the LORD, saying, We have sinned against thee, both because we have forsaken our God, and also served Baalim.

11 And the LORD said unto the children of Israel, Did not I deliver you from the Egyptians, and from the Amorites, from the children of Ammon, and from the Philistines?

12 The Zidonians also, and the Amalekites, and the Maonites, did oppress you; and ye cried to me, and I delivered you out of their hand.

13 Yet ye have forsaken me, and served other gods: wherefore I will deliver you no more.

14 Go and cry unto the gods which ye have chosen; let them deliver you in the time of your tribulation.

15 And the children of Israel said unto the LORD, We have sinned: do thou unto us whatsoever seemeth good unto thee; deliver us only, we pray thee, this day.

16 And they put away the strange gods from among them, and served the LORD: and his soul was grieved for the misery of Israel.

17 Then the children of Ammon were gathered together, and encamped in Gilead. And the children of Israel assembled themselves together, and encamped in Mizpeh.

18 And the people and princes of Gilead said one to another, What man is he that will begin to fight against the children of Ammon? he shall be head over all the inhabitants of Gilead.

JUDGES 11:4-6, 32, 33

4 And it came to pass in process of time, that the children of Ammon made war against Israel.

5 And it was so, that when the children of Ammon made war against Israel, the elders of Gilead went to fetch Jephthah out of the land of Tob:

6 And they said unto Jephthah, Come, and be our captain, that we may fight with the children of Ammon.

. . . .

32 So Jephthah passed over unto the children of Ammon to fight against them; and the LORD delivered them into his hands.

33 And he smote them from Aroer, even till thou come to Minnith, even twenty cities, and unto the plain of the vineyards, with a very great slaughter. Thus the children of Ammon were subdued before the children of Israel.

KEY VERSE

[The Israelites] put away the strange gods from among them, and served the LORD: and his soul was grieved for the misery of Israel. —**Judges 10:16**

GOD INSTRUCTS HIS PEOPLE

Unit 2: Listening for God in Changing Times

LESSONS 6–10

LESSON AIMS

After participating in this lesson, each student will be able to:

1. Summarize the story of Jepthah's deliverance of the Israelites.

2. Explain why wholehearted devotion to God was important for Israel and remains important today.

3. Acknowledge and repent of a less than wholehearted devotion to God.

LESSON OUTLINE

Introduction

A. The Sin of Syncretism

One definition of *syncretism* is "the union of conflicting beliefs, especially religious beliefs." Syncretism is sinful for the exclusive Jewish belief system of the Old Testament and the Christian belief system of the New Testament. God is one, and there is no other (Deuteronomy 6:4). "There is . . . one Lord, one faith, one baptism, one God and Father of all, who is above all, and through all, and in you all" (Ephesians 4:4-6). Yet sometimes Christians commit the sin of syncretism without realizing it.

A few years ago, a book titled *The Prayer of Jabez* appeared, and it became a massive best seller. Many Christians came under its spell. While I do not attribute evil intent to the author, the result nevertheless was a syncretistic moment in the life of the church at large. The book promoted a "health and wealth" gospel message using a certain interpretation of the prayer of Jabez as its basis (1 Chronicles 4:10). Although God granted Jabez "that which he requested," there is no "health and wealth" gospel here. That is incompatible with biblical faith, both ancient and modern. God is not a cosmic vending machine who automatically dispenses goodies whenever we pray just the right words and do just the right things. To bring such a viewpoint into Christianity is syncretism.

Ancient peoples tended to have a primary god for each nation (1 Kings 11:7, 33). Nations tended not to change their primary gods (Jeremiah 2:11), although they might "pile on" other gods as well. Israel was to be a notable exception. She was supposed to have unchanging allegiance to the one and only true God. But ancient Israel was taken in by the fertility gods of Canaan.

These nature gods were thought to bring blessing or harm to the people, and it was thought foolish to neglect them. Some Israelites undoubtedly continued worshiping the Lord while "piling on" these other gods. This is syncretism. Practically speaking, however, the result is abandonment of Yahweh God altogether (Judges 10:6, 10), since God does not share His glory (Isaiah 42:8; 48:11).

B. Lesson Background

Our lessons in Judges to this point have made us familiar with the sin cycle of God's people. Today's lesson takes us to God's provision of Jephthah as the delivering judge. We date the exploits of Jephthah to the six-year period 1086–1080 BC. Jephthah was "a mighty man of valour," as was Gideon several decades previously (Judges 11:1; compare 6:12). Jephthah was an outcast to his family, for he was born of a harlot (11:1) and was spurned by his half brothers (11:2).

Jephthah fled to settle in Tob, about 15 miles north of Ramoth Gilead, in eastern Manasseh (11:3). Stated differently, Tob is about a dozen miles east of the Sea of Galilee. There Jephthah gathered a small army of malcontents ("vain men") who raided and fought together (Judges 11:3; compare David's band of men, 1 Samuel 22:2).

As our lesson opens, it has been about 320 years since the Israelites took possession of the promised land. The appointment of Saul as Israel's first king is only about 36 years in the future as the disturbing period of the judges moves toward its close.

I. Crisis
(JUDGES 10:10-18; 11:4-6)

All the action of the story of Jephthah takes place in the transjordan area between Gilead and Ammon in the tribal territory of Gad. This area is bounded by the Jabbok River to the north and the city of Aroer in the south.

A. Cry and Admission (v. 10)

10. And the children of Israel cried unto the LORD, saying, We have sinned against thee, both because we have forsaken our God, and also served Baalim.

It is interesting how hard times can penetrate a people's hard hearts and prick their consciences about sin. In Israel's case, the Ammonites have oppressed God's people for 18 years in the transjordan area in Gilead (Judges 10:8). The Ammonites have grown bold enough to raid across the Jordan River (10:9). Finally, at the end of that 18-year period, the Israelites realize their error in worshiping the gods around them (10:6).

True confession recognizes the offended party. Thus the Israelites address God as Yahweh (LORD), His personal name, and call him *our God*. One cannot serve both fictitious pagan gods and the one true God. That is syncretism.

> **What Do You Think?**
> What is your reaction when a repeat offender repents? What should your reaction be?
> *Talking Points for Your Discussion*
> - Issues of healthy and unhealthy skepticism
> - Issues of personal involvement (being the one who was wronged)

B. Fact and Suggestion (vv. 11-14)

11, 12. And the LORD said unto the children of Israel, Did not I deliver you from the Egyptians, and from the Amorites, from the children of Ammon, and from the Philistines? The Zidonians also, and the Amalekites, and the Maonites, did oppress you; and ye cried to me, and I delivered you out of their hand.

The deliverances of God are impressive! Deliverance from the Egyptians is the subject of Exodus 7–14. The Amorites are defeated in the transjordan area in Numbers 21:21-31. The reference to deliverance *from the children of Ammon* (that is, the

HOW TO SAY IT

Amalekites	*Am*-uh-leh-kites or Uh-*mal*-ih-kites.
Ammonites	*Am*-un-ites.
Amorites	*Am*-uh-rites.
Aroer	Uh-*row*-er.
Gilead	*Gil*-ee-ud (G as in *get*).
Jephthah	*Jef*-thuh (*th* as in *thin*).
Manasseh	Muh-*nass*-uh.
Maonites	*May*-on-itz
Minnith	*Min*-ith.
obeisance	oh-*bee*-suntz.
Othniel	*Oth*-ni-el.
Philistines	Fuh-*liss*-teenz or *Fill*-us-teenz.
Ramoth	*Ray*-muth.
syncretism	*sin*-kruh-*tih*-zem.
Zidonians	Zye-*doe*-nee-uns.

Ammonites) may be confusing, since they are the present oppressor. But they were allied with King Eglon of the Moabites in the past (Judges 3:12, 13), also defeated. Shamgar, a judge, had delivered Israel from the Philistines for a while (3:31).

The Israelites were supposed to have driven out the Zidonians. But the Israelites didn't get the job done (Joshua 13:2-4; Judges 1:31). The Zidonians probably had been allied with Jabin and Sisera more recently (Judges 3:3; 4:2, 3). The Amalekites, who seem to be perpetual enemies of Israel, had allied themselves with both the Moabites (3:12, 13) and the Midianites (6:3); the Maonites may be a variant reference to the Midianites.

Whenever Israel cries out in distress, God answers with a deliverer. We speculate that the numbering of the oppressors at seven stands for "completeness," for there are other enemies not mentioned (notably the Moabites and Canaanites). The sevenfold listing of oppressors here is balanced by the sevenfold listing of gods that the Israelites have worshiped per Judges 10:6.

13. Yet ye have forsaken me, and served other gods: wherefore I will deliver you no more.

Up to this point in the narrative of the book of Judges, there have been four major judges (Othniel, Ehud, Deborah, and Gideon) and three minor ones (Shamgar, Tola, and Jair). These seven deliverers have not been able to keep Israel faithful to her covenant relationship with God. Instead, the people revert to their multigod mind-set each time a judge dies, worshiping all the fertility and nature gods that surround them.

God has had enough. Thus He declares: *I will deliver you no more.* Does grace have its limits? Perhaps we can say that God does not deal in "cheap grace," a term made famous by Dietrich Bonhoeffer (1906–1945) in his book *The Cost of Discipleship.*

❧ WHOSE FAULT? ❧

I recently read a novel about a businessman who had become very successful in his line of work. But he had also become negligent in teaching his son about self-control and self-discipline. The son grew up lacking nothing. His life was a continual round of partying, girls, and escapades. Dad always bailed him out, gave him whatever spending money he wanted, and cleaned up the "problems" as well as he could. When a school expelled the son for rowdy behavior, dad took him on a vacation.

On this vacation, the father finally realized how irresponsible his son had become. After a firm talk, the son agreed to go back to college and finish a degree. When the son got in trouble once more, his dad took him out of school and made him get a job to earn his own spending money. It took a while, but the son finally learned the lesson. We might see certain similarities between the son in this story and the Israelites: the Israelites had been given a land flowing with milk and honey, but they abused this privileged position.

On the other hand, there is at least one vital difference here between the earthly father and the heavenly one. The earthly father was functioning as what we call *an enabler.* This means that this father shared the blame for much of the son's behavior since the father did not let the son suffer the consequences for misbehavior. When God said, "I will deliver you no more," He was serious about not being an enabler! At this point in the story line, God has allowed the consequences for misbehavior (idolatry) to be experienced for 18 years. God knows how to act in our best interest, and He always does. —J. B. N.

14. Go and cry unto the gods which ye have chosen; let them deliver you in the time of your tribulation.

We get the unmistakable impression that God is "fed up"! If the Israelites think their preferred gods are so worthy, then they should try getting their deliverance from them. In reality, such gods are "nothings." Such gods cannot deliver even if the Israelites believe that they can. Perhaps the Israelites are already reaching this conclusion because of the oppression they suffer!

On the other hand, the true God is quite capable of delivering. But will He do so this time? The apostle Paul recounts how God gives sinful people over to their own sins: "Wherefore God also gave them up to uncleanness . . . God gave them up unto vile affections . . . God gave them over to a

Return to God's Ways

reprobate mind" (Romans 1:24, 26, 28). This will be the state of any nation or country that persists in sinning against God (compare Jeremiah 44:25).

C. Request and Repentance (vv. 15, 16)

15. And the children of Israel said unto the LORD, We have sinned: do thou unto us whatsoever seemeth good unto thee: deliver us only, we pray thee, this day.

Israel has already confessed her sin (v. 10, above). However, following God's response of "I will deliver you no more" (v. 13, above), the Israelites submit themselves to God on unconditional terms. They accept His punishment. But they plead still again: *Deliver us only, we pray thee, this day.* In Hebrew, the phrase *we pray thee* is expressed by one little sound—*na*. In the ears of the Hebrew, it may be equivalent to our "please," or as a small child might draw it out, "pleeeease!" This is Israel's desperate appeal.

> **What Do You Think?**
> What was a time when suffering consequences for a bad or sinful decision helped you make better decisions later?
> *Talking Points for Your Discussion*
> - In handling money
> - In personal relationships
> - At work

16. And they put away the strange gods from among them, and served the LORD: and his soul was grieved for the misery of Israel.

Even though Israel is at the mercy of God and has no promise of deliverance, she nevertheless truly repents. This involves putting away the pagan gods listed in Judges 10:6. Most of these are "household" gods—small figurines set in special places in the house so that obeisance could be made on a regular basis (compare Judges 18:14, 17, 18, 20).

Instead, the people vow to serve the true God, and God responds! God's compassion is far beyond any human compassion. How many times will we forgive—seven times (Matthew 18:21, 22)? God's compassion begins to be manifested in the series of events that follow.

> **What Do You Think?**
> What does this passage teach us about repentance?
> *Talking Points for Your Discussion*
> - Affirmations as they lead to actions
> - Actions as they lead to affirmations
> - God's response to affirmations and actions

D. Confrontation and Search (vv. 17, 18)

17. Then the children of Ammon were gathered together, and encamped in Gilead. And the children of Israel assembled themselves together, and encamped in Mizpeh.

The Ammonites have gathered to make war. The territory of Gilead, the site of their camp, is centrally located between Bashan in the north and the southern tableland on the east side of the Jordan River. The Israelites counter with their own war assembly at Mizpeh, which means "watchtower." This can refer to several locations. It seems best to locate this Mizpeh a few miles south of the Jabbok River and fairly close to the assembly of the Ammonites in Gilead.

The capital of the Ammonites is Rabbah (modern-day Amman), about 15 miles southeast of Mizpeh. Presumably this is at the end of the 18-year oppression of Judges 10:8. The war councils begin.

18. And the people and princes of Gilead said one to another, What man is he that will begin to fight against the children of Ammon? He shall be head over all the inhabitants of Gilead.

In the case of Gideon, he first was designated as the leader, then he collected an army. In the case before us, the reverse is true. An army first is gathered, but it is leaderless. The people and elders of Gilead apparently realize their need for someone with military experience. To attract such an individual, they promise this person a high position among them. In the three verses that follow (not in today's text), the narrative offers a parenthetical account of Jephthah's troubling family life (see the Lesson Background). The purpose is to show the ironic and humiliating appeal the leaders of Gilead have to make to Jephthah.

What qualities should you look for in choosing a leader? During the American Revolution, the Continental Congress faced exactly this task. After the British raid on Lexington and Concord, thousands of Massachusetts militiamen gathered around Boston, hemming the British in. But the militia had no overall military organization. Members of Congress had the responsibility of choosing the leader, and they selected George Washington.

Washington had military experience going back over 20 years, and he was a colonel in the Virginia militia. He was known to be fervently committed to the patriot cause. He was mild in demeanor, not given to excessive boasting or outbursts of temper. In addition, having a Virginian supervise the New England forces would create a political tie to bind north and south together for the difficult struggles ahead. All in all, it was a good choice.

The Gileadites were also looking for a military leader with a reputation. They were smart enough not to let Jephthah's "lowly" background (Judges 11:1-3) disqualify him. Remember, "For ye see your calling, brethren, how that not many wise men after the flesh, not many mighty, not many noble, are called: But God hath chosen the foolish things of the world to confound the wise; and God hath chosen the weak things of the world to confound the things which are mighty" (1 Corinthians 1:26, 27).   —J. B. N.

E. War and Leadership (11:4-6)

4. And it came to pass in process of time, that the children of Ammon made war against Israel.

This statement resumes the narrative from the end of chapter 10. It also places the Ammonites as the aggressors.

5. And it was so, that when the children of Ammon made war against Israel, the elders of Gilead went to fetch Jephthah out of the land of Tob.

The Israelites must find a warrior-leader for their forces. No one is qualified among their immediate number to be this leader. But Jephthah apparently has built a reputation for his ability to fight (Judges 11:3). So *the elders of Gilead* appeal to him.

6. And they said unto Jephthah, Come, and be our captain, that we may fight with the children of Ammon.

The appeal of the leaderless leaders seems to be a temporary one—to lead in battle only. In Judges 11:7 (not in today's text), Jephthah rebukes the Gileadites for their part in his expulsion from the area many years before. The Gileadites sweeten the appeal by offering him headship over all Gilead if he is successful in battle (11:8). Jephthah seems to take a little revenge against his own people as they swear an oath to make him head of the Gileadites as well as captain over the fighting forces (11:8-11). It is either all or nothing! The sting of illegitimacy now becomes tolerable as Jephthah contemplates his change in circumstances.

> **What Do You Think?**
> What are some ways God has used a negative experience in your life to benefit others?
> *Talking Points for Your Discussion*
> - From loss of a job
> - From failing to achieve a goal
> - From unfair criticism
> - From family background or circumstances

II. Resolution

(Judges 11:32, 33)

Jephthah first tries diplomacy, asking the Ammonite king why his troops are attacking (Judges 11:12). The king responds by noting his desire to regain territory lost more than 300 years previously (11:13; compare Numbers 21:24). Jephthah responds skillfully (Judges 11:14-27), but the Ammonite king does not care about Jephthah's well-developed arguments (11:28). God's Spirit comes upon Jephthah and moves him into action (11:29).

A. Deliverance (v. 32)

32. So Jephthah passed over unto the children of Ammon to fight against them; and the LORD delivered them into his hands.

Diplomacy doesn't work, so now it's time to fight. The resulting battle is described only in general terms (v. 33, below). It takes a warrior-leader like Jephthah who is brave enough to fight the

Ammonites after their long oppression. Even so, both Jephthah and the leaders of Gilead realize it is the Lord's victory (see Judges 11:9, 10: 12:3).

B. Devastation (v. 33)

33. And he smote them from Aroer, even till thou come to Minnith, even twenty cities, and unto the plain of the vineyards, with a very great slaughter. Thus the children of Ammon were subdued before the children of Israel.

Aroer is located on the King's Highway, the main north-south trade route in the transjordan area. While there is another Aroer much farther south, that is not the one in view here. This Aroer is the one near Rabbah (Joshua 13:25) and close to the river Arnon. Minnith is about 10 miles due south from there. Archaeologists have found many settlements with watchtowers in this area, and it is probable that many of the 20 cities noted here are included in those. Jephthah not only pushes the Ammonites out of Gilead, he also invades the territory of Ammon proper to destroy the fighting ability of the Ammonites and their king.

The story of Jephthah's victory is marred by two sad epilogues: a rash vow involving his own daughter (Judges 11:30, 31, 34-40) and the slaughter of fellow Israelites from the tribe of Ephraim (12:1-6). When the Ephraimites challenge Jephthah for their "honor" (as they had done with Gideon in 8:1-3), Jephthah does not turn them away with a "soft" answer as Gideon did (12:1-3). Instead, Jephthah's Gileadite army slays 42,000 Ephraimites.

There is no record of peace with Jephthah's victory. The text records only that "Jephthah judged Israel six years. Then died Jephthah" (Judges 12:7). The deterioration of the period of the judges will continue with the call of Samson.

Visual for Lessons 9 & 10. *Point to this visual as you ask, "How has God worked through one of your weaknesses to advance His kingdom?"*

Conclusion

A. The Compassion of God

God demonstrated compassion toward ancient Israel on many occasions. Time and time again the Israelites committed apostasy by following the fictitious gods of the surrounding nations during the period of the judges. And God delivered the people repeatedly. Yet they continued in their sin of apostasy due to syncretism. "I will deliver you no more" (Judges 10:13) could have stood. But God had great compassion and again relented.

Without a compassionate God, we would all perish. Let us strive to put aside all forms of syncretism in our private lives as well as our corporate life in the church. In these hard times for the church, both culturally and politically, let us strive to uphold God's standards of belief and behavior.

B. Prayer

Our Father, thank You for being compassionate and forgiving. Take away our bent toward mixing the world's values with Your values, the world's behavior with Your standards of behavior. Help us to return to Your ways rather than go our own way. And as You are compassionate toward us, may we be so toward others. In Jesus' name, amen.

C. Thought to Remember

Syncretism is deadly.

INVOLVEMENT LEARNING

Some of the activities below are also found in the helpful student book, Adult Bible Class.
Don't forget to download the free reproducible page from www.standardlesson.com to enhance your lesson!

Into the Lesson

Recruit a female actor to present the following short monologue to introduce Jephthah. Introduce her as Jephthah's daughter.

"My father knew what it was to be rejected by family, for our own kin had driven him away from home. They did not want him, the son of a prostitute, to share in their inheritance. This rejection probably made my father cherish me, his only child, all the more. I was sad to see him go to war, especially on behalf of those who had rejected him. How joyful I was to hear him returning victorious! Yet my joy was short-lived. Father had made a foolish vow of sacrifice to God, and he was a man of his word. You know my fate. Even so, my father loved me, and I loved him."

This short recitation will give you an opportunity to introduce some of the biographical information about Jephthah. See especially Judges 11:1-3, 7, 30-40.

Into the Word

Read the lesson text aloud. Then give each learner a handout with a table of three columns and four rows. The top row will have the three column headings of *God, Jephthah,* and *Israel.* The other three rows will be blank. Underneath the table put the following list of words: *compassionate, desperate, destroyer, exiled, faithless, forsaken, grieved, humbled, leader.* Have these directions on the handout: "Put the nine words into the nine blanks, one word per blank. Your selections should be the 'best' description of the name that is in the column head above it. Each word can be used exactly once. Some words may well fit more than one column, but decide which column each best fits." The anticipated answers are compassionate, forsaken, and grieved for God; destroyer, exiled, and leader for Jephthah; desperate, faithless, and humbled for Israel. Allow a few minutes, then ask learners to defend their choices.

Recruit in advance two learners for a father/son (or mother/daughter) telephone conversation. Provide telephones as props. Have your actors either stand or sit in such a way that they are not facing each other. Say, "I want you to listen in on this telephone call. I think you'll find it interesting."

છ છ છ

Son [while dialing]: Things are just really going bad for me right now. Dad will bail me out.

Father [looking at the caller ID]: Well, would you look at that. It's my good-for-nothing son. Wonder what he wants now. [answering] Hello, son.

Son: Dad, I'm in big trouble. I need your help.

Father: So, what else is new? Let's count the number of times I've rescued you already. There was that suspension from high school, there was that DUI, there was that credit card thing . . .

Son [interrupting]: I know, Dad. You have always been there and I . . .

Father [interrupting] Not anymore! Why don't you go to your current low-life friends for help?

Son [with desperation]: They won't help me, and that's a lesson I never learn. Can I come see you?

Father: Believe it or not, there's nothing I would like more. See you soon. [both hang up]

છ છ છ

Have someone read aloud Judges 10:6-15 (of which verses 10-15 are in today's text). Ask, "What are the close parallels between the telephone conversation and these verses? What elements between the phone conversation and the text are not parallel?" This can be a small-group discussion.

Into Life

Download the reproducible page and distribute copies of one or both of its activities. The Alternatives exercise will challenge learners to consider their behavior in various circumstances. Since this involves personal decisions, you may wish to use it as a take-home activity. The second part of the Tough Questions exercise, also rather personal, can also be a take-home activity after you cover the first part of the exercise in class.

Return to God's Ways

WALK IN GOD'S PATH

BACKGROUND SCRIPTURE: **Judges 13; 21:25**
PRINTED TEXT: **Judges 13:1-8, 24, 25**

JUDGES 13:1-8, 24, 25

1 And the children of Israel did evil again in the sight of the LORD; and the LORD delivered them into the hand of the Philistines forty years.

2 And there was a certain man of Zorah, of the family of the Danites, whose name was Manoah; and his wife was barren, and bare not.

3 And the angel of the LORD appeared unto the woman, and said unto her, Behold now, thou art barren, and bearest not: but thou shalt conceive, and bear a son.

4 Now therefore beware, I pray thee, and drink not wine nor strong drink, and eat not any unclean thing:

5 For, lo, thou shalt conceive, and bear a son; and no razor shall come on his head: for the child shall be a Nazarite unto God from the womb: and he shall begin to deliver Israel out of the hand of the Philistines.

6 Then the woman came and told her husband, saying, A man of God came unto me, and his countenance was like the countenance of an angel of God, very terrible: but I asked him not whence he was, neither told he me his name:

7 But he said unto me, Behold, thou shalt conceive, and bear a son; and now drink no wine nor strong drink, neither eat any unclean thing: for the child shall be a Nazarite to God from the womb to the day of his death.

8 Then Manoah intreated the LORD, and said, O my Lord, let the man of God which thou didst send come again unto us, and teach us what we shall do unto the child that shall be born.

. . . .

24 And the woman bare a son, and called his name Samson: and the child grew, and the LORD blessed him.

25 And the Spirit of the LORD began to move him at times in the camp of Dan between Zorah and Eshtaol.

KEY VERSES

The woman bare a son, and called his name Samson: and the child grew, and the LORD blessed him. And the Spirit of the LORD began to move him. —**Judges 13:24, 25**

GOD INSTRUCTS HIS PEOPLE

Unit 2: Listening for God in Changing Times

LESSONS 6–10

LESSON AIMS

After participating in this lesson, each student will be able to:

1. Identify key points in the Lord's preparation to send Samson as a deliverer.

2. Identify some principles in the Lord's instructions to Samson's parents that are reliable child-rearing principles for today.

3. Make a list of ways that parents and the church can foster spiritual growth in children.

LESSON OUTLINE

Introduction

A. Raising Up Leadership

Every Christian family ought to think in terms of raising up children for eventual leadership in the church, whether that is full-time ministry or volunteer ministry. It is not easy with our present culture of individualism and materialism with its pervasive influence through television, movies, music, and the Internet. Even so, there are some basic principles that Christians should model for their children and grandchildren in order to help them develop leadership qualities.

First, consistently live the Christian life before your children and grandchildren. Second, assist your children and grandchildren in getting biblical teaching from a variety of persons and places. Third, cultivate in your children and grandchildren a healthy self-image from a biblical perspective by being positive and encouraging. Fourth, discipline your children and grandchildren with love. Fifth, use a child's failure as a teaching opportunity. Finally, pray for your children and grandchildren daily and lean on the Holy Spirit to do His work in them.

These principles should guide us as we help our children and grandchildren walk in God's path. Even so, there is no guarantee of success, since God gives us free will. Samson's parents probably did their best to help their son walk in God's path, although Samson revealed many character flaws in his life. Even so, Samson's parents honored God by their efforts.

B. Lesson Background

Vows were a regular part of life in ancient Israel, and much instruction was given on how to make vows (Leviticus 27). One such vow was the Nazarite vow (see Numbers 6:1-21). Anyone could make this vow. It was a special separation and consecration to God for any time period. Its purpose was to experience the "life of God" for a time and to be a symbol of this "fullness of life" to others.

Three basic prohibitions characterized the Nazarite vow. First, no food or drink made from grapes could be consumed (Numbers 6:4). No grape jelly on your biscuit! Second, there could be no cut-

Walk in God's Path

ting of the hair (v. 5). Hair had to be allowed to grow as long as the vow was maintained. Third, there was to be no touching of a dead body or carcass (vv. 6, 7). All three prohibitions had this one thing in common: they represented life. Red wine represented blood. Since "the life of the flesh is in the blood" (Leviticus 17:11), such wine reminded one of life. As long as a person lives, that person's hair grows. By letting hair grow, one was protecting the "life" of the hair. Staying away from dead bodies also affirmed life.

Under special circumstances, a person could become a Nazarite for life. Such was the life of Samson (Judges 13–16), son of the parents whom we are studying today. Lifetime Nazarites had no choice in the matter, for one or both parents made the vow for the child. The cases of Samson, Samuel (1 Samuel 1:11, 22, 28), and John the Baptist (Luke 1:15) involved vows for the yet-to-be-born as God intervened on behalf of barren mothers.

Jephthah, the subject of last week's lesson, judged Israel for 6 years before he died (Judges 12:7). Then came the minor judges Ibzan, Elon, and Abdon; they judged Israel for a total of 25 years (12:8-15). This is where today's text picks up.

I. Revelation
(JUDGES 13:1-5)
A. Setting (v. 1)

1. And the children of Israel did evil again in the sight of the LORD; and the LORD delivered them into the hand of the Philistines forty years.

HOW TO SAY IT

Aegean	A-*jee*-un.
Askelon	*Ash*-ke-lon or *As*-ke-lon.
Bethshemesh	Beth-*she*-mesh.
Jephthah	*Jef*-thuh (*th* as in *thin*).
Laish	*Lay*-ish.
Manoah	Muh-*no*-uh.
Mycenaean	*My*-suh-**nee**-un.
Shephelah	She-*fuh*-lah.
theophany	the-*ah*-fuh-nee.
Zorah	*Zo*-ruh.

The fact that the Israelites commit *evil again in the sight of the Lord* is a sadly familiar refrain by this point in the book of Judges. Because of this evil, the Lord allows the Philistines to dominate the Israelites for 40 years, from about 1115 to 1075 BC. This sin cycle begins again with apostasy and oppression, but the cycle doesn't go any further with Samson. He will not deliver the Israelites from oppression; he will only begin the process (Judges 13:5, below). Character issues may be in play here: Samson will demonstrate an unholy interest in the opposite sex, and he will break every part of his imposed Nazarite vow (Judges 14–16).

The threat to Israel in last week's lesson had come from the east. The oppression we see now comes from the west. The Philistines had been a migrating sea people from the region of the Aegean Sea and Asia Minor; they finally settled on the coastline of Palestine (the area called Gaza today). They established five capital cities: Askelon, Ashdod, Ekron, Gath, and Gaza (Joshua 13:3; 1 Samuel 6:17). These people are considered more "advanced" (reflecting the Mycenaean culture) than the Israelites, who are forced to live in the Shephelah (hill country). The Philistines protected their technological advantage in ironworking (1 Samuel 13:19-22).

B. Barrenness (v. 2)

2. And there was a certain man of Zorah, of the family of the Danites, whose name was Manoah; and his wife was barren, and bare not.

Zorah is located in the Shephelah, the hill country near the northern border of Judah in the eastern Sorek Valley, close to Bethshemesh (Joshua 15:10; 19:41; 21:16). If that's too confusing, just think of Zorah as being about 15 miles due west of the Mount of Olives. The Danites' original allotment of land is here. The allotment runs northward to the Yarkon River along the coast of the Mediterranean Sea. With pressure from the Philistines, many of the Danites migrate north and take over ancient Laish (see Judges 18). They call it *Dan*. It is located at the foot of Mount Hermon.

Manoah, whose name means "rest," has a wife who is infertile. God will often use our limitations to His advantage and produce outcomes that stagger the imagination. Manoah's wife, unnamed in the text, is one of several barren women who become able to bear children in order to bring a special child into the world. Think of Sarah (Genesis 21), Rebekah (Genesis 25), Rachel (Genesis 30), Hannah (1 Samuel 1), and Elisabeth (Luke 1).

What Do You Think?

What are some ways that God works in the midst of stressful family situations today? How will you make yourself available to be God's instrument in that regard?

Talking Points for Your Discussion
- Situations involving childlessness
- Situations involving prodigal children
- Situations involving blended families
- Situations involving "releasing" children
- Situations involving being single or single again

C. Son (v. 3)

3. And the angel of the LORD appeared unto the woman, and said unto her, Behold now, thou art barren, and bearest not: but thou shalt conceive, and bear a son.

The appearance of *the angel of the Lord* is what we call *a theophany,* which means "a manifestation of God." The phrase *angel of the Lord* appears dozens of times in the Bible. Often it is clear that this being represents God himself, thus being a theophany. For example, *the angel of the Lord* seems to refer to God personally in Exodus 3:2-4 and Zechariah 12:8. Later in our text, Manoah's wife will describe in more detail what she sees.

To be bereft of children is a shameful condition for an Israelite woman. Thus the words *thou shalt conceive, and bear a son* are the most beautiful words she will ever hear! Being startled and not really knowing who is speaking to her, she begins to listen to his instructions.

D. Future (vv. 4, 5)

4. Now therefore beware, I pray thee, and drink not wine nor strong drink, and eat not any unclean thing.

Manoah's wife receives a strict warning against certain drink and food. Such warnings are not new, however. The restrictions in Leviticus 11; Numbers 6:3, 4; etc. are hundreds of years old by this point. Is this reminder of these ancient restrictions a little prenatal care by the angel of the Lord? Are Manoah and his wife in the habit of drinking wine and eating unclean food? We simply do not know. Perhaps the warning is to keep the woman as healthy as possible to give birth to this son who is destined to become Israel's next deliverer. Perhaps she is to identify with her son as much as possible. Regardless, she pays attention.

5. For, lo, thou shalt conceive, and bear a son; and no razor shall come on his head: for the child shall be a Nazarite unto God from the womb: and he shall begin to deliver Israel out of the hand of the Philistines.

The details concerning the Nazarite vow come from Numbers 6:1-21 (see the Lesson Background). In Acts 18:18, we see Paul fulfilling a vow that involves the cutting of hair. What we see here, however, is a permanent prohibition against getting a haircut. This Nazarite vow will be for life. We also notice a divine call before birth (compare Isaiah 52:13–53:12; Jeremiah 1:4, 5). Very few people are bound with such lifetime vows before birth (Samson, Samuel, and John the Baptist).

What Do You Think?

What are some things that churches and parents can do to foster spiritual growth in children?

Talking Points for Your Discussion
- Deciding when to use secular resources, if ever
- Achieving consensus on needs/expectations
- Evaluating the effectiveness of children's ministry programs

This son is to *begin to deliver Israel out of the hand of the Philistines.* The author of Judges is well aware that Samson only "begins" the process, which will continue with Samuel, Saul, and Jonathan, culminating with David. This thought gives full understanding to the repeated theme of Judges: "In those days there was no king in Israel . . . every man did that which was right in his own eyes" (Judges 17:6; 21:25). Among other things, the oppression of the Philistines is not overcome until there is a king over Israel.

II. Retelling

(JUDGES 13:6, 7)

A. Visitor Described (v. 6)

6. Then the woman came and told her husband, saying, A man of God came unto me, and his countenance was like the countenance of an angel of God, very terrible: but I asked him not whence he was, neither told he me his name.

Manoah's wife calls the mysterious visitor *a man of God,* which is a term for prophets (see Deuteronomy 33:1; Joshua 14:6; etc.). However, she knows he is something more than a prophet. She describes his appearance to be that of *an angel of God,* and literally from the Hebrew "very fearful" or *terrible* (meaning "causing terror").

But she has not asked where he comes from or what his name is. In ancient culture, the request for one's home and/or name is important for hospitality's sake. But names can be used for magical purposes as well. Thus, to give one's name is a favor to the host, but it also makes one vulnerable. The third commandment forbids using God's name in any magical way, among other things (Deuteronomy 5:11). Later, Manoah will ask the angel of God his name, but it will not be revealed (see Judges 13:17, 18; compare Genesis 32:29).

❧ *RECOGNIZABLE?* ❧

How do you recognize a "man of God"? How would you know one if you saw one? Manoah's wife had no problem in this regard, since the extreme appearance of "the angel of the Lord" allowed her to draw no other conclusion.

But sometimes a "man of God" will be recognizable not by appearance, but by word and deed. One of the most significant in this regard was Boniface, the famous missionary to eighth-century Germany. When he appeared in Geismar, the locals ignored him because they were devoted to Thor, whom they worshiped at a "sacred" oak tree. Boniface chopped down the tree, cut the wood into lumber for a chapel, and converted the local population. He came as a man of God.

Boniface was invited into the neighboring kingdom of Frankland (later known as France). There the clergy was corrupt, nobility ruled churches as their private possessions, and discipline was lax throughout the country. Boniface reformed the clergy, removed the churches from the nobility's possession, and straightened out the church. He came to them as a man of God.

Perhaps today you can speak God's words to your family and your neighbors. You can stand for what is right and resist corruption. You can trust in the Lord and break the addictive power of sin in your own life as well as the lives of others. You can be a man or woman of God. When you are, others will notice.   —J. B. N.

> **What Do You Think?**
> How will you be a man or woman of God today in such a way that others will notice?
> *Talking Points for Your Discussion*
> - In word
> - In deed

B. Promise Related (v. 7)

7. But he said unto me, Behold, thou shalt conceive, and bear a son; and now drink no wine nor strong drink, neither eat any unclean thing: for the child shall be a Nazarite to God from the womb to the day of his death.

Manoah's wife retells the promise in a summarized fashion. However, at the last phrase concerning his being a Nazarite to God from the womb, she adds *to the day of his death,* as if to emphasize the lifetime commitment. She also does not mention the purpose for the birth of this son—the beginning of the deliverance of Israel from Philistine oppression. Surely this is communicated to her husband at some time during these anxious moments, although not recorded in the story.

> **What Do You Think?**
> What "essentials" do you think should guide churches and parents as they partner to prepare children for Christian service?
> *Talking Points for Your Discussion*
> - Spiritual issues
> - Physical issues
> - Emotional issues

III. Responsibility

(JUDGES 13:8, 24, 25)

A. Help Requested (v. 8)

8. Then Manoah intreated the LORD, and said, O my Lord, let the man of God which thou didst send come again unto us, and teach us what we shall do unto the child that shall be born.

After hearing his wife's testimony concerning the mysterious visitor, Manoah makes a specific petition to God. He calls God *my Lord,* thus posturing himself as a servant and God as master. He wants God to resend the messenger. At the end of the verb *come,* Manoah uses a polite word of entreaty that essentially means "please" (pronounced *na;* see the use of this word also in the discussion of Judges 10:15 in last week's lesson).

Negatively, we might view Manoah as a skeptic who needs firsthand experience with *the man of God* to be convinced. Viewed from a more positive angle, Manoah simply may want to be sure he "gets it right" regarding how to rear a child who is destined to confront Philistine oppression. Thus Manoah makes the specific petition a polite one in hopes of learning from the man of God how to raise a Nazarite so that he may accomplish God's purposes on earth. The prayer *teach us what we shall do unto the child that shall be born* is one that all expectant parents should pray!

> **What Do You Think?**
> If an expectant parent were to pray Manoah's prayer today, how might he or she evaluate the result as being a response from God?
> *Talking Points for Your Discussion*
> - The test of Scripture
> - The test of personal experience
> - The test of logic

Verses 9-23, not in today's text, narrate how the angel of the Lord reveals himself to Manoah and his wife. Also addressed are Manoah's question about how to raise the son to be born and to what purpose, the angel's instructions, how the angel goes up into the flames of the sacrifice, and finally the response of Manoah and his wife.

B. Son Blessed (v. 24)

24. And the woman bare a son, and called his name Samson: and the child grew, and the LORD blessed him.

Thus the promise is fulfilled just as the angel of the Lord had said. Why his name is called *Samson* is a mystery, for Samson comes from a Hebrew word that means "sun." The village of Bethshemesh ("House of the Sun," or temple of the god Shemesh) is located only a couple of miles from Samson's home in Zorah. Sun worship is not unknown among the Israelites (see 2 Kings 23:11; compare Deuteronomy 4:19). Regardless, the child grows, and God blesses him as He does other special children (1 Samuel 2:26; Luke 2:52).

C. Spirit Stirs (v. 25)

25. And the Spirit of the LORD began to move him at times in the camp of Dan between Zorah and Eshtaol.

The mission of Samson is "a divine thing." Samson can never accomplish his purpose in life without the Spirit's guidance and movement (see for other judges: Judges 3:10; 6:34; 11:29; compare 1 Samuel 16:13 for David).

Reference to *the camp of Dan* suggests temporary dwellings, for the people seem to be living in tents. Zorah and Eshtaol are only a mile apart, and there is a spring running between them. This is the place where the Spirit begins to move Samson; this seems to be preliminary to the Spirit's actions in Judges 14:6.

We recognize that the faithfulness and carefulness of Samson's parents do not account for the reckless and irresponsible manner in which Samson later conducts himself (Judges 14–16). But in spite of Samson's breaking of every Nazarite vow, God still begins to deliver Israel from the Philistines through Samson. Probably the 20 years of Samson's "ministry" (Judges 16:31) are the last 20 years of Philistine oppression, thus being contemporary with Samuel's early ministry. Samuel's victory at Ebenezer (1 Samuel 7:10-13) is likely the Philistines' last grab for power after Samson's defeat of them at the time of his death. In spite of all that, it will take King David's military victories to eliminate this threat (2 Samuel 5:17-25).

I do not consider myself to be a charismatic, and I rarely use the phrase, "The Lord showed me . . ." At the same time, I willingly and gladly acknowledge that the Lord moves in mysterious ways to accomplish His purposes. The probable result is that I have been slow to say "the Lord has done this" when the Spirit of the Lord has worked through various circumstances.

Martin Luther (1483–1546) realized that there were numerous applications of late medieval Catholicism that needed reforming. The Spirit of the Lord worked through him, giving him the courage and tenacity to work for a purer church. Thomas Campbell (1763–1854) saw the numerous problems of sectarian denominationalism in America. So he worked to eliminate this divisiveness by emphasizing the unity of the church based on the simple teachings of the New Testament. The Spirit of the Lord had moved him. Billy Graham began in the late 1940s to preach an evangelical message of revival that led him to become a world figure in preaching crusades. The Spirit of the Lord had moved through him.

How is the Spirit of the Lord trying to work through your life today? How could the Spirit of the Lord move more efficiently and effectively if you were completely devoted to Him? —J. B. N.

Conclusion

A. Need for Leadership

There is always a need for proper leadership in the church. In fact, we need good leadership at all levels of society. Where will this leadership come from? The best source is from committed Christian parents who will raise up their children by Christian principles. Encouragement should be given to these young people to attend Christian educational institutions that specialize in biblical teaching, Christian worldview studies, and ministry/mission training.

On the other hand, God can raise up leadership from unexpected places. Personally, I came from a purely pagan background. I had no hope of being in Christian leadership except for a little lady in a black Nash (a brand of automobile dis-

Visual for Lessons 9 & 10. *Point to this visual as you ask, "What are famous examples of people being used by God in spite their having a disability?"*

continued in the 1950s), who gave my sister and me a ride to Bible school each Sunday for about five years. That is what it took to lead me to Christ and Christian ministry.

One of my students had a terrible family background. His father was a drug addict who was imprisoned several times; his mother was not much better. He spent much of his early childhood in foster homes. A leader in a local church befriended him, eventually leading him to Christ and baptizing him. This leader encouraged him to attend a Bible college, and he did. Now this student is a youth minister in his hometown church. He is a dedicated, committed, and growing minister of the gospel.

God can raise up leadership from any place. But there must be churches and individuals committed to searching for potential leaders. Christian men and women should encourage not only their own children, but also the lost children of others to become the leaders they ought to be.

B. Prayer

Our Father, it is difficult at best to rear children properly in a culture of godless materialism. Help us to help our children and grandchildren to respond to the call of leadership and to seek spiritual maturity. In Jesus' name, amen.

C. Thought to Remember

Teach the next generation.

INVOLVEMENT LEARNING

Some of the activities below are also found in the helpful student book, Adult Bible Class.
Don't forget to download the free reproducible page from www.standardlesson.com to enhance your lesson!

Into the Lesson

Before class, divide your learning space into two sections with obvious signs *Good Parents* and *Bad Parents*. Assure learners as they arrive that the designations are for an activity, not to label class members themselves! Begin class by saying, "As you notice the section you are in, answer this question: 'What characterizes the kind of parent of the sign you are under?'" Jot responses on the board. Responses will no doubt include some entries you can relate to Manoah and his wife, as today's study progresses.

Into the Word

Read aloud Judges 13:1-8, 24, 25. Then work through the text in the following groupings.

Verse 1, Philistine oppression. Review briefly the sin cycle of the period of the judges, as given in previous lessons of this quarter. Identify where Samson fits in the timeline of the judges.

Verse 2, a barren woman. Distribute to half the class handouts with these six scrambled words: *AAHRS, ABEEHKR, ACEHLR, AAHHNN, ABEEHILTS.* To the other half of the class, assign the following six text-clusters: Genesis 21:1-3; Genesis 25:21, 24-26a; Genesis 29:31; 1 Samuel 1:2, 20; Luke 1:7, 13. Ask the first group to begin unscrambling the words (give the hint that they are women's names); ask the other group to find and read their texts.

As the first group begins to identify the names *Sarah, Rebekah, Rachel, Hannah,* and *Elisabeth,* have the second group read the related verses. After all are identified, ask, "Why did I not include the name of the barren woman of Judges 13:2?" The answer, of course, is that Samson's mother goes unnamed in the Scriptures.

Verse 3 and 6, angel of the Lord. Summarize the lesson writer's observations. *Option:* To expand this section, use an online concordance to create a handout that lists some "angel of the Lord" passages (there are over five dozen in the Bible). Discuss a few of these, but don't let this section drag out.

Verses 4, 5, 7, the Nazarite vow. Stress that understanding the concept of the Nazarite vow is important for full comprehension of Samson's life. Recruit two or more of your good oral readers to read aloud Numbers 6:1-21, alternating verses. Then ask, "What inconveniences and burdens does this Nazarite vow present to the one who is a Nazarite for life?" Let the class summarize, but note, among other things, the problem of not being able to participate in the burial ceremony of a parent who dies. Point out that this vow was taken for Samson by Samson's parents, not by Samson himself.

Verses 8, 24, 25, the context of Samson's early life. Use this segment to compare and contrast the responsibilities of Samson's parents with those of parents today.

Into Life

Note that God in His Word has direction for parents, with Manoah and his wife as potential examples. Ask your class to suggest principles of parenting from today's text. The following may be offered: 1. Know that every child is a gift from God (v. 3). 2. Mothers-to-be need to keep themselves healthy (v. 4). 3. Parents need to discuss the role of God in the life of their yet-to-be-born child (vv. 6, 7). 4. Seeking the wisdom of God for parenting skills is always appropriate (v. 8). 5. Watching for the blessing of God as the child grows should be natural (vv. 24, 25).

Finish by distributing *Congratulations on the New Baby* cards that you or a class member have created. Suggest that class members look for an opportunity in the week ahead to share an idea from today's lesson with an expectant or new parent. (Note: use this idea with sensitivity if there are members of your class who are childless.)

Distribute copies of both activities on the reproducible page as take-home work.

Walk in God's Path

MAKING A CHOICE

BACKGROUND SCRIPTURE: Ruth 1
PRINTED TEXT: Ruth 1:8-18

RUTH 1:8-18

8 And Naomi said unto her two daughters in law, Go, return each to her mother's house: the LORD deal kindly with you, as ye have dealt with the dead, and with me.

9 The LORD grant you that ye may find rest, each of you in the house of her husband. Then she kissed them; and they lifted up their voice, and wept.

10 And they said unto her, Surely we will return with thee unto thy people.

11 And Naomi said, Turn again, my daughters: why will ye go with me? are there yet any more sons in my womb, that they may be your husbands?

12 Turn again, my daughters, go your way; for I am too old to have an husband. If I should say, I have hope, if I should have an husband also to night, and should also bear sons;

13 Would ye tarry for them till they were grown? would ye stay for them from having husbands? nay, my daughters; for it grieveth me much for your sakes that the hand of the LORD is gone out against me.

14 And they lifted up their voice, and wept again: and Orpah kissed her mother in law; but Ruth clave unto her.

15 And she said, Behold, thy sister in law is gone back unto her people, and unto her gods: return thou after thy sister in law.

16 And Ruth said, Intreat me not to leave thee, or to return from following after thee: for whither thou goest, I will go; and where thou lodgest, I will lodge: thy people shall be my people, and thy God my God:

17 Where thou diest, will I die, and there will I be buried: the LORD do so to me, and more also, if ought but death part thee and me.

18 When she saw that she was stedfastly minded to go with her, then she left speaking unto her.

KEY VERSE

Ruth said, Intreat me not to leave thee, or to return from following after thee: for whither thou goest, I will go; and where thou lodgest, I will lodge: thy people shall be my people, and thy God my God. —**Ruth 1:16**

GOD INSTRUCTS HIS PEOPLE

Unit 3: A Case Study in Community

LESSON AIMS

After participating in this lesson, each student will be able to:

1. Summarize the exchange between Naomi and her daughters-in-law.

2. Explain why Ruth's choice to stay with Naomi was both caring and costly.

3. Suggest a series of practical steps on how to minister to someone going through a difficult circumstance.

LESSON OUTLINE

Introduction

A. Mistakes in the Bible

The July 2008 issue of *Reader's Digest* included an article titled "41 Secrets Your Doctor Would Never Share (Until Now)." The comments were obtained from two dozen physicians, both general practitioners and specialists. Some of the observations were humorous, but many revealed an extreme degree of frustration over certain aspects of the medical profession. Said one respondent, "In many ways, doctors are held to an unrealistic standard. We are never, ever allowed to make a mistake. I don't know anybody who can live that way." In truth, no one can live "mistake free."

The Bible's recording of the "mistakes" or sins of the people is one of the qualities that makes the Bible the timeless, ever-relevant treasure that it is. Yes, there are "mistakes in the Bible," to use the heading of this section, but we're not talking about mistakes of a factual nature. Rather, what we're talking about is the Bible's brutal honesty about the failures of the people it describes. From Abraham to David to Peter, the Bible is consistent in recording the mistakes and inconsistencies of even its "heroes."

What is true of individuals is also true in the record of the history of Old Testament Israel. Sadly, that history is pockmarked with Israel's sinful mistakes in failing to obey God. His faithfulness to His people was exemplary; theirs to Him was woefully deficient. This is well illustrated by contrasting the accounts in the books of Joshua and Judges. Albert Baylis's assessment of their contents is true: "If the book of Joshua is a flowing stream, fresh and invigorating with direction and power, then in Judges the river turns sluggish and muddy, its polluted water ultimately spiraling down a storm drain."

And yet, in the midst of the pollution of the period of the judges emerges a story that provides a welcome breath of fresh air—the story of Ruth.

B. Lesson Background

The book of Ruth is set "in the days when the judges ruled" (Ruth 1:1). The period of the judges covers the years of approximately 1373 to 1050 BC.

The account of Ruth may have occurred in the latter portion of the 1100s BC, since Ruth was the great-grandmother of David, who began his rule as king in 1010 BC. The four generations from Ruth to David fit within the time thus designated.

The book of Ruth begins with a choice made by a man named Elimelech, a resident of Bethlehem, to leave his homeland of Judah because of a famine. He took his wife, Naomi, and sons Mahlon and Chilion to Moab, located south and east of the Dead Sea (a journey of perhaps 50 miles). At some point, Elimelech died (Ruth 1:3). Tragedy struck again about 10 years later when Mahlon and Chilion died (1:4, 5; the cause of death is not stated). They had married Moabite women: Mahlon married Ruth, and Chilion married Orpah (1:4; 4:10). Ruth 1:5 captures the sense of loss: "and the woman was left of her two sons and her husband." Naomi was in an especially vulnerable position. Not only was she a widow, she was a widow in a foreign land.

Eventually word came to Naomi that the famine in Judah had come to an end (Ruth 1:6). Naomi determined that she would return to Judah. Her daughters-in-law decided to travel with her (1:7). They formed a rather curious trio. Though mother-in-law and daughters-in-law came from different religious and social backgrounds, they were bound by the common thread of their tragedies: each woman's husband had died. Each faced a very uncertain and troubling future.

I. First Plea

(RUTH 1:8-10)

A. Tender Words (vv. 8, 9a)

8. And Naomi said unto her two daughters in law, Go, return each to her mother's house: the LORD deal kindly with you, as ye have dealt with the dead, and with me.

We do not know how far the three women travel before Naomi urges her two daughters-in-law to return to Moab. Nor do we know what the trio may discuss as they journey. But at some point Naomi realizes that it is better for Orpah and Ruth to return to their homes in Moab rather than continue with her to Judah.

So Naomi encourages Orpah and Ruth to return *each to her mother's house*. It seems, from other Old Testament passages, that the usual practice is for a widow to return to her father's house (as in Genesis 38:11; Leviticus 22:13), not her mother's. Naomi's words may reflect the existence of a custom whereby marriages are arranged in the mother's house, since remarriage is what she desires for her daughters-in-law, as the next verse indicates.

In the blessing Naomi offers to Orpah and Ruth, Naomi acknowledges the kindness of those two to this point. They do not have to accompany Naomi to Judah, but they want to. Naomi's statement recognizes that they have also dealt in a similar manner with the dead (that is, their husbands) by not abandoning the husbands' mother after the deaths.

Acting with kindness is one of the key themes in the book of Ruth. Later Naomi will note the Lord's "kindness" after hearing of the way Boaz has treated Ruth by allowing her to glean in his field (Ruth 2:20). Still later, at the threshing floor, Boaz will acknowledge Ruth's "kindness" in recognizing his position as a kinsman and approaching him about fulfilling that role (3:10).

> **What Do You Think?**
> What are some kind deeds others have done for you in a difficult time? What are some that were counterproductive? How do these experiences influence your deeds for others?
>
> *Talking Points for Your Discussion*
> - The role of listening
> - "Counseling" vs. "giving advice"
> - The helper's focus: on the other or on self?

9a. The LORD grant you that ye may find rest, each of you in the house of her husband.

Naomi specifies the nature of the "kindness" she desires the Lord to show to her daughters-in-law. The concept of *rest* carries with it the idea of security. The plight of widows in the ancient world is especially difficult. They are often taken advantage of by unscrupulous people in positions of power. This is true in Jesus' day (Luke 20:47). The Law of Moses includes special commands regarding the care of widows (Exodus 22:22-24; Deuteronomy

14:28, 29; 24:19-22). The prophets often call attention to violations of such commandments and to God's disapproval (Isaiah 1:17, 23; Jeremiah 7:5-7; Zechariah 7:8-10). Compassion toward widows (and other neglected groups) is to characterize followers of Jesus (Acts 6:1-3; 1 Timothy 5:3-8, 16; James 1:27).

❧ WHAT KIND OF REST? ❧

Many decades ago, I saw a cartoon that has remained in my memory. It showed two mountaineers relaxing on a front porch smoking their corncob pipes. In the background was a woman bending over a washboard scrubbing clothes in sudsy water. One mountaineer was saying to the other, "I'd like to get something for my wife, but she has just about every convenience imaginable."

On the American frontier of the nineteenth century, the labor required of a woman to maintain the home was daunting, to say the least. All cooking had to be done over an open fire. Water had to be brought in by pails from a well or a nearby creek. Clothing was made by hand. All washing also was done by hand. The men did the plowing, but the women milked the cows, churned the butter, tended the vegetable garden, slopped the hogs, fed the chickens, gathered the eggs, and saw to the "book learning" of the younger children.

All these duties would have been common for women in biblical times as well. So when Naomi talked of her daughters-in-law finding "rest" in the home of a husband, she was not talking about a life of leisure! Rather, she was talking about security and protection. It is in this sense that Jesus says we will find rest for our souls in Him (Matthew 11:29). This is not referring to physical lei-

sure, for we all have work to do for the kingdom of God. The eternal security and protection Jesus offers is the best kind of rest there is! —J. B. N.

B. Touching Response (vv. 9b, 10)

9b, 10. Then she kissed them; and they lifted up their voice, and wept. And they said unto her, Surely we will return with thee unto thy people.

The initial reaction of both daughters-in-law appears firm. They cannot bear to leave Naomi to fend for herself.

II. Second Plea
(RUTH 1:11-14)
A. Naomi's Desperation (vv. 11-13)

11. And Naomi said, Turn again, my daughters: why will ye go with me? are there yet any more sons in my womb, that they may be your husbands?

Naomi attempts to reason with Orpah and Ruth, encouraging them to think of the big picture. Is Naomi, at her age, in a position to have sons whom the two eventually can marry?

Naomi's words reflect the existence of what is often called *the levirate law* in Old Testament Israel. (The word *levirate* comes from the Latin *levir,* meaning "brother-in-law.") Under this provision (described in Deuteronomy 25:5, 6), if a married man dies without fathering any children, his brother is to marry the widow. The firstborn of this union will be considered the child of the man who died childless.

This law has a twofold purpose: (1) it is meant to provide a measure of security or protection for a widow, and (2) it ensures that the deceased's family line will continue. Naomi's two sons died childless, and she recognizes that her age precludes her from having any more sons who can become husbands for Orpah and Ruth.

12, 13a. Turn again, my daughters, go your way; for I am too old to have an husband. If I should say, I have hope, if I should have an husband also to night, and should also bear sons; would ye tarry for them till they were grown? would ye stay for them from having husbands?

Naomi continues her appeal by creating a hypothetical situation. Even if she could somehow find and marry a man that very night and bear sons through him, it would be foolish to expect Orpah and Ruth to wait until these sons are in a position to marry them. The phrase *stay for them from having husbands* conveys a similar meaning. Orpah and Ruth should not be expected to stay unmarried while waiting *for them* (Naomi's hypothetical sons) to reach the age of marriage.

13b. Nay, my daughters; for it grieveth me much for your sakes that the hand of the LORD is gone out against me.

Naomi concludes her appeal by voicing the bitterness she feels concerning her status. The plight of all three women is indeed desperate, but more so for Naomi because of her advanced age. At least Orpah and Ruth are young enough that they can remarry and find the rest, or security, that appears unattainable in Naomi's case.

It is interesting to consider Naomi's words *the hand of the Lord is gone out against me* in comparison with her earlier references to the Lord's kindness (v. 8, above). Here she contends that the Lord has been anything but kind to her. Rather than seeing some kind of contradiction in Naomi's words, it may be best to recognize her very human frustration with her circumstances and with how God is working in all of this. Anyone who has experienced bereavement and the resulting turmoil of emotions can likely see himself or herself in Naomi at this point.

What Do You Think?

What was a time you had a negative attitude toward God because of a difficult circumstance? How did you grow spiritually as a result?

Talking Points for Your Discussion

- Biblical examples of complaints: Numbers 14:1-4; 1 Kings 19:4, 10, 14; Jonah 4:2, 3, 9
- God's responses to complaints: Numbers 14:26-29; 1 Kings 19:11-13, 15, 16; Jonah 4:4, 10
- Responding in faith despite doubt: Mark 9:24; Luke 5:5

B. Orpah's Departure (v. 14)

14. And they lifted up their voice, and wept again: and Orpah kissed her mother in law; but Ruth clave unto her.

More weeping results from Naomi's anguished words, but this time it is followed by action—at least on Orpah's part. She kisses her mother-in-law farewell. Ruth, however, is not persuaded. She clings to Naomi. The Hebrew word translated *clave* is the word rendered as "cleave" in Genesis 2:24, which describes the bond that God intends to exist between a husband and wife. Such is the strength of Ruth's devotion to her mother-in-law.

III. Third Plea
(RUTH 1:15-18)

A. Naomi's Counsel (v. 15)

15. And she said, Behold, thy sister in law is gone back unto her people, and unto her gods: return thou after thy sister in law.

With the departure of Orpah, Naomi now has some additional leverage with which to strengthen her appeal to Ruth: *thy sister in law is gone back unto her people, and unto her gods*. Naomi's argument includes two important parts of one's identity in the ancient Near East: one's people and one's gods.

The first one appeals to Ruth's sense of national identity; she should return to her people—the culture and surroundings with which she is most familiar. The second appeals to Ruth's religious identity. Naomi earlier had asked the Lord's (her God's) blessing on Ruth and Orpah (vv. 8, 9, above); here she acknowledges the importance of the religion that is a part of Ruth's upbringing. The Moabites are worshipers of many gods, though they paid homage to a chief god known as Chemosh (called "the abomination of Moab" in 1 Kings 11:7).

B. Ruth's Commitment (vv. 16-18)

16. And Ruth said, Intreat me not to leave thee, or to return from following after thee: for whither thou goest, I will go; and where thou lodgest, I will lodge: thy people shall be my people, and thy God my God.

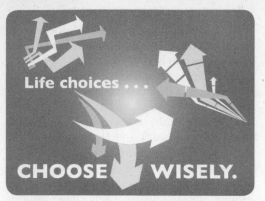

Visual for Lesson 11. *Point to this visual as you ask, "What was a life choice you made that seemed minor at the time, but had major consequences?"*

Ruth's expression of devotion to Naomi is often used in wedding ceremonies at the point when bride and groom express their commitments to one another. This is not an inappropriate use of these words, but the original setting in which these sentiments are uttered should not be forgotten. Ruth is declaring that she has come to a new chapter in the story of her life. She is breaking ties with her heritage and establishing a new identity: Naomi's people (the Israelites) will now be her people and Naomi's God (the Lord) will be her God. For Ruth, this is a kind of "Good Confession" of faith.

One should not overlook the fact that this is a very costly, sacrificial decision for Ruth to make. She is choosing to share in Naomi's plight, which, as Naomi has already stated, is virtually hopeless. Although Naomi has not been speaking very favorably about her God (v. 13, above), Ruth nonetheless affirms a clear allegiance to Him!

> **What Do You Think?**
> What are some ways to connect with people of other nationalities or religious backgrounds so that they might come to faith as Ruth did?
> *Talking Points for Your Discussion*
> ▪ Issues of "where" (Acts 17:17)
> ▪ Issues of "transparency" (1 Corinthians 2:1-5)

17. Where thou diest, will I die, and there will I be buried: the LORD do so to me, and more also, if ought but death part thee and me.

Ruth adds yet a further demonstration of the degree of her commitment. In ancient times, the place of one's burial is a matter of great significance. One's final resting place makes a statement regarding the location with which he or she wants most to be identified (Genesis 47:29-31; 50:24, 25). Ruth, however, has no family members buried in the place where Naomi will be buried (other than Naomi herself). This is another way for Ruth to claim Naomi's people as hers.

Ruth concludes her declaration of loyalty with an oath: *the Lord do so to me, and more also, if ought* [meaning "anything"] *but death part thee and me*. This kind of "till death do us part" devotion is the likely reason why Ruth's words continue to be included in wedding ceremonies.

18. When she saw that she was stedfastly minded to go with her, then she left speaking unto her.

Naomi now realizes that Ruth will not be swayed from her decision. Like Abraham, Ruth has chosen to leave her people and her household behind and travel to a new chapter of her life. Naomi's God will be the author of whatever lies ahead.

> **What Do You Think?**
> In a mobile society, what are some ways to "go with" others? Why is it important to do so?
> *Talking Points for Your Discussion*
> ▪ Benefits and limitations of technology: e-mail, Facebook, Twitter
> ▪ Impact of our choices
> ▪ Long-distance spiritual "connection" (Colossians 2:5)
> ▪ God's role

❧ WHEREVER YOU GO . . . ❧

We think of Ruth as the devoted daughter-in-law who committed herself to stay with Naomi. But what does Ruth's devotion say about Naomi? What kind of person was Naomi that Ruth would make this commitment to her? Perhaps Naomi represented a magnetic lifestyle of love that inspired Ruth to want to follow her literally to the ends of the earth.

Making a Choice

Another person with a magnetic personality was Francis of Assisi (1181/82–1226). The son of a wealthy cloth merchant, Francis felt a call to live a simple life of poverty and sacrifice for the benefit of others. So he abandoned his father's wealth, became a hermit monk, and lived by begging for the leftovers from other people's meals. With his own hands he began the repair of several decrepit churches around Assisi and was soon involved in various acts of mercy. His actions inspired other young men to commit themselves to his leadership and lifestyle. They formed a monastic order that today we know as the Franciscans.

Naomi's attitude and lifestyle drew Ruth to want to share them. The same was true of Francis and his followers. What kind of example will you set today that will have others wanting to follow in your footsteps? —J. B. N.

Conclusion

A. More Than a Case Study

The three lessons from Ruth in this quarter are being considered under the topic "A Case Study in Community." If one thinks of a community as simply a group in society, then there are many "communities" that are part of one's life.

We enter a community known as a family the moment we are born. As we grow and mature, we are placed in other communities where we have very little choice in the matter (a school, for example). Eventually, however, we find ourselves in a position to be more selective about those communities with which we choose to identify. Most people find that such communities provide a feel-

ing of companionship and camaraderie that helps one cope with the demands and pressures of daily living. Many in our society are hungry for such a sense of belonging; unfortunately, some turn to dishonest sources (gangs, for example) to fill that void.

One summer, I watched a softball game in which my younger son was playing. As the game neared its end, players from the teams who were to play in the next game began to gather. Some of the players' wives or girlfriends had come along to watch. One girl stood off to the side. She was obviously upset about something and appeared to be on the verge of tears. Another girl sitting in the bleachers with some of her friends noticed the girl standing alone and called out to her. "Hey, it looks to me like you need to vent. Why don't you come over to my house later and vent? My friends come to my place all the time, and all they do is vent. You'll fit right in." Slowly the girl made her way over to the others in the bleachers, and before long she was laughing with the rest of them. She had found a "community" that would help her get through whatever it was that bothered her.

Such an attitude of openness, love, and acceptance should characterize the church. Tragically, it seems that at times groups such as softball teams seem to grasp the concept of real fellowship better than followers of Jesus do! The pagan world takes the initiative at reaching out and showing community, while the church stays on the sidelines, doing little or nothing to touch hurting people.

The story of Ruth needs to be more than just *a case study*. It should be *a care study*—one that challenges us to action, to establish community with others, to choose to care as Jesus did.

B. Prayer

Father, it is easy for us to remain isolated and distant from the needs of those around us and to think of reasons for doing so. Help us not to live by such a standard; help us instead to live by a higher standard—Yours. In the name of Jesus who left Heaven's glory to save us, amen.

C. Thought to Remember

Reach out to others as Jesus did.

HOW TO SAY IT

Assisi	Uh-*sih*-see.
Boaz	*Bo*-az.
Chilion	*Kil*-ee-on.
Elimelech	Ee-*lim*-eh-leck.
Judah	*Joo*-duh.
levirate	*leh*-vuh-rut.
Mahlon	*Mah*-lon.
Moab	*Mo*-ab.
Orpah	*Or*-pah.

INVOLVEMENT LEARNING

Some of the activities below are also found in the helpful student book, Adult Bible Class.
Don't forget to download the free reproducible page from www.standardlesson.com to enhance your lesson!

Into the Lesson

Download the reproducible page and put copies of the Choices activity in chairs for learners to begin working on as they arrive. As class begins, say, "Some choices are very important; other choices less so. Some choices are easy; some are difficult. Some have heavy consequences; some do not. Today's study is all about 'Making a Choice,' and the choices involved are serious: moving, changing cultures, and embracing a different religious viewpoint." To set the context for this lesson and the next two, recruit two of your good oral readers to read Ruth 1:1-7 before the class, alternating either verses or paragraphs.

Into the Word

Have on display several cardboard boxes of various sizes. Comment: "There is a word of six letters that implies lots of physical exertion and emotional distress. That word is M-O-V-I-N-G! When moving, we have to make choices regarding what to take and what to leave behind."

Have one box clearly labeled *LEAVE* and another box labeled *TAKE;* don't display those labels until this point in the lesson. Draw an invisible line down the middle of your class, and give the two sides these directions, as you indicate sides: "You on the *LEAVE* side are to look at today's text and context and tell us what Naomi and her daughters-in-law were leaving behind as they departed Moab. You who are on the *TAKE* side are to look at today's text and context and tell us what Naomi and her daughters-in-law were taking on their move." Stress to your learners that they should not think solely in terms of tangible things. (*Option:* If your class is large, use small groups and give duplicate assignments.)

Allow groups time to read the text and make their choices. Alternate between sides as you call for answers. As a suggestion is made, jot it on a sheet of paper and "pack" it in the appropriate box.

Expect a variety of ideas. Here is a sampling: *leave*—Naomi leaves Orpah (v. 14); Orpah leaves Naomi (v. 14); Ruth leaves the possibility of marrying a Moabite husband (v. 16); Ruth leaves the gods/religion of her culture (v. 16); at least Naomi and Ruth leave behind the graves of their husbands; *take*—Orpah takes/keeps the familiarity of Moab (v. 14); Ruth takes a firm commitment to the God of Israel (v. 16); Ruth takes/keeps a deep love for Naomi (vv. 16, 17); Naomi takes a conviction that God is working against her (v. 13).

Into Life

Conduct a "What Would You Say to Encourage . . . ?" discussion. Ask that question three times, using the names of Naomi, Ruth, and Orpah once each. Let the class respond.

At the end, ask the class to generalize responses to the question, "Without being flippant or superficial, what would you say to encourage someone who is going through difficult circumstances, based on the principles learned from today's study?" Accept learner responses. Some possibilities include: "Challenge the individual to make a willful, personal decision" (v. 8a); "Petition God's blessing, even as you give your own" (v. 8b); "Suggest positive possibilities" (v. 9); "Be realistic, but optimistic" (vv. 12, 13a); "Resist the temptation to blame God" (v. 13b); "Once decisions and commitments are made, accept them and move on" (v. 18). You might decide simply to introduce these principles and let the class reflect the basis for each from the text.

Note that Naomi considered herself a victim of God's displeasure. That is the reason she calls herself *Mara* ("Bitter") in verses 20, 21 (not in today's text). Ask the class to explain how circumstances can be interpreted in more than one direction. Distribute the Naomi or Mara? activity from the reproducible page as a take-home exercise so your learners can examine this idea further.

EMPOWERING
THE NEEDY

BACKGROUND SCRIPTURE: Ruth 2, 3; Leviticus 19:9, 10
PRINTED TEXT: Ruth 2:8-18

RUTH 2:8-18

8 Then said Boaz unto Ruth, Hearest thou not, my daughter? Go not to glean in another field, neither go from hence, but abide here fast by my maidens:

9 Let thine eyes be on the field that they do reap, and go thou after them: have I not charged the young men that they shall not touch thee? and when thou art athirst, go unto the vessels, and drink of that which the young men have drawn.

10 Then she fell on her face, and bowed herself to the ground, and said unto him, Why have I found grace in thine eyes, that thou shouldest take knowledge of me, seeing I am a stranger?

11 And Boaz answered and said unto her, It hath fully been shewed me, all that thou hast done unto thy mother in law since the death of thine husband: and how thou hast left thy father and thy mother, and the land of thy nativity, and art come unto a people which thou knewest not heretofore.

12 The LORD recompense thy work, and a full reward be given thee of the LORD God of Israel, under whose wings thou art come to trust.

13 Then she said, Let me find favour in thy sight, my lord; for that thou hast comforted me, and for that thou hast spoken friendly unto thine handmaid, though I be not like unto one of thine handmaidens.

14 And Boaz said unto her, At mealtime come thou hither, and eat of the bread, and dip thy morsel in the vinegar. And she sat beside the reapers: and he reached her parched corn, and she did eat, and was sufficed, and left.

15 And when she was risen up to glean, Boaz commanded his young men, saying, Let her glean even among the sheaves, and reproach her not:

16 And let fall also some of the handfuls of purpose for her, and leave them, that she may glean them, and rebuke her not.

17 So she gleaned in the field until even, and beat out that she had gleaned: and it was about an ephah of barley.

18 And she took it up, and went into the city: and her mother in law saw what she had gleaned: and she brought forth, and gave to her that she had reserved after she was sufficed.

KEY VERSE

The LORD recompense thy work, and a full reward be given thee of the LORD God of Israel, under whose wings thou art come to trust. —**Ruth 2:12**

GOD INSTRUCTS HIS PEOPLE

Unit 3: A Case Study in Community

LESSONS 11–13

LESSON AIMS

After participating in this lesson, each student will be able to:

1. Describe the kindnesses that Boaz showed to Ruth while she was gleaning in his field.

2. Compare and contrast the manner in which Ruth was enabled to provide for herself and her mother-in-law with programs by which the government and/or the church help the poor today.

3. Suggest a way the class or church can empower the poor as Ruth was empowered.

LESSON OUTLINE

Introduction

A. The Day After

While working on these lessons during September of 2008, the city where I live (Cincinnati) experienced the impact of Hurricane Ike. The storm did most of its damage in the Galveston, Texas, area, then moved northward and entered the Ohio Valley. There Ike's winds struck with a force not experienced by most who live in this part of the country. Damage was extensive, with approximately 90 percent of the Greater Cincinnati area losing power because of Ike.

The day after the winds passed through, residents in our neighborhood spent most of the time cleaning up from the storm. Many could not go to work because their workplaces had no power. The conversations and interaction between neighbors as they talked about the storm and assisted one another with the cleanup was nice to see—but also, sad to say, unusual. Truth be told, most of us in our neighborhood do not take much initiative to visit or stop and chat. It often takes some kind of a dilemma to bring people out and get them talking with each other.

While it should not take a crisis to promote community, situations of need can provide special opportunities for this to occur. Today's lesson highlights the concern God's people should have for those in need by citing Boaz's example of kindness to Ruth. His initiative and his "second mile" helpfulness exemplify the kind of spirit followers of Jesus should demonstrate.

B. Lesson Background

Last week's study concluded with Ruth's determination to accompany her mother-in-law, Naomi, in traveling to Judah following the tragedies that had befallen them while living in Moab. The two women came to Bethlehem "in the beginning of barley harvest" (Ruth 1:22).

Apparently not long after their arrival, Ruth approached Naomi about going to the fields where the harvesting was taking place to gather "after him in whose sight I shall find grace" (Ruth 2:2). Ruth's request reflected a familiarity with one of the Israelite laws that provided for the needs of the impov-

Empowering the Needy

erished or of groups such as widows (including Naomi and Ruth), who had very few means of supporting themselves. The Law of Moses instructed Israelite farmers that special provisions were to be made to allow the needy to gather some of the harvest while harvesting was under way (Leviticus 19:9, 10; 23:22; Deuteronomy 24:19-22).

Naomi encouraged Ruth to follow through with her plan. Ruth proceeded to a field that belonged to a man named Boaz, who had been introduced previously in Ruth 2:1. There he is described as "a kinsman of her [Naomi's] husband's, a mighty man of wealth, of the family of Elimelech."

At some point after Ruth began her gleaning, Boaz arrived from Bethlehem. Before long, he inquired concerning the stranger in his field. He was informed that the woman had returned from Moab with Naomi. She had asked for permission to gather grain and had diligently carried out her task ever since her arrival. Curious to know more, Boaz approached the woman.

I. Boaz's Instruction
(RUTH 2:8-10)
A. Assurance (vv. 8, 9)

8. Then said Boaz unto Ruth, Hearest thou not, my daughter? Go not to glean in another field, neither go from hence, but abide here fast by my maidens.

What a pleasure it must be to work for Boaz! The first words he speaks in the book of Ruth are words of greeting to his reapers: "The Lord be with you" (Ruth 2:4). One must keep in mind that this account takes place during the time of the judges, when "every man did that which was right in his own eyes" (Judges 17:6; 21:25). Clearly Boaz is an exception to this rule (or lack of rules). The response of his reapers ("The Lord bless thee," v. 4) reflects a mutual respect.

Boaz's character is further demonstrated by his treatment of the stranger who has come to glean in his field. As previously noted, the Law of Moses required that during the time of reaping a landowner is to make special allowances for the needy to gather some of the harvest. The landowner is not required to speak to these individuals, yet

Boaz takes the initiative to assure Ruth that she, though a foreigner from Moab, will not be subjected to any kind of abuse or mistreatment. Perhaps he is aware that Ruth may be the target of verbal taunts or even physical harm because of her background. He tells her to *abide here fast* [close] *by my maidens.* She will not be left alone where she can be more vulnerable to harm.

9. Let thine eyes be on the field that they do reap, and go thou after them: have I not charged the young men that they shall not touch thee? and when thou art athirst, go unto the vessels, and drink of that which the young men have drawn.

Here is evidence of Boaz's "second mile" attitude. He repeats his directive that Ruth stay in his field and go with his servant girls. To provide further reassurance, he also informs Ruth of his instructions to the young men regarding their disposition toward her. The Hebrew word translated *touch* can have certain negative connotations and probably does in this passage. If Ruth has any fears about any mistreatment from the harvesters, Boaz desires to dispel them.

Boaz then takes his kindness a step further in providing water. Again, such a gesture as this is above and beyond what the Law of Moses requires. As a foreigner, Ruth probably expects to be commanded to draw water for the Israelites around her; instead, Boaz invites her to drink from the water that the Israelites have drawn!

> *What Do You Think?*
> Under what situations should we and should we not have a "second mile" attitude? Why?
> *Talking Points for Your Discussion*
> - Work, church, and family situations
> - Issues of discernment and enabling (Matthew 5:41; 7:6; 10:16; 2 Corinthians 8:13; 11:20, 21; 2 Thessalonians 3:10; Hebrews 13:2)

❧ CAN'T TOUCH THIS! ❧

In the colonial days of America, procuring agents for the British navy would often search through the forests of South Carolina looking for tall, straight pine trees. They needed trees of such quality to use as masts for British warships. When they found good specimens, they would put the king's royal mark on the trunk. Anyone cutting down such a marked tree was subject to heavy penalties, for the tree was protected by law and the king's identifying seal.

Boaz placed Ruth under similar protection. She did not have a physical mark placed upon her, but Boaz gave his servants instructions that she was under protection. Anyone troubling her would suffer consequences. She was "a marked woman," but certainly not in the negative sense of that phrase!

We too are "marked people." Consider our status in Christ: "ye heard the word of truth, the gospel of your salvation: in whom also after that ye believed, ye were sealed with that holy Spirit of promise" (Ephesians 1:13). It is this mark or seal that guarantees that we "are sealed unto the day of redemption" (Ephesians 4:30). The seal of the Holy Spirit ensures that we are under God's protection from evil throughout eternity. Hallelujah!
—J. B. N.

B. Amazement (v. 10)

10. Then she fell on her face, and bowed herself to the ground, and said unto him, Why have I found grace in thine eyes, that thou shouldest take knowledge of me, seeing I am a stranger?

Ruth's initial reaction is astonishment at the degree of grace, or kindness, extended to her as a complete stranger in this land. Perhaps no such practice of extending kindness to strangers exists in her native Moab, so she finds such treatment from Boaz to be particularly striking.

II. Boaz's Insight
(RUTH 2:11-13)

A. Perception (v. 11)

11. And Boaz answered and said unto her, It hath fully been shewed me, all that thou hast done unto thy mother in law since the death of thine husband: and how thou hast left thy father and thy mother, and the land of thy nativity, and art come unto a people which thou knewest not heretofore.

At some point, Boaz has heard the story behind Ruth's coming to Bethlehem with her mother-in-law. He has been informed of the kindness she has demonstrated to Naomi, even though Ruth's own husband had died.

Boaz is also aware of the sacrifice Ruth has made—to leave her father and mother and native land to identify with a people of whom she has little or no knowledge prior to her marriage to Naomi's son. At a time in Israel's history when selfishness is the dominant character trait, the example of Ruth (a foreigner no less!) shines brilliantly.

B. Prayer (v. 12)

12. The LORD recompense thy work, and a full reward be given thee of the LORD God of Israel, under whose wings thou art come to trust.

Earlier Naomi had asked a blessing on Ruth (along with Orpah), that each receive kindness from the Lord and find "rest" in the home of another husband (Ruth 1:8, 9). At this point, Naomi's words have come true, at least partially, for Ruth. The Lord blesses by allowing Ruth to experience the gentleness and graciousness of Boaz. And in the future, Boaz will become that husband in whom Ruth will find rest (although there is no indication of that occurring yet).

In the meantime, Boaz pronounces another blessing on Ruth. He uses an interesting phrase to picture the care that the Lord provides for those who seek a refuge in Him by describing the Lord as the one *under whose wings thou art come to trust*. Not only is this phrase the source of a famous hymn ("Under His Wings"), but it possesses an important link to something that happens later in the book of Ruth.

When Ruth approaches Boaz at the threshing floor later in chapter 3, she tells him, "I am Ruth thine handmaid: spread therefore thy skirt over thine handmaid; for thou art a near kinsman" (Ruth 3:9). The Hebrew word translated *skirt* is the same word translated as *wings* in the present verse. When Boaz follows Ruth's bidding (which amounts to a proposal of marriage), it is in effect the answer to Boaz's prayer of blessing in the present verse.

Boaz's "wings" (of his garment) thus will become God's "wings." That is, God uses Boaz to shelter Ruth and give her rest and security through her marriage to Boaz.

C. Plea (v. 13)

13. Then she said, Let me find favour in thy sight, my lord; for that thou hast comforted me, and for that thou hast spoken friendly unto thine handmaid, though I be not like unto one of thine handmaidens.

Humbly Ruth accepts the favor granted to her by Boaz. She expresses her desire to continue to find favor in the eyes of Boaz, even as she acknowledges she is not worthy of such treatment. She realizes that she does not have the standing usually associated with such treatment.

Such a grateful attitude reminds us of that which is shown by the prodigal son as he prepares to return home to his father (Luke 15:17-19). It also models the attitude of every Christian who realizes that he or she has done nothing whatsoever to earn God's gracious favor that comes to us through the death and resurrection of Jesus.

III. Boaz's Invitation
(RUTH 2:14-18)
A. Offer (v. 14)

14. And Boaz said unto her, At mealtime come thou hither, and eat of the bread, and dip thy morsel in the vinegar. And she sat beside the reapers: and he reached her parched corn, and she did eat, and was sufficed, and left.

When mealtime comes, Boaz offers Ruth yet another gesture of hospitality. He is not compelled to do this by law; his act is yet another reflection of a compassionate spirit that is willing to go beyond the law's requirements. He invites Ruth to join the harvesters for lunch. Once again, she is treated as an equal, not as a foreigner.

The vinegar into which Ruth is to dip her bread is probably a vinegar-based sauce. The word *corn* does not refer to "corn" in the sense of "maize" as we understand it today. That food is unknown in Boaz's time and place. Rather, *parched corn* is a general reference to "roasted grain." This may well be some of the barley that is currently being harvested (Ruth 1:22). Ruth doesn't leave the table hungry. The word *left* indicates that she has some grain left over, which she later takes home to Naomi (v. 18, below).

❧ *A SIGN OF FAVOR* ❧

Our diets today are very different from those of the ancient world. This fact may make it easy to overlook references that may not mean much to us, but that may have been significant to ancient people. Take, for example, Boaz's gift of "parched corn," which is some kind of roasted grain. I have eaten roasted grain. Frankly, I didn't care for it all that much. Even so, I would rate it a bit higher than rice cakes, which seem like eating Styrofoam.

Yet parched grain was part of the normal ration for Roman soldiers. On the American frontier, about the only trail rations Indians and settlers had was parched corn. Indians normally dry-roasted it; settlers usually panfried it. In the ancient world, parched grain was considered a near delicacy. One Jewish source likens parched grain to today's candy. Other Jewish references comment on parched grain as an inducement for children to come into a store or to keep them awake while the story of the Passover is recited.

Some advocates of "natural" food today consider parched grain a hearty, nutritious snack. But in the ancient world it was more than that. Boaz's gift of parched grain to Ruth was a sign of considerable favor. Keep in mind that the world may not understand some of God's gifts to us as signs of His favor. We have to explain. —J. B. N.

B. Orders (vv. 15, 16)

15, 16. And when she was risen up to glean, Boaz commanded his young men, saying, Let her glean even among the sheaves, and reproach her not: and let fall also some of the handfuls of purpose for her, and leave them, that she may glean them, and rebuke her not.

Once more Boaz takes precautions to make sure that Ruth is treated with dignity. In yet another "second mile" gesture, he gives his permission for Ruth to *glean even among the sheaves,* that is, to take grain that is already harvested and bundled. His reapers are not to challenge her as she does this. (They likely would do so under normal circumstances, since allowing such additional gleaning is not required by the Law of Moses.) Furthermore, he tells the reapers to *let fall also some of the handfuls of purpose for her.* In other words, they are to allow some of what they glean to fall to the ground intentionally for Ruth.

C. Output (vv. 17, 18)

17. So she gleaned in the field until even, and beat out that she had gleaned: and it was about an ephah of barley.

Ruth is certainly industrious! Following the midday mealtime, she gleans *in the field until even* (or sunset). But she doesn't stop work. Most likely, Ruth uses a club or stick to thresh the grain, separating the husks from the kernels and thus reducing the load to carry home.

The ephah of grain she ends up with is roughly six-tenths of a bushel, weighing about 29 pounds. This is quite an output for one day's efforts; it testifies both to Ruth's hard work and to Boaz's generosity toward her.

> **What Do You Think?**
> Under what circumstances should we expect an impoverished person to do some work before we give them food as opposed to giving the person a straight handout?
>
> **Talking Points for Your Discussion**
> - Physical and mental abilities of the recipient to do some work
> - Enabling laziness (2 Thessalonians 3:10-12)
> - Enabling self-worth (1 Thessalonians 4:11)
> - Enabling the recipient to do likewise (Ephesians 4:28)

18. And she took it up, and went into the city: and her mother in law saw what she had gleaned: and she brought forth, and gave to her that she had reserved after she was sufficed.

Naomi had earlier stated on her return to Bethlehem, "I went out full and the Lord hath brought me home again empty" (Ruth 1:21). Now Ruth comes back "full" after leaving Naomi's house "empty" at the start of the day.

The verses that follow reveal that Naomi is greatly encouraged by Ruth's productive day.

HOW TO SAY IT

Bethlehem	*Beth*-lih-hem.
Boaz	*Bo*-az.
Deuteronomy	Due-ter-*ahn*-uh-me.
Elimelech	Ee-*lim*-eh-leck.
ephah	*ee*-fah.
Judah	*Joo*-duh.
Leviticus	Leh-*vit*-ih-kus.
Moab	*Mo*-ab.

Empowering the Needy

And when she learns who Ruth's benefactor is, she becomes especially excited—the most excited she has been since the book began! She recognizes that Boaz is "one of our next kinsmen" (Ruth 2:20). At a time that Naomi believes is right, she will instruct Ruth on how to present herself to Boaz in such a way as to encourage him to fulfill his duties as a kinsman, marry Ruth, and preserve the family line of Naomi's husband, Elimelech. Thus in one day Naomi's desperation has been replaced by a glimmer of hope.

Conclusion

A. Gleaning Truth (Not Grain) from Boaz

Boaz serves as an example of the attitudes we should possess toward those in need. Let's consider what he did.

First, Boaz approached Ruth. Sometimes it can be difficult for Christians to take the initiative with the needy, especially if it requires us to move out of our comfort zone. Most of Boaz's reapers probably ignored the stranger in the field, although apparently some wanted to take advantage of her in some way (thus Boaz's warning of which he told Ruth in Ruth 2:9).

Second, Boaz was willing to go the second mile. The kindnesses he extended to Ruth went far beyond the requirements of the Law of Moses. Genuine love and compassion are not limited by the letter of the law (compare Matthew 5:41).

Third, Boaz desired to maintain Ruth's dignity. He did all he could to make her feel a part of the community of reapers. Boaz exhibited similar respect for Ruth in the social setting of the midday meal. Our ministry to the needy today must not be limited to surroundings where they must come to us to be helped; we must go where they are and get to know them in "nonchurch" settings.

In today's world, where government programs are often seen as the source of assistance to those in need, Boaz's example is extremely timely. He reminds us that it is up to all followers of the Lord to do what we can to address the hurts of those around us. Community programs are helpful and have their place, but nothing ministers in the name of the Lord (and nothing establishes genuine

Visual for Lesson 12. *As you discuss verse 12, point to this visual and ask, "How are God's 'wings' similar to those of parents? How are they different?"*

community) more than the individual who goes the second mile to tell someone, "I care." Will you be a Boaz in the neighborhood where you live?

B. Similar Gleanings from Ruth

Ruth's example is also noteworthy. She was not lazy. She took the initiative to ask Naomi about gleaning. She worked hard from the moment of her arrival in the field.

Of course, not everyone we try to help will be like Ruth. Sometimes we become frustrated at the lack of initiative people demonstrate. Perhaps they have become accustomed to receiving "handouts" without accountability. Some may be offended if we try to do more than just apply a bandage to their situations by addressing larger issues.

A congregation should look closely at its surroundings and prayerfully consider creative ways to address needs. The Old Testament law desired to strike a balance between helping those in need and respecting their dignity by encouraging self-reliance and initiative. So should we.

C. Prayer

Father, help us to see the needy as You see them. May we be people of compassion. May we remember that James's words are still true, that faith without works is dead. In Jesus' name, amen.

D. Thought to Remember

Treat others as God treats you.

INVOLVEMENT LEARNING

Some of the activities below are also found in the helpful student book, Adult Bible Class.
Don't forget to download the free reproducible page from www.standardlesson.com to enhance your lesson!

Into the Lesson

Wear old, raggedy clothes (even if over your clothes you normally wear for church). Stand by the entrance to your classroom with a container to receive "alms," clearly labeled *Please Give.* Set a sign up by you with words to the effect *Need Help!* Your learners will show a variety of responses as they enter; most will be amused.

Once class assembles, ask, "How do most people react to such solicitation of help as I demonstrated?" and "Why do we tend to react in those ways?" Let learners respond freely.

After a brief discussion, say, "Today we are looking at the Old Testament pattern for helping those in need. As we study, be thinking about the advantages and disadvantages of such a system for today. Think also about the ways we deal with the needy in our culture and in our church."

Into the Word

For today's lesson, it is important for your learners to be familiar with God's directions for providing for the needy in ancient Israel. Have two of your good oral readers read these passages: (1) Leviticus 19:9, 10; 23:22; and (2) Deuteronomy 24:19-22. In those passages, God specifies the ways that agricultural provisions are to be made to the poor in ancient Israel for their survival.

Divide your class into two or more groups (even pairs). Label each as either *Ruth* or *Boaz.* Give one the word *SPECIAL*; give the other the word *TREATMENT.* Give all groups this direction: "Use the letters of your word to make an acrostic related to the ways Boaz gave special treatment to Ruth in today's text. Note to the group with the word *treatment:* "You may skip one E and one T to equalize the count at seven letters for everyone." Tell the groups that they may list single words for each letter, words that represent elements of Boaz's dealings with Ruth, or they may write phrases or complete statements beginning with the letters.

Though your learners will offer a variety of appropriate responses, here is one sample for each letter: *S*—seeks the Lord's blessing on her (v. 12); *P*—praises her nobility and character (v. 11); *E*—eats with her (vv. 14, 15); *C*—calls her "daughter" (v. 8); *I*—invites her to work with his servants (v. 8); *A*—addresses her (vv. 11, 12); *L*—lets her drink from the water already drawn (v. 9); *T*—talks to her personally (v. 8); *R*—restricts his men (vv. 9, 15); *M*—meals made available (v. 14); *N*—nice, Boaz was nice to her (v. 13). If your learners need help getting started, give one of the above as an example. This activity should clearly demonstrate the carefulness and grace of Boaz in dealing with Ruth (and other poor neighbors).

Alternative: Instead of the above, download the reproducible page and distribute copies of the Boaz the Benevolent activity. You can use small groups or study pairs to complete this.

Into Life

Ask learners if they are familiar with the term *workfare.* Allow someone to define it; be sure the definition includes the idea that *workfare* designates a system that requires a certain amount of work on the part of the one receiving government assistance.

Ask the class to compare and contrast the modern concept of *workfare* with the Old Testament system in which Ruth participated. (Don't allow a political diatribe against common governmental benevolence programs.) Ask, "How does the church practice benevolence without encouraging dependency and laziness?" After discussion and suggestions, ask the more personal question, "How do you and I do so individually without being condescending or hard-hearted?"

Have learners complete the The Christian and Benevolence activity from the reproducible page. This exercise calls for an examination of benevolence principles based on New Testament texts.

CARING FOR
ONE ANOTHER

BACKGROUND SCRIPTURE: Ruth 4
PRINTED TEXT: Ruth 4:1-10

RUTH 4:1-10

1 Then went Boaz up to the gate, and sat him down there: and, behold, the kinsman of whom Boaz spake came by; unto whom he said, Ho, such a one! turn aside, sit down here. And he turned aside, and sat down.

2 And he took ten men of the elders of the city, and said, Sit ye down here. And they sat down.

3 And he said unto the kinsman, Naomi, that is come again out of the country of Moab, selleth a parcel of land, which was our brother Elimelech's:

4 And I thought to advertise thee, saying, Buy it before the inhabitants, and before the elders of my people. If thou wilt redeem it, redeem it: but if thou wilt not redeem it, then tell me, that I may know: for there is none to redeem it beside thee; and I am after thee. And he said, I will redeem it.

5 Then said Boaz, What day thou buyest the field of the hand of Naomi, thou must buy it also of Ruth the Moabitess, the wife of the dead, to raise up the name of the dead upon his inheritance.

6 And the kinsman said, I cannot redeem it for myself, lest I mar mine own inheritance: redeem thou my right to thyself; for I cannot redeem it.

7 Now this was the manner in former time in Israel concerning redeeming and concerning changing, for to confirm all things; a man plucked off his shoe, and gave it to his neighbour: and this was a testimony in Israel.

8 Therefore the kinsman said unto Boaz, Buy it for thee. So he drew off his shoe.

9 And Boaz said unto the elders, and unto all the people, Ye are witnesses this day, that I have bought all that was Elimelech's, and all that was Chilion's and Mahlon's, of the hand of Naomi.

10 Moreover Ruth the Moabitess, the wife of Mahlon, have I purchased to be my wife, to raise up the name of the dead upon his inheritance, that the name of the dead be not cut off from among his brethren, and from the gate of his place: ye are witnesses this day.

KEY VERSE

Then said Boaz, What day thou buyest the field of the hand of Naomi, thou must buy it also of Ruth the Moabitess, the wife of the dead, to raise up the name of the dead upon his inheritance. —Ruth 4:5

441

GOD INSTRUCTS HIS PEOPLE

Unit 3: A Case Study in Community

LESSONS 11–13

LESSON AIMS

After participating in this lesson, each student will be able to:

1. Tell how Boaz secured the right to marry Ruth and to become the source of security for her and Naomi.

2. Tell why it was important for Boaz to follow the complicated procedure that qualified him to become the kinsman.

3. Commit to following procedures more carefully when trying to do something positive in the community.

LESSON OUTLINE

Introduction

A. "Give Care"

At the church where my wife and I worship, the service we attend often concludes not with the frequently heard expression "Have a great day!" but with the challenge, "*Give* a great day!" Worshipers are thus encouraged to continue their service outside the walls of the church building. In a similar manner, one could alter the expression "Take care" (often used just before parting company with someone) to "*Give* care." That phrase comes closer to expressing a Christian's outlook and the theme of today's study: "Caring for One Another."

Our lesson today, the final one from the book of Ruth, focuses on how Boaz carried out a selfless act as Ruth's "kinsman." What he does in today's Scripture text is consistent with his "second mile" attitude throughout the book and reflects a life characterized by caring for others.

B. Lesson Background: Kinsman

Much of the background to today's study is the same as that of the previous two lessons; thus that material need not be repeated here. Instead, we will provide a bit of background on the concept of *kinsman* in Old Testament Israel, an important role of Boaz in today's lesson.

The work of a *kinsman* or *redeemer* is set forth in the Law of Moses. There it is seen to include buying back family land that had been sold because of financial need (Leviticus 25:25), buying back a relative who had become a slave to another because of financial need (Leviticus 25:47-49), and avenging the killing of a relative (Numbers 35:16-21). In short, the kinsman stood up for family members who might be vulnerable to mistreatment because of difficult circumstances that had befallen them.

Naomi was quite pleased when she learned that Boaz was the man in whose field Ruth had gleaned, for Naomi recognized him to be "one of our next kinsmen" (Ruth 2:20). Later Naomi encouraged Ruth to prepare herself and approach Boaz with the idea of having him carry out the role of a kinsman by marrying her. This would preserve the family line of Elimelech (Naomi's deceased husband) through the children of Boaz and Ruth.

Caring for One Another

The Law of Moses does not say anything about marriage as one of the duties of the kinsman. Even so, it seems that this would have been one of the responsibilities that a kinsman could carry out as part of his obligation to help a family member in a desperate situation. Having no heirs to carry on one's name was "bad news" in the ancient world.

After Ruth had in essence "proposed" to Boaz on the threshing floor (Ruth 3:9), Boaz pointed out that there was another kinsman who was a closer relative than he to the family of Elimelech (3:12). Boaz, being a man of integrity, would not bypass the other kinsman to fulfill Ruth's request.

Thus Boaz told Ruth, "If he will perform unto thee the part of a kinsman, well; let him do the kinsman's part: but if he will not do the part of a kinsman to thee, then will I do the part of a kinsman to thee, as the Lord liveth" (Ruth 3:13). When Ruth reported to Naomi what had occurred at the threshing floor, the insightful mother-in-law recognized that Boaz would address such an important matter as soon as possible (3:18). This is exactly what Boaz proceeded to do in today's printed text.

C. Lesson Background: Intercultural Marriage

Before diving into today's text, perhaps some comments should be added regarding the marriage of Boaz (an Israelite) to Ruth (a Moabitess). She was not part of the covenant people. Did this marriage violate the Law of Moses? The law did include certain restrictions about a Moabite not being part of "the congregation of the Lord" (Deuteronomy 23:3), thus limiting their participation in worship. Marrying a Moabite, however, was not specifically prohibited by the law.

HOW TO SAY IT

Boaz	*Bo*-az.
Chilion	*Kil*-ee-on.
Elimelech	Ee-*lim*-eh-leck.
Israelites	*Iz*-ray-el-ites.
Mahlon	*Mah*-lon.
Moabitess	*Mo*-ub-*ite*-ess.
Pharez	*Fair*-ezz.
Tamar	*Tay*-mer.

During the time of Ezra centuries later, "mixed marriages" between Israelites and such peoples as the Moabites were considered offensive and a threat to the purity of the covenant people. Thus action was taken to dissolve such marriages (Ezra 9:1, 2; 10:1-5; compare Nehemiah 13:23-37). It must be remembered that at that time in Israel's history, following the Babylonian captivity, it was crucial that God's people remain separate from the idolatrous influence of peoples such as the Moabites. This separation would help ensure that the Israelites would not become guilty (again) of the sins that had led to the captivity.

With Ruth's marriage to Boaz, the danger of being swayed by idolatrous practices did not exist. Ruth had affirmed without reservation her allegiance to the God of Israel and had severed ties with her Moabite background. One might say she had been "converted" to the covenant people. Thus, despite her Moabite nationality, there was no danger of the family line of Elimelech being "tainted" by Boaz's marriage to Ruth. Because of their common bond of faith in the God of Israel, Boaz and Ruth were not, to use Paul's language, "unequally yoked" (2 Corinthians 6:14).

I. Preparations Executed
(RUTH 4:1, 2)
A. Speaking to the Kinsman (v. 1)

1. Then went Boaz up to the gate, and sat him down there: and, behold, the kinsman of whom Boaz spake came by; unto whom he said, Ho, such a one! turn aside, sit down here. And he turned aside, and sat down.

As Naomi had predicted (Ruth 3:18), Boaz wastes no time in arranging to meet the other *kinsman of whom* he had spoken to Ruth. So Boaz goes to the town gate, most likely of Bethlehem. In the ancient Near East, important transactions are conducted at the gate of a city, probably because people frequently pass by such an area. It might be considered the equivalent of a town hall (compare Joshua 20:4; 2 Chronicles 32:6; Proverbs 31:23).

There Boaz waits until the kinsman passes by. Apparently, Boaz knows the man by sight, since Boaz calls out to him when he sees him.

B. Speaking to the Elders (v. 2)

2. And he took ten men of the elders of the city, and said, Sit ye down here. And they sat down.

What is about to happen will require witnesses. Thus Boaz rounds up 10 elders. Why 10 are chosen is not indicated, and the Old Testament does not mention a certain number of elders being necessary for conducting the kind of business described here. Perhaps this simply reflects a local custom. We should note that Boaz is careful to respect the proper legal procedure of his day.

> **What Do You Think?**
> Other than the situation of Matthew 18:16 and 1 Timothy 5:19, when is it a good idea to involve witnesses in church issues? What procedures can be used? When is having witnesses a bad idea? Why?
>
> *Talking Points for Your Discussion*
> - Counseling situations
> - Visiting situations
> - Video recording as a "witness"

II. Plan Explained
(Ruth 4:3-6)
A. Naomi's Situation (v. 3)

3. And he said unto the kinsman, Naomi, that is come again out of the country of Moab, selleth a parcel of land, which was our brother Elimelech's.

Boaz first mentions an issue concerning a plot of land. Issues concerning land are, after all, a part of a kinsman's primary duties. Naomi is selling some land that had belonged to her deceased husband, Elimelech. (The term *brother* here is used in a broad sense of "fellow townsperson or Israelite.")

Naomi's selling of her property can involve two possible scenarios. One is that she owns the land, but because of her impoverished situation, she is being forced to sell it; the kinsman is the one responsible for making sure the land stays within the family. The other possibility is that Elimelech had sold the land before his family left for Moab. According to the Law of Moses, however, Naomi retains the right of redemption to buy it back (Leviticus 25:25-27). Since she lacks sufficient resources,

the kinsman is the one who will purchase it, in this case, exercising the "right of redemption."

> **What Do You Think?**
> When does discussing someone's need with others cross the line into being an invasion of privacy? How can we avoid crossing that line?
>
> *Talking Points for Your Discussion*
> - Motive: gossip versus seeking godly counsel
> - Discussing group needs vs. an individual's needs (Acts 6:1-6)
> - Getting permission from the person whose need is to be discussed
> - Legalities of "privileged communications"

B. Boaz's Solution (v. 4)

4. And I thought to advertise thee, saying, Buy it before the inhabitants, and before the elders of my people. If thou wilt redeem it, redeem it: but if thou wilt not redeem it, then tell me, that I may know: for there is none to redeem it beside thee; and I am after thee. And he said, I will redeem it.

Boaz explains his desire to carry out the role of a kinsman, but he also acknowledges his awareness of the kinsman who is more closely related to the family of Elimelech. If that kinsman declines to buy back the land, then Boaz is next in line after him to do so. The kinsman, however, states his desire to redeem the land.

C. Kinsman's Struggle (vv. 5, 6)

5. Then said Boaz, What day thou buyest the field of the hand of Naomi, thou must buy it also of Ruth the Moabitess, the wife of the dead, to raise up the name of the dead upon his inheritance.

Now Boaz informs the kinsman of an additional but crucial detail: there is more to the kinsman's obligation than just the purchase of land! The nearest relative must also carry out the responsibility of marrying Ruth *(the wife of the dead)* so that the name of Elimelech (through his son Mahlon, Ruth's deceased husband) and his property can be maintained. This responsibility falls to the kinsman with whom Boaz is conversing.

Caring for One Another

What Do You Think?

What are the problems and opportunities, from both scriptural and practical perspectives, of intercultural marriages?

Talking Points for Your Discussion

- Motives of those involved
- Opening or closing doors of ministry
- Impact on the extended families
- Genesis 27:46—28:2; Numbers 12:1; Ezra 9, 10; Acts 16:1; 2 Corinthians 6:14-17

6. And the kinsman said, I cannot redeem it for myself, lest I mar mine own inheritance: redeem thou my right to thyself; for I cannot redeem it.

It is easy to miss the high drama that follows Boaz's declaration in the previous verse. What will the kinsman do? If he accepts Boaz's offer, then all of Ruth's planning (not to mention Naomi's) will be for nothing. We do not know how much time elapses between verses 5 and 6; perhaps several seconds pass as the kinsman weighs the implications of Boaz's proposal.

When the kinsman speaks, he states his fear that, in effect, if he has a son through Ruth and if that son is his sole surviving heir, then his own property will eventually go to the family of Elimelech. This is likely what he means by the phrase *lest I mar mine own inheritance.*

What Do You Think?

Under what circumstances, if any, would it be proper to put up one's house as collateral in order to bail someone out of jail? Why?

Talking Points for Your Discussion

- Responsibility to care for one's family (1 Timothy 5:4, 8)
- The example of Jesus leaving His heavenly home to suffer for us
- Risking necessities vs. risking nonnecessities

❧ MISPLACED CONTEMPT? ❧

It is easy to feel contempt for the man who declined Ruth's hand in marriage. Ruth was a woman of high character, and the man who got

her also got a piece of property. What could be wrong with that? But think about the reverse—the man who got the property also got Ruth and the obligations that went with her. For the kinsman to marry Ruth had great potential for creating legal headaches in terms of inheritance should he and Ruth produce offspring.

Adding a wife to the household also carried the possibility of disrupting a happy home if the man was already married. Perhaps the man was familiar with all the problems of the multi-wife household in Genesis 29:15–30:34. Who could blame the man for wanting to dodge that bullet?

Boaz indeed became a hero of the story. But there is no indication that he was already married (the text doesn't say), so he may not have had the legal and practical concerns that the kinsman had. Boaz did indeed have a "second mile" attitude. But that doesn't mean that the kinsman to whom Boaz spoke was the selfish villain of the story. Evaluating motives should be approached with a great deal of caution!   —J. B. N.

III. Property Exchanged
(RUTH 4:7-10)
A. Custom Described (vv. 7, 8)

7. Now this was the manner in former time in Israel concerning redeeming and concerning changing, for to confirm all things; a man plucked off his shoe, and gave it to his neighbour: and this was a testimony in Israel.

With Boaz now in a position to accept the responsibility of kinsman, the biblical writer pauses to explain the act by which this will be made legally binding. The removal of a shoe in confirming a transaction is mentioned in Deuteronomy 25:7-10. There the transaction described involves the refusal of a man to accept the responsibility of marrying his brother's wife if that brother dies without having any children.

As part of confirming such a decision, the widow is to approach her brother-in-law, remove one of his shoes, spit in his face, and declare, "So shall it be done unto that man that will not build up his brother's house" (Deuteronomy 25:9). Thus the reputation of the brother-in-law becomes rather tarnished because of his refusal to assist his deceased brother.

Here, however, the primary purpose of this transaction involves the transfer of property (or redemption) rights. The widow (Ruth) does not spit in the other kinsman's face; in fact, she is not even present on this occasion. (Perhaps this is because of her Moabite background, but nothing is said in the text about this.) Still, the shoe is used in conducting the transaction. This is appropriate for any land or property transfer, since the shoe is to be considered the part of one's clothing that last touched the property being transferred. Thus giving the shoe to the new owner signifies the transfer of the land.

This verse concludes by noting that *this was a testimony in Israel.* In other words, this practice is a standard way to make all transactions in Israel official, whether they involve land or not.

8. Therefore the kinsman said unto Boaz, Buy it for thee. So he drew off his shoe.

Both the words of the kinsman and his action *(he drew off his shoe)* confirm the transfer of responsibility.

What Do You Think?
Under what circumstances is it proper, if ever, for Christians to create legally binding agreements among themselves as opposed to merely "giving one's word"? Why?

Talking Points for Your Discussion
- Spiritual maturity levels of those involved
- Achieving "a meeting of the minds"
- Requirements of the laws of the country
- Jeremiah 32:8-16; Matthew 5:37; 1 Corinthians 6:1-8

B. Consequences Declared (vv. 9, 10)

9. And Boaz said unto the elders, and unto all the people, Ye are witnesses this day, that I have bought all that was Elimelech's, and all that was Chilion's and Mahlon's, of the hand of Naomi.

Now it is Boaz's turn to speak. In so doing, he affirms what has just transpired before witnesses.

10. Moreover Ruth the Moabitess, the wife of Mahlon, have I purchased to be my wife, to

raise up the name of the dead upon his inheritance, that the name of the dead be not cut off from among his brethren, and from the gate of his place: ye are witnesses this day.

With this additional declaration comes the most noteworthy part of the transaction. Boaz has acquired Ruth as his wife in order to keep the family line of her deceased husband Mahlon (and thus of Elimelech, his father) from disappearing. To be *cut off . . . from the gate of his place* may mean having no one to speak for that person in a place of authority. Some believe that Elimelech, when he was alive and living in Bethlehem, may have been one of the elders who met at the gate for considering issues such as the one Boaz has just raised. Now, through the offspring of Boaz and Ruth, his place will not remain vacant.

Just as Boaz began his remarks with the declaration *ye are witnesses this day* (v. 9), so also he concludes his remarks. All those present proceed to voice their agreement (v. 11, not in today's text). They also add a blessing to their assent, asking that "the woman" (Ruth) be blessed as Rachel and Leah whose sons became the source of the tribes of Israel.

Another blessing is added: "And let thy house be like the house of Pharez, whom Tamar bare unto Judah, of the seed which the Lord shall give thee of this young woman" (v. 12, not in today's text). This is an appropriate blessing, since Pharez's birth to Judah and Tamar produced a son for a deceased family member—although the circumstances of that conception were certainly far from noble (Genesis 38). The story of Boaz and Ruth, by contrast, is quite noble. As a result of their marriage, Naomi, who earlier lamented her emptiness (Ruth 1:21), is made full beyond her wildest dreams (4:13-17). So is the nation of Israel, because the great-grandson of Boaz and Ruth will be David, Israel's greatest king (4:18-22).

❧ WITNESSES ❧

In court trials, people are called to give testimony regarding what they have seen. Such people are called *witnesses.* Sometimes a person having expertise in a particular subject matter is called in to give an evaluation regarding the facts of a case;

Caring for One Another

this person is referred to as an "expert witness." I have been called twice to appear as just such a witness. Witnesses of integrity are the backbone of any sound legal system. We are incensed by accounts of false witnesses (1 Kings 21:13; Matthew 26:60).

The concept of *witness* is vital in the Bible, with various forms of that word occurring dozens of times. The truth of the gospel is established by credible eyewitnesses (Luke 24:48; Acts 2:32; 3:15; etc.). When we pass along that truth to others, we witness for Jesus. This is sometimes called "testifying" or "giving testimony" (2 Timothy 1:8; 1 John 4:14). Even though our witness and testimony is true, not everyone will like it. Christians are sometimes killed because of their witness (Revelation 20:4).

We wonder if the witnesses in the case of Boaz were reluctant or willing to be in that role. Would being such a witness result in making an enemy of someone? Was being a witness in that legal proceeding thought to be a nuisance? Did those witnesses have "better things to do," wishing to be elsewhere? Remember: Jesus expects us to be His witnesses today. Just by definition, we *never* have anything "better to do" than to be His witness.

—J. B. N.

Visual for Lesson 13. *Point to this visual as you ask, "What are some ways our class can serve God together with Boaz's 'second-mile attitude'?"*

Conclusion

A. Caring but Cautious

These three lessons from Ruth have highlighted the importance of caring for others. Boaz's initiative and "second mile" spirit are certainly worth imitating.

Today's lesson reveals another way in which Boaz serves as a model for us: he takes care to follow proper channels in accomplishing his goal of helping Ruth. There is no "the end justifies the means" attitude here. Boaz did not simply spring into action without considering how best to carry out his plan. Today's Scripture passage reflects careful attention to detail—going to the town gate, waiting for the other kinsman to arrive, convening 10 of the elders, and then clearly laying out in the presence of witnesses what he had in mind to do.

Our enthusiasm for Christ should not prevent us from paying proper attention to laws, regulations, or anything else that falls under the category of "the right way to do things." Our respect for those matters is part of our testimony for Christ. Paul's advice in 2 Corinthians 8:21 still applies: "Providing for honest things, not only in the sight of the Lord, but also in the sight of men."

B. Boaz and Jesus

Many have commented on how Boaz's actions as a kinsman or "redeemer" foreshadow those of Jesus as the Redeemer of humanity. The New Testament itself makes no such link, thus one should be cautious about pressing any connection too rigidly. However, when the position of redeemer is considered in light of Old Testament descriptions of the Lord as Redeemer (Psalms 19:14; 130:8; Isaiah 59:20; 63:16), the links can be justified. Of course, Jesus' work as Redeemer far outweighs anything Boaz could ever achieve. Boaz went the second mile for Ruth's earthly well-being; Jesus made an immeasurable journey, from Heaven to earth, to redeem lost humanity for eternity.

C. Prayer

Father, thank You for the beautiful story of Boaz and Ruth, which shines brightly in the midst of a dark time in the history of God's people. And thank You for our Redeemer, Jesus. May our lives shine for Him. In His name, amen.

D. Thought to Remember

Go the second mile with integrity.

INVOLVEMENT LEARNING

Some of the activities below are also found in the helpful student book, Adult Bible Class.
Don't forget to download the free reproducible page from www.standardlesson.com to enhance your lesson!

Into the Lesson

Have the question *How careful are you?* displayed on the board as your learners arrive. Say, "Let's see how careful you are with laws, rules, and societal expectations." Distribute handouts with the following quiz. (Tell learners that no one will have to reveal his or her score, and that the quizzes will not be collected.) 1. Do you violate the "15 items or fewer" rule in a checkout lane? 2. Do you leave your cell phone on when signs say it should be off? 3. Do you park in spaces restricted to drivers other than yourself? 4. Do you enter through an exit or exit through an entrance? 5. Do you violate the *Don't Walk* sign at crosswalks? 6. Do you follow seat-belt laws?

After a few minutes, comment, "Today's study in Ruth 4 is of an exercise of carefulness in matters of God's law and the traditions that had arisen in social exchange. Boaz was careful all the way to the letter L!"

Into the Word

Download the reproducible page and distribute a copy of the Ten Witnesses activity to each learner. Say, "This activity calls for finding 10 attention-to-detail elements in Boaz's legal transaction. There may be more than 10, so we're going to see who can find the most."

Divide the class into study pairs or small groups of no more than three. Allow adequate time for pairs or groups to research the entire text of today's lesson and jot their conclusions. Call for team answers, jot them on the board, then compare and contrast results. Expect some good-natured banter about "what doesn't count," ideas that overlap too much, etc. Use the lesson commentary to expand on ideas that you think are important or that the class finds intriguing.

Wrap up by saying, "C-A-R-E-F-U-L . . . Boaz was careful and precise in matters of business, careful and precise in matters of God's law, careful and precise in matters of relations with the opposite sex. Because he is full of care, he is fully careful."

Into Life

Download the reproducible page and distribute copies of the Headlong, Headstrong, or Just Plain Wrong? activity. This activity will require your learners to think personally about their own degree of carefulness in various matters. Since it calls for personal responses, don't put anyone "on the spot" to answer. Learners may be more willing to open up with one another if you have them complete this exercise in small groups.

Next, distribute handouts titled *Steps to Success* that features a diagram of a series of eight "stair steps," numbered one to eight from the bottom up. Ask your learners to write down one positive change they would like to see in your community or congregation. Then say, "Consider carefully what steps are necessary and/or advisable to seeing that change accomplished. Write the sequence of what should happen on your 'steps,' as a challenge to get started wisely on facilitating the desired change."

If you think it helpful, you can try one such listing as a whole class. For example, you could ask your class to think about how to go about improving the landscaping around your church building to make it more attractive and aesthetically pleasing. Some of the procedural steps (not necessarily listed here in the ideal order) could be deciding what specifically needs to be done, distinguishing between safety and aesthetic issues, addressing budget limitations, involving church leadership, involving community leadership, recruiting workers for a periodic maintenance, checking legal ramifications of property alterations, and soliciting permission for certain changes.

The idea is to help your class see the importance of attention to procedure, as Boaz did, rather than just "diving in" (compare 1 Corinthians 14:40).